Coire Sois

Coire Sois

The Cauldron of Knowledge

A COMPANION TO EARLY IRISH SAGA

TOMÁS Ó CATHASAIGH

EDITED BY MATTHIEU BOYD

University of Notre Dame Press

Notre Dame, Indiana

University of Notre Dame Press
Notre Dame, Indiana 46556
www.undpress.nd.edu
All Rights Reserved

Copyright © 2014 by University of Notre Dame
Published in the United States of America

Library of Congress Cataloging-in-Publication Data

Ó Cathasaigh, Tomás.
Coire Sois, The Cauldron of Knowledge : a Companion to Early Irish Saga /
Tomás Ó Cathasaigh ; edited by Matthieu Boyd.
    pages cm
Includes bibliographical references and index.
ISBN 978-0-268-03736-9 (pbk.) — ISBN 978-0-268-03736-9 (hardback)

1. Irish literature—To 1100—History and criticism.
2. Irish literature—Middle Irish, 1100–1550—History and criticism.
3. Epic literature, Irish—History and criticism.
I. Boyd, Matthieu, editor of compilation. II. Title.
PB1321.O34   2013
891.6'209001—dc23

2013029855

∞ *The paper in this book meets the guidelines for permanence
and durability of the Committee on Production Guidelines
for Book Longevity of the Council on Library Resources.*

Contents

Foreword by Declan Kiberd	ix
Preface by Matthieu Boyd	xv
Acknowledgments	xxi
Abbreviations	xxv
Maps	xxviii

1	Introduction: Irish Myths and Legends (2005)	1

PART 1. THEMES

2	The Semantics of *síd* (1977–79)	19
3	Pagan Survivals: The Evidence of Early Irish Narrative (1984)	35
4	The Concept of the Hero in Irish Mythology (1985)	51
5	The Sister's Son in Early Irish Literature (1986)	65
6	Curse and Satire (1986)	95
7	The Threefold Death in Early Irish Sources (1994)	101
8	Early Irish Literature and Law (2006–7)	121

PART 2. TEXTS

The Cycles of the Gods and Goddesses

9	*Cath Maige Tuired* as Exemplary Myth (1983)	135
10	The Eponym of Cnogba (1989)	155
11	Knowledge and Power in *Aislinge Óenguso* (1997)	165
12	"The Wooing of Étaín" (2008)	173

The Ulster Cycle

13	*Táin Bó Cúailnge* (2002)	187
14	Mythology in *Táin Bó Cúailnge* (1993)	201
15	*Táin Bó Cúailnge* and Early Irish Law (2005)	219
16	*Sírrabad Súaltaim* and the Order of Speaking among the Ulaid (2005)	238
17	Ailill and Medb: A Marriage of Equals (2009)	249
18	Cú Chulainn, the Poets, and Giolla Brighde Mac Con Midhe (2005)	259
19	Reflections on *Compert Conchobuir* and *Serglige Con Culainn* (1994)	271

The Cycles of the Kings

20	"The Expulsion of the Déisi" (2005)	283
21	On the LU Version of "The Expulsion of the Déisi" (1976)	293
22	The Déisi and Dyfed (1984)	301
23	The Theme of *lommrad* in *Cath Maige Mucrama* (1980–81)	330
24	The Theme of *ainmne* in *Scéla Cano meic Gartnáin* (1983)	342
25	The Rhetoric of *Scéla Cano meic Gartnáin* (1989)	352

	Contents	vii
26	The Rhetoric of *Fingal Rónáin* (1985)	376
27	On the *Cín Dromma Snechta* Version of *Togail Brudne Uí Dergae* (1990)	399
28	*Gat* and *díberg* in *Togail Bruidne Da Derga* (1996)	412
29	The Oldest Story of the Laigin: Observations on *Orgain Denna Ríg* (2002)	422
30	Sound and Sense in *Cath Almaine* (2004)	439

The Fenian Cycle

31	*Tóraíocht Dhiarmada agus Ghráinne* (1995)	449
	The Pursuit of Diarmaid and Gráinne (translated by the author, 2011)	466
Further Reading (compiled by Matthieu Boyd)		484
Notes		501
Bibliography of Tomás Ó Cathasaigh		551
Works Cited		555
Index		589

Foreword
Declan Kiberd

Tomás Ó Cathasaigh is one of a generation of scholars whose intellectual formation owes as much to French poststructuralism as to native interpretative traditions. His early essays appeared not only in *Éigse* but also in *The Crane Bag*, a journal of ideas whose very title encapsulated that moment when old Irish legend was invoked under the sign of continental literary theory. Repeatedly in the following pages, he cites the work of Georges Dumézil on the three functions of warrior and hero mythology in Indo-European narrative: sacred sovereignty; physical force; fertility and food production. Yet, unlike many scholars who found a guru and a method when Paris dictated fashions in cultural analysis, Ó Cathasaigh cheerfully admits at an early stage of his application that Dumézil's approach may well be superseded; for the present, he concludes, it is the theory that accounts most fully for the workings of the texts under scrutiny.

There is an equally delicious moment in another essay when Ó Cathasaigh offers two quotations from that *maître à penser*, Claude Lévi-Strauss, on the structure of ancient myth: the sentences quoted are rather at odds with one another, but Ó Cathasaigh is content to note the discrepancy as an element in the range of possible interpretations, leaving resolution for some other time.

This is typical of his method with his own predecessors in the study of early Irish texts. In often-packed paragraphs, he offers reviews of the various mythological, historical, and linguistic approaches to Cú Chulainn or Fionn. These reviews sometimes hint at the conflicts between famous scholars without ever accusing them of fanaticism and without remarking that such monomania was of just that warlike kind warned against by many monkish redactors of the old tales.

As a gifted teacher, Ó Cathasaigh has the gift of explanation rather than simplification. He feels the need to acquaint his students with the range of past approaches, even as he develops his own method. There is a mellow, amused, sometimes vaguely regretful note in his surveys of the scholarly battlefield, but also an insistence on saying his piece, even though in saying it he will usually concede that there will be many more analyses to trump his own. That note of tentative, enquiring reverence for the text under discussion and of respect for all scholars past and future is still unusual enough in the field to be worthy of celebration.

Why did early Irish literature become, rather like Shakespeare's texts in the nineteenth century, a happy hunting ground for zealotry and fanaticism among commentators? Some of this could be put down to the vanity of gifted pioneers in a developing discipline; more again might be attributed to the strident patriotism of certain nationalist interpreters of "the matter of Ireland"; but the main reason for such repressive analyses may have been a puritanical fear of art, the sort of panic that often overwhelms a mind confronted by the uncontrollable nature of literary texts. Many scholars were rather like patients in the early years of psychoanalysis who aborted the analysis not long after it had begun. Fearing the potent force of stories rich in emotional and symbolic power, they retreated into a merely linguistic or historical analysis, treating those texts as a means of establishing the rules of grammar or syntax or of understanding the surrounding world picture. The idea that each text might be the passionate utterance of a literary artist was the last thing most wanted to think about.

Ó Cathasaigh is quite trenchant and steadfast about this: "In general we can say that an appreciation of the conceptual framework which underlies early Irish narrative is an essential element in the criticism of individual works. But whereas, in this respect as in others, the historian can cast light on the early texts by virtue of his knowledge and interpretation of other (non-literary) sources, there are strict limits to the amount of historical information which may be extracted from what are, after all, literary texts." That is a modest and timely warning to Celtic scholars of the autonomy of the creative imagination. Even the criticism of modern Irish texts, restricted to a largely linguistic analysis in the first half of the twentieth century, ran in the second half of that century the equal risks of reducing literature to fodder for historians. While it was certainly a good thing that some historians were now competent enough in Irish to use its materials, some of them, in taking the figurative promises of lovers over-literally, may have inferred a degree of material comfort in Gaelic society of the eighteenth century that did not widely exist. With much the same reservation in mind, it has to be said that a great lament like *Caoineadh Airt Uí Laoghaire* ("The Lament for Art O'Leary") was something more than an exercise in rural sociology or indeed an example of composition by a group. As one reads and admires Ó Cathasaigh's attempts to restore and respect the artistic nature of the foundational texts under his scrutiny, one is struck by a singular irony: the period in which he wrote many of these essays was one in which scholars of modern Irish-language texts often performed a reverse maneuver on, say, *Caoineadh Airt*, seeking to highlight it as an example of communal tradition rather than individual talent.

Ó Cathasaigh remarks that writers of English have turned to the legends and sagas for inspiration far more often than writers of modern Irish. That is undeniable—the achievements of a Yeats, Synge, or George Russell in recasting the story of Deirdre and the Sons of Uisneach are proof enough of that. Yet the persistence of this story as the most popular of *Trí Truaighe na Scéalaíochta* ("The Three Sorrows of Storytelling"), while a sign of its artistic brilliance, must also have answered a felt need in more modern societies, wracked not only by emigration but also by guilt at the treatment of those migrants intrepid enough to return. It might even be said that the *gae bolga*, which explodes on entering the skin, was taken by more modern tellers as a prefiguration of the dum-dum bullet; or that accounts of the periodic bouts of depression overtaking heroes prefigure the jaded state of a society deprived of hope or innovation. Indeed, the obsession in so many tales and poems with the loss of sovereignty by flawed leaders must strike any young student now reading them in Dublin as a prophecy of an Ireland that they will, in all likelihood, have to leave. Although all the classic texts must be allowed to breathe in their own time and setting, there is every reason for current writers to want to make them live again as exempla of continuing crises in Irish culture.

And there is evidence that contemporary writers of Irish, such as Nuala Ní Dhomhnaill, are turning for inspiration and guidance to texts that were once of great interest to the revival generation. Ó Cathasaigh, with characteristic modesty, suggests that many students may prioritize the study of modern Irish over early Irish literature; but, if anything, the reverse is true—the early texts provide one of the great literatures of Europe, beside which the writings in the modern Irish language, however brilliant, read like something of a coda.

The essays in this volume will be gratefully read by scholars of Irish literature in English for the light that they cast on such topics as the relation between god and man as mediated through a hero-figure, or for the ways in which they illuminate the difference between the story of Cú Chulainn (about his integration into Ulster society) and Fionn (expressing his extra-social status as a mercenary warrior for hire). If religion mediates man's relation with destiny, morality deals with the attempts by mortals to regulate their dealings with one another—and it is on the cusp between these zones that the hero-figure comes into his own. Ó Cathasaigh has his own way of suggesting that the religious and moral impulse may clash with and destroy one another in the end: he finds in *Tochmarc Étaíne* ("The Wooing of Étaín") a narrative commentary on "the relationship between god and man, between the denizens of the *síde* and the men and women living on the surface of Ireland."

There is much to learn from these pages, whose insights might assist even readers of *Finnegans Wake*. Ó Cathasaigh laments at one point that Giambattista Vico's comment (that the first science to be learned should be the interpretation of fables) has left little impression upon the intellectual life of Ireland—but it certainly fascinated James Joyce, whose last work is an attempt to locate all knowledge from the Christian Gospels to the *Annals of the Four Masters* within a narrative that spans Vico's ages of gods, heroes, and peoples. That said and admitted, it would of course be wrong if Irish legend were to be seen simply as (in Ó Cathasaigh's phrase) "a quarry for modern creative writers." The whole burden of these essays is that it constitutes a great literature in its own right and not a mere backdrop to the study of any other.

Ó Cathasaigh's emphasis on the text serves as a corrective in his mind to a possible over-emphasis on the life of a writer, the accompanying world picture, or even the implied readers and audiences. (Borrowing from M. H. Abrams, he uses the terms "the work," "the artist," "the universe," and "the audience.") In this he may reflect something of the protocols of close reading, which came to prominence in the middle decades of the twentieth century, especially in English literary studies, under the influence of major thinkers like Abrams, W. K. Wimsatt, or, indeed, Denis Donoghue (who had a huge following in the lecture-halls of University College Dublin when Ó Cathasaigh was a young scholar). To those nativists who might object that such protocols are of little relevance to a literature produced out of very different conditions, the answer must surely be: why not? The work, as Ó Cathasaigh says, "is our point of departure, and to it we must always return." But there are pressing reasons, other than the mid-twentieth-century fashion of treating texts as autonomous artifacts, for taking a severely literary approach: "There are, of course, literary critics who would in any case argue the primacy of work-based criticism on theoretical grounds, but in regard to early Irish literature we need only appeal to the purely practical consideration that the work is virtually all that we have at our disposal in the way of evidence." Writing brilliantly of the *Táin*, Ó Cathasaigh marvels that, despite the limited but interesting range of interpretations, commentators have chosen to ignore rather than contest what literary criticism exists. Most of the essays here are a plea to fellow scholars to look up from their grammatical dictionaries and to engage in the wider debate. Nor should scholars of modern Irish feel excluded from the discussion, which might lead some of them to question some of Ó Cathasaigh's own analyses. For instance, he disputes the suggestion that Cú Chulainn is a Christ-like personage, but a figure who combines pagan ferocity with a death while strapped to a pillar will continue to strike many of us as a prefiguration of muscular Christians, a sort of English public-schoolboy in the drag of Celtic hero.

Ó Cathasaigh's invitation to scholars is pressing in its pragmatism but also in its confidence in the artistic value of the works to be studied. Earlier scholars who mined texts for their philological or historical learning were in all likelihood often lacking in such confidence: without ever quite realizing it, they may have feared that early Irish literature was often inferior as literature. It is a noteworthy and welcome development that in recent decades some of the leading commentators on modern Irish-language literature, such as Seán Ó Coileáin and Philip O'Leary, have themselves written on the early Irish tales in a manner that vindicates Ó Cathasaigh's methods. For his own part, Ó Cathasaigh (again following Abrams) is supremely interested in the rhetorical devices of voice and authorial address that seem to conjure in turn an implied reader of a certain kind, trained in such literary devices. Yet he also remains grateful for the continuing work of historians and grammarians: "It has to be said that an immense amount of work remains to be done on early Irish literature: most of the texts stand in need of competent edition and translation, not to speak of interpretation and evaluation."

Despite that need, the discipline of early Irish studies stands currently, in Irish universities at any rate, in real danger of collapse. The main source of that danger is a Higher Education Authority (and its agents in campus administrations) determined to introduce "business methods" to the study of the humanities and, in so doing, to count the number of students in every classroom. There is reason to believe that the rather cranky methods adopted by some scholars of Old Irish may have turned bright young people away from it to work in other areas. If that is true, then Ó Cathasaigh's exciting, open-minded approach to narrative as art provides a perfect antidote along with the promise of revival. There may never be huge numbers studying Old Irish in Dublin or other cities, but it is no exaggeration to say that the health of their discipline provides a reliable indication of the true state of both academia and the nation. If ancient kings were enjoined to protect the sovereignty of the polity, placing duty to that order above short-term considerations, there ought to be a similar constraint on today's education authorities and university presidents. Otherwise, the work of all academics is in vain; and the *ces noínden* (period of debility) that immobilized the men of the *Táin* may last even longer in our time than it did in theirs. A people without a clear sense of the past will cease to form a conception of the future. Ó Cathasaigh quotes a famous bardic poem that suggests that if the old texts are allowed to die, then people will know nothing more than the name of their own fathers. The warning may be even more apposite now than when Giolla Brighde Mac Con Midhe issued it.

Preface
Matthieu Boyd

For over thirty years, Tomás Ó Cathasaigh has been one of the foremost interpreters of early Irish narrative literature *qua* literature. His method combines a rare philological acuity with painstaking literary analysis.

Ó Cathasaigh broke new ground with his insistence that the extraordinarily rich and varied corpus of early Irish literature "cannot be properly understood except as literature, with due allowance being made for its historical dimension." In "Pagan Survivals: The Evidence of Early Irish Narrative" (1984), the item in this volume that gives the fullest attention to scholarly trends, he remarked: "the tendency has been to conduct the discussion of Irish texts principally in terms either of the artists who have produced them or of the universe which is reflected in them, so that there is a pressing need to analyze the extant texts as literary works in their own right." Later, in his study of "The Rhetoric of *Fingal Rónáin*," he added frankly that "Irish studies has not had enough of the cultivation of literary scholarship as an intellectual discipline."

If he was correct in this, the phenomenon can partly be explained by the initial difficulty posed by the language of the texts and by the time and effort needed to develop the linguistic tools that literary critics would require. The Royal Irish Academy *Dictionary of the Irish Language*, begun in 1913, was only completed in 1976, and the *Lexique étymologique de l'irlandais ancien*, begun in 1959, remains unfinished. Even now, despite considerable progress in the last three decades, the field continues to feel the lack of modern editions and translations of important works.

However, there was also a question of attitudes. Previously, the literary texts had been treated as repositories of linguistic forms, historical data, and mythological debris to be exploited by philologists, historians, and mythologists, often for predetermined purposes. They were invariably seen as the products of mere scribes or redactors rather than self-conscious literary artists. Some scholars, like T. F. O'Rahilly, went so far as to consider the texts to be in error vis-à-vis their theories. Ó Cathasaigh's point was that, regardless of the origins of a particular text, it could be profitably studied in the form in which it has come down to us, with respect to the rhetorical strategies employed, or the sustained development of key themes either within a single text (as in "The Theme of *lommrad* in *Cath Maige Mucrama*" [1980–81]), or in a number of texts (as in "The Semantics of *síd*" [1977–79]). His studies revealed a hitherto unsuspected degree of narratorial art and thematic consistency within and among the sagas to which he gave his attention. He sometimes achieved this through the judicious application of theoretical frameworks such as Dumézil's trifunctional approach to Indo-European myth, which he was among the first to bring to bear. He was not shackled to literary criticism, however, and was also able to produce outstanding historical research (e.g., in "The Déisi and Dyfed" [1984]) and technical studies of manuscript redactions and early Irish grammar.

After nearly two decades of such work, it was natural that Ó Cathasaigh should have been asked to survey "Early Irish Narrative Literature" in the volume on *Progress in Medieval Irish Studies* edited by Kim McCone and Katharine Simms (see Ó Cathasaigh 1996b, a valuable snapshot of the field); but with characteristic modesty he said hardly anything there about his own contributions. Patrick Sims-Williams, in his 2009 John V. Kelleher Lecture at Harvard University, "How Our Understanding of Early Irish Literature Has Progressed," was not so reticent. He identified two major advances of the past few decades: (1) the realization that early Irish literary texts are attuned to the political conditions in which they were redacted, and can be analyzed as propaganda; and (2) the realization that early Irish literary texts can be analyzed as works of literature, on their own terms. The first approach is exemplified by the work of Donnchadh Ó Corráin and Máire Herbert; the second by that of Ó Cathasaigh.

It is no longer necessary to justify a literary-critical approach to early Irish texts. Ó Cathasaigh was swiftly joined in this by Kim McCone, Joseph Nagy, Philip O'Leary, Joan Radner, William Sayers, and others. They in turn have been followed by a new generation of scholars. One thing that consistently distinguishes Ó Cathasaigh's work is the respect in which it is held by scholars on both sides of ideological divides, such as the well-known nativist/antinativist tension that became acute upon the publication in 1990 of Kim McCone's *Pagan Past and Christian Present in Early Irish Literature*. Often, Ó Cathasaigh's reading of an early Irish saga is the basis for all subsequent work.

Medievalists in other areas, treading (perhaps unconsciously) in the tracks of nineteenth-century Celtic enthusiasts like Ernest Renan and Matthew Arnold, too often have an unfortunate tendency to treat early Irish literature as exotic, mystical, and mystifying, calling it (for instance) "extremely rich in color, fresh and sensuous description and imagery, a delight in nature, and a delight in the play of language" but at the same time "weak in consistent or logical narrative force, devoid of character development, and lacking in subtlety" (Colish 1997, 85). Ó Cathasaigh's body of work is a definitive rebuttal of such perceptions. The way he makes us see both the subtlety and the logic in this literature lays a strong foundation for comparative study and opens early Irish saga to the appreciation of the wider world.

With the exception of his book, *The Heroic Biography of Cormac mac Airt* (1977)—which Patrick K. Ford, his future Harvard colleague, described as "the best and most solid piece of comparative analysis of early Irish literature to appear in some time" (1979, 836)—Ó Cathasaigh has chosen to express himself through articles in scholarly journals and edited collections. It may be said that the lasting fame of journals such as *Celtica*, *Éigse*, and *Ériu* is due in no small part to his contributions.

This volume brings together Ó Cathasaigh's most important articles published over a period of some thirty years. For most of this time, he was employed at University College Dublin, where he attained the rank of Statutory Lecturer. In 1995, he became Henry L. Shattuck Professor of Irish Studies at Harvard University, where he remains in 2013.

The book is by no means a definitive collection of Ó Cathasaigh's oeuvre. He has important contributions currently in press and many others still to be written. Nevertheless, the articles appearing here are proven classics, or "instant classics" of unmistakable value, and having them at last between two covers will not only make them more accessible to those who are already used to citing them, but also help a new audience to discover them and the fascinating literature that they discuss.

HOW THIS BOOK IS ORGANIZED

The contents of this book are subdivided into "Themes" (studies on overarching or recurrent issues in the field) and "Texts" (studies on individual literary works). An article like "The Theme of *lommrad* in *Cath Maige Mucrama*," which is an elucidation of a single saga, appears under "Texts." "Texts" has been further subdivided into the conventional Cycles: the Cycles of the Gods and Goddesses (to use Ó Cathasaigh's preferred designation, as against "the Mythological Cycle"); the Ulster Cycle; the Cycles of the Kings; and the Fenian Cycle.

Articles are in chronological order within each group, except that "Texts" articles on the same subject (*Táin Bó Cúailnge*, "The Expulsion of the Déisi," *Scéla Cano meic Gartnáin*, and *Togail Bruidne Da Derga*) appear together for ease of reference, and have sometimes been reordered to begin with the most general or accessible treatment, followed by more focused or specialized discussions.

The volume opens with "Irish Myths and Legends," Ó Cathasaigh's 2005 Anders Ahlqvist Lecture, which introduces the Cycles and many of the major topics that the articles explore in more detail. It is the work of a mature scholar presenting his subject through the lens of his own expertise.

At the end of the volume are a few suggestions for "Further Reading" relating to each article, which are intended to show the current state of scholarship with respect to the text or theme that Ó Cathasaigh discusses. These suggestions are not meant to be exhaustive, nor do they include sources that Ó Cathasaigh himself has cited; rather, they emphasize new work and conflicting interpretations. The scantiness of the Further Reading in some cases indicates that very little has been done on Ó Cathasaigh's subject since he wrote about it—these may be especially productive topics for future research.

New editions and translations of early Irish texts are normally not mentioned in the Further Reading section. Rather, this information can be found in the list of Works Cited; for every edition that Ó Cathasaigh cites, the entry also identifies any more recent editions that have appeared, which then have their own entries in the Works Cited.

EDITORIAL INTERVENTION

Obvious misprints in the original publications (on the order of "Rawlinson 5 B02" for "Rawlinson B 502" or "kinship" for "kingship") have been silently corrected. Further corrections have been made only with the author's knowledge and approval. When a statement in the original article is no longer true, a correction appears in square brackets.

British English spellings have been changed to American English, except in quotations. The occasional Irishism has been amended for the benefit of North American readers.

The spelling of proper nouns such as names and titles of Irish texts has been standardized across the volume, except in quotations from the secondary literature. The spellings are those that Ó Cathasaigh currently prefers: *Cúailnge* instead of *Cúailgne* is one example. The spelling of names does occasionally vary according to the date of the text under discussion; thus the spellings *Finn* and *Óengus* are used for the characters in Old and Middle Irish texts, as opposed to *Fionn* and *Aonghus* for the characters in Early Modern Irish texts such as *The Pursuit of Diarmaid and Gráinne*.

Bibliographic references originally appeared in a variety of formats. All are now expressed in parenthetical notation. However, in order to preserve the original numbering, it was not thought advisable to eliminate any notes. In one case ("*Gat* and *díberg* in *Togail Bruidne Da Derga*") the notes had to be renumbered, as the numbering restarted on every page in the original.

Ó Cathasaigh's works are listed in a separate bibliography in advance of the Works Cited.

A NOTE ON THE TITLE

As explained in the text known as "The Caldron of Poesy" (L. Breatnach 1981; compare Kelly 2010), the Cauldron of Knowledge, *Coire Sois* (pronounced approximately "Corra Sosh"), is generated upside-down within a person, and knowledge is distributed out of it. At earlier stages—the Cauldrons of *Goiriath* and *Érmae*, which represent basic and intermediate study—the cauldron has to be set upright so that it can fill with knowledge; it is converted into *Coire Sois*, the highest stage, by the action of either sorrow or joy. Included in this joy (*fáilte*) is *fáilte dóendae* 'human joy,' of which there are four kinds, the third of which is "joy at the prerogatives of poetry after studying it well." This description, of both the knowledge-distributing cauldron and what is needed to create it, seems appropriate for Tomás Ó Cathasaigh, a consummate teacher whose official rank of professor would be expressed in Modern Irish as *ollamh*, the old word for the highest grade of *fili* or poet. The *fili*'s remit was not simply poetry but also the knowledge of history, law, philology, place-name lore, and narrative literature—diverse competencies exemplified by the essays assembled in this book.

The subtitle, "A Companion to Early Irish Saga," should not be construed as a claim of exhaustiveness. Not every early Irish saga extant is even mentioned in these pages, let alone comprehensively discussed. However, the book is a wise and dependable guide to the corpus: it covers the Cycle groupings, key terms, important characters, recurring themes, rhetorical strategies, and the narrative logic that this literature employs, and thus constitutes exemplary preparation to read almost anything in the field.

Acknowledgments

The contents of this book have been reproduced from other sources, which are gratefully acknowledged here.

"Irish Myths and Legends: The First Anders Ahlqvist Lecture," first published in *Studia Celtica Fennica* 2 (2005): 11–26, appears with the kind permission of the editor of *Studia Celtica Fennica*, Dr. Riitta Latvio.

"The Semantics of *síd*," first published in *Éigse* 17, no. 2 (1978): 137–55, appears with the kind permission of the editor of *Éigse*, Prof. Pádraig Breatnach.

"Pagan Survivals: The Evidence of Early Irish Narrative," first published in P. Ní Chatháin and M. Richter (eds.), *Ireland and Europe: The Early Church*, 291–307 (Stuttgart: Klett-Cotta, 1984), appears with the kind permission of the publisher, Klett-Cotta Verlag.

"The Concept of the Hero in Irish Mythology," first published in R. Kearney (ed.), *The Irish Mind: Exploring Intellectual Traditions*, 79–90 (Dublin: Wolfhound Press, 1985), appears with the kind permission of the volume editor, Prof. Richard Kearney.

"The Sister's Son in Early Irish Literature," first published in *Peritia* 5 (1986): 128–60, appears with the kind permission of the editor of *Peritia*, Prof. Donnchadh Ó Corráin.

"Curse and Satire," first published in *Éigse* 21 (1986): 10–15, appears with the kind permission of the editor of *Éigse*, Prof. Pádraig Breatnach.

"The Threefold Death in Early Irish Sources" was first published in *Studia Celtica Japonica* n.s. 6 (1994): 53–75.

"Early Irish Literature and Law: Lecture Presented at the Annual Meeting of the Finnish Society of Sciences and Letters, April 27, 2007," first published in *Sphinx* (2007): 111–19, appears with the kind permission of the editor of *Sphinx*, Prof. Peter Holmberg, and the Finnish Society of Sciences and Letters.

"*Cath Maige Tuired* as Exemplary Myth," first published in P. de Brún, S. Ó Coileáin, and P. Ó Riain (eds.), *Folia Gadelica: Essays Presented by Former Students to R. A. Breatnach*, 1–19 (Cork: Cork University Press, 1983), appears with the kind permission of the publisher, Cork University Press.

"The Eponym of Cnogba," first published in *Éigse* 23 (1989): 27–38, appears with the kind permission of the editor of *Éigse*, Prof. Pádraig Breatnach.

"Knowledge and Power in *Aislinge Óenguso*," first published in A. Ahlqvist and V. Čapková (eds.), *Dán do oide: Essays in Memory of Conn R. Ó Cléirigh*, 431–38 (Dublin: Linguistics Institute of Ireland, 1997), appears with the kind permission of Prof. Anders Ahlqvist on behalf of the volume editors.

"Myths and Sagas: 'The Wooing of Étaín,'" first published in B. Ó Conchubhair (ed.), *Why Irish? Irish Language and Literature in Academia*, 55–69 (Galway: Arlen House, 2008), appears with the kind permission of the volume editor, Prof. Brian Ó Conchubhair.

"*Táin Bó Cúailnge*" (spelled "*Táin Bó Cúailgne*"), first published in A. D. Hodder and R. E. Meagher (eds.), *The Epic Voice*, 129–47 (Westport, CT: Praeger, 2002), appears with the kind permission of the publisher's parent, ABC-CLIO.

"Mythology in *Táin Bó Cúailnge*," first published in H. L. C. Tristram (ed.), *Studien zur Táin bó Cuailnge*, 114–32, ScriptOralia 52 (Tübingen: Gunter Narr Verlag, 1993), appears with the kind permission of the publisher, Gunter Narr Verlag.

"*Táin Bó Cúailnge* and Early Irish Law: The Osborn Bergin Memorial Lecture V (Endowed by Vernam Hull); Lecture Delivered 31st October 2003" was first published by the Faculty of Celtic Studies, University College Dublin (2005).

"*Sírrabad Súaltaim* and the Order of Speaking among the Ulaid," first published in B. Smelik et al. (eds.), *A Companion in Linguistics: A Festschrift for Anders Ahlqvist on His Sixtieth Birthday*, 80–91 (Nijmegen: Stichting

Uitgeverij de Keltische Draak, 2005), appears with the kind permission of Dr. Rijcklof Hofman on behalf of the volume editors and the publisher, Stichting Uitgeverij de Keltische Draak.

"Ailill and Medb: A Marriage of Equals," first published in Ruairí Ó hUiginn and Brian Ó Catháin (eds.), *Ulidia 2: Proceedings of the Second International Conference on the Ulster Cycle of Tales*, 46–53 (Maynooth: An Sagart, 2009), appears with the kind permission of the publisher, Prof. Pádraig Ó Fiannachta (An Sagart).

"Cú Chulainn, the Poets, and Giolla Brighde Mac Con Midhe," first published in J. F. Nagy and L. E. Jones (eds.), *Heroic Poets and Poetic Heroes in Celtic Tradition: A Festschrift for Patrick K. Ford*, 291–305, *CSANA Yearbook* 4–5 (Dublin: Four Courts Press, 2005), appears with the kind permission of then-editor of the *CSANA Yearbook*, Prof. Joseph Nagy, and of the publisher, Four Courts Press.

"Reflections on *Compert Conchobuir* and *Serglige Con Culainn*," first published in J. P. Mallory and G. Stockman (eds.), *Ulidia: Proceedings of the First International Conference on the Ulster Cycle of Tales*, 85–89 (Belfast: December Publications, 1994), appears with the kind permission of Prof. J. P. Mallory on behalf of the volume editors and the publisher, December Publications.

"The Expulsion of the Déisi," first published in the *Journal of the Cork Historical and Archaeological Society* 110 (2005): 68–75, appears with the kind permission of the guest editor, Dr. Kevin Murray, and of the Council of the Cork Historical and Archaeological Society.

"On the LU Version of 'The Expulsion of the Déisi,'" first published in *Celtica* 11 (1976): 150–57, appears with the kind permission of the editors of *Celtica*, Prof. Fergus Kelly and Prof. Malachy McKenna, and of the publisher, the Dublin Institute for Advanced Studies.

"The Déisi and Dyfed," first published in *Éigse* 20 (1984): 1–33, appears with the kind permission of the editor of *Éigse*, Prof. Pádraig Breatnach.

"The Theme of *lommrad* in *Cath Maige Mucrama*," first published in *Éigse* 18, no. 2 (1981): 211–24, appears with the kind permission of the editor of *Éigse*, Prof. Pádraig Breatnach.

"The Theme of *ainmne* in *Scéla Cano meic Gartnáin*," first published in *Celtica* 15 (1983): 78–87, appears with the kind permission of the editors of *Celtica*, Profs. Fergus Kelly and Malachy McKenna, and of the publisher, the Dublin Institute for Advanced Studies.

"The Rhetoric of *Scéla Cano meic Gartnáin*," first published in D. Ó Corráin, L. Breatnach, and K. R. McCone (eds.), *Sages, Saints and Storytellers: Celtic Studies in Honour of Professor James Carney*, 233–50 (Maynooth: An Sagart 1989), appears with the kind permission of the publisher, Prof. Pádraig Ó Fiannachta (An Sagart).

"The Rhetoric of *Fingal Rónáin*," first published in *Celtica* 17 (1985): 123–44, appears with the kind permission of the editors of *Celtica*, Profs. Fergus Kelly and Malachy McKenna, and of the publisher, the Dublin Institute for Advanced Studies.

"On the *Cín Dromma Snechta* Version of *Togail Brudne Uí Dergae*," first published in *Ériu* 41 (1990): 103–14, appears with the kind permission of the editors of *Ériu* and the Royal Irish Academy.

"*Gat* and *díberg* in *Togail Bruidne Da Derga*," first published in A. Ahlqvist et al. (eds.), *Celtica Helsingiensia: Proceedings from a Symposium on Celtic Studies*, 203–13, Commentationes Humanarum Litterarum 107 (Helsinki: Societas Scientiarum Fennica, 1996), appears with the kind permission of Prof. Anders Ahlqvist on behalf of the volume editors.

"The Oldest Story of the Laigin: Observations on *Orgain Denna Ríg*," first published in *Éigse* 33 (2002): 1–18, appears with the kind permission of the editor of *Éigse*, Prof. Pádraig Breatnach.

"Sound and Sense in *Cath Almaine*," first published in *Ériu* 54 (2004): 41–47, appears with the kind permission of the editors of *Ériu* and the Royal Irish Academy.

"*Tóraíocht Dhiarmada agus Ghráinne*," first published in *Léachtaí Cholm Cille* 25 (1995): 30–46, appears with the kind permission of the editor of *Léachtaí Cholm Cille*, Prof. Pádraig Ó Fiannachta. The translation is by the author, Tomás Ó Cathasaigh.

We are immensely grateful to Prof. Declan Kiberd for the foreword, and to Prof. Thomas Charles-Edwards and Dr. Fiona Edwards for creating the maps.

Abbreviations

Abbreviations used in only one article are defined within that article.

Anecd.	Osborn Bergin et al., eds. 1907–13. *Anecdota from Irish Manuscripts.* 4 vols. Halle a. S.: Max Niemeyer.
BBCS	*Bulletin of the Board of Celtic Studies*
BUD	*Orgain Brudne Uí Dergae* (Nettlau 1893, 151–52; Thurneysen 1912–13, 1:27; V. Hull 1954a; S. Mac Mathúna 1985, 449 f.)
CA	*Cath Almaine* (Ó Riain 1978)
CCC	*Compert Con Culainn* (van Hamel 1933)
CCSH	*Comparative Studies in Society and History*
CConch	*Compert Conchobuir* (V. Hull 1934)
CDS	*Cín Dromma Snechta(i)* (lost ms.)
CMCS	*Cambridge/Cambrian Medieval Celtic Studies*
CMM	*Cath Maige Mucrama* (O Daly 1975)
CMT	*Cath Maige Tuired* (Stokes 1891b; Gray 1982)
DIAS	Dublin Institute for Advanced Studies
DIL	E. G. Quin (gen. ed., 1953–75) et al. 1913–76. *(Contributions to a) Dictionary of the Irish Language.* Dublin: Royal Irish Academy. Compact ed. (1983). Online version at http://www.dil.ie.
ÉC	*Études Celtiques*

ED	"The Expulsion of the Déisi"
Eg.	Egerton (classification of mss. held by the British Library)
gen.	genitive case
IEW	Julius Pokorny, ed. 1948–69. *Indogermanisches etymologisches Wörterbuch*. Bern: Francke.
IT	Whitley Stokes and Ernst Windisch, eds., trans. 1880–1909. *Irische Texte mit Übersetzungen und Wörterbuch*. 4 vols. Leipzig: S. Hirzel.
ITS	Irish Texts Society
JCHAS	*Journal of the Cork Historical and Archaeological Society*
JIES	*Journal of Indo-European Studies*
K	Kinsella (1970)
KZ	*Kuhns Zeitschrift (Zeitschrift für vergleichende Sprachforschung)*
LEIA	J. Vendryes, ed. 1959–. *Lexique étymologique de l'irlandais ancien*. 7 vols. Dublin: DIAS/Paris: Centre National de la Recherche Scientifique.
LL	R. I. Best, Osborn Bergin, M. A. O'Brien, and A. O'Sullivan, eds. 1954–84. *The Book of Leinster, formerly Lebar na Núachongbála*. 6 vols. Dublin: DIAS.
LU	*Lebor na hUidre* (Royal Irish Academy MS 23 E 25)
LU	R. I. Best and Osborn Bergin, eds. 1929. *Lebor na hUidre: Book of the Dun Cow*. Dublin: DIAS.
Met. Dind.	E. J. Gwynn, ed., trans. 1903–35. *The Metrical Dindshenchas*. 5 vols. Dublin: DIAS.
NUI	National University of Ireland
PBA	*Proceedings of the British Academy*
PHCC	*Proceedings of the Harvard Celtic Colloquium*
PMLA	*Proceedings of the Modern Language Association*
PRIA	*Proceedings of the Royal Irish Academy*
RC	*Revue Celtique*
SC	*Studia Celtica*
SH	*Studia Hibernica*
SLH	*Scriptores Latini Hiberniae*
SPAW	*Sitzungsberichte der Königlich Preussischen Akademie der Wissenschaften*
TBC I	Cecile O'Rahilly, ed., trans. 1976. *Táin Bó Cúailgne: Recension I*. Dublin: DIAS.

TBC LL	Cecile O'Rahilly, ed., trans. 1967. *Táin Bó Cúalgne from the Book of Leinster*. Dublin: DIAS.
TBDD	*Togail Bruidne Da Derga* (Knott 1935)
TE1	*Tochmarc Étaíne*, part 1 (Bergin and Best 1934–38)
Thes.	Whitley Stokes and John Strachan, eds., trans. 1901–3. *Thesaurus Palaeohibernicus: A Collection of Old-Irish Glosses, Scholia, Prose and Verse*. 2 vols. Cambridge: Cambridge University Press.
Ulidia	J. P. Mallory and Gerard Stockman, eds. 1994. *Ulidia: Proceedings of the First International Conference on the Ulster Cycle of Tales*. Belfast: December Publications.
Ulidia 2	Ruairí Ó hUiginn and Brian Ó Catháin, eds. 2009. *Ulidia 2: Proceedings of the Second International Conference on the Ulster Cycle of Tales*. Maynooth: An Sagart.
W	Welsh
YBL	The Yellow Book of Lecan (Trinity College Dublin MS 1318 [=H 2.16]).
ZCP	*Zeitschrift für Celtische Philologie*

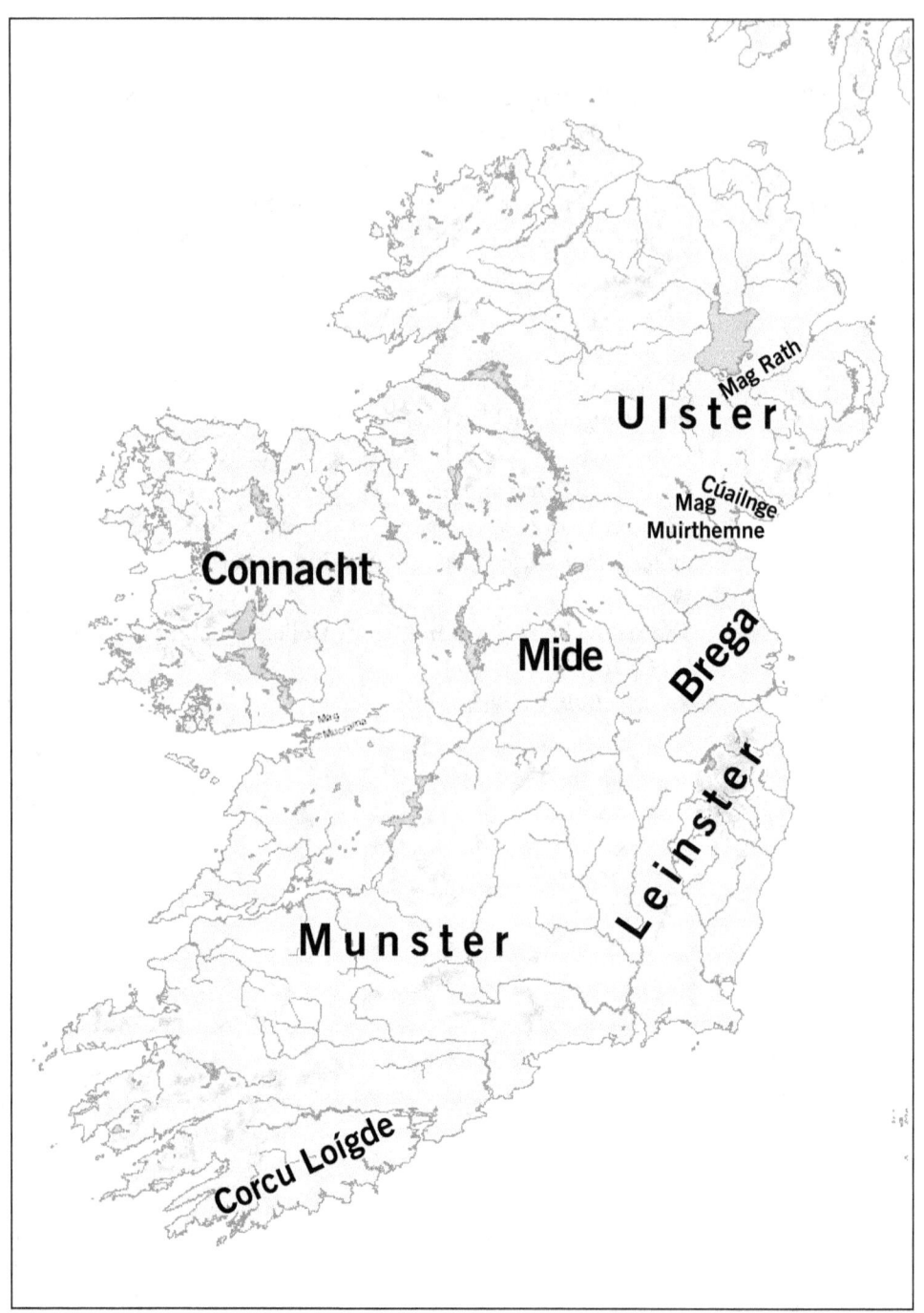

Map 1. Provinces and regions of early Ireland.

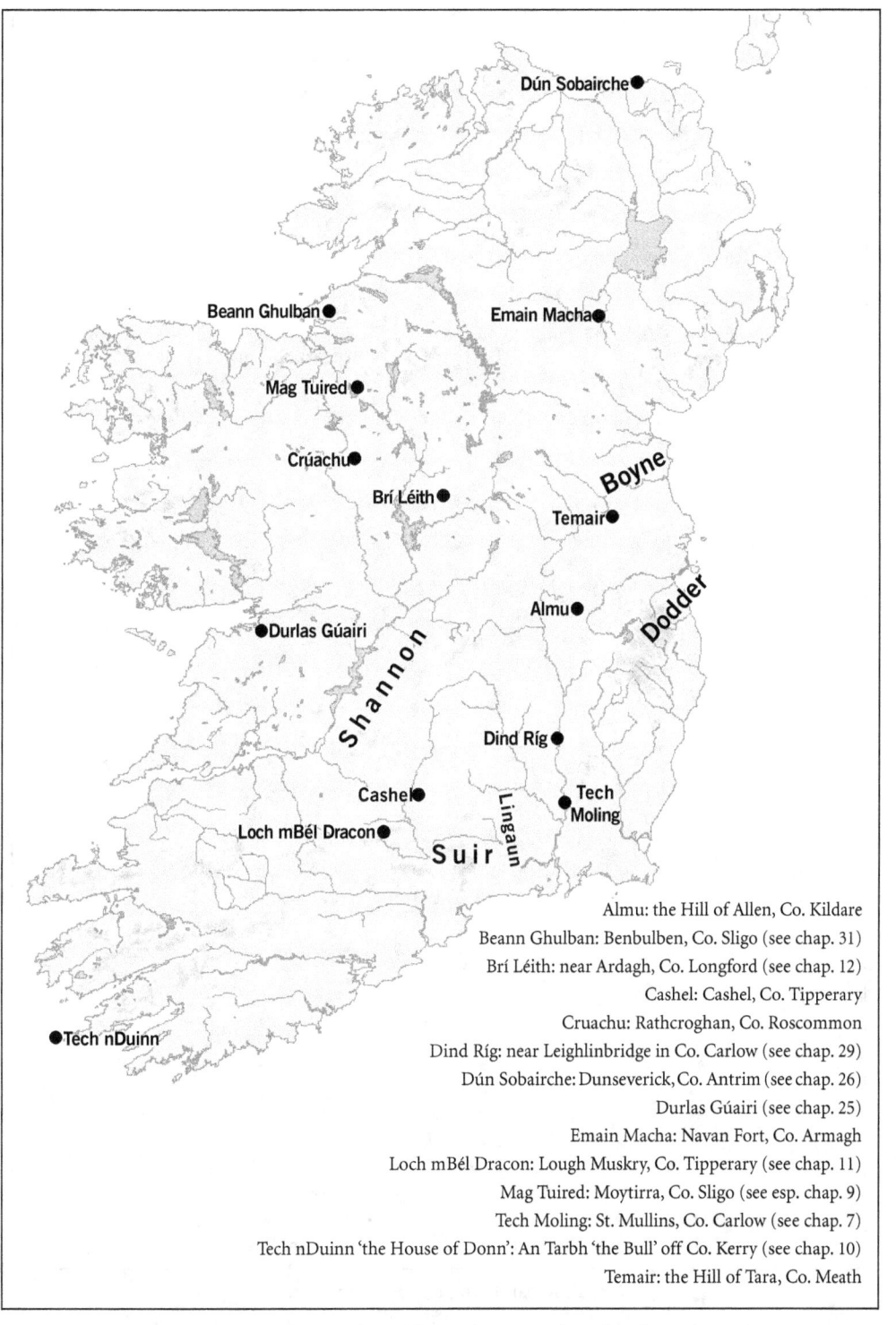

Map 2. Rivers and significant places mentioned in the text.

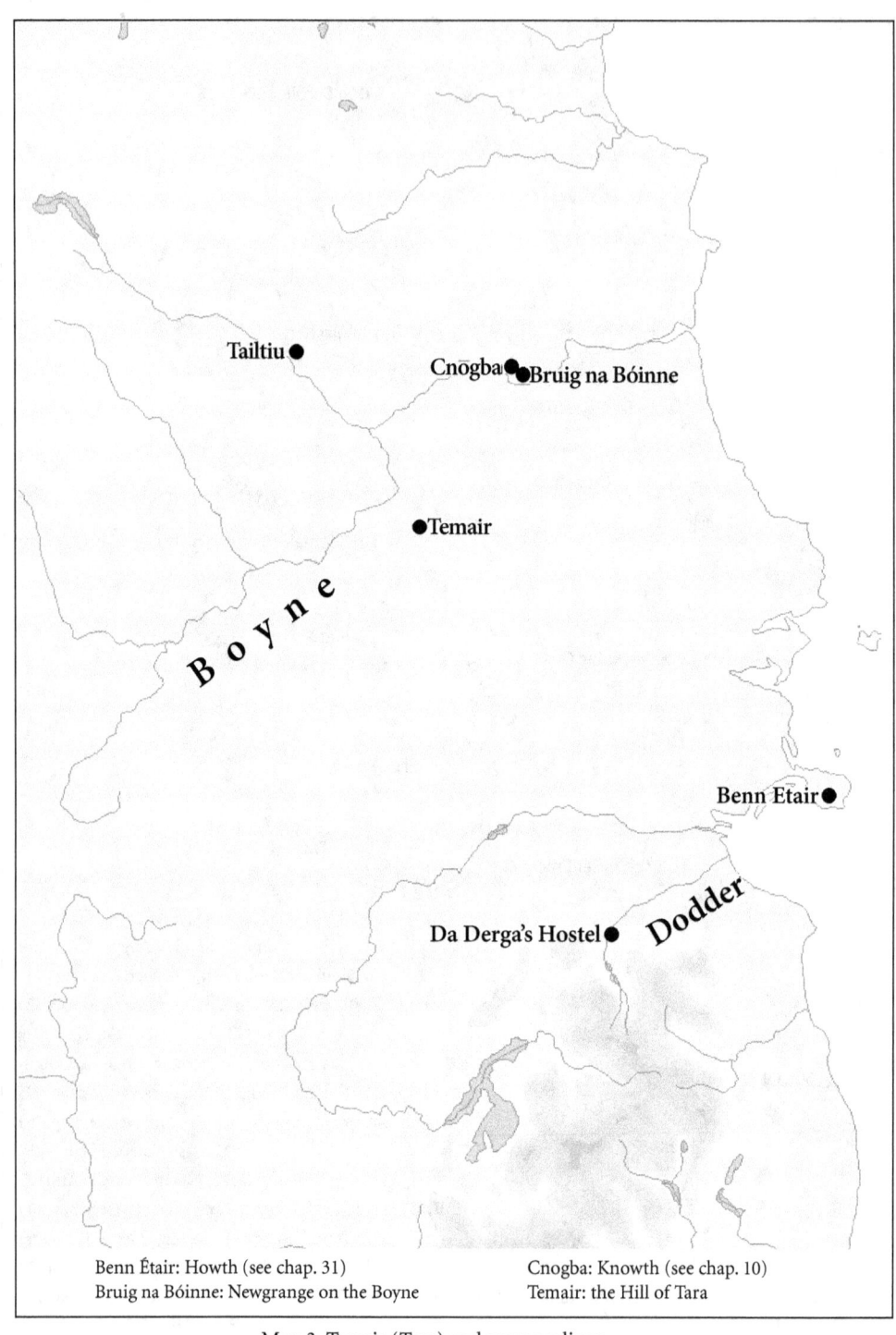

Benn Étair: Howth (see chap. 31)
Bruig na Bóinne: Newgrange on the Boyne
Cnogba: Knowth (see chap. 10)
Temair: the Hill of Tara

Map 3. Temair (Tara) and surroundings.

1

Introduction
Irish Myths and Legends

(2 0 0 5)

An immense body of narrative lore has come down to us in Irish manuscripts, and the earliest surviving tales are probably to be dated to the seventh or the early eighth century. Literacy in the vernacular came early to Ireland. We know that there were Christians in Ireland in 431 A.D. for Pope Celestine sent them a bishop in that year. These Irish Christians must have had men among them who were literate in Latin. Some degree of literacy in the Irish language was present even earlier than the fifth century, however: evidence for this is found in the nature of the ogam alphabet. The oldest surviving records of the Irish language are ogam inscriptions incised in stone. Something under four hundred of these inscriptions survive, and they generally consist of a personal name in the genitive case, accompanied, more often than not, by the name of that person's father or other ancestor.

The earliest inscriptions probably date to the fifth and sixth centuries, and some may belong to the fourth (McManus 1991, 40). The invention of the ogam alphabet cannot be later than the fourth century (McManus 1991, 41), and Anders Ahlqvist (1983, 10) has suggested that it may date to the end of the second century or the beginning of the third. We know nothing of the identity of the inventor of this alphabet, but we can be sure that he knew Latin and that his invention entailed an analysis of the Irish language. It is possible that ogam may have been used to inscribe on wooden tablets what D. A. Binchy (1961, 9) called "an elementary type of written literature," but nothing of the kind survives. The only such tablets that we have are six that were found in Springmount Bog (near Ballymena, County Antrim) in 1913: they have been dated to the later years of the sixth century (Ó Cuív 1984, 87) and bear portions of the psalms in Latin.

The literature that survives from the early Irish period, in Irish and in Latin, is the product of an intellectual elite that included ecclesiastical scholars and learned poets (*filid*, singular *fili*). The *filid* were the most prestigious of the *áes dána* ("men of art") in early Ireland: they were highly trained and their power largely resided in their role as purveyors of praise and blame. The *filid* seem to have arrived at an early accommodation with the church. The sixth-century monastic saint Colum Cille (Columba) is traditionally represented as a defender of the *filid*, and this seems to have an historical basis. In the life of Colum Cille written in the seventh century by his kinsman Adomnán, Colum Cille is depicted as a patron of the Irish-language poets: he would entertain them and invite them to sing songs of their own composition. Colum Cille was the subject of the *Amra Choluim Chille* 'The Eulogy of Colum Cille,' which is attributed to the *fili* Dallán Forgaill and is generally considered to have been composed shortly after the saint's death.

Another poet who is considered to be emblematic of "the fusion of native tradition and Christianity in sixth-century Ireland" (Watkins 1976a, 275) is Colmán mac Lenéni (died ca. 606). Colmán was a *fili* who became a cleric late in life. Some fragments of his work have been preserved, and in one of the surviving quatrains clearly dating from his time as a cleric, Colmán uses legal language to say that his poem has not been composed for earthly reward, but rather for the grace of God (Watkins 1976a, 274–75). The word used for "grace" in this connection is not (as one might expect) a borrowing from Latin, but rather a native Irish word *rath* that is used of the fief given by a lord to his vassal or "client." Colmán's talent and skill as a *fili*, which he had been using in the service of secular kings, will henceforth be devoted to praise of God.

The indications are that in early Ireland storytelling was a function of the *filid*, but we cannot say what the relationship may have been between the stories narrated by the *filid* and those that survive in the manuscripts. Some scholars have emphasized those features of the material that reflect an inheritance from Celtic or even Proto-Indo-European culture, while others have chosen to highlight the innovative character of the tales, and the ecclesiastical and Latin influences on their formation. These need not be mutually exclusive positions. In what I have to say, I shall refer from time to time to inherited features of the material, but I shall also be at pains to point to ways in which the narrative literature is at one with the laws and the wisdom literature.

Irish tales were classified according to their titles. Some of these have to do with major events in the life of an individual, such as *comperta* ("conceptions"), *aitheda* ("elopements"), *tochmarca* ("wooings"), *echtrai* ("expeditions [to the Otherworld]"), *immrama* ("sea-voyages"), and *aitte/aideda* ("violent deaths"). Others relate momentous or cataclysmic events in the social and political history of population groups, such as *catha* ("battles"), *tomadmann* ("eruptions [of lakes or rivers]"), *tochomlada* ("migrations"), *oircne* ("slaughters, destructions"), *togla* ("destructions"), and *tána bó* ("cattle raids").

Modern commentators have found it convenient to classify the material according to cycles. The Mythological Cycle deals with the gods and goddesses, and I would prefer to speak of it as the Cycles of the Gods and Goddesses (cf. "*Cath Maige Tuired* as Exemplary Myth," chap. 9 in this volume). The Ulster Cycle depicts a Heroic Age in Ireland's past, and celebrates the acts of a warrior caste. The Fenian Cycle also recounts the heroic deeds of fighting men, but these are hunter-warriors, and the Ulster and Fenian Cycles "differ profoundly in their characters, their milieu, their ethos and their provenance" (Rees and Rees 1961, 62). The Cycles of the Kings focus on the lives of prehistoric and historic kings, and have to do as well with the activities of saints and poets. The Irish church also produced a formidable number of Saints' Lives, first in Latin and then in Irish.

What I propose to do in this introduction is to focus on a few of the more important texts. The account which I shall give of the material will be a somewhat personal one, and I have no doubt that my biases will be readily apparent. I begin with *Cath Maige Tuired*, "The Battle of Mag Tuired" (E. Gray 1982), which is by common consent the most important of our mythological tales. The text that has come down to us would seem to be a composite work put together by an eleventh- or twelfth-century redactor mainly from ninth-century material (Murphy 1955a, 19), and it deals with a conflict between the Túatha Dé Danann and the Fomoiri, culminating in a great battle at Mag Tuired (Moytirra, County Sligo) in which the Túatha Dé Danann are victorious. This battle is included in the schema of legendary prehistory which came to be known as *Lebor Gabála Érenn*, "The Book of the Taking of Ireland," often referred to as "The Book of Invasions," and which tells of six prehistoric invasions of Ireland (Rees and Rees 1961, 104). It is also concerned with the origin of physical features, boundaries, and names, and with the genesis of Irish customs and institutions. The last three "invasions" were those of the Fir Bolg, the Túatha Dé Danann, and the Children of Míl or Gaels. The "first" battle of Mag Tuired was fought between the Túatha Dé Danann and the Fir Bolg. Our text is concerned with the "second" battle, in which the Túatha Dé Danann vanquished the Fomoiri.

The Túatha Dé Danann ("The Tribes of the Goddess Danu") are in large measure Irish reflexes of the gods of the Celts, and it is possible to see among them some intimations of a Celtic pantheon (Mac Cana 1970, 23–41). The Fomoiri, whose name derives from *fo* 'under' + *mor* 'specter,' are malevolent and somewhat shadowy personages. The hero of the Túatha Dé Danann, the young god who leads them to victory at Mag Tuired, is Lug, the Irish reflex of a Celtic god who is commemorated in numerous Continental place-names, and whose Welsh equivalent is called Lleu. According to *Cath Maige Tuired*, the Túatha Dé Danann king of Ireland, Núadu, had an arm lopped off in battle. He had to relinquish the kingship, for an Irish king was required to be unblemished. He was succeeded—at the behest of the womenfolk of the Túatha Dé Danann—by Bres, whose relationship to the Túatha Dé Danann was through his mother. His father was of the Fomoiri: he had come over the sea to Ireland, impregnated Bres's mother, and left her. Bres proved to be a thoroughly unworthy king, and the Túatha Dé Danann forced him to abdicate. Núadu in the meantime had been fitted with a silver arm, and he again became king. Bres went into exile, and gathered together a great army to invade Ireland.

In *Cath Maige Tuired*, Lug comes as a stranger to Tara, traditionally the seat of the kings of Ireland, and seeks admittance to Núadu's court. He is opposed by an official of Núadu's, who asks him repeatedly to name a skill that would entitle him to enter Tara. Lug names a remarkable number of skills, one by one, and is told each time that there is already a practitioner of that skill in Tara. He is not to be bested, however: he asks whether there is anyone in Tara who possesses all of those skills, and of course there is no such person. The king then decrees that Lug should be admitted to Tara. At first Lug sits in the sage's seat, but Núadu decides that Lug will be just the one to liberate the Túatha Dé Danann from the depredations of the Fomoiri. He therefore changes places with Lug, who thus becomes king.

Lug's father was Cían of the Túatha Dé Danann and his mother was a daughter of Balar of the Fomoiri. Balar had a destructive eye that would disable an entire army if they looked at it. In the decisive act of the battle, Lug casts a sling stone at Balar's eye that carries it through his head, so that it is the Fomoiri that look at it. Balar dies, and by killing his own maternal grandfather, Lug ensures victory for the Túatha Dé Danann. He goes on to spare Bres's life, and in return Bres has to reveal the secrets of ploughing, sowing, and reaping.

Cath Maige Tuired is the Irish version of the War of the Gods, an Indo-European theme that is well known from Greek and Scandinavian mythology and can be seen in Indian and Persian mythology as well. Georges Dumézil has interpreted this theme in terms of the tripartite structure that he posited for Proto-Indo-European ideology. This comprises three functions: the sacred, including sovereignty; physical force; and a third function, fertility, that includes food production.[1] In the War of the Gods Dumézil sees a contest between a group which is competent in the first and second functions and one which is competent in the third. The first of these groups vanquishes the second and incorporates it, thus achieving competence in all three functions. In the Irish version, the Túatha Dé Danann did not actually incorporate the defeated Fomoiri, but they did acquire competence in agriculture when the battle was over and Lug wrested the secrets of ploughing, sowing, and reaping from Bres (Dumézil 1968, 289–90). Moreover, Lug achieves victories over Núadu (who tries to exclude Lug from the seat of kingship at Tara), Balar (on the battlefield), and Bres (who is obliged to yield up the secrets of agriculture in exchange for his life): in this sequence he establishes his preeminence in kingship, physical force, and food production, thereby encompassing all three of the domains which belong to the tripartite structure (see "*Cath Maige Tuired* as Exemplary Myth," chap. 9 in this volume).

Bres's reign stands in contrast to that of Lug. His relationship with the Túatha Dé Danann is a contractual one, and, as Dumézil (1943, 230–41) has seen, his failure to fulfil his obligations to his people signals the breakdown of the social contract: a king is obliged to show generosity to his subjects, and Bres declines to do so. What is in question here is the relationship between *rí* and *túath*. There was a hierarchy of kings in early Ireland, but even the most powerful of kings was basically ruler of a single *túath* (Byrne 1973, 41). The reciprocal pair *túath* and *rí* is of Indo-European origin: the small tribal unit (**teutā-*) ruled by a powerful chieftain (**reg-*) belongs to the reconstructed lexicon of Indo-European (Watkins 2000, xxxiv). In *Cath Maige Tuired* the Túatha Dé Danann are variously called Túatha Dé or Túath Dé, but in those parts of the text that recount the reign of Bres, the singular is always used. Moreover, the election of Bres to the kingship is described in technical legal language: for the obligations that the king must discharge to his people the word used is *folad*, and it is his failure in this respect that prompts his *túath* to depose him (see further "The Sister's Son in Early Irish Literature," chap. 5 in this volume). Thomas Charles-Edwards (1994) has shown that the Irish law tract *Críth Gablach* describes a contract between king and people: the king has obligations (*folad*) to his people, and they have obligations to him. He observed that the contractual approach to kingship in *Críth Gablach* is unlikely to have its roots in canon law, "nor is it to be explained by any influence from Greek or Roman political thought for it stems from native ideas of lordship and contract" (Charles-Edwards 1994, 119). We may add here that those very same "native ideas of lordship and contract" find narrative expression in the account of Bres's reign in *Cath Maige Tuired*.

An equally important ideological concern in *Cath Maige Tuired* is that of kinship, and the contrast between Lug, who is related to the Túatha Dé Danann through his father, and Bres, who is related to them through his mother. Bres is what is known as a "sister's son" and the Túatha Dé Danann are his maternal kin. The eighth-century poet Blathmac son of Cú Brettan son of Congus of the Fir Rois in what is now County Monaghan wrote at length about Christ in verse that he addressed to Christ's mother, Mary (Carney 1964). For him Jesus was a "sister's son" of the Israelites and their slaying of him was *fingal*, which is the crime of slaying a member of one's own kindred. This was a particularly heinous crime in early Ireland, as it was the duty of the kindred to avenge the death of one of their members, and this would not be practicable if the perpetrator of the crime was himself a kinsman. In *Cath Maige Tuired*, Bres fails his maternal kinsmen; in Blathmac's presentation of the story of Christ, the Israelites fail their sister's son. I may add that Blathmac also sees their slaying of Christ as a repudiation of their legal obligation to him as lord (see again "The Sister's Son," chap. 5 in this volume).

The conceptual framework of *Cath Maige Tuired* is reflected in the way in which an eighth-century Irish poet interpreted and presented the life of Christ, and also in *Críth Gablach*, which Charles-Edwards (1986, 73) has described as "one of the few outstanding pieces of social analysis in early medieval Europe." At least some of the contents of *Cath Maige Tuired* were inherited from oral tradition, but the ideology that it expresses was clearly of vital concern in the literate Christian community of early Ireland.

The Ulster Cycle celebrates the exploits of the warriors of the Ulaid (Ulstermen), and especially those of Cú Chulainn. The king of Ulster is Conchobor, and his court is at Emain Macha (now Navan Fort, near Armagh). There is a state of endemic warfare between the Ulstermen and the people of Connacht who are ruled by Ailill and Medb; their court is at Crúachu (now Rathcroghan in County Roscommon). The traditional date of the Ulster heroes is the century before Christ. The centerpiece of the cycle is *Táin Bó Cúailnge*, "The Cattle-Raid of Cooley," often referred to as the *Táin* (*TBC I*; Kinsella 1970). It tells of an invasion of Ulster by a great army ("the men of Ireland") led by Medb and Ailill; its purpose is to carry off the Brown Bull from the Cooley peninsula in what is now County Louth. The raid lasts for the three months of winter; during this time the men of Ulster are debilitated, and its defence falls to Cú Chulainn. Clustered around the *Táin* there is a group of foretales (*remscéla*), which provide background information on the circumstances in which the raid took place and the personages who were involved on either side.

One of the foretales is *Compert Con Culainn*, "How Cú Chulainn Was Begotten" (trans. Kinsella 1970, 21–25). Cú Chulainn had a divine father, Lug, and a human one, Súaltaim. According to his birth-tale some birds visited Emain Macha and devoured its vegetation to the very roots. The Ulstermen pursued the birds, which led them to Bruig na Bóinne (Newgrange and associated monuments at the bend of the Boyne). In early Irish literature Bruig na Bóinne is a localization of the Otherworld. A child was born during the night, and Conchobor's sister Dechtine took the child back to Emain. The child died, and Lug appeared to Dechtine in a dream telling her that he was the father of the child, and had implanted the very same child into her womb. He told her that the boy would be called Sétantae. When Dechtine was visibly pregnant, Conchobor betrothed her to Súaltaim. She was ashamed to go pregnant to her husband's bed, and she aborted the boy. Then she slept with Súaltaim: she conceived again and bore a son, Sétantae, who was later given the name Cú Chulainn.

This is one of the most remarkable of the many Irish *comperta* (Rees and Rees 1961, 213–43). The hero has a threefold conception. He is first begotten at Bruig na Bóinne by Lug upon his unnamed Otherworld consort; then at Emain by Lug upon Dechtine; and finally by Súaltaim upon Dechtine. In the first conception, the parents are both divine; in the third they are both human. In the second conception the father is divine and the mother human. We see in this sequence how the hero mediates the opposition between god and man.

It has been shown that the lives of many traditional heroes follow a largely uniform plot or pattern, which is sometimes called the heroic biography. The conception and birth of the hero is an essential part of the pattern. Other episodes in Cú Chulainn's heroic biography are his "Boyhood Deeds," which are recounted in the course of the cattle-raid in the *Táin*; *Tochmarc Emire*, "The Wooing of Emer," which tells how he overcame formidable obstacles to win the hand of Emer in marriage; *Serglige Con Culainn*, "The Wasting Sickness of Cú Chulainn," dealing with his adventures in the Otherworld; and the story of his violent death.

We have seen that Cú Chulainn's father Lug was a hero among the gods, and that he distinguished himself as a king, as a warrior, and in the domain of food production. Cú Chulainn, on the other hand, is a martial hero. The old words for such a hero "express the notions of fury, ardour, tumescence, speed. The hero is the furious one possessed of his own tumultuous and blazing energy" (Sjoestedt 1949, 58–59). This aspect of the hero is most dramatically expressed in Cú Chulainn's *ríastrad*, the physical distortion that seizes him when he is angered, and for which Kinsella uses the inspired term "warp-spasm." The martial ethos of the Ulster Cycle is also seen in the wolf-cult which underlies the names: the king, Conchobor, is the "Hound/Wolf-Desiring One," the great warrior Conall (Cernach) is the "Hound-/Wolf-Powerful One," and Cú Chulainn himself is the "Hound/Wolf of Culann." One of the initiatory episodes in the "Boyhood Deeds" tells how Sétantae faced a fierce mastiff and slaughtered it with his bare hands. The hero assumes the role and name of the vanquished hound: henceforth he is "The Hound of Culann."

Cú Chulainn received his training as a warrior from the Amazonian Scáthach. He is a supreme master of the martial arts, with a formidable repertoire of "feats" (*TBC I*, 173). In the course of his defence of Ulster, Cú Chulainn faces a number of opponents in single combat, but the greatest of them is his foster-brother Fer Diad. He too was trained by Scáthach, and in their encounter in the *Táin* the foster-brothers perform the feats that they learned from her. In the end, Cú Chulainn achieves victory by using a feat which was taught only to him: the deployment of a strange weapon known as the *gae bolga* which enters a body as a single barb, but once inside becomes twenty-four. He is remarkable for his words as well as his deeds: in the single combats, he shows his verbal dexterity as well as courage and skill. He craves fame above all else: provided that his name live after him he will be content with a short life. But his motivation in the *Táin* is far from being purely egotistical. He is fiercely loyal to his mother's brother. The men of Ulster are at one with Cú Chulainn in their *condalbae* (love of kindred), and that I believe is what determines the outcome of the cattle-raid, bringing victory to the Ulstermen over the invaders.

Finn mac Cumaill (Mod. Ir. Fionn Mac Cumhaill) is the leader of a band (or bands) of hunter-warriors. The Irish word for such a band was *fían*, and it is from this that the Fenian Cycle (Early Ir. *fíanaigecht*, Mod. Ir. *fiannaíocht*) derives its name. It recounts Finn's exploits, and those of his followers, as they hunt, fight, conduct raids, and live an open-air nomadic life. It is sometimes called the Finn Cycle, and yet another name for it is the Ossianic Cycle, after Finn's son Oisín, the Scottish Gaelic form of which is Oisean. The oldest texts, which are very short, date from the seventh century onwards. The twelfth century saw the composition of *Acallam na Senórach*, "The Colloquy of the Ancient Men," and the formation of a ballad literature about the Fíana. *Acallam na Senórach* has recently been translated by Ann Dooley and Harry Roe as *Tales of the Elders of Ireland* (1999). Ballads and poems continued to be composed after the twelfth century and there were also new prose tales. The Fenian material is abundantly represented in the folk tradition of the twentieth century.

This was to become the best known of the cycles outside Ireland and Scotland, thanks to the Scotsman James Macpherson. He published two works, *Fingal* (1762) and *Temora* (1763), and claimed that they were translated from epic poems composed by "Ossian" in the third and fourth centuries A.D. While a vigorous debate was to ensue as to the authenticity of these works, they did enjoy an enormous vogue in Romantic Europe, and the names of Fingal (Macpherson's version of Finn), Ossian, and Ossian's son Oscar were widely known in the nineteenth century (Knott and Murphy 1966, 145–46).

Finn was assigned a place in the synthetic history that was concocted in the Irish schools: he is there said to have been captain of the professional soldiery of Cormac mac Airt in the early third century A.D. Gerard Murphy points out (Knott and Murphy 1966, 147–48) that both the oldest stories about Finn and modern folklore point definitely to Finn's having been originally a mythological figure, and he shows that Finn is comparable in some important respects to the god Lug. Just as Lug opposes the one-eyed Balar, whose eye used to burn up whatever it looked on directly, Finn likewise has for his chief opponent Áed who was nicknamed Goll: Áed means "fire" and Goll means "one-eyed." Finn's opposition to what Rees and Rees have called "a supernatural malevolent burner" (1961, 66) is a recurrent element in the cycle. One of the manifestations of this burner is Aillén mac Midna who, blowing fire from his mouth, burned Tara every Samain (Halloween). Finn kills Aillén as he is about to escape into a *síd* 'Otherworld Dwelling' (Dooley and Roe 1999, 52–54). Another point of comparison, which has been noted by Alwyn and Brinley Rees, is that Finn ousts from the *síd* of Almu his maternal grandfather, Tadg son of Núadu, who was responsible for the slaying of Finn's father by Goll/Áed, and that in tales recorded in the modern period, Balar (who, it will be remembered, is Lug's maternal grandfather) is responsible for the death of Lug's father.[2]

Like Cú Chulainn, Finn is credited with a number of "Boyhood Deeds" (Nagy 1985, 209–18), for which we depend upon what Murphy describes as the "poorly constructed but valuable account" of an incomplete text in a manuscript of the fifteenth century (Knott and Murphy 1966, 156). Finn, we are told, was born after the slaying of his father, and he was brought up secretly in the wild by two women-warriors (*fénnidi*) because his life was in danger. He is triumphant in contests with other boys, shows himself superior to his elders at deer hunting, and acquires arms and vanquishes a wild beast. He avenges his father's killing and acquires his father's treasure. He then goes on to acquire wisdom: he studies the craft of poetry under Finn Éices ("Finn the Poet"). One day he burns his thumb on the "salmon of wisdom" and when he bites his thumb truth is revealed to him. The "thumb of wisdom" is his from then on. A further defining adventure awaits him: he slays Aed, son of Fidga, with a poisonous spear that he has acquired from Fíacail ("Tooth") son of Conchenn ("Doghead"), a spear that, if left in the *síd*, could cause rabies in the land. This is Finn's Samain adventure: he acts when the *síde* are open and the murderous Aed is passing from one *síd* to another. Finn acquires the spear as a reward for his wonderful deed.

The "Boyhood Deeds" of Cú Chulainn and of Finn define them as heroes. And we see from these adventures that the heroism of one will be very different from that of the other. As Nagy (1984) has shown, Cú Chulainn's "Boyhood Deeds" have to do with the integration of the hero into Ulster society, whereas those of Finn emphasize his extra-social character. Sjoestedt drew a distinction between "the hero of the tribe" (Cú Chulainn) and "the heroes outside the tribe" (the *fían*-warriors). This distinction has won wide acceptance, and it is appropriate to quote Sjoestedt's remarks at some length:

> Passing from the legend of Cú Chulainn to the legends of the Fíana, one has the impression of entering a heroic world which is not only different from that in which the tribal hero moves, but irreconcilable with it. The two bodies of tradition have some conceptions in common: the same fusion of warrior and magician in the person of hero-magicians, the same constant coming and going between the world of men and the world of the *Síde*, between sacred and profane. But in other respects the contrast seems complete. It is not merely a difference of formal character, details of manners, techniques of warfare, here on foot or on horseback, there in a chariot; it is a difference of function, ... of the position which the hero occupies in society and in the world. Cú Chulainn finds his place quite naturally, though it is a dominant place, in Celtic society as we know it not only from the sagas but from history.... Finn with his bands of warriors (*fíana*) is by definition outside the tribal institutions: he is the living negation of the spirit which dominates them. (Sjoestedt 1949, 81)

Recent scholarship has explored the extent to which *fiannas*, the activity of the *fían*, lies outside the tribal institutions, and this exploration has focused primarily on *díberg*, which has the meaning "brigandage," and in Old Irish denotes in particular the activity of organized bands of killers that had their own code of conduct, entailing a vow of evil and the wearing of diabolical marks. McCone (1986, 6) suggests that "*fiannas* denoted *fían*-activity in general, whereas *díberg* had a more specialized reference to a particularly nasty aspect of it that early churchmen were prone to emphasize in order to discredit the institution as a whole." He has also noted that in some sources no significant difference is made between membership of a *fían* and the practice of *díberg* (McCone 1986, 4–5). One of those sources is "The Destruction of Da Derga's Hostel," which I shall discuss presently.

Among the many kings who feature in the Cycles of the Kings, Cormac mac Airt and Conaire Mór, two legendary kings of Tara, are of especial interest. Cormac, son of Art and grandson of Conn of the Hundred Battles, is a prestige ancestor of the Uí Néill and the ideal king of Irish tradition (Ó Cathasaigh 1977). In his birth-tale we are told that he was conceived on the eve of the prehistoric Battle of Mag Mucrama, in which Art and his Munster ally Éogan were slain by Lugaid Mac Con, who thereupon seized the kingship of Tara. The child is abducted by a she-wolf, who rears him with her whelps. He is later rescued and returned to his mother along with the whelps. One day Lugaid Mac Con pronounces a false judgment. The Queen's garden has been stripped of its woad by some sheep owned by another woman. Lugaid decrees that the sheep should be forfeit. Cormac mac Airt, who is present, demurs, saying that only the wool should be forfeit, on the principle of "one shearing for another": the woad will grow again, and so should the wool. Cormac's judgment exemplifies *fír flathemon*, "the truth and justice of a ruler," and he is elected to the kingship of Tara in place of Lugaid. Cormac's reign is a Golden Age of peace and plenty in Ireland.

The central role of *fír flathemon* in the Irish ideology of kingship, which is expressed in narrative form in the tales on Cormac, is also reflected in the laws and in the wisdom texts, and above all in *Audacht Moraind*, "The Testament of Morann" (Kelly 1976). This is a seventh-century example of the genre known as *Speculum Principum* ("Mirror of Princes"). It consists of advice supposedly sent by the legendary judge Morann mac Moín to Feradach

Find Fechtnach, who is about to be made king. Much of what Morann has to say concerns *fír flathemon*: it keeps plagues and lightning from the people, and it ensures peace and prosperity in the realm, as well as abundance of milk and corn and fish, and fertility among the people.

The tragic story of Conaire Mór ("the Great") is told in *Togail Bruidne Da Derga*, "The Destruction of Da Derga's Hostel" (trans. Gantz 1981, 60–106), a composite text compiled, probably in the eleventh century, from earlier materials, perhaps including two ninth-century versions of the story. Much of the tale is devoted to the circumstances leading to Conaire's death in the Otherworld abode (*bruiden*) of Da Derga, but it is nevertheless a biography of Conaire, dealing in turn with his conception and birth, his boyhood, his elevation to kingship, the golden years of his reign, and the events leading to his death. The circumstances of Conaire's conception and birth indicate that he is destined for greatness. The hero's mother is a virgin, lowly of status but not of descent, who is deliberately rendered difficult of access. She is nevertheless overpowered by a bird that assumes human shape. He sleeps with her and tells her that a son, Conaire, will be born of their encounter. And so it comes to pass. Meanwhile, Etarscélae, king of Tara, has taken the woman as his wife, and Conaire is brought up as Etarscélae's son. He is fostered with the three sons of a *fían*-warrior named Donn Désa.

When Etarscélae dies, Conaire is visited by Nemglan, a bird-man who declares himself to be king of Conaire's father's birds. He instructs Conaire to go to Tara naked and bearing a sling. Conaire does so, and in the meantime it has been revealed to the wise men there that the future king will arrive at Tara in this way. The people of Tara question the revelation, on the grounds that Conaire is too young to be king. Conaire satisfies them that his youth is no obstacle, and they then enthusiastically accept him as their king.

At this point we are given a list of the taboos of Conaire Mór, listing certain actions that he should avoid in his reign. The early years of Conaire's reign are described as a golden age of great bounty. But a threat to these paradisal conditions arises when Conaire's foster-brothers, the sons of Donn Désa, yearn for the thieving and robbery and brigandage and murder which their father and grandfather used to commit. They test the mettle of the king by indulging in theft. When this is brought to the attention of the king, he declines to punish them. And so they are emboldened to advance in crime from theft to brigandage (*díberg*). Now one of the taboos laid upon Conaire was that there should not be any *díberg* during his reign. He has brought about the infraction of one of his taboos by failing to take action against his foster-brothers when they had engaged in the lesser crime of theft.

Conaire makes further difficulties for himself when his foster-brothers and their companions in the crime of brigandage are brought before him for judgment. He decrees that his foster-brothers should be set free, but that the others should die. He immediately recognizes that this is a false judgment, and reverses it. He banishes all of the brigands overseas. As soon as the king's judgment has been given and the brigands have departed, we hear that the perfect peace that had been enjoyed during Conaire's reign has broken down. Conaire finds himself in circumstances that impel him to transgress his remaining taboos. He takes a path that leads him to his doom in the *bruiden*. He encounters a number of malevolent Otherworld beings along the way, and in the meantime his foster-brothers and their allies return to Ireland and assail Conaire in the *bruiden* which they set on fire three times. Conaire's head is cut off, and when at length the severed head is given a drink of water, Conaire dies.

Conaire's tragedy is that he allowed his love of his foster-brothers to deflect him from his duty as king. In this respect he stands in contrast to them: they love him too, but their first concern is their inherited calling as brigands, and their primary loyalty is to their fellow-brigands, who insist that Conaire be put to death. Conaire's placing of his personal feelings above the requirements of his office also contrasts with Cú Chulainn's willingness in the *Táin* to slay his beloved foster-brother Fer Diad when the interests of Ulster are at stake.

The early Irish storytellers were fascinated by the transcendental mysteries of birth and death. I should like to end with an anecdote of threefold death that is recounted (in Latin) in Adomnán's Life of Colum Cille:

> Once, this priest called Findchán, a soldier of Christ, brought with him from Ireland to Britain a man of the race of Ulster and of royal stock yet wearing a cleric's habit. His name was Áed Dub, and it was intended that he should remain for a number of years as a pilgrim in Findchán's monastery. This Áed Dub had been a very bloody man and had killed many people, among them Diarmait mac Cerbaill, ordained by God's will as king of all Ireland. This same Áed, having spent some time in pilgrimage, was ordained priest in Findchán's monastery, but the ordination was invalid even though a bishop had been brought. This was because the bishop had not dared to place his hand on Áed's head

until Findchán (who had a carnal love for Áed) had first laid his right hand on his head in confirmation.

When this ordination was later made known to the saint, he took it ill, pronouncing thereupon this fearful judgment on Findchán and Áed, now ordained, saying: "That right hand which Findchán, against the law of God and of the Church, laid on the head of a son of perdition will soon grow rotten. It will give him great pain, and be dead and buried before him though he will live many years after his hand is buried. Áed, however, who was ordained unfittingly, will return as a dog to his vomit; he will again be a bloody murderer and in the end, killed by a spear, he will fall from wood into water and die drowning. He deserved such an end to life long ago for killing the king of all Ireland."

The blessed man's prophecy concerning both of them was fulfilled. First, the right fist of the priest Findchán became rotten and preceded him into the earth, being buried on the island called Ommon. The man himself, in accordance with St Columba's words, lived on for many years. Áed Dub, priest in name only, returned to his old wickedness and, being pierced by a treacherous spear, he fell from the prow of a ship into the waters of a lake and perished. (Sharpe 1991a, 138–39)

In Irish tales of threefold death an offence is committed, there is a prophecy that the delinquent will die in three different ways, and in due course the prophecy is fulfilled. In this short anecdote Áed Dub offends in no less than four ways: he commits regicide, he is improperly ordained, he has a great deal of blood on his hands, and he commits a sexual sin. These offences can be interpreted in terms of the Dumézilian functions: regicide and improper ordination are sins in the domain of the sacred; excessive use of physical force is a sin of the second function; and sexuality is assigned to the third. And the punishment fits the crime: a good deal of evidence supports the view that falling through the air, being pierced by a spear, and drowning also belong to the first, second, and third functions (Sayers 1992; see also "The Threefold Death," chap. 7 in this volume). This anecdote is interesting in all sorts of ways, but not the least of them is the use of a symmetrical trifunctional anecdote of threefold death as evidence of the prophetic power of a great Irish saint. Colum Cille, as we have seen, is especially associated with confluence of native tradition and monastic culture. It is appropriate that the Life written about a century after his death should contain such a remarkable product of that confluence.

THEMES

2

The Semantics of *síd*

(1977-79)

The occurrence in Old Irish of the formally identical pair *1 síd/síth* 'Otherworld hill or mound,' and *2 síd/síth* 'peace,' naturally invites speculation as to whether they are etymologically related. Stokes[1] suggested plausibly that the words may have come from the same root (**sed-*), but he did not go so far as to claim that they were ultimately one and the same. Pokorny[2] seems to have been the first to claim that these homonyms were originally identical, and he compared English *settlement*. The matter has been taken up again in the recent fasciculus of the etymological dictionary:[3] the editors note the suggestion that the two words are identical in origin, but (like the editors of *DIL*, s.vv.) they do not commit themselves for or against it. They do go on to say that the homonymy has given rise in the native tradition to "jeux de mots," referring by way of example to *LU* line 9999. Here they are following Thurneysen,[4] both in making the point and in adducing this example, which is a sentence from the early Old Irish text *Echtrae Chonnlai*.⁵ This text is of first importance as an expression of the Irish conception of the Otherworld, and the sentence in question will provide a convenient starting point for a study of the semantics of our two homonyms. But it needs to be considered afresh, since the existence of the pun which Thurneysen saw in the text is not acknowledged by either of its modern editors;⁶ regrettably, neither of them gives his reasons for rejecting it.

The relevant sentence occurs in the opening sequence of the text. What happens is that Connlae sees "a woman in wonderful attire" approach him, and he asks her whence she has come. This is her reply:⁷

> I come from the Lands of the Living, a place in which there is neither death nor sin nor transgression. We enjoy lasting feasts without toil and peace (*caínchomracc*) without strife. *Síd már i táam, conid de suidiu no-nn-ainmnigther áess Síde.*

If this last sentence were divorced from its context, one would certainly translate *síd* as "Otherworld (dwelling)" or the like, and that is indeed how Pokorny takes it: "Ein grosser Elfenhügel ist's, in dem wir wohnen, deshalb nennt man uns das Síd-Volk."⁸ The "jeu de mots" arises from allowing the context to dictate a different interpretation of *síd* here, as in Thurneysen's translation: "wir leben in grossem frieden (*síd*); deshalb nennt man uns síd-leute."⁹ Thus, following Pokorny, *síd* can be taken as a gloss, as it were, upon "The Lands of the Living," and in fact the Otherworld domain in question is called Síd mBoadaig later in the text (§5). Thurneysen's rendering, on the other hand, implies that *síd már i táam* extends the reference to "peace without strife." It is impossible to be absolutely sure about the author's intentions, but there are good reasons for supposing that there is a deliberate pun here. First, there is the general point that the Irish literati were much given to wordplay, especially in explanation of names, so that the very possibility of a pun in an "etymological" context of this kind is enough to suggest that it is deliberate. Second, it is likely that the author of *Echtrae Chonnlai* would have wished to exploit the ambivalence of *síd*, since the Otherworld is a major theme of his story: Oskamp argues that its "main motif" is "the opposition between this world and the otherworld, and between mortals and immortals."¹⁰ Finally, it is the purpose of this note to show that there is a semantic nexus between the two denotations of *síd*, and this could scarcely be unfamiliar ground to one as well-versed in Irish tradition as the author of *Echtrae Chonnlai* would have been. In any case, he does explicitly and unambiguously identify peace (*caínchomracc cen debuith*) as a condition of the Otherworld, so that to deny him a pun here would be as much as to say that he was unaware of the ambivalence of *síd*.

I suspect that the original pun was on *áess síde* as Otherworld people and people of peace, and that *síd már i táam* may not have stood in the original text. The reading *de suidiu*, upon which both Thurneysen and Pokorny base their interpretation of the sentence, is well founded in the manuscripts of Version I. On the other hand, two of the manuscripts of that version read respectively *desuidib* (YBL[2]) and *ti suigib* (Egerton 88, for *di suidib*), while both manuscripts of Version II have *desuidib*. This indicates that *de suidib* may be the original reading. Moreover, it is difficult to see why *de suidib* should have been substituted for *de suidiu* in this context, whereas the opposite change can easily be explained. I would retrace the development as follows. (1) The woman's description of the Lands of the Living was as translated above, and was followed by *conid de suidib* . . . , "It is on account of those . . . ," where *suidib* refers to the feasts and the peace enjoyed in the Otherworld. (2) *Síd már i táam* was inserted as a gloss on *caínchomracc lenn cen debuith*. The Irish mania for glossing texts was no less marked than their devotion to wordplay, and items which originated as glosses were frequently embodied in the texts by subsequent copyists. *Síd* occurs elsewhere as a gloss on *caínchomracc*,[11] and apart from that the glossator might have felt that *áess síde* was not explained with sufficient clarity or explicitness by the unglossed text. Furthermore, such an origin for *síd már i táam* could account for its peculiar syntax.[12] (3) Once this gloss became embodied in the main text, it would have been natural to regard *síd* here as an explanation of *áess síde*: hence the substitution of *de suidiu* 'on that account.'

Whichever way we choose to read the text, a connection between peace and the Otherworld is clearly stated in *Echtrae Chonnlai*, and while the *áess síde* are doubtless so called because they are denizens of the Otherworld, it will be seen in what follows that "people of peace" would be no less apt a designation.

As well as being an Otherworld tale, *Echtrae Chonnlai* belongs to the literature of kingship, at least in being attached to Dál Cuinn: Connlae is son of the eponymous Conn, who also plays his part in the story. The key to the semantics of *síd* is to be found in the central role of the king in Irish political ideology, a fairly consistent view of which emerges from the sagas, the laws, and the wisdom literature.[13] The king is the center of the cosmos: the distinguishing characteristic of the just and righteous king is called *fír flathemon* (lit., "prince's truth"), and when the king is possessed of this all is right with his world. The doctrine on *fír flathemon* is set out in the celebrated wisdom text *Audacht Moraind*, of which the earliest recension, believed to be of seventh-century date, has been edited by Fergus Kelly.[14] Much the same doctrine finds narrative expression in some of the king-tales, notably those of the legendary kings of Tara, Cormac mac Airt and Conaire Mór. Two points are relevant to the present discussion: first, that legitimate kingship has its source in the Otherworld, and, second, that the reign of the righteous king is marked by peace (as well as plenty) in the land. That is as much as to say that *1 síd* denotes the source of *fír flathemon*, and *2 síd* its symptom.

It is not, of course, at all remarkable that a state of internal peace should be expected to characterize a land ruled over by a worthy king, and we find due reference to this in *Audacht Moraind*: "It is through *fír flathemon* that the ruler secures peace (*síd*), tranquility, joy, ease and comfort."[15] While this may seem commonplace enough as a general observation, I shall argue below that the detailed descriptions of the state of peace secured through *fír flathemon* are of particular significance. But first, having seen the evidence of *Audacht Moraind* that *2 síd* was a symptom of *fír flathemon*, I must establish that the Otherworld was considered to be its source. *Audacht Moraind* itself is silent on this point, but the Otherworld dimension of kingship is abundantly documented elsewhere in Irish literature. For reasons of space, I shall limit myself here to discussing two texts which, though very different in character, both show the king as deriving his legitimacy from the Otherworld. They are *Echtrae Chormaic* and *Togail Bruidne Da Derga*, and they relate respectively to Cormac mac Airt and Conaire Mór, two kings who "exemplify in a special fashion the function of the prehistoric kings of Tara."[16]

Cormac's Otherworld adventure, *Echtrae Chormaic*,[17] tells how Cormac sets out in pursuit of a stranger who has taken off Cormac's daughter, son, and wife. A great mist falls and Cormac finds himself alone on a plain. Having witnessed a number of marvels, Cormac goes into a palace where he is welcomed by a handsome warrior and a beautiful girl. In the evening a man arrives with a pig which can be roasted only if a truth be told for each quarter. Three truths are told, and then it is Cormac's turn. Cormac tells the story of his wife, son, and daughter, and the whole pig is then found to be done. Cormac's family are restored to him, the warrior gives him a golden cup which distinguishes truth from falsehood, and he gives him a magic branch. He reveals that he is Manannán mac Lir, king of *Tír Tairngiri* 'The Land of Promise,' and that it was to show Cormac *Tír Tairngiri* that he brought him there. On the next morning when Cormac rises, he finds himself at Tara with his wife, son, and daughter, and the golden cup and the branch.

There could be no clearer account, in terms of Irish tradition, of the Otherworld dimension of kingship. The quality (*fír*) which characterizes the worthy king reigns supreme in the Otherworld: the roasting of the pig exemplifies the Act of Truth, based on a belief in the magic power of truth.[18] Cormac is subjected to a test, and by telling a true story he proves himself worthy of kingship. Moreover, in acquiring a magic cup which can distinguish truth from falsehood, and which we are told does not survive after Cormac's death, he acquires his functional attribute as a worthy and righteous king. Finally, Cormac's wife, Eithne Thóebḟota,[19] is a version of the chthonic goddess of sovereignty, so that in taking her back from the Otherworld, Cormac is in effect validating his title to kingship.[20] I may add that in *Baile in Scáil*[21] the theme of the Otherworld as source of kingship is found in relation to Cormac's grandfather Conn, and in *Echtrae Airt*[22] it is associated with Cormac's father, Art.

The account of the Otherworld origin of Conaire Mór's kingship, as we find it in *Togail Bruidne Da Derga* (*TBDD*),[23] is very different from the foregoing, but its general import is the same. Although much the greater part of *TBDD* is devoted to his downfall, the tale is really a biography of Conaire, dealing in turn with his conception and birth, his boyhood, his elevation to kingship, the golden years of his reign, and turning only then to the tragic story of his doom. Conaire is already marked out for greatness by the manner of his conception and birth. Although he is brought up as son of Etarscélae, king of Tara, the latter is not his biological father. His mother Mess Búachalla is granddaughter of King Echaid Feidlech and the beautiful Étaín who was born in a *síd*. On the night before she marries Etarscélae, Mess Búachalla sees a bird on the skylight coming to her. The bird leaves his "bird-skin" on the floor and ravishes her. He tells her that she will be pregnant by him and bear a son (who must not kill birds), and that Conaire should be his name. The prophecy is fulfilled. And later, when Etarscélae dies and a successor must be chosen for him, the young Conaire is instructed by Nemglan, "the king of your father's birds," and, having acted accordingly, Conaire is proclaimed king. Thus, it is the bird-man—clearly an Otherworld personage—who calls Conaire to his destiny as king. Nemglan lays a number of injunctions (or "taboos") upon Conaire, and these constitute in effect a contract with the Otherworld. So long as Conaire observes these injunctions his reign (*ind énflaith*, "the bird-reign") is prodigiously prosperous, being marked by abundance, by peace and amity among his people, and by good weather.

The *TBDD* account of the election of Conaire Mór, as I hope to show in a future article, reflects a ritualistic scenario comprising three parts: designation by the gods, recognition by the wise men, and acceptance by the people. This is the structure also of the election of the ancient Hindu king Prthu, as analyzed by Dumézil.[24] The comparison does not end there, since Prthu, like Conaire, consults the wise men, is instructed in the duties of a king, and his reign too was a Golden Age. For present purposes, however, it has been sufficient to isolate for attention the Otherworld intervention in Conaire's elevation to kingship.

Both our kings, then, are depicted as having had their kingship sanctioned by Otherworld personages—Cormac by Manannán mac Lir, Conaire by Nemglan. And they are both explicitly credited with bringing about a state of *síd* 'peace': of Cormac it is said that there was *síth n-oll co rían ina ré*, "great peace as far as the sea in his reign";[25] of Conaire we are told in *TBDD* that there was perfect peace in his reign (*lánsíth i nÉrinn i flaith Conaire*, line 229). These kings exemplify the source and symptom nexus of which the homonymy of *síd* provides the lexical correlative. A further connection between *1 síd* and *2 síd* arises at this point, for the kingdom which enjoys internal peace mirrors in some measure the conditions of the Otherworld as they are set forth in such texts as *Echtrae Chonnlai* and *Immram Brain*.[26] The ideal conditions enjoyed during the reign of Conaire Mór are described as follows in *TBDD* (lines 182 ff.):

> Now there were in his reign great bounties, that is, seven ships in every June of every year arriving (?) at Inber Colbtha, and oak-mast up to the knees in every autumn, and . . . such abundance of peace (*caínchomracc*) that no man slew another in Ireland during his reign. And

to every man in Ireland the voice of his fellow seemed as sweet as harp-strings. From mid-spring to mid-autumn no wind disturbed a cow's tail. His reign was neither thunderous nor stormy.

There is a similar description later in the text (lines 487 ff.), where the good weather and natural abundance of his reign are again described. Here it is said that "[i]n his reign it seems to every man in Ireland that the voice of his fellow is as sweet as harp-strings because of the excellence of the law and the peace (*ar febus na cána 7 in tsída 7 in chaínchomraic*) which obtain throughout Ireland."

These passages describe the Golden Age enjoyed in the mythical past. It is significant that neither of them is modelled stylistically on the classic accounts of the Otherworld: if they were, we would be entitled to suspect that we had to do with a literary topos, taken over from the *echtrai* and *immrama*. As well as the stylistic differences, certain Otherworld features are lacking in this Golden Age—here there is, inevitably, no talk of immortality, nor is there any explicit mention of sin. What we are given in these passages in *TBDD* is an account of the ideal conditions enjoyed in the mythical past, which is independent of literary descriptions of the Otherworld, but shares with them their paradisal character. The Golden Age is separated in time, the Otherworld in space from the storyteller and his audience: they are different responses to the yearning for an ideal world. The essential congruence of these two expressions of the paradisal state is explicitly recognized in a text on Cormac mac Airt which does draw upon the literary descriptions of the Otherworld: there it is said that "Ireland became a Land of Promise during his reign" (*Dorigne tra tir tairngire d'Erinn ana ré*).[27] This might almost be a gloss on the description already quoted from another text of the conditions in Ireland during Cormac's reign: *síth n-oll co rían ina ré*. The state of peace secured by the kings of the mythical past, whose kingship was sanctioned by the Otherworld, is seen as a re-creation in this world of the paradisal condition. Thus, in its highest form, *2 síd* is a simulacrum of *1 síd*.

The Otherworld interventions in the affairs of men are not always benign, and the Otherworld dimension of kingship has its dark side. What the gods bestow, they can also take away, and the story of Conaire's downfall in *TBDD* shows a succession of malevolent Otherworld beings drawing him inexorably to his doom in the *bruiden* of Da Derga, which is itself, as O'Rahilly persuasively argued, a localization of the Otherworld.[28] But Conaire brings all this upon himself by failing to check the unlawful activities of his beloved foster-brothers, thereby transgressing one of the injunctions laid upon him at the beginning of his reign by Nemglan the birdman. Some time after Conaire's elevation to kingship his foster-brothers take to thieving. This they do in order to see what punishment the king might inflict upon them and how the theft in his reign might damage him. The victim of their crime complains to the king each year, but Conaire refuses to punish his foster-brothers. They are therefore emboldened to advance in crime from thieving (*gat*) to marauding (*díberg*). This is a disastrous development for Conaire, for one of the injunctions laid upon Conaire by Nemglan was that there should not be *díberg* in his reign: by failing to punish his foster-brothers for their earlier and less serious crime of theft he causes the violation of one of his own taboos. Conaire further departs from the path of just and righteous kingship when his foster-brothers and their companions in crime are brought before him, for he delivers a false judgment, decreeing that the others should be killed by their fathers but that his foster-brothers should be spared.[29] This is accepted by Conaire's subjects, but he himself sees its injustice, and he revokes it, saying, "The judgment I have given is no extension of life to me": he ordains that all the marauders should be spared and banished overseas to Alba. Ironically, even this revised judgment proves "no extension of life" to Conaire, for in due course the marauders whom he has spared return to add their efforts to those of the malevolent Otherworld beings in bringing about the destruction of Conaire Mór.

Conaire's offence here has two parts: he offends against the Otherworld in transgressing a taboo, and against *fír flathemon* in giving a false judgment. This provides us with an Irish example of an old Indo-European theme, what Dumézil has called "the single sin of the sovereign": "single but irreparable, for it destroys either the raison d'être of sovereignty, namely the protection of the order founded on truth . . . , or the mystical support of human sovereignties, namely the respect for the superior sovereignty of the gods and the sense of the limitations inherent in every human delegation of that divine sovereignty. The king falls prey to one or the other of these risks, which . . . are at bottom reducible to the same thing."[30] This formulation, written without any reference to Conaire Mór, nevertheless stands as an excellent summary of the central theme of *TBDD*, save that in this case the king falls prey to both of the "risks" described by Dumézil. In giving the false judgment, he destroys the protection of the order founded on truth (*fír*), while the transgression of the taboo destroys the respect of the Otherworld beings who have delegated sovereignty to him.

The result of Conaire's sin is similarly in accord with Dumézil's account of "[t]he blow, administered without delay and with no possibility of redress, which destroys all the roots and fruits of a most excellent good fortune."[31] In *TBDD*, no sooner has the king's judgment been given and the marauders banished than we hear that the perfect peace (*lán-síth*) that had been enjoyed during Conaire's reign has broken down, and Conaire, in violation of another of Nemglan's injunctions, sets out to restore peace. When he seeks to return to Tara he finds that he cannot do so, for the lands round about are full of bands of raiders coming from every side, men roam about naked, and the land is all on fire. He is told that this is a sign that the law has broken down there (*isí in cháin ro mebaid and*). And so Conaire turns away and, successively transgressing further taboos, he travels along the path which leads him to his doom in the *bruiden*.

It may be noted in passing that the end of the Golden Age, which is the result of Conaire's sin, is stated in terms of the break-down of *síth* and *cáin* ("law") in the land. The word for 'peace' in Modern Irish is *síocháin* (< *síthcháin*), a compound of *síd/síth+cáin*.[32] *DIL* takes the first element to be *1 síd* (that is, the Otherworld *síd*). It is an interesting conceit, and cannot altogether be ruled out in view of my argument that the Otherworld is the source of *fír flathemon* and hence of peace, and further that a kingdom at peace mirrors the Otherworld. For all that, I suspect that it is no more than a slip on the part of the editors of *DIL*, and that they may have intended to write *2 síd*. The latter is given as the first element in *LEIA* R-S (122), and this seems the more likely explanation. The compound may be taken to underline the connection between strong and just rule on the one hand, and peace on the other.

The texts which I have chosen show a clear relationship between the Otherworld and peace, mediated in the person of the king. I have not concerned myself with the date of these texts, for late as they may be in their extant forms, they do reflect ancient tradition. Both in its account of the accession to kingship of Conaire Mór, and in that of his downfall, *TBDD* reflects with remarkable fidelity Indo-European themes which have been established by Dumézil on the basis of other texts. Elsewhere I have given reasons for supposing that *Echtrae Chormaic* may reflect the adaptation of the old and widely distributed Bear-son legend to the Irish ideology of kingship.[33] What we find in these and many other Irish texts is an ancient ideology refracted through literature. To quote Dumézil once more: "A literary work does not have to set forth a theory: it is the hearer's or the reader's task to perceive the providential design which has arranged the events in the order in which the work presents them and with the results it describes. Yet it is the design that justifies these events and results, and gives them a meaning."[34] The providential design which underlies these texts is that expressed in the doctrine of *fír flathemon*. Dillon has argued persuasively that this doctrine is an inheritance from Indo-European culture, one of a number of items preserved in Ireland, on the margin of the Indo-European area, though lost in most other regions of the West.[35] Wagner concedes the antiquity of *fír flathemon*, but he dissents from Dillon's view of its Indo-European character.[36] It will be clear from my recourse to Dumézil that I am accepting the Indo-European hypothesis, and indeed my analysis of *TBDD* adds a further item to the already formidable body of correspondences which have been adduced in support of Dillon's view. The Otherworld of Irish tradition must also have its roots in ancient ideas;[37] what is to the point here is that the Otherworld dimension of kingship, expressed in narrative form in *Echtrae Chormaic* and *TBDD*, is likewise of great antiquity, and must be seen as an integral part of the ideology of kingship.

There is another connotation of *síd* which bears upon the relationship of the king to the Otherworld, and in particular the consecration of the king. We have seen that the kingdom aspires to the ideal condition of the Otherworld, and that only a just and righteous king, endowed with *fír flathemon*, can satisfy these aspirations. The ideology of kingship is matched by the symbols and rituals which surround the office, and especially by those attending the election and consecration of the king. All the studies of the inauguration of Irish kings, from John O'Donovan's classic account of 1844,[38] to Myles Dillon's lecture published posthumously in 1973,[39] show the truth of F. J. Byrne's remark that "the ceremonies which attended the inauguration of Irish kings may have been as old as the tumuli on which they were performed."[40] I have chosen this quotation because it refers to inauguration on tumuli; compare the observation of Edmund Spenser: "They use to place him that shall be their Captain upon a stone, always reserved for that purpose, and placed commonly upon a hill."[41] Many of these

2. The Semantics of *síd*   29

tumuli or hills will doubtless have been *síde*, so that their use as inauguration sites furnishes the physical or material correlative of the abstract connections which I have been pursuing.

The connection between the Otherworld and conditions in this world, as mediated in the person of the king, is deeply embedded in the very ground-rock of Irish mythology and literature. It will be necessary now to turn to a closer consideration of the lexical situation, since it may be objected that the semantic nexus which I have been trying to establish is not fully borne out by the actual usage of *síd* in early Irish, insofar as *1 síd* is but one of a number of designations of the Otherworld, and *2 síd* but one component of the Golden Age secured by an ideal king. These facts cannot be ignored, but they will seem less weighty when it is remembered that we are talking about a homonymy which does exist. In any case, it seems only reasonable to regard *2 síd*, which denotes a state of peace, as an adequate general designation of the conditions of an ideal reign. It is in relation to *1 síd* that the real difficulty arises—not unnaturally, since the Irish conception of the Otherworld, as it is expressed in the literature, is extraordinarily complex. The character and nomenclature of the Otherworld show an admixture of native and ecclesiastical elements. A case in point is *Tír Tairngiri*, which came into Irish as a translation of *terra repromissionis* (the Promised Land of the Old Testament),[42] but which, as we have seen, is used in a thoroughly pagan context in *Echtrae Chormaic* as the name of the Otherworld domain presided over by Manannán mac Lir. Amidst all the confusion, however, *síd* enjoys a special status as a term for the Otherworld: it is the normal generic term which can be used without further definition to denote the Otherworld. It differs in this important respect from *Mag Mell*, *Tír na mBéo*, etc., which are descriptive terms.[43] It is true that, when used of a particular localization of the Otherworld, *síd* seems almost invariably to refer to a mound or tumulus, though *Echtrae Chonnlai* has provided us with an apparent exception in Síd mBoadaig.[44] These were doubtless the most vividly conceived of the Otherworld abodes, as they were certainly the most immediate and visible on the landscape. But when used less specifically in collocations such as *ben síde* it must mean simply "(the) Otherworld": thus, *ben síde* (or *ben a sídib*) 'goddess, woman of the Otherworld,' *fer síde* 'god, man of the Otherworld,' *áess síde* 'Otherworld folk, the gods.'

The most plausible explanation of this state of affairs is that the meaning of *síd* (or its etymon **sēdos*) has partly shifted from the general

(Otherworld) to the particular (hollow hill). We may compare Greek ἕδος, which in the meaning "seat, abode, dwelling place" is used especially of gods.[45] Latin *sēdes* 'id.' is used also of the temple and seat of the gods.[46] On the basis of the etymological evidence, it may be conjectured that the semantic prehistory of 1 *síd* was one of progressive specialization of meaning, narrowing from abode in general to abode of the gods in particular, and then from abode of the gods in general to hollow hill in particular.[47]

The use of this word, or of one based on it, to denote peace could logically have arisen at any stage in this progression. For an unsettled or migrant people, the notion of abode or settlement might readily be linked with that of peace. And this simple association of ideas could account not only for the Irish homonymy, but also for the occurrence of Latin *sēdāre* 'to appease,' beside *sēdes* 'abode,' and, coming nearer home, of Welsh *hedd* 'peace,' beside *sedd* 'seat.' But however the Irish homonymy originated, it must have become rooted at an early stage in the ideology of kingship which links the Otherworld with peace. And I shall end this note with a brief consideration of the Welsh pair, *sedd* and *hedd*, which, if I am not mistaken, will show that the relationship between them is conditioned by the same Indo-European (and a fortiori Common Celtic) ideology which underlies Irish *síd*.

The Otherworld of Welsh tradition (Annwfn) has much the same character as that depicted in Irish texts,[48] and while Irish influence may be detected in certain details of the Welsh accounts,[49] there can be little doubt that for the most part the Welsh conception of Annwfn derives independently from the Celtic Otherworld.[50] The Welsh *gorsedd* is etymologically a near-match for Irish *forad*,[51] and they have a somewhat similar range of meanings,[52] but *gorsedd* has in addition the Otherworld connotations of Irish *síd*.[53] As for the institution of kingship, Binchy has shown, by confronting the somewhat exiguous evidence of the innovative and dynamic Welsh texts with the more abundant testimony of the conservative and archaic Irish sources, that we may speak of a "Common Celtic" type of kingship.[54] Given that there are Welsh reflexes of the Celtic Otherworld and of Celtic kingship, we might hope to find, in Wales as in Ireland, literary expressions of the Otherworld dimension of kingship. And we have not far to seek, for the first part of *Pwyll* (the First Branch of the *Mabinogi*) supplies themes of kingship of the type we have seen in the Irish texts, and especially in *Echtrae Chormaic*.

The first part of *Pwyll* (*Pwyll I*, as it was dubbed by W. J. Gruffydd)[55] is an *echtrae* in all but name.[56] Pwyll Prince of Dyfed encounters Arawn king of Annwfn, and unwittingly offends him. In order to win Arawn's friendship, Pwyll is required to change places with him for a year, each of them taking the form of the other, and at the end of the year Pwyll must face Arawn's enemy Hafgan in single combat, and strike him one (and only one) fatal blow. Pwyll agrees to these terms and he is conveyed to Annwfn by Arawn. He spends the year there in Arawn's place, but each night when he goes to bed with Arawn's wife he chastely turns his back to her. At the year's end, he does as he was bidden, and defeats Hafgan in single combat, as a result of which Hafgan's realm is united with Arawn's. The next day Pwyll returns to Arawn, who thanks him for what he has done, restores his form and takes back his own. Each of them then returns to his own kingdom. Arawn learns from his wife how Pwyll had been faithful to him, and Pwyll in turn discovers that his land of Dyfed was ruled better than ever before when Arawn was there in Pwyll's guise. From that time on the friendship between Pwyll and Arawn increases. The name Pwyll Prince of Dyfed falls into disuse, and he is called Pwyll Head of Annwfn ever after.

The motifs used in the composition of this tale are for the most part not those of *Echtrae Chormaic*, although of course they are all drawn from a common store. But the basic pattern of the two stories is identical: the sojourn of the hero (Cormac, Pwyll) in the Otherworld (Tír Tairngiri, Annwfn) is brought about by its king (Manannán, Arawn). Cormac and Pwyll are tested in the Otherworld, and they are not found wanting. They then return to their own kingdoms, where they are enabled to rule prosperously.

The tests to which the heroes are submitted—Cormac must tell a truth (*fír*), Pwyll must face an adversary in single combat—serve one and the same function in this scenario, but the affinity of the two tests lies deeper than that. Thomas Charles-Edwards has shown that Pwyll's duel with Hafgan is to be compared with the Ordeal by Battle described in Irish texts and known in Irish as *fír fer* (lit., "men's truth").[57] This Ordeal by Battle, like Cormac's Act of Truth, reflects a belief in the all-embracing power of truth;[58] the emphasis in the one case is on valor, in the other on truthfulness. It can scarcely be fortuitous that there is a parallel difference of emphasis between the Cauldron of the Head of Annwfn and Cormac's Cup. We have already seen that Cormac's Cup, which Manannán bestowed upon him in the Otherworld, can distinguish between truth and falsehood; according to the early Welsh poem "The Spoils of Annwfn,"[59] the Cauldron of the Head of Annwfn "will not boil the food of a coward."[60] The similarity between these two "testing talismans" has been noted by Loomis,[61] although he does not mention the association of the Irish cup with Cormac, something which is crucial to the present argument. Since Pwyll has the title Head of Annwfn, the Welsh talisman could well be called "Pwyll's Cauldron." Thus, the comparison between Pwyll and Cormac is reinforced by the fact that the Welsh cauldron is sensitive to courage, and the Irish cup to truthfulness, since this difference reflects precisely that between the tests to which the two heroes are subjected in the Otherworld. Rachel Bromwich has suggested that there may have been a group of stories in Welsh which connected a number of heroes with Otherworld visits, from which they returned, like Cormac mac Airt, with magic treasures.[62] Unhappily, although there is a tantalizing reference in "The Spoils of Annwfn" to "the story of Pwyll and Pryderi," no tale has come down to us of how Pwyll won the cauldron from the Otherworld.

If the hero of *Pwyll* differs from Cormac in returning from the Otherworld without a magic treasure, he nevertheless does not return empty-handed, for he has secured the lasting friendship of the king of the Otherworld. The Welsh term (*cerennyd*) used for the "friendship" which Pwyll wins from Arawn by killing Hafgan suggests a formal legal relationship, a treaty between Dyfed and the Otherworld securing peace between them.[63] Pwyll, like Cormac, will now be in a position to rule prosperously, and the benefits which accrue to Dyfed are made clear in an important passage in the text. This occurs when Pwyll has returned from Annwfn and asks his men (who know nothing of Pwyll's absence) how his rule had been over them during the past year compared to what it had been before that. "Lord," they reply, "never was thy discernment so marked; never wast thou so lovable a man thyself; never wast thou so free in spending thy goods; never was thy rule better than during this year." Pwyll then explains what has happened. "Aye, lord," they say, "thank God thou hadst that friendship; and the rule we have had that year, surely, thou wilt not withhold from us?" "I will not, between me and God," answers Pwyll.[64] This passage shows that Dyfed had the benefit of Otherworld rule under Arawn, and that it will continue to do so under Pwyll, whose very name suggests that he is endowed with "discernment."⁶⁵ Because of Pwyll's sojourn in the Otherworld and his pact of friendship with its king, Dyfed now takes on something of the character of the Otherworld, and in this respect it bears comparison with Ireland in the reign of Cormac mac Airt, and in the reign of Conaire Mór before he broke faith with the Otherworld by transgressing one of his taboos.

All of this provides a context within which we may consider *sedd, hedd*. These are both from **sed-*, being differentiated by the initial and by gender.⁶⁶ The regular development of Proto-Indo-European *s-* in British is to *h-*, and *sedd* is one of a small number of exceptions to this rule. Jackson says of these exceptions that their history "suggests the capricious workings of various analogies."⁶⁷ It has possibly been retained (or restored) here on the analogy of the compound *gorsedd*, where the retention of *-s-* is regular, and this may have been prompted by a desire to establish (or maintain) a clear distinction between the two words.⁶⁸ In gender, *sedd* is feminine, *hedd* masculine, and they have been traced respectively to **sedā, *sedo-s*.⁶⁹ But *hedd* could just as well come from neuter **sedo-n*: Welsh offers no criterion for choosing between the two. We may therefore have recourse to the Irish evidence, and we find that Irish has several compounds (*cétad, forad*, etc.), all of them originally neuter *o*-stems. This tilts the balance in favor of neuter for Welsh also. There are then two possibilities: either the distinction of gender was originally feminine/neuter, or the distinction arose only when the neuter gender broke down in Welsh, and was originally feminine/masculine. If the latter is the correct explanation, British would have originally been at one with Goidelic in using the same word for "abode (of the gods)" and "peace"; it may be assumed, on the evidence of *gorsedd*, that *sedd* had Otherworld connotations.

The possibility that the original distinction was between feminine and neuter cannot be discounted, for it would represent a tendency, inherited from Indo-European, to exploit the semantic value of gender. Meillet⁷⁰ has adduced a large number of examples from various Indo-European languages in support of his argument that the basis of gender in the parent language was the distinction between animate and inanimate: "la catégorie du genre avait sa pleine valeur en indo-européen, c'est-à-dire dans la langue d'un peuple qui opposait d'une manière systématique et constante l'animé à l'inanimé."⁷¹ The animistic views which inform Meillet's discussion are not, so far as I know, now much in vogue, but they are perfectly appropriate to the opposition *sedd* (*gorsedd*) : *hedd*, which contrasts the Otherworld, peopled by personages who intervene decisively from time to time in the affairs of men, with the condition of peace which is in the gift of the Otherworld.

Whichever of these explanations is preferred, it can be said that the present contrast between *sedd* and *hedd* obscures an earlier situation which confirmed the evidence of the Welsh and Irish texts linking the notion of peace with the Otherworld. *Síd*, on the other hand, continued for a long time to denote both notions, and, on the evidence, it must be accounted (with *fír*) one of the most important items in the religiopolitical vocabulary of Old Irish.

3

Pagan Survivals
The Evidence of Early Irish Narrative

(1 9 8 4)

In 1902, W. G. Wood-Martin said: "Christianity is generally supposed to have annihilated heathenism in Ireland. In reality it merely smoothed over and swallowed its victim, and the contour of its prey, as in the case of the boa-constrictor, can be distinctly traced under the glistening colours of its beautiful skin. Paganism still exists, it is merely inside instead of outside."[1] The image of the boa-constrictor is striking, not to say startling, but the claim which it supports cannot be fully sustained: it is too much to say that the contour of pre-Christian Irish heathenism can be distinctly traced. On the other hand, Christianity is not now generally supposed to have annihilated heathenism in Ireland. So far as the early literature is concerned, opinions differ as to the balance between survival and innovation, but there can be no doubt that it is heavily indebted to the pagan tradition of pre-Christian

Ireland. Early medieval Ireland is, of course, by definition premodern, and so it is not at all surprising that such evidence as we have for the period should show that the manners and customs of the country were of a kind which we tend to find in premodern societies generally. What is remarkable about the Irish situation is the extent and richness of the vernacular literature which has come down to us from the early medieval period. Much of this literature is firmly rooted in ancient myth and remains robustly pagan in character; it has been used, along with other evidence, to build up at least a partial picture, not only of the pagan religion of the Irish, but also of that of the Celts, and it has even been laid under contribution in the comparative study of Indo-European mythology.

It has to be said that an immense amount of work remains to be done on early Irish literature: most of the texts stand in need of competent edition and translation, not to speak of interpretation and evaluation. The narrative material is only a part of this literature, but it is a considerable part; in treating such a subject in a short paper one must obviously be selective. I shall not attempt either to give an overview of early Irish narrative,[2] or to describe the considerable body of evidence on paganism which can be gleaned from it.[3] What I propose to do is to give some account of the ways in which the study of early Irish narrative has proceeded, to touch upon some of the problems which have arisen in the course of that study, and to exemplify these with reference to a short excerpt from what is perhaps our most important mythological text.

A framework of some kind is required so that we may order the critical theories and perspectives which have been brought to bear on early Irish narrative, and the one which I have chosen is that which was used by Meyer Abrams in his study of Romantic criticism,[4] and which comprises four co-ordinates: these he terms the *work*, the *artist*, the *universe*, and the *audience*.[5] One should perhaps explain what is meant by *universe* in this context. As Abrams puts it, "the work is taken to have a subject which, directly or deviously, is derived from existing things—to be about, or signify, or reflect something which either is, or bears some relation to, an objective state of affairs."[6] It is for this element, "whether held to consist of people and actions, ideas and feelings, material things and events, or super-sensible essences,"[7] that he uses the term *universe*. The other terms are self-explanatory, but it should be noted that for early Irish narrative, *artist* is to be taken as a generic term which denotes all those who have had an active role in the composition and transmission of the work.

3. Pagan Survivals

Among the four co-ordinates which have been mentioned, the work, being our primary datum, enjoys a privileged status: it is our point of departure, and to it we must always return. There are, of course, literary critics who would in any case argue the primacy of work-based criticism on theoretical grounds, but in regard to early Irish literature we need only appeal to the purely practical consideration that the work is virtually all that we have at our disposal in the way of evidence. Yet the tendency has been to conduct the discussion of Irish texts principally in terms either of the artists who have produced them or of the universe which is reflected in them, so that there is a pressing need to analyze the extant texts as literary works in their own right. For present purposes, however, it must be acknowledged that the co-ordinates which have been attended to are central to the question of pagan survival, since the artists are the agents of survival and the universe contains its elements. I begin, then, with authorship and transmission, and pass on in turn to the universe, the audience, and the work.

AUTHORSHIP AND TRANSMISSION

We are dealing with a literature whose authors are not known to us by name, and which is in that sense anonymous. Two points of fact must be made at the outset. In the first place, none of our early narrative texts survives in a manuscript written before the latter part of the eleventh century.[8] In the Irish manuscript tradition, the processes of composition and transmission cannot always be absolutely distinguished from one another, for the composition in writing of early Irish narrative can be seen as a continuous process, comprising the expansion and contraction, reshaping and redaction of matter, much of which must have been received into the literature from indigenous oral tradition, but some of which is of learned ecclesiastical provenance. It is often possible, on linguistic grounds, to assign an approximate date to the composition of a relatively unitary text, and the same can sometimes be done for a stratum or for strata of a compilatory text. But we can never hope to recover the pristine condition of any of our early texts.

Secondly, it should be noted that even to the extent that we can strip away accretions and arrive at a text approximating the form in which a given work was first written out, we still have not got so much as a single pre-ecclesiastical text. We know that it was under the aegis of the Church that the art of writing and the skills involved in the production of manuscripts were brought to Ireland, and that it was the churchmen who adapted Latin orthography to the Irish language. For these and other reasons we have to consider the extent to which ecclesiastics may have contributed to the formation and development of early Irish narrative literature.

Kenney observed that "the great majority of the written sources for the history of Ireland in the early middle ages are due to two sets of institutions, the monastic churches and the secular orders of learning,"[9] and there can be no dispute about that. On the other hand, the evidence would not seem to support the rigid division of labor implied by Kenney's listing, first of "the chief classes of texts which were produced or preserved in the monasteries,"[10] and secondly of "the chief classes of texts composed or transmitted by the *filid*."[11] Kenney credits the monastic churches only with matter of ecclesiastical interest, and of the imaginative literature he allows them only "imaginative religious literature, including voyage and vision tales and semi-apocryphal matter, to which may be added prophecies."[12] All the rest is attributed to the secular orders of learning. But the ecclesiastical contribution to the secular literature cannot be dismissed out of hand. Binchy says: "As we have them, [the native lore, the old sagas, the poems] are all of monastic provenance; they were usually written in monasteries, where they received a certain dressing-up from the scribes and redactors."[13] Where opinions would now diverge is on the character and extent of what Binchy somewhat dismissively calls "dressing-up." James Carney has treated the Irish sagas as literary compositions by men working in a Christian literate community,[14] and while Carney may overstate the specifically ecclesiastical character of some of the compositions which he has studied,[15] it seems to me that the evidence supports his general contention that the early texts as we have them were indeed composed in a Christian literate community.

This brings us to the related question of the relationship between the texts which were being written out in the manuscripts, and the oral tradition. If Irish literature contains survivals from Common Celtic and Indo-European culture—and the comparative evidence shows that it does—then clearly these elements must have been transmitted orally until such time as they were transferred into the written record. Calvert Watkins went so far as to say: "Ireland has the oldest vernacular literature in Europe; our earliest monuments go back to the sixth century. And it is not the beginnings of a literature that we see then, but the full flowering of a long tradition, pre-Christian, pre-literate and uninfluenced by the Graeco-Roman world."[16] The oral tradition was indeed for a long time pre-Christian, pre-literate, and uninfluenced by the Graeco-Roman world, but we have no direct access to that tradition. It is true that Watkins was writing in the particular context of a discussion of early Irish poetics and that he pointed to an impressive number of inherited features in its vocabulary and cultural context.[17] Moreover, while prose is the main vehicle of narrative in the early texts, the old poetical tradition is represented in them by the species of metrical composition known as *roscada*,[18] and these latter are presumably the "archaic passages" to which Binchy refers when he remarks that "the compilers (doubtless monastic) of saga texts in the eighth and ninth centuries, though in general they adopted the linguistic and expository techniques established by the glossators of late Latin texts, also transcribed, with varying degrees of accuracy, archaic passages derived from oral tradition."[19] When all that has been said, however, what has been preserved in the manuscripts is by definition a written literature; the introduction of writing was an innovation on the part of people who were Christian, literate, and influenced (in some degree) by the Graeco-Roman world; and what we see, already in the seventh century,[20] but especially in the eighth and ninth centuries, is "the beginnings of a literature," however much it may owe to the vigorous oral tradition which not only preceded it, but continued to flourish alongside.

It has been said that "the oral-literary question has been to Irish literary scholarship what the Patrician problem has been to historians of early Ireland. It has probably received more attention than any other question relating to the early literature without the achievement of anything approaching a consensus, except perhaps for the negative one of justified ignorance and bewilderment in the face of conflicting attitudes and theories, of inadequate evidence, and of inadequate examination of the evidence."[21] In the absence of a consensus one must give one's own view, and it seems safe to make the following general observations. First, the comparative evidence shows that much of the matter in early Irish narrative derives from oral tradition, this being true in particular of survivals from Common Celtic and Indo-European culture. Secondly, the indications are that the written literature had its beginnings in the monasteries and continued to flourish in them throughout the early medieval period.[22] The ecclesiastics' contribution to that literature was therefore crucial and continuing: its nature and extent remain to be precisely established, though a start has been made in that direction by Carney and others. In sum, then, we may say that early Irish narrative literature owes much to the vigorous oral tradition which not only preceded it but continued unabated alongside, and that the creation and survival of that literature show that the early Irish churchmen were not only open to, but deeply involved in, the extra-ecclesiastical lore of their country.

THE UNIVERSE

With regard to the universe of early Irish narrative, in the sense already defined, there are, I think, three main orientations to be discerned in the criticism, and these may be described in turn as mimetic, mythological, and textualist.

The mimetic stance is that of the critics who see in the literature a reflection of events which really happened or of a state of affairs which actually existed—the universe of the work is the society in which it was produced. The most extensive and influential body of mimetic criticism devoted to early Irish literature is that of H. M. and N. K. Chadwick and their disciples, who have treated the Ulster Cycle as a celebration of a lost Heroic Age.[23] There is ample justification for regarding the Ulster Cycle in this light, but the theory of the Heroic Age has its pitfalls. One of these is a tendency to apply the theory in a reductionist way. Thus, in introducing his valuable reading of the Ulster Cycle as "a window on the Iron Age," Kenneth Jackson says of the material that it "contains very little that can reasonably or safely be taken for myth, or ought to be interpreted as such."[24] There is, on the contrary, a good deal in the Ulster Cycle that can reasonably and safely be taken for myth: one need only mention, among much else, the life-crises of its great hero, Cú Chulainn,[25] or the winter sleep which afflicts the Ulidians,[26] or the two great bulls which confront one another in *Táin Bó Cúailnge*.[27]

Another pitfall of the theory of the Heroic Age lies in overestimating the historicity of the literature. It could be argued that the theory is founded on such an overestimation: the claim that "in matter and in the structure of its narrative [Heroic literature] is almost everywhere the same"[28] could well give rise to suspicion that we may be dealing in some measure with the diffusion of literary conventions rather than with an independently uniform set of literary responses to more or less identical societies. (The identity of these societies might in turn be attributed, in varying degrees, to cultural diffusion or independent development.) But even if we take leave to lay aside such suspicion and accept the proposition that "where there is heroic literature, it may ... reasonably be inferred that a Heroic Age preceded it, and that the general traits of that Age, perhaps even some of its persons, are presented to us in that literature,"[29] this inference relates merely to the mimetic origin of Heroic literature. It is quite another matter to use the Heroic literature as evidence for the duration of a given Heroic Age. The battle of Allen, fought between the Uí Néill and the Laigin in 722, is described in Heroic terms in *Cath Almaine*,[30] and it has therefore been suggested that in Ireland the Heroic Age lasted until the eighth century.[31] It seems to me, however, that *Cath Almaine* has more to tell us about the durability of literary conventions than about the conditions in Ireland at the time when the battle was fought.

Here we must leave the question of the Heroic Age, and turn briefly to a consideration of the historical information which may be extracted from early Irish narrative.[32] F. J. Byrne has said that "early Irish literature cannot be properly understood except as historical documentation,"[33] and he has drawn extensively on the literature for historical purposes, notably in *Irish Kings and High-Kings* (1973). There is a mass of literature dealing with the origins of Irish population-groups and dynasties, their territorial distribution, and their status; there are also numerous tales dealing with the careers of kings, some of whom are prehistoric (and may or may not be figments of the imagination), while others are known from reliable sources to have lived in the historical period. Literary works of this kind purport to be historical and they make political claims; it is right that their historicity should be assessed and their claims measured. If, however, we cannot control this material with reliable contemporary documentation—and this, more often than not, is the position in which we find ourselves—then our verdict on the historicity of the texts must be speculative, and it cannot go much beyond considerations of consistency and plausibility. As for the political claims of the texts, these may not always reflect the state of affairs as it really existed, but they can at least be interpreted as expressing the political aspirations of the population group or dynasty in question.

It can also be claimed that early Irish tales embody and express the ideology and value-system of the community, and here we find many elements which have been inherited from pre-Christian culture. This line of approach has not often been taken in the study of early Irish narrative, except insofar as it pertains to the mythological criticism which will be discussed presently. A recent example, however, is the analysis by Thomas Charles-Edwards of the well-known early Irish tale *Fingal Rónáin*[34] in relation to the role of honor and status in early Irish society,[35] and it is an example which shows very clearly how valuable this kind of analysis can be. In general we can say that an appreciation of the conceptual framework which underlies early Irish narrative is an essential element in the criticism of individual works. But whereas, in this respect as in others, the historian can cast light on the early texts by virtue of his knowledge and interpretation of other (non-literary) sources, there are strict limits to the amount of historical information which may be extracted from what are, after all, literary texts.

The mythological interpretation of early Irish narrative had its chief exponent among modern scholars in T. F. O'Rahilly.[36] Gerard Murphy must also be mentioned here, since he attempted to uncover a mythological basis for the Fenian Cycle.[37] The mythological criticism of early Irish narrative has received a new lease of life from the work of Georges Dumézil on Indo-European comparative mythology. Dumézil has himself considered some Irish material, and his theory has been more extensively applied to it by others, notably by Alwyn and Brinley Rees.[38] Dumézil is not without his critics, and there are those who would question the very basis of his theory.[39] The validity of the theory must ultimately be judged by comparatists. Within the more limited perspective of Irish studies, it may be said in Dumézil's favor that, given the comparative theoretical framework within which he operates, it is his practice to address himself to the extant material as we have it. One of the major weaknesses of O'Rahilly's procedure is that he had a high-handed attitude to the transmitted texts: time and again he found it necessary to contest the testimony of the manuscript texts as being at variance with his theory, and in effect to rewrite the tales in order to make them fit that theory.[40] It is axiomatic that any theory is valid only insofar as it accounts for the facts, and O'Rahilly's theory falls short on this score.[41] Dumézil's work, on the other hand, has illuminated a number of Irish texts which were hitherto shrouded in obscurity. His treatment, for example, of *Cath Maige Tuired*[42] "has the not inconsiderable merit of recovering order and purpose from apparent chaos."[43] It may be necessary in the future to refine Dumézil's theory, or even wholly to replace it; in the meantime its practical value in the elucidation of Irish narrative literature has by no means been exhausted. Quite apart from its pragmatic value, however, there remains the consideration that, in any account of pagan survivals in Irish narrative, the reflexes of Indo-European myth must be attended to.

Besides the mimetic and the mythological approaches to the universe of early Irish narrative, I have mentioned another, for which I used the term *textualist*. It might seem that textualist criticism should come up for consideration under the rubric of the work rather than that of the universe, but we must distinguish here between intra-textual and inter-textual criticism. Intra-textual criticism, concerned as it is with analysis of a given text, is properly to be assigned to the rubric of the work. Moreover, the same could be argued of that variety of inter-textual criticism which confines itself to analysis of the versions and recensions represented by the extant manuscript texts of a given tale.[44] There is also, however, a good deal of inter-textual criticism where the primary concern is with the relationship between and among works of literature, rather than their relationship to the world or to myth. Literature is thus deemed to be autonomous: its universe comprises other works of literature, or the constituents of those works, such as motifs or tale-types. Thurneysen's great study of the Ulster Cycle treats the manuscript tradition of Irish narrative as a closed system, and the extant texts of the cycle are described in terms of their relationship to one another.[45] The Finnish "historical-geographical" method has not been widely used in the study of early Irish narrative: no scholar has done for Irish tradition what Kenneth Jackson did for the Welsh in *The International Popular Tale and Early Welsh Tradition*.[46] The great monument of the "historical-geographical" school in our field is Tom Peete Cross's *Motif-Index of Early Irish Literature*,[47] a work which can be useful even to those who do not subscribe to the theory on which it is based.[48]

While the international popular tale may have had a relatively poor showing in the criticism of early Irish narrative, certain other tale-types have been pursued with some vigor and in a manner which is akin to that of the Finnish school. One may instance the numerous analogues which have been adduced of the Tristan-story.[49] D. A. Binchy has taken a dim view of this kind of work, remarking in his introduction to *Scéla Cano Meic Gartnáin*: "It was, I think, unfortunate that Thurneysen should have entitled his translation [of *Scéla Cano Meic Gartnáin*] 'An Irish Parallel to the Story of Tristan,' for ever since there has been a tendency to judge our text according to whether this parallel stands or falls. The hunt for the '*Ur*-Tristan' goes merrily on, and as there does not seem to be the remotest likelihood of his ever being caught, we may expect that the relationship between Cano and Créd will continue to be scrutinized for arguments on one side or the other."[50] This seems too harsh a view: research of this kind would seem to find ample justification in the very nature of the early literature, for there is no doubt that its authors felt free to borrow from such works as were available to them.[51]

So far as our theme is concerned, it may be said in general that the textualist critic *qua* textualist is not greatly concerned with the survival of paganism, for he is operating within a closed system. (Even when critics see reflexes of Celtic myth in medieval romance, they are, I think, positing vestiges rather than survivals.) On the other hand, the mythological critics are dedicated to the pursuit of survivals. The mimeticists are more difficult to characterize in this respect, and space does not allow a detailed discussion here. It may be said, however, that the crux of the matter is whether they are talking of the survival of literary conventions whose origins were anterior to the composition of the extant texts, on the one hand, or of a mirroring of a contemporary state of affairs or set of events, on the other.

THE AUDIENCE

We may pass on to the question of the audience, which Abrams defines as "the listeners, spectators, or readers to whom the work is addressed, or to whose attention, at any rate, it becomes available."[52] It would seem that the *fili* was expected to relate—or perhaps rather, as Seán Mac Airt has suggested,[53] to expound—traditional tales to his patron, but what audience, what "listeners, spectators, or readers" were the monastic traditors catering for? This is a question which can be addressed in two ways, the one historical and the other literary. The literary approach will rely upon the intention of the work, as discerned from analysis of its contents. A. G. van Hamel[54] has sought to establish the existence in Irish (and Celtic) tradition of what he called "exemplary myth," explaining that "the adjective 'exemplary' . . . as applied to heroes or traditions, means a hero or tradition that had to be regarded in the early Celtic society as an example which must be imitated by them. . . ."[55] Van Hamel's treatment of the Irish evidence is unsatisfactory,[56] but his inadequate advocacy of his case does not compel us to reject the proposition that early Irish narrative may have been exemplary in intention. I have argued elsewhere that *Cath Maige Tuired* is exemplary myth in van Hamel's sense:[57] as such it would be deemed to have had "palpable designs" upon its audience. It has been indicated above that certain extant works are political in their purpose and content, and it is reasonable to hold that manifestly propagandistic literature implies an audience which will be swayed by it.

So much for the intention which is implicit in the content of the works. The historian would also wish to have evidence on the actual reception of these works which would show that we are dealing with communication rather than mere expression, or even the use of literary conventions which may have been taken over from the work of the *filid*. Francis John Byrne is in no doubt as to the social significance of Irish mythology: "The importance of mythology for the historical understanding of an early society cannot be overstressed. The Irish concept of kingship, for example, is rooted in mythology. Myth in turn counteracts upon history. If life may be said to imitate art, it is even more true that if in early Ireland we can isolate a characteristic myth of kingship we shall find historical kings attempting to live up to the demands of that myth."[58] It can certainly be said that the modern scholar who seeks to understand the mythology and ideology of kingship in early Ireland must do this by examining the extant narrative texts, together with the laws and the wisdom literature. What remains in question is the degree to which the mythology and the ideology were propagated and perpetuated outside the monasteries by means of texts which were written out within the monastic scriptoria.

THE WORK

Some years ago, James Carney wrote: "Much close work remains to be done on Irish literature, and meanwhile generalisations are very dangerous,"[59] and, further, "every saga requires careful analytic study, and every other saga, anecdote or tradition used to elucidate it must itself be subjected to scrutiny and analysis."[60] It is true, of course, that the studies which have already been done on early Irish literature have all been intended to elucidate the material in one way or another. Thus, much of the theorizing on the relationship between orality and literacy in Irish tradition has arisen from a desire to account for what have been taken to be inadequacies (or at best peculiarities) in the extant texts. The mimetic, mythological, and textualist approaches to the universe of Irish narrative have to do with the content of the texts, and consideration of the audience of the tales throws light on their function in society. For all that, however, the kinds of criticism which we have been considering all share the tendency to divert attention away from the need to interpret early tales as literary works.

A distinction was made above between inter-textual and intra-textual criticism. Even the latter variety tends, as it is practiced in our field, to shy away from the rigorous analysis of the literary properties of the work. The usual procedure is the "geological" one of isolating strata in the manuscript text or texts of a given work, and of striving thereby to describe its genesis. Whatever contention there may be about the manner in which criticism of this kind has hitherto been conducted,[61] it must be conceded that, issuing as they have from a continuous process of composition and transmission, our manuscript materials conduce by their very nature to "geological" criticism.

All that need be said is that the attempt to rediscover the process whereby a given work of literature came into being is a valid exercise, but that it does not exhaust the critic's task: there must also be elucidation and interpretation of the product itself. What is now most urgently required in the study of early Irish narrative literature—apart from the edition and translation of texts—is the careful analysis of individual works, and, in particular, the kind of study which, as Abrams put it, would analyze each work "as a self-sufficient entity constituted by its parts in their internal relation."[62] An approach of this kind would not be intended to replace existing criticism, but rather to complement and balance it.

A SPECIMEN OF EARLY IRISH NARRATIVE

It has not been possible in the space at my disposal to illustrate the discussion with excerpts from the Irish texts. By way of compensation for this, a short excerpt is given here in translation from *Cath Maige Tuired*,[63] the story of the war between the Túatha Dé Danann and the Fomoiri which culminated in a great battle said to have been fought at Mag Tuired (now Moytirra in County Sligo). The background to the passage given here is that Núadu, king of the Túatha Dé Danann, had lost an arm in battle, and had therefore to relinquish the kingship, since a king must be without physical blemish. This excerpt will serve as a minor specimen of the imaginative literature which was being written out in the monastic scriptoria, and it is followed by a brief commentary showing the relevance of the passage to the matters which have been discussed in the course of this paper.

> Now Núadu was being treated [for his disability], and a silver hand was put on him by Dían Cécht with the motion which every hand has.
> But Dían Cécht's son Míach disapproved of that. He went to fetch the hand [which had been struck off Núadu] and he said: "Joint to joint of it, sinew to sinew!" And he healed Núadu in the course of three periods of three days. For the first three days he put it up against his side and it became covered with skin. For the second three days he put it on his breast. During the third three days he would cast white bundles (?) of black bullrushes when they had been blackened in a fire.
> Dían Cécht disapproved of that remedy. He hurled a sword into the crown of his son's head so that it cut the skin down to the flesh on his head. The lad healed that by exercising his skill. Dían Cécht struck him again and cut his flesh as far as the bone. The lad healed this by the same means. Dían Cécht struck a third blow and reached the membrane of his brain. This too the lad healed by the same means. Dían Cécht then struck a fourth blow and cut out the brain, so that Míach died, and Dían Cécht said that no physician could heal himself of that stroke.
> Then Míach was buried by Dían Cécht, and three hundred and sixty-five herbs, in accordance with the number of his joints and sinews, grew through the grave. Airmed[64] then spread out her cloak and she piled up those herbs in their proper order. But Dían Cécht came to her, and he mixed up the herbs so that their proper curative uses were not known, unless the Holy Spirit should teach them afterwards.
> And Dían Cécht said: "If Míach be not alive, Airmed shall survive."

Commentary

Cath Maige Tuired survives in only one late manuscript,[65] but it nevertheless provides a good example of the continuous process of composition and transmission in Irish manuscript tradition. The extant text is in a sixteenth-century vellum manuscript, BL Harley 5280, and it was written out by one Giolla Riabhach Ó Cléirigh.[66] We have no external evidence on the genesis of Giolla Riabhach's text; the internal evidence suggests that we have to do with a "composite work put together by an eleventh- or twelfth-century redactor mainly from ninth-century material."[67] While we have no information on those who preceded Giolla Riabhach in the composition and transmission of this tale, the presumption on present evidence must be that its manuscript life began in a monastic scriptorium in the Old Irish period (600–900), and continued in the monasteries until the twelfth century, when the custody of the manuscript literature passed into lay hands.[68] The language of our excerpt would indicate that it was first written down within the Old Irish period.

Cath Maige Tuired abounds in pagan survivals, and one of them occurs in our excerpt in the person of Núadu, who is the Irish reflex of the Celtic god known in British as Nodons (or Nodens), and in Welsh as Nudd (and Lludd, owing to assimilation of the initial to that of the epithet *Llaw Ereint* 'of the Silver Hand').[69] Núadu's name, his epithet *Airgetlám* ('of the Silver Hand'), and perhaps something of his role in *Cath Maige Tuired*[70] are traceable to Common Celtic, and must therefore have come into the written record from oral tradition. The same route was doubtless followed by the magical charm which Míach uses in healing Núadu.[71] In our text this charm is thoroughly pagan, but it is to be found in a Christianized form in the later oral tradition.[72] We are reminded, however, of the ecclesiastical dimension by the reference in our excerpt to the Holy Spirit.

Gerard Murphy said of *Cath Maige Tuired* that "its juxtaposition of Old Irish and Middle Irish matter and its tendency to record stray scraps of lore about the characters mentioned, rather than to concentrate on episodes essential to the theme, remind one forcibly of the museum type of arrangement . . . which is so common in manuscript texts of our older saga-tradition."[73] Here Murphy is referring to his theory that "medieval Irish manuscripts would seem indeed to be related to living storytelling much as the museum today is related to living material culture."[74] In positing significant difference between oral and written culture, Murphy is at one with James Carney: "I find it impossible for many reasons to believe that the form of any of the fictions or entertainments preserved in our medieval manuscripts is in any way close to the form in which they would be told when they existed (in so far as they actually did) on a purely oral level."[75] They diverge radically, however, in that for Murphy "any artistry in the sagas redounds to the credit of the oral storytellers; any defects are ascribable to the written tradition,"[76] whereas Carney is inclined to attribute the literary qualities of the Irish texts to what he calls "the external element." The evidence upon which Carney bases his contention that "those features [of *Táin Bó Cúailnge*] which are part of the epic scale of presentation must be due to imitation of the classics or of Christian developments of them"[77] includes a small number of items in the *Táin* which are comparable to the mention of the Holy Spirit in our text. *Cath Maige Tuired* also displays an epic scale of presentation, but a stray reference to the Holy Spirit is not sufficient reason for attributing this to external influence.

This excerpt might not appear fertile ground for the mimetic critic, but Wolfgang Meid has suggested that the Celts could fit artificial limbs, his evidence being the name of a third-century Caledonian chief, one Argentocoxos ("Silver Foot").[78] As this suggestion is, to say the least, extremely improbable, we may pass on to the mythological and textualist critics. The dispute between Dían Cécht and his son is a version of the Generation Conflict, and there has been a deal of discussion, first as to the origin and history of the Generation Conflict in general,[79] and secondly as to the origin of the Irish versions in particular.[80] Schultz adduced the Ulster version of the Generation Conflict in support of his contention that Thurneysen underestimated the mythological component of the Ulster Cycle,[81] and there are good grounds for seeing the Conflict as an Indo-European myth.[82] On the other hand, Tom Peete Cross argued that the Irish *literati* borrowed the Conflict from the Anglo-Saxons,[83] and while his case is less than compelling, it cannot be disproved.

Whatever one may think about the origin of the Generation Conflict as it occurs in Irish literature—my own inclination is to see it as a survival rather than a borrowing—one must also attend to the manner in which it is used in this text. It is found in the anecdote about Dían Cécht and Míach, and this anecdote is told in the course of a story about Núadu's successor, Bres, which is itself a version of the Generation Conflict.[84] The authors of our manuscript tales were not hidebound by considerations of linear exposition: thematic iteration is a common feature of their work, and in the present excerpt we have an example of the sandwich structure in which one realization of the Generation Conflict is slotted into another.[85] The story of how Dían Cécht killed his son may be what Murphy called "a scrap of lore," but in our text it is integrated into a work of literature, and not treated as a mere museum-piece.

In conclusion it may be said that early Irish literature is not the detritus of a lost mythology, nor yet a new phenomenon, born, like Athena, fully grown. It is the creation of a society which had two sets of cultural institutions, one indigenous, and oral in its medium, the other ecclesiastical and literate. These were sometimes hostile, sometimes amicable, but between them they contributed to the formation of a literature which combined matter drawn from the oral tradition with other elements and transmuted them into something new. It is a remarkable literature, and it must be accounted a significant achievement, not only of Ireland, but of Western Christendom.

4

The Concept of the Hero in Irish Mythology

(1985)

Giambattista Vico claimed, as long ago as 1725, that "the first science to be learned should be mythology or the interpretation of fables."[1] Vico's words, and the work of modern mythologists in many fields—anthropology, depth psychology, the history of religions, and literary criticism—have left little impression on the intellectual life of Ireland. Yet our manuscripts contain mythological texts whose abundance and archaic character make them unique in Western Europe. Insofar as our mythology has been at all rediscovered, credit must rest largely with our creative writers, and notably with Yeats, whose use of myth in the creation of literature was hailed as "a step toward making the modern world possible in art."[2] The use of myth by Anglo-Irish writers stands in marked contrast to the practice of modern writers in the Irish language. There is a chiastic pattern here: Anglo-Irish writers trying to create a national literature in English have drawn upon the resources of the indigenous tradition, whereas those writers whose aim has been to create a modern European literature in Irish have for the most part turned away from traditional themes. Perhaps in their case the burden of the past was too strong in the language itself to allow them to exploit Irish myth for their own purposes.

But it is not primarily as a quarry for modern creative writers that Irish mythology lays claim upon our attention, but rather as a rich and complex body of material which is there and which calls for elucidation and interpretation. It is in that mythology that we can discover the native ideology of Ireland, for although the early Irish material includes a valuable wisdom literature the abstract formulation of philosophical and theological theories was not the Irish way. It was in their myths that they explored the nature of men and the gods, and a central task of criticism must be to uncover and to restate in abstract terms the configuration of the ideological patterns which underlie the myths. As the great French mythologist Georges Dumézil put it: "A literary work does not have to set forth a theory: it is the hearer's or the reader's task to perceive the providential design which has arranged the events in the order in which the work presents them and with the results which it describes. Yet it is the design that justifies these events and results, and gives them a meaning."[3]

This "providential design" must be established by close study of the texts, but the general observation may be made that Irish myth is concerned above all with the relationship between man and the gods, and that the myth of the hero is used as a vehicle for exploring this relationship. In this respect, Irish myth shares the character of mythological systems in general. The situation can be stated in structuralist terms: a basic opposition in Irish myth is between man and god, and this opposition is mediated in the person of the hero. "Opposition" is used here in the sense of the discrimination of paired categories, and it is the structuralist view that every mythical system is built upon a sequence of such oppositions which are mediated by a third category which is abnormal or anomalous.[4] The hero belongs to this third category: he is at once the son of a god and of a human father; he is mortal and he lives out his life among men, but Otherworld personages intervene at crucial moments in his life. The myth of the hero is exceptionally well represented in Irish sources, and the space at my disposal here allows only a selective treatment. It seemed best to choose two of the more remarkable heroes of Irish tradition for extended discussion, and the two who are dealt with are the martial hero, Cú Chulainn, and the king-hero, Conaire Mór. In each case I concentrate on a single tale: for Cú Chulainn I restrict myself in the main to the early version of his "Conception Tale," and for Conaire Mór to "The Destruction of Da Derga's Hostel." The necessarily summary account of these two texts may perhaps give some indications of the thematic content of the Irish versions of the myth of the hero, while the commentary is intended to elucidate the ideological framework within which they may be interpreted. Having considered the two texts, we go on to two other topics, one of which is thoroughly pagan, while the other shows an admixture of pagan and Christian elements. The first of these is the role of the god Lug in relation to mortal heroes, the second the election to kingship of Corc of Cashel.

The early version of *Compert Con Culainn* ("The Conception of Cú Chulainn," henceforth *CCC*)[5] tells how a flock of birds repeatedly grazed to the roots the plain of Emain Macha, the ancient capital of Ulster. The warriors of Ulster gave chase to the birds and pursued them in nine chariots, Conchobor's daughter Dechtine serving as his charioteer. In the evening, three of the birds led the pursuers to the edge of Bruig na Bóinne (Newgrange), where night came upon the Ulstermen. It snowed heavily and the Ulstermen sought shelter. They found a new house where they were made welcome by a couple. The man of the house told them that his wife was in labor. Dechtine went to her and a boy-child was born. At the same time, a mare outside the house dropped two foals, and these were given to the child. By morning both the house and the birds had disappeared, and all that remained with the Ulstermen at the edge of Bruig na Bóinne were the child and the two foals. With these the warriors returned to Emain Macha.

Dechtine reared the child but he fell ill and died. Then a man came to Dechtine in her sleep and said that he was Lug son of Eithniu. He told her that she would be pregnant by him; it was he who had brought her to Bruig na Bóinne, it was with him she had stayed the night, and the boy she reared was his son. It was that boy he had placed in her womb, and his name would be Sétantae.

Conchobor betrothed Dechtine to one Súaltaim mac Roich, but she was ashamed to go to Súaltaim's bed while pregnant and carried out an abortion. Then she slept with Súaltaim: she conceived again, and bore a son, Sétantae, who was later given the name Cú Chulainn.

The theme of the "Waste Land," with which *CCC* opens, occurs frequently in Irish tradition: the laying waste of the land is the ultimate sanction of the gods. In *CCC* the land is laid waste by Otherworld birds; in other texts this is done by Otherworld horses and pigs; and the fruits of the earth will of themselves dry up when the land is ruled by an unrighteous king, who is unpleasing to the gods. The theme of the Waste Land implies the need for a fecundating hero who will restore vegetation to Emain Macha. In Irish tradition the fecundating role of the hero is seen most clearly in the lives of the king-heroes, who ensure the fertility of land and beast and man by their wise and judicious rule: we shall presently see that Conaire Mór exemplies this. Cú Chulainn, on the other hand, is essentially a martial hero, the defender of his people against the enemy invader. But it has been argued that in the *Táin*, when he defends Ulster against the ravages of its Connacht enemies while Conchobor and the Ulstermen are undergoing their winter sleep, Cú Chulainn exemplifies the vigorous young male as the vital force in nature, and that this scenario represents an ancient vegetation myth, the basic theme of which is "the triumph of life and fecundity over death and decay, as suggested by seasonal change."[6] The occurrence of the theme of the Waste Land in *CCC* lends weight to that interpretation. In the immediate context of *CCC*, however, the theme presages the decisive intervention by the Otherworld in the affairs of Ulster. It also has the function of inducing the Ulstermen to give chase to the birds, which lead them to Bruig na Bóinne.

Bruig na Bóinne is a localization of the Otherworld, one of the *síde* to which the gods were consigned when men came to share dominion of the land in Ireland. Thus, these *síde* (the singular is *síd*) were the abodes of the gods: they were located in the mounds of the earth (both natural formations and prehistoric tumuli), under the lakes, and on the islands of the ocean. The world of the *síde* was distinct from that of men, but contact between the two was frequent, especially at Samain (November 1) when the *síde* were believed to be open, and their denizens free to wander abroad at will—beliefs which have persisted down to modern times. The prominence of the *síde* on the landscape doubtless contributed to the constant awareness among Irish country people of the imminence of the Otherworld. Bruig na Bóinne, in particular, was originally the whole necropolis on the Boyne, but the name became specially attached to Newgrange, which is but one of the tumuli there. In our text, the lord of Bruig na Bóinne is Lug, the Irish reflex of a Celtic god who is commemorated in the names of a number of continental cities such as Lyons (from an earlier *Lug(u)dunum*), Laon, and Leiden. We have seen that when he later comes to Dechtine in her sleep, Lug explains that it was he who brought her to Bruig na Bóinne. And he brought her there, not on an errand of doom, but so that Sétantae might be brought into the world. Thus, Bruig na Bóinne is here the telluric womb from which emerges the savior-hero of Ulster.

Cú Chulainn shares with mythical personages everywhere the characteristic of dual paternity: he is at once the son of a god (Lug) and of a human father (Súaltaim). What is remarkable in the case of Cú Chulainn is that he is conceived three times: in one manuscript text of *CCC* he is said to have been "the son of three years." The number three is of course everywhere invested with symbolic significance, and triplicity of gods and heroes is a very common theme in Irish myth. Cú Chulainn's threefold conception is one of the many expressions of this notion. Another one which may be noted here is the theme of threefold death, of which we have a number of examples in Irish texts and which will be mentioned again in connection with Conaire Mór. Triplicity is a feature also of Celtic iconography, both in Ireland and on the continent, its most striking expression being the head with three faces. In the particular case of Cú Chulainn, his triplicity is related to his destiny as a warrior, for his martial career is marked by a number of encounters with triple adversaries of one kind or another. One such encounter is his initiatory combat in which he ventures forth and defeats the three formidable sons of Nechta Scéne. This has been identified as a variant of an ancient mythical exploit in which a god or hero slays an adversary who is endowed with some form of triplicity: Dumézil compares Heracles, who conquers the three-headed Geryon, and who was conceived in one night three times as long as normal.[7]

But perhaps the most interesting feature of the threefold conception in *CCC* is its structural sequence. The boy is first begotten in the Otherworld by Lug upon his Otherworld consort; then at Emain by Lug upon Dechtine; and finally by Súaltaim upon Dechtine. There is thus a progression from fully divine to fully human parentage: in this sequence the hero recapitulates in his own life the history of man, since, if we may judge from the occurrence of deity names in their pedigrees, the Irish apparently believed themselves to be descended from the gods. Furthermore, this sequence gives us a singularly clear example of the manner in which the hero mediates between the gods and men: the second (or middle) conception, linked to the first and third by Lug and Dechtine respectively, mediates the opposition between the divine and the human. In this case at least the "meaning" of the triplicity of the hero is inseparable from the structure of the narrative.

The manner of Cú Chulainn's conception and birth marks him out for greatness. He is destined to save his people from the ravages of war: how he accomplishes this is shown in the *Táin*. There is a whole cycle of texts about Cú Chulainn telling how he was initiated into warrior status, how he overcame great obstacles to win Emer as his wife, how he journeyed to the Otherworld, how he killed his only son, and, finally, how he met his tragic death. Taken together, these episodes make up Cú Chulainn's heroic biography from conception and birth to death. Rather than follow up these texts here, however, we turn now to our second hero.

Conaire Mór (Conaire the Great) is depicted in our sources as a prehistoric king of Tara. His biography is heroic, and it follows much the same basic pattern as that of Cú Chulainn. But Conaire is destined to be king, and, in contrast to the martial ethic which informs the cycle of Cú Chulainn, Conaire's life is presented in terms of the pacific ethic which was the basis of the Irish ideology of kingship. I have already referred to the fecundating role of the king who ensures the fertility of man and beast and land by his wise and judicious rule. The characteristic of the king which ensured fertility in this way was known as *fír flatha* ('Prince's truth,' alternatively called *fír flathemon* 'ruler's truth'). "Truth" in this context is a broad term, embracing the notions of wisdom and justice, and, as well as fertility, it also secures seasonable weather and amity among men. In short, it is a cosmic force, and the doctrine of *fír flatha* places the king at the center of the cosmos. This is the doctrine which is expressed in heroic terms in the life of Conaire Mór.

Our text for Conaire Mór is *Togail Bruidne Da Derga* (*TBDD*).[8] The title is conventionally translated "The Destruction of Da Derga's Hostel," but the *bruiden* or "hostel" in question is a localization of the Otherworld. (It may be noted in passing that this *bruiden* gave its name to Bohernabreena, near Tallaght in County Dublin.[9]) It is in Da Derga's hostel that Conaire met his death, and the title of our tale is in keeping with the fact that much the greater part of it is devoted to that event and to those which led up to it. *TBDD* is nonetheless a biography of Conaire, dealing in turn

4. The Concept of the Hero in Irish Mythology   57

with his conception and birth, his boyhood, his elevation to kingship, the Golden Age enjoyed in Ireland during his reign, and turning only then to the tragic story of his death. All of this resolves itself into three sections, which we shall consider in turn: the making of a king, the golden age, and the tragedy of a king.

THE MAKING OF A KING

Conaire's mother Mess Búachalla was brought up in humble circumstances, but she was the daughter of a king and a beautiful goddess who was born in a *síd*. Mess Búachalla married Etarscélae king of Tara, but on the night before her marriage she saw a bird on the skylight coming to her. The bird left his "bird-skin" on the floor and ravished her. He told her that she would bear his son and that he should be called Conaire. So it came to pass, and Conaire was brought up as the son of Etarscélae. He was reared with three foster-brothers. Now Conaire had three "gifts" (*búada*)—the gift of hearing, the gift of seeing, and the gift of calculation—and he shared these gifts with his foster-brothers, giving one gift to each of the three.

When Etarscélae died and a successor was to be chosen, Conaire was told by his foster-father to go to Tara. He set out and when he reached Dublin he saw great speckled birds, which he pursued as far as the sea and onto the waves. They then cast off their bird-skins, and one of them identified himself to Conaire as Nemglan, "the king of your father's birds." Nemglan instructed Conaire to go along the road to Tara stark naked, bearing a stone and a sling. Meanwhile, it had been prophesied at a "bull-feast" (a solemn divinatory rite) that the person who arrived in this way would be the future king. So when Conaire appeared he was recognized as king. His nakedness was covered with royal raiment, he was placed in a chariot, and he bound the hostages of Tara (an act which signifies their submission to him). But the people of Tara objected to him, since he was young and beardless. Conaire refuted this objection, however, saying that a king was not disqualified by youth, provided that he be generous, and that it was his right from father and grandfather to bind the hostages of Tara. This utterance was greeted with enthusiasm by the people ("'Wonder of wonders,' they cried"), and Conaire was invested with the kingship. Then the taboos of Conaire's reign are listed: these are prohibitions which were laid upon

Conaire (perhaps by Nemglan, but the text is ambiguous at this point), and so long as they are honored Conaire's reign is marked by prodigious peace and prosperity.

The begetting of Conaire Mór represents an Otherworld intervention in the affairs of Tara. We are reminded of the Otherworld birds in *CCC*, who summon the Ulstermen to Bruig na Bóinne. In *TBDD* the birds have a more direct role: Conaire is begotten by a god who appears in the guise of a bird; he is called to his destiny by the king of his father's birds, Nemglan; and his reign is called "the bird-reign" (*énflaith*). This Otherworld intervention is an integral part of the election of Conaire to kingship, and it seems right to compare the sequence summarized above with the scenario which Dumézil has traced in the traditions concerning the primitive Hindu king Pṛthu: designation by the gods, recognition by the wise men, and acceptance by the people.[10] These three elements occur in *TBDD*: Conaire is designated by the very manner of his conception; he is recognized as king when he arrives on the road to Tara in fulfilment of the diviner's prophecy; and he is accepted by the people when he successfully meets their objection to his youth and beardlessness. Each of these stages has its proper place in the structure, but it is in the last one that Conaire establishes his right to the kingship. This he does by delivering a true judgment on the matter of his own eligibility for kingship, a judgment which reveals his understanding that it is essential for a ruler (*flaith*) to be generous—a notion which is reflected in the Modern Irish *flaithiúil* 'generous.' This true judgment shows Conaire to be possessed of *fír flatha*, which, as we have seen, is the distinguishing characteristic of the rightful king.

THE GOLDEN AGE

TBDD describes the state of peace and plenty which was enjoyed in Ireland during the reign of Conaire Mór. The ideal conditions which characterized his reign (and also that of Cormac mac Airt) are reminiscent of the Otherworld in its beneficent aspect as it is depicted in Irish texts. They represent two different responses to the paradisal yearning, the Otherworld being separated in space, the Golden Age in time from the storyteller and his audience. In Old Irish the word for "peace" is *síd*, which is a homonym of the word which (as we have seen) denotes a habitation of the gods. These homonyms were originally one and the same: I have argued elsewhere that the homonymy reflects the nexus between the Otherworld and conditions in this world, as mediated in the person of the king. The Otherworld is the source of the king's cosmic truth (*fír*) and peace is its symptom; the state of peace secured by the kings of the mythical past, whose kingship was sanctioned by the Otherworld, is seen as a re-creation of the paradisal condition; and, as a material correlative to these abstract connections, the king would seem often to have been consecrated upon a *síd*.[11]

THE TRAGEDY OF A KING

The Golden Age of peace and plenty depicted in *TBDD* is a measure of the beneficent role of the rightful king. In fulfilling this role the king is constrained by his *gessi* (taboos), and by the requirement to maintain the order based on cosmic truth. Conaire's tragedy is that he is faced with a conflict between his duty in these respects and his love for his foster-brothers, and that he puts love before duty. What happened is that Conaire's foster-brothers took to thieving in order to see what punishment the king might inflict upon them and how the theft in his reign might damage him. Conaire repeatedly refused to punish them. They were therefore emboldened to advance in crime from theft to marauding, the significance of this being that one of the taboos laid upon Conaire was that there should be no marauding during his reign. By failing to punish his foster-brothers for their earlier and less serious crime, Conaire caused the violation of one of his own taboos. And then, when the foster-brothers and their companions in crime were brought before him on the charge of marauding, Conaire delivered a false judgment, decreeing that the others should be slain by their fathers, but that his foster-brothers should be spared. Conaire saw the injustice of his judgment and revoked it, saying, "The judgment which I have given is no extension of life for me." He ordained instead that all the marauders should be spared and banished overseas. Ironically, even the revised judgment proved "no extension of life" to Conaire, for in due course the marauders whom he had spared returned to destroy him in the *bruiden* of Da Derga.

All of this provides us with an Irish example of what Dumézil has called "the single sin of the sovereign," which "destroys either the raison d'être of sovereignty, namely the protection of the order founded on truth ... or the mystical support of human sovereignties, namely the respect for the superior sovereignty of the gods and the sense of the limitations inherent in every delegation of that divine sovereignty.... The king falls prey to one or the other of these risks, which are at bottom reducible to the same thing."[12] Dumézil was not aware of the occurrence of this theme in Irish tradition, but his formulation stands as an excellent summary of Conaire's "sin" in *TBDD*, save that Conaire falls prey to both of the "risks" described by Dumézil. The taboos which have been laid upon him constitute in effect a contract with the Otherworld, and his transgression of one of these taboos destroys the respect of the Otherworld personages who have delegated sovereignty to him. In failing to punish his foster-brothers, and later in delivering a false judgment, Conaire destroys the respect for the order founded on truth.

No sooner has the king's judgment been given and the marauders banished than we hear that the perfect peace has broken down which had been enjoyed during Conaire's reign. The Otherworld now takes on its malevolent aspect, and Conaire proceeds to transgress all the taboos which have been laid upon him. He sets out from Tara and finds that he cannot return, for the lands round about are full of raiders coming from every side, men roam about naked, and the land is all on fire. This is a sign that the law has broken down there. And so Conaire turns away and he takes the path which leads him to his doom in the *bruiden*. He encounters a number of malevolent Otherworld beings on his way to the *bruiden*, and in the meantime his foster-brothers and their allies return to Ireland. They assail Conaire in the *bruiden*, which they set on fire three times. Conaire's head is cut off, and the severed head is given a drink of water which has been taken by his servant Mac Cécht from Uarán Garaid on the plain of Croghan in County Roscommon after a tour of the rivers and lakes of Ireland. The severed head thanks Mac Cécht, and Conaire dies.

Conaire dies by decapitation, but the elements of fire and water are also present: the *bruiden* is set on fire, and Conaire dies only after water has been poured into his throat and gullet. I suspect that we have a variant here of the motif of threefold death (see further, "The Threefold Death in Early Irish Sources," chap. 7 in this volume). This is well represented in Irish sources, and in its classic form comprises death by wounding, drowning, and burning. Although Conaire is not drowned and it is not explicitly stated that he is burned, the elements of iron, water, and fire are brought into play in the account of his death.

There is another instance of triplicity in *TBDD* which is made explicit, and which has a bearing on the interpretation of the text, namely the fact that Conaire's foster-brothers are three in number. Irish tradition presents examples of trios which are merely triplications of a single personality. Perhaps the best known of these is the trio in the Deirdre story: the three sons of Uisliu are at all times found together, and among them only Noísiu has a definite personality. Áinle and Ardán are but shadows of Noísiu, and they die when he dies.[13] The three foster-brothers in *TBDD* (who are themselves blood-brothers) are a somewhat different trio, for they are identical in appearance and dress, not only among themselves, but also with Conaire: the text says that all four were identical in their clothing, their weapons, and the color of their horses. Moreover, it will be recalled that Conaire distributed his gifts (*búada*) to them: each one of them represents an aspect of his triple self and together they are his equal. These three personages are cast in Conaire's image, and in *TBDD* they use his own "gifts" to destroy him: it is scarcely too much to suggest that they may be taken to represent the evil side of his nature. In this way they are a projection in corporeal form of "the enemy within." They too die at the destruction of the *bruiden*.

The "providential design" (to use Dumézil's term) which gives meaning to the tragic events of *TBDD* is that of the Irish ideology of kingship, and it will be clear by now that the Otherworld is central to that ideology. Many Irish texts give expression to the Otherworld legitimation of sovereignty, but this notion is nowhere more explicitly stated than in *Baile in Scáil* ("The Phantom's Vision").[14] This tells how Conn Cétchathach was brought to an Otherworld abode where he met a couple—a girl sitting on a chair of crystal and wearing a golden crown, and a man sitting on a throne. The man identifies himself to Conn as Lug and tells him that he has come to Conn to tell him the span of his sovereignty and of that of every prince that will come of him in Tara forever. The girl is identified as the Sovereignty of Ireland, and she has a golden cup from which she gives Conn a drink of ale at Lug's instructions. And then she asks who next should be given a drink from the cup, and Lug names Conn's successor, and so the dialogue continues and we are given a list of those who will follow Conn in the kingship of Tara.

This text is a version of the sovereignty myth, which has to do with the espousal of a king to the goddess of sovereignty, and it shows that the kingship of Conn and his descendants at Tara has been conferred at the behest of the god Lug. It will be remembered that Lug was the divine father of Cú Chulainn, and now we find him presented as legitimator of the Dál Cuinn kings of Tara. The key to Lug's role is to be found in the story of the battle of Mag Tuired (now Moytirra, in County Sligo), *Cath Maige Tuired*.[15] This tale tells of the war of the gods, and in it we see Lug successively attaining pre-eminence in the domains of sovereignty, martial vigor, and agricultural practice: those who are acquainted with Dumézil's work will recognize here the three terms of the tripartite structure which that scholar has established for Indo-European ideology.

Lug may be described as the hero among the gods. His heroic deeds in relation to kingship, martial vigor, and agricultural practice were performed in the time of the gods, which preceded the appearance of man in Ireland. When men did come to share dominion of the land, the gods, as we have seen, retreated to the *síde*. Thenceforth, great deeds were to be performed by mortal heroes, such as Cú Chulainn, who differ from Lug in that, however great their achievements in life, they must die, and when they are dead they are dead.

What then is the relationship between the mortal hero and his divine predecessor who still inhabits the *síde*? It can be said, in the first place, as de Vries has argued, that the hero raises himself to the level of the gods.[16] Having performed his deeds in the time of the gods, Lug is by definition anterior to the mortal heroes: it follows that the other heroes are perceived within the system as replicating (in some measure) the heroic achievements of Lug. In the field of kingship, the great hero is Cormac mac Airt, who is the exemplary model of *fír flatha*; the Golden Age which was enjoyed in his reign was not brought to an end by any sin of the kind committed by Conaire Mór. In the field of martial vigor, Cú Chulainn is the outstanding figure. But the connection between Lug and Cú Chulainn or Cormac is not solely that of exemplary model and replicator. We know from *CCC* that Lug was progenitor to Cú Chulainn. And *Baile in Scáil* attests to a connection of a somewhat different kind between Lug and Cormac. The latter was one of the Dál Cuinn kings of Tara, and one of those upon whom the drink of sovereignty was conferred at Lug's behest. In this act, Lug effectively bestows his Otherworld consort, the Sovereignty of Ireland, upon Cormac for a stated period of years. As her spouse for the time being, Cormac is Lug's surrogate as king of Tara, while Cú Chulainn, for his part, is an incarnation of Lug.

What we find in the early Irish narrative texts is mythology and ideology refracted through literature, and it is worth noting that this literature would not have come down to us were it not for the labors of monastic scribes.

Early Irish literature stems from the fruitful interplay of two sets of institutions, the native orders of learning and the monastic schools. The texts contain many survivals from Celtic and Indo-European culture, and these elements clearly must have been transmitted orally until such time as they were transferred into the written record. The written literature had its beginnings in the monasteries in the seventh century, and continued to flourish in them until the twelfth, and what survives to us today is the remains of that literature. The early Irish texts owe much to the vigorous oral tradition which not only preceded the written literature but continued unabated alongside, but the ecclesiastics' contribution to their extant condition must have been crucial and continuing. The creation and survival of the early Irish narrative texts show that the early Irish churchmen were not only open to, but deeply involved in the extra-ecclesiastical lore of their country.

It will be appropriate, therefore, to end with an instance of syncretism: this is an account of the election to the kingship of Cashel of Corc mac Láire (Corc son of the Mare), in which the basic pattern is similar to that of the election of Conaire in *TBDD*, but which is realized in partly Christian terms.[17] The designation by the gods here takes the form of designation by angels; the recognition of Corc by the wise men is here entrusted to swineherds to whom it has been revealed in a vision, though there is also a druid who discovers that Corc is to be king by means of druidic divination; the people assent to Corc's accession by answering "Amen" to his response to a blessing. As Dillon pointed out, this blessing, apart from a pious invocation, "is rather pagan than Christian in expression." This blessing and the king's solemn response to it show the power of the spoken word, as did Conaire's pronouncement on his eligibility to kingship. Finally, we may note that the king is bound to preserve his prescriptions, namely that he have truth and mercy; such a prescription (*búaid*) "is a thing or act which brings good luck, and which is therefore a duty or prescribed conduct, the reverse of *geis*";[18] we are reminded of the *gessi* which were laid upon Conaire.

The story of Corc also bears comparison with *Baile in Scáil*, for here the angels reveal the names of the kings who are to succeed Corc in the kingship of Cashel. In contrast to *Baile in Scáil*, however, this text shows the kings to have been legitimated by God, of whom the angels are of course messengers.

Corc of Cashel mediates between his people and God. The other texts which I have been discussing exemplify some of the ways in which Irish tradition presents the destiny of the hero who mediates between man and the pagan gods. The worldview of these texts is an anthropocentric one: man is the center of the cosmos, and the fruits of the earth and the workings of the elements are contingent upon the physical and moral excellence of the king—and, in texts where the martial ethic prevails, upon that of the champion. But the hero is subject to constraints from within and without, and Otherworld personages intervene at all the crucial moments in his career. These interventions may be benevolent or malevolent, reflecting the contradictory aspects of the Otherworld. A benevolent god may function as progenitor and helper, a malevolent one as villain and destroyer. The burden of heroism is a heavy one, and is ultimately unenviable. While celebrating the achievements of the hero, Irish myth asserts the precariousness of man's position in the cosmos.

5

The Sister's Son in Early Irish Literature

(1986)

In the early Irish poem "Tair cucum, a Maire boíd" ("Come to me, loving Mary"),[1] which is ascribed, in the sole surviving manuscript, to one Blathmac son of Cú Brettan son of Congus of the Fir Rois,[2] the poet invites Mary to join him in keening her crucified son. In doing this, the poet, who must surely have been a cleric, shows no sign of embarrassment at the fact that keening was an offence for which penances were prescribed in the Irish penitentials:[3] according to the Old-Irish Penitential, if a cleric happens to commit such an offence, "he has double penance, compared with a married woman."[4] So far from paying any heed to the attitude to keening which is embodied in the penitentials, the poet confidently expects to be rewarded for his labors with a long life and eternal salvation (lines 553–56), and those who recite his keen will likewise be saved from Hell (lines 557–64). Christ must be keened because every splendid household keens its lord; the poet remarks how distressing it was that the Jews did not suffer that Christ should be keened by his own people (lines 493–96, 509–12): "no cry meeting cry was raised over the body of Christ" (lines 499 f.), "beating of hands over the body of pure Christ was not permitted to apostles" (lines 503 f.). The poet is here applying the norms of Irish society to the aftermath of the crucifixion: in an Irish household cries of lamentation are raised and hands are beaten over the body of a deceased lord, and that is therefore what the apostles, had they been permitted, would have done over the body of Christ.

The Irish manner of keening the dead is but one of the norms of his own society which inform the poet's presentation of the life of Christ. As Carney has said, "he deals with Palestine in the beginning of the Christian era, but his vision is essentially a vision of Ireland."[5] The relationship between Christ and the Jews is expressed in terms of the Irish social code, and it is twofold: there is the bond of kinship, since Jesus is related to the Jews through his mother, and there is also the bond of clientship, which is the contractual relationship between the Irish *flaith* (lord) and *céle* (client). The contractual relationship between Jesus and the Jews has its origin in the covenant (*cotach*) which God made with Abraham (lines 309–12), and in fulfilment of which he granted them the Promised Land, *Tír Tairngiri* (lines 357 f.). The poet says that God "endowed them with the best country in the world" (*rosn-ír thír as deg din bith,* line 381), and it is significant that the verbal form *-ír* which occurs here is the preterite of *ernid* 'grants,' which is used in particular of a lord's granting of a fief or a gift to a client.[6] For the Jews to oppose Christ, the son of God, therefore, was *rind fri giallnai,* literally, "spear-point against base clientship" (line 394): the poet explains that in Ireland it would be described as *sénae iar n-aitite,* "denial after recognition," which evidently refers to the repudiation of a contract which has been solemnly entered into (lines 395 f.).[7] The contract which is in question at this point is that with God the Father, but the poet goes on to imply that the Jews were also clients of Christ: he granted them many wonderful requests (lines 413–16). The verbal form used here is again *-ír,* the preterite of *ernid,* and in this context Christ is said to be *ar ruiri rígrathach.* Carney translates this as "our royal gracious king," but *ríg-rathach* could be taken to mean "kingly in the bestowal of gifts," a rendering which would suit the context very well, since *rath* is the verbal noun of *ernid* and is used of the feoff or gift given by the lord to the client.[8] In any case, everything that Christ bestowed on the Jews in return for their clientship was "wealth to slaves"; they violated their counter-obligations, *ro-coillset a cobfolaid* (line 424). The grammatical problem posed by the ending *-aid* of *cobfolaid* has been fully discussed by Binchy,[9] and here we need only concern ourselves with its meaning, which is identical with that of *frithfolad*, the prefix *cob-* having been substituted for *frith-* in order to provide alliteration with *-coillset*. *Frithfolad* is the converse of *folad*, and the semantics of these two words has been greatly illuminated by Binchy.[10] Since the meaning of these words is not only relevant to our poet's perception of Christ's relationship with the Jews, but will also arise in our discussion of Bres son of Elatha, it will be helpful at this point to quote at some length from what Binchy has to say on the juridical use of *folad/frithfolad*:

> Perhaps the word which comes nearest to covering all [the] various meanings [of *folad*] is the English term "consideration" in the law of contracts. Both in the singular and (more frequently) in the plural *folad* stands for the "values" which one side grants to or gets from the other as a result of their mutual relationship, whether this be contractual, political, economic (lord and client), religious (Church and tribe) or domestic (man and wife, father and son, etc.). In every such relationship the values to which either party is entitled invest him with a "right" by imposing a corresponding "duty" on the other, so that semantically *folad* is an ambivalent word . . . : sometimes it can mean "rights, dues," sometimes "liabilities, duties," depending on the context. . . . The converse of *folad* is *frithfolad*. . . . Invariably O. Ir. *frithfolad* (sg. or pl.) presupposes the delivery of his *folad* by one or other of the parties to the relationship; it arises only in circumstances which are described in English legal terminology as "consideration executed on one side." As Thurneysen put it, "*frithfholad* ist, was für ein *folad* gegeben wird," and the phrase of *Cáin aigillne* which he is explaining runs: *cach folad cona fhrithfholud*, "each *folad* along with its counter-*folad*," i.e. "every grant entails a return gift."[11]

The poet's charge against the Jews is that they did not meet the obligations imposed upon them when they accepted the gifts given to them.

One of the bonds which existed between Christ and the Jews, then, and which was violated by them, was that of Lord and clients. The other was that of kinship. The doctrine of the conception of Christ is set out in a quatrain:

> Prímgein Dé Athar fri nem
> do mac, a Maire ingen;
> ro-láithreth hi combairt glain
> tri rath spirto sechtndelbaig.

Carney translates: "The first-born of God, the Father, in Heaven is your son, Mary, virgin: he has been begotten in a pure conception through the grace of the Septiform Spirit" (lines 21–24). Time and again in the poem we are reminded that Christ was "son of the living God," "son of God, the Father in Heaven." Emphasis is also laid on Christ's kinship, through his mother, with the Jews. The reward which they gave him for his healing of bodies and of souls "was not a fitting thing in blood-relationship" (*nibu choindfe chobfolo*, lines 175 f.). Mary's own people (*cenél*) seized her son and flogged him (lines 181 f.). His very mother-kin (*a fírmáithre*) crucified the man who had come to save them (lines 186–88).

Taking up the theme again, the poet says that it was "from that people" (*din tuaith sin*) that God "chose a virgin to conceive his white lamb" (lines 385 f.). The story of Christ's crucifixion is told "for the purpose of censuring the Jews; for they have crucified . . . the body of Christ, their sister's son" (*dég ro-crochsat . . . corp Críst, maic a ndeirbsethar*, lines 399 f.). The significance of Christ's status as sister's son of the Jews is spelt out in the following quatrain:

> Ainbli gnúisi, condai fir
> ro-fersat in fingail-sin;
> céin ba diïb a máthair
> ba diäll for fírbráthair.

Carney translates: "Of shameless countenance and wolf-like were the men who perpetrated the kin-slaying; since his mother was of them it was treachery towards a true kinsman" (lines 409–12).

The general import of these quotations is clear enough: Jesus was related to the Jews through his mother, so that in crucifying him they were killing their own kin. But the deeper significance and resonance of the quatrain which we have just quoted can be appreciated only in terms of the position of the sister's son in early Irish ideology. In a mainly patrilineal society, how and in what precise circumstances does a man come to be described as a true kinsman (*fírbráthair*) of his mother's kin? If Jesus is accurately described as a *fírbráthair* of the Jews then his killing was indeed kin-slaying (*fingal*), and it has been pointed out that in Irish law *fingal* "was the most dreadful of crimes, for it was the duty of a murdered man's kin to exact either vengeance or compensation from the killer; but if the murderer himself belonged to the kin, human justice faltered."[12] Likewise, we shall see that *condai* 'wolf-like' is a peculiarly apt epithet for men who perpetrate the crime of kin-slaying. Everything hinges, then, on the central question of the sister's son as *fírbráthair*, and that question will be addressed presently.[13]

It must be acknowledged at this point that the themes of kinship and clientship are interwoven in the text, whereas for our purposes we have looked at them as separate strands. Moreover, the gift-giving nexus, which is predominantly seen as that of lord and client, is also taken to be that of king and *túath*.[14] The main lines of the social "message" of "Tair cucum, a Maire boíd" become clear when we reunite these themes, for the relationship between Christ and the Jews would have remained sound only if they had honored the obligations imposed upon them by Christ's kinship and lordship and kingship. The focus of the present article is upon the role and status of the sister's son in early Irish ideology, but we shall find confirmation in other literary sources that the relationship of the sister's son to his mother's kin could flourish only when it was properly integrated into the wider web of relationships which formed the basis of social order.

A significant relationship between mother's brother and sister's son, known as the avunculate, is a feature of many societies. One of the best-known accounts of the avunculate is that of the great ethnographer, Tacitus, who observed such a relationship among the Germans:

> The sons of sisters are as highly honoured by their uncles as by their own fathers. Some tribes even consider the former tie the closer and more sacred of the two, and in demanding hostages prefer nephews to sons, thinking that this gives them a firmer grip on men's hearts and a wider hold on the family.[15]

The modern successors of Tacitus have revealed the avunculate to be a widespread institution in primitive societies. They have also shown that, where the avunculate occurs, societies differ with respect to how sister's son and mother's brother feel about and behave towards one another. In some societies the relationship is one of affection, which in some cases is a "joking relationship," marked by licensed ragging and disrespect; in others it tends towards hostility, the uncle being a stern disciplinarian who is held in awe by his nephew.[16] Lévi-Strauss has pointed out that "because the relationship between nephew and maternal uncle appears to have been the focus of significant elaboration in a great many primitive societies, anthropologists have devoted special attention to it."[17] Elsewhere, he has been disparaging of this "special attention": "The special relationship of tenderness or of fear which exists in innumerable cultures between the nephew and the maternal uncle, has fascinated sociologists to such a point that too often they plunge headlong at it like the bull at the matador's cape, without concerning themselves with the exact nature of the reality that it covers."[18] It is unnecessary for present purposes to choose among the different explanations of the avunculate which have been offered. It is worth mentioning, however, that it has long been established that the occurrence in a given society of the institution of the avunculate does not have any value whatever as evidence that that society is (or ever was) matrilineal or matriarchal.[19]

The avunculate has been discussed in the context of the comparative study of the kinship terminology of the Indo-European languages, and in particular the attempts to discover the nature of the Proto-Indo-European kinship system. One of the major problems of Proto-Indo-European kinship terminology is presented by the words for uncle and nephew, sometimes specifically mother's brother and sister's son.[20] Old Irish *nia* 'sister's son' is the regular reflex of Proto-Indo-European *nepōts*. According to the language, *nepōts has given the word for 'grandson, descendant' (as in Indo-Iranian); 'nephew' (as in Middle Welsh *nei*, Old English *nefa*, Old High German *nevo*), and specifically 'sister's son' in Old Irish *nia* and Serbian *ne ak*; and both 'grandson' and (later) 'nephew' in Latin *nepos*. Old Irish *amnair* 'mother's brother' is not normally brought into the discussion by the comparatists, and its etymology has not yet been established. [No longer true; on *amnair*, see now McCone (1992).] In many Indo-European languages, however, the word for 'uncle,' sometimes specifically 'mother's brother,' represents an "enlargement"[21] of one kind or another of *awos. From *awos (without enlargement) we get the words for grandfather in Latin (avus), Hittite, and Armenian; from various enlargements (such as *avius, *avonkelos, *avīnos, *awentros) words for 'mother's brother' (like Latin avunculus) or 'uncle' (like Welsh ewythr).[22]

The occurrence in some of the Indo-European languages of terms for 'mother's brother' and/or 'sister's son' suggests that the avunculate was part of the kinship-system of the speakers of these languages. Supporting evidence is provided by indications in their texts of close relationships between nephews and their maternal uncles.[23] From Irish literature, the bond between Cú Chulainn and his maternal uncle Conchobor, as it is depicted in the Ulster sagas, offers a case in point.[24] The problem remains as to whether the avunculate was developed separately in the different language-groups or was inherited from the common culture. Recent writers have tended to opt for an Indo-European avunculate.[25]

There is also the more fundamental problem of the comparability of relationships implicit in the kinship terms. There must have been an analogy between the relationships of ego to mother's brother and that of ego to grandfather, to account for the derivation of words like *avunculus* from *awos, and there must also have been a perception of identity or close comparability between ego's relationships with his grandson and his sister's son, to account for the use of *nepōts for both 'grandson' and 'sister's son.' It is one thing to draw these inferences, and quite another to explain the evident comparability of the relevant relationships. Such attempts as have been made at explanation, in terms of cross-cousin marriage or Omaha-style kinship, have been cogently criticized by Beekes and Szemerényi.[26] Fosterage has also been discussed in this connection,[27] and in early Irish sources adoption seems relevant to the avunculate, but the comparability of relationships would hardly seem to find a sufficient explanation in fosterage or adoption. Szemerényi bases his approach on a radical reassessment of the Indo-European avunculate, but there are serious flaws in the solution which he offers.[28]

The problem which we have been considering is one for comparatists, and it cannot be solved on the sole basis of the Irish material. What the Irish evidence does show, however, is that the comparability of relationships, which is inferred from the comparative data, continued to exist in Ireland well into the historical period. The evidence I refer to comprises, first, an ambivalence regarding Cú Chulainn's relationship to Conchobor, and, secondly, the later history of Old Irish *gormac* 'adopted son, sister's son.'

Cú Chulainn's relationship to Conchobor has been mentioned above as an example of the avunculate, and that is consistent with the way in which the relationship is generally depicted in the sagas. There were, however, two traditions regarding Cú Chulainn's relationship to Conchobor, each of them being represented in a version of *Compert Con Culainn* (Cú Chulainn's Birth-tale).[29] In both versions, Cú Chulainn's mother is Dechtine (or Dechtire), but in Version I she is Conchobor's daughter, in Version II his sister. According to Version I of his birth-tale, therefore, Cú Chulainn was grandson, rather than sister's son, of Conchobor. It has been suggested that the relationship between Conchobor and Dechtine was changed by the redactor of Version II because he was confused by the kinship terminology of Version I,[30] but the argument does not stand up, since the passage which is said to have occasioned the confusion does not actually occur in Version I.

Taken on its own, the ambivalence regarding Cú Chulainn's relationship with Conchobor might seem merely to show the existence of two different versions of Cú Chulainn's pedigree. It is the history of *gormac* which indicates that it is doubtless significant that the variation is between sister's son/maternal uncle and grandson/grandfather.

Gormac is a compound of *mac* 'son, boy,' and the modifier *gor*. The meaning of *gor* has been elucidated by Binchy.[31] The *mac gor* is the 'dutiful son,' who carries out the duty of filial obedience, particularly support of his parents in old age. Such duty is denoted by the abstract *goire*. The compound *gormac* denotes an adopted son, a son, that is, who has been adopted for the purpose of maintaining the adopter; as well as 'adopted son' it means 'sister's son,' and this is taken as an indication that a sister's son would normally be adopted for this purpose.[32] The terminology thus points to the social role of the sister's son.

The Modern Irish reflex of *gormac* is *garmhac* 'grandson.' This meaning is not listed for *gormac* in *DIL*, and no early example is known to me. It may be that the duty of maintenance sometimes devolved upon a grandson. In *Táin Bó Cúailnge* we are told that Iliach, grandfather of Lóegaire Búadach, was (in Cecile O'Rahilly's translation) "being cared for with filial piety by his grandson" (*buí icá gairi la húa*).[33] This use of *gaire* (dat. *gairi*), which is the later form of Old Irish *goire*, may reflect the social context of the shift of meaning from 'sister's son' to 'grandson,' which we see in the use of Modern Irish *garmhac*. The shift seems to be a relatively late one in the history of Irish, and it would therefore indicate that the relevant relationships long remained comparable in Ireland.

The use of *gormac* for 'sister's son' is an innovation in Old Irish; the inherited word, as we have seen, is *nia*. The prehistory of *nia* has been considered in an important article by Thomas Charles-Edwards.[34] His view, which has been accepted by Szemerényi,[35] is that its Common Celtic etymon **neūss* (Indo-European **nepōts*) meant 'grandson,' and that it acquired the meaning 'sister's son' only at a relatively late stage in Common Celtic. On the contrary, I think that his painstaking presentation and analysis of the evidence can be used to show that in all probability the meaning 'sister's son' for **neūss* was either inherited from Indo-European, or developed at an early stage in Common Celtic.

Having noted the variations among Indo-European languages in the meanings of words from **awos* and **nepōts*, respectively, Charles-Edwards goes on to say: "The fact that the variations are widely distributed in the Indo-European world does not, however, prove that they go back to the period when the Indo-Europeans formed a single people, but, rather, that they are connected with features of society common to most Indo-European peoples at a later period."[36] He then proceeds to a systematic consideration of the relevant Celtic terms of kinship. His discussion is of some complexity, and must of course be read in full; in what follows, I shall take note only of the points which have to do with **neūss* (and hence with *nia*).

Charles-Edwards adduces evidence from Brythonic to show that Common Celtic *neūss* must have had the meaning 'grandson,' 'descendant,'[37] and he assumes that it at first had no other meaning. What must then be accounted for is how it came to mean 'sister's son' (Old Irish *nia*) or 'nephew' (Middle Welsh *nei*, Modern Breton *ni*). He argues that this development may have occurred in three stages. **Awos* was inherited from Indo-European, and from it **awios* was formed in Celtic to mean 'grandson';[38] this is the word which gave Old Irish *aue* 'grandson,' 'descendant' (and of course Modern Irish *ó*). Celtic would thus have both **neūss* and **awios* for 'grandson.' In the first stage of development suggested by Charles-Edwards, **awios* acquires the meaning 'nephew.' (The Celtic languages offer no direct evidence for this development, and it seems to me to be inadequately motivated.)[39] At this stage, therefore, **awios* would have meant 'grandson' or 'nephew,' and **neūss* 'grandson' only. In the second stage, **neūss* changed its meaning. The social context of this change was that certain men belonged to the kindred of the mother, rather than that of the father. Such was the position, as we shall see presently, of the sister's son of early Irish law (and early Irish literature). A similar situation is posited for the period of Common Celtic, and it is invoked in support of the notion that in this second stage "**awyos* retained its old meaning, but **neūss* came to mean 'maternal grandson-nephew within his maternal kindred.' **Neūss* now referred to the man who was a member of his maternal kindred."[40] In the third stage, "the last which can be assigned to Common Celtic, **awyos* still kept its old meaning, but **neūss* came to mean 'sister's son who belongs to his maternal kindred.'"[41]

After the period of Common Celtic, Irish *aue* came to mean simply 'grandson,' 'descendant,'[42] while *nia* (<**neūss*) retained the meaning which it had finally acquired in Common Celtic. In Brythonic, **awios* was lost, and *neīs* (<**neūss*) was generalized to mean 'nephew in general,' thus accounting for Middle Welsh *nei*, Modern Breton *ni*.[43]

There are some difficulties in Charles-Edwards's view of the development within Common Celtic. First, it is not clear why **awios* should have been coined for 'grandson,' if an unambiguous **neūss* already existed with this meaning. Secondly, there is no evidence that **awios* ever meant 'nephew' as well as 'grandson.' Thirdly, there is the very considerable difficulty, which is admitted by Charles-Edwards,[44] that, on grounds of general probability, if there were two words **awios* 'grandson' or 'nephew,' and **neūss* 'grandson,' then the unambiguous **neūss* is the one which would have been likely to retain the meaning 'grandson,' leaving the ambiguous **awios* to be specialized in the sense 'sister's son.'

It seems to me that the data can be better explained if we take two facts into account. First, we know, thanks to Charles-Edwards,[45] that **neūss* must have meant both 'grandson' and 'sister's son' at some stage in its history, since it has given words in the Celtic languages which have, or imply, one or the other of these meanings. Secondly, some of its congeners in other Indo-European languages show evidence of a like ambiguity. It is reasonable to assume, therefore, that this ambiguity was inherited in Common Celtic, or, at the very least, that there was an inherited tendency towards it. The comparative evidence indicates that the social conditions which gave rise to the use of **neūss* for 'sister's son'—in a word, the avunculate—existed in

5. The Sister's Son in Early Irish Literature

Indo-European times, though, *pace* Szemerényi, not necessarily at the earliest period.[46] They can therefore be assumed a fortiori to have existed at the earliest stage of Common Celtic. The history of **neūss*, then, could be reconstructed as follows: (1) Common Celtic **neūss* meant 'grandson' or 'sister's son.' (2) A new word **awios* was coined for 'grandson.' (3) **Neūss* ceased to mean 'grandson' and retained the meaning 'sister's son.' The subsequent developments in the daughter languages were as outlined by Charles-Edwards, and summarized above.

The evidence of the kinship terms, on the reading of it which has been presented here, indicates that social recognition of the sister's son was inherited in Ireland from the period of Common Celtic, and ultimately from Indo-European times. A question which arises in relation to Old Irish is why, beside *nia*, a second term, *gormac*, should have been used for 'sister's son.' The answer may lie, partly at least, in what I have already said about *gormac*. It will be recalled that the *gormac* is the son who is adopted for the purpose of maintaining the adopter, and that its use of the sister's son in particular is taken to indicate that he would be the one normally adopted for this purpose. The sister's son thus came to be known by a term which denoted his function in the kindred to which he belonged through his mother, and in which he had a special relationship with his mother's brother. This development in the terminology of kinship may have been helped along by the fact that the primary word, *nia*, had a homonym in Old Irish, and was therefore ambiguous. DIL distinguishes *2 nia* 'sister's son' from *1 nia* 'warrior, champion,' of which it says that it is "apparently used sometimes of a recognized or professional champion in attendance on a king or chief."[47] The two words are etymologically distinct: *2 nia*, as we have seen, is the reflex of an Indo-European kinship-term, while *1 nia* is apparently from **neit-s*, which contains the root **nei* 'to be excited, to shine.'[48] The distinction is maintained in the genitive singular in ogam inscriptions (NIOTTA 'sister's son,' NET(T)A(S) 'champion'),[49] and perhaps in archaic manuscript-forms (*nioth* and *néth*, respectively).[50] But the words seem to have influenced one another from an early time, and eventually the nominative and other cases fell together. When we find names like *Maccnio* and *Cathnio*, it is not possible to be sure which of the homonyms is represented in them.[51] Pokorny attributes the falling together of the two words to the confusion which could have occurred when they were used in the formation of names and their original meaning was obscured.[52] It is likely, however, that there was a semantic overlap between the words. We have only to consider the case of Cú Chulainn, who is the representative *par excellence* in Irish saga both of the sister's son and of the professional champion in attendance on a king. We shall see that the story of Bres in *Cath Maige Tuired* suggests that it was unwise (and perhaps improper) to elevate a sister's son to the kingship. It may be that the proper role of a sister's son, such as Cú Chulainn, whose uncle was king, was that of the professional champion: he should not aspire to the succession, but he could assume the prestigious office of the professional warrior who defended the domain of his maternal uncle. In any case, the inherited kinship-term *nia* became homonymous with the word for a functionary, and it is exiguously attested in the literature. On the other hand, *gormac*, as we have seen, started off as a word for a person who performed a certain function, and came to be used as a kinship term synonymous with 2 *nia*.

The correlative of the sister's son is the mother's brother. Old Irish has the word *amnair* for 'mother's brother,' but it is attested only twice in the manuscripts. In the St. Gall Priscian, it glosses *auunculus*, and is itself explained as *bráthair máthar* 'mother's brother.'[53] The second example is in the Old-Irish Life of Brigit, where we find *amnair in druad*;[54] that this means 'the druid's maternal uncle' is certain, since he is also called *bráthair máthar in druad* and *avunculus magi*.[55] M. A. O'Brien[56] observes that the word was probably rare in the time of the St. Gall glossator, since he deemed it necessary to explain it further, and this is probably true also of the author of the Life of Brigit, as he uses it in a context in which its meaning is made abundantly clear. So far as our written sources go, then, *amnair* is already obsolescent in the ninth century;[57] henceforth, a person's maternal uncle will be referred to as his 'mother's brother.' (It is all the more remarkable, therefore, to find the Modern Irish reflex of *amnair* being used of the maternal uncle in the present century among Irish speakers on Tory Island off Donegal.)[58]

It is perhaps worth noting that *amnair* is in both examples given as the equivalent of *bráthair máthar*, which could be translated 'mother's kinsman,' since Old Irish *bráthair* can be used of a kinsman as well as of a male sibling. *Bráthair máthar* can refer to the maternal uncle, as when Art mac Cuinn is said to have been *bráthair máthar* to Éogan mac Ailella, who was son of Art's sister Sadb.[59] It is nevertheless conceivable that the Irish equivalent of the Latin *avunculus* could have been any adult male of the mother's kindred. There is certainly an inherent ambiguity in the notion of 'sister's son' as it is found in early Irish literature. *Nia* and *gormac* are glossed *mac sethar*,[60] which could be translated 'son of a kinswoman,' since *siur* (gen. *sethar*) can mean 'kinswoman' as well as 'sister' (in the literal sense of 'female sibling'). In the literature, the *nia* or *gormac* is considered to be 'sister's son' to the mother's kindred, or indeed to greater groups to which he has gained access through his mother. In *Mesca Ulad*, "The Intoxication of the Ulstermen," Celtchar mac Uthechair expresses his disapproval of Cú Chulainn by saying, "Alas for Ulster that the *gormac* who gives the advice was ever born."[61] This has been explained as a reference to the fact that Cú Chulainn was son of Conchobor's sister Dechtine,[62] but the context would suggest that Cú Chulainn is being regarded as *gormac* of the Ulaid as a whole. We shall find a clear case presently in Bres, who is brought up among his mother's people (*máithre*), the Túatha Dé Danann, and who is described as their sister's son (*gormac*). An instance of a similarly extended usage of *nia* is found in the prophecy which Cú Chulainn is said to have made of the coming of Christ, where he says *nia doíne ticfa*, "a sister's son of mankind will come."[63] This is the passage which Cormac mac Cuilennáin cites in his glossary to illustrate the use of *nia*: *Nia, mac sethar, ut dixit Cu Chulaind profetans de Christi adventu.... Nia duine tiucfae (.i. mac sethar duine)*, "*Nia*, sister's son (or kinswoman's son), as Cú Chulainn said, prophesying the coming of Christ, 'a *nia* of mankind will come,' that is, a sister's (or kinswoman's) son of mankind."[64] As Charles-Edwards points out, "this is an Irish legal interpretation of 'et incarnatus est de Spiritu Sancto ex Maria virgine.'"[65] Christ belongs to the human race through Mary, his mother, and he is in that sense a sister's son to mankind. The same notion informs the Blathmac poem with which we started out, save that there Christ is sister's son (*mac deirbsethar*) to his very mother-kin (*fírmáithre*), the Jews (lines 400, 412).

It is worth noting here that the name Cairbre Nia Fer is to be explained along similar lines. In the Book of Armagh we find *in regno Coirpri Nioth fer*:[66] *nioth* is the expected reflex in Old Irish of the genitive singular of the word for sister's son, corresponding, as we have seen, to ogam NIOTTA. MacNeill held that *nioth* must be the genitive of *1 nia* 'champion,' the form being taken over from *2 nia*. The latter word he rejects on the grounds that

C. Nia Fer "cannot mean 'C. nephew of men'"![67] The probability is that Cairbre was deemed to have a supernatural father,[68] and to have belonged to the human race through his mother. Hence the name "Cairbre, Sister's Son to Man (lit. 'of men')."

What was the legal status of the sister's son? Or, more specifically, was there a legal basis for the poet's claim that Jesus was a true kinsman (*fírbráthair*) of his mother's kin, and that in killing him they committed the crime of kin-slaying (*fingal*)?[69] To answer this question, we must consider the relationship in law of a man to his maternal kin. Here we can draw upon Binchy's paper on family membership of women, which is primarily concerned with the mother, but deals also with the position of the son.[70] The general rule was that the children of a recognized marriage belonged to the father's family. The maternal kin had certain limited rights with regard to them: they might intervene if the proper education of the sons was neglected or insufficiently carried out by the husband; if one of the sons had been unlawfully slain, the maternal kin were entitled to payment of one-seventh of the wergild. Otherwise the maternal kin had "no share in the sons" of a recognized marriage, except for the son of a *cú glas* or an *ambue*,[71] both of whom, as we shall see, were immigrants into the woman's *túath*.

There were certain unions which "were of so transitory a nature as to involve no change in the woman's family membership."[72] The sons of some unions of this kind belonged to the mother's family, and this may have been true of all of them.

The situation of the *cú glas* and the *ambue* has been explicated by Charles-Edwards.[73] In early Irish society, the legal and jurisdictional unit is the petty kingdom, the *túath*, and the rights and obligations of a freeman are contained within that unit. If a man marries outside his own *túath*—if, as a legal text puts it in a contemptuous way which is echoed in *Táin Bó Cúailnge*, he "follows the buttocks of his wife across a boundary"[74]—he loses the rights which he had enjoyed in his own *túath*, and depends for his status upon the status of his wife. If he comes from a *túath* within Ireland, he is an *ambue* (literally, "one who possesses no cattle");[75] if he comes from outside Ireland, which would normally mean that he was an *Albanach* or Briton, he is a *cú glas* ("wolf").[76] Since such a father is without the legal capacity of a freeman, the son becomes a member of his maternal kindred, and from them receives the *orbae niad*, "the inheritance of a sister's son."

So far as I know, no mention is made in the laws of the *amnair* 'mother's brother.' But, as Charles-Edwards says, "it is likely that one of the maternal uncles took over the rights and duties of the father."[77] Binchy has pointed out that in the early tale *Imathchor Ailello ocus Airt*[78] the mother's brother acts as representative of the maternal kindred: Ailill Ólomm has abandoned his wife Sadb, because she has borne him twins, a boy and a girl, whom she is forced to bring up without assistance from him. Her cause is taken up by her brother Art, who impleads Ailill before the judge Olldam.[79] Charles-Edwards has proposed a solution to the problem posed by the ogam inscription containing NIOTTA (genitive of 'sister's son'), which would cast light on the role of the mother's brother.[80] The inscription reads DUMELI MAQI GLASICONAS NIOTTA COBRANOR[IGAS], which may be translated "[the stone] of D., son of G., sister's son of C."[81] Charles-Edwards[82] compares inscriptions of the type DEBRANI MAQI ELTI AVI OGATOS, "of D., son of E., *aue* of O.,"[83] which gives the paternity (son of E.) and the kindred membership (*aue* of O.) of the dead man. He proposes that the function of NIOTTA in the first inscription, like that of AVI in the second, is to give the kindred membership: D. is son of G., but belongs to the kindred of his mother's brother, C.

Charles-Edwards's proposal in relation to this inscription is not limited to the formula, important though that is. He would translate, "the stone of Dumelas, son of a *cú glas*, sister's son of Cobranoris," with GLASICONAS (genitive) taken as the equivalent of Old Irish *con glais* (genitive of *cú glas*), and as having the elements reversed in composition.[84] This is a very attractive suggestion: even if it were insisted upon that GLASICONAS should be taken as a name, the nominative of which would be *Glaschú* in Old Irish,[85] it could be interpreted as a nickname given to an immigrant from overseas. This interpretation would be entirely consistent with the evidence in the laws that the son of such an immigrant belongs to his mother's kindred.

There seems, then, to be some evidence to support what is implicit in the very existence of the words *amnair* and *nia*, which is that the avunculate was an institution in early Ireland. What emerges most clearly is that the *nia* was a son who belonged to his maternal kindred. Where I would disagree with Charles-Edwards is that he limits such sons to those of exiles, of an *ambue* or a *cú glas*.[86] Binchy is surely correct in including the sons of transitory unions, and this is borne out by the evidence of the literature. The description of Christ as a *nia* is a case in point: he is the son of a transitory union, and Charles-Edwards is hardly correct when he says that Christ "is thought of as the son of an exile from heaven."[87] Bres son of Elatha, *gormac* of the Túatha Dé Danann, the circumstances of whose begetting are set out below, is also the son of a transitory union.

As a *nia*, Christ would have been a member of his mother's kindred, and he would have been a *fírbráthair*, as Blathmac put it, of the members of that kindred; if any of them were to kill him, it would be *fingal* on their part. What we have in the Blathmac poem, then, is the application of the model of kindred to the Jews as a whole.

The Blathmac poem offers a clear demonstration of the presence of a set of concepts relating to the sister's son in the ideological matrix within which the poet apprehended the story of the life of Jesus. This set of concepts is an inherited one: it is reflected in the kinship terms, in the laws, and in the literature. In what follows I shall examine some of the ways in which concepts relating to the sister's son are encoded in early Irish narrative.[88]

We may begin with the gods, since themes of kinship play a crucial part in the material which has come down to us concerning them. I shall confine myself to *Cath Maige Tuired*, "The Battle of Mag Tuired,"[89] which deals in explicit terms with the relationships of certain personages to their maternal kin. *Cath Maige Tuired* tells the story of the contention between the Túatha Dé Danann and the Fomoiri, which culminated in a battle which is said to have been fought at Moytirra (Mag Tuired) in County Sligo, in which the Túatha Dé Danann vanquished the Fomoiri. The Túatha Dé Danann are a group of deities which are presented in Irish texts as one of the successive sets of prehistoric invaders of Ireland, while the rather shadowy Fomoiri never appear as settlers in Ireland, and have strong associations with the sea and the islands.[90] The struggle between these two groups, as it is depicted in *Cath Maige Tuired*, is a version of the Indo-European myth of the war of gods. It has recently been argued that conflicts between groups of gods such as the Túatha Dé Danann and the Fomoiri, which represent the Indo-European myth, are to be interpreted "in terms of structural conflicts between different principles of kinship in the social organisation of Indo-European society; descent versus alliance, succession through the mother versus succession through the father, etc."[91] There is in fact a web of relationships linking individuals of the Túatha Dé Danann with those of the Fomoiri, as J. G. Oosten has shown.[92] For our purposes a brief résumé of the relevant parts of *Cath Maige Tuired* will suffice to show how the social implications of kinship are explored in the tale.

The story begins at a time when yet another group, the Fir Bolg, held sway in Ireland. The Túatha Dé Danann made an alliance (*caratrad*) with the Fomoiri, and Balar grandson of Nét of the Fomoiri had given his daughter Eithne to Cían, son of Dían Cécht of the Túatha Dé Danann. Lug was born of the union of Cían and Eithne.[93] Thus Lug, whose role is to be decisive in the contention between the Túatha Dé Danann and the Fomoiri, is of mixed parentage, his father being of the Túatha Dé Danann, and his mother of the Fomoiri.

Bres son of Elatha is another person of mixed parentage, and the circumstances of his conception and birth are told as an anecdote in *Cath Maige Tuired*. Elatha, king of the Fomoiri, came to Ériu, a woman of the Túatha Dé Danann, as an uninvited stranger from across the sea; he importuned her, and had intercourse with her. Having done so, he revealed his identity to her, prophesied that a boy would be born of their encounter, and told her what to call the boy. Elatha then went back to the Fomoiri, while Ériu returned to her home, and in due course gave birth to Bres (§§15–23). Bres is thus the antithesis of Lug, his father being of the Fomoiri, and his mother of the Túatha Dé Danann. Since Bres lives with his mother's kin, he is a *gormac*, and he is so called in the text.

The Túatha Dé Danann came to Ireland to take it by force from the Fir Bolg. They defeated the Fir Bolg in a great battle, killing their king. But Núadu, king of the Túatha Dé Danann, had an arm amputated in battle and, being blemished, was ineligible to retain the kingship. Contention arose between the Túatha Dé Danann and their womenfolk as to who should succeed Núadu as king. The women argued that the Túatha Dé Danann should give the kingship to Bres son of Elatha, their own sister's son (*gormac*), on the grounds that giving him the kingship would bind the alliance (*caratrad*) of the Fomoiri with them, since his father Elatha was of the Fomoiri. The Túatha Dé Danann yielded to their womenfolk and bestowed the kingship of Ireland upon Bres. To his maternal kin (*máithre*), the Túatha Dé Danann, Bres gave seven hostages as a guarantee that he would restore the sovereignty should any failure on his part to discharge his obligations to them so give cause (*ma forfertís a mifholtae fesin*, §§9–11, 14, 24).

Bres proved utterly disastrous as king. The Fomoiri imposed tribute on Ireland "so that there was no smoke from a house in Ireland for which they were not paid tribute"; the Túatha Dé Danann were put to work for Bres, performing menial tasks. He was duped into giving a false judgment, thereby showing himself unworthy of the kingship. Moreover, the Túatha Dé Danann (here again said to be his *máithre*) greatly complained about him, for he failed to discharge his obligations of hospitality and entertainment to them. The Túatha Dé Danann, for their part, ceased to render service or payment to Bres. Cairbre son of Étaín, poet of the Túatha Dé Danann, came to Bres for hospitality on one occasion, and was ungenerously received. For this, he satirized Bres, who was blighted from that time on (§§24–32, 36–39).

After that the Túatha Dé Danann went to speak to their *gormac*, Bres son of Elatha. They asked him to honor the guarantees that he had given them, and he restored the sovereignty to them. But he was not then able to discharge his obligations to them (*nibo sofoltach friu di sin*), and he asked that they wait for him for seven years. This they granted on certain conditions, which he accepted (§40).

The real reason why Bres asked for this respite was that he was unwilling to be ejected from the kingship, and wished to gather the warriors of the Fomoiri to take the Túatha Dé Danann by force as soon as he had achieved an invincible advantage. He repairs, then, to the land of the Fomoiri, and there meets his father, Elatha, for the first time. Lest there be any lingering doubt about the nature of his reign, Bres tells Elatha that what has taken him out of Ireland is his own injustice (*anfír*) and arrogance (*anúabar*): he has deprived the Túatha Dé Danann of their valuables and possessions and of their food. He nonetheless announces his intention of taking Ireland by force, and sets about gathering a great army among the Fomoiri (§§41–51). It is that army which in due course invades Ireland and is defeated by the Túatha Dé Danann at Mag Tuired.

Bres is not assigned to any named maternal uncle in *Cath Maige Tuired*: the terms of the discussion of his kingship are *gormac* and *máithre*. His land he receives from his mother (§24), and we have seen that it is on the advice of the womenfolk that he is made king. The clear burden of the narrative is that the Túatha Dé Danann erred in taking this advice, and that it is not appropriate for a sister's son to be elected to kingship.

Bres's kinship with the Túatha Dé Danann is only one side of the coin. We have seen how Blathmac treated of both Christ's kinship with the Jews and the contractual nexus which bound them to him as their lord and king.

5. The Sister's Son in Early Irish Literature 83

Cath Maige Tuired likewise combines the theme of kinship with themes of kingship, and in particular with an account of the contractual nature of Bres's relationship, as king, to the Túatha Dé Danann. In an earlier article, drawing on the work of Dumézil, I have discussed the events of Bres's reign in terms of a breakdown of the social contract,[94] and all I wish to do here is to consider two aspects of the matter which I neglected in that article.

First, there is the designation of Bres's maternal kindred. In mentioning them above, I have followed convention in calling them *Túatha Dé Danann*. In the text of *Cath Maige Tuired*, however, they are normally referred to as either *Túath Dé* or *Túatha Dé*, showing a variation between the singular and plural of *túath*. In those parts of the text which recount the reign of Bres, the singular is always used. What is in question here, therefore, is essentially the relationship between king and *túath*.

Secondly, I should like to say a word about the two excerpts from the Irish text which have been included in the above résumé. In the first of them, Bres gives seven hostages to his maternal kin as a guarantee that he would restore the sovereignty *ma forfertís a mifholtae fesin*, which I would translate as "should any failure on his part to discharge his obligations [to them so] give cause" (§24).[95] In the second excerpt, the Túatha Dé Danann have asked Bres to honor the guarantees he had given them, and he restores the sovereignty to them. But[96] *nibo sofoltach friu di sin*, and he asks that they wait for him for seven years. The Irish here I translate as "he was not then able to discharge his obligations to them" (§40).[97] These renderings differ somewhat from those of previous translators but, while I cannot insist upon the precise wording, I believe they convey the essence of what is being said in the original. *Folad* is the element common to *mifholtae* and *sofoltach*:[98] I have already quoted extensively from Binchy on *folad*, and here I may add for good measure that Thurneysen says of it that it "can hardly be rendered by a single word. It denotes that which constitutes the essence of a thing . . . in the case of lords and clients the essence of their relationship, the correct discharge of their mutual obligations."[99] What is true of lords and clients is evidently true too of king and *túath*. Bres enters into a solemn contract upon his election as king, and gives seven hostages as a guarantee that he will fulfil his obligations. It is the duty of a king to exercise moderation, to show truth and justice (*fír*), and to offer hospitality and entertainment to his people. It is the discharge of these duties which constitutes Bres's *folad*, and we have seen that he falls down in every respect. That is why they ask him to restore the sovereignty, and he is obliged to accede to their request. His *mífholta* have indeed given cause for the restoration.

The second reference to *folad* must be considered in the light of the first, since both of them are made in connection with the notion of restoring the kingship. A question mark hangs over the precise import of the second reference, however. The use of *di sin*, which I have translated as "then," but which would more literally be "thenceforth,"[100] forbids us to take it as referring to the events of Bres's reign. One possibility is that the reference is to whatever residual obligations Bres may have to the Túatha Dé Danann after relinquishing the sovereignty over them. Another, intriguing one is that Bres is not now an acceptable candidate for re-election to kingship, and that what he is requesting is that he might try again in seven years' time.

We know, however, that his real intention is to win back the sovereignty by force of arms. Having failed as king, Bres repairs to his father's people, from whom he raises an army with which to return to Ireland and make war on his maternal kin.

Bres's tenure of office as king is thrown into sharp relief by the career of Lug. In structural terms, Bres and Lug are cross-cousins: as we have seen, Lug's father is of the Túatha Dé Danann, his mother of the Fomoiri.[101] The marriage of which Lug was born sealed the alliance between the Túatha Dé Danann and the Fomoiri. The election of Bres to kingship was intended to strengthen that alliance, but issued instead in warfare between the two groups. It was Lug who mobilized the Túatha Dé Danann against the impending invasion of the Fomoiri, and it was he who led his father's people to victory over his maternal relatives.

When Bres had departed for the land of the Fomoiri, his predecessor Núadu was restored to the kingship, his hand having been restored to him in the meantime. Núadu held a great feast at Tara in the course of which Lug, in typical heroic fashion, arrived there, uninvited and evidently unknown to those within. Núadu attempted to exclude him from Tara, but Lug was eventually admitted on the grounds that he was master of so many arts that his like had never before been seen in Tara. Núadu goes on to cede the kingship to Lug, who in turn sets about preparing the Túatha Dé Danann for battle (§§53–74).

The preparations are described at length. An attempt is made by the Túatha Dé Danann to keep Lug away from the battle, so that he might remain unblemished. But he contrived to reach the battlefield, and took his place at the head of the Túatha Dé Danann. He urged the Túatha Dé Danann, here called "the men of Ireland," "to fight the battle fervently, so that they should no longer be in bondage. For it would be better for them to die defending their *athardae* [paternal kin] than to be in bondage and under tribute as they had been" (§129).

The decisive incident in the battle is Lug's victorious encounter with his maternal grandfather, Balar of the Fomoiri, who had already slain Núadu. Balar had an evil eye which was never opened save on a battlefield. Four men used to lift up the lid of the eye with a handle through the lid. A host, however numerous, which beheld the eye could not resist warriors. There is a dialogue between Lug and Balar, and then Balar commands that his eyelid be raised. But when this has been done, "Lug cast a sling-stone at him, so that the eye went (back) through his head. And so it was his own army that looked at it." After that, the battle became a rout, and the Fomoiri were beaten back to the sea (§§133–35).

Lug comes upon his cross-cousin, Bres son of Elatha, after the battle. Bres implores Lug to spare him. Lug agrees to do so on condition that Bres answers three questions: "How shall the men of Ireland plough? How shall they sow? How shall they reap?" Bres does so, and he is spared (§§149–161).

Lug is the defender and savior of his *athardae*, his paternal kin. In fulfilling this role, he is brought into conflict with his maternal kin. His slaying of Balar, which is a version of the mythical killing of a king by his sister's or daughter's son (his **nēpots*),[102] saves Ireland, and the Túatha Dé Danann, from the Fomorean menace.[103] By wresting from Bres the secrets of ploughing, sowing, and reaping, he ensures that the Túatha Dé Danann will henceforth have control over the fruits of the earth.[104] Bres, for his part, having proved a disastrous king of his maternal kindred, is the instigator of the battle in which his paternal kindred are routed. Bres was a *gormac*, and the essence of his fault lay in a failure of *goire*—a failure, that is to say, to show the proper filial care for his maternal kin to whom, as sister's son, he belonged.[105]

The antithesis of Bres in the matter of *goire* is the Ulster hero, Cú Chulainn, for he is the most prodigiously filial of sister's sons in relation to his maternal kindred. Cú Chulainn, moreover, is the son of Bres's cross-cousin, Lug.

Cú Chulainn was conceived three times: he was first begotten in Bruig na Bóinne (the necropolis at the bend of the Boyne in County Meath) by Lug upon his Otherworld consort; then at Emain Macha (Navan Fort in County Armagh, seat of Conchobor's court in the Ulster sagas) by Lug upon Dechtine; and finally by Súaltaim upon the same Dechtine.[106] This manner of coming into the world puts the mark of a hero on Cú Chulainn, and he answers the call to heroism in the epic *Táin Bó Cúailnge*.[107]

The *Táin* is the centerpiece of the Ulster Cycle. It tells of a great cattle-raid carried out upon Ulster by the Connachta, with the assistance of numerous allies from all around Ireland, and of some exiled Ulstermen, notably Fergus, who had once been king of Ulster. The raid was instigated by Medb, who was queen of the Connachta and Fergus's lover. It was mounted at a time when the men of Ulster were afflicted by the *ces noínden*, which was a winter sleep or torpor affecting the adult males of Ulster and extending from *Samain* (1 November) to *Imbolc* (1 February).[108] Súaltaim, being an outsider (he resided at Mag Muirthemne, which was in Conaille), was immune to the *ces*, and so was his son Cú Chulainn.[109] Thus it fell to Cú Chulainn to ward off the invaders single-handed, and much of the *Táin* is devoted to his spectacular exploits in so doing, until the Ulstermen arose from their torpor to vanquish the Connachta, who returned to their own land, while the Ulstermen went in triumph to Emain Macha.

There is a section of the *Táin* which deals with Cú Chulainn's boyhood deeds (*macgnímrada*), and this is essentially a description in sequence of the boy's initiation as a warrior.[110] It is the first stage in this sequence (*TBC I*, lines 399–456) which is of particular relevance to our theme. I should point out that at this stage the boy is called Sétantae; it is only later, in the course of his initiation into warrior status, that he acquires the name Cú Chulainn.

The young Sétantae, who is being raised by his father and mother in Mag Muirthemne (in County Louth), has heard of the boy-troop of king Conchobor at Emain Macha, and sets out to join them in defiance of his mother's wishes. Sétantae does not know that anyone who wishes to join the boys in their playing field must bind them over to protect him, and when he arrives at Emain Macha he comes on to the playing field without securing their protection. All 150 boys attack him, but he successfully wards them off and then goes on the attack himself. He has knocked down fifty of the boys when Conchobor seizes him and upbraids him for his treatment of the boys. The dialogue continues as follows (lines 440–54):

"It was right for me (to treat them so), master Conchobar," said he. "I came to play with them from my home, from my father and mother, and they were not kind to me."

"What is your name?" said Conchobar.

"I am Sétanta the son of Súaltaim and Deichtire, your sister. It was not to be expected that I should be tormented here."[111]

"Why were the boys not bound over to protect you?" asked Conchobar.

"I did not know of (the need of) that," said Cú Chulainn. "Undertake to protect me against them."

"I agree," said Conchobar.

But then he turned again and attacked the boys throughout the house.

"What have you got against them now?" asked Conchobar.

"Let me be bound over to protect them," said Cú Chulainn.

"Undertake it then," said Conchobar.

"I agree," said Cú Chulainn.

As Lug had at Tara, Sétantae arrives at Emain Macha uninvited and unknown to those within.[112] He is not therefore a *nia*, in the strict sense of a sister's son who belongs from his birth to his mother's kindred. The above scenario represents the adoption of a sister's son by his mother's brother, and it is interesting to see not only the manner in which it is done, but also the language which is used. The word for "protecting" in the Irish text is *fóesam*, and the form translated as "I agree" is *atmu*, the first person singular of *ad-daim* 'acknowledges.' What is in question here is the solemn acknowledgement of the obligation to provide *fóesam*, and the solemnity of the utterance is duly reflected in the grammar of *atmu*.[113] This throws light on a phrase which I have already quoted from Blathmac: the poet says that in Ireland the killing of Christ would be described as *sénae iar n-aitite* (Carney 1964, line 396), which Carney translates as "denial after recognition." *Aititiu* (here in the dative *aitite*) is the verbal noun of *ad-daim*, and the context would support the view that the reference is to the repudiation of a solemn contract of reciprocal obligation of the kind entered into by Conchobor and Sétantae. As for Sétantae himself, the expression *mac fóesma* is used of the adopted son,[114] and that is precisely what Sétantae has become as a result of his exchange with Conchobor. Sétantae will henceforth be obliged to show *goire* to his mother's brother.

We saw that in the accounts of Cú Chulainn's conception and birth there are two versions of his relations with Conchobor. In the *Táin*, however, he is consistently sister's son to the king. It is this relationship which allowed him to expect that he would be well received in Ulster, as is clear from the dialogue printed above. The relationship also governs the response to him not only of the king, but of the men of Ulster in general. Culann the smith welcomes him *fo déig cridi do máthar*, "for your mother's sake" (line 591), and when the boy has come close to death "a great alarm was raised by them at the thought that the son of the king's sister had almost been killed" (lines 589 f.). Conchobor has an intimate relationship with the boy: when he returns from the foray in which he has blooded his weapons, he sits at Conchobor's knee "which was his resting-place always after that" (lines 802 f.). Cú Chulainn's loyalty to Conchobor is manifest in his deeds, but he expresses it also in his words. When the Connachta send an emissary to offer terms to Cú Chulainn, he identifies himself to the emissary only as a *céile* of Conchobor's; and when he hears the terms that would be offered, he says that Cú Chulainn "will not exchange his mother's brother for another king" (lines 1264 f.).

In characterizing Cú Chulainn's relationship to the people of Ulster, Sjoestedt says "he is their defender and their champion. He is the ideal type of youth, of fighter, at once the glory and the living rampart of his tribe."[115] For her, Cú Chulainn is the type of "the hero of the tribe," as distinct from "the hero outside the tribe," who is typically a member of a *Männerbund* or *fían*. The marginal status of the *fían*-warrior, and the disruptive nature of his activities, has been well brought out in recent studies.[116] McCone points out that "there is evidence to suggest that clerical manipulation may have glossed over more intimate links between the two types of warrior in real life,"[117] but, whatever its source, the ideological distinction between them is clear in the literature.

The highest condition that a society can aspire to is one of perfect peace and prosperity; the yearning for this condition is a paradisal one, and it finds expression in the literature in the descriptions of the Golden Age said to have been enjoyed in the reigns of Cormac mac Airt and Conaire Mór.[118] But in the real world it was required of a king to be brave in battle, a point which has recently been documented from the laws and the literature.[119] In a world where the king was expected to prove his mettle by making a cattle-raid, known as *crech ríg*,[120] the professional warrior had his due place.

5. The Sister's Son in Early Irish Literature 89

It has been said that "one might almost describe the endemic warfare of early Ireland as 'harmless,' for, while it could be barbarous, its primary aim was not unlike that of the modern riot weapon: to sting and to stun but not to kill.... Like the later faction fight it had a strong element of ritual, but it was essentially less destructive because it was less rigidly patterned and because in the long run its purpose, at least in theory, was to uphold the social order and to bond the tribal kingdom."[121] Needless to say, this is a far cry from what we find in *Táin Bó Cúailnge*, where the fighting is on an epic scale and the impact of the invasion is summed up in the words of Súaltaim: "Men are slain, women carried off, cattle driven away!" (line 3425). Another summation of the events of the cattle-raid, "fury destroys the world" (line 4076), has been chosen as the title of an article by Radner, in which she questions the received view of the Ulster sagas as a celebration of a lost heroic age: "Thematically, the Ulster Cycle as a whole tends to present the tragic breakdown of those relationships on which early Irish society was founded: the relationship between host and guest, between kindred, between foster-brothers, between men and women, between lords and clients and kings and overkings, between the human world and the gods."[122]

This cannot altogether be gainsaid. Even the participants in the raid say nothing to justify the enterprise. Before they set out from Crúachain, Medb says, "All those who part here today from comrade and from friend will curse me, for it is I who have mustered this hosting" (lines 25 f.). And when the final battle has been lost, her ally and lover, Fergus, speaks disparagingly, and with transparent metaphor, of "a herd of horses led by a mare. Their substance is taken and carried off and guarded as they follow a woman who has misled them" (lines 4123 f.). Werewolving, more usually associated with *fian*-warriors, makes its appearance here too: Fergus prophesies that "warriors' blood will be spilt on the ground by this army of curs in human shape" (*la slúag inna ndunechon*, line 2420). Evidence of the breakdown of social order is all about us in *Táin Bó Cúailnge*.

Yet it is impossible not to see in *Táin Bó Cúailnge* a celebration of the martial heroism of Cú Chulainn: of his courage and ingenuity, his mastery of the martial arts, his unswerving loyalty. The epic theme of the *Táin* is Cú Chulainn's single-handed defence of Ulster: as his divine father, Lug, was to the Túatha Dé Danann, so is Cú Chulainn to the Ulstermen—their defender and savior. If Conchobor owes the protection of his realm to his sister's son, his daughter's son also plays a crucial part. Perhaps the most touching passage in all the *Táin* is the following one in which Fergus describes the arrival on the scene of the final battle of Erc, son of Cairbre Nia Fer and of Conchobor's daughter (lines 3827 ff.):

> I should think it likely that those might be the men of Tara with the fine, noble lad who is Erc, the son of Cairpre Nia Fer and of Conchobar's daughter. . . Without asking permission of his father, that boy has come to the assistance of his grandfather. It is because of that lad that you will be defeated in battle. He will experience neither dread nor fear as he makes for you in the middle of your army. Bravely will the warriors of Ulster roar as they hew down the army before them, rushing to rescue their beloved lad. They will all feel the ties of kinship (*Do-icfe uile ell condolba*) when they see the boy in that great conflict. Like the baying of a bloodhound will be heard the sound of Conchobar's sword as he comes to the boy's rescue. Cú Chulainn will cast up three ramparts of (dead) men around the battle as he rushes towards the little lad. Mindful of their kinship (*condalb*) with the boy, the warriors of Ulster will attack the vast (enemy) host.

The theme of *condalbae* (kin-love) is a recurrent one in the *Táin*. Fergus who, on Conchobor's own admission, was driven by him "into exile to dwell with wolves and foxes" (lines 4050 f.), is affected by kin-love: because of it (*ar chondalbi*) he sends a warning to the Ulstermen before the raiders set out (line 216), and takes the raiders on a detour as they make their way to Ulster (line 229). When it is put to him in the course of the final battle that he exerts too much force on his own people (*túath*) and race (*cenél*), he turns his sword upon the hills rather than strike his own people (lines 4068 ff.).

It is the strength of kin-love, then, which ultimately defeats the destructive forces which are unleashed upon Ulster in *Táin Bó Cúailnge*. The collapse of social order is stemmed and ultimately reversed, thanks to the prodigious efforts of a sister's son who responds to the needs of his maternal kin, and who discharges the obligations which were laid upon him when he entered into a contractual relationship with his mother's brother.

The destructive possibilities of the avuncular relationship are also represented in the Ulster Cycle. According to one version of his pedigree, Noísiu was another sister's son of Conchobor's.[123] It was Noísiu who eloped with Deirdriu, who had been reared at Conchobor's behest as a wife for himself. The lovers eventually returned to Ulster under Conchobor's protection, with Fergus and others as sureties. But Conchobor arranged that Noísiu and his brothers should be slain, and it was this treachery on Conchobor's part which led to the exile of Fergus and his fellow-sureties.[124] The rivalry in love of Conchobor and his sister's son finds correspondence in the story of Tristan and Iseult, for Tristan was sister's son to Mark.[125]

One of the best-known confrontations in the Ulster Cycle is that of the Ulsterman Conall Cernach with the Connachtman Cet mac Mágach, as each of them stakes his claim for the "champion's portion" in the "Story of Mac Da Thó's Pig."[126] It is said that Conall Cernach was sister's son to Cet. Even before Conall was conceived, it was prophesied of him that no child would be more unfilial (*ingaire*) than he to his mother's kin, the Connachta. Cet nonetheless protected his sister until she brought forth her son. It was once again prophesied of the boy that he would be unfilial, and Cet then drew the little boy towards him, and put him under his heel, and bruised his neck, but did not break his spinal marrow. The mother said, "Wolfish (*conda*) is the treachery (*feall*) you perform, o brother!" Cet acknowledged as much, and said that the boy should be called Conall (or *con-fheall*).[127]

This anecdote does not reveal the actual etymology of *Conall* (see Thurneysen 1946, 89 §140) but, in its use of *conda* of an injury done to a sister's son, it is reminiscent of Blathmac's poem, where the same word is used of those who crucified Christ (Carney 1964, line 409). Cet's wolfish deed was prompted by the prophecy that Conall would be unfilial; Christ on the other hand was filial (*gor*) in his relations with the Jews (line 121), and indeed, in his second poem, Blathmac says that it is from Christ that true filial piety (*fírgaire*) is to be learned (lines 689–90). It is true that in this latter instance the reference is to Christ's filial demeanor to his father in heaven. Likewise, the reference to the filial character of Christ's kin-love (*ba gor... in chondalbae*, lines 738–39) seems to have to do with the household of heaven. But the notion that Christ is the exemplar of *goire* is clearly established, and the repudiation of this *goire* makes the crucifixion all the more wolfish.

A similar application of the notion of wolfishness is found in relation to Lugaid Mac Con and Ailill Ólomm of the Éoganachta. The cycle of tales dealing with the intertwined genealogy and fortunes of the legendary kings of Dál Cuinn, of the Éoganachta, and of the Corcu Loígde, is a rich source for themes of kinship and related matters, including the theme of *goire*.[128] I shall confine myself here to two aspects of the latter theme. Lugaid Mac Con is said to have been foster-son of Ailill Ólomm and his wife Sadb. After his victory in the battle of Mag Mucrama, Lugaid became king of Tara. But in due course he was ousted from the kingship of Tara, and he then repaired to Ailill to offer him filial care (*dia gorigud*, O Daly 1975, line 341). Ailill welcomes Lugaid, and accepts his offer, saying, "Come to me that we may come to an agreement, that you may make me (your) father and that I may make you (my) son for I have no sons with me to maintain me (*dom gaire*)" (lines 343 ff.). They then embrace, but Ailill touches Lugaid with a poisonous tooth which he had, and as a result of this Lugaid's cheek melts away (lines 346 ff.). In another account of the same incident, Sadb tells Lugaid that it is a wolf's tooth (*fiacail maic thíre*) which has lacerated him (lines 346 ff.).

At an earlier stage in his career Lugaid had learned that Ailill had a wolfish heart (*cride fáelda*, line 753). He nevertheless offers himself, in effect, as *gormac* to Ailill, but all that he gets in return is the laceration of a wolf's tooth.

The other aspect of the treatment of *goire* in this cycle which I should like to mention here is the extension of the concept to include patriotic duty in relation to Ireland as a whole. Lugaid Mac Con spends some time in exile from Ireland before he returns with the army which he leads to victory at the battle of Mag Mucrama, thereby acquiring for himself the kingship of Tara. He expresses his love for Ireland when he says, ironically as it turns out, that "he would rather be devoured by the wolves of Ireland than remain any longer away from his country" (lines 250–51). Yet the sentence which is given in Irish in the following passage shows that it is the narrator's view that Lugaid's invasion of Ireland was not the act of a patriotic Irishman: "Lugaid came then with that army and with that great and mighty host to avenge his wrong on the men of Ireland. He who brought them was no dutiful son (*Nírbo gor in mac dos-n-uc*). They invaded Ireland and many submitted to him" (lines 161 ff.). There is no personal correlative of *mac gor* either in the immediate context as quoted, or in the wider context of the passage. This, together with the mention of Ireland both before and after the narratorial comment, makes it clear that what is in question here is a lack of *goire* with regard to Ireland.

It is the element of wolfishness in the repudiation of *goire* which link this cycle of tales to the others which we have been discussing. The rich symbolism of the wolf in Irish ideology has been explored in a number of papers by McCone.[129] For present purposes, it is sufficient to note that the opposition between wolf and man is mediated by werewolves, the *cú glas*, and others who, though they are in some sense human, are excluded from society and belong to the wild. It is mediated also by the domesticated dog, a case in point being Culann's hound in *Táin Bó Cúailnge*, which is said by its master to be a *fer muintire* 'servant,' literally "a man of the household" (line 595). Now it is incumbent upon man in society to be *gor*; to fail in this, and more particularly to repudiate the *goire* of one's kindred, is to reduce oneself to the condition of a wolf.

But what of Cú Chulainn, who is nothing if not *gor* in his demeanor, and is yet the hound of Culann? He slays Culann's hound in an initiatory combat, and takes on the role as well as the name of the hound which he has destroyed (lines 598 ff.). But he has already been integrated into Ulster society. The role he assumes is that of the wolf as defender and protector of the master's domain, which in his case is the realm of his maternal uncle. It is true that on occasion his wild side, his *furor heroicus*, can get the better of him, as it does when he returns from an initiatory foray, undertaken for the purpose of blooding his newly acquired weapons. He proclaims that unless some man is found to fight with him, he will shed the blood of everyone in the fort. The women bare their breasts to him, and, as he averts his gaze, the warriors of Emain Macha seize him and cast him into a tub of cold water. This is done three times, and then the queen puts fresh garments on him, and he sits at Conchobor's knee which is his resting-place always after that (lines 808 ff.). He has been re-incorporated into society: his wolfish ferocity and strength will henceforth be subordinated and indeed harnessed to his social role as *gormac*.

This study of the sister's son in early Irish literature is not intended to be all-embracing. What emerges from it is this: the relationship between sister's son and maternal kindred is an important theme in the literature;

the relationship can be amicable or hostile, and can accordingly be greatly beneficial to society, or greatly destructive of social order; the sister's son must be integrated into society by means of a solemn contract; and the social good will be served only if the obligations imposed by that contract are duly discharged on both sides. The social role of the sister's son can be summed up in the word *goire*, and this is reflected in *gormac*, which came to replace the inherited *nia* as the designation of "sister's son."[130]

6

Curse and Satire

(1986)

Old Irish *maldacht* 'curse' is a loan from Latin, and can broadly be taken as the ecclesiastical equivalent of native *áer* 'satire.' The precise range of the two words, and the extent to which they may overlap, remain to be determined. In an appendix to his valuable study of satire,[1] Robert C. Elliott discusses the curse. He finds it impossible to distinguish formally between magical satire and the curse,[2] and suggests that "perhaps the best approach is to look at both curse and satire as relatively undifferentiated responses to the threats and possibilities of a hostile environment. Behind them both is the will to attack, to do harm, to kill—in some negative way to control one's world."[3] One of the items discussed by Elliott in this context is the account of how St. Patrick cursed Bécán: "Patrick . . . uses the formula 'I ordain' and winds a spell around the name of a victim in a fashion indistinguishable from that of the magician-satirists."[4] This curse of Patrick's is recounted in an anecdote in *Acallam na Senórach*,[5] and the purpose of the present note is to juxtapose that anecdote with the one in *Cath Maige Tuired* which deals with "the first satire that was made in Ireland," in which the *fili* Cairbre son of Étaín similarly winds a spell around the name of his victim, Bres.[6] We shall see that Patrick's curse and Cairbre's satire are effective instruments, which are used to bring about the deposal of an unrighteous king.

We may begin with a summary of the Patrician anecdote. Patrick and his companions were approached by a young man who deposited a lapful of nuts and apples at Patrick's feet. The young man was questioned by Patrick and declared himself to be Falartach son of Fergus; he said that his heritage was the kingship of Brega, Mide and Déisi Temrach, but that he was engaged in plunder and marauding upon his brother Bécán. (From this we are apparently to understand that Bécán has usurped Falartach's heritage; this inference finds support later on in the anecdote.)[7] Patrick promises to restore Falartach's heritage to him within the year. The discussion then turns to Ros mic Treoin, from which Falartach has brought the fruit, and which is the subject of a poem here delivered by Caílte.

As night approaches, Patrick enquires about supper, and Falartach tells him that he could get supper at the house of Falartach's brother, Bécán, in the *túatha* of Brega and Mide. Some clerics go ahead to Bécán's house, but, although he has a hundred and twenty milch herds, Bécán refuses to give them any food. When Patrick hears of this, he utters an imprecation, ordaining that not one of Bécán's cattle or people shall remain alive on the morrow.

And that came to pass, *ut dixit Patricius*:

> *Bécán,*
> *ní rab ilar a tredan!*
> *Oiret rabh grian ar deiseal,*
> *ní rabh seiser d'óibh Bécán!*

> (Bécán, / may there not be many of his fastings! / As long as the sun travels right-handwise, / may there not be six descendants of Bécán!)[8]

Then all at once the earth swallows up Bécán and his people, and all his wealth, both animal and human. Falartach then offers to provide supper for Patrick that night from the twenty-nine cows which have served to feed the band of fighters whom he has hitherto employed in plunder and marauding. Patrick promises to grant the kingship from midday on the morrow to Falartach, and to his descendants after him until such time as they will oppose the church. And in that way Bécán is consigned to the earth, and Patrick bestows kingship on Falartach.

The context for Cairbre's satire in *Cath Maige Tuired* begins with a dispute which arose among the Túatha Dé Danann as to who should be king in succession to Núadu, who has become ineligible to retain the office owing to the loss of an arm in battle. The womenfolk among them succeed in having the kingship bestowed upon Bres, whose mother was of the Túatha Dé Danann, with the result that they in turn withhold from him their service and the payment of fines and tribute.

Then one day Cairbre, son of Étaín, *fili* of the Túatha Dé Danann, comes to seek hospitality at Bres's house. Cairbre is given miserable accommodation and a paltry ration of food.

> The next day he arose, and he was not pleased. As he went over the rampart, he said:
>
> *Cen colt for crib cernine,*
> *cen gert ferbba fora n-asa aithrinni,*
> *cen adba fir iar ndruba disoirchi,*
> *cen díl daimi rissi, rob sain Brisse!*
>
> ---
>
> (Without food speedily on a platter, / without a cow's milk on which a calf thrives, / without a man's habitation after the staying of darkness, / without payment of a band of storytellers, / let that be Bres's lot!)[9]

"Bres's wealth, then, is no more," said he.
That came to pass. There was nothing but decay on him from that time.
And that is the first satire that was made in Ireland.

The Túatha Dé Danann then went to speak to Bres. They demanded their sureties from him, and he restored the sovereignty to them.

The role of Cairbre, the *fili*, as magus, in *Cath Maige Tuired*, corresponds to that of Patrick, the saint, in *Acallam na Senórach*. It is true that the anecdotes are not comparable in every respect. The most noteworthy difference between them is that Cairbre's role is the purely negative one of satirizing Bres, whereas Patrick not only curses Bécán, but also bestows the kingship upon Falartach. Furthermore, the ecclesiastical element in the Patrician anecdote is expressed in the stipulation that Falartach and his descendants will hold the kingship as long as they do not oppose the church. Such differences as these, however, do not detract from the remarkable similarities between the two anecdotes. These similarities are set out in what follows.

1. *The initial situation in each instance is the incumbency of an unrighteous king.* Bres was elected, after some contention, at the behest of the womenfolk. He was not descended in the male line from the Túatha Dé Danann; his father was Elatha of the Fomoire, and Bres was chosen in the mistaken belief that such a choice would strengthen the alliance which had been forged between the Túatha Dé Danann and the Fomoire. His conduct of the office showed him to be an unworthy king. As for Bécán, it is not stated in so many words that he was a usurper, or even that he held the kingship of the *túatha* of Brega, Mide, and Déisi Temrach. Falartach does claim that this kingship is his own rightful heritage, but that he is engaged in plunder and marauding against his brother Bécán. (In the corresponding portion of the Modern Irish version of the *Acallam*, Falartach expounds on his situation at greater length, explaining that his brother Bécán has banished him to the wild and does not allow him to visit his patrimonial lands.[10] But even here we are not quite told that Bécán has taken the kingship for himself.) Later we learn that Bécán is in the *túatha* of Brega and Mide, and that he is very wealthy, being the possessor of a hundred and twenty milch herds. It is after the death of Bécán as a result of Patrick's curse that the saint grants the kingship to Falartach. It is a fair inference from all of this that Bécán has been enjoying the kingship until he is cursed, and that it is his removal from the scene which creates the vacancy which can now be filled by Falartach.

2. *The king is opposed.* In *Cath Maige Tuired* the social contract which binds the king to his people breaks down. He fails to provide them with food and entertainment, and they in turn withhold from him their service and the payment of fines and tribute. In the *Acallam*, Falartach engages in plunder (*fogail*) and marauding (*díberg*). The occurrence of these activities, and of *díberg* in particular, signifies the breakdown of law and order in the land. In Irish literature, the locus classicus for the evil effects of

díberg in society is *Togail Bruidne Da Derga*: it is enjoined as a *geis* on Conaire Mór that there be no *díberg* in his reign; when Conaire Mór fails to punish his foster-brothers for the lesser crime of *gat* ("theft"), they go on to engage in *díberg*, and thus set in motion the chain of events which leads to the loss of peace, the collapse of law and order, and the death of Conaire Mór.[11] The practice of *díberg* was strongly condemned by the church,[12] and this may lend added significance to the ecclesiastical dimension of the Patrician anecdote: by restoring his proper heritage to Falartach, Patrick brings an end to the evil practice of *fogail* and *díberg* in which Falartach has hitherto been engaged.

In these different ways, then, both Bres and Bécán are opposed. In both instances, however, resolution of the problems posed by the unrighteous king awaits the decisive intervention of a magus, in one case a *fili*, in the other a saint.

3. *The magus seeks hospitality of the king, who fails to show due generosity.* Bres treats Cairbre in a niggardly fashion, while Bécán altogether declines to afford hospitality to Patrick. The king's ungenerous demeanor provides the occasion for the malediction of the magus.

4. *The malediction takes the form of an incantatory verse wound around the name of the king.* Both the *fili* and the saint spell out the effects of the malediction: Patrick ordains that not one of Bécán's cattle or people shall remain alive on the morrow; Cairbre declares that Bres's wealth is at an end.

5. *The malediction brings about the deposal of the king.* Patrick also causes the death of Bécán; while there is nothing but decay on Bres after the satire, his life is prolonged for good narrative reasons—he has yet to initiate, fight, and lose the battle of Mag Tuired.

The accounts of Patrick's curse and Cairbre's satire are embedded in and adapted to narrative contexts of different kinds. For all their differences of surface realization, however, the two episodes have a common underlying structure comprising the five items outlined above. Moreover, the maledictions which are at their core are alike both in form and in function. To call one of them a curse and the other a satire is a matter of nomenclature only: we tend to use *curse* for the malediction of a saint, and *satire* for that of a *fili*, but these magical maledictions of Patrick and Cairbre belong to the common ground shared by curse and satire. As I have said, the extent of the overlap between the two categories remains to be determined. We have been looking at only two examples. And it is as well to emphasize here that these examples are culled from literary texts. The portrayal in literature of saints and *filid* is not necessarily to be taken as an accurate representation of the practices of ecclesiastics and poets in society at large. It is nonetheless worth recalling here an event which shows the ritual sanctions available to churchmen and *filid* being recognized and invoked as instruments of public order in sixteenth-century Ireland. A treaty was entered into by O'Donnell of Tyrconnell and O'Connor of Sligo in 1539. "As guarantors appear the archbishop of Tuam and other ecclesiastics, who promise to excommunicate O'Connor should he break the treaty; and three members of the poetic families of Ward and O'Clery—Conchobar Ruadh Mac an Bháird, Ó Cléirigh, and Fearghal mac Domhnaill Ruaidh Mac an Bháird—who undertake on behalf of the poets of Ireland to satirize him at O'Donnell's behest."[13] The public use of the ritual sanctions of churchman and *fili*, which is invoked as a threat in this treaty, finds literary exemplars, among others, in the cursing of Bécán by Patrick and the satirizing of Bres by Cairbre.

7

The Threefold Death in Early Irish Sources

(1994)

Irish versions of the threefold death have been the subject of scholarly interest since 1940, when Kenneth Jackson published his article "The Motive of the Threefold Death in the Story of Suibhne Geilt." He introduced the topic as follows: "The motive of the Threefold Death is a popular tale of the well-known international type current in Europe in medieval and modern times. A prophet foretells that a certain man will die in three different ways (generally including by fire and water). This is thought to be incredible and to prove him no true seer, so that the man feels quite secure. In the sequel the prophecy comes true" (Jackson 1940, 535).

The morphology of the motif has been more fully set out by Joan Radner in "The Significance of the Threefold Death in Celtic Tradition" (1983, 183 f.):

In its most fully realized form, it has five parts—five distinct ordered stages that serve to advance the action:

(1) The future victim commits an offense.
(2) There is immediately a prophecy, almost always delivered by a cleric, that the offender will be punished for his offense by a threefold death.
(3) Disbelief in the prophecy is expressed.
(4) The events of the story bring about a reversal, and *belief* may be explicitly expressed.
(5) The prophecy is fulfilled and the offender/victim is killed.

Jackson's article was concerned with the occurrence of the motif in material which has to do with "the well-known Irish legend" of Suibne Geilt (Jackson 1940, 536), and with the relationship of this with material concerning Myrddin/Merlin and Lailoken, who are British figures of the Suibne type. The version of the Suibne legend which furnished Jackson with an instance of the motif was not the well-known *Buile Suibne* (O'Keeffe 1913; 1931), but rather a poem beginning *A ben Graig is graccda sain*[1] (Stokes 1908, 26–28), which is one of a set of five poems concerning St. Moling and Suibne, the language of which "seems to point strongly to the eleventh century" (Jackson 1940, 538). These poems are referred to as the *Anecdota* poems, after their place of publication. Jackson prefaced his treatment of this material with a list of instances of the motif from other sources, medieval and modern, including two early twelfth-century Latin poems, two modern Welsh versions, and various "modern Esthonian folk versions." The Irish material mentioned by Jackson comprises accounts of the deaths of four men:

(1) The death of Áed Dub (Áed the Black) of the Cruithin, murderer (in the year 565) of Diarmait mac Cerbaill, who was of the Southern Uí Néill and king of Tara, is recounted in Adomnán's seventh-century Life of Columba (Anderson and Anderson 1991, 64–67).
(2) Diarmait mac Cerbaill's death, which is not described in detail by Adomnán, is the subject of *Aided Diarmata Meic Cerbaill* (O'Grady 1892, 1:72–82; 2:76–88; Rayner 1988, 17–31), which is tentatively dated by Jackson (1940, 535) to the eleventh century.

(The threefold death of Diarmait mac Cerbaill is also recounted in the Irish Life of St. Brendan of Clonfert [Plummer 1922, 1:44–95 at 88–90; 2:44–92 at 85–87]; there is an incomplete account in *Stair ar Aed baclámh* [O'Grady 1892, 1:66–72; 2:70–76].)

(3) The death of Muirchertach mac Erca, a Northern Uí Néill king of Tara, is the subject of *Aided Muirchertaig Meic Erca* (Nic Dhonnchadha 1964; Cross and Slover 1969, 518–32; Guyonvarc'h 1983). The text is late Middle Irish or early Modern Irish; Jackson (1940, 535) suggests that it may be as late as the fourteenth century. Muirchertach is said to have been slain in 534, but Francis John Byrne (1973, 102) observes that his "absolute historicity" is open to question.

(4) The death of Grác, St. Moling's herdsman, and murderer (in the seventh century) of Suibne Geilt, is recounted, as we have seen, in the *Anecdota* poems; there is a prose account in the Middle Irish Life of Moling (Stokes 1907, 32–36).

There are, as we shall see, many other cases of threefold death in early Irish sources, but it is in the death-stories of these four men that Radner's morphology is most fully realized. The five elements are not present in all of the texts,[2] but each of them contains an offence, a prophecy, and fulfilment of the prophecy. The offence is of crucial importance in these tales, and this element, as Bo Almqvist has pointed out to me, distinguishes them from folk-versions of the motif. Radner remarks that "whatever other ramifications it may have, the offense that results in the death prophecy is always committed by a *secular* figure against the laws or clergy of the Church" (Radner 1983, 187), and she observes that "the threefold death motif, in Celtic tradition, belongs to a fictive Christian world in which there is conflict among sacral personages—that is[,] among people who control and embody sovereign or religious power" (183). In terms of the tripartite ideology posited by Dumézil, in which the first "function" has to do with the sacred, the second with physical force, and the third with fertility,[3] she says of the motif that it seems to be "primarily concerned with first-function power relationships in Christian society" (Radner 1983, 183).

The tripartite ideology has been invoked in a different way by Donald Ward (1970); in his view the three deaths reflect modes of human sacrifice which correspond respectively to the three functions. In the Irish stories, all three modes function simultaneously, and Ward argues that this reflects an Indo-European trifunctional sacrifice. A recent article by William Sayers (1992) also interprets the threefold death in trifunctional terms.

In what follows I shall take a fresh look at the Irish material, paying particular attention to the offences committed by the four delinquents who suffer the threefold death. I hope to show that the offences committed by Áed Dub and Muirchertach mac Erca are trifunctional in character; we shall see that a somewhat similar claim has been made by David J. Cohen (1977) with regard to the sins of Suibne in *Buile Suibne*. It will be necessary then to consider the nature of the threefold death as it is depicted in the Irish sources, and it will be argued that, in the case of Áed Dub at least, each of the functions is represented in turn by one of his deaths, so that there is a functional symmetry between death and punishment.

Much the earliest of our stories of threefold death is narrated in Adomnán's *Vita Columbae*, a Life, in Latin, of the sixth-century St. Columba, known in Irish as Colum Cille, which was completed before 704. Adomnán divided his subject-matter into prophecies, miracles, and angelic visitations, and it is among the prophecies that the death of Áed Dub is recounted. The following translation is taken from Anderson and Anderson (1991, 65–67):

> The blessed man's prophecy concerning the priest Findchán, founder of the monastery that is in Irish called *Artchain*, in the land of Eth [Tiree].
>
> At another time, the above-mentioned priest Findchán, a soldier of Christ, brought with him in clerical garb, from Ireland to Britain, Áid, surnamed the Black, Cruithnian by race, and of royal lineage, intending that he should for some years be a pilgrim with him in his monastery. This Áid the Black had been a very bloody man, and a slayer of many men; he had also killed Diormit, Cerball's son, who had been ordained, by God's will, as the ruler of all Ireland. This same Áid, then, after passing some time in pilgrimage, was ordained as priest, although not rightly, in the above-mentioned Findchán's monastery, a bishop being summoned for the purpose. But the bishop dared not lay his hand upon Áid's head, until first Findchán (whose love for Áid was earthly) laid his right hand upon Áid's head, for confirmation.

7. The Threefold Death in Early Irish Sources

When the ordination thus made was afterwards reported to the holy man, he was much displeased. Thereupon he pronounced the following terrible sentence upon that Findchán, and upon the Áid who had been ordained, saying: "That right hand which, contrary to divine law and the law of the church, Findchán has laid upon the head of a son of perdition will presently rot, and after torments of great pain will precede him into the earth in burial; and surviving after his hand has been buried he will live for many years. And Áid, unworthily ordained, will return like a dog to his vomit, and he will again be a bloody killer, and at last, pierced with a spear, will fall from wood into water, and die by drowning. He has deserved such an end much sooner, who has slaughtered the king of all Ireland."

This prophecy of the blessed man was fulfilled in regard to them both. For the right hand of the priest Findchán decayed first, and preceded him into the earth, being buried in the island that is called Ommon. But he himself, according to the word of St. Columba, lived for many years afterwards. And Áid the Black, priest only in name, returned to his former evil deeds, and, pierced with a spear by treachery, fell from the prow of a ship, into the water of a lake, and perished.

Jackson said that this instance of the motif is incomplete. It is true that only three of Radner's five stages are here: the offence, the prophecy, and fulfilment of the prophecy. There is no suggestion that the prophecy was not believed, and hence no question of conversion from disbelief to belief. This was not what Jackson had in mind, however; his view was that one of the deaths is lacking in Adomnán's story, and this view was shared by Radner, who describes Áed Dub's death as "twofold" (1983, 180), and by the Andersons, who call it a "double death" (1991, 67). But Jackson did say that Áed Dub's fall from the prow of a ship may be compared with the fall from a tree into water which is a component of the threefold death in two of the non-Irish versions mentioned by him. I think we can see how the problem arose for Jackson. In his summary of Adomnán's story the prophecy includes a fall from a tree into water, whereas the death includes rather a fall from the prow of a ship. This discrepancy between the prophecy and the event is not present in the Andersons' translation where what is prophesied is taken to be a fall from wood—the word is *lignum*. We can take it therefore that what is prophesied is a threefold death, by wounding, falling from wood, and drowning, and that this is what Áed Dub suffers.

It remains to consider the offence for which Áed Dub is punished. Columba's prophecy is prompted by the news that Áed Dub has been "unworthily ordained," but he remarks that Áed Dub deserved his end much sooner, having "slaughtered the king of all Ireland." We have already been informed by the narrator that Áed Dub has slain the king who had been ordained, by God's will, as the ruler of all Ireland. We are also told that Áed was a very bloody man, and a slayer of many men. Moreover, the account of Áed Dub's ordination includes the detail that he loved Findchán carnally—the Andersons' rendering of *carnaliter* as "earthly" is rather less transparent than Picard's "of the flesh" (Picard 1989, 372).

There are no less than four offences here: regicide, improper ordination, bloodshed, and sexual sin. If we seek to classify them we can see that they fit neatly into the tripartite framework espoused by Dumézil. Áed Dub sins doubly against the first function, the sacred, which embraces kingship and the priesthood, the bloodshed for which he is condemned relates to the second function, physical force, while his sexual sin offends against the third function, fertility.

Áed Dub, having sinned against the sacred, and in the improper use of martial force and sexuality, is punished with a threefold death. I believe that the same can be argued of Muirchertach mac Erca, according to the version of his death recounted in *Aided Muirchertaigh Meic Erca*. Muirchertach is hunting one day at the edge of Bruig na Bóinne, and when he has been left alone on his hunting-mound a beautiful young woman appears beside him and he loves her so much on sight that he would give the whole of Ireland if he could have her for one night. She says that she has come to find him, and that she will be his lover on condition that he never utters her name, that his wife Duaibsech shall not be in her sight, and that clerics shall never be in the same house with her. Muirchertach accepts these conditions. She tells him her names: Sigh, Sough, Storm, Rough Wind, Winter-night, Cry, Wail, Groan (?). (The third of these, Sín 'Storm,' is the name used of her in the tale.)

Muirchertach and Sín go to his dwelling, Tech Cletig ("the house of Cleitech") on the Boyne, and after a great feast Muirchertach's wife Duaibsech, his children, and his Uí Néill associates are expelled. Duaibsech repairs to her confessor, Cairnech, and tells him that she fears death that night for she has been visited by a woman from the *síd* (Otherworld). Cairnech blesses her. He takes the leaders of the Northern Uí Néill to Tech Cletig, but Sín keeps them away. Cairnech then curses Muirchertach and says that his life and his reign are at an end. Cairnech blesses the Northern Uí Néill, however, oversees a treaty between them and the descendants of Tadg mac Céin, and returns to his monastery.

Sín is now Muirchertach's consort—he sits on his throne and she sits on his right. She claims to be able to work miracles and she demonstrates this by bringing forth two great battalions who slaughter one another, and by making wine of the water of the Boyne and enchanted pigs of ferns. Muirchertach observes the contest between the battalions, and then drinks the wine and eats the meat. He thinks them the best he has ever had. On the morning after this magical feast, however, he is like a man suffering from a wasting sickness. But Sín makes blue men of the stones and others with heads of goats, and Muirchertach wearies himself fighting them. And so he spends his days fighting phantom warriors, and his nights drinking the magical wine and eating the magical pork. One day the clerics come to his assistance; he comes to his senses and realizes that all he has been doing is hacking the stones and sods of the earth. He confesses his sins: we could characterize his misdeeds in Adomnán's words about Áed Dub, and say that he has been "a bloody man and killer of many men"; one detail which should be mentioned is that he confesses (Nic Dhonnchadha 1964, lines 560 ff.) to having killed his grandfather, Loarnd.

But he returns to Cleitech and to Sín, and once more is in thrall to her. He again partakes of the magic feast. This is the Tuesday after Samain, and the seventh night of Sín's magic. She conjures up a great storm which causes the king to say her name. Then he sleeps and dreams that Cleitech will be set on fire, and that he and his people will be too weak to resist. When he awakens he again says her name. She says he will die, and accuses him of having slain many people. He admits that he has done so, and says that his death is near, and that it was prophesied of him that his death, like that of his grandfather Loarnd, would be by burning.

When he sleeps after that he has another dream: "He went in a ship to sea, and his ship foundered, and a taloned griffin came to him and carried him into her nest, and then the nest was burnt around him, and the griffin fell with him" (Nic Dhonnchadha 1964, lines 730 ff.).

Once again he sleeps, and on this occasion Sín forms by magic many hosts around the house, and she sets fire to the house. When the king wakes up, he tries to escape the burning house, but a spear pierces him in the chest. He goes back into the house, but as the fire intensifies he gets into a cask of wine, in which he is drowned. Then the fire falls on his head and five foot of him is burnt; but the wine keeps the rest of his body without burning.

Muirchertach is given Christian burial, and Cairnech recites his necrology; reference is once again made to his *fingal* ("kin-slaying") of his grandfather. Duaibsech keens her husband in the traditional way, and then she dies of grief for him.

Sín approaches the clerics, and when Cairnech accuses her of killing the king of Tara, she admits that she has done so and asks for salvation for her soul. Cairnech tells her that if she confesses and repents she will be forgiven. She then reveals her identity: "Sín is my name and Sige son of Dían son of Trén is my father. Muirchertach mac Erca killed my father, my mother and my sister in the Battle of Cerb on the Boyne, and he also beheaded in that battle the Old Tribes of Tara and all my paternal kin" (Nic Dhonnchadha 1964, lines 902 ff.). She confesses and repents and goes in obedience to Cairnech, and dies forthwith of grief for Muirchertach. Cairnech prays for Muirchertach and his soul is released from Hell.

It had long been thought that the death suffered by Muirchertach in this tale was the twofold one of drowning and burning, but Tomás Ó Concheanainn (1973–74a) has shown that the apparent absence of the third death arose through editorial error, and that the text does say that the king was also pierced by a spear.[4]

In all of our tales the threefold death follows a curse or prophecy by a cleric. Muirchertach is cursed by Cairnech, but although his death is predicted by Cairnech, the manner of it is not. Muirchertach dreams that he will die by fire, which he says has been prophesied of him. Jackson (1940, 535) suggested that the original story contained three dreams instead of one, the implication being that the others would have been of death by wounding and death by drowning. Be that as it may, we have seen that Muirchertach had another dream, in which his ship founders at sea, a griffin carries him into her nest, which is burnt, and the griffin falls with him. This seems to be a prophecy of threefold death, involving drowning, burning, and falling (from a tree, presumably). It is reminiscent of the death suffered by Áed Dub, save that here there is burning instead of wounding.

An allegorical interpretation of the dream is given in the tale by a druid: "The ship in which you were is the ship of sovereignty steered by you on the sea of life. The ship that foundered is your sovereignty coming to an end,[5] and your life coming to an end. The taloned griffin that has carried you into her nest is the woman who is your consort, making you intoxicated, taking you with her into her bed, and detaining you in Tech Cletig so that it will be burnt over you. And the griffin falling with you is the woman dying because of you" (Nic Dhonnchadha 1964, lines 734–44).

The druid takes the dream to be a premonition of Muirchertach's death, but while all three elements are interpreted allegorically, the burning is the only one which is linked by the druid to the actual circumstances of the death. The death of Muirchertach is amply prefigured in the tale: in Cairnech's prophecy; in Muirchertach's dream of the fire at Tech Cletig, which prompts him to recall an earlier prophecy that he will die by fire; and in the dream of the ship and the griffin. It is only in the latter that we have a prediction, as it seems, of threefold death, and even this prediction is diluted in the druid's allegorical interpretation. In the event, the burning of Muirchertach in the conflagration at Tech Cletig is preceded by wounding and drowning in a vat, but that particular form of threefold death has not been prophesied in the tale.

The offence for which Cairnech curses Muirchertach is that he has taken Sín instead of his wife, Duaibsech, and that, at Sín's behest, he has banished Duaibsech and her children by him, and repudiated the clerics. Sín's role is crucial here, and Kim McCone (1990, 133) has said of her that "far from punishing any previous misdemeanour of the king's, Sín leads a hitherto flawless sovereign astray out of personal malice." But if we look at the events of Muirchertach's career in the order of their occurrence, rather than of their revelation in the tale, a different picture emerges. Muirchertach has killed his maternal grandfather Loarnd, as he himself confesses; Cairnech, as we have seen, also refers to this act of *fingal* in his necrology of the king. This is not only a kin-slaying, it is also regicide, for Loarnd was a king in Alba. In the second place, he has by his own confession lived a violent and murderous life. Moreover, it is this aspect of his career which motivates Sín in her seduction and destruction of him: he has killed her father, her mother, her sister, and all her paternal kin. It is after he has offended in these ways that Sín comes to him, and he sins sexually with her.

Muirchertach's sins, like those of Áed Dub, span the three functions, the sacred, physical force, and fertility; and like Áed Dub he sins doubly against the sacred, in his case by regicide and by repudiation of Cairnech.

Radner (1983, 200) offers a different analysis of Muirchertach's offence:

(1) Muirchertach abandons church and family for the *síd* woman, Sín.
(2) Muirchertach has committed *fingal* by burning his grandfather.
(3) Muirchertach violates Sín's *geis* by saying her name.

The third item here, the violation of the naming-taboo placed upon him by Sín, is not, I suggest, of the same order as Muirchertach's other offences. The taboo is a condition of the contract entered into by Muirchertach and Sín: if he infringes it he will lose her, and also, as it turns out, lose his life. We may compare the *geisi* laid upon Conaire in *Togail Bruidne Da Derga* (Knott 1936, lines 168 ff.). They too constitute a contract with the Otherworld (see "The Semantics of *síd*" and "The Concept of the Hero," chaps. 2 and 4, respectively, in this volume), and when Conaire infringes them he is led to his doom in Da Derga's hostel. One of the portents of doom which marks his journey to the hostel is a visitation from the hideous Cailb, who bears comparison with Sín (Rees and Rees 1961, 348), and who has been aptly described as "the personification of death, woe, and destruction" who "invites the reluctant hero to make her his ultimate bride" (Rees and Rees 1961, 338). There is nevertheless a crucial difference in the role of taboo in the lives of Conaire and Muirchertach. Conaire's *geisi* are laid upon him as he is about to enter upon his reign; Ireland enjoys a Golden Age of peace and plenty, and Conaire is a "flawless sovereign" so long as he keeps faith with the Otherworld.[6] Muirchertach, on the other hand, has already committed regicide and led a violent life before Sín arrives on her mission of destruction. His offence with regard to her lies in entering into a contract with her, whereby he is to enjoy her sexual favors on terms set by her. Sín devises the circumstances in which he is certain to infringe the taboo; it is a means of ensuring his death, rather than its ultimate cause.

It will be recalled that one of the crimes committed by Áed Dub was the murder of Diarmait mac Cerbaill, but that Adomnán does not tell us how it was done. The fullest account is given in Diarmait's death-tale, *Aided Diarmata Meic Cerbaill*. It opens with an Origin-Legend of Clonmacnoise, and with events which, whether historical or otherwise, are deemed to have occurred in 544, this being the year of death of Túathal Máelgarb, who is said to have succeeded Muirchertach mac Erca as king of Tara, and to have been Diarmait mac Cerbaill's immediate predecessor. Diarmait is in exile from Túathal and he comes upon Ciarán, who is in the act of establishing his church at Clonmacnoise. Ciarán is assisted by Diarmait, and promises in return that Diarmait will be king. Within a week, Túathal Máelgarb has been killed and Diarmait is elected king.

Diarmait bestows land on Ciarán in gratitude for having attained kingship through his benediction. But Diarmait proceeds to kill an enemy of his, one Flann mac Díma, on that very land: he sets Flann's house on fire; Flann is wounded in the house and gets into a bath-tub, in which he dies.

This is a violation of Ciarán's sanctuary, and hence of his honor. He upbraids Diarmait and tells him that the death he shall suffer is that which Flann has received at his hands: to be wounded and drowned and burnt. Diarmait attempts to buy off the cleric, but to no avail. "And hence it was that Diarmait's death was indeed brought about as had been prophesied."

This sequence constitutes a threefold-death tale of the structure which we have seen in *Vita Columbae*: offence, prophecy, and fulfilment. The offence is homicide in violation of a cleric's sanctuary; the prophecy is threefold death; we are told that the prophecy was fulfilled, but the fulfilment does not in fact occur for many years. The sequence is accommodated within a larger narrative in which Diarmait's violation of sanctuary and the prophesying of his death recur.

Despite what has happened, Diarmait and Ciarán go on to attend an assembly which the king has convened at Uisnech. Ciarán performs a miracle there, saving them all from drought, and Diarmait submits himself and his descendants to him. Diarmait then reigns prosperously for many years. Some years later, his death is prophesied by a seer, Bec mac Dé, who says that Diarmait will be killed by Áed Dub, whose father, Suibne, king of Dál nAraide, has been slain by Diarmait. Áed Dub is thereupon banished from Ireland. Diarmait later violates the sanctuary of St. Rúadán at Lothra, by taking into captivity the king of Uí Maine, who has taken refuge with the saint. Rúadán and his monks chant psalms, strike their bells, and fast against Diarmait, finally cursing the kingship of Tara and predicting that the ridgepole of Diarmait's house will fall on his head and kill him. Diarmait later slays a Connacht prince who was under the protection of Colum Cille, and the saint ensures Diarmait's defeat at the battle of Cúl Dreimne. After the battle Diarmait's death is again foretold. And there are further prophecies, culminating in that uttered by Diarmait's druids, in which they tell him that he will die by wounding (*marbad*), by drowning (*bádudh*), and by burning (*loscad*). But they predict that this will happen in such seemingly impossible circumstances that Diarmait is confident that he can survive, even though the circumstances predicted by the druids have earlier been foretold by Bec mac Dé.

All the prophecies are eventually fulfilled. Diarmait accepts an invitation to a feast from a stranger called Banbán, although he is warned by his wife not to do so. Diarmait sleeps with Banbán's daughter, and she acts in such a way as to create the circumstances which have been prophesied for Diarmait's death. He then tries to leave the house, but Áed Dub strikes him with a spear; he turns back to the house, but it has been set on fire; he enters a vat of ale. The roof tree falls on his head, and so he dies.

This could be described as a fourfold death, for it adds the impact of the ridgepole, which had been prophesied by Bec mac Dé and Rúadán, to the threefold death by wounding, drowning, and burning which had been foretold by Ciarán and Diarmait's druids. Diarmait's sexual sin, his adultery with Banbán's daughter, is the immediate prelude to his death. Áed Dub's role in the scenario is motivated by vengeance for the slaying of his father, which was itself an act of regicide on Diarmait's part, since Áed Dub's father was king of Dál nAraide. There is a further intimation of the punishment fitting the crime in the story of the killing of Flann, in which the threefold nature of Flann's death is replicated in the death prophesied for Diarmait by Ciarán. But the killing of Flann is punished not only because it was a violent act in itself, but also because it violated Ciarán's sanctuary. The violation of sanctuary is to the fore in this tale, and Radner (1983, 193) has pointed out that "it is certainly no coincidence that sanctuary rights were a major issue in Church-state relations in the eleventh century." As her analysis shows, this is a text about what we would call Church-State relations.

The versions considered so far have to do with the Uí Néill—Diarmait and Muirchertach were Uí Néill kings, and Áed Dub murdered an Uí Néill king in the person of Diarmait—and the events are set in the sixth century. The death of Grác, on the other hand, is set in the seventh century and has no connection with the Uí Néill. There are three versions of the death of Grác, but he suffers threefold death in only two of them. Grác is described in one of the *Anecdota* poems as the saint's cowherd (Stokes 1908, 25). In the next poem, *A ben Graig is graccda sain*, Moling tells Grác's wife the story of his death. A woman had wrongfully accused Suibne to Grác of seducing Grác's wife, and Grác attacked and wounded him. Suibne made his way to Moling's oratory and was buried by him. Then Grác tested Moling: he came to him in disguise and asked how he would die. Moling, who did not recognize Grác, said he would die by wounding. The next day, Grác came again and Moling said he would die by burning. On the third day, Moling said he would be drowned. In the event, someone wounded Grác with a spear when he was climbing a tree, and he fell down into a fire, and then drowned.

The offence committed by Grác here is the murder of Suibne, which, since it is also an affront to Moling, may be compared to Diarmait mac Cerbaill's violation of sanctuary. In the account of Grác's death in the Irish Life of Moling, Suibne does not appear. Grác is a marauder who steals a cow which has been given by Moling to Ruadsech, wife of Gobbán Saer who is building Moling's oratory. Moling makes Ruadsech three promises: to send his people to slay Grác; to have him burned; and to have him drowned. His promises are greeted with derision by Ruadsech, who suspects Moling of being responsible for Grác's crime. But Moling tells his people to kill Grác; in an attempt to escape them, Grác climbs a tree, but he is wounded, falls into a fire, and thence into the river Barrow, in which he drowns.

In this version of Grác's death, the stealing of the cow bestowed by Moling is the final offence of a wicked person (*mac mallachtan*, lit. "son of a curse") who has been pillaging (*fogail*) and marauding (*díberg*); getting the better of such persons is a common theme in Irish hagiography (Sharpe 1979, 80–85; McCone 1990, 219). Here, as elsewhere, the threefold death is part of "a fictive Christian world."

The earliest version of the Grác story (V. Hull 1930b), which is probably of the ninth century (Jackson 1940, 541), refers neither to Suibne nor to the threefold death. In this version, Grác, who is a "bad neighbor" to Moling, is beheaded; there seems to be a vestige of this in the third quatrain of *A ben Graig is graccda sain*, where Moling thanks Christ that Grác has lost his head. Carney (1955, 142) suggests that the threefold death which Grác suffers in the later versions was taken from "the original story of Suibne," the victim there having been Suibne himself.

While we do not have direct access to "the original story of Suibne," there is a detailed account of his death in *Buile Suibne*, which is generally believed to have been composed in its present form in the twelfth century. Having wandered in his madness throughout Ireland, Suibne comes to Tech Moling, the church of St. Moling (St. Mullins in County Carlow), and is welcomed by the saint, who says that Suibne is destined to die there. Moling has Muirgil, wife of his herdsman, Mongán, give Suibne milk each night: she would make a hollow in cowdung with her foot and fill it with milk, and Suibne would come warily and drink it. One night a woman taunts Muirgil about Suibne's visits, accusing her of preferring Suibne to her husband as a lover. This is overheard by Mongán's sister, and the next morning, when she sees Muirgil setting out with Suibne's milk, she goes to Mongán and tells him that his wife is with another man. Mongán in jealousy takes a spear, and as Suibne lies drinking his milk Mongán thrusts his spear into him, breaking his back. (Here we are told that in another version, the herdsman had placed a deer's horn under Suibne in the spot where he used to take his milk out of the cowdung, so that he fell on it, and that he met his death in that way.) Moling is sent for, and Suibne is given the sacraments. He declares himself innocent of any wrongdoing against Mongán. Moling curses the repentant Mongán, dooming him to shortness of life in this world and hell in the next. Suibne dies against the doorpost of Moling's church, and is buried.

This is described by Carney (1955, 141) as "a disguised version of that which we know from the *Anecdota* poems." It is a much more circumstantial account, but otherwise it differs from that in the *Anecdota* poems in two respects:[7] first, the name of Moling's herdsman here is Mongán rather than Grác, and his wife's name is Muirgil;[8] secondly, Mongán, unlike Grác, does not suffer the threefold death. The two accounts clearly derive from a common source; we cannot say how much that source may have contained of the matter which is found only in *Buile Suibne*.

Carney (1955, 142) remarks that "the peculiar circumstances" of Suibne's death in *Buile Suibne* "where he is pierced by a spear while lying on the ground drinking milk out of a hole is somewhat reminiscent of the instances of threefold death where the victim dies by a spear, a fall, and by drowning." The reminiscence is even stronger in the alternative version cited by the narrator of *Buile Suibne*: as Frykenberg (1984, 107) observes, we seem to have in this "an instance of the 'Threefold Death' motif involving falling, piercing on a point projecting out of liquid, and drowning." It may be added that Suibne himself predicts that he will die at Tech Moling by being pierced by an antler (O'Keeffe 1931, lines 1218 f.).

Suibne is slain for an offence that he did not commit: he is innocent of adultery with Muirgil. But of course he has not led a blameless life. In the opening episode of *Buile Suibne*, St. Rónán is marking out a site for a church on Suibne's territory. When Suibne hears the saint's bell, he attacks him and throws his psalter into a lake. Suibne's assault upon Rónán is interrupted by a summons to the battle of Mag Rath, but Rónán curses him to wander and fly stark-naked throughout the world, and to die at spear-point. At Mag Rath, Rónán acts as guarantor to both sides that fighting would be restricted to an appointed period each day, but Suibne persistently violates the saint's guarantee. Then when the day for the great battle comes, and Rónán is sprinkling holy water on the combatants, Suibne kills one of the saint's psalmists, and casts a spear at Rónán himself, which is deflected by the saint's bell. Rónán curses Suibne in much the same terms as before. Finally, as the two great armies face one another, they raise three mighty roars. When Suibne hears these sounds, he looks up into the heavens, is seized by madness, and flies away "like any bird of the air."

Suibne's sins in *Buile Suibne* have been seen by Cohen (1977) as a reflex of the theme of the three sins of the warrior, which Dumézil (1983) has identified in Indian, Greek, and Germanic narratives. In this scenario the warrior sins against each of the functions in turn. With his outrages against Rónán, Suibne sins against the first function. His cowardly flight from battle is a sin against the second. The third sin is represented by the adultery with which Suibne is charged; he does not actually commit it, but his death results from the imputation that he did so. Within the context of the Irish tales of threefold death, then, Suibne shares with Áed Dub and Muirchertach mac Erca a trifunctional sin, save that in his case the sin against the third function is present only by imputation. The prophecy is of death by piercing with spear-point or stag's antler. The death, when it comes, is reminiscent of the wounding, falling, and drowning suffered by Áed Dub, rather than the death by wounding, drowning, and burning which is suffered by Muirchertach mac Erca, Diarmait mac Cerbaill, and Grác, and which has come to be regarded as "the characteristically Irish form of the threefold death" (Radner 1983, 181).

The combination of wounding, drowning, and burning occurs in a wide variety of Irish sources (Ó Cuív 1973–74). The earliest extant Irish allusion to a threefold death is probably that identified by Brian Ó Cuív (1973–74,

150) in the seventh-century text *Baile Chuinn,* "The Vision of Conn" (Murphy 1952). This text contains a list, cast in the form of a prophecy, of the kings who will rule Ireland in succession to the eponymous Conn Cétchathach. As its editor, Gerard Murphy, has pointed out, each of the kings named in *Baile Chuinn* is clearly identified down to Fínnachta, who reigned from 675 to 695, whereas, from Fínnachta on, the kings are identified by vague kennings. Having dealt with Fínnachta, the text continues as follows: "Rule from Níall to Níall; the descendant of Níall is everyone's Níall: hostages are pledged; fire approaches thee; through him bracken shall be red and rough; in the third month over a year he shall surely die by the sea: great the gloom and loss to the world's generation" (Murphy 1952, 149).[9] As Ó Cuív (1973–74, 150) remarks: "Despite the vagueness of the language this text does seem to contain direct reference to two of the elements of the threefold death, namely fire (*tein*) and water (*muir*), while the third, wounding, is implied in the phrase *rúadgarg raithnech lais* ('through him bracken shall be red and rough'). If this interpretation is correct we have here the prophecy element of the threefold death motif without the *dénouement.*" It should be noted that the prophecy is devoid of any narrative context in *Baile Chuinn.* It is nevertheless of interest to find what seems to be a prophecy of death by fire, wounding, and water in what is one of the very earliest literary texts extant in Irish.

This passage is taken by Ó Cuív (1973–74, 150) to refer to "a king who, it is prophesied, will rule Ireland." It seems to me, however, that in the words "rule from Níall to Níall; the descendant of Níall is everyone's Níall," Níall is used generically in all but the third occurrence, the reference in the latter being of course to Níall Noígiallach, ancestor of the Uí Néill. The meaning would then be that after Fínnachta descendants of Níall Noígiallach will rule, one after the other ("rule from Níall to Níall"), and that each of them will be for his subjects a surrogate for Níall Noígiallach ("the descendant of Níall is everyone's Níall"). The use of Níall as a generic may be compared with the similar use, in *Aided Muirchertaig Meic Erca,* of Conall and Éogan as designations, respectively, of descendants of Níall's sons of those names (Nic Dhonnchadha 1964, lines 174, 185). Francis John Byrne has suggested to me, in an oral communication, that the reference in *Baile Chuinn* may indeed be to a Níall who may have ruled during an interruption in Fínnachta's reign. This would not impose a different interpretation of "the descendant of Níall is everyone's Níall"; it would simply suggest that this utterance is prompted by the fact that Niall's own name was borne by this particular descendant of his. But the matter would have a crucial bearing on our reading of the prophecy of threefold death in this text. If this prophecy is to be taken as relating to Niall as a generic, it would indicate that the Uí Néill kings of Ireland will die by wounding, drowning, and burning. On the other hand, if the reference is to a particular individual named Niall, the prophecy would be confined to him. Indeed, it might even be taken as being addressed to him in person, if the transmitted text is sound in using the second person singular pronoun in "fire approaches thee," as contrasted with the third person of "through him bracken shall be red and rough," and of "he shall surely die by the sea."

A generic interpretation is required in a similar prophecy in *Aided Diarmata Meic Cerbaill*, which may be based ultimately on that in *Baile Chuinn*. Diarmait asks the prophet Bec mac Dé to tell him how his kingdom will be after his death. In the course of his reply, Bec says: "These are the rulers who will succeed you: from Niall to Niall, from land to land, a Niall by sea, a Niall in slaying, a Niall in fire" (O'Grady 1892, 1:80, 2:85). In translating this cryptic passage, O'Grady inserted "(The kingdom shall revolve)" before "from Niall to Niall." There can be no doubt that the meaning here is that Diarmait will be succeeded by Uí Néill kings. The components of the threefold death are represented here as sea, slaying, and fire. It is not clear from the wording whether they should be taken separately as prophecies of three different forms of violent death, or together as prophecies of threefold death.

The Uí Néill kings of Ireland are associated with the threefold death in a genealogical text (M. O'Brien 1962, 125) which has been discussed by Brian Ó Cuív (1964–66; 1973–74); it says that, of the Christian kings of Ireland from Niall Noígiallach's son Lóegaire (d. 461) to Brian Bórama (d. 1014), twenty-five were burned and drowned and slain, the phrase used being *ro loisced 7 ro báided 7 ro gonad*; in an accompanying poem, which lists their names, it is said that they were killed by fire and sea and wounding. Two of the twenty-five kings listed are Muirchertach mac Erca and Diarmait mac Cerbaill. Of the other twenty-three, Ó Cuív (1973–74) has observed that the combined evidence of the annals, genealogical material, regnal lists, and literary sources indicates that twenty-two of them died in battle or at the hands of a rival, so that for them the term *ro gonad* would be correct; that *ro báided* would be correct in the case of the remaining one, Niall Caille; and that *ro loisced* does not apply to a single one. Ó Cuív (1973–74, 145) suggests that "it is not necessary to assume that the *senchaide* believed that all of the twenty-five kings suffered such a fate. It seems to me that the terms proper to the threefold death motif were being used by the genealogists to indicate a range of violent deaths which were in contrast to death from non-violent causes which was the fate of the other twenty kings of Ireland in the period in question."

The notion that Uí Néill kings will be likely to suffer violent death seems to be present as early as the seventh-century *Baile Chuinn*, where it already involves wounding, drowning, and burning. These three types of death are mentioned together in a range of other texts; of one of these items Ó Cuív says that it may be "almost formulaic," of another that it may reflect an indulgence to some extent in "literary colouring." He also notes that drowning, burning, and wounding are the most obvious ways of meeting a violent death. Triadic formulations are endemic in Irish tradition; the persistence and pervasiveness of this particular triad doubtless owes something to the real risk that there was of dying in one or other of these violent ways, but it can scarcely be dissociated from the popularity in Ireland of tales of threefold death. Radner (1983, 199) plausibly suggests that the three forms of death are mentioned in the genealogical material "as a literary formula, appropriate here because of its acquired traditional resonances: in the Christian era, violent death is God's punishment for a king's violent life."

The literary formula which acquired these resonances in the Christian era may have had its origins in the Celtic or even in the Indo-European past. Mention has already been made of Donald Ward's argument that the Irish threefold death is based on an Indo-European sacrifice. He says:

> The material that has been adduced for Celtic religion reveals a striking agreement with the situation found in Germanic religion. In each case, there is a triad of divinities representing the three social classes, and each of the gods is honored by a separate kind of human sacrifice. Moreover, the pattern for Celtic tradition is remarkably similar to that found in Germanic tradition. In the latter, the three means of doing away with the victim were by noose, fire, and water. And as in the Germanic sources, the noose was associated with the first-function sacrifice, and water with the third-function sacrifice. Only in the case of

the second function does one find an apparent inconsistency. In Germanic religion the weapon was used, whereas in Celtic religion fire was preferred. The two methods of sacrificing a victim are apparently in complementary distribution. That is, killing by weapon and by fire represent variants of a single class of sacrificial practice. (Ward 1970, 135)

To this we may add that in certain German-speaking areas burial alive is found instead of drowning (Ward 1970, 130). We can say, therefore, that, if Ward's reading of the material is correct, the three forms of sacrifice are (1) hanging, (2) slaying or burning, and (3) drowning or burial, and that they relate respectively to Dumézil's first, second, and third functions.

The death of Áed Dub by falling from wood, wounding, and drowning corresponds reasonably well to Ward's formulation. It is also consistent with the suggestion by William Sayers (1992, 67) that the Irish wounding, drowning, and burning have replaced a paradigm in which death occurs simultaneously and successively in three fields of action, (1) the heavens, (2) the earth's surface, and (3) the underneath, in its marine and subsurface dimensions. The death occurs through (1) aerial movement such as falling, (2) the earth-bound movement of men wielding forged arms or other means of martial aggression like fire, and (3) various kinds of interaction with liquids and the earth itself as realized in submersion and interment. Sayers locates this paradigm within a complex pattern of trifunctional homologies; for present purposes it will be sufficient to note that the numbers supplied above correspond to those of the functions. In support of his paradigm, Sayers adduces a variety of evidence ranging from the tale of the multiple death of Lóegaire mac Néill to the eighth-century account of Christ's death by the poet Blathmac. He also shows that the hanging and falling motif occurs in marginal form in the tales of death by wounding, drowning, and burning.

One of the items cited by Sayers is a triad in the Irish Laws which offers us a tantalizing glimpse of penal practice in early Ireland. In "an early (9th century?) gloss on a legal fragment" (Kelly 1988, 217), it is stated that "three deaths are recognized as being carried out by the laity: slaying and the pit and hanging; one death by the Church i.e. hanging only."[10] The commonest form of execution, according to Kelly (1988, 217), seems to have been hanging (*crochad*) from a gibbet (*gabul*). He points out that the most obscure of these three forms of execution is *góla* 'the pit,' and says that "it appears that the condemned person—presumably in chains or fetters—is left to die of starvation and exposure in a pit" (Kelly 1988, 218). He cites a reference to the punishment pit (*cuithe*) in a ninth-century poem in which a clerical author includes "a foul dripping pit" (*cuithe salach súg*) among the methods of subduing peoples and bringing about peace.[11]

The triad—slaying, the pit, and hanging—can be read disjunctively as three different forms of execution, possibly imposed as a punishment for different crimes. On the other hand, Kelly (1988, 219) observes that "a spell in the pit may of course be a prelude to death by other means. A Middle Irish poem . . . refers to the criminal who is brought from the fetters to the pit (*ó gebind co cuthi*) and from the pit to the gallows (*ó chuthe co croich*)." This raises the possibility that the triad comprises three stages in a ritual form of execution which the Church may have wished to reduce to the single act of hanging. In any case, the three deaths carried out by the laity exemplify Sayers's paradigm, and they also collectively correspond to the death of Áed Dub, given that interment and drowning are in complementary distribution in the paradigm.

The evidence suggests that the death suffered by Áed Dub is trifunctional, and we have seen that the same is true of his offence. This, the earliest of our stories of threefold death, is the only one of them which shows an unambiguously trifunctional symmetry between offence and death. It may be a realization of an inherited narrative pattern. On the other hand, Dumézil (1983, 5) has observed that "the idea that a warrior, man or god, successively commits a spectacular sin in each of the three areas (social, moral, even cosmic) defined by the three functions, is not so unique that it could not have been reinvented independently in several places, in several societies where the ideology of the three functions remained alive and dominant." As early as the seventh century, the trifunctional offence and death are linked by the prophecy of a saint, and the prophecy, sentence, or curse of a cleric is an integral part of all the later tales. The authors of these tales inherited a trifunctional ideology, and the background to their literary compositions includes ritual sacrifice, penal practice, and a tradition of oral storytelling. In the foreground, as Radner has shown, there were considerations of what would now be called relations between Church and State.[12]

8

Early Irish Literature and Law

(2006–7)

THE LAWS

"Law," it has been said, "was one of the greatest achievements of the Irish in the early middle ages,"[1] and it may be added that the study of early Irish law is today one of the most vibrant areas of Irish scholarship. A large corpus of law survives in the manuscripts: there are something like fifty Old Irish law tracts, together with numerous fragments, and we find references to many texts that are now lost to us. Linguistic evidence shows that the texts were compiled in the seventh or eighth centuries. They survive for the most part in manuscripts from the fourteenth to the sixteenth centuries, and most of them are accompanied by later glosses and commentary. Many of the texts were made available, with translation, in *The Ancient Laws of Ireland* (6 vols., Dublin: Alexander Thom, 1865–1901), but for various reasons this is unreliable. Some individual texts were published in good editions in the twentieth century, and in 1978 an edition by D. A. Binchy of the entire corpus was published (without translation) in six large quarto volumes.[2] Binchy's edition is austere, to say the least, and yet the current flowering of early Irish legal scholarship followed upon its publication, and is hugely indebted to it. Fergus Kelly has given us a lucid and authoritative overview of the legal system,[3] and Liam Breatnach has provided a "companion" to Binchy's edition of the corpus,[4] which admirably succeeds in its stated aims of guiding the reader "through the vast and multifarious corpus of mediaeval Irish law tracts."

The law tracts were in continuous use in Irish-speaking parts of Ireland until the native system was broken up early in the seventeenth century. The law was administered by *brehons* (< Irish *breitheamh* 'judge,' pl. *breitheamhain*), and the system as a whole is often known as brehon law. This is an apt description in more ways than one, since the tracts themselves generally contain judge-made law.

THE ARCHAISM OF THE LAWS

Many scholars would agree with Binchy's observation that "the main interest of Irish law for the student of early institutions is that it shows how a legal system based, not on State sanctions, but on the power of traditional custom, formulated and applied by a learned professional caste[,] could function and command obedience."[5] For his own part, however, Binchy was especially interested, throughout his career, in what he saw as the archaic character of the material. An excellent statement of his views will be found in a lecture on "The Linguistic and Historical Value of the Irish Law Tracts,"[6] which he delivered to the British Academy in 1943. Here, as elsewhere in his writings, he stressed the survival of archaisms in the language of the early law texts. He argued that the content of the texts was also archaic:

> [The Irish tracts] offer the student of legal antiquities a wealth of evidence which confirms, supplements and occasionally modifies the conclusions arrived at from other sources. The conservatism which philologists have often noted as a feature of the Irish language is paralleled in

Irish law. . . . Indeed, the writings of the Irish jurists are something more than a faithful record of customs of the conquering Goidelic tribes: they also furnish detailed information about certain legal institutions which are but dimly reflected in the most ancient records of cognate legal systems.[7]

The "Goidelic tribes" were the people who brought with them to Ireland the Celtic dialect from which the Irish language developed over the centuries, and the "cognate legal systems" were of course those "found in the early law of all those peoples whose language belongs to the Indo-European family."[8] The following makes this clear:

The customary law which the Goidelic conquerors brought with them to Ireland was "Indo-European" in basis and origin. How far it had already been modified by external influences, such as racial admixture, is a question too difficult to be discussed here; but at all events it had retained the principal institutions found in the early records of Hindu, Greek, Roman, Germanic, and Slavonic law.[9]

Ireland never came within the political and administrative framework of the Roman Empire. The conversion of Ireland to Christianity did of course bring an important external influence to bear on the native legal system, but Binchy argued that the wording of the law texts, which received their definitive form after the law schools had long been Christian, had led scholars to exaggerate the revolution Christianity had effected in Irish law. He points out that "the Irish tracts show, on certain fundamental points, an obstinate refusal to conform to Christian teaching."[10]

THE NEW VIEW

Recent research on the laws, however, has revealed the extent to which the laws are imbued with Christian teaching, and the emphasis has shifted away from the remote origins of the law to a consideration of the content of what are now seen as very sophisticated texts. Moreover, there has been a growing consensus that the learned establishment of early Ireland comprised ecclesiastical and lay scholars and men of letters working together or at least in harmony with one another. It is to members of that establishment that we owe not only the vernacular law tracts of which we have been speaking, but also the corpus of Canon Law that was recorded in Latin in Ireland, and it is now clear that both bodies of law influenced the other in various ways. The intellectual and creative ferment that followed upon the coming together of native and ecclesiastical elements in Ireland also saw the production of a vibrant and exuberant literature in the vernacular (as well as in Latin), and what I would like to do below is to say a little about the relationship between literature and law in early Ireland.

THE *FILID* AND THE LAWS

We may begin with the *fili* (pl. *filid*), who was at once a man of letters and a professional academic. The conventional English equivalent is "poet," but this word, as we understand it today, is a poor enough equivalent of the Irish. The *fili* had a legally recognized status and role in early Irish society. He was credited with supernatural wisdom and had at his disposal two powerful instruments in the form of satire and eulogy. He was expected to be competent in the law; the chief poet (*ollam*), who was recognized in law as the highest grade of *fili*, was required, *inter alia*, to "be knowledgeable in the jurisprudence of Irish law."[11] The *filid* had an important role in the transmission and teaching of customary law. So much is made clear in question and answer format in the Introduction to the collection of tracts known as *Senchas Már* 'The Great Tradition': "What has preserved the tradition of the men of Ireland? The joint memory of the ancients, transmission from ear to ear, the chanting of poets (*filid*), its being augmented by the law of Scripture, its being founded on the law of nature."[12]

While it now receives less attention than it used to, there can be no denying that oral tradition contributed to the formation of the law texts. Even if we leave aside the question of Indo-European survival, certain technical terms in the laws attest to a Common Celtic heritage that must have been part of the oral tradition before the law texts were written. In general, however, the oral component in the surviving law texts cannot easily be separated out from the rest of what are, after all, written texts.

The *filid* were also involved in the composition of law texts. The oldest datable law text, *Cáin Fhuithirbe* 'The Law of Fuithirbe,'[13] which was completed some time between 678 and 683, was commissioned and drafted by four named persons, three of whom were clerics, and the fourth a *fili*.[14] The first of the two tracts that bear the title *Bretha Nemed* 'Judgments Concerning Privileged Persons,' written in the second quarter of the eighth century, is ascribed to three kinsmen, one of them a bishop, the second a *fili*, and the third a judge.[15] Most of our law texts are anonymous, but such evidence as we have suggests that "the early Irish law texts were written in a context of cooperation between ecclesiastics and lay academics, which also included the involvement of practicing members of the legal profession."[16] The ways in which the *filid* contributed to the textualization of the customary law would include the more traditional elements in its content.

The texts are sometimes written in prose and sometimes in a mixture of prose and verse. The prose is frequently alliterative, and the verse is for the most part the rhymeless alliterative verse known as *roscad*. The stylistic, metrical, and even grammatical features of this form of verse would have been part of the curriculum of the *filid*, and its use in the law texts is clear evidence of their involvement.

The *filid* were also custodians of the rich narrative literature of early Ireland. As they progressed through their courses of study, the grades of *fili* acquired progressively larger numbers of traditional tales, culminating in the repertoire of the *ollam*, which comprised no less than three hundred and fifty tales. Now the law texts frequently used traditional tales as "leading cases." As Binchy put it:

> The Irish legal records abound in references to the ancient mythology of the race. . . . Like their modern successors, the Irish lawyers were great sticklers for precedent. They were always anxious to have a "leading case" on which to hang a particular rule or institution; only they searched for such cases, not in the Law Reports, but in the sagas of the heroic age. Hence the origin of well-known rules—and more particularly of innovations in the law . . . —is traced back to the actions of some famous mythological figure and thus invested with the sanction of hallowed antiquity.[17]

Irish narrative literature is now classified in cycles: the Mythological Cycle, the Ulster Cycle, the Fenian Cycle, and the Cycles of the Kings, and personages from all of these cycles figure in stories preserved in the law texts.[18]

The *filid*, then, left their mark on the form and content of the law texts. They also had a role in court procedure. An important early document on this latter topic indicates that judgment was arrived at and expounded by a judge or judges. There was a back court in which sat the king, the bishop, and the chief poet, and these dignitaries are collectively described as "the cliff which is behind the courts for judgment and for promulgation." The judgment, therefore, was evidently promulgated by the king or other dignitary, or at least announced in his presence and with his approval, and consequently supported by his power and prestige.[19] Where there was a legal dispute relating to poets or poetry, the matter was brought before the king, the king then went to the chief poet, and the king and the chief poet decided the case.[20]

THE *FILID* IN THE LAWS

The laws tell us a great deal about the early Irish learned classes, and particularly about the *filid*. This is especially true of the texts that, according to Binchy, emanated from a poetico-legal school in Munster. These include the *Bretha Nemed*, and two tracts that deal with status: the first of these, the *Uraicecht Becc* ("Small Primer"), is especially concerned with the status of "privileged persons," including the *filid*; the second, *Uraicecht na Ríar* ("The Primer of Stipulations") has to do with the "grades" of poets. I shall confine myself here to the latter text. It lists the seven grades and three sub-grades within the profession. These grades represent successive stages in a progression that an individual might make in his lifetime, and the distinction among them was one of learning rather than of function or office. The exception is the highest grade, the *ollam* or chief poet, who held an office within one of the many small kingdoms that were the jurisdictional units of early Ireland. He is frequently mentioned along with the king and the bishop, and we have seen above that he sat with them in courts of law.

The profession of poetry was hereditary. The *fili* had to complete a prescribed course of training, and it is clear from *Uraicecht na Ríar* that he was required to maintain a high standard of personal as well as professional conduct. A few lines from the text may serve to exemplify how the *filid* are discussed in the laws:

> How is a grade conferred on a poet? It is not difficult: he shows his compositions to an *ollam*, who has the seven grades of knowledge, and

the king receives him in the fullness of his grade, in which the *ollam* declares him to be on the basis of his compositions, and his guiltlessness, and his purity, that is, purity of learning, and purity of mouth, and purity of hand and marital union, and purity consisting of being innocent of theft and plunder and illegality, and purity of body, that he have only one wife, for one perishes through dark (illicit) cohabitation aside from one chaste (woman) on lawful nights.[21]

In the conferral of a grade upon a poet, as described here, the king and the *ollam* each has his role: the *ollam*, having assessed the candidate and assigned him to the appropriate grade, presents him to the king who accepts him into the fullness of that grade. The *ollam*'s assessment of the candidate covers his professional attainments and certain aspects of his personal and professional conduct. The same standard of conduct would seem to have been required of all poets, whatever their grade; the kind of thing which is set out in the text would not be subject to gradation. The particular grade to be conferred must have been determined on the basis of professional attainments. Of these only the poet's "compositions" are mentioned here. The evidence suggests that this refers to the candidate's expertise in the traditional narratives, the extent of which (as we have seen) depended on the grade in question.

While no indication is given of how the poet's personal and professional conduct is gauged, his professional attainments are assessed by examination: "he shows his compositions to an *ollam*." The examination may very well have been an oral one: the Irish original uses a form of the verb *do-aisféna* 'shows, displays, exhibits,' which can be used of oral revelation, such as the confession of sins. The conduct of the poet is described in terms of guiltlessness (*ecnae*) and purity (*idnae*). On the face of it we seem to be confronted with six kinds of purity, but the list can almost certainly be reduced to four: "purity of hand" is very probably the same as "purity consisting of being innocent of theft and plunder and illegality," while "purity of marital union" is obviously the same as "purity of body," which, we are told, requires that he marry only one, virtuous wife, and that even with her his intercourse be confined to "lawful nights." Moreover, the wording of another legal text suggests that the "guiltlessness" required of him is to be equated with "purity of hand and marital union." The purity of learning and of mouth, on the other hand, may be considered to pertain particularly to the poet's professional conduct. "Purity of learning," we are told elsewhere, "cleanses the impurity of all types of poetry."[22] As for "purity of mouth," this may refer to avoidance of unjustified or illegal satire. This would be consistent with the observation of the admittedly very much later scholar Dubhaltach Mac Firbhisigh: "The grades of the poets were required to be free of the taint of theft and killing, defamation (*aoradh*) and adultery and from everything that was harmful to their learning."[23]

MYTHICAL OR LEGENDARY LAW-GIVERS

The law tracts, in whole or in part, are sometimes attributed to mythical or legendary figures. One of these is the legendary king of Tara, Cormac son of Art and grandson of Conn, who, as Binchy has remarked, is portrayed in the literature as the Numa Pompilius of Irish law. In *Geneamuin Chormaic Uí Chuinn* 'The Birth-Tale of Cormac Ua Cuinn,'[24] which is actually a brief biography of the king, we are told that "a great din of thunder came into the air at the birth of the boy." The boy in question, known from his father as Cormac mac Airt or from his grandfather as Cormac Ua Cuinn, is in many ways the ideal king of Irish tradition, and it comes as no surprise that the conditions that will be enjoyed in Ireland during his reign should be prophesied at his birth. Responding to the thunder, the man who is to be Cormac's foster-father says:

> Noise of thunder
> The birth of a king
> Increase of corn
> Extinction of falsehood
> A ship's stern of sense
> Inspiration of truth
> Darkening of every utterance

We must supply the connectives that are implied here. Noise of thunder greets (and reveals) the arrival of a boy who will be king, and as a result of his birth, crops will be more abundant, falsehood and injustice will be extinguished, truth and justice will prevail, and utterances will be obscure. (On the face of it, we might think that this latter prediction is something of a letdown, since the other effects of the boy's reign are clearly beneficent. But obscurity was prized by the *filid*: in an early text on poetry, "darkening of speech" is mentioned in an entirely positive context.[25]) The boy is called "a ship's stern of sense," which refers to the "ship of state," a metaphor that is taken up in a prophecy further on in the text in which the same foster-father says:

> You are the son of the true prince, that is, son of Art son of Conn Cétchathach, and it is prophesied of you that you will succeed your father at the helm, for there will be no corn nor milk nor mast nor fish nor weather in season until you enjoy dominion in Tara.

Here too we have an echo of the "increase of corn" foretold in the earlier prophecy, and abundance of corn, milk, fruit, and fish was attributed in early Ireland to the incumbency of a righteous king. Specifically, it was the king's truth and justice—in Irish, *fír flathemon*—that ensured this abundance, and this is something that is emphasized again and again in the laws, the wisdom texts, and the tales. In this respect, Cormac's biography, as it is recounted in his birth-tale and elsewhere, reflects in narrative form the ideology of kingship that is expressed in the legal and wisdom texts.[26] In yet another prophecy of his foster-father's in the birth-tale, we find the following:

> He will bestow just law upon the lands of Ireland
> There will be a court over Ireland
> His great judgments will be cited (?) on this island until the end of the world.

LAW IN THE TALES

The tales of Cormac belong to the Cycles of the Kings, and it is scarcely surprising that the law should loom large in tales of this kind, concerned as they are with the deeds of legendary or historical kings. But legal concepts pervade tales from all the cycles. Tales of the gods tell of the origins of institutions and customs, and serve as exemplary texts.

Cath Maige Tuired 'The Battle of Mag Tuired'[27] is perhaps the most important of our mythological tales, and it presents the war of the gods in terms of the early Irish social code. Its depiction of early Irish kingship as a contract between king and people is wholly consistent with what we find in the laws. A knowledge of the law also helps us to understand what is going on in *Tochmarc Étaíne* 'The Wooing of Étaín,'[28] a trilogy of tales that tell how the god Midir sought and, after many vicissitudes, ultimately won the hand of the goddess Étaín. The gods have magical powers, and enchantment is an important component in the saga. Yet Midir's wooing of Étaín unfolds as a series of transactions—of promises, pledges, purchases, wagers, and so on. The exercise of magical power is in great measure subject to legal or quasi-legal constraints. A case in point concerns the greatest of the gods, the Dagdae, who "used to work wonders for them and control the weather and the crops." When he decided that the time had come for him to bestow upon his son Óengus the great megalithic mound now known as Newgrange, and which was in the possession of another god, Elcmar, the Dagdae devised an ingenious (and underhanded) way of doing so that entailed a judgment on the legal claims of Óengus and Elcmar. Again, when Óengus's foster-father Midir takes Étaín home as his bride, his earlier wife Fúamnach uses her magical powers to separate the lovers—she transforms Étaín into a pool of water—and she can do this because she has the legal protection of the gods. It is only when she breaks the law by violating Óengus's precinct at Newgrange that she forfeits the protection of the gods, and Óengus is at liberty to assail her. He follows her to her father's house and cuts off her head.

The greatest of the early Irish tales is *Táin Bó Cúailnge* 'The Cattle Raid of Cooley,' which deals with the epic defence of the province of Ulster by the young Cú Chulainn, against an army of invaders bent upon securing possession of the great bull of Cooley. This tale too is replete with legal terminology, and indeed there are several passages in it that give us clear indications of a law of war, and which supplement the somewhat meager testimony on this matter in the laws themselves.[29] We cannot be sure that the indications given to us in *Táin Bó Cúailnge* on such matters as the conduct of war correspond precisely to the actual law of early medieval Ireland, but we can at least say that the circumstantial accounts in the tale are compatible with the laconic statements of the laws. And we can say without any shadow of doubt that an understanding of the language and concepts of early Irish law enriches our reading of *Táin Bó Cúailnge*, and of early Irish literature as a whole.

TEXTS

THE CYCLES OF THE GODS AND GODDESSES

9

Cath Maige Tuired as Exemplary Myth

(1 9 8 3)

The myth of the War of the Gods, also known as the theomachy, is represented in Irish tradition by the contention between the Túatha Dé Danann and the Fomoiri, which culminated in a battle said to have been fought at Moytirra in County Sligo, in which the Túatha Dé Danann vanquished the Fomoiri. The fullest account of this contention is to be found in the early version of *Cath Maige Tuired*, which is preserved in the sixteenth-century British Library manuscript Harley 5280, where it is entitled *Cath Maige Turedh ocus genemain Bres meic Elathain ocus a ríghe*, "The Battle of Moytirra, and the birth of Bres son of Elathan and his reign."[1] This text, which has been written out in notoriously aberrant spelling, "would seem to be a composite work put together by an eleventh or twelfth-century redactor mainly from ninth-century material."[2] In the present essay, all references to *CMT* are to the Harley text.[3]

The momentous battle fought at Moytirra finds its place in the schema of legendary prehistory which was shaped and propagated by the literati, and which came to be known as *Lebor Gabála Érenn*. According to the literati, the Túatha Dé Danann won two great battles at Moytirra, and it was in the second of these that they vanquished the Fomoiri, having already defeated the Fir Bolg in the first battle of Moytirra.[4] It may be that each of these encounters rests on a foundation of ancient myth,[5] but it has long been suspected that Irish tradition originally knew only one battle of Moytirra, of which the other must in some measure be a duplicate.[6] T. F. O'Rahilly held that "the story of the first battle of Mag Tuired was in existence before that of the second, to which it served as a model."[7] In O'Rahilly's view "the second battle is merely a pseudo-historical expansion of a mythological theme, the 'slaying' of the god Balar by Lug; under the influence of the story of the first battle the duel between these supernatural personages becomes a battle between two armies."[8] The antiquity of the myth of the War of the Gods, however, has been amply demonstrated,[9] so that there can be no good grounds for stripping *CMT* down to the centerpiece of the battle, which is the confrontation of Lug and Balar. As for the thesis that the story of the first battle served as a model for that of the second, Gerard Murphy has made a cogent case against it,[10] and, on present showing, primacy must be accorded to the tradition that the battle of Moytirra was fought between the Túatha Dé Danann and the Fomoiri.

Nearly half a century ago, A. G. van Hamel[11] tried to establish the existence in Irish (and Celtic) tradition of what he called "exemplary myth," explaining that "the adjective 'exemplary' . . . as applied to heroes or traditions, means a hero or tradition that had to be regarded by people in the early Celtic society as an example which must be imitated by them, or of whose example the deeds of other men must be regarded as a reflexion."[12] Van Hamel's treatment of the Irish evidence is somewhat unsatisfactory, and he drew what Gerard Murphy called "rash conclusions."[13] But the notion that Irish myth could be exemplary in character is not to be dismissed merely because of the weakness of van Hamel's advocacy of his case. On the contrary, this notion has been rehabilitated by some of the more recent work on *CMT*:[14] what I propose to do here is to take a fresh look at *CMT* with this notion in mind, and to set out the different ways in which this tale can be interpreted as an exemplary myth.

It will be useful at this point to give a broad outline of the story that is told in *CMT*, with some commentary on the episodes which are relevant to our theme. The story begins with the coming of the Túatha Dé Danann to Ireland, and tells how they made an alliance with the Fomoiri. Núadu was at that time king of the Túatha Dé Danann, but he lost one of his arms in battle, and, being blemished, he had to relinquish the kingship. The Túatha Dé Danann had then to elect a new king, and they chose Bres, whose mother Ériu was of the Túatha Dé Danann, but whose father Elatha was of the Fomoiri. The circumstances of Bres's conception and birth are set out in the text (§§15 ff.), as promised by the mention of *genemain Bres meic Elathain* in the title. Here it will be sufficient to say that it is a "birth" of the usual heroic type.[15] Bres is thus by definition a hero, but in the event we shall see that he is a hero who is doomed to failure.

In electing Bres, the Túatha Dé Danann thought that he would cement their alliance with the Fomoiri, but what happened was that the Fomoiri held Ireland under tribute and the Túatha Dé Danann were obliged to perform humiliating and menial tasks for Bres. And so they conspired against Bres and tricked him into giving a false judgment. The story then shifts to Núadu: he was first fitted with a silver hand by Dían Cécht, but then his own hand was restored to him by Míach son of Dían Cécht. In this way Núadu was made whole. But although Núadu would have been eligible to resume the kingship, it is not stated at this point that he did so. Rather does the storyteller give us another version of the story of Bres's reign, commencing *Gapuis tra Bres an flaith* (§36). Stokes translated this: "So Bres held the sovereignty," but this can hardly be correct: *gabais in flaith* must surely mean "he assumed the sovereignty,"[16] and what we have here is another account of the reign. According to this account, Bres was a niggardly king, as we are told in the much-quoted passage: "His mother's kin, the Túatha Dé, greatly complained about him, for their knives were not greased by him; though they often visited him, their breaths did not smell of ale" (§36). Because of this inhospitable treatment on Bres's part, the Túatha Dé Danann ceased to pay him tribute. Then one day their poet Cairbre son of Étaín sought hospitality from Bres and was shabbily treated, and so he satirized Bres and "nothing but decay was on Bres from that time." And that, we are told, was the first time ever that satire was made in Ireland (§39).

Then the Túatha Dé Danann ejected Bres from the kingship, and he repaired to his father's kin, the Fomoiri, and among them he met his father Elatha for the first time. The dialogue which ensued between Bres and his father has a bearing on the interpretation of the events of Bres's reign. Elatha asked Bres what had brought him out of the land which he ruled. Bres replied: "Nothing has brought me save my own injustice and arrogance" (*m'anfhír 7 m'anuabhar fesin*, §45), and he admitted that he had stripped the Túatha Dé Danann of their wealth and that he did not receive tribute from them. And Bres went on to tell his father that he had come to him for warriors, for he wished to take Ireland by force. His father responded: "You should not take it by injustice if you do not take it by justice" (*Ni rogaba la hainbfír mani gaba la fír*, §48). Nonetheless, the champions of the Fomoiri came together and they set out for Ireland to subdue the Túatha Dé Danann.

All of this explains how the Túatha Dé Danann and the Fomoiri came to fight the battle of Moytirra. This early part of *CMT* is to all intents and purposes the story of Bres, his *genemain* and his *ríge*: we meet him again at the end of the tale, when Lug and Bres have a highly significant confrontation. It will be worth our while here to consider the events of Bres's reign in some detail, not only because they carry an important part of the meaning of *CMT*, but also because they are relevant to the question of the exemplary character of the tale.

There are, as I have already indicated, two different accounts of Bres's reign in *CMT*: these have been set together rather clumsily, providing us with yet another example of what Myles Dillon called "patchwork,"[17] which is such a common feature of our literary texts. In the first version, Bres displeases the Túatha Dé Danann by his overbearing arrogance, and so they bring about a situation in which he gives a false judgment, and thereby offends against the truth—against the *fír flatha* ['Prince's truth'] which distinguishes a worthy king. The point is made for us in the text, for when Bres has given his judgment, the Dagdae upbraids him: "What you utter, o king of the warriors of the Féni, is not a Prince's Truth" (*Ni fíor flathu deit, a rí óc fénei, a n-udbere*, §29). We have seen that Bres later admits to his own *anfír*, and that his father presses the point home when he tells Bres that he should not take Ireland by *anfír* if he did not take it by *fír*.

Dumézil has established the existence of an Indo-European theme which he calls the single sin of the sovereign, and which takes the form of a sin against the truth or a sin of pride.[18] Although Dumézil, who has drawn frequently on *CMT* in his comparative work, says that "the Celts present nothing of this sort, it seems,"[19] I believe that Bres's false judgment is in all probability a reflex of the single sin of the sovereign. It is true that the Irish word *fír* embraces the notion of "justice" as well as that of "truth," so that when Bres confesses *anfír* we cannot assume that he is referring specifically to the Act of Untruth which he has made in giving a false judgment. Moreover, it might be asked, if Bres is a generally overbearing king, how can we speak of a "single" sin? The answer lies in the nature of *fír*, which, as Calvert Watkins describes it, is "an intellectual force, *verbally expressed*, which ensures the society's prosperity, abundance of food, and fertility, and its protection from plague, calamity, and enemy attack."[20] It is the verbal expression, the act of public utterance, which is crucial here, for in it resides the power for good. The opposite of *fír flatha* is *gáu flatha*: this too is verbally expressed, and its power for ill lies in the verbal utterance. As an illustration of this principle, we may cite the interdiction placed by the Ulaid upon their king, Conchobor mac Nessa: they would not allow him to give judgment, so that he might not give a false one, so that the crops would not be the worse for it.[21] If the king is precluded from giving any judgments, he cannot give a false one, and so the people are spared the dire consequences which would follow such a pronouncement. We can see, therefore, why the Túatha Dé Danann should resort to a ruse to make Bres give a false judgment: it is necessary that his unworthiness as a ruler should be made manifest in a public utterance.

The locus classicus of *gáu flatha* in Irish literature is *Cath Maige Mucrama*, where we find a description of the false judgment given by the king of Tara, Lugaid Mac Con, and of its dramatic aftermath. When Lugaid pronounces his judgment, the side of the house in which the judgment was made collapses; Lugaid continues in office for a year, but the crops do not grow; the men of Ireland expel Lugaid from the kingship as being an "unlawful ruler" (*anflaith*); and he goes to Munster, where he is slain by Ailill Ólomm.[22] In this scenario, the fact that Lugaid's judgment is a false one is made manifest by the collapse of the side of the house; the cosmic effect of his untruth is seen in the failure of the crops; and the retribution which is visited upon Lugaid is swift and sure: the men of Ireland withdraw their consent from his rule, and he goes to his death.

The account of Bres's judgment in *CMT* is not carried through in such a thorough-going fashion as that of Lugaid in *Cath Maige Mucrama*. Thus, although Bres does concede the falsehood of his judgment by reversing it (§30), there is no external manifestation of its falsehood to compare with the collapse of the side of the house brought on by Lugaid's judgment. The retribution which is visited upon Bres is not as swift as we would expect, and the narrator does not explicitly connect it with the judgment. The fact, however, that we are told at this point how Núadu was released from his ineligibility for the kingship suggests that Bres would here have been deposed, to be succeeded by Núadu. But the story of the judgment has to be accommodated to that of the satire, and the deposal of Bres follows the satire in the narrative. For all that, however, Bres is thoroughly punished in *CMT*, and the punishment which he suffers would appear to retain the essential lineaments of the retribution which attaches to the single sin of the sovereign. For, if we may here anticipate the rest of the story, we shall find that Bres is punished in three stages: he is deprived of the kingship, his army is routed by the Túatha Dé Danann, and he is finally forced to yield up the secrets of ploughing, sowing, and reaping to Lug. This sequence spans the three domains or "functions" of sacral kingship, martial force, and agriculture. In offending against the truth, Bres commits a sin of the first function since sacral kingship is characterized by *fír flatha*, and yet he is punished successively in respect of all three. Now the examples which Dumézil has adduced of the sin of the sovereign show a comparable "asymmetry": the sin is depicted in terms of the first function, whereas the retribution extends to all three.[23] The conclusion must be that the theme of the single sin of the sovereign is one of the strands which have been woven into the fabric of *CMT*.

The second account of Bres's reign in *CMT* also invokes the spoken word, this time in the form of the satire pronounced by Cairbre son of Étaín, *fili* of the Túatha Dé Danann. The sequence of events is well known, since it is invariably recounted in modern discussions of the role of the *fili* as satirist in Gaelic Ireland. The story of Cairbre's satire is told also as an independent anecdote;[24] the text of the satire is given there, and also in the commentary on *Amra Choluim Chille*.[25] In *CMT* itself only the first four words of the satire are quoted, but in Stokes's edition the remainder is supplied from the commentary on the *Amra*.

Dumézil has provided an extended and very valuable discussion of this portion of *CMT*.[26] Having examined the careers of two mythical kings, the

Indian Pṛthu and the Roman Servius Tullius, Dumézil turned to the Irish material in search of a myth equivalent to those of Pṛthu and Servius, "un mythe exposant dramatiquement et justifiant par un exemple fameux, par un premier exemple, et la technique de l' 'appréciation qualifiante' et la nécessité de l'échange des prestations entre le roi et ses sujets."[27] In the story of Cairbre's satirizing of Bres, Dumézil finds such a myth, "mais dans une forme inattendue, en négatif": here we are dealing with a myth, not of accession, but of deposal; the qualificatory appraisal is realized, not as praise, but as censure; the appraising poet acts, not as a panegyrist and the inventor of praise, but as a satirist and the author of the first satire; instead of abundance and generosity we find scarcity and avarice. Here then we are shown the risks entailed in transgressing the rules, rather than the benefits which flow from abiding by them.[28]

The "rules" which are in question here have to do with the exchange of prestations between the king and his subjects—or rather those of his subjects who are of sufficient status to participate in such an exchange. This exchange of prestations is the primitive system of gift/counter-gift which, D. A. Binchy suggests, is reflected in Irish in the opposition *folad/frithfolad*, and "on which the entire structure of 'obligations'—legal, political, religious and domestic—was based in early pre-literate societies before the development of cities, courts of justice and coinage; in other words the primitive system from which our modern law of contract derives its origin."[29]

It is in terms of the social contract that Dumézil interprets what happens in *CMT*. Having levied rent on the Túatha Dé Danann, Bres fails to provide them with hospitality; and so they withhold service and wergild from him.[30] The bond between the king and his people has been broken: as Dumézil puts it: "le circuit vital—impôts montant du peuple au roi; générosités, et principalement générosités alimentaires, descendant du roi au people—ne se ferme pas."[31]

But this state of affairs is allowed to continue until the *fili* intervenes: he is empowered—indeed, he inaugurates the exercise of his power—to express the public sentiment in the form of a satire. In his satire he puts into words the "démérite alimentaire du roi." And his satire is an effective instrument: after the satire has been pronounced, Cairbre says: "Bres's wealth, then, is no more!" and the text goes on: "That came to pass. There was nothing but decay on Bres from that time" (§39). The Túatha Dé Danann then demand that Bres abdicate.

Dumézil lays stress on the crucial role of the *fili* in this scenario, and in a recent article Kim McCone has likewise drawn attention to the importance of the verbal utterance here: even though the evil effects of the king's niggardliness have been felt for some time, a *ráiteas sollúnta* ("solemn statement") is required to confirm the king's fault before the crisis comes which will ultimately eject the king from the sovereignty.[32] McCone also remarks that in its demonstration of the power of the word, Cairbre's satire may be compared with the false judgment of Lugaid Mac Con.[33] It is interesting to note in this context that Dumézil argues that the power of the poet is founded on the truth, and that the efficacy of his utterances is contingent upon their veracity: thus, the praise or censure expressed by the poet must be justified by the facts.[34] As far as censure goes, Irish tradition offers support for Dumézil's contention,[35] and of course we have seen that in *CMT* Cairbre's satire is amply justified by Bres's conduct.

If we can compare Cairbre's satire to Lugaid's judgment, then we can also compare it to Bres's judgment in *CMT*. The indications are, as we have seen, that the judgment episode has been foreshortened in *CMT*, and if that is so the two accounts of Bres's reign can be said to be homologous:

1. king arrogant	1. king niggardly
2. false judgment	2. satire
3. —	3. decline in fortunes
4. deposal, defeat, loss of agricultural supremacy	4. deposal

One of these episodes, therefore, is redundant. In much of Irish narrative there is a tension between the cumulative tendency on the one hand, and linear exposition on the other. In the story of Bres, as we have it in *CMT*, the cumulative tendency wins out, and so we have both a false judgment and a satire. Either of these would have been sufficient to bring about the deposal of the king, as we know from the story of Lugaid in the case of judgment, and of Caier[36] in the case of satire. It could perhaps be said in the storyteller's favor that he thereby teaches two lessons rather than one: he teaches the necessity for the king to observe the prince's truth, and he also teaches the need for the king to show that generosity which was so much a mark of the worthy ruler that *flaithiúil* remains to this day a common word for "generous."

9. *Cath Maige Tuired* as Exemplary Myth   143

If the early part of *CMT* is largely devoted to Bres, the rest (and much the greater part) of it belongs to Lug. In summarizing *CMT* above, we left it at the point when the army of the Fomoiri sets out for Ireland to subdue the Túatha Dé Danann. The storyteller then turns his attention to the affairs of the latter (§§52 ff.). Núadu, we are told, is again in sovereignty over the Túatha Dé Danann after Bres, and he holds a great feast for them at Tara: and then the coming of Lug is described in a well-known passage. Lug arrives unannounced at Tara, "a young warrior, fair and shapely, wearing the crown of a king," and leading a band of strangers. His name is announced to the doorkeeper, and he asks Lug what art he practices, for none without an art enters Tara. Lug says that he is a wright. The doorkeeper replies, "We do not need you. We have a wright already, one Luchtae son of Luachaid." Then Lug says that he is a smith; but the doorkeeper's response is as before: they do not need him, they already have a smith. The dialogue goes on like this for a long time, Lug naming his various skills and the doorkeeper rejecting him. Finally Lug says: "Ask the king whether he has a single man who includes all these arts, and if he has I shall not enter Tara." Núadu says that Lug should be admitted and he then goes into the fortress and sits in the sage's seat, for he is a sage in every art. Then Núadu decides to change seats with Lug, and so Lug goes to the king's seat. For thirteen days, Núadu "rises up before" Lug in homage.

    That is how Lug becomes king of Tara. This is to be seen as Lug's first victory in *CMT*, for, in effect, he has ousted Núadu from the kingship and had himself instated in his stead. Lug comes to Tara as a stranger, an outsider, wearing the crown of a king; an attempt is made to exclude him; but he establishes his right to enter Tara and shows himself worthy of the kingship itself. Lug's confrontation with the doorman enables the storyteller to give a catalogue of the Túatha Dé Danann; it also serves to reveal the omnicompetence of Lug—Lug *ildánach* or *samildánach*. But its function in the plot is that it enables Lug to establish his right to enter Tara: it is by appealing to his omnicompetence that Lug defeats the attempt to exclude him. Just when it seems that there is no art that Lug could possess which is not already represented among the Túatha Dé Danann at Tara, he outwits the doorman by asserting (in what is essentially a rhetorical question) that it is unique to possess so many arts at the one time. The doorman is acting in Núadu's interest, so that Lug's victory over the doorman is effectively a defeat for Núadu. Lug's ousting of Núadu is achieved peacefully without resort to arms: he reveals his wisdom in establishing his right to enter Tara, and he does this in the form of a verbal utterance. There is an analogy here with the true judgment whereby Cormac mac Airt shows himself worthy of kingship.[37] Moreover, Núadu yields voluntarily to Lug, just as in the early version of the story of Cormac mac Airt's accession to kingship, Lugaid Mac Con yields peacefully to Cormac, once the latter has given his true judgment.[38] We may compare also the accession of Conaire Mór to the kingship of Tara, as it is described in *Togail Bruidne Da Derga*: Conaire has been designated by the gods, and recognized by the wise men, but the people object to him on the grounds of his youth. But Conaire refutes this, saying that a king is not disqualified by youth provided that he be generous. This utterance is accepted with enthusiasm and Conaire is invested with the kingship.[39]

Lug's utterance fulfils the same function as those of Cormac and Conaire, and it can be classed as a true judgment. The content of these judgments is not to be dismissed as irrelevant. Cormac's judgment concerns *lommrad* 'laying bare,' a matter which, as I have argued elsewhere, pertains to the relationship between the king and the fertility of the land.[40] Conaire's case is that what is essential for a king is that he be generous, and we have seen the truth of this in the story of Bres. What we learn from Lug would seem to be that a king should be omnicompetent. When Núadu beholds Lug's many powers he considers whether Lug could put away from the Túatha Dé Danann the bondage they suffer from the Fomoiri (§74), and, once he has been made king, that is what Lug goes on to do.

Lug sets about the preparations for battle and these are described at length in the text (§§75 ff.), but I must pass over them here. The battle too is described in detail. The Túatha Dé Danann attempt to keep Lug from the battle so that the beauty of his body might not be impaired, and for that reason they keep him under guard (§95). But Lug escapes and goes to the battlefield, where he speaks to the warriors to give them strength. And then he adopts a magical posture, going round the Túatha Dé Danann on one foot and with one eye open and chanting to them. They then give battle. The decisive encounter is that between Lug and Balar, who, though he is of the Fomoiri, is Lug's maternal grandfather.[41] Balar, who has already slain Núadu, has an evil eye which is never opened save on a battlefield. Four men used to lift up the lid of the eye with a handle through the lid. A host, however numerous, which beheld that eye could not resist warriors (§133).

There is a dialogue between Lug and Balar, and then Balar commands that his eyelid be raised. But when this has been done, "Lug cast a sling-stone at him, so that the eye went (back) through his head. And so it was his own army that looked at it" (§135). After that the battle becomes a rout, and the Fomoiri are beaten back to the sea.

That then is Lug's second victory in *CMT*: the first is achieved by means of guile, and (as I have argued) by giving a true judgment, as is appropriate in the domain of kingship; the second by martial means, as befits a champion.

An important incident occurs after the battle. Lug comes upon Bres, who implores Lug to spare him. Lug agrees to do so on condition that Bres answers three questions: "How shall the men of Ireland plough? How shall they sow? How shall they reap?" (§158). Bres answers the questions and he is spared.[42] Lug has wrested the secrets of ploughing, sowing, and reaping from Bres: henceforth, the Túatha Dé Danann will have control over the fruits of the earth. Dumézil has noted that before the battle, the Túatha Dé Danann did not have all the competences necessary in a sedentary community: they had command of druidic magic, warrior prowess, all the arts and crafts, and the techniques of medicine and smithcraft, but they lacked competence in agriculture. This deficiency is made good after the battle in that they acquire the secrets of agricultural practice. In this Dumézil[43] sees a reflex of the Indo-European theomachy, which he interprets as a war between representatives of the first two functions and those of the third, leading to the incorporation of the latter into the community of the former.

In this respect, what was true of the Túatha Dé Danann in general was also true of Lug in particular: he was king and champion, and master of all the arts, but he had no competence in agriculture until he wrested its secrets from Bres. In doing this Lug achieved his third victory in *CMT*, and indeed it is the one which continued to be celebrated in the harvest-festival of Lughnasadh, the survival of which into our own time has been shown and documented by Máire MacNeill.[44] Writing of *CMT*, MacNeill gave it as her view that Núadu, Balar, and Bres are three aspects of Lug's opponent,[45] but I would prefer to see Lug's successive victories over this trio as a sequence in which he establishes his pre-eminence in the domains of kingship, martial prowess, and agriculture. This fits in neatly with the tripartite structure which Dumézil has posited for Indo-European ideology: in *CMT*, Lug is the omnicompetent hero, but he is also the hero who encompasses all three of the domains which belong to the tripartite structure.

We can now turn to a consideration of the exemplary status of *CMT*. Van Hamel's description has already been quoted (p. 136 in this volume) of an exemplary hero or myth as one "that had to be regarded by people in the early Celtic society as an example which must be imitated by them, or of whose example the deeds of other men must be regarded as a reflexion." In this van Hamel is making what I take to be a valid distinction between two ways in which a myth can be deemed to be exemplary, the first of them having to do with the social function of myth, and the second with the place of a given myth in the mythological system to which it belongs. If we say that myth provides an exemplar which is to be imitated by people as they live out their lives, then we are speaking of the social function of myth; if we think that a myth provides a model for the deeds of personages as they are recounted in other tales, then we are positing an exemplary or paradigmatic role for that myth within the mythological system. We shall see that these two aspects of the exemplary status of myth are relevant to the interpretation of *CMT*, in other words that it has an exemplary function both on the social plane and within the mythological system. The bulk of what follows is devoted to the systemic aspect of the matter, but for the sake of completeness I begin with a brief account of the social function of *CMT*.

Such a function is clearly predicated of a hero or tradition that "had to be regarded by people in . . . society as an example which must be imitated by them." This formulation is not quite satisfactory, since a hero is such only insofar as he is different from the common man, and it follows that his specifically heroic deeds cannot be imitated by ordinary mortals.[46] But a man may seek to emulate the achievements of a hero or even of a god, even if he must ultimately fail to raise himself to their level. It may well be that a man would be spurred on to such emulation by listening to the recitation of a tale at the appropriate time. In the Irish tale-lists, the material is classified according to events or deeds, such as "Battles," "Cattle-raids," and "Voyages," and Alwyn and Brinley Rees have suggested that there may have been a tendency to tell these tales in the circumstances that corresponded to them in real life. Thus, it may be that "it was 'Battles' in particular that were related to kings about to embark upon war, that 'Cattle-raids' were told before undertaking a cattle-raid, 'Voyages' on setting out to sea,"[47] and so on. We might also expect that the instruction of a king would include the narration and explication of the tales about mythical (and historical) kings, and there could be no more suitable material for this purpose than that pertaining to Bres and Lug.[48]

It may be, then, that van Hamel's formulation is not too wide of the mark, though "emulation" might be better than "imitation." Van Hamel claimed further that "an exemplary story is intended to impart the actual power of imitating its hero."[49] The Irish evidence will not carry us quite so far, but it does attest to a belief, which is parodied in *Aislinge Meic Conglinne*, that to listen to a tale will bring life, offspring, and prosperity.[50] It is said of *Táin Bó Cúailnge*, for example, that he who hears it recited will enjoy a year's protection.[51] Here, as with the judgment of a king and the eulogy/satire of the poet, we see the power of the truth, verbally expressed: the story "works like a charm, because in the belief of the narrator it tells what has truly happened."[52]

As far as the content of a myth is concerned, we can say that an exemplary myth embodies in a dramatic way the ideology and value system of the community, and that it validates these in the course of the narrative. This can be done negatively, as we have seen in the story of Bres, who suffers dearly for his arrogance and neglect of the truth, and also for his breach of the social contract. Or it can be done positively, as it is with the sagacious and resourceful Lug, whose beneficent career is articulated in terms of the tripartite ideology which was part of Ireland's Indo-European heritage.

As well as its function in reinforcing the ideology and value system of the community, myth can also be used more specifically to explain the origins and justify the continuation of particular customs and practices. (It can also be used, as Binchy points out, in respect of innovations in the customary law, which are "always traced back to the action of some famous mythological figure and thus invested with the sanction of hallowed antiquity."[53]) The use of mythical precedent in this way is a universal feature of pre-modern cultures: "life is meaningful in as much as it is an imitation or re-enactment of what the gods did in the beginning."[54] In *CMT*, as we have seen, we are told of the first satire that was composed in Ireland. So too are we given the circumstances of the first *caíned* in Ireland: "Brigit came and keened her son. She shrieked first, she cried at last. And crying and shrieking were then heard for the first time in Ireland" (§125).[55]

Even if the first occasion of a custom is not mentioned, it can be explained as being practiced now because it was practiced then: we do it now because it was done by the gods. Thus, in *CMT* the storyteller explains a contemporary custom in terms of what was done "at that time," that is at the time when the battle was fought at Moytirra, the time of the gods.[56] The story goes that the warrior Ogmae found the sword of Tethra, king of the Fomoiri: "Ogmae unsheathed the sword and cleansed it. Then the sword told everything that had been done with it, for it was the custom of swords at that time that (the warriors) would unsheath them (and the swords) would then relate the deeds that had been done with them. That is why swords are entitled to the tribute (*cīos*) of cleansing them after they have been unsheathed. Hence also charms are preserved in swords thenceforward" (§162).

The explanation offered in that passage for the preserving of charms in swords brings to mind that two charms, of which variants have been recorded in Scotland in modern times, are embedded in the narrative of *CMT*. The first of these is that spoken by Dían Cécht's son Míach as he restores Núadu's hand: *ault fri halt di, 7 fēith fri fēth*, "joint to joint of it, and sinew to sinew" (§33).[57] The other is Bres's reply to Lug's questions about ploughing, sowing, and reaping: *Mairt a n-ar, Mairt hi corad sīl a nguirt, Mairt a n-imbochdt*, "On a Tuesday their ploughing, on a Tuesday their casting seed into a field, on a Tuesday their reaping."[58] The survival of these two charms is a remarkable testimony to the conservatism of Gaelic culture. It is probable that the memory of their use in the time of the gods has faded long since, just as has the connection of the widely celebrated Lughnasadh with its eponymous god. Some (though by no means all) of the gatherings at Lughnasadh have been Christianized, and this has also been done, on occasion, to our two charms.[59] At a time, however, when the mythological literature enjoyed currency in the Gaelic world, the efficacy of these charms would doubtless be attributed to their having been used and sanctioned by the gods. This would be in accord with the mentality which we have seen reflected in §162, and with the other ways in which *CMT* serves to underpin the received "manners and customs."

So much for the social function of *CMT*. When we come to consider the systematic role of the tale in providing a mythological model for the deeds of other personages in myth and literature, the main question to be considered is that of the status of Lug in relation to other heroes: in other words, is Lug the divine prototype of human (or semi-human) heroes such as Cú Chulainn, Finn mac Cumaill, Cormac mac Airt, and Conaire Mór? I have considered this opinion elsewhere, in connection with the mythological theories of T. F. O'Rahilly.[60] My argument was to the effect that the existence of a biographical pattern (the "heroic biography") is well established, and that the lives of Irish heroes such as those just mentioned are realizations of that pattern. In considering the status of Lug in relation to the other heroes we must distinguish between the questions as to whether (1) the others have been modelled on Lug, and (2) the hero raises himself in his heroic biography to the level of a god. The first of these questions must be left open, since we have no evidence that the lives of these heroes were composed on the model of that of Lug. As for the second question, however, I sinned against the light in giving short shrift to the notion, which had been espoused by de Vries,[61] that a hero raises himself to the level of the gods.[62] For the fact is that Lug, who performed his heroic deeds in the time of the gods, is by definition anterior to heroes who, even if they lived in the dim and distant past, nevertheless performed their heroic deeds in the time of man. It follows that the other heroes are perceived within the system as replicating (in some measure) the achievements of Lug. Moreover, there is evidence in the extant texts that certain heroes are unambiguously connected with Lug: we shall see that this is true of the Dál Cuinn kings of Tara (such as Cormac mac Airt) and of Cú Chulainn, and that Finn mac Cumaill has "some kinship" with Lug.

It will be noted that these heroes come from the main cycles according to which the bulk of early Irish narrative is nowadays generally classified. The material on Cormac belongs to the Cycles of the Kings, that on Cú Chulainn to the Ulster Cycle, and that on Finn to the Fenian (or Ossianic) Cycle. The cycle to which *CMT* belongs is known as the Mythological Cycle, but a happier choice of title would be the Cycle—or Cycles—of the Gods, since mythical personages and themes have a place in all the cycles. This classification into cycles is open to criticism—for one thing, it does not accommodate all the material[63]—but it has the practical advantage of being known and understood.

There are three points to be made about these cycles which are relevant to our theme. First, tales such as *CMT* in the Cycles of the Gods have to do with the personages and events of the time of the gods, whereas the other cycles deal with the time of man. The events of the Cycles of the Gods are therefore, as we have seen, anterior to those of the other cycles.

Secondly, there is the fact that the actors in the Cycles of the Gods have a different status from that of the mortal actors in the other cycles. However heroic these latter may be, they are more or less rigidly contained within their own proper cycles: thus we would not expect an Ulster hero, for example, to turn up in a Fenian tale. And setting aside the Cycles of the

Gods, if the other cycles were to overlap in any way we would recognize this as exceptional and as requiring special explanation. In short, the categories are established, and if the boundaries are breached we discern this because we know the boundaries.

This limitation does not apply to the gods and goddesses: they are not confined within the Cycles of the Gods, but appear also in other cycles, where they impinge on the heroes by intervening at crucial moments in their careers, as, for example, in *Táin Bó Cúailnge* when Lug comes to succor Cú Chulainn,[64] or in *Tóraíocht Dhiarmada agus Ghráinne*[65] when Aonghus comes to the aid of Diarmaid Ó Duibhne. These examples, from the Ulster and the Fenian Cycles respectively, are of the god as helper, but the gods may intervene in the life of the hero either benevolently as progenitor and helper or malevolently as villain and destroyer. The events and mortal personages of these cycles are those of the time of man, when the gods no longer hold sole and sovereign sway over Ireland. And since the heroes of these cycles are mortal, it follows that, however formidable their achievement in life, they must ultimately die and be no more.[66] These cycles, then, have to do with the relationship between man and the gods when men lived on the surface of Ireland, and the gods inhabited the *síde*, from which they were apt to emerge from time to time to intervene in the affairs of man.[67]

The third observation which is to be made about the sorting of material into cycles is that this should not be allowed to obscure the presence in all of them of a measure of common thematic content. This presence is of course implicit in the classification of the tales into "Battles," "Cattle-raids," "Voyages," and so on. Themes of kingship and sovereignty, for example, are not confined to the Cycles of the Kings, but occur in all of them. The same is true of the life-pattern of the hero: in all of these cycles, and among the tales of saints and poets, there are heroes whose lives represent a realization, in whole or in part, of the heroic biography. In this way, the cycles reinforce one another, presenting the same "message" in a variety of ways.

Lug's first victory in *CMT* was the replacement of Núadu as king of Tara, and so we may turn to the relationship between Lug and the Dál Cuinn kings of Tara. Here the key text is *Baile in Scáil*.[68] This tells how Conn Cétchathach is brought to an Otherworld abode where he meets a couple—

a girl sitting on a chair of crystal and wearing a gold crown, and a man sitting on a throne. The man identifies himself to Conn as Lug and tells him that he has come to Conn to tell him the span of his sovereignty and of that of every prince that will come of him in Tara forever. The girl is identified as the Sovereignty of Ireland and she has a golden cup from which she gives Conn a drink of ale at Lug's instructions. And then she asks who next should be given a drink from the cup, and Lug names Conn's successor, and so the dialogue continues and we are given a list of those who will follow Conn in the kingship of Tara.

As O'Rahilly pointed out,[69] this is a version of the sovereignty myth, the myth which R. A. Breatnach discussed in "The Lady and the King,"[70] and which has to do with the espousal of the king to the goddess of kingship. Of the two elements of carnal contact and the dispensing of liquor only one is given here, but in such a context as this the one implies the other. In any case, it is likely that "the acceptance by the bridegroom of a draught of liquor handed to him by the bride signified mutual consent to the marriage."[71] It seems clear then that Conn is being espoused to the Sovereignty of Ireland, and the same is true of all the other kings mentioned.

In this way, Lug is shown to validate the Dál Cuinn kings of Tara (and Lugaid Mac Con as well) by instructing his Otherworld consort to give them the drink which symbolizes sovereignty for the term of years specified by Lug. We can carry the interpretation of this text a step further and say that this means, in effect, that each of them in turn will be wedded to Lug's consort, and in that important sense take the place of Lug, and be his surrogate for the time being in the kingship of Tara.

It must be said that T. F. O'Rahilly's discussion of *Baile in Scáil* in *Early Irish History and Mythology* (1946) amounts to a dismissal of the text as it now stands. According to O'Rahilly, Conn is really the god of foreknowledge and prophecy, but here he "is merely king of Tara, and as a mortal he no longer possesses the power of seeing into the future; hence it is necessary to transport him to the Otherworld in order that the future may be revealed to him."[72] Lug's role in the story is "a mythological impossibility, and marks a redactor's mishandling of the original story."[73] But the text makes perfectly good sense as it stands and explains how the king-heroes of the Dál Cuinn (and hence of the Uí Néill), such as Cormac mac Airt and Niall Noígiallach, stood in relation to Lug. To take Cormac as an example (since in the literature he is the most outstanding of Conn's descendants), we can regard him as a surrogate for Lug in his role as spouse of the Sovereignty of Ireland, and we can see Cormac's accession to the kingship of Tara as a re-enactment in human time of the primordial accession of Lug. Cormac, like Lug, is particularly associated with fertility: his reign was a Golden Age and Ireland took on the character of the Otherworld during his reign.[74]

Lug's relationship with Cú Chulainn is that of progenitor, as we learn from *Compert Con Culainn*.[75] This tells how Cú Chulainn was conceived three times: he was first begotten in Bruig na Bóinne by Lug upon his Otherworld consort; then at Emain Macha by Lug upon the human Dechtine; and finally by the human Súaltaim upon the same Dechtine.[76] And so, like many another hero, Cú Chulainn has both a divine and a human father, and in his case the divine father is Lug. The manner (not to say the number) of his conceptions marks him out for greatness, and his destiny is fulfilled in *Táin Bó Cúailnge*. It has been argued that in the *Táin*, when he defends Ulster against the ravages of its enemies while Conchobor and the Ulstermen are undergoing their winter sleep, Cú Chulainn exemplifies the vigorous young male as the vital force in nature, and that this scenario represents "the triumph of life and fecundity over death and decay, as suggested by seasonal change,"[77] and there is some support for this view in *Compert Con Culainn*. The tale opens with the theme of the Waste Land: the plain of Emain Macha has been grazed to the roots by a flock of Otherworld birds. It is the pursuit of the birds which leads the Ulaid to Bruig na Bóinne, where they encounter Lug and his consort. The laying waste of the land shows the need for a fecundating hero, and such a one is provided by Lug in the shape of his own son. And that son goes on to reinvigorate Ulster and to save the Ulaid from their foes, as Lug saved the Túatha Dé Danann from the invading Fomoiri in *CMT*.

In sum, then, Cormac (who, as spouse for the time being of the Sovereignty of Ireland, is a surrogate for Lug) represents Lug in his kingly aspect, and Cú Chulainn (who is an incarnation of Lug) represents him in his martial aspect. Cormac accedes to the kingship of Tara by making a true judgment, and in this he re-enacts Lug's defeat of Núadu. Cú Chulainn's many victories in single combat, brought about by courage, strength, and resourcefulness, and by exercise of *fír catha* ("truth of battle"), recall Lug's defeat of Balar.

9. *Cath Maige Tuired* as Exemplary Myth

The nature of the relationship between Lug and Finn is more difficult to establish. The similarities in the traditions of the two personages have been thoroughly set out by Gerard Murphy,[78] and the core of the argument is as follows: "Lugh ('The Bright One') was the fighter of battles with otherworld beings and had for his chief opponent the one-eyed Balar, whose eye used to burn up whatever it looked on directly. Fionn ('The Fair One') likewise is the fighter of battles with otherworld beings and has for his chief opponent Aed who was nicknamed Goll: Aed means 'fire' and Goll means 'one-eyed.'"[79] Elsewhere, Murphy says that "the similarity between Fionn and Lugh might be explained on the hypothesis that Fionn was another name for the God Lugh,"[80] and he also speaks of "an original identity or quasi-identity of Fionn with Lugh and of Goll with Balar,"[81] and of "Fionn's having been originally a mythological figure possessing some kinship with the god Lugh."[82] (In O'Rahilly's system, of course, Finn is ultimately identical with Lug.)

The parallelism between Lug and Finn is impressive, and it would appear too that both of them are Irish versions of mythological personages who were known and celebrated by the continental Celts.[83] As far as the Irish narrative material is concerned, both Lug and Finn are depicted in terms of the heroic biography but they share certain details which are lacking in at least some of the other realizations of the pattern. While there is no good reason to suppose that one of them is modelled on the other, there may well have been some influence, in matters of detail, in one direction or the other. But whatever may be the origins of the extant traditions about Lug and Finn, there is one important difference between them which is not taken into account in Murphy's analysis, and that is that Lug is a divine hero, whereas Finn is not: Lug is a hero among the gods, and lives on in a *síd* after the coming of man to Ireland, whereas Finn dies, and when he is dead he is dead. When this distinction between the two of them is recognized, the hypothesis may be proposed that Finn's confrontation with Áed/Goll is perceived as a re-enactment in human time of Lug's primeval confrontation with Balar. Perhaps this hypothesis is lent some support by the clear evidence that Cú Chulainn and Cormac were presented as re-enacting the primordial deeds of Lug.

It is not only the good deeds which replicate those of the gods: there is divine precedent too for evil and harmful acts.[84] Bres's sin against the truth is re-enacted in human time by Conaire Mór,[85] and, as we have seen, by Lugaid Mac Con. His inhospitable treatment of the poet is re-enacted by the Connacht king Caier, who is duly satirized for it.[86] We will not follow up these personages here, for we have already seen that Irish narrative can teach its lessons negatively as well as positively. O'Rahilly saw Bres as "ultimately a double of Lug,"[87] and it is true that they are both heroes, and king-heroes at that. But they are heroes of a different type: Bres commits the single sin of the sovereign, whereas Lug's career is altogether unblemished. O'Rahilly also expressed the view that Cormac mac Airt and Conaire Mór were identical,[88] but here too we must recognize two different types. If Cormac's triumphant and beneficent kingship of Tara is rightly to be seen as a replication in history of the primordial kingship of Lug, then it seems reasonable to regard the tragic history of Conaire Mór as a replication of the ill-fated reign of Bres.

One of the conclusions which emerges from an analysis of myth, and of Irish myth in particular, is the operation of the principle of redundancy. This principle can operate within texts or among them, can be intratextual or intertextual. As an example of intratextual redundancy in *CMT* we may cite the ways in which the magical potency of the spoken word is demonstrated: we see it in the judgment, in the satire, and in the charms. And among the texts of the different cycles we find the same kind of life being lived by various heroes, differing in detail but always based on a common pattern. They reinforce one another: the career of Cormac proves that of Lug, the story of Conaire Mór is evidence for that of Bres, and so on. In a sense, therefore, all heroic tales have an exemplary function in society. But the events of *CMT* happened "in the beginning": Lug is the first king to encompass all three functions, and Bres is the first to suffer satire. They are the paradigmatic figures, and *Cath Maige Tuired* is our most considerable exemplary text.[89]

10

The Eponym of Cnogba

(1989)

Cnogba (Knowth) is part of the necropolis of Bruig na Bóinne, at the bend of the River Boyne in County Meath.[1] In the Dinnshenchas of Cnogba, we are told that it is properly Cnoc Buí, the Hill of Bua or Buí, who was daughter of one Ruadrí Ruad and wife of Lug mac Céin; she was buried there, and the great mound was constructed over her body.[2] Much the same information is given in the Dinnshenchas of Nas: Cnogba is the Hill of Buí "of the battles"—she lived and was buried there;[3] she is also referred to as Buí in Broga, "Buí of Bruig (na Bóinne)."[4] Buí and Nas were daughters of Ruadrí, here said to have been king of Britain, and each of the two sisters was married to Lug.[5] While Lug mac Céin, otherwise known as Lug mac Eithlenn, is one of the best-known figures in the Irish pantheon, his relationship with Buí is poorly documented. To the references in the Dinnshenchas, we can add that the Banshenchas mentions Bua, daughter of

Ruadrí, king of the Britons, as one of Lug's wives,[6] and that in an anecdote preserved in YBL, Lug is said to have been married to Buach, daughter of Dáire Donn.[7] (We shall see that Buach may be taken as a variant of Buí.) Lug is also said to have been married to Echtach, daughter of Daig, and to Englecc, daughter of Elcmar.[8]

The form *Cnogba* cannot be explained as a reflex of *Cnoc Buí*. It might be assumed, therefore, that Buí was simply drawn into the Dinnshenchas in order to provide a plausible etymology for Cnogba, and that the notion that she was married to Lug was prompted by his known associations with Bruig na Bóinne. This assumption may be correct, as far as it goes, but it leaves us far short of the whole story. Buí's dual role as eponym of Cnogba and spouse of Lug is part of a larger design, and the purpose of the present article is to trace that design by drawing data on Lug and Buí from a number of disparate sources.

The crucial step towards an understanding of Buí's character was taken by T. F. O'Rahilly when he identified the eponymous Buí of the Dinnshenchas with the personage known in Irish literature and folklore as the Hag of Beare (Caillech Bérri, modern Cailleach Bhéarra).[9] He contended that in "The Lament of the Old Woman of Beare,"[10] dated by Murphy to the late eighth or early ninth century, the *caillech*'s name is given as Buí, and he drew attention to "other references to her as Boí, Buí, Bua" in an anecdote in LU,[11] and in the Dinnshenchas. O'Rahilly's observations, as reported by Gerard Murphy, are not backed up by argument, and it is therefore necessary to state the case for them. There are two issues to be considered: first, the interpretation of a line in "The Lament" as giving the *caillech*'s name as Buí, and secondly the identification of the *caillech* with the Buí of the Dinnshenchas, and of the anecdote in LU. We shall see that O'Rahilly's interpretation of the relevant line has been accepted by Murphy, but that it has been silently rejected by the other scholars who have subsequently translated the poem. On the other hand, the identification of Caillech Bérri with the eponym of Cnogba is presented by F. J. Byrne[12] and Proinsias Mac Cana[13] as part of the conventional wisdom, without acknowledgment of O'Rahilly.[14]

In his 1963 edition of "The Lament," Murphy printed the fifth line as *Is mé Caillech Bérri Buí*, and translated, "I am the Old Woman of Beare, beside Dursey"; he was probably influenced by the fact that Oileán Baoi Bhéarra was the "old name" for Dursey.[15] In *Early Irish Lyrics*, in deference to O'Rahilly, the line is printed *Is mé Caillech Bérri, Buí*, and translated "I am Buí, the Old Woman of Beare." Carney translates "I am the hag of Buí and Beare";[16] Greene and O'Connor "I am the Nun of Béarra Baoi."[17]

While there is no need to doubt that Buí is a personal name in this as in other texts, the question is whether to take it as an eponym, or, with O'Rahilly, as the name of the *caillech*. In favor of the former is the occurrence of Buí as the eponym of a number of places in the Beare peninsula;[18] we have seen that Dursey was called Oileán Baoi Bhéarra, and we shall see that two of the rocks off Dursey were Inis Buí and Bó Buí. Bérre Buí cannot be ruled out as a placename. Moreover, it seems that the name Buí for Caillech Bérri, if known, was not universally accepted: in the prose introduction to "The Lament" in one of the manuscripts, her name is given as Dígde;[19] in a shorter form of this account of her, the name is given as Digi, with Duinech as an alternative.[20] Nevertheless, there is a *caillech* called Buí in the LU anecdote on Corc Duibne which is discussed below; she is the eponym of Inis Buí and Bó Buí, off Dursey, which is itself off the Beare peninsula; we can be virtually certain that she is indeed Buí, the *caillech* of Beare.

The connection of Caillech Bérri with Bruig na Bóinne, whenever and by whomever it was first mooted, has lived on in folklore. She is presented as a "megalith-builder" in her own right: the megalithic monuments of Meath are supposed to have been dropped by her from her apron.[21] She is said to have lived near Oldcastle in Meath:[22] the reference is doubtless to the cemetery at Loughcrew, which is known as Sliabh na Caillí (The Hag's Mountain).[23] The *caillech* who is associated with the megaliths of Meath, and, as *caillech* and under the name Buí, with the Beare peninsula, is surely the Buí who is claimed in the Dinnshenchas as eponym of Cnogba.

What is to be made of the espousal, according to the Dinnshenchas, of Buí to Lug? F. J. Byrne has said:[24] "That she should here be connected with the more civilised figure of the Celtic god Lug mac Céin means no more than that she was the mother-goddess of the local peoples...."[25] By process of rationalisation therefore the *Dindshenchas* has 'married' her to Lug, a god particularly associated with the Louth area, and almost certainly identical with Tadg mac Céin, ancestor of the Ciannachta of Ferrard and Duleek baronies as well as of the Gailenga and related tribes throughout Meath."[26] Buí's role as a mother-figure may well have contributed to her position in the Dinnshenchas, but there is more to the marriage of Lug and Buí than is allowed in Byrne's own "rationalisation" of it. Proinsias Mac Cana says of the marriage that "it brings us directly within the crucial mythic complex of sovereignty centred on the god who personified it and the goddess who legitimised it."[27] Mac Cana, I believe, is in the right area here, but he has gone strangely astray: there is every indication that the marriage of Lug and Buí has to do with sovereignty, but consideration of the evidence will show that it is Buí, not Lug, who may have personified sovereignty.

In his name as well as in some of his characteristics, Lug is a reflex of a Celtic god. His virtual omnicompetence is reflected in his sobriquet *samildánach*, and in the manner in which he is said to have secured entry to Tara.[28] He is particularly associated with kingship, with martial prowess, and with fertility, as we see in *Cath Maige Tuired*, where he achieves the kingship of the Túatha Dé Danann, leads them to victory in battle, and secures for them the secrets of ploughing, sowing, and reaping.[29] He is the divine father of Cú Chulainn,[30] and in the course of Cú Chulainn's defence of Ulster in *Táin Bó Cúailnge*, Lug comes to his assistance from the Otherworld (*a ssídib*).[31] In *Baile in Scáil*,[32] he is presented as legitimator of the Dál Cuinn (and hence also of the Uí Néill) kings of Tara.

According to the Middle-Irish *Senchas na Relec*, Bruig na Bóinne was the burial ground of the Túatha Dé Danann.[33] Lug's connection with Bruig na Bóinne is early, for it is there, as the Old-Irish *Compert Con Culainn* has it, that Cú Chulainn was begotten by Lug.[34] He is also specifically associated with Cnogba: in a thirteenth-century poem, the cave (*uaim*) on Cnogba is said to be an entrance to Emain Ablach, where Lug was reared.[35]

Lug's consort in *Baile in Scáil* is the goddess of sovereignty. Conn Cétchathach is brought to an Otherworld abode where he meets a couple—a girl sitting on a chair of crystal, and a man sitting on a throne. The man identifies himself to Conn as Lug, and says that he has come to Conn to tell him the span of his sovereignty and of that of every ruler of his descent that will be in Tara until the end of time. The girl is identified as the Sovereignty of Ireland (*Flaith Érenn*), and she has a golden cup from which she gives Conn a drink of ale at Lug's instructions. And then she asks who next should be given a drink from the cup, and Lug names Conn's successor, and so the dialogue continues, and we are given a list of those who will follow Conn in the kingship of Tara.[36]

As O'Rahilly pointed out, this is a version of the myth in which a king marries the goddess of kingship: the sexual element is not explicit in this version, the wedding being symbolized rather by the dispensing and acceptance of liquor.[37] It is Lug who names the successive kings of Tara, and instructs his consort to give them the drink, which symbolizes sovereignty, for the term of years specified by him. I have suggested that, in doing so, Lug decrees that each of those named will be wedded to his consort, and in that sense take Lug's place, and be his surrogate for the time being in the kingship of Tara.[38]

Niall Noígiallach, ancestor of the Uí Néill, is among the Dál Cuinn kings nominated by Lug in *Baile in Scáil*, but there is another story of how Niall received the sovereignty from the goddess.[39] Niall and his brothers were rivals. One day they went hunting, and when they had caught and eaten of their quarry, they became thirsty. Each of the brothers in turn went in search of water and found a well, guarded by an ugly *caillech* who demanded sexual contact in exchange for the water. Only Niall was prepared to comply, and as he did so the *caillech* became a beautiful young woman, who revealed that she was the sovereignty (*flaithes*), and that Niall and his descendants would be kings.

The central motif here is that of the *puella senilis*:[40] upon sexual union with one who is to be king, the ugly hag is transformed into a young woman of great beauty, and declares herself to be the sovereignty. It may be noted here that the descriptions of the woman, in her contrasting manifestations as hag and as maiden, include her covering of hair and/or clothing. The hag has a wild cropped scorched bald pate; she is gray-haired; she has gray bristly hair like the tail of a wild horse.[41] The maiden is golden-haired; her locks are like Bregon's buttercups; she wears a beautiful green mantle; or she wears a costly full-purple mantle.[42] The relevance of these descriptions to Buí will be seen when we come to discuss "The Lament of the Old Woman of Beare."

The sovereignty-figure appears alone in Niall's story, and Lug is given no part in the proceedings. There is a connection with Cnogba, however, in one version of the story, which tells that the hunt which leads to Niall's encounter with the *caillech* takes place "in the mound of Cnogba" (*a Cnogba chuirr*).[43] With this piece of the jigsaw in place, we can now see the following picture in outline: Lug and Buí are man and wife; Buí resides at Cnogba, and the "cave" of Cnogba is also an entrance to Emain Ablach, with which Lug is associated; Lug has as Otherworld consort a personage described as the Sovereignty of Ireland; access to that personage is gained at Cnogba. It is a reasonable extrapolation from all of this that Buí is another name for the personage known as the Sovereignty of Ireland. It remains to consider whether this extrapolation finds support in what we know of Buí from other texts.

Our quest for further information on Buí will take us to Corcu Loígde in West Munster. It is therefore worth noting that Corcu Loígde personages share with Dál Cuinn (and Uí Néill) the distinction of having received the favor of the Sovereignty of Ireland. According to *Baile in Scáil*, Dál Cuinn rule at Tara is to be interrupted by the reign of Lugaid Mac Con of Corcu Loígde, who is the third king nominated by Lug for receipt of the ale of sovereignty. The story of the *puella senilis* is also attached to them. In a tale told in the Dinnshenchas of Carn Máil,[44] and in *Cóir Anmann*,[45] the sons of Dáire, ancestor of Corcu Loígde, are confronted by a hideous *caillech*, demanding sexual intercourse. Only Lugaid Loígde is prepared to comply. The hag becomes a beautiful woman; in the Dinnshenchas, she announces that she is the sovereignty of Scotland and Ireland (*flaithius Alban is Hérend*), and that the high-kings sleep with her; in *Cóir Anmann*, she says that she is the sovereignty (*in flaithius*), and prophesies that the kingship of Ireland will be obtained by Lugaid Loígde.[46] In the Dinnshenchas, the sovereignty-figure says that, although she has revealed herself to Lugaid Loígde, nothing further will come of their encounter; it is with his son Lugaid Mac Con that she will sleep. Dáire then prophesies that Lugaid Mac Con will be king of Ireland and Scotland. This twist in the story is consistent with the claim, made in *Baile in Scáil* and elsewhere, that Lugaid Mac Con was the Corcu Loígde king of Ireland.[47]

A valuable source of information about Buí is an anecdote, which is recounted in the LU version of "The Expulsion of the Déisi," and which tells how Corc Duibne was cleansed of congenital pollution under the care of a *caillech* called Boí/Buí.[48] In the course of their search for a home, the Déisi come to Tech nDuinn, off Dursey; Corc Duibne (whose name is evidently a back-formation from Corcu Duibne) tells them that he was reared there, and the anecdote is then told. Corc was born of the incestuous union of Cairbre Músc with his own sister. The crops failed as a result of the incest, and when the boy was born, the men of Munster demanded that he be killed, in order to remove the shame from the land. But a druid offered to achieve this end by removing Corc from Ireland, and he took him to an island, where he entrusted him to Buí. For a full year, Corc was washed each morning on the back of a white red-eared cow, and then the cow was turned into a rock in the sea. The name of the rock was Bó Buí, and that of the island Inis Buí. Corc was then taken back to Ireland.

Tech nDuinn is represented in Irish texts as an abode of the dead.[49] What Corc Duibne undergoes, however, is a purificatory rite: the pollution which attaches to him is gradually transferred onto a cow, and when that has been done the cow is turned into a rock. Corc Duibne is then fit to be incorporated into society, and he is returned to Ireland. The mention of Tech nDuinn in connection with this rite indicates that Corc's exile-and-return is conceived, symbolically at least, as death and rebirth.

It is significant that it was a cow that was sacrificed as a "scapegoat" at the culmination of the rite. The modern name for Tech nDuinn is An Tarbh (The Bull), and the two adjacent rocks are known as The Cow and The Calf. The use of "The Bull" as equivalent of "Donn's House" has given rise to the plausible notion that the eponymous Donn is to be identified with the great bull known as In Donn Cúailnge.[50] *Dáire* is a taurine name; the ancestor of the Corcu Loígde is also called Dáire Donn, and seems to be identical with Donn.[51] In an anecdote in YBL, Lug is said to have been married to Buach, daughter of Dáire Donn.[52] Bergin suggested that Buach was originally genitive of *Boí/Buí*. While the extant sources do not show any clear inflectional pattern for Buí and its variants, the likelihood is that we have to do with reflexes of two separate formations on the root **Bow-* 'cow'; *Boí/Buí* would be a guttural formation, and would have had *Buach* as genitive, while *Bua*, earlier disyllabic **Buë*, would be an *ia*-stem formation.[53]

Buí's ministrations to Corc Duibne are performed on Inis Buí, and the petrified cow becomes known as Bó Buí. It is not stated in the text that Inis Buí is the same as Tech nDuinn, and it may simply have been in its vicinity. Given that Buí is a bovine name, it is likely that Inis Buí is The Cow, and Bó Buí The Calf.

The association of the *cailleach* with the sea informs the imagery of "The Lament of the Old Woman of Beare," which is our oldest source for Buí.[54] The poem opens with a complaint that ebb-tide has come to her, as to the sea, and in the penultimate stanza she contrasts her condition with that of an island in the sea, to which flood-tide comes after its ebb. "The

Lament" was first published by Kuno Meyer, who characterized it as "the lament of an old hetaira who contrasts the privations and sufferings of her old age with the pleasures of her youth, when she had been the delight of kings."[55] The dominant mood is of anger and regret at the passing of her youth, but this changes on occasion to resigned acceptance of her decline. She describes her clothing and her physical condition—she used to wear "a smock that was ever renewed" (*no meilinn léini mbithnuí*), but now she is so thin that she cannot wear even a cast-off smock (quatrain 2); her arms are bony and thin (8, 9); she does not speak sweetly (11); her hair is scant and grey. She contrasts her mood with that of the joyous maidens at Mayday (10). She says that she envies no one old, excepting only Feimen (a plain in County Tipperary): "I have worn an old person's garb; Feimen's crop is still yellow" (13); she also contrasts her lack of a new cloak with the delightful cloak of green which God has spread over Drummain (unidentified; 20 f.).

She says that her arms used to embrace glorious kings (quatrain 8), and that she had her day with kings, drinking mead and wine (23). This explains why Meyer calls her a "hetaira," and why Greene and O'Connor describe her as "ex-mistress of the kings of Munster."[56] It is probable, however, that the woman's apparent promiscuity is of the political kind, and that it reflects the *caillech*'s role as goddess of sovereignty.[57] We find some support for this view in the pervasiveness in the poem of references to the *caillech*'s covering of hair and clothing; we have seen that such references are to be found in descriptions of the sovereignty-figure, in both her ugly and her beautiful manifestations. Buí used to wear "a smock that was ever renewed," but now she envies the plain of Feimen, whose crop (*barr*) is still yellow (*buide*); we are reminded of the transformed hag who was golden-haired (*mongbuide*).[58] Similarly, her contrast of her own clothing with the cloak of green (*brat uaini*) over Drummain recalls the matchless green mantle (*óenbrat úainide*) which covers the transformed hag.[59] Her comparison of her own covering with the verdure of the countryside gains in force when we consider that fertility of the land is secured when the rightful aspirant to kingship mates with the sovereignty-figure. Buí's tragedy is that she now expects "neither nobleman nor slave's son" to visit her (15): she is a *caillech* who is destined to die because she will never again be transformed into a beautiful young woman.

What we have here, as Seán Ó Coileáin has suggested,[60] is a particular political application of the myth of sovereignty. The power of the Corcu

Loígde has waned, owing to the ascendancy of the Éoganachta; the sovereignty goddess has therefore had her day. This is why she contrasts her condition with that of the plain of Feimen, near Cashel: as Ó Coileáin puts it, "to the author royalty in contemporary terms meant the Éoganachta kingship and it is of the enduring nature of this and places such as Mag Femin associated with it, that the Caillech is envious."[61]

"The Lament" has a mythico-political dimension, then, but it is also a Christian poem. The *caillech* makes several references to God, as when she says, "When the Son of God deems it time, let Him come to carry off His deposit" (7). It is her King who has spread the cloak of green over Drummain, and, in a splendid metaphor, she compares his action in so doing to the fulling of cloth: "Noble is He who fulls it: He has bestowed wool on it after rough cloth" (21). It may be that the poet was influenced, as B. K. Martin has argued, by *de contemptu mundi* literature,[62] though the *caillech* herself is less than wholehearted in her embrace of *contemptus mundi*. The *caillech*'s contrast of her decline with the continuing vigor in external nature may owe something to the contrast, which is classical and literary in origin, "between the single life of men and the renewed life of nature."[63] It is the use of that contrast, whatever its origins, which invites comparison with the Irish literature of sovereignty. As Martin says of "The Lament," "the work cannot, it appears, be fully understood in terms of any single tradition, no more in terms of simple *contemptus mundi* than of native Celtic saga."[64]

The author of the prose introduction which is given in one of the manuscripts of "The Lament"[65] was well aware that the *caillech* was a complex figure. He presents her as a foster-mother, and as ancestress of people and races. He says that "she passed into seven periods of youth, so that every husband used to pass from her to death of old age." (Seán Ó Coileáin reports an attractive suggestion of John Kelleher's, that "her seven periods of youth may refer to the seven Corco Loígde kings of Osraige whom she may be understood to have wedded."[66]) The introduction also claims that she received the veil (*caille*) from Cuimíne, and that she wore it for a hundred years. As Murphy puts it, this justifies the title *caillech*, and "in quatrains 11, 12 and 22 of the poem, the Old Woman of Beare is clearly looked upon as a nun."[67]

Caillech in Old Irish has the meanings "nun; old woman; hag."[68] It is derived from *caille* 'veil' (a borrowing of Latin *pallium*), and its literal meaning is "veiled one." We are thus brought back once again to the prominence given in descriptions of the sovereignty figure to her covering. A. H. Krappe adduced instances from other countries of "The Veiled (or 'Veiling') One" being used as an appellation of a personage who is at once chthonic goddess and goddess of death, and he argued that Cailleach Bhéarra should be added to their number.[69] It is difficult to say how much of the character of the Cailleach Bhéarra in folklore derives from her namesake in the early literature: we cannot be sure, for example, that the bovine character of Buí is reflected in the magical cow associated in folklore with the *caillech*.[70] What we can say is that the notion of the *caillech* as chthonic goddess and goddess of death fits what we have learnt of Buí from our various sources: the role of the earth-goddess in relation to sovereignty informs the imagery of "The Lament"; in the Corc Duibne anecdote, Buí performs a rite of death and rebirth; and she is presented as the eponym of Cnogba, which, being a mound in Bruig na Bóinne, is at once an abode of the dead, and, as in *Compert Con Culainn*, a telluric womb.

11

Knowledge and Power
in *Aislinge Óenguso*

(1 9 9 7)

Aislinge Óenguso[1] is one of the most engaging of the early Irish sagas. It tells how Óengus, son of a god and goddess, the Dagdae and the Boann, falls in love with a beautiful woman whom he has seen in his dreams; he loses his appetite and becomes emaciated. When his "disease" has been diagnosed, the gods traverse Ireland in search of the woman. She is at length identified as Cáer Iborméith, daughter of Ethal Anbúail, who is king of Síd Úaman, an Otherworld habitation in Connacht; she lives in a lake in Munster, spending one year as a swan and the next in human form. When Óengus is taken to the lake, Cáer is in human form; Óengus recognizes her, but he cannot make contact with her. Óengus returns to the lake when Cáer is in the form of a swan. He summons her to him, and they make love; they sleep in the form of two swans and then circle the lake three times and fly to Óengus's home at Bruig na Bóinne, where Cáer remains with him as his wife.

The linguistic evidence suggests that *Aislinge Óenguso* was composed in the eighth century.[2] It survives in a single vellum manuscript, London, British Library MS Egerton 1782, written, for the most part in 1517, by members of the Ó Maoilchonaire family; in all probability, it was written for Art buidhe Mac Murchadha Caomhánach, who died while it was in progress.[3] Egerton 1782 contains a large number of early Irish tales, including *Táin Bó Cúailnge* and a group of tales which are connected in one way or another with the *Táin*, and which are described in some sources as *remscéla* (prefatory tales). *Aislinge Óenguso* is one of this group in Egerton 1782. In the course of the *Aislinge*, Ailill, king of Connacht, and his wife, Medb, help Óengus in the arduous task of winning his beloved Cáer, and at the end of the tale it is explained that this is why Óengus had an alliance with Ailill and Medb, on basis of which Óengus accompanied them on the cattle-raid which is the subject of the *Táin*. Now none of the surviving recensions of the *Táin* refer to Óengus, and it has therefore been suggested that the link which is made at the end of *Aislinge Óenguso* with the events of TBC "is probably an artificial one."[4] Shaw discussed the matter at some length and claimed that "we may conclude with certainty that the text had originally no connection with the great epic, that the last paragraph is a later addition and a forgery, added to the text about two centuries after the date of the original composition."[5] On the other hand, Carney contended that five tales, *Táin Bó Fraích, Táin Bó Dartada, Táin Bó Regamain, Táin Bó Flidais*, and *Aislinge Óenguso*, show a common relationship to the events of *Táin Bó Cúailnge*: "Ailill and Medb are about to embark upon the great military expedition celebrated in TBC. But it is first necessary for them to gain allies, and cattle to feed the army on the march."[6] He points out that all of the tales "are necessarily prior in time of action to TBC,"[7] and adds that "the general pattern is (a) a love interest involving someone closely associated with Ailill by blood or by alliance, (b) the securing for Ailill, as a result of the particular romantic situation, of either cattle or allies, or both."[8]

It is possible that in a version of the *Táin* which has not survived, Óengus came to the assistance of Ailill and Medb. In any case, we probably owe the survival of *Aislinge Óenguso* to the fact that the compilers of Egerton 1782 classified it as a prefatory tale to the *Táin*, and hence included it in the set of these tales which they transcribed. Thanks to the enlightened patronage of Art buidhe Mac Murchadha Caomhánach, and to the scholarship and industry of the Ó Maoilchonaire family, we have a sixteenth-century transcription of an eighth-century tale. The text has inevitably undergone some changes in the course of transmission, so that, in Shaw's words, "the language of the text as preserved in the manuscript may be said to be Old Irish with a very strong leaven of early and late Middle Irish forms."[9] In his edition, Shaw has normalized the text to an Old Irish standard; quotations in the present paper are from the normalized text, except where a different form is imposed by what has become known about Old Irish since 1934.

The tale opens with the dream which gives it its title. Here is Jackson's translation:[10]

> Oenghus was asleep one night,[11] when he saw a girl coming towards him as he lay on his bed. She was the loveliest that had ever been in Ireland. Oenghus went to take her hand, to bring her to him in his bed. As he looked, she sprang suddenly away from him; he could not tell where she had gone. He stayed there till morning, and he was sick at heart. The apparition which he had seen, and had not talked with, made him fall ill. No food passed his lips. She was there again the next night. He saw a lute in her hand, the sweetest that ever was; she played a tune to him, and he fell asleep at it. He remained there till morning, and that day he was unable to eat.
>
> He passed a whole year while she visited him in this way, so that he fell into a wasting sickness.

What follows in the body of the tale is an account of the wooing and, ultimately, the winning of Óengus's teasing visitant. But it is, for much of the time, a vicarious wooing and winning, since Óengus is in no condition to act on his own behalf. The woman who appears to him engages his interest but he is unable to detain her, and he does not know where she disappears to: he lacks the power and the knowledge which would enable him to cope with the situation into which he has been thrust. Indeed, having failed to make contact with the woman, Óengus "was sick at heart" (*nipo slán laiss a menmae*, §1); "he fell ill" (*do-génai galar ndó*, §1); and "no food passed his lips" (*nícon luid biad inna béolu*, §1). On the day after the woman's second appearance "he was unable to eat" (*nícon ro-proind*, sic leg, §1). At the year's end he has become afflicted with a wasting sickness (*serg*, §2). Later on in the tale, his father the Dagdae says to Óengus, *Ní ségdae dúnn ná cumcem do socht* (§9). Jackson translates, "We feel it to be discourteous that we cannot content you,"[12] but this fails to convey the sense of the Irish text, and in particular of the word *socht*. Shaw in the glossary to his edition (s.v.) says that the meaning of *socht* is obscure, but in the meantime the word has been elucidated by Calvert Watkins,[13] who points out that in the Old Irish period its basic meaning is "stupor," and observes that "this 'stupor' is . . . a pathological state imposed impersonally from outside on one."[14] In the light of this, the Dagdae's words may be translated, "It is unfortunate for us that we cannot deal with your stupor."

Óengus's love for Cáer is visited upon him; he has neither hand nor part in bringing it about. (It is interesting in this respect to recall Shaw's observation that "the most striking characteristic of the style of *Aislinge Óenguso* is the writer's strongly marked predilection for passive and impersonal constructions."[15]) Deprived though he is of his appetite and his strength, Óengus nevertheless ultimately succeeds in consummating his love for Cáer. What I propose to do in this paper is to analyze the successive stages in the process whereby this consummation is achieved. The key to the success of Óengus's amorous enterprise is the acceptance, by him and by others, of the deferral of his goal. Over a period of four years, the plot advances through a sequence of delegated functions. The emphasis, both in the language and in the action, is on various kinds and degrees of knowledge and of power, and these are orchestrated in such a way as to lead, step by step, to the union of Óengus and Cáer.

The first step that must be taken in relation to Óengus's illness is diagnosis. The reader knows the cause of Óengus's illness, but the members of his household do not, and he does not tell them (*nícon epert fri nech*, §2), because, as we later learn (§4), he did not dare to do so. In this early part of the tale, the emphasis is on knowledge, and on the lack of it. Óengus "could not tell where she had gone" (*nícon fitir cia arluid húad*, §1), and "no one knew what was wrong with him" (*ni fitir nech cid ro mboí*, §2). When the physicians of Ireland were brought together, "even they did not know what was wrong with him in the end" (*nícon fetatar-som cid ro mboí asendud*, §2). Fergne, physician to Conchobor king of Ulster, is then sent for. Fergne, who in other texts is invariably called Fíngen,[16] has magical diagnostic powers: he can tell from a man's face what his illness is, and he can tell from the smoke which comes from a house how many people are ill in it. He recognizes that Óengus has fallen in love with someone who is absent from him. The diagnosis is confirmed by Óengus, who tells Fergne how he has been seeing the woman every night in his dreams. Óengus has now been liberated from the dread of speaking about the cause of his illness, and he can seek help, which Fergne advises him to do. In response to Óengus's confirmation of his diagnosis, Fergne says, "It does not matter. It has been destined for you to make love to her. And send a request to your mother the Boann that she come to speak with you" (*"Ní báe,"* ol Fíngen, *"ro-tocad* (sic leg.)[17] *duit cairdes frie; ocus foítter úait cossin mBoinn, cot máthair, co tuidich dot accaldaim,"* §3).

Fergne's words here help us to understand what happens in this tale. The use of the phrase *ní báe* ("it does not matter") may seem odd, in view of the seriousness of Óengus's condition, but its significance derives from what immediately follows it, which is the reassurance that Óengus is destined to achieve union with the woman. The phrase *ní báe* appears, as we shall see, at a number of points in the tale, always as an expression of refusal to be daunted by difficulties which might seem to threaten the achievement of the consummation of Óengus's love. It is followed on each occasion by words or actions which take the hero forward towards his ultimate goal. Fergne, for his part, does not suggest that Óengus should passively await the fulfilment of his destiny; his advice is rather that the Boann should be asked to help.

The Boann is summoned to Óengus's side; she is told of his condition, and asked by Fergne to have the whole of Ireland scoured to see if she can find a young woman to answer the description of the one whom Óengus has seen. The Boann spends the second year of Óengus's illness doing this, but she has no success. (We discover later in the tale that the young woman was in the form of a swan for the whole of that year.) Fergne is summoned again, and he recommends that they seek help of the Dagdae. This the Boann does, but the Dagdae says that he knows no more than she does (*Ní móo mo éolas in-dáthe-si*, §5). Fergne says that the Dagdae does indeed know more, for he is the king of the *síde* of Ireland. He goes on, however, to suggest that they send to Bodb, king of the *síde* of Munster, for his knowledge is much spoken of throughout Ireland (*is deilm a éolas la hÉirinn n-uili*, §5).

The Dagdae's emissaries say to Bodb: "We do not know (*nícon fetammar*) where in Ireland is the woman whom he has seen and loved" (§6), and they tell him that he is bidden by the Dagdae to seek the woman throughout

Ireland. Bodb agrees to do so, asking for a year's delay "to find out the facts of the case" (*co fessur fis scél*, §6). By the end of the year, which is the third one of Óengus's illness, Bodb has found the woman at Loch Bél Dracon (Lough Muskry) in Crotta Cliach (the Galtee Mountains), and he asks that Óengus come to him so that they may find out whether Óengus recognizes the young woman when he sees her. When Óengus comes to Bodb's *síd*, and has been duly welcomed, Bodb asks him to come with him to see if he would recognize the girl, and he adds, "even if you do recognize her, I have no power to give her to you (*ní-s-cumcaim-si*), and you may only see her" (§7). They went to the lake, and "they saw three times fifty grown girls, and the young woman herself among them. The girls did not reach above her shoulder. There was a chain of silver between each couple; and a necklet of silver round her own throat, and a chain of refined gold" (§8). When Óengus tells Bodb that he recognizes the young woman, Bodb says, "I can do no more for you" (*ní-m thá-sa cumacc deit . . . bas móo*, §8). Óengus is not disturbed by this: "That does not matter then, since I have seen her; I cannot take her this time" (*"Ní báe són ém . . . óre as sí ad-condarc; ní cumcub a breith in fecht so,"* §8). Óengus has made an important advance: the young woman whom he loves, but whom he has known only from his dreams, has been located, and he has seen her in the flesh. He accepts that Bodb does not have the power to bestow the young woman upon him. But he has one further demand to make on Bodb's knowledge, which is the name and identity of the woman. "I know it truly (*Fetar* [sic leg.] *écin*)," says Bodb, "she is Cáer Iborméith, daughter of Ethal Anbúail from Síd Úaman in the land of Connaught" (§8).

All of this is duly related to the Dagdae, who responds by expressing regret that he has no power to help Óengus (*Ní ségdae dúnn . . . ná cumcem do socht*, §9). Bodb advises the Dagdae to go to Ailill and Medb as the young woman is in their province.

The Dagdae goes to Connacht and receives a lavish welcome. The Dagdae tells Ailill that he has come to see whether they would bestow the daughter of Ethal Anbúail upon Óengus. Ailill says that they have no power over her (*ní linni a cumacc*, §10), but that if they had such power (*dia cuimmsimmis*, §10) she would be given to him. The Dagdae then proposes that Ailill summon Ethal to him, but when Ethal is sent for he divines Ailill's intentions, and declines to go, saying that he will not give his daughter to the Dagdae's son. Ailill is told that Ethal "cannot be made to come, (for) he

11. Knowledge and Power in *Aislinge Óenguso*

knows why he is summoned" (*"Ní étar fair a thuidecht; ro-fitir aní dia congarar,"* §11). "No matter (*Ní báe*)," says Ailill, "he shall come, and the heads of his warriors shall be brought with him" (§11). There follows the harrowing of Síd Úaman by the combined forces of the Dagdae and Ailill: they bring out three score heads and Ethal is taken in captivity to Crúachu.

Ailill demands that Ethal give his daughter to Óengus, but Ethal says, "I cannot (*ní cumcaim*); her magic power (*cumachtae*) is greater than mine" (§12). When asked by Ailill what great *cumachtae* she has, Ethal says that she spends every other year in the shape of a bird, and the other years in human shape. Ailill next tries to find out what year she is in the shape of a bird; Ethal declines to answer, but under threat of beheading he finally does so, announcing that at the next Samain she will be at Loch Bél Dracon in the shape of a bird with thrice fifty swans. He adds that he has prepared a feast for them. The Dagdae intervenes at this stage and says, *Ní báe lemm-sa íarum, óre ro-fetar a haicned do-s-uc-so* (§12). The first part of this is clear: it means "it does not matter to me, then," or, as Jackson has it, "I do not care, then," but what is the meaning of the second part? Shaw says that "the meaning of this sentence is not quite clear"; he proposes that *do-s-uc-so* be taken as 2sg. present subjunctive with 3sg. feminine infixed pronoun, and he translates, "since you know her nature, let you bring her";[18] compare Jackson's "since you know her nature, do you bring her."[19] This interpretation is formally possible, provided we take *do-uc* as imperative rather than subjunctive. But it does not seem to me to be at all compatible with the context. I suggest rather that we translate, "since I know her nature, do you take her." On this reading, the Dagdae is saying that he is satisfied with the knowledge which he has now acquired of the woman's nature, and that he is happy that Ethal proceed with his Samain feast for her and her companions. In other words, he is not demanding that the woman be handed over to him at this time.

Then a treaty is made between them, between Ailill and Ethal and the Dagdae, and Ethal is released. The Dagdae goes home and fills Óengus in on what has happened, and he tells him to go at the next Samain to Loch Bél Dracon, and to call Cáer to him from the lake. And so we come to the final scene, in which the consummation of Óengus's love for Cáer is preceded by what is essentially a contract between the two. Óengus calls Cáer to him, and she says, "I will go, if you will undertake on your honor that I may come back to the lake again." He pledges his honor.

> She goes to him then, and he embraces her. They fall asleep in the form of two swans, and go round the lake three times, so that there should be no loss of honor for him. They go away in the form of two white birds till they come to Bruig Maic ind Óaic, and sing a choral song so that they put the people to sleep for three days and three nights. The young woman stays with him after that.[20]

In this transaction, Óengus guarantees to maintain the integrity of what we now know to be the woman's nature and magic power, her *aicned* and *cumachtae*, and he redeems his promise by joining her in assuming the form of a swan. And he is duly rewarded when the young woman stays with him.

Fergne, as we have seen, had prophesied that Óengus would be united with Cáer, his words being *ro-tocad* (sic leg.) *duit cairdes frie* (§3). *Cairdes* in this context doubtless means "sexual union," but the word can also denote a treaty of friendship; it is used of the treaty between the Dagdae and Ailill and Ethal (§13), and of the alliance between Óengus and Ailill and Medb which, according to our tale (§15), led to Óengus's participation in the cattle-raid which is the subject of *Táin Bó Cúailnge*. The crucial role of allies in the achievement of ends is clear in *Aislinge Óenguso*. Having availed himself of the knowledge and power of a number of personages, Óengus is able to approach his beloved, and, having accepted and abided by the terms laid down by her, he is united with her and takes her to Bruig na Bóinne as his wife.

12

"The Wooing of Étaín"

(2008)

Irish has a long history, stretching from the ogam inscriptions of the fifth century up to the present day. In a colloquium devoted to the study of Irish, Modern Irish language and literature may well be accorded pride of place. But Early Irish also offers a very rewarding field of study, as Calvert Watkins (2008) shows. What I want to do is to say a little about the splendid heritage of myth and saga that survives in Irish, and specifically in Early Irish, which can be taken in this context to include Old and Middle Irish, the language respectively of 600–900 and 900–1200. I should point out that we also have some accomplished tales from the later period—*Tóraíocht Dhiarmada agus Ghráinne* 'The Pursuit of Diarmaid and Gráinne'[1] may be mentioned as an especially fine specimen—but for the most part it is the tales of the Early Irish period that appeal to us today. Much of what I have to say in what follows will focus on *Tochmarc Étaíne* 'The Wooing of Étaín,'[2] a trilogy of tales that tell how the god Midir sought and, after many vicissitudes, ultimately won the hand of Étaín. This is one of the most remarkable works of Irish storytelling, and it is my hope that readers will be inspired to look at it for themselves, and also seek out some of the other tales that have come down to us in the manuscripts.

Early Irish narrative literature was one of the products of a powerful intellectual and artistic elite that combined the energy and resources of ecclesiastical scholars, authors, and artists with those of traditional Irish-language poets, jurists, and storytellers. The accommodation of the clerical and native learned classes in Ireland was made possible by the circumstances in which the country was converted to Christianity. Early in the fifth century—in the year 431, to be precise—Pope Celestine sent a bishop to the Irish "who believed in Christ." The fact that there were Christians in Ireland at that time indicates that there was some degree of Latin literacy in the country. As Ireland never became part of the Roman Empire, the churchmen had to come to terms with a political structure and an intellectual tradition that were very different from those of Rome. At a very early stage, the clerics began to use and write the vernacular, and it was not long before they took an active interest in the native storytelling tradition. The earliest surviving tales date from the seventh century and they must have been written—and in some sense composed—in ecclesiastical settings. On comparative grounds, the content of many of these tales can be shown to be indebted to an oral tradition stretching back to the Common Celtic era, and even beyond it, to that of Proto-Indo-European. The manuscripts do not name the authors of these tales, but we must be thankful to them for what they have given us. The narrative literature is extensive, and inevitably somewhat variable in quality. At its best, it is robust, vibrant, and exuberant. It can also be subtle and ingenious in its use of language, and very rich in its thematic content.

It has become conventional in modern times to classify the material in cycles. The so-called Mythological Cycle—which I prefer to call the Cycles of the Gods and Goddesses—recounts the adventures of the *Túatha Dé*, "The Peoples of the God(s)/Goddess(es)," also known as *Túatha Dé Danann*, "The Peoples of the Goddess Danu." These adventures have to do with the relations of the *Túatha Dé* among themselves, with other divinities or quasi-divinities such as the *Fomoiri* or Fomoreans, and even on occasion with the human inhabitants of Ireland.

12. "The Wooing of Étaín"

The Ulster Cycle has to do with the martial activities of a warrior aristocracy centered at the court of King Conchobor at Emain Macha (Navan Fort in County Armagh), and subsisting in a state of endemic warfare with the Connachta, who are ruled by Ailill, with more than a little help from his wife Medb, and centered at Crúachu (Rathcroghan in County Roscommon). The great hero of this cycle is Cú Chulainn, and its centerpiece is *Táin Bó Cúailnge* 'The Cattle-Raid of Cooley,'[3] in which the hero defends the province of Ulster against the invading forces of Ailill and Medb at a time when the adult warriors of Ulster are stricken with a debility that puts them out of action for three months. The army mustered by Ailill and Medb is described as "the men of Ireland": it includes battalions from Munster and Leinster beside those from Connacht, and for good measure includes a number of formidable Ulstermen who have gone into exile following an unforgivable violation of their personal honor by King Conchobor.

The Ossianic or Fenian Cycle also celebrates the heroic deeds of fighting men, but they are quite different from the warriors of the Ulster Cycle. In the Ossianic Cycle, Finn mac Cumaill presides over a *fían* or band of warriors that is available for hire and lies outside the bounds of society. In early tales of the cycle, Finn confronts and defeats an Otherworld adversary. He acquires wisdom, and becomes a poet. He is a warrior, a hunter, and a seer, and comprehends within himself the competencies required for the functioning of society. Cú Chulainn and the other Ulster warriors are "heroes of the tribe"; the *fían*-warriors are outside the tribe, and frequently at odds with it.

The Cycles of the Kings recount the adventures of various Irish kings. There are some very fine short sagas among them, but the greatest of them is *Togail Bruidne Da Derga* 'The Destruction of Da Derga's Hostel,'[4] which tells the tragic tale of Conaire the Great, whose reign as king of Tara ushered in a Golden Age of peace and prosperity in Ireland, but who was ultimately hounded to an ignominious death in the "hostel" or *bruiden* of the red god called Da Derga.

An older system of classification was based on the titles of the tales. Some of them have to do with major events in the life of an individual, such as *comperta* ("conceptions"), *aitheda* ("elopements"), *tochmarca* ("wooings"), *echtrai* ("expeditions [to the Otherworld]"), *immrama* ("sea-voyages"), and *aitte/aideda* ("violent deaths"). Others relate momentous or cataclysmic events in the social and political history of population groups, such as *catha* ("battles"), *tomadmann* ("eruptions [of lakes or rivers]"), *tochomlada* ("migrations"), *oircne* ("slaughters, destructions"), *togla* ("destructions"), and *tána bó* ("cattle raids").

These tales give us access to imagined worlds that are full of danger and of opportunity, and where wonderful things can and do happen. One characteristic of the material that I should like to mention here, however, is that very often the tales give expression in narrative form to a view of the world, and of mankind's place in it, that also informs the laws and the wisdom texts. One of the great tales in the Cycles of the Gods is *Cath Maige Tuired* 'The Battle of Mag Tuired,'[5] which depicts the epic defence of Ireland by the god Lug against an invading army led by Bres son of Elatha, who had been king of Ireland but was deposed by the Túatha Dé Danann when he proved himself unworthy to hold the office. The tale lingers at length on the ill-fated rule of Bres, and in its depiction of Lug and Bres provides us respectively with positive and negative paradigms of kingship. Its description of early Irish kingship as a contract between king and people is wholly consistent with what we find in the early Irish laws. Its exploration of various aspects of the relationship between a man and his kindred is similarly on all fours with what we find in other Early Irish sources.

Cath Maige Tuired is in many respects our most important mythological text. Yet, as Gerard Murphy has said,

> The otherworld atmosphere which gives its special beauty to [the Mythological] cycle is . . . better illustrated in other tales, such as the ninth-century *Tochmarc Étaíne* or "Wooing of Étaín," which tells how Étaín, wooed and won by Midir in the otherworld, was transformed into a brilliantly coloured fly by her rival Fúamnach, who blew her into this world, where, swallowed in a drink by an Ulster queen, she was reborn as a human. Wooed once more in human shape by the king of Tara, she was ultimately won back to the otherworld by Midir as the result of a rash stake made by the king in a game of *fidchell*.[6]

What I would like to do in the space that remains to me is to introduce you to *Tochmarc Étaíne*, which has rightly been called "the most extraordinary of all early Irish 'wooings.'"[7]

In the first of the three tales in *Tochmarc Étaíne*, Midir wins the hand of Étaín with the assistance of his foster-son Óengus, but his scorned earlier wife Fuamnach soon deprives Midir of his new bride. These early adventures take place in the Otherworld, which in Irish tradition mainly comprised a number of *síde* or hollow hills dotted around Ireland. These include the *síd* at Bruig na Bóinne (Newgrange in the necropolis at the bend of the river Boyne in County Meath), where Óengus presides; Midir's dwelling at Brí Léith in Tethba (west of Ardagh in County Longford); and Mag nInis (in south-east County Down, around Downpatrick in Ulster), the home of Étaín's father, Ailill (and also, it would seem, of none other than Bres, son of Elatha, who played such an inglorious part in *Cath Maige Tuired*). When Fuamnach blows the fly into Ireland, she lands in a house in Ulster and falls into the cup of the (unnamed) wife of a warrior named Étar. Étar's wife swallows the fly, which is then conceived in her womb and is born as Étaín, daughter of Étar. And "it was a thousand and twelve years from the first begetting of Étaín by Ailill until her last begetting by Étar" (*TE1* §21). In the second tale, Echaid Airem, king of Ireland, takes Étaín as his wife. The king's brother Ailill falls in love with Étaín, and becomes dangerously ill. In order to cure Ailill of his love sickness, she agrees to sleep with him, but the person she actually meets in Ailill's guise is Midir. When Midir reveals his true identity to her and invites her to go away with him, she declines, but says that she would willingly do so if bidden by Echaid. In the third part, Midir again presses his suit upon Étaín, and she says that she will go only if Midir obtains her from her husband. When Midir wins the game of *fidchell*, Echaid is obliged to allow him to embrace and kiss Étaín. Echaid refuses to sell Étaín to Midir, but he permits him to embrace her, and when Midir does so he bears her up and out through the skylight of Echaid's heavily fortified dwelling at Tara, and the couple fly in the form of two swans to an Otherworld dwelling in Munster.

Midir's great and abiding love for Étaín is the overarching subject of *Tochmarc Étaíne*. The gods have magical powers, and enchantment is an important component in the saga. Yet Midir's wooing of Étaín unfolds as a series of transactions—of promises, pledges, purchases, wagers, and so on. The exercise of magical power is in great measure subject to legal or quasi-legal constraints. These considerations are established in the opening episodes of the saga, which have to do with the conception and birth of Midir's foster-son Óengus, the assumption by Óengus of the lordship of Bruig na Bóinne, and the circumstances which lead to Óengus's involvement in the initial wooing of Étaín.

Tochmarc Étaíne begins with the primeval mating of the Dagdae, king of the Túatha Dé (Danann), and Boann, eponymous goddess of the river Boyne; and the conception and birth of their son Óengus. The opening lines have to do with power:

> There was a famous king of Ireland of the race of the Tuatha Dé, Eochaid Ollathair was his name. He was also named the Dagda [i.e. good god], for it was he that used to work wonders for them and control the weather and the crops. Wherefore men said he was called the Dagda. (*TE1* §1)

The Dagdae wants to make love to Boann, but she is married to Elcmar who is lord of Bruig na Bóinne (literally, "the land of [the river] Boann"), and although she would happily yield to the Dagdae's suit, she fears her husband's great power (*cumachtae*). The Dagdae sends Elcmar away on an errand, and works great spells (*tincheadla mora*) on him. Elcmar declares his intention of returning before nightfall (literally, "between day and night"), but the Dagdae ensures that nine months go by in what seems to Elcmar no more than one day. In the meantime the Dagdae has slept with Boann, and she has borne him a son, Óengus. He is known also as *In Mac Óc* ("The Young Son") "for his mother said: 'Young is the son who was begotten at the break of day and born betwixt it and evening'" (*TE1* §2). When Elcmar returns Boann is her old self, and Elcmar remains unaware of her sexual adventure with the Dagdae.

Óengus is sent into fosterage with Midir at Brí Léith. Since Midir brings him up as his own son, Óengus is completely unaware of his biological parentage until he is taunted one day on the playing field by what we would call the captain of the opposing team, and who describes Óengus as "a hireling whose father and mother are unknown" (*TE1* §4). Following this incident, Midir tells Óengus who his parents are, whereupon Óengus demands to be taken to his father to try to get him to acknowledge Óengus as his son. Midir takes the boy to Uisnech in the center of Ireland, where the Dagdae resides and where he is holding court. Midir speaks for Óengus, saying that the boy wishes to be acknowledged by his father and for land to be given him. The Dagdae readily acknowledges his son: *Is mac dam*, "He is my son" (TE1 §5). But he says that Bruig na Bóinne, the land that he wishes to bestow upon Óengus, is not yet available, for it is in the possession of

Elcmar, and the Dagdae does not wish to annoy him further. Midir presses the Dagdae to give him advice for Óengus, and the Dagdae proposes a course of action that entails taking what, on the face of it at least, seems rather an unfair advantage of a lack of vigilance on Elcmar's part. The Dagdae's advice is that Óengus should approach Elcmar in Bruig na Bóinne at *Samain* (November 1). That, we are told, "is a day of peace and amity among the men of Ireland, on which none is at enmity with his fellow" (*TE1* §6). Elcmar will therefore be unarmed, and Óengus is to threaten to kill him, promising to spare him, however, if Elcmar grants him what he demands. What Óengus is to demand is that he be king for a day and a night in Bruig na Bóinne. When Elcmar comes to reclaim the land Óengus is not to return it: he is to say that the land is now his in perpetuity, for he has been given the kingship for a day and a night, and "it is in days and nights that the world is spent" (*TE1* §6). He is to insist that the matter be submitted to the Dagdae for his adjudication.

Óengus follows the Dagdae's advice to the letter. In the face of great threats from Elcmar when he comes to reclaim the land, Óengus declines to give it up until the matter is put to the Dagdae for his adjudication in the presence of the men of Ireland. The Dagdae finds in favor of Óengus, and in addressing Elcmar he adds the detail that Elcmar gave his land for mercy shown him, for his life was dearer to him than his land. He sweetens the pill, however, by promising him land that will be no less profitable to him than Bruig na Bóinne:

> "Where is that?" said Elcmar. "Cleitech," said the Dagda, "with the three lands that are round about it, thy youths playing before thee every day in the Brug, and thou shalt enjoy the fruits of the Boyne from this land." "It is well," said Elcmar, "so shall it be accomplished." (*TE1* §8)

Elcmar goes to Cleitech and builds a stronghold there, and Óengus remains in the Bruig.

Midir comes to visit Óengus a year later, and in the course of an incident one of his eyes is knocked out. This blemish will prevent him from returning to the land of which he is king, but Óengus arranges for the god of medicine to heal the eye. Óengus then invites him to remain at Bruig na Bóinne for a year. Midir will do so only if he is paid for it. The payment (*lóg*) that he demands comprises a worthy chariot, a suitable cloak, and "the fairest maiden in Ireland" (*TE1* §8). Óengus has no problem with the chariot and the cloak, but he wonders who this maiden is that according to Midir "surpasses all the maidens in Ireland in form." Midir lets him know:

> "She is in Ulster," said Midir, "Ailill's daughter Étaín Echraide, daughter of the king of the north-eastern part of Ireland. She is the dearest and gentlest and loveliest in Ireland." (*TE1* §11)

And so Óengus sets out to seek her hand from Ailill at Mag nInis.

I have dwelt at some length on these episodes because they introduce certain themes that are taken up and developed in various ways in the course of the trilogy. There is the matter of magic power, which we are told both the Dagdae and Elcmar possess, though only the former is seen to exercise it here. We may note in passing the contrast between the Dagdae's opportunistic sexual desire for Boann and Midir's overweening love for Étaín. The taking of the Bruig is cast in legal terms: the Dagdae, as the text has it, "adjudged each man's contract in accordance with his undertaking" (*Concertasidhe cor caich amal a indell*, *TE1* §8). The question of time is all-important in *Tochmarc Étaíne*: for Elcmar, nine months are spent in what seems to be one day; Óengus is conceived at the break of day, and born between the end of the day and the beginning of the night; all time (we are told) is spent in days and nights. In the second tale, the simple matter of one day following another is used by Étaín to console her husband's distraught brother. The difference between appearance and reality, which we see in Elcmar's perception of the passing of time, is at the very heart of the second tale, and has a crucial bearing on the aftermath of Midir's wooing of Étaín in the third. It is related in both of them to the question of identity, something that also arises in the case of the young Óengus. Land is a matter of great concern in this tale: the inheritance and possession of it, the ruling of it, and, most fundamentally, the very shaping of it.

Let us return now to the price that Midir has demanded for remaining as Óengus's guest at Bruig na Bóinne. Óengus offers to buy Étaín from her father Ailill, who in turn exacts a heavy price. He requires Óengus to clear twelve plains and to drain the land by making twelve rivers flow from it to the sea. It is the Dagdae who accomplishes these tasks for Óengus. Since their accomplishment is for the general good, Ailill then demands for himself Étaín's weight in gold and silver. When the price has been paid,

Óengus returns to Bruig na Bóinne. Étaín sleeps with Midir that night, and on the next morning a mantle befitting him and a chariot are given to him. He is pleased with his foster-son and stays with him in the Bruig for a full year.

The mention together here of chariot, cloak, and wife is not to be taken as mere zeugma. The bestowing of a chariot and a cloak upon a man is part of the ritual of making a king. We see this in the scene depicting the election of the king of Tara in *Togail Bruidne Da Derga*: the lesser kings see the young Conaire approaching them in a manner that has been prophesied, and they put upon him the clothing of a king and place him in a chariot (*do-bertatar étach ríg dó imbi 7 da-bertatar i carpat*).[8] As for the fairest maiden in Ireland, there are clear indications, as T. F. O'Rahilly noted, that Étaín is the goddess of sovereignty.[9] To be married to Étaín, therefore, is to be king. We recall that when Midir is blinded he laments that he cannot return to the land of which he is king. The allusion here is to the requirement that an Irish king must be without physical blemish: Midir has become ineligible to retain sovereignty. Óengus not only ensures that his sight is restored, but he enhances Midir's sovereignty by winning for him the hand of Étaín and presenting him with the trappings of kingship in the form of a chariot and cloak.

When his year at Bruig na Bóinne is up, Midir returns with Étaín to his own land at Brí Léith. As they set out, Óengus warns Midir to beware of the dreadful, cunning woman who awaits him. The woman in question is Midir's wife Fuamnach, who had been reared by a druid, Bresal, and "was wise and prudent and skilled in the knowledge and magic power of the Tuatha Dé Danann" (*TE1* §15). She is evidently free to exercise her magical power (*cumachtae*), because, as Óengus warns Midir, she has Óengus's "word and warranty before the Tuatha Dé Danann" (*TE1* §15). When Midir returns home with his new wife, Fuamnach welcomes them, but it is not long before she strikes Étaín with a wand, so that she turns into a pool of water. Fuamnach returns to her foster-father, Bresal, and Midir leaves the house to the water into which Étaín has turned. Midir is now without a wife. But then another transformation occurs:

> The heat of the fire and the air and the seething of the ground aided the water so that the pool that was in the middle of the house turned into a worm, and after that the worm became a purple fly. It was as big

as a man's head, the comeliest in the land. Sweeter than the pipes and harps and horns was the sound of her voice and the hum of her wings. Her eyes would shine like precious stones in the dark. The fragrance and the bloom of her would turn away hunger and thirst from any one around whom she would go. The spray of the drops she shed from her wings would cure all sickness and disease and plague in any one round whom she would go. She used to attend Midir and go round about his land with him, as he went. To listen to her and gaze upon her would nourish hosts in gatherings and assemblies in camps. Midir knew that it was Étaín that was in that shape, and so long as that fly was attending upon him, he never took to himself a wife, and the sight of her would nourish him. He would fall asleep with her humming, and whenever any one approached who did not love him, she would awaken him. (*TE1* § 17)

Here the cosmic forces that transform the pool of water into a magic fly trump the malevolent power wielded by Fuamnach. The cosmos, as traditionally envisaged by the Irish, is tripartite, its three components being *nem, talam, muir* 'heaven, ground, and sea,' or more precisely the heavens, the surface of the earth, and the underneath (whether marine or subsurface).[10] These three components, in the shape of the heat of the fire and the air, and the seething of the earth and the water, combine to liberate Étaín from her inanimate entrapment. Her beneficent effect as she accompanies Midir around his territory, dispelling hunger and thirst and curing the sick, reminds us of the doctrine that is expounded in the wisdom literature and reflected in both the laws and the sagas, that the king who was wise and just brought about the physical well-being of his people.

The love and contentment that Étaín, in the shape of a fly, has brought to Midir and his people are not destined to last. Fuamnach visits Midir, bringing with her as sureties Lug, the Dagdae, and Ogmae, here described as the three Gods of Danu (*Dé Danann*). They now have the right and duty to protect Fuamnach, a role that had earlier been assumed by Óengus. Fuamnach has brought powerful incantations from Bresal and she uses her power to stir up a magical wind that drives the fly into the air where she moves around for seven years until she alights on the breast of Óengus at Bruig na Bóinne. Óengus cares for her so that her good spirits return to her. But Fuamnach uses a ruse to have Óengus removed from the scene and she once more uses her powers to blow Étaín away, this time sending her to the house of Étar in Ulster.

Fuamnach oversteps the mark on this occasion. At Bruig na Bóinne, Étaín is under Óengus's protection, and in assailing her there, Fuamnach violates Óengus's honor. Her powerful sureties will be of no avail to her now. Óengus follows her traces to Bresal's house, and he cuts off her head and brings it with him to Bruig na Bóinne.

Myles Dillon said of *Tochmarc Étaíne* that "there is a strange beauty there which perhaps no other Irish story shares."[11] We can see something of that in the first story; it is amplified in the other two, which I cannot discuss in detail here. Dillon went on to say: "The temper of love is there and the power of magic—this is a pure fairytale—and a happy ending."[12] To say that *Tochmarc Étaíne* is a pure fairytale, however, is to do less than justice to the thematic content of the tale. And it has a happy ending only in a limited sense. It is true that Midir is reunited with Étaín at the end, but there is trouble in store for the people of Ireland. Echaid is not content to let matters rest when Midir has taken Étaín away from him. He sets out with his men to recover Étaín, and they are determined to dig up every *síd* in Ireland until they find her. When they assail the *síd* of Brí Léith, Midir appears before them. He rebukes Echaid, but promises to return Étaín. The next morning fifty women appear at Tara all like Étaín in form and dress. Echaid chooses one of them and the rest depart. The men of Ireland are well satisfied with what Echaid has done to rescue the woman from the beings of the *síde*. Some time later, however, Midir appears to Echaid and tells him that his wife was pregnant when Midir took her from him, and that she bore a daughter, and it is the daughter that Echaid now has as his wife. To make matters worse, Echaid's daughter is pregnant by him, and she bears him a daughter. Echaid decrees that his incestuous child be thrown into a pit of wild beasts. But his men leave her instead in a kennel at the house of the herdsman of Tara. The herdsman and his wife rescue the girl and bring her up in secret. Etarscélae—the king of Tara—hears about her, and he takes her away by force; she remains with him thereafter as his wife. She is the mother of Conaire son of Etarscélae, also known as Conaire Mór: the story of his tragic downfall is told, as we have seen, in *Togail Bruidne Da Derga*. In that text Conaire is described as "the king whom phantoms banished."[13] Elsewhere it is said that because Conaire was descended (through his mother) from Echaid: "he was killed for Echaid's crimes, for it is the beings from the *síd* of Brí Léith who mustered [for] the slaying [of Conaire] because their *síd* had been broken up by Echaid as he sought Étaín."[14] Conaire, and the people of Ireland, were to pay a heavy price for Echaid's harrowing of Midir's Otherworld abode.

Of the two great works in the Cycles of the Gods and Goddesses, *Cath Maige Tuired* has to do with the relations of the gods among themselves and with other divine or quasi-divine personages, whereas *Tochmarc Étaíne* concerns itself with both the relations of the gods among themselves and their dealings with the human inhabitants of Ireland. The relationship between god and man, between the denizens of the *síde* and the men and women living on the surface of Ireland, is a central and abiding feature of Irish saga, and it is explored in a variety of ways in each of the cycles. The major tale-types are also shared among the cycles. I have noted above that some of the tale-types have to do with major events in the life of an individual, and that others relate momentous or cataclysmic events in the social and political history of population groups. *Tochmarc Étaíne* fits both descriptions. Midir's wooing of Étaín is clearly the most significant event— or rather sequence of events—in his life, and in hers. But we are also presented here with cosmogonic myth: the tasks laid upon Óengus in the first tale, and performed by the Dagdae, entail the clearing of the plains and the drawing out of the rivers of Ulster; those laid directly upon Midir in the third tale have to do with the formation of the midlands of Ireland.

THE ULSTER CYCLE

13

Táin Bó Cúailnge

(2002)

> "Every man has kindly feelings for his own people."
> —*The Táin*

Táin Bó Cúailnge 'The Cattle-Raid of Cooley,' often referred to simply as the *Táin*, tells of an invasion of Ulster by a great army led by Medb and her husband, Ailill, who is king of Connacht (in the north-west of Ireland); its purpose is to carry off the Brown Bull from the Cooley peninsula in what is now County Louth (in the north-east). Medb is the instigator of the raid, and hers is one of the strongest and most insistent voices in the tale. I shall be attending to some of her utterances in what follows, and the words of hers which I have used as epigraph point to the theme of love of one's kindred which will be the primary focus of what I wish to say here about the *Táin*. When the mighty army assembled by Medb and Ailill is about to set out from their court at Rathcroghan, Medb displays an acute awareness of what she has taken upon herself when she says to her charioteer: "All those who part here today from comrade and friend will curse me for it is I who has mustered this hosting" (126; K 60).[1] It is typical of Medb that she does not allow this insight to influence her actions in any way. As her ill-fated enterprise proceeds, her words as well as her deeds expose her as the arrogant, heartless, dishonest, cynical—and endlessly fascinating—manipulator that she is. Her character is of course revealed cumulatively, but here perhaps one example will suffice to show the kind of person we are dealing with. In the course of the invasion, Medb and Ailill are obliged to seek one warrior after another who will be brave (or foolhardy) enough to face the apparently invincible Cú Chulainn in single combat, since for a long time he is the only one who stands between the invaders and the achievement of their goal. When it has been decided that a certain Cúr mac Da Lath should be asked to take on this task, Medb remarks: "If he kills Cú Chulainn it means victory. If he is himself killed, it will be a relief to the host. It is not pleasant to consort with Cúr eating and sleeping" (172; K 127). She seems to feel that the death of the individual who continues to thwart them is of no greater moment than ridding themselves of the hapless Cúr, one of their own warriors, whose table manners and sleeping habits are not to her liking.

Medb remains her wayward and irrepressible self through all the vicissitudes of the raid until, at last, her allies desert her, and her army is vanquished. She then finds herself at Cú Chulainn's mercy, and all she can do is utter the simple and humble words "Spare me!" (236; K 250). Cú Chulainn lets her know that she deserves to die, but he does spare her. Her last, brief, words are to Fergus: they are evidently an admission of defeat—the tentative translation is "Men and lesser men (?) meet here today, Fergus" (236; K 251). In any case, Fergus issues a stunning rebuke: "That is what usually happens to a herd of horses led by a mare. Their substance is taken and carried off and guarded as they follow a woman who has misled them" (237; K 251). She is reduced to silence, and even the subsequent contest of the bulls, which is watched by all the survivors of the battle, draws no comment from her.

The *Táin* begins with the mustering of an army, which is so great that it is often referred to as "the men of Ireland." As they are about to set out on the raid, and just after Medb has predicted that she will be cursed by the troops, she meets the prophetess Fedelm, who warns her that her expedition will be a bloody one. Medb comforts herself in the knowledge that the Ulster king Conchobor, as she declares, "lies in his debility in Emain together with the Ulstermen and all the mightiest of their warriors" (126; K 61). This "debility" is one to which adult Ulstermen are peculiarly prone; it lasts for "the three months of winter"—from the first of November to the first of February—and during that time they are too weak to engage in the defence of their province. There is, however, one young man living in Ulster who is not stricken with the debility: this is of course Cú Chulainn ("The Hound of Culann"), and the reason for his immunity is that his kinship with the Ulstermen is through his mother—his father Súaltaim is also immune from the debility. Cú Chulainn greatly impedes the invaders as they make their way across the country, but they do eventually reach Finnabair in Cooley and from there they "spread out over the province [of Ulster] in quest of the Bull" (128; K 65). They are unsuccessful at first: "the army scattered and set the country on fire. They gathered all the women, boys, girls and cows that were in Cooley and brought them all to Findabair" (152; K 100), but they did not find the bull. Having harried Cooley, the army goes southward to Conaille, driving the cattle before them. When they arrive in Conaille, Cú Chulainn kills so many of them that Ailill makes terms with him. It is agreed that each day Cú Chulainn will engage a warrior in single combat at a ford, and that in the meantime the army will not take the cattle away (160; K 117). Cú Chulainn vanquishes a great number of opponents in this way; and even when the invaders capture the bull and take it into their encampment (167; K 126), Cú Chulainn remains an obstacle in their path. A small number of Cú Chulainn's combats are described in detail, culminating in the killing of his beloved foster-brother, Fer Diad.

The cattle-raid leads ultimately to a great battle between Connacht and Ulster, but owing to the debility of the Ulstermen, the warfare between the provinces is asymmetrical: we begin with the muster of the Connachta and their allies, and we do not reach the muster of the Ulstermen until more than three-fourths of the tale has been told (218; K 220). Somewhat earlier, as the three months of winter come to an end, individual Ulstermen begin to recover their vigor, and they come to challenge the invaders. When the Ulstermen are finally free of their debility, they muster a huge force and meet and vanquish the Connachta in the great battle.

This asymmetry in the *Táin* is what calls Cú Chulainn to the single-handed defence of Ulster: the temporary disablement of the men of Ulster requires (and allows) him to assume the role of an epic hero. That Cú Chulainn is destined for greatness is already clear in the story of his birth. This is told, not in the *Táin*, but in one of the "prefatory" or "preliminary" tales (Irish *remscéla*) associated with it, and which inform us about some of the personages in the *Táin* and help us to understand the circumstances in which they find themselves. The story of Cú Chulainn's birth is a variation on a common heroic pattern, and shows him to have a divine father, Lug, as well as a human father, Súaltaim. Each of them, as we shall see, is assigned a role in the *Táin*. Cú Chulainn is a precocious hero, as the invaders soon discover. While they are still in the initial stages of their journey from Connacht to Cooley, Fergus sends a warning of the forthcoming invasion of the Ulstermen. This is received by Cú Chulainn and Súaltaim. They go to watch out for the invaders, and Cú Chulainn has a premonition that they will arrive that very night. This poses a difficulty for him, as he has an assignation with a woman, which he is honor-bound to keep. He takes elaborate (and successful) steps to delay the invaders while he goes to meet his lover. Medb and Ailill are curious to know more about the formidable foe who has contrived to stop them in their tracks, and it is in that context that we are given "The Eulogy of Cú Chulainn" and the long section devoted to his "Boyhood Deeds."

By way of introduction to "The Eulogy," and in response to a question from Ailill, Fergus says of Cú Chulainn: "In his fifth year he went to the boys in Emain Macha to play. In his sixth year he went to learn feats of arms to Scáthach and went to woo Emer. In his seventh year he took up arms. At the present time he is seventeen years old" (135; K 75). Medb then asks, "Is he the most formidable among the Ulstermen?" and this elicits the following eulogy:

> "More so than any of them," answered Fergus. "You will not encounter a warrior harder to deal with, nor a spear-point sharper or keener or quicker, nor a hero fiercer, nor a raven more voracious, nor one of his age to equal a third of his valour, nor a lion more savage, nor a shelter in battle nor a sledge-hammer for smiting, nor a protector in fighting, nor doom of hosts, nor one better able to check a great army. You will not find there any man his equal in age like unto Cú Chulainn in growth, in dress, in fearsomeness, in speech, in splendour, in voice and appearance, in power and harshness, in feats, in valour, in striking power, in rage and in anger, in victory and in doom-dealing and in violence, in stalking, in sureness of aim and in game-killing, in swiftness and boldness and rage, with the feat of nine men on every spear-point." (135–36; K 75–76)

I thought it was worth quoting this in full, partly to compensate for the fact that I will not have a lot to say about Cú Chulainn's extraordinary feats in the *Táin*, which vindicate Fergus's florid tribute, but mainly because otherwise it would be difficult to appreciate the sheer audacity of Medb's response: "'I reck little of that,' said Medb. 'He has but one body; he suffers wounding; he is not beyond capture. Moreover he is only the age of a grown girl and as yet his manly deeds have not developed.'" The notion that Cú Chulainn is not yet ready for his task is contested by Fergus: "'Nay,' said Fergus. 'It were no wonder that he should perform a goodly exploit today, for even when he was younger, his deeds were those of a man'" (136; K 76). He then launches into an account of the first of Cú Chulainn's "Boyhood Deeds," telling how he went to join the boys in Emain Macha, an episode to which, as we have seen, Fergus has already briefly alluded.

In her curt dismissal of Fergus's words, Medb seriously underestimates the hero, disregarding the evidence of her eyes and ears. It is of course literally true that Cú Chulainn has but one body, and while he is never captured, he is grievously wounded in the *Táin*. The full extent of Medb's misjudgment becomes clear only as the raid progresses, but it is already about to be adumbrated in "The Boyhood Deeds." These episodes from Cú Chulainn's childhood and youth show him arriving, unbidden, at Emain Macha, and his gradual incorporation into Ulster society. The feats that he performs as he goes through successive stages of initiation into warrior status show how well fitted he is for the role that befalls him in the *Táin*. Most dramatically, we discover that his containment within that "one body" of his is sometimes alarmingly precarious. When his heroic fury is aroused he suffers what Thomas Kinsella has called his "warp-spasm." This condition, which earns him the sobriquet "The Distorted One," first occurs in "The Boyhood Deeds," and is described at length in a later passage which begins:

> Then a great distortion came upon Cú Chulainn so that he became horrible, many-shaped, strange and unrecognizable. All the flesh of his body quivered like a tree in a current or like a bulrush in a stream, every limb and every joint, every end and every member of him from head to foot. He performed a wild feat of contortion with his body inside his skin. (187; K 150)

Cú Chulainn is in many respects a man apart, but he is not altogether alone. For one thing, he has an important and multi-faceted relationship with his charioteer, Lóeg, who saves his life on at least one occasion (179; K 138). What I want to explore, however, is the significance of kinship in his performance of his heroic role, and it is time now to return to Medb's observation on kin-love that I quoted at the outset. This is made when she has contrived to persuade Fer Diad to take up arms against Cú Chulainn: she commends Fer Diad, saying, "Every man has kindly feelings for his own people. So is it any more fitting for him to work for Ulster's weal since his mother was of Ulster, than for you to seek the good of Connacht, for you are the son of a Connacht king?" (197; K 170). In a way which is entirely characteristic of Medb, this is a rather perverse observation, since the preceding exchange between Fer Diad and Medb contains nothing to suggest that he is motivated by love for his people. Fer Diad seems rather to be solely concerned with his personal honor. It is out of fear of being satirized (and thus losing his honor) that Fer Diad responds to Medb's summons to him to go to the invaders' camp in the first place. He declines to go with the messengers she first sends to fetch him, and she then dispatches "poets and artists and satirists who might satirise him and disgrace him and put him to shame, so that he would find no resting place in the world until he should come to the tent of Medb and Ailill" (196; K 168). When he arrives at the camp, Medb's daughter Finnabair sets about seducing him and plying him with drink. Once he is suitably "sated and cheerful and merry" Medb asks him whether he knows why he has been summoned there. He affects not to know of any particular reason other than that it is perfectly appropriate for him to receive the hospitality that is being enjoyed by the other "nobles of the men of Ireland." She tells him that he has been summoned there so that she might bestow gifts upon him, gifts which she then lists, and which include great riches, enhanced status, Finnabair's hand in marriage, and Medb's sexual favors. Fer Diad, rendered sober perhaps by the seriousness of the situation in which he finds himself, divines Medb's true intentions (if indeed he was not already aware of them). He informs her that great as the gifts are he will not accept them from her as the price of fighting his foster-brother. In order to set him at odds with Cú Chulainn, she claims that the latter has boasted that he would defeat Fer Diad in combat. It is quite likely that Medb, who is no stranger to deceit, has made this up, but the alleged insult is enough to persuade Fer Diad that he must be the first to face Cú Chulainn in single combat on the following day.

Fer Diad's fierce concern for his honor is in keeping with the social code that informs the *Táin*. In the "Boyhood Deeds," Cú Chulainn goes so far as to say, "Provided I be famous, I am content to be only one day on earth" (143; K 85). But Fer Diad differs from Cú Chulainn in that his defence of his honor seems to be entirely self-centered, whereas Cú Chulainn's fame is acquired by dint of his defence of Ulster, and in particular of his own homeland, Mag Muirthemne. Moreover, Fer Diad's tragedy is that, having been told by Medb that his foster-brother has spoken ill of him, he feels obliged to redeem his honor in a way that, in the event, leads to his death. For Cú Chulainn, once he has heard that Fer Diad is to oppose him, does indeed make the kind of boast Medb has imputed to him: "I swear the oath of my people that his every joint and limb will bend beneath my sword-point as pliantly as a rush in mid-stream, if he once appears before me on the ford" (200; K 173). This, however, is not spoken as a challenge to Fer Diad. It is rather a response to Fer Diad's challenge to him, which arises only because Fer Diad has been foolish enough to take heed of Medb. Cú Chulainn makes good his boast and slays Fer Diad at the ford.

Following her observation on the universality of kin-love, Medb asks, "So is it any more fitting for him to work for Ulster's weal since his mother was of Ulster, than for you to seek the good of Connacht, for you are the son of a Connacht king?" This rhetorical question shows a form of litotes, so that it actually implies that it is more fitting for Fer Diad, who is the son of a Connacht king, to work for the good of Connacht, than it is for Cú Chulainn, who is related to the people of Ulster through his mother, to work for the good of Ulster. Just as Medb overstates Fer Diad's loyalty to his father's people, she gravely underestimates Cú Chulainn's devotion to his maternal kindred. When the future hero arrives in Emain Macha to join the boys, he announces to Conchobor that he is the son of Súaltaim and of Conchobor's sister Deichtine and indicates that he expects to be treated accordingly. He develops a close relationship with Conchobor, and the Ulstermen generally have a special affection for him because of his mother. Cú Chulainn, for his part, shows his loyalty to Conchobor in his deeds, but he also expresses it in his words. When an emissary comes to offer terms to Cú Chulainn, he identifies himself to the emissary only as someone who acknowledges Conchobor as lord; and when he hears the terms that would be offered he says that Cú Chulainn "will not exchange his mother's brother for another king" (160; K 116).

Yet, in her own way, Medb unerringly puts her finger on what ultimately determines the outcome of the struggle, when she says that "every man has kindly feelings for his own people." In the Irish text, this concept is conveyed by the adjective *condolb*, which means "mindful of kin, kindly" (*DIL*, s.v.) and which in essence has to do with love of one's kind (in its original sense). The same can of course be said of the abstract, *condalbae*, defined in *DIL* as "affection for kindred, love, sympathy, kindness," and which has also been variously translated "kin-love" and "feelings of patriotism." We shall see that the text is quite explicit in stating that *condalbae* underlies the response of the Ulstermen to the assault on their province.

The asymmetry in the contest between Ulster and Connacht is offset to a degree by the presence among the invaders of a group of Ulster exiles. A good half of the description of the muster of the invading army is devoted to the arrival at Rathcroghan of Conchobor's son Cormac Conn Loinges. His sobriquet Conn Loinges means "head of the exiled forces," but Fergus is much the most commanding figure among the Ulster exiles in the *Táin*. The reason for their departure from Ulster is explained in one of the "prefatory tales," which is entitled "The Exile of the Sons of Uisliu" (trans. K 8–20), but is often popularly referred to as "The Deirdre Story": it has to do with the violation by Conchobor of solemn guarantees of safe conduct given by Fergus and Cormac Conn Loinges. When Conchobor meets Fergus in the battle at the end of the *Táin*, he taunts him by identifying himself as "[o]ne who drove you into exile to dwell with wolves and foxes, one who today will hold you at bay in the presence of the men of Ireland by dint of his own prowess" (234; K 247). Fergus, for his part, claims responsibility for the raid in an address to Cú Chulainn: "It was I who, in requital for the wrong done to me by the Ulstermen, collected and brought these forces to the east. With me the heroes and the warriors came from their own lands" (200; K 174).

Fergus and his fellow-exiles are a constant presence in the invading army. When they have all set up camp at Cúil Silinne—the first stop on their eastward journey—the four men who share Ailill's tent are all exiled Ulstermen. We are soon reminded of their independent status when Fergus intervenes in a row that has developed between Ailill and Medb. Having conducted a survey of the army, Medb tells Ailill and Fergus that one of the divisions, the Gailióin, has set up camp and conducted its business more efficiently than any of the others. She expresses the view that it would be pointless for the rest of them to proceed with the raid if the Gailióin were also to go, "for it is they who will take credit for the victory of the army"

(129; K 66). Nor is she content that they should stay behind. She demands that they be killed. Ailill denounces this as "a woman's counsel," but Fergus responds more forcefully, saying, "It shall not happen unless we are all killed, for they are allies of us Ulstermen." Medb claims that she could do it in any case, since she has her own two divisions and the seven divisions of her sons, but once again Fergus is resolute in his response: "'That will not be,' said Fergus, 'There are here seven kings from Munster allies of us Ulstermen, and a division with each king. I shall give you battle in the middle of the encampment where we now are, supported by those seven divisions, by my own division and by the division of the Gailióin'" (130; K 66–67).

As it happens, no blood is shed over this matter: Fergus resolves it by proposing that the division of the Gailióin should be broken up and distributed among the other divisions, and Medb is content with that. Fergus has nevertheless made it clear that as an Ulsterman, he has a mind of his own, and the strength to back it up. We can now see that when Fergus said to Cú Chulainn that it was he who "collected and brought these forces to the east," it was not altogether an idle boast, especially if we interpret it in the light of his further observation that with him "the heroes and warriors came from their own lands." He is effectively the commander of that half of the army that is not from Connacht: the Ulster exiles, the Gailióin from Leinster, and the seven divisions of Munstermen. The significance of this is seen in the final battle: when Fergus and his division withdrew from the fray, "the men of Leinster and the men of Munster went away too, and nine divisions, those of Medb and Ailill and of their seven sons, were left in the battle" (236; K 249).

Fergus is given the task of guiding the raiders to their destination. At first he leads them astray, and as we have seen, he sends a warning to the Ulstermen. In the first instance in the tale of a narratorial intrusion telling us what motivates one of the characters, we learn that Fergus sent the warning *ar chondalbi*, "for the sake of kinship" (131; "old friendship" K 68). Another such intrusion quickly follows: "Then Fergus was given the task of leading the army along the path. He went far astray to the south to give the Ulstermen time to complete the mustering of their army. This he did out of affection for his own kin (*ar chondailbi*)" (131; "old friendship" K 69). Ailill and Medb notice that they are taking a strange route, and they begin to fear that Fergus will betray them. Medb tells him that he should no longer lead them if he feels the pull of kinship (*condailbi*), and he indignantly denies that there is any hint of treachery in what he is doing: the purpose of the detour is to avoid Cú Chulainn, "the great one who guards Mag Muirthemne."

The invaders cannot avoid Cú Chulainn for long. When they do meet, Fergus acts as intermediary between them, and we are in no doubt as to where Fergus's true sympathies lie. Let me give as an example Fergus's reaction to what happens when Cú Chulainn is fighting Lóch Mac Mo Femis. The Morrígan comes to Cú Chulainn in the form of an eel that twines itself round his feet so that he falls prostrate athwart the ford, allowing Lóch to inflict injuries upon him. Fergus is aghast at Cú Chulainn's performance, and he commands that one of his own men taunt Cú Chulainn "lest he fall in vain" (180; K 135). This is duly done, and Cú Chulainn is sufficiently re-energized to defeat Lóch.

The conduct of warfare in the *Táin* is governed by a set of conventions or code of conduct known collectively as *fír fer*, literally "the truth of men," but usually translated "fair play." This is frequently mentioned, but not always observed, in the *Táin*. On one occasion when the terms of fair play were broken against Cú Chulainn, Fergus, we are told, "demanded of his sureties that Cú Chulainn should get fair play" (182; K 139). This is evidently a demand, with the force of law, that in their conflict with Cú Chulainn, Fergus's Connacht allies act according to the conventions of *fír fer*, and for a time they actually do so—until Medb again loses patience and sends a hundred men to attack Cú Chulainn.

Of the many meetings between Cú Chulainn and Fergus in the *Táin*, the most significant is that which happens when Fergus has supposedly been persuaded to engage the younger man—here said to be his foster-son—in single combat. It is quite clear from their conversation on that occasion that neither one of them has the slightest intention of fighting the other. But a certain formality must be observed:

> "Retreat a step from me, Cú Chulainn."
> "You in turn will retreat before me," said Cú Chulainn.
> "Even so indeed," answered Fergus.
> Then Cú Chulainn retreated from Fergus as far as Grellach Dolluid so that on the day of the great battle Fergus might retreat before him. (194; K 165)

When Fergus confronts his old enemy, Conchobor, in the battle, he is understandably out for vengeance. The successive pleas of three of his fellow Ulstermen persuade him to stay his hand. His companion in exile, Conchobor's son Cormac Conn Loinges, grasps his arm as he is about to aim a vengeful blow at Conchobor. He begs Fergus to remember the honor of Ulster: "it will not be lost unless it be through your fault today" (235; K 248). Fergus turns aside, and Conchobor leaves the scene. Fergus nevertheless goes on to kill a hundred Ulstermen, and then he meets another of his fellow-exiles, Conall Cernach. Conall upbraids him for following a "wanton woman" and exerting force against his own "people and race." On Conall's advice he turns his sword on the hills, and with three blows shapes what are now "the flat-topped hills of Meath." These great blows alert Cú Chulainn and he approaches Fergus. He declares himself to be Cú Chulainn son of Súaltaim and son of Conchobor's sister, and he demands that Fergus hold back from him. Fergus agrees to do so, thus redeeming the promise he made when Cú Chulainn declined to encounter him in single combat (236; K 249).

Cú Chulainn owes much to Fergus and to others among the Ulster exiles who are ostensibly his enemies. He is also assisted by the interventions of his human father, Súaltaim, and of his divine father, Lug. Both of them intervene sparingly, Súaltaim making two appearances, Lug only one; but each of them in his way profoundly affects the course of events.

Lug comes to Cú Chulainn from one of the habitations of the gods, which in Irish are called *síde* (singular *síd*), and which O'Rahilly here translates as "fairy mounds" (183; K 142). He brings him the balm of sleep, and he cures him of his wounds. He stiffens his son's resolve for battle by reciting an incantation beginning, "Arise, O son of mighty Ulster, now that your wounds are healed."

While the hero sleeps, the youths of Ulster come south from Emain Macha to fight the invaders. They fight bravely and well, but in the end they are all slain. Cú Chulainn is dismayed when he hears about the death of the youths: "Alas that I was not in my full strength, for had I been, the youths would not have fallen as they did, nor would Fallamain have fallen." Lug consoles him as follows: "Fight on, little Cú, it is no reproach to your honour, no disgrace to your valour." But when Cú Chulainn invites him to stay, so that together they might avenge the boys:

"Indeed I shall not stay," said the warrior, "for though a warrior may do many valorous and heroic deeds in your company, the fame and glory of them will redound not on him, but on you. Therefore I shall not stay. But exert your valour, yourself alone, on the hosts, for not with them lies any power over your life at this time." (185; K 147)

Lug gives expression here to the heroic ideal, which is the exercise of valor in the pursuit of honor and fame and glory; in this he echoes Cú Chulainn's avowed commitment to the pursuit of fame. We might also find it unsettlingly reminiscent of Medb's reasoning with regard to the Gailióin: as we have seen, she demanded that they be put to death, for otherwise they would claim credit for the invading army's victory. Medb, however, was concerned with the collective conduct of a division in an army, whereas Lug and Cú Chulainn are focused on the single warrior. The distinctive attitudes of Lug and Cú Chulainn have to do with different loyalties. Lug has no interest in Ulster; his concern is for the welfare of his son. Cú Chulainn, on the other hand, is unswerving in his loyalty to his mother's brother and the province of which he is king.

Cú Chulainn's defence of Ulster is framed by two interventions on Súaltaim's part, both of which are described as warnings. The first occurs when Cú Chulainn and Súaltaim have received Fergus's message about the forthcoming invasion. Cú Chulainn asks his father to take a warning to the Ulstermen, while he himself sets about delaying the invaders. We hear nothing further of this first warning of Súaltaim's to the Ulstermen. We might well ask ourselves why Cú Chulainn should have dispatched him at all, given that Súaltaim and himself are the only two Ulstermen who are not stricken by the debility. There seems to be no point in delivering a warning to persons who are in no position to act upon it.

The answer, I think, lies in what we are told about Súaltaim's second appearance, which is recounted in the section entitled "The Repeated Warning of Súaltaim." This occurs as Cú Chulainn lies prostrate from his wounds, which were such that "there was not on Cú Chulainn's body a spot which the tip of a rush could cover which was not pierced, and even his left hand which the shield protected bore fifty wounds" (217; K 218). Súaltaim has returned to his abode in Mag Muirthemne when he has intimations of an assault upon Cú Chulainn. He cries out: "Is it the sky that cracks, or the sea that overflows its boundaries, or the earth that splits, or is it the loud cry of my son fighting against odds?" He then goes to Cú Chulainn, who for all his wounds, is not pleased to see his father, for he knows that Súaltaim "would not be strong enough to avenge him." So he immediately sends his father off to Emain to deliver a message to the Ulstermen. We can assume that on the earlier occasion as well, Cú Chulainn sends his father away in the knowledge that he should not be expected to take a fighting role.

The charge given to Súaltaim on the second occasion is of the utmost seriousness: "'Go to the men of Ulster,' said Cú Chulainn, 'and let them give battle to the warriors at once. If they do not, vengeance will never be taken on them'" (217; K 218). Súaltaim goes to Emain and cries out: "Men are slain, women carried off, cattle driven away." In what is clearly a ritual, he shouts out this warning in three different parts of the court. A druid asks, "Who carries them off? Who drives them? Who slays them?" Súaltaim's answer to these questions is a succinct, if chilling, summary of what has happened so far in the *Táin*:

> "Ailill mac Máta slays them, carries them off, drives them away, with the guidance of Fergus mac Róig," said Súaltaim. "Your people have been harassed as far as Dún Sobairche. Their cows, their women-folk, and their cattle have been carried off. Cú Chulainn has not let them come into Mag Muirthemne and Crích Rois during the three months of winter. Bent hoops (of wood) hold his mantle (from touching him). Dry wisps plug his wounds. He has been wounded and bled profusely (?)." (217; K 219)

The druid accuses him of inciting the king and says that he should die for it; the king concurs with the druid in this sentence, and the people concur with the king. With regard to the substance of Súaltaim's warning, however, the king adjudges him to have spoken the truth.

In view of the urgency of his mission, we might well expect Súaltaim to be appalled at the lugubrious pace of this quasi-juridical procedure. He is in any case dissatisfied with the answer he has got; he rushes forth, and falls on his shield, the scalloped rim of which cuts off his head. He has apparently been attempting to flee Emain on horseback, for we are told that his horse brought the head back into Emain on the shield. In a final dramatic act, Súaltaim's severed head utters the same warning once more.

In Conchobor's response, Súaltaim is at once maligned and vindicated: "'Too loud was that shout indeed,' said Conchobor. '(I swear by) the sea before them, the sky above them, the earth beneath them that I shall restore every cow to its byre and every woman and boy to their homes after victory in battle'" (217; K 219). He is critical of Súaltaim's shout, but he unwittingly echoes Súaltaim's portentous words about the sky, the sea, and the earth, and he vows to act. True to his word, he immediately sets about the muster of the men of Ulster. Súaltaim's warning has the desired effect, and the wrongs inflicted upon Ulster and upon its defender, Súaltaim's own son, will soon be avenged in battle.

Each of the characters in this epic subsists in a complex web of alliances and relationships, and this affects their actions at crucial times. The contest between Ulster and Connacht takes place within the framework of a code of conduct which, as I have said, is frequently mentioned, but often breached. Rules of engagement are agreed, and ad hoc arrangements of one kind and another are made from time to time. Medb and Ailill have gathered a mighty army, with allies from Ulster, Leinster, and Munster, as well as their own province of Connacht. Cú Chulainn in his defence of Ulster shows all the virtues of the martial hero—courage, ingenuity, physical prowess—in abundance. When all is said and done, however, it is the power of kin-love among the Ulstermen that brings them victory in this epic.

In the translation of Medb's statement implying that it would be more fitting to work for the good of one's paternal rather than one's maternal kin, "more fitting" translates the comparative of *cóir*, a word which has a strong legal resonance. It is worth noting that, in law at least, the paternal kindred would generally command one's primary loyalty in early Ireland. What stands to Conchobor in the *Táin* is that he is supported by those who are related to him through their mothers as well as those who are Ulstermen in the male line, and I shall close with a quotation which gives expression to this point. In what is perhaps the most touching passage of all in the *Táin*, Fergus describes the arrival on the scene of the final battle of Erc, son of Cairbre Nia Fer and of Conchobor's daughter:

> Without asking permission of his father, that boy has come to the assistance of his grandfather. It is because of that lad that you will be defeated in battle. He will experience neither dread nor fear as he makes for you in the middle of your army. Bravely will the warriors of Ulster roar as they hew down the army before them, rushing to rescue their beloved lad. They will all feel the ties of kinship [*condolba*] when they see the boy in that great conflict. Like the baying of a bloodhound will be heard the sound of Conchobor's sword as he comes to the boy's rescue. Cú Chulainn will cast up three ramparts of (dead) men about the battle as he rushes towards the little lad. Mindful of their kinship with the boy [*condalb*], the warriors will attack the vast (enemy) host. (228; K 234–35)

14

Mythology in *Táin Bó Cúailnge*

(1993)

Táin Bó Cúailnge is a work of some complexity, and it should therefore be amenable to a wide range of critical approaches, literary, linguistic, historical, and mythological. The complex character of the *Táin* is sometimes overlooked by individual critics, but it is reflected in the diversity of the criticism which has been devoted to it. While that criticism is as yet quite modest in extent, the *Táin* has been discussed, in whole or in part, separately or as part of the Ulster Cycle, from a number of viewpoints, all of them having some implications for the general theme of orality and literacy. The Ulster Cycle was considered by the Chadwicks and their disciples as a reflection of a lost Heroic Age;[1] it has also been discussed, by Ó Corráin and Aitchison, in terms of the historical circumstances in which it was given shape.[2] The mythological components in the *Táin*, and in the Cycle generally, have been considered by O'Rahilly, Sjoestedt, Rees and Rees, and others.[3]

James Carney held that the *Táin* was a work of literature, created in a mixed culture, and he agreed with Thurneysen that it was deliberately imitative of the classics.[4] John Kelleher argues that the *Táin* was created in response to certain historical circumstances, but he implies that its dominant figure, Cú Chulainn, was based on the model of Jesus Christ.[5]

In view of all this it will be helpful to begin our discussion of the *Táin* with the question "Cid so?"; in other words to ask ourselves "What is it?" The answer is "not difficult": *Táin Bó Cúailnge* is an epic, and it follows that its primary claim on our attention must be as a work of literature. It is useful to make this point at the outset, because there has been a tendency to discredit the literary status of early Irish narrative texts, to see them, not as works in their own right, but rather in relation to myth or history or oral tradition. This tendency can be put down to the fact that the serious study of early Irish literature has historically (and necessarily) been the domain of philologists, who have understandably fought shy of the concerns and methods of literary critics. This is usually done without explanation or apology, but one eminent philologist, Jaan Puhvel, makes the case for his own discipline by expressing undisguised disdain for literary criticism:

> Modern literary myth-critics, armed with ungainly ritualist and psychoanalytic panoplies, may indeed set to work on any ancient epic, as well as take apart to their own satisfaction a work by James Joyce or Scott Fitzgerald: they will never get any closer to the core of one than the other, because in their butcher shop all carcasses hang equal. If we are to make any headway in studying Indo-European epic as a narrative genre, philology alone will help us along.[6]

Our knowledge of early Irish literature we owe in large measure to philologists, and in the case of the *Táin* we are especially indebted to the late Cecile O'Rahilly for her remarkable editorial achievement;[7] it is therefore with no disrespect for philology that I say that it alone, as traditionally practiced, will not suffice if we are to understand our texts. There is of course nothing amiss in viewing the *Táin* within a mythological or historical perspective, nor would I suggest for a moment that it is not a suitable case for consideration within the general topic of this series of colloquia. All that I am saying is that we should always bear in mind what it is that we are dealing with. If that is done, we need not, and should not, exclude any critical approach to the *Táin* which remains faithful to the transmitted texts, and which helps to illuminate them.

Commentators on the *Táin* have ignored, rather than reviled, literary criticism, but the result is that we are still very much in the dark as to how the *Táin* is constituted as a work of literature. Moreover, one of the weaknesses of much of the commentary on the *Táin* has been the reductive way in which theories have been applied to it: thus T. F. O'Rahilly, being satisfied that the Ulster tales "are wholly mythical in origin," contends that "they have not the faintest connexion with anything that could be called history, apart from the fact that traditions of warfare between the Ulaid and the Connachta have been adventitiously introduced into a few of them, and especially into the longest and best-known tale, 'Táin Bó Cualgne.'"[8] Kenneth Jackson, on the other hand, states that the Ulster Cycle "belongs to the genre of literature of entertainment and contains very little that can reasonably or safely be taken for myth or ought to be interpreted as such."[9] It is in no such reductive spirit that I begin my paper with a brief consideration of the *Táin* as epic.

For a general description of epic, we may turn to M. H. Abrams, who says that "in its strict use by literary critics the term 'epic' or 'heroic poem' is applied to a work that meets at least the following criteria: it is a long narrative poem on a great and serious subject, related in an elevated style, and centered on a heroic or quasi-divine figure on whose actions depends the fate of a tribe, a nation, or the human race."[10] Setting aside the fact that it comprises a mixture of prose and verse, the *Táin* meets the criteria set out by Abrams: it is a long narrative work, related for the most part in an elevated style; its subject matter, the invasion and defence of Ulster, is great and serious; it is centered on the heroic figure of Cú Chulainn, on whose actions the fate of Ulster depends. The difference between the *Táin* and short sagas such as *Scéla Mucce Meic Da Thó* ("The Story of Mac Da Thó's Pig") is not merely, or even mainly, a matter of relative length; the difference in scale, in subject matter, and in treatment of subject matter bespeaks a difference of genre between the *Táin* and the short sagas. This is not something which we can pursue here. For our purposes it is enough that the identification of the *Táin* as an epic helps us to put its mythic content into focus, and to see how what may seem to be quite disparate mythic strands are woven into a literary work which is simple in its general outline, but remarkably complex in its detail; single-minded in the achievement of its purpose, but multifarious in the means so used.

A question of literary history arises at this point. Was the *Táin* composed in deliberate imitation of classical epic, of Homer's *Iliad* or Vergil's *Aeneid*? Or is it rather a "primary epic," a type which, as Abrams puts it, would have been "shaped by a literary artist from historical and legendary materials which had developed in the oral traditions of his nation during a period of expansion and warfare"?[11] Thurneysen detected what he claimed were reminiscences of classical epic in the *Táin*, and he was inclined to assign these to the *Grundtext*, in which, as it seemed to him, an Irishman had for the first time attempted to compile a single extensive narrative from the "short narratives and episodes as the storytellers were accustomed to relate them," and which would compare with classical epic.[12] Thurneysen's view has been endorsed by James Carney,[13] but Gerard Murphy and Proinsias Mac Cana have argued against it.[14] Very briefly one might say that whereas Carney holds that the *Táin* was composed in imitation of Homer, Murphy rejects this and offers two other explanations for such similarities as exist between the *Iliad* and the *Táin*, the first being "a common Indo-European tradition," the second "the natural resemblance of manners in any Heroic Age."[15] It is important to note that when Carney says that the *Táin* "consists in part of traditional material, in part of imaginative reconstruction of the remote pagan Irish past in form and terms that belong to the mixed culture of early Christian Ireland," he recognizes the presence in the *Táin* of elements derived from oral narrative.[16] Murphy, for his part, goes some of the way to meet Carney, saying that "when Carney warns us against regarding Christian elements in Irish stories about pagan times as 'interpolation' he is on firm ground. The pagan stories are available only in Christian versions, and the Christian element is as definitely a part of them as the Christian language in which they are told."[17] What is in question, therefore, is the role of those who gave the *Táin* written form. Neither Murphy nor Carney would support Mac Cana's remarkable assertion that "it is . . . very possible—indeed probable—that an oral version of the *Táin* not radically different from the first written version was already in existence during the seventh century."[18] The notion that the early writers of Irish saga were passive traditors of oral narrative is dismissed by Carney, who sees them as "literary authors rather than scribes."[19] I agree in general with this view of Carney's, which now commands increasing consent among scholars,[20] but I have to say that, whatever may have motivated or influenced the composition of the *Táin*, it has not as yet been demonstrated that the content of the *Táin* is derived in any significant measure from classical epic. It has also become necessary, in view of what has recently been happening in Irish studies, to mention the possibility of biblical influence, but again it remains to be shown that the content of the *Táin* is significantly indebted to the Bible.[21]

The *Táin*, as Cecile O'Rahilly puts it, "tells of a foray made by Medb of Connacht into the territory of the Ulaid for the purpose of carrying off the bull Donn Cúalgne from the district of Cúalgne, present-day Cooley, Co. Louth." As O'Rahilly remarks in this context, "plundering raids, especially cattle-raids, are a characteristic feature of Irish heroic saga";[22] we are reminded too of *Scéla Mucce Meic Da Thó* in which contention of the Connachta and the Ulaid for a gigantic pig is framed by their contention for an extraordinary hound. We cannot say whether this cattle-raid represents an ancient invasion-myth which here provides the kernel of an epic. What we can say is that the object of the quest, the Donn Cúailnge, is a creature of mythical proportions; his role in the *Táin* is complemented by that depicted or alluded to in other Irish texts; his Celtic congeners are represented in iconography and nomenclature; and he is the Irish reflex of an Indo-European male bovine, whose primary role in a myth of cosmogony by dismemberment is reflected in the *Táin* and in one of its associated *remscéla* ("prefatory tales"), *De Chophur in da Muccida* 'The Quarrel of the Two Swineherds.' Our knowledge of Donn Cúailnge is thus greatly extended by attending to the comparative data.

The mythological study of early Irish narrative has been conducted in two main ways, one of them being concerned with Celtic mythology, the other being the wider discipline of comparative mythology. The two are not always kept apart, but they nevertheless represent different orientations in the mythological study of Irish texts. Each of them, in its way, has light to cast on Donn Cúailnge.

In the narrower field of Celtic mythology, the texts are interpreted in conjunction with evidence from other sources for Celtic religion. An account of this kind of work is given by Anne Ross in the introduction to her *Pagan Celtic Britain*,[23] where she discusses the three kinds of evidence which are available: the evidence of archaeology, the testimony of Greek and Roman commentators, and the vernacular literatures of Ireland and Wales.

Ross points out that "the evidence for native cults is ... very much of an archaeological nature, but its interpretation is another matter. The material evidence is suggestive of certain patterns of belief, but an understanding of these apparent patterns cannot be based on archaeology alone" (1967, 2); for such an understanding we must turn to the other two varieties of evidence. As for the comments of Greek and Roman writers, these "are too insubstantial and fragmentary to do more than point the way in certain instances. Moreover, it is only too easy to misinterpret archaeological evidence, and in complex societies such as those which existed in Celtic countries during the period of Roman occupation, where classical and exotic cults became fused and confused with the more homely native equivalents, we are indeed in the middle of a quagmire" (2–3). Much more abundant than the testimony of Greek and Roman commentators is the evidence of vernacular narrative, which Ross characterizes as being "on the one hand more elusive, and on the other more reliable than the two sources already discussed" (3). Our assessment of the reliability of Irish narrative as a source for Celtic mythology will depend, of course, on our view of the nature and extent of the oral component in the transmitted texts. Ross's view is that "we may suppose that certain cult legends, changed in a Christian milieu into hero tales or topographical legends, may have circulated for centuries until they found written form under the sympathetic aegis of the Irish church" (3); indeed I would say that her work presupposes that the cult legends *must* have circulated for centuries until they "found written form." Comparison of the narrative with the other sources can be helpful in two ways: "The other sources can assist in getting the mythology contained in these early literary traditions into perspective, and the literary material can act as an invaluable yard-stick against which the conclusions the archaeological material allows us to draw can be compared and measured." The fruits of this kind of work are described with some modesty: "And when, as is not infrequently the case, the three sources can all be shown to point in the same direction, then we may feel justified in concluding that, for a little while, and in a very limited fashion, we have managed to check the constantly shifting and changing patterns of Celtic religion, and have penetrated a little below the confusing, moving surface, to discover something of the permanent core which underlies the unstable picture which normally confronts us" (3).

What we tend to get in this way is a thematic skeleton, derived in large measure from the archaeological evidence, but fleshed out with stories from Irish and, to a lesser extent, Welsh manuscripts. The narrative material is

14. Mythology in *Táin Bó Cúailnge*

indeed brought into perspective, but there must be some doubt as to the validity of that perspective. The criticism of Ross's book by Liam de Paor should be borne in mind: he reminds us that the Celts were an essentially non-literate people, and says that "if we wish to study the Celts at all, we are forced to see them as a half-Hellenised or half-Romanised people—because they are shown to us in the framework of Greek or Roman ideas—or we are forced to try to understand the society and ideas of one people, such as the Gauls or Britons of pre-Roman times, through the writings (about themselves) of another people, the Irish of a thousand years later."[24] Ross's work is nevertheless valuable as a work of reference: the material which she has gathered, for example, about the bull shows the importance of this animal in Celtic iconography and nomenclature, and tends to confirm the impression which we get from the Irish literary sources that the Donn Cúailnge has its origins in a bull-cult.[25]

The second way in which the mythological content of the texts can be studied is that of comparative mythology. The work which we have been considering is of course comparative, insofar as it entails the comparison both of different kinds of evidence, and of the narrative texts of Ireland and Wales. But the study of comparative mythology differs from that of Celtic mythology in taking a wider canvas, either within a general science of comparative religion, in which typological comparisons are made, as in the work of Mircea Eliade, or a comparison of the myths and literatures of speakers of Indo-European languages, where similarities are deemed to spring from a genetic relationship among the items compared. Here we are comparing text with text; in this we are perhaps on firmer ground than when the comparison is of text with icon or other item of material culture. But it must be remembered that the reading of any given text is to some degree interpretive, and, in the case of early Irish narrative, the hypothesis is that we are dealing with mythology refracted through literature.

In the nineteenth century, comparative mythology was practiced by philologists, but criticism of their theories led, by the end of the century, to what has been aptly called "the eclipse of solar mythology."[26] Comparative mythology had something of a second coming in Ireland in the work of T. F. O'Rahilly: he criticized John Rhŷs for having applied "'solar' methods of interpretation in all directions with incredible recklessness,"[27] but he was able, for his own part, to see a solar deity in the type of personage which he called the "Otherworld God," and of which he names as examples, among many others, both Donn Cúailnge and Culann's Dog, who is slain and replaced by Cú Chulainn.[28] In France, in the meantime, Georges Dumézil was rehabilitating the comparative study of mythology on a foundation which combined anthropological and sociological considerations with those of philology.[29]

Two aspects of Dumézil's work are relevant to our topic. In the first place he has uncovered a number of story-patterns which can be taken to have their origins among the speakers of Proto-Indo-European. Secondly, he has discerned in numerous texts in the Indo-European languages a common ideology which he has also attributed to the speakers of the original language. We shall consider the matter of ideology somewhat later, but here I want to draw attention to an Indo-European story-pattern which Bruce Lincoln has uncovered in the *Táin*.[30] Lincoln analyzes what he calls the Indo-European myth of the first sacrifice, of which independent Indian, Iranian, Germanic, and Roman versions can be located, in addition to Greek, Russian, Jewish, and Chinese versions "that seem to be the result of secondary diffusion."[31] In each of the primary texts, a primordial being is killed and dismembered, and from his body the cosmos is fashioned.[32] On the basis of comparative reconstruction, Lincoln argues that the Proto-Indo-European myth is one which is characteristic of pastoralists. It tells of the creation of the world through the primordial sacrifice of a man and an ox or a bull, and it establishes a pattern for all future sacrifice and for all future creation.[33] Two major variants of the Indo-European myth are reconstructed, one Indo-Iranian and the other European.[34]

Now Lincoln sees a reflex of this myth in the confrontation of the bulls at the end of the *Táin* and in the prefatory tale *De Chophur in da Muccida*.[35] (The latter tells that the bulls originated as pig-herds, and went through a series of transformations as various creatures before they reached their final condition; there is an allusion to this story in the *Táin* itself when Dubthach prophesies: "There will come a leader of armies who will try to recover the cattle of Murthemne. Because of the companionship of the two swineherds, ravens of the battle-field will drink men's blood."[36]) Lincoln remarks:

> This Irish variant of the Proto-Indo-European myth has been much transformed. Relegated to a position as prologue and postscript to an epic tale of battle and adventure its characters and values are thoroughly subjugated to those of the epic. Its heroes become retainers and servants of epic kings, or alternatively, the bulls sought by those kings

as booty. Its central act of sacrifice becomes an epic duel between those noble bulls. For all these transformations, it remains recognizable nonetheless and provides valuable confirmation of the authenticity of the Indo-Iranian versions of the myth on numerous points.[37]

Here, then, we have an example of myth refracted through literature. In this respect the *Táin* and its prefatory tale belong to the category which Jaan Puhvel has recently described as follows:

> Yet equally important is the next level of transmission, in which the sacred narrative has already been secularized, myth has been turned into saga, sacred time into heroic past, gods into heroes, and mythical action into "historical" plot. Many genuine "national epics" constitute repositories of the tradition where the mythical underpinnings have been submerged via such literary transposition. Old Chronicles can turn out to be "prose epics" where the probing modern mythologist can uncover otherwise lost mythical traditions. Such survival is quite apart from, or wholly incidental to, the conscious exploitative use of myth in literature, something that Western civilization has practiced since artful verbal creativity began.[38]

There are some questions here for the comparatist: for example, is it not possible to think of an Indo-European epic hero, of which Cú Chulainn is to some degree a reflex? I, for one, find it hard to credit that he is an Indo-European god who has been transformed into an Irish hero. But the general point that an epic like the *Táin* constitutes a repository of tradition is well illustrated by Lincoln's findings.

Enough has been said about the great bull which was the object of the raid. Let us turn now to consider some of the other mythological components of the epic, and we may begin with a look at the *cess* or "debility" with which the Ulstermen were afflicted; this is a necessary condition of the raid, since it renders the Ulstermen unable to defend their territory. This *cess* has been much discussed, and the most plausible interpretation of the way it is presented in the *Táin* seems to me to be that of Tomás Ó Broin, who sees it as "a death or winter sleep" of the kind represented in seasonal myth and ritual.[39] The effects of the winter sleep are overcome by the actions of Cú Chulainn; the basic idea is "the triumph of life and fecundity over death and decay."[40]

We first hear of the "debility" of the Ulstermen before the raiders set out from Connacht. Medb encounters Fedelm, a poetess who is possessed of the power of prophecy called *imbas forosnai*, and asks her to prophesy the fate of Medb's expedition. Fedelm's chilling prophecy is: "I see it blood-stained, I see it red." But Medb is nothing daunted: "'That is not true,' said Medb, 'for Conchobor lies in his debility in Emain together with the Ulstermen and all the mightiest of their warriors, and my messengers have come and brought me tidings of them.'"[41] The expedition sets out "on the Monday after Samain."[42] Fergus sends a warning to the Ulstermen "who were still suffering from their debility, all except Cú Chulainn and his father Súaltaim";[43] it was apparently they who received Fergus's warning, and it was Cú Chulainn in particular who acted upon it. The reason for Cú Chulainn's immunity is later hinted at by Fergus. He is recounting one of Cú Chulainn's Boyhood Deeds, and he says: "On another occasion, the Ulstermen were in their debility. Among us women and boys do not suffer from the debility nor does anyone outside the territory of Ulster, nor yet Cú Chulainn and his father."[44] Cecile O'Rahilly points out[45] that this particular passage seems to derive from the tale *Noínden Ulad*, which purports to explain the origin of the debility, and which explicitly states that Cú Chulainn did not suffer from the debility because he was not an Ulsterman (*ar nírbo do Ultaib dó*).[46]

There are clear indications in the *Táin* that the debility lasted for the three months from Samain (November 1) to Imbolc (February 1), which in Ireland are the three months of winter. So much is implied in Recension II,[47] while in Recension I we are told that Cú Chulainn fought single-handed "from the Monday after Samain until the Wednesday after the festival of Spring" (*ón lúan íar Samain cosin cétaín íar n-imolg*);[48] we are also told twice that he fought for the three winter months (*trí mísa gaimrid*).[49] Ó Broin's notion that the debility is a winter sleep is obviously consistent with these indications as to its duration.

A difficulty which must be considered is the surprise expressed by Fergus at the duration of the debility in the *Táin*: "'And I find it strange,' said Fergus, 'that they are so long in recovering from their debility'" (*"Ocus machdad lim-sa," ol Fergus, "a fot co tecat-side assa cessaib"*).[50] We would expect Fergus, of all people, to know the facts of this matter. It is conceivable that this utterance of his is intended to deceive the Connachta, whom he is addressing on this occasion. We have clear evidence of the duplicitous side of his character in the passage of the *Táin* in which he takes the invading Connachta on a detour to give the Ulaid time to complete the mustering

14. Mythology in *Táin Bó Cúailnge*   211

of their army.[51] The narrator tells us about this, adding for good measure that Fergus acted "out of affection for his own kin" (*ar chondalbai*).[52] When Medb challenges Fergus and suspects that he may be feeling "the pull of kinship," he denies his treachery.[53] Whatever about Fergus's intentions in relation to the Connachta, however, his expectation that the Ulaid would have time to complete the mustering of their army is scarcely compatible with their debility, and it suggests therefore that Fergus was unaware that they were in that condition. Perhaps we should simply remember that absolute consistency is not to be expected on matters of this kind. By way of illustration in the *Táin* itself, we may compare the clear implication, to which I have already alluded, that Cú Chulainn was immune to the debility because he was not an Ulsterman with the remark made by Follomon son of Conchobor when the young Cú Chulainn (then called Sétantae) came as a stranger to Emain Macha: "The boy insults us ... Yet we know he is of the Ulstermen (*sech rafetamár is di Ultaib dó*)."[54] In any case, even if Fergus's avowed surprise at the duration of the debility is to be taken as genuine, it may indicate a certain instability in the tradition relating to the matter, but it does not negate the clear statement in the *Táin* that on this particular occasion the Ulstermen were afflicted for three months.

Cecile O'Rahilly points out that there is also in Recension I "a suggestion that the attack of *cess* was intermittent":

> In a long passage denoted by the scribe as *córugud aile* containing many *roscada* and obviously belonging to the oldest stratum of *TBC* we are told that Cú Chulainn goes to Conchobor to warn him of the enemy's attacks, but Conchobor tells him that the warning is useless and comes too late: *Indiu tonánic ar tinorcuin in chétnae* (1219–20), "Today we have been smitten (by the *cess*) as before." The H-interpolator later takes up the same point and borrows the word *tinnorcain* when he tries to explain how the Ulsterman Munremar can come to fight with Cú Roí. "At this point the *noénden Ulad* came to an end. According as they awoke (from their *cess*) a band of them kept attacking the (enemy) host until they were once more smitten (by their *cess*)" ... (1629–30).[55]

The remark of Conchobor's which O'Rahilly quotes would not seem to be very telling one way or the other: it could simply be a way of saying that the Ulstermen are still afflicted by the debility. As for the narrator's words as given by the H-interpolator, they certainly indicate that a temporary remission from the debility was considered possible. This is not necessarily incompatible with the notion of a winter sleep: we could say in seasonal terms that spring has seemed to come early, but that it is a false spring, and quickly yields once more to the sleep of winter.

Ó Broin has been accused of distorting the textual evidence,[56] but it is quite clear that the *cess* is presented in the *Táin* as a winter sleep. In accepting this, however, it is not necessary to follow Ó Broin in his theory that the *cess* is based on a fertility ritual.[57] The seasonal character of the debility does suggest a connection with fertility, however, and we shall see presently that the circumstances of Cú Chulainn's conception imply that he is a fecundating hero. The *cess* in the *Táin* is also symptomatic of the collapse of social order. As Joan Radner has said in a different context:

> Thematically, the Ulster Cycle as a whole tends to present the tragic breakdown of those relationships on which early Irish society was founded: the relationship between host and guest, between kindred, between fosterbrothers, between men and women, between lords and clients and kings and overkings, between the human world and the gods.[58]

It is Cú Chulainn, in Sjoestedt's words, "their defence and their champion ... at once the glory and the living rampart of his tribe"[59] who saves Ulster from final disaster, and so I turn now to a brief consideration of what has been called the Myth of the Hero, as it is represented in the Ulster Cycle, and in the *Táin* in particular.

We have seen that an epic is said to be "centred on a heroic or quasi-divine figure on whose actions depends the fate of a tribe, a nation or the human race."[60] In the *Táin*, Cú Chulainn is that figure: the world celebrates his martial heroism, his courage and ingenuity, his mastery of the martial arts, his unswerving loyalty. In short, he is an epic hero, the epic theme of the *Táin* being his single-handed defence of Ulster. When we look at his life as a whole, however, we find that it is a realization of the heroic biographical pattern common to Indo-European and Semitic tradition.[61] This pattern is not confined to epic heroes, but in Cú Chulainn's case it is realized in martial terms that are altogether appropriate to epic.

It is characteristic of the heroic biography that the birth of the hero is anomalous, and Cú Chulainn is no exception. The early version of his conception-story[62] opens with the theme of the Waste Land: the fruits of Emain

Macha are consumed to the roots by birds. The Ulidians set out in pursuit of the birds, and they are led to Bruig na Bóinne, the great necropolis at the bend of the Boyne, and a site of singular importance in Irish myth. There Sétantae was born, and he was brought back to Ulster; he died, but he was conceived again. The parents of his first conception were the god Lug and his (unnamed) Otherworld consort, those of his second Lug and Dechtine, sister to the Ulster king, Conchobor. Sétantae was not born of his second conception, but was conceived for a third time, his parents now being the human Súaltaim and Dechtine. (Sétantae later went on to acquire the name Cú Chulainn, in circumstances which are recounted in the *Táin*.)

The theme of the Waste Land implies the need for a fecundating hero, an element which is of course consistent with Ó Broin's interpretation of the debility of the Ulstermen as a winter sleep, from the effects of which Ulster is rescued by this vigorous young male as the vital force in nature. Cú Chulainn shares with many sacred or mythic personages the characteristic of dual paternity: he is at once the son of a god (Lug) and of a human father (Súaltaim). As I have already said, anomalous birth is a predictable feature of the heroic biography. It is therefore quite unnecessary to assume that the numerous Irish examples of this phenomenon are based on the life of Christ. John Kelleher, however, has noted that Irish annalists placed the death of Cú Chulainn at 2 A.D., and, having made the unexceptional point that "the choice of that date—like 33 A.D. for the death of Conchobor—was clearly to associate these heroes with Christ,"[63] he goes on to say: "Thus the lives of Christ and Cú Chulainn overlap by one year—to which may be added that each of them has a life-span divisible by three; each has a divine father but is known as the son of a mortal father; each dies for his people, erect and pierced by a spear. By such manipulations the pre-eminence of the *Táin* was again asserted."[64] The implication is that just as the death of Cú Chulainn was dated to overlap with the life of Christ, so also the other features of his biography mentioned by Kelleher were "manipulations" whereby Cú Chulainn was associated with Christ.

This seems to me to be extremely far-fetched. Cú Chulainn's role in the *Táin* is indeed that of savior of his people, but he is a very different kind of personage from Jesus Christ. Moreover, while he shares with Christ, and with many other heroes, the characteristic of dual paternity, he differs from them in having a triple conception, which shows a sequence from fully divine, through mixed divine and human, to fully human parentage. I have elsewhere said of this sequence that in it the hero recapitulates in his own life the history of man, since, if we may judge from the occurrence of deity names in their pedigrees, the Irish apparently believed themselves to be descended from the gods. Furthermore, this sequence gives us a singularly clear example of the manner in which the hero mediates between the gods and men: the second (or middle) conception, linked to the first and third by Lug and Dechtine respectively, mediates the opposition between the divine and the human. In this case at least the "meaning" of the triplicity of the hero is inseparable from the structure of the narrative.[65]

Kim McCone, who accepts Kelleher's views on Cú Chulainn, writes as follows about the conception-story:

Going as it does well beyond the standard requirements of heroic liminality, this genesis of the Ulster hero *par excellence* can hardly be understood except as an orthodox allegory and "native" typology of Christ's mysterious incarnation as set forth in the New Testament.[66]

One has to say, however, that the narrative also goes well beyond what might reasonably be required of an orthodox allegory and "native" typology of Christ's incarnation. The three-fold conception of Cú Chulainn is not directly based on the story of Christ, and it must be seen rather in the light of the prevalence of triplicity of gods and heroes in Irish literature, and of the occurrence of triplicity in Celtic iconography. Perhaps this is what McCone has in mind when he speaks of "native" typology, but it can be understood as such without recourse to the hypothesis of Christian allegory. Moreover, there are good comparative grounds for holding that Cú Chulainn's triplicity is an inherited feature which is inextricably bound up with his destiny as a warrior. Cú Chulainn's warrior initiation is achieved by successful combat with the three sons of Nechta Scéne;[67] taken together, his conception and his initiatory combat exemplify the Indo-European theme which Dumézil has summed up in the formula "the third kills the triple."[68]

We have wandered away from the *Táin* in our treatment of Cú Chulainn as hero, but with the three sons of Nechta Scéne we have returned, not, it is true, to the three-month time frame of the great raid, but to Cú Chulainn's "Boyhood Deeds," which are recounted to the invaders by exiled Ulstermen. There is evidence in the Book of Leinster of some disagreement as to the status of the "Boyhood Deeds" in relation to the *Táin*; we are informed that they were classified by some people as "prefatory tales," but that they are in fact narrated in the body of the *Táin*.[69] Daniel Melia has pointed out, however, that we have no version of the *Táin* which lacks the "Boyhood Deeds," and he is doubtless correct in saying that they "were considered a part of the *Cattle Raid of Cooley* from the time that it was put together as an entity."[70]

The episodes which constitute Cú Chulainn's "Boyhood Deeds" are successive stages in the development of the martial hero and of his incorporation into society. Melia has shown that many of them share the pattern of arrival, opposition, and final acceptance: Cú Chulainn enters from outside; he asserts himself against the men of Ulster; and he is accepted by the Ulstermen as a warrior (several times by Conchobor himself). Within the framework of this recurrent pattern we find a cumulative exposition of heroic themes, which have been well treated by Alwyn and Brinley Rees.[71] We can regard them as mythical in origin, but it is instructive also to consider their place in the epic.

The "Boyhood Deeds" present Cú Chulainn as a precocious hero: "one can say that for the purpose of the larger story his precocious heroism cannot simply be stated but must be illustrated graphically."[72] The Connacht army—and the reader—are being prepared for Cú Chulainn's prodigious feats in the *Táin*, and those very feats are lent a degree of verisimilitude by the accumulation of eye-witness accounts of his youthful exploits. Within the framework of the *Táin*, then, the "Boyhood Deeds" arouse expectations, and in a way authenticate Cú Chulainn's subsequent actions in all their extravagance. The narrative device which is used—that of the so-called "flashback"—enables the narrator to escape from the tyranny of linearity, and to appropriate for his purpose events which lie outside the temporal frame of the cattle raid. One of the major themes of the *Táin* is martial heroism, and the portrayal of the hero is deepened by the details of the "Boyhood Deeds."

Much of the ideological content of the *Táin* is centered on the heroic figure of Cú Chulainn. Proinsias Mac Cana has drawn a contrast between the king tales and those devoted to martial heroes:

> The king tales taken as a whole have a social orientation, centred as they are on the paramount institution in Irish society. By contrast,

when we turn to the heroic literature *pur sang* we find by and large that each protagonist stands as an individual rather than as a kind of surrogate for society. The hero *par excellence* is the hero alone.[73]

There can be no gainsaying that the martial hero *par excellence* is the martial hero alone; indeed, the best example we have is Cú Chulainn who stands alone against the invaders of Ulster. Yet in doing so he is a kind of surrogate for society, and in particular for the men of Ulster who lie stricken by their debility. But this is scarcely what Mac Cana has in mind: the social orientation of the king tales is seen in their ideological content, and this is presumably what Mac Cana thinks is lacking in the tales of martial heroism. The fact is, however, that the ideology of warfare is richly explored in the *Táin*, and in other tales of the Ulster Cycle. Important work on this aspect of the material has been published by Philip O'Leary.[74] I would also mention here the way in which kinship is presented in these tales, and especially Cú Chulainn's status as a sister's son to Conchobor (and to the Ulaid as a whole).[75] There is no lack of social orientation in the Ulster Cycle: what we need is further detailed analysis of the ideological content of the texts.

T. F. O'Rahilly discerned two basic myths in the Irish material, the Myth of the Birth of the Hero, and the Myth of the Rival Wooers. The latter, more prosaically known as the eternal triangle, is represented in the *Táin* by Medb, her husband Ailill, and her lover Fergus. Medb shows many of the characteristics of the goddess of sovereignty, but we see little of this in the *Táin*. It has been suggested that the three essential attributes of a king—justice, victory, and the power to give fruitfulness to the earth and health to mankind—are reflected in Medb's requirements in a husband: he must be without jealousy, without fear, without niggardliness.[76] There is also an ideological dimension in the relationship between Fergus and Medb, the essential notion being that, by yielding to Medb's attractions, Fergus is unmanned, and betrays his own kith and kin.

The unmanning of Fergus is expressed in terms of the taking of his own sword from its scabbard. This is done by Ailill's charioteer while Fergus and Medb are engaged in intercourse. When Fergus discovers his loss, he fashions a wooden sword as a replacement.[77] Cú Chulainn later speaks derisively of Fergus's "empty rudder."[78] Conall Cernach upbraids Fergus for assailing his own people "for the sake of a woman's buttocks."[79] These sentiments are echoed by Fergus himself when he finally speaks of the folly of following a woman's buttocks.[80] In general, this is an expression of the inappropriateness of following a woman into battle: we may compare Ailill's contemptuous dismissal of *banchomhairle* (woman's counsel).[81] More precisely, however, the sexual nature of Fergus's relationship with Medb is in contrast with Cú Chulainn's response to the advances of a beautiful young woman (who in reality is the Morrígan in disguise): he rejects them, saying that it was not for a woman's buttocks that he had undertaken his task.[82] The warrior is single-minded in pursuit of his aims, and is not to be distracted by sexual temptation. It is true that Cú Chulainn had earlier abandoned his post for an encounter with Fedelm Nóichride, but he does this in fulfilment of a pledge which he has already given, and he takes precautions to ensure that the raiders will not be able to take advantage of his absence.[83]

A further layer of meaning is encoded in the allusion by Conall Cernach, Fergus, and Cú Chulainn to a woman's buttocks. Thomas Charles-Edwards has pointed out that these allusions echo the account given in the laws of the circumstances in which a freeman forfeits his legal rights: he "follows the buttocks of his wife across a boundary,"[84] and henceforth depends for his status upon the status of his wife. This is obviously regarded with disdain: loyalty to kindred is an absolute value, and it is love of kindred which saves Ulster in the *Táin*.[85] In all of this we have further evidence of the "social orientation" of the heroic literature.

It has not been possible to do more in the space at my disposal than to touch upon some aspects of the mythological component in the *Táin*. We can claim, however, that some of the personages, some of the story-patterns, and some incidental details in the *Táin* reflect the Celtic, and even the Indo-European, heritage of Ireland. To the extent that they do so, credit must be divided between the oral traditors who made them available to the epic's authors, and those authors in turn for having used them in their literary work. Out of fairness to these authors, it must be stressed that the *Táin* is no mere "repository of tradition," still less a "dessicated husk."[86] By way of illustration, we may take Cú Chulainn's role as sister's son, which I have already mentioned as part of the ideology of kinship which is presented in the *Táin*. The role of the sister's son, which is also a central concern of *Cath Maige Tuired*, is part of the ideological framework within which the Irish accommodated the story of Christ: so much is clear from the manner in which his life and death are narrated by the eighth-century Blathmac. His work "offers a clear demonstration of the presence of a set of concepts relating to the sister's son in the ideological matrix within which the poet apprehended the life of Jesus. This set of concepts is an inherited one: it is reflected in the kinship terms, in the laws, and in the literature."[87] The ideology which is expressed in the *Táin* includes inherited elements, then, which cannot be dismissed as mere baggage, retained for the purposes of a literature of entertainment. That the ideology which underlies the *Táin* was charged with meaning for the Irish people in the eighth century is shown by Blathmac's recasting of the life of Christ within the framework of that ideology.

Recent scholarship has fruitfully attended to the specifically ecclesiastical elements in early Irish literature. It is important that this new emphasis should not lead to a devaluation of the material which derives from extra-ecclesiastical sources. I have remarked elsewhere that

> early Irish literature is not the detritus of a lost mythology, nor yet a new phenomenon, born, like Athena, fully grown. It is the creation of a society which had two sets of cultural institutions, one indigenous, and oral in its medium, the other ecclesiastical and literate. These were sometimes hostile, sometimes amicable, but between them they contributed to the formation of a literature which combined matter drawn from the oral tradition with other elements and transmuted them into something new.[88]

Ulster's epic, *Táin Bó Cúailnge*, is one of the works of literature which was thus brought into being.

15

Táin Bó Cúailnge and Early Irish Law

(2005)

Táin Bó Cúailnge 'The Cattle-Raid of Cooley' tells of the invasion of Ulster by a great army assembled by Ailill and Medb of Connacht. The army is sometimes referred to as "the men of Ireland": of its eighteen divisions, nine were from Connacht, seven from Munster, and one from Leinster. The remaining division was composed of Ulster exiles, under the leadership of Fergus mac Róich, who had left the province following a dispute with their king, Conchobor mac Nessa. When the invaders set out, on the Monday after *Samain* (November 1), the men of Ulster are disabled by a debility that will last until the beginning of February. The young Cú Chulainn, whose relationship with the Ulstermen is through his mother, is immune from the debility, and much of the tale is devoted to his heroic defence of the province. The invaders wreak terrible destruction upon Ulster but they fail of their primary purpose, which is to secure the Brown Bull of Cooley. And

Cú Chulainn continues to keep them sufficiently at bay until the Ulstermen rise from their torpor and Conchobor leads them to victory in a great battle.

The language of the *Táin* is rich in legal vocabulary. And this is by no means confined to any one stratum in the tradition. The *Táin*, as Thomas Kinsella has put it, is "the work of many hands."[1] It has a long history, much of it no longer recoverable. There are two main recensions.[2] The first of them is a compilation of material, some of it from the ninth century or earlier, and some at least as late as the eleventh; the second recension dates from the twelfth century. Legal language occurs prominently in both of these recensions; it is already very much to the fore in one of the precursors of the *Táin*, a poem attributed to the seventh-century author Luccreth Moccu Chíara, and which, as James Carney has said, "gives us a side-glimpse into the emotional and political background to *Táin Bó Cúailnge*."[3] The legal dimension is foregrounded in the opening sequence of the poem, and we are alerted to it in the first line, *Conailla Medb míchura*, "Medb enjoined evil contracts."[4]

A striking example of the use in the *Táin* of legal terminology will serve to introduce my topic. As the invasion proceeds, Medb is greatly perturbed by the number of her warriors that are slain by Cú Chulainn and she decides upon a plan to bring about his defeat.[5] She arranges with him that they should meet the next day to parley, insisting that he come unarmed to the meeting, since (as she claimed) she would be coming alone, save for her women attendants. Her real intentions are otherwise: she proposes to instruct some of her best warriors to attack Cú Chulainn even as she makes "mock peace" with him. Cú Chulainn, however, takes her at her word and agrees to do as she has asked. Happily for Cú Chulainn, his failure to divine Medb's duplicity is not shared by his charioteer, Lóeg:

"Ced ón, cinnas as áil duit-siu techt i ndáil Medba i mbárach, a Chú Chulainn?" or Láeg.

"Amal conniacht Medb dano," ol Cú Chulaind.

"At móra glonna Medbi," ol in t-ara. "Atágur lám ar cúl aci."

"Cinnas as dénta dún samlaid?" for sé.

"Do chlaideb fót choim," ol in t-ara, "arnachat fagthar i mbáegul, ár ní dlig láech a enecland dia mbé i n-écmais a arm. Conid cáin midlaig no ndlig fón samail sin."

"Déntar amlaid íarom," ol Cú Chulaind.

"How do you intend to go and meet Medb tomorrow?" asked Láeg.

"As Medb asked me," said Cú Chulainn.

"Many are Medb's treacherous deeds," said the charioteer. "I fear that she has help behind the scenes."

"What should we do then?" said he.

"Gird your sword at your waist so that you may not be taken unawares. For if a warrior is without his weapons, he has no right to his honour-price, but in that case he is entitled only to the legal due of one who does not bear arms."

"Let it be done so then," said Cú Chulainn.[6]

When Medb comes to the meeting she sets fourteen warriors in ambush for Cú Chulainn, and when he arrives they all rise up to attack him. He fights back, however, and kills all fourteen of them.

It is no surprise that the older and more worldly-wise Lóeg should press caution upon Cú Chulainn, who is as reckless here in his unwonted pursuit of peace as he is ordinarily impetuous in combat. What is remarkable is that, having commented on Medb's character, the charioteer goes on to coach the warrior in a point of law, telling him how he is putting himself at risk of losing his honor-price. In early Ireland, an individual's honor-price (*eneclann* or *lóg n-enech*) was the measure of his status in what was a highly stratified society; it determined the limits of his legal capacity, and it had to be paid as compensation for serious offences against him. A person could lose some or all of his honor-price if he conducted himself in a way that was inappropriate to one of his rank or office. The Laws tell us how this can happen to a king, and how it can happen to a lord. Two of the ways in which a king might lose his honor-price may be cited here. He will lose it if he goes off hunting by himself, the reason being that a king should always be accompanied by a retinue.[7] A king who does manual work with mallet, spade, or axe has his honor-price reduced to that of a commoner.[8] The Laws do not tell us, as far as I know, how a warrior may suffer the loss or diminution of his honor-price, but what Láeg has to say on the matter in the *Táin* reveals the same kind of thinking as that which we find in the Laws in relation to the king.

The burden of Láeg's remarks is that it is perfectly proper for a warrior to go alone to parley with the enemy. If he does so, however, he must recognize that he is entering into a situation of potential danger, and he should prepare for the worst, at least to the extent of arming himself. If he fails to take this elementary precaution, the compensation due to him for any treachery perpetrated upon him will be based on the honor-price of a mere *midlach*. The general sense of *midlach* in the literature appears to be "a coward, weakling," but its original meaning may be "one incapable of bearing arms, below the status of warrior."[9] It must have this latter sense here, since what is in question is the loss of status. Presumably, any compensation owing in such circumstances would be exacted when hostilities end and the parties make peace.

We have clear intimations here of a law of war. I shall argue presently that there are other indications in the *Táin* that the conduct of war was governed by certain conventions that have the force of customary law. Whether they correspond to the actual law of early medieval Ireland must remain an open question, but the very least that can be said is that they provide a legal framework for the events of the *Táin*. It has of course not gone unnoticed that certain legal concepts are represented in the *Táin*, and I propose now to look all too briefly at five episodes which turn upon or entail points of law. Two of these are included in "The Boyhood Deeds of Cú Chulainn." In the early stages of the raid, the exiled Ulstermen tell their companions stories of Cú Chulainn's extraordinary feats as a boy. In the first of them he goes to join Conchobor's court at Emain Macha (Navan Fort in County Armagh). Still at this stage named Sétantae, he has been living with his father and mother in Mag Muirthemne (in County Louth) when he hears about the king's *macrad* ("[troop of] boys"). In defiance of his mother, he sets out alone on the hazardous journey to Emain Macha to join them. As soon as he arrives, he rushes in among the boys, not knowing that he cannot be admitted to the *macrad* until its members have been enjoined to protect him (*co n-arnastá a fóesam forro*).[10] A fight ensues, and Conchobor eventually seizes Cú Chulainn by the arm:

"Ní maith airráilter in macrad," ol Conchobar.
    "Deithbir dam-sa, a phopa Chonchobair," ol sé. "Dosroacht do chluichiu óm thaig, óm máthair is om athair, 7 ní maith ro mbátar frim."
    "Cia th'ainm-seo?" ol Conchobar.
    "Sétanta mac Súaltaim atomchomnaic-se 7 mac Dechtere do phethar-su. Níba dóig mo chonpére sund."

"Ced náro nass do fóessam-su dano forsna maccu?" ol Conchobar.

"Ni fhetar-sa aní sin," ol Cú Chulaind. "Gaib it láim mo fóesam airtho didiu."

"Atmu," ol Conchobar.

"The boys are not well treated," said Conchobar.

"It was right for me (to treat them so), master Conchobar," said he. "I came to play with them from my home, from my father and mother, and they were not kind to me."

"What is you name?" said Conchobar.

"I am Sétanta the son of Sualtaim and of Deichtire, your sister. It was not to be expected that I should be tormented here."[11]

"Why were the boys not bound over to protect you?" asked Conchobar.

"I did not know of the need of that," said Cú Chulainn. "Undertake to protect me against them."

"I agree (*Atmu*)," said Conchobar.[12]

Thomas Charles-Edwards sees in this episode evidence that in early Ireland a boy, before he took up arms, might form part of a *macrad* in a royal household, and he adds that the *Táin*, "whatever the particular exaggerations it may contain, agrees with the laws that even the games of boys were defined and controlled by law; and both imply the existence of a distinct stage of life governed by such rules."[13]

It should be noted that Cú Chulainn, once he finds out about the rule, sets himself above it. The requirement is that the protection of the new member be bound upon the boys: the wording here, which in the present indicative would be *naiscthir fóesam* X *for* Y, "the protection of X is bound upon Y," is quite clear. To put it another way, Y (the boys) would be enjoined to protect X (Cú Chulainn). But what Cú Chulainn demands, and receives, is something quite different: he is to be protected *against* the boys by the king. In accepting this obligation, Conchobor uses a grammatical form, *atmu*, which indicates that a formal, legally binding, relationship is now being established between Cú Chulainn and Conchobor.[14] Since they are respectively sister's son and mother's brother, the relationship between them is in effect that known as the avunculate, which is an important component of the early Irish kinship system and is richly represented in early Irish literature.[15] Cú Chulainn has now achieved much, but he is not yet finished; he makes a further demand, which must also be out of the ordinary, since it comes as a surprise to the king:

> La sodain doella-som forsin macraid sethnón in taige.
> "Ced taí dano dóib innossa?" ol Conchobar.
> "Coro nastar a fóesam-som form-sa dano," ol Cú Chulaind.
> "Gaib it láim didiu," ol Conchobar.
> "Atmu," ol Cú Chulaind.
>
> ———
>
> But then he [Cú Chulainn] turned again and attacked the boys throughout the house.
> "What have you got against them now?" asked Conchobar.
> "Let me be bound over to protect them," said Cú Chulainn.
> "Undertake it then," said Conchobar.
> "I agree (*Atmu*)," said Cú Chulainn.[16]

So far from needing the protection of the boys, Cú Chulainn now has a formal, legally binding role as their protector.

In interpreting this passage, I have differed somewhat from Thomas Charles-Edwards's understanding of it. But I agree with his characterization of Cú Chulainn here as "a sharp-witted lawyer prepared to bandy legal niceties and exchange correct legal formulae with the king of the Ulstermen himself."[17]

If we might now move forward for a moment to the events of the cattle-raid, we shall find that Cú Chulainn sees his relationship with Conchobor in legal terms as *céilsine* ("clientship, vassalage"). Ailill has begun to fear that the army will not last long with Cú Chulainn killing so many of them, so he sends an emissary to offer him terms (*coma*). He is prepared to offer great gifts to Cú Chulainn in order to induce him to abandon Conchobor and to accept Ailill as his lord instead: "And let him take service with me, it is better for him than to be in the service of a princeling" (*ocus táet im chélsine-sea.*[18] *Is ferr dó oldás célsine óctigern*).[19] The emissary, Mac Roth, goes to the spot where Fergus says that he will find Cú Chulainn, and he addresses the charioteer:

> Imcomairc Mac Roth do Láeg cia díambo chéli.
> "Céle dond fïr uccut tís," or Láeg.

Boí Cú Chulaind i sudiu isin tsnechtu co rrici a dí leiss cen mether imbi oc escaid a léine. Atbeir dano Mac Roth fri Coin Culaind cia díarbo chocéle.

"Céle Conchobair meic Nessa," or Cú Chulaind.

"Indad fil slondud bas derbu?"

"Is lór sin," or Cú Chulaind.

"Anáu cia airm sund hi tá Cú Chulaind?" ol Mac Roth.

"Cid asbérthá fris?" or Cú.

Adfét dó in n-imarchor n-ule amal asrubartmár.

"Cía no beth Cú in n-occus ni dingned insein. Ní rriri bráthair a máthar ar ríg n-aile."

Mac Roth asked Láeg whose vassal he was.

"Vassal to yonder man below," said Láeg.

Cú Chulainn was sitting stark-naked in the snow which reached up to his thighs, examining his shirt for lice. So Mac Roth asked Cú Chulainn whose vassal he was.

"Vassal of Conchobor mac Nessa," said Cú Chulainn.

"Have you no more definite description?"

"That is sufficient," said Cú Chulainn.

"Where is Cú Chulainn then?" asked Mac Roth.

"What would you say to him?" said Cú Chulainn.

So Mac Roth told him the whole story as we have (already) related.

"Even if Cú Chulainn were near at hand, he would not agree to that. He will not exchange his mother's brother for another king."[20]

In this passage, the naked warrior will not even confess that he is Cú Chulainn. He will admit of only one cultural trait: his legal relationship as *céile* to his mother's brother, Conchobor. Lóeg, for his part, sees himself as *céile* to the warrior, suggesting that the relationship between the fighter and his charioteer is legally that of a reciprocal pair, what in Irish would be called *lánamain*. That the lord and his client form such a pair is explicitly stated in the Laws;[21] in this particular case the bond is strengthened immeasurably by Cú Chulainn's undying loyalty to the brother of his mother Dechtine.

Another one of the Boyhood Deeds tells how Sétantae acquired the name Cú Chulainn ("The Hound of Culann"). Conchobor accepts an offer of hospitality from a smith named Culann. He forgets that he has arranged that Sétantae should join them later, and Culann unleashes a fierce guard dog. Sétantae approaches the guard-dog fearlessly, and kills him with his bare hands. Culann is devastated, as he has been depending on the dog to guard his home and livestock. The boy tells him that he will rear a hound of the same breed, and until the hound is grown and fit for action, he will himself be a hound to protect Culann's cattle and his person. Cathbad the druid thereupon confers the name Cú Chulainn upon the boy.

Sétantae's combat with the hound has been seen, quite rightly, as a stage in his initiation into warrior-status, and as an expression of inherited martial ideology. Sétantae's response to Culann's difficulties, on the other hand, as Liam Breatnach has recently shown, "is in accord with the requirements of early Irish legal practice."[22] The law required a person who killed a dog that guarded its owner's livestock to pay a fine and supply a dog of the same breed. A Middle-Irish commentary adds that the person should undertake the functions of the dog until the substitute is trained. As Breatnach has said, Cú Chulainn responds in explicitly legal terms in the second recension:

"Nádbad lond-so etir a mo phopa Culand," ar in mac bec. "Dáig bérat-sa a fírbreth sin." "Ca breth no bérthasu fair, a meic?" for Conchobar. "Má tá culén do ṡíl in chon út i nHérind ailébthair lim-sa gorop inengnama mar a athair. Bam cúsa imdegla a almai 7 a indili 7 a feraind in n-ed sain." "Maith rucais do breth, a meic bic," for Conchobor. "Nís bérmais ém," ar Cathbath, "ní bad ḟerr."

"Be not angry at all, master Culand," said the little boy, "for I shall deliver a true judgment in this matter." "What judgment would you deliver on it, my lad?" said Conchobor. "If there is a whelp of that hound's breeding in Ireland, he will be reared by me until he be fit for action like his sire. I shall myself be the hound to protect Culand's flocks and cattle and land during that time." "A good judgment you have given, little boy," said Conchobor. "I would not have given a better myself," said Cathbad.[23]

I should like to look now at two episodes in the *Táin* that seem to exemplify acts that are mentioned laconically in the Laws. One of these has to do with a satirist named Redg. Ailill and Medb are continually looking for ways to outwit Cú Chulainn. On one occasion, they decide that if Cú Chulainn were deprived of his spear, he would no longer be a formidable foe. Ailill instructs Redg to ask Cú Chulainn for his spear.

"Tuc dam-sa do gaí," or in cánte.
"Acc óm," or Cú, "acht dabér seótu dait."
"Nád géb-sa ón," ar in cáinte.
Gegna-som dano in cáinte úair nad fáet a targid dó, 7 asbert in cánte na bérad a enech mani berad in cletíni. Focheird Cú Chulaind íarom in cletíne dó co lluid triana chend forstarsnu.
"Is tolam in sét se ém!" ol in cáinte.

"Give me your spear," said the satirist.
"No indeed," said Cú Chulainn, "but I will give you treasure."
"I shall not accept that," said the satirist.
So he wounded the satirist since he did not accept what was offered him, and Redg said that he would bring dishonour on him (by satire) unless he got the javelin. So Cú Chulainn threw the javelin at him and it went right through his head.
"This treasure was quickly delivered indeed," said the satirist.[24]

Here we see that, having unsuccessfully tried to buy off the satirist by offering him treasure instead of the spear, Cú Chulainn finds himself in what seems to be an impossible situation: if he parts with his weapon, he will no longer be able to defend Ulster, but if he fails to comply with the satirist's demand he will lose his honor, which is more precious to the warrior than life itself. Cú Chulainn, as we might expect, solves the problem brilliantly: he throws the spear at the satirist and it goes right through his head.

Fergus Kelly has pointed out that in the law text on privileged and professional persons known as *Bretha Nemed toísech*, one of the three qualifications required of the satirist is given as *ailges do ceanduibh co nimderctar gruaide*, which Kelly translates as "an extempore request which causes a blush."[25] Kelly aptly draws attention to Redg's demand in this connection.[26] It is the satirist's business in life to purvey shame, which is physically manifest in a "blush" (literally, "reddening of cheeks"), and this is what would have been visited upon Cú Chulainn, had he not been so swift and inventive of thought and so deft of action. I may draw attention in passing to the play on *sét* 'treasure' in this passage. The satirist asks for the javelin, but is offered "treasures" (*seótu*)[27] instead; when he rejects the offer he nonetheless receives "a treasure" (*sét*), but it is in the form of the javelin and it kills him. This treasure satisfies the satirist's original demand, but does not enrich him any more than it impoverishes Cú Chulainn. Moreover, since

Cú Chulainn is in a position to retrieve his javelin, he is neither dishonored nor disarmed.

The surviving fragments of the seventh-century law text *Cáin Ḟuithirbe* have recently been edited and elucidated by Liam Breatnach.[28] One of the verse-passages in the text has to do with the right of a lord to use violence in certain circumstances, one of which is in response to *géim n-áilgeso*.[29] Breatnach takes this to be "a shout of importuning."[30] The word *áilges* we have already seen in connection with the satirist's extempore request (*áilges di chennaib* in normalized spelling); according to *DIL* (s.v.) it has the "legal sense 'demand, request' (usually made by a poet)," and "the general sense '(importunate) wish or request.'" I suggest that the shout of importuning is exemplified in the *Táin* in the episode entitled *Sírrabad Súaltaim* 'Súaltaim's Long Warning.' Cú Chulainn sends his father Súaltaim to Emain to inform the Ulstermen about what has been happening while they have been debilitated. Three times, from different locations in Emain, he cries out, *Fir gontair, mná brattar, baí agthar!* ("Men are slain, women carried off, cattle driven away").[31] A druid questions him, and he gives a graphic account of the raiders' depredations. Next comes the druid's response:

"Ba huise," ol in draí, "a bás ind fir ro gresi ind ríg."
"Is deithbir dó," ol Conchobar.
"Is dedbir dó," ol Ulaid.
"Is fír a canas Sualdaim," ol Conchobar. "Ón lúan aidche samnai co ricci lúan aidchi imbuilc ocor n-indred."

"It were right," said the druid, "that one who so incited the king should die."
"It is right that he should," said Conchobar.
"It is right," said the Ulstermen.
"What Súaltaim says is true," said Conchobar. "From the Monday on the eve of Samain until the Monday on the eve of Spring we have been ravaged."[32]

The response to Súaltaim's words shows the following order of speaking: the judge pronounces judgment, the king responds to what the judge has said, and the people respond to the king. I have argued elsewhere that a scenario of this kind is to be found in other early Irish sources, both legal and literary.³³ Here we may note how ironic it is that having agreed that Súaltaim should die, Conchobor accepts the truth of what Súaltaim has said, and goes on to act upon it by mustering the men of Ulster. Súaltaim's tragedy is that his desperate plea is adjudged to be an incitement of the king. We could hardly hope to find a better example of "a shout of importuning" than this.

The first recension of the *Táin* opens abruptly with an account of the muster by Ailill and Medb of their "great army"—it is evidently assumed that the reader will have a general acquaintance with their reason for doing so. The second recension, on the other hand, has an elaborate prologue narrating the sequence of events that led up to the cattle-raid. It resolves itself into three parts. In the first of them, the "Pillow Talk," Ailill and Medb argue about the nature of their marriage, and the role of each of them within it. They go on to compare their respective movable wealth, and find that they are equal in every respect save that Medb possesses no bull to correspond with the white-horned bull (Finnbennach) which is in Ailill's possession. Medb then sends an emissary to Cúailnge to obtain a loan for one year of the bull known as Donn Cúailnge. The mission does not succeed, and Medb decrees that the bull should be taken by force.

Ailill and Medb both have recourse to legal terminology as they argue about their marriage. Medb's father left no sons; she claims to have inherited the province of Connacht from him, and to have acted in her own right in contracting the marriage and in giving a dowry (*coibche*) to Ailill.³⁴ She charges Ailill with being *fer for tinchur mná* ("a man dependent on a woman's marriage-portion"). In early Irish law, *tinchor* is used of the property brought into the marriage by either partner: *lánamnas fir for bantinchur* 'a union of a man on woman-property' refers to a marriage to which a man contributes little or nothing.³⁵ In a commentary on this episode, Donnchadh Ó Corráin takes Medb at her word, and says that Ailill is here humiliated.³⁶ But in the text, Ailill offers a very different view of the marriage: he has two brothers among the provincial kings of Ireland, and he says that he ceded kingship to them because they were older. He goes on to claim that "they were no better in bounty and the bestowal of gifts than I" (*níptar ferra im rath nó thidnacul andú-sa*).³⁷ The bestowal of bounty— specifically *rath*—entails the enfeoffing of clients, which is the basis of a lord's rank. Ailill's boast is that in this respect he was the equal of a provincial king before ever he married Medb. Moreover, as the son of a Connacht princess, he claims to have assumed the kingship there in virtue of his mother's rights.

Medb and Ailill make claims that would not be sustainable in Irish law. Being the daughter of a man who has left no sons, Medb is a *banchomarbae* 'female heir,' and as such she could inherit a life-interest in her father's land.[38] But no king would own the land of an entire province, and it follows that Medb could not inherit the province of Connacht. Ailill, for his part, could not assume kingship in virtue of his mother's rights. We are dealing here with an imagined past. And it is worth noting that Ailill's account of the situation is consistent with what we find in the Leinster genealogies, where it is said that Medb went with the Connachtmen to Leinster and that they took Ailill back with them as their king because his mother was one of them (*ar ba díb a máthair*).[39] What we are given in the Pillow Talk is an argument: there are two views of the marriage, and there is no reason why one of them should be privileged above the other. Medb does not demur at Ailill's rejection of her characterization of the marriage: in fact, they arrive at a resolution of their difficulty in every respect except the narrow one of which of them now possesses the greater wealth. A balanced view of the argument would be that, legally at least, theirs is a marriage of equals. In property terms, as we have seen, the only difference between them is that Ailill possesses a bull and Medb does not: it is in order to remove this discrepancy that Medb instigates the raid on Ulster to secure the Brown Bull of Cooley.

This brings us to a consideration of the cause of war. The opening words of the first recension are *Tarcomlad slóiged mór la Connachtu .i. la hAilill 7 la Meidb*, "A great army was mustered by the Connachtmen, that is, by Ailill and Medb." As it happens, the Laws tell us the circumstances in which a king may legitimately require his subjects to answer a call to a *slóiged* 'muster.' According to *Críth Gablach*, there are three of them;[40] it will suffice here to say that a cattle-raid on another jurisdiction is not among them. The list is doubtless indicative rather than comprehensive, but the omission of cattle-raiding is surely deliberate. A. T. Lucas has said of cattle-raiding that "nothing in Irish society is better documented over so long a period. It is the most typical and abiding event recorded in the annals down the centuries and it pervades almost every branch of Irish literature."[41] Lucas failed to find any mention of the practice in the texts of the Laws, although he pointed to some references in the later commentaries. The Church was strongly opposed to cattle-raiding. One of the *Penitentials* states that "cattle seized in a raid are not to be taken by Christians whether in trade or as gifts: for what Christ rejects how shall the soldier of Christ receive?"[42] This is suitably high-minded, but Fergus Kelly suggests that the Church's attitude may have been partly motivated by its own extensive farming interests.[43] The position in any case is that cattle-raiding was not countenanced by the law and was condemned by the Church, but nevertheless seems to have been much practiced by otherwise estimable persons in society. An analogy from relatively recent times that comes to mind is the illicit making and marketing of *poitín*.

I now wish to consider what the *Táin* has to tell us about the conduct of war. Before the army sets out on its illegal raid, Medb receives a prophecy that there will be much bloodshed. This does not faze her: "for in every muster and in every army assembled in a great encampment there are quarrels and strife and bloody woundings" (*ar bít imserga 7 círgala 7 fuili fordergga i cach slúag 7 i cach thaurchomrac dúnaid móir*).[44] And indeed the first thing that happens when the army have camped after the first stage of their journey is a quarrel, instigated by Medb, and which threatens to engulf the entire army "in strife and bloody woundings." Medb is alarmed when she notices the general efficiency of the division of the Gailióin (from Leinster), and she says that they should be slain. Fergus opposes this: "It shall not happen unless we are all killed, for they are allies of us Ulstermen (*is áes comchotaig dúinni 'nar nUltaib*)."[45] As the argument proceeds, it emerges that the seven kings of Munster, each of whom has a division, are similarly allied (*comchotach*)[46] to the exiled Ulstermen. If battle is to be joined then and there among the invaders, as Fergus threatens, the nine divisions of the Connachtmen will face nine divisions under Fergus's command. As it happens, Fergus proposes a compromise that diffuses the row: the Gailióin will be distributed among the other divisions. But the inherent instability of the invading army has been shown up. Fully half of it is expected to respond to Fergus's command. The nature of the *comchotach* (lit. "mutual covenant") is clarified for us in Recension II, where Fergus declares: "I myself am bond and surety and guarantee for them since they came from their own lands, and me shall they uphold in this day of battle" (*Messi dano as chor 7 as glinni 7 trebairi friu ó tháncatar ó crichaib dílsib fadesin, 7 lim congébat 'sind ló bága sa*).[47] What is perhaps of greatest significance about the covenant is that it is made with Fergus and his companions *as Ulstermen*. This is something that Cú Chulainn will be able to exploit in the course of the raid. For example, when the Munster king Lugaid mac Nóis visits him, Cú Chulainn reminds Lugaid of his alliance (*cocéle*) with the men of Ulster, and Lugaid in turn asks for a truce (*cairte*) for his company. Cú Chulainn agrees to grant this to Lugaid and to Fergus, and also to the physicians, provided that they swear to preserve his life and send him food every night.[48]

Fergus has an especially affectionate relationship with Cú Chulainn, who is his foster-son.[49] This is seen at various points in the story, but nowhere more tellingly than at the final battle, when Fergus honors an agreement to stand back from Cú Chulainn, just as Cú Chulainn had done when he faced Fergus earlier in the course of the raid. Thereupon, "Fergus and his division of three thousand went away. The men of Leinster and the men of Munster went away too, and nine divisions, those of Medb and of Ailill and of their seven sons, were left in the battle" (*Luid Fergus as íarom in tan sin cona thríchtaib cét. Lotar didiu in Gaileóin 7 na Muimnich, 7 fácbaid noí tríchaid cét Medba 7 Ailella 7 a secht mac isin chath*).[50] The game is now up for Ailill and Medb: Cú Chulainn comes to the battle at midday, and by sundown he has overcome the last of the invaders.

Fergus reveals his loyalty to Ulster almost immediately after the difficulty over the Gailióin has been sorted out. The army is led astray across bogs and streams until they reach Granard in County Longford. Fergus is then asked to lead the army, but he takes them far astray to the south on what Medb calls a *fordul*.[51] He does this out of love for his own kin (*condalbae*),[52] and it is *condalbae* too which motivates him to send a warning to Ulster about the impending raid.[53] I have argued elsewhere that *condalbae* is what ultimately determines the outcome of the cattle-raid, bringing victory to the Ulstermen over the invaders.[54] Here I would merely add that the Laws also show awareness of the power of *condalbae*: it is not right for a king to retain among his mercenary soldiers a man whom he spares in battle "lest he betray him through feelings of grievance or patriotism (*condalbae*)."[55]

Cú Chulainn receives Fergus's warning, and goes to Iraird Cuillenn (six miles from Kells in County Meath) to watch out for the invaders. On the very night when he expects them to arrive, he feels obliged to go to his concubine, as he has pledged to do. He forms a branch into a hoop, fixes it with a peg, and with one hand throws it over a pillar stone. On the peg of the hoop he leaves an inscription in ogam saying that none of them should pass until one of them, other than Fergus, should likewise succeed in throwing such a hoop over a pillar stone.

This act—described in the text as "containment of chiefs" (*astúd rurech*)⁵⁶—does give the army pause, and we shall see that it contains a crucial indication as to how the invaders should conduct themselves. Two similar acts follow. First, Cú Chulainn cuts and throws a forked branch with one hand, and leaves an inscription saying that they should not pass unless one of them, other than Fergus, can equal that feat. This is when the invaders rest, and the Boyhood Deeds of Cú Chulainn are related. Secondly, Cú Chulainn cuts down an oak-tree in the army's path and writes an ogam inscription on it, saying that none should go past it until a warrior should leap across it in a chariot. Thirty horses fall in the attempt, and thirty chariots are broken. Cú Chulainn has not made an exception of Fergus on this occasion and it is Fergus who leaps across the oak-tree in his own chariot. The cattle-raid can now proceed in earnest.

Let us return now to the throwing of the hoop, and the response of the invaders. Fergus reads out the inscription, and questions the druids about it. One of the druids responds:

Crephnas churad caur rod lá
lánaingces for erreda,
astúd rurech ferg i ndá
óenfer co n-óenláim ro lá.

In nách diá réir slúag ind ríg
inge má ro choilled (v.l. ro choillset) fír
conid ro lá úaib nammá
óenfer amal fer ro lá
Nocon fetur acht insin
Ní frisi corthe in t-id.

———

A hero cast it there, the swift cutting (?) of a hero, a source of perplexity to warriors, containment of chiefs with their followers.⁵⁷
One man cast it there with one hand.

Does not the king's army obey him unless they have broken faith?
I know no reason why the withe was cast there save that one of you should cast a withe even as one man did.⁵⁸

In mentioning what O'Rahilly translates as "breaking faith," the druid adds significantly to what Fergus has said about the inscription. He does so politely, in the form of a question: there is no "shout of importunity" here. But the burden of what he has to say will not be lost on anyone who is acquainted with early Irish ideology. The word *fír* has to do with what is just and true. It is used of solemn utterances, notably judgments and oaths, and of the ordeal, in which the immediate judgment of the deity is secured. Kinsella's translation at this point, "the rule of war," gets the point across quite effectively. What the druid is saying, surely, is that if the invaders do not comply with Cú Chulainn's demand they will have acted unjustly and improperly, and in the present context this means that they will have broken the law of war. A provision in *Cáin Ḟuithirbe* may be relevant here: it states that a lord is justified in using violence when there is *cath cen lethroí fír*.[59] Breatnach translates, "a battle without the other side having a just cause."[60] I have no argument with this translation, but I would suggest that it could also mean "a battle in which the other side does not act according to the law of war." The conduct, no less than the cause, of war must accord with *fír*.

This brings us to the matter of *fír fer*, literally "truth of men."[61] The first mention of this in the *Táin* comes relatively early, when three warriors together with their three charioteers go to do battle with Cú Chulainn, and he kills all of them "for they have broken the terms of fair play" (*úair ro brisiset fír fer fair*).[62] It comes up again in the highly charged discussion that follows the cuckolding of Ailill by Fergus: "'Let me go in front with the banished Ulstermen,' said Fergus, 'to make sure that the lad gets fair play with the cattle before us and the army in our rear, and the women folk behind the army'" (*"Rom lécid-sa com loingis hi tossuch," or Fergus, "ar náro brister fír fer forin gillae, 7 na baí riund 7 in slúag inar ndeóid 7 na mná ina ndíaid-side"*).[63]

I have already mentioned that an emissary was sent by Ailill to offer terms to Cú Chulainn. The outcome was that Ailill's various offers were rejected. The emissary finally asks:

"In fil na aill didiu?"

"Fil," ol Cú Chulaind, "7 ní epér frit-su. Dothíasar fair má atchosse nech dúib."

"Rafetar-sa," or Fergus. "Dam-sa ararocles in fer a ḟoilsigud, 7 immorro ní less dúib-si. Ocus iss ed inso in choma," or Fergus. ".i. áth forsi ngénathar a gléo 7 a chomrac fri óenfer arná ructhar ind éit de sin láa co n-aidchi dús in táir cobair Ulad fóo. . . ."

"Is assu ém dúinni," or Ailill, "in fer cech laí andás a cét cach aidchi."

"Is there anything else then?"

"There is," said Cú Chulainn, "but I shall not tell you. It will be agreed to if some one (else) tell you."

"I know what it is," said Fergus. "The man has arranged that I should make it known. But indeed it is of no advantage to you. These then are the terms: that for a day and a night the cattle shall not be taken away from the ford on which he shall fight in single combat, in the hope that help may come from the Ulstermen to him...."

"It is better for us indeed," said Ailill, "to lose one man every day than a hundred men every night."[64]

Fergus reports back to Cú Chulainn: terms of engagement have now been agreed. It is not altogether clear from the passage that I have just quoted that Ailill and Medb give Fergus sureties for the agreement. It becomes evident later when Fergus demands on the strength of his sureties that *fír fer* not be violated against Cú Chulainn.[65] Once again the second recension is more explicit. In describing Fergus's role in negotiating the agreement they quote him as saying:

"Co tartar cuir 7 glinni, rátha 7 trebairi imm airisium arna comai sin 7 'ma tabairt di Choin Chulaind." "Ataimim-si ém," ar Medb, 7 aurnaidmis Fergus fón samail cétna foraib.

"Let pledges and covenants, bonds and guarantees be given for abiding by those terms and for fulfilling them to Cú Chulainn." "I agree to that," said Medb, and Fergus bound them to security in the same way.[66]

It has to be said that Ailill and Medb show no real commitment to the terms that they have negotiated. Medb does not hesitate to send her warriors to attack Cú Chulainn in numbers: "Attack him vigorously ... over the ford from the west, so that ye may cross the river, and let terms of fair play be broken against him" (*"Berid grem catha chuci ... tarsin n-áth aníar co ndigsid taris, 7 brister fír fer fair"*).[67] Time and again, the narrator charges Ailill and Medb with violating *fír fer*. Medb's use of the phrase suggests that they are well aware of the nature of their transgression, and this is borne out in an episode in the second recension when the invaders agree to send Calatín Dána with his sons and grandson against Cú Chulainn:

bad fíadnaisi d'Fergus ra naidmthea sain, 7 ra fémmid tiachtain taris. Dáig iss ed ra ráidsetar corbo chomlund óenfir leó Calatín Dána cona sécht maccaib fichet 7 a úa Glass mac Delga, dáig iss ed ra ráidset corbo ball dá ballaib a mac 7 corbo irrand dá irrandaib 7 combad ra Calatín Dána sochraiti a chuirp fadessin.

This agreement was made in the presence of Fergus but he was unable to dispute it; for they said that they counted it as single combat (that) Calatín Dána and his twenty-seven sons and his grandson Glas mac Delga (should all engage in the fight), for they asserted that his son was (but) one of his limbs and one of his parts and that the issue of his own body belonged to Calatín Dána.[68]

The concept of *fír fer* seems to operate at two levels in the *Táin*. In the first place, there is a legal requirement for numerical parity in combat. The law privileges single combat. It is true that in *Gúbretha Caratniad*,[69] an exception is allowed, but as O'Leary remarks, this text—"The False Judgments of Caratnia"—"makes its points by having Caratnia appear to rule against the most fundamental Irish legal concepts."[70] In other words, the exception very much proves the rule. Caratnia generally offers a sound reason for his departure from the general rule, but his justification for departing from the rule of numerical parity is so weak that Thurneysen dismissed it as a juridical joke.[71]

Secondly, the general requirement is formalized in the terms of engagement proposed by Cú Chulainn, accepted by Ailill and Medb, and guaranteed by Fergus. It is also formalized to varying degrees in the verbal exchanges accompanying so many of the combats described in the *Táin*. Ward Parks[72] has examined the contractual dimension of exchanges of this kind in the Homeric and Old English traditions, and Bernard Martin[73] and William Sayers[74] have looked at the *Táin* in the light of Parks's work. For reasons of space, I must pass over this material here. All I can do is to point out that, taken together, Cú Chulainn's encounters with his opponents entail a very great deal of legal activity, including on occasion the solemn renunciation of a bond (*cotach*) which had existed between the combatants,[75] and in the case of Fer Diad an elaborate contract (*córaidecht*) between the individual warrior and those for whom he fights.[76]

We can now throw more light on Cú Chulainn's ogam inscriptions. While they are not invitations to single combat, they represent a challenge from one warrior to any one of the invaders to equal what the challenger has achieved. It is comparable to the single combat in that it allows an individual to prove himself in the face of overwhelming odds. Numerical strength may bring victory, but a victory that is true and just will depend on the superiority of one warrior pitched against another. It is in that sense that *fír fer* is an ordeal by single combat.

I do not suggest that the ways in which legal concepts are observed in the *Táin* necessarily correspond in precise detail to what is presented in the law texts. The *Táin* is a work of literature—an epic—and the focus is on the heroism of an individual in circumstances that would not be replicated in the "real world." The account that I have given of my topic is by no means exhaustive, and yet I hope that it will now be clear that some understanding of the language and concepts of early Irish law enriches our understanding of what happens in *Táin Bó Cúailnge*.

16

Sírrabad Súaltaim and the Order of Speaking among the Ulaid

(2005)

Ba airmert di Ulltaib ní labrad nech díb acht fri Conchobar, ní labrad Conchobar acht ressna tríb druídib. "It was the practice (?) of the Ulstermen that any one of them would speak only to Conchobor, and Conchobor would speak only to the three druids." (Irish text, *TBC I*, 104; translation mine)

Is amlaid ro bátar Ulaid, geiss d'Ultaib labrad rena ríg, geis don ríg labrad rena druídib. "This is how it was with the Ulstermen: it was tabu for them to speak before their king and it was tabu for the king to speak before his druids." (*TBC LL*, 111 [text]; 246 [translation])

These sentences are taken respectively from the first and second recensions of *Táin Bó Cúailnge* 'The Cattle-Raid of Cooley' (henceforth the

16. *Sírrabad Súaltaim* and the Order of Speaking among the Ulaid 239

Táin), which recounts a prehistoric raid upon Ulster at a time when the Ulstermen suffer a debility that prevents them from defending their province. For three months the defence of Ulster falls to the young Cú Chulainn who, together with his father Súaltaim, is immune from the debility. The text I have given is in each case that of the standard edition, as is the translation from Recension II. Reasons for rejecting O'Rahilly's translation of the passage in Recension I will be set out below, and it will further be suggested that an earlier state of the Irish text of the passage is recoverable from the manuscript readings.

The observation occurs in each case as a narratorial intrusion in the episode entitled *Sírrabad Súaltaim* ("Súaltaim's Long Warning"), which comes at a point in the *Táin*[1] when Cú Chulainn has defended Ulster for the duration of the Ulstermen's debility and lies prostrate from his wounds. Súaltaim has had no part in the defence of Ulster, but at his home in Mag Muirthemne he now receives intimations of an assault upon Cú Chulainn. He cries out: "Is it the sky that cracks, or the sea that overflows its boundaries, or the earth that splits, or is it the loud cry of my son fighting against odds?" He goes to Cú Chulainn, who dispatches him to the court of Conchobor king of Ulster at Emain Macha: "'Go to the men of Ulster,' said Cú Chulainn, 'and let them give battle to the warriors at once. If they do not, vengeance will never be taken on them.'" Súaltaim goes to Emain and delivers his "warning" to the men of Ulster in the words, "Men are slain, women carried off, cattle driven away." This he does three times. He receives no immediate answer, and the narratorial observation is intruded at this point by way of explanation. The druid questions Súaltaim, who responds with a succinct, if chilling, summary of the events of the cattle-raid. The druid charges him with inciting the king, and sentences him to death for it. The king concurs in this, even though he adjudges the substance of Súaltaim's warning to be no more than the truth. The assembled Ulstermen add their consent.

Súaltaim rushes out, but he falls on his shield, the rim of which cuts off his head. His horse brings the head back into Emain on the shield, and in a final dramatic act the severed head utters the same warning as before.

Conchobor now speaks at greater length, in words which at once malign and vindicate Súaltaim: "'Too loud was that shout indeed,' said Conchobor. 'The sea is before them, the sky above them, the earth beneath them. I shall restore every cow to its byre and every woman and boy to their homes after victory in battle.'"[2] He is critical of Súaltaim's shout but unwittingly echoes his portentous words about the sky, the sea, and the earth. He promises to act and, true to his word, immediately sets about mustering the men of Ulster. Súaltaim's warning has had the desired effect, and the wrongs inflicted upon Ulster and upon its defender, Súaltaim's own son, will soon be avenged in the "great battle."

This remarkable episode, framed by the cosmic motif of earth, sky, and sea that has been discussed by Sayers (1986) and L. Mac Mathúna (1999), is of the first importance in the plot of the *Táin*. What I propose to do now is to focus on what Súaltaim says to the Ulstermen, and on their response to him, according to the account given in Recension I. Súaltaim's intervention has all the appearance of being a ritual warning. That it is received and responded to in a quasi-juridical manner should be clear in the following analysis, in which I intersperse my own comments (in italic) with the text of this part of *Sírrabad Súaltaim*, as translated by O'Rahilly (*TBC I*, 217).

1. *Submission: Súaltaim calls out three times, in three phrases, from three different parts of Emain.*

    Súaltaim came to Emain and called out to the men of Ulster:
    "Men are slain, women carried off, cattle driven away!"
    His first shout was from the side of the court, his second from the ramparts of the royal residence, his third from the Mound of the Hostages in Emain.

2. *Examination: Súaltaim is questioned by a druid.*

    No one answered, for it was tabu for the Ulstermen that any of them should speak before Conchobor, and Conchobor spoke only before the three druids.
    "Who carries them off? Who drives them away? Who slays them?" asked the druid.

3. *Detailed submission: Súaltaim responds to the druid.*

    "Ailill mac Máta slays them, carries them off, drives them away, with the guidance of Fergus mac Róig," said Súaltaim. "Your people have been harassed as far as Dún Sobairche. Their cows, their women-folk, and their cattle have been carried off. Cú Chulainn has not let them come into Mag Muirthemne and Crích Rois during the three months of winter. Bent hoops (of wood) hold his mantle (from touching him). Dry wisps plug his wounds. He has been wounded and bled profusely (?)."

4. *Sentence: the druid says that Súaltaim should die.*
    "It were right," said the druid, "that one who so incited the king should die."
5. *The king concurs with the druid.*
    "It is right that he should," said Conchobor.
6. *The people concur with the king.*
    "It is right," said the Ulstermen.
7. *Substantive judgment: the king accepts the truth of Súaltaim's submission.*
    "What Súaltaim says is true," said Conchobor. "From the Monday on the eve of Samain until the Monday on the eve of spring we have been ravaged."

The version of the *Sírrabad* in Recension II is at once longer and less complete than that of the first. Several touches have been added in this version such as the amusing remark that "Sualtaim was not a coward but neither was he a valiant warrior but only a middling one."[3] The first four stages that we have discerned in the first version—submission, examination, detailed submission, and sentence—are found here. The fact that Súaltaim "got not the answer that sufficed him from the Ulstermen" is emphasized here, and the detailed response to the druid's examination is longer and more provocative than that in the first version. It ends with an ultimatum, "And unless ye avenge this at once, ye will never avenge it until the end of doom and life." This is no more than an echo of Cú Chulainn's words to Súaltaim when he was sending him on his way, but it is perhaps understandable that a poor view was taken of it at Emain. The text continues as follows:

"More fitting is death and destruction for the man who so incites the king," said Cathbath the druid. "That is true indeed," said all the Ulstermen. Sualtaim went his way in anger and wrath since he had not got the answer which sufficed him from the Ulstermen.

Here we have the fourth and sixth stages—the druid's sentence and the concurrence of the people—but stage five, the king's concurrence, is lacking. Conchobor has no part in this exchange; he only speaks when Súaltaim's severed head repeats the warning for the fourth time. As the narrative stands, then, the people infringe the *geis* by speaking immediately after the druid, instead of waiting for the king to have his say.

The ritualistic character of Súaltaim's warning is immediately evident in the fact that he delivers it three times, in three phrases, from three different parts of Emain Macha. In its threefold structure, Súaltaim's warning is reminiscent of a *rabad* in *Scéla Cano Meic Gartnáin* 'The Story of Cano son of Gartnán' (Binchy 1963, 2–4). Cano has come to Ireland to escape from his enemy Áedán mac Gabráin, and is enjoying the hospitality of the joint-kings of Tara, Diarmait and Blathmac, when a secret delegation from Áedán offers them a reward for Cano's head. The joint-kings seem happy to entertain this offer. A daughter of Diarmait's, who has fallen in love with Cano, overhears their conversation, and goes to alert Cano. She takes a switch in her hand, and positions herself on the lintel of the entrance to the residential enclosure. Cano then makes to leave the enclosure, armed with a single spear. Speaking in verse, Diarmait's daughter tells him that he is inadequately armed, and warns him to be wary. The warning is in three parts. The first is a quatrain, addressed to Cano as he comes out of the house in which he has been staying, and the second a quatrain spoken as he passes through the gateway of the enclosure. The third part of the warning comprises three quatrains that she recites to him as he goes away from her. Diarmait's daughter uses the switch to accompany her words: as Cano passes under the lintel she places the switch on his head, and as he comes out she deals him a blow. Cano's response to all of this is to say: "This is a warning (*robad*),[4] girl," to which she replies: "If it is a warning there is a reason for it. Silver which is to be given as a reward for killing you is being weighed in that house over there." I have suggested elsewhere that the *rabad* given in *Scéla Cano* is "a ritual warning, delivered in verse, and divided into three parts (1 + 1 + 3) by the use of simple actions with a switch, these actions being in themselves an inherent part of the ritual" ("The Rhetoric of *Scéla Cano Meic Gartnáin*," p. 368 in this volume). Cano's response, which at first sight seems rather bathetic, is an acknowledgement that he has been the recipient of a solemn ritual warning.

The warning given to Cano, for all its solemnity, is a private communication. Súaltaim, on the other hand, delivers a warning to the king in his court, and (according to the first recension) the druid, king, and people respond in that order. The second recension states that they are bound by *geis* to do so, and there is a similar comment in *Mesca Ulad* 'The Intoxication of the Ulstermen': *Óen do gessib Ulad labrad ríana ríg 7 óen do gessib in ríg labrad ríana druídib* (Watson 1941, 11); "One of the prohibitions of the men of Ulster was to speak before their king, and one of the prohibitions of the king was to speak before his druids" (Watson 1942, 8). It must be said that this *geis* does not appear to loom large in the everyday life of the Ulstermen as it is depicted generally in the sagas: they frequently speak before their king does, and the king, for his part, does not often seem constrained to wait for a druid to speak before him. There is no contradiction here, once we recognize that the *geis* applies only in certain circumstances.

In *Mesca Ulad*, the requisite order of speaking is revealed by the narrator in the context of an agreement that Conchobor and his retinue should attend two banquets in succession on the one night. The first of them is to be hosted until midnight by Fintan son of Niall Niamglonnach, the second thereafter by Cú Chulainn. While the Ulstermen are enjoying Fintan's hospitality, Cú Chulainn sends his charioteer, Lóeg, to observe the stars and to find out when midnight will come; when it does so, Lóeg addresses Cú Chulainn:

> "It is midnight now, O hound of feats," said he.
> When Cú Chulainn heard it he told Conchobar; Cú Chulainn was in the hero's seat before him. Conchobar arose with the speckled bright horn of a buffalo. Mute and silent were the men of Ulster when they saw the king standing. Such was their silence that if a needle fell from roof-tree to floor it would be heard.
> One of the prohibitions of the men of Ulster was to speak before their king, and one of the prohibitions of the king was to speak before his druids.
> Then said Cathbad the noble glorious druid: "What is that, O illustrious high king of Ulster, O Conchobar?"
> "It is Cú Chulainn; he thinks it is time to go and drink his banquet."
> "If he wished to earn the blessing of the men of Ulster all together and to leave our weak ones and our women and our youths behind!"
> "I should wish it," said Cú Chulainn, "provided that our heroes and our champions and our men of battle, our musicians and poets and minstrels come with us." (Watson 1942, 8)

It is clear in this passage that the order of speaking becomes relevant only once Cú Chulainn has spoken and Conchobor has risen to his feet. Cú Chulainn evidently does not infringe the prohibition by speaking to

Conchobor in the first place. The dramatic character of Conchobor's response to Cú Chulainn's petition presumably arises from the circumstances in which it is delivered as much as from its content: speaking to the king from the hero's seat, Cú Chulainn demands that the Ulstermen interrupt their revelry, and travel (as previously agreed) to Cú Chulainn's home to partake of a second feast.

This is a serious request made to the king in public, and it initiates a solemn, or at least a formal, procedure. The king takes the first step, when he rises to his full height with the drinking horn[5] in his hand. While this silences the assembled Ulstermen, it is evidently a signal to the druid to ask the king what the matter is. Conchobor passes on Cú Chulainn's petition. The king makes no substantive response to the petition: it falls to the druid to give a judgment, which is that the petition should be granted on certain conditions. Cú Chulainn accepts these conditions. Contrary to what we have seen in *Sírrabad Súaltaim*, neither king nor people make any comment on the druid's judgment. That the acquiescence of the king would be required goes without saying. And the concurrence of the people is implicit in the terms in which the druid speaks to Cú Chulainn: he tells him what he must agree to do if he is to receive "the blessing of the people of Ulster."

The prescribed order of speaking is mentioned, both in the *Táin* and in *Mesca Ulad*, in relation to a formal response made to a public address or submission to the king. It is a reasonable inference that it applies only in such situations.

I turn now to the wording of the narratorial comment in Recension I of the *Táin*. Of the four manuscripts that preserve texts (all of them incomplete) of this recension, only *Y* (The *Yellow Book of Lecan*) and *C* (*O'Curry* MS 1) contain *Sírrabad Súaltaim*. The readings (including the immediately preceding sentence) are as follows:

Y: Ní frecart nech. Ba airmert di Ulltaib ní labrad nech díb acht fri Concobar, ní labrad Concobar acht ressna tríb druídib. (*TBC I*, lines 3428–29; Strachan and O'Keeffe 1913, lines 2987–89; the first *acht* is in the margin, the second added later under the line)

C: Ni freccart nech do Ultaib. Ua hairmbert di Ultaib ni di lapradh acht fri Concobor. Ni laprad Conchobar acht fri nech dinaib trib druithibh. (Ó Fiannachta 1966, lines 2556–58)

Neither of these readings is entirely satisfactory. The parallelism in *C* between *fri Concobor* and *fri nech* is superior to *Y*, which has *fri Concobar*, but *ressna tríb druídib*. On the other hand, *C* has the clearly erroneous *ni di lapradh* in the second sentence. On the face of it, an eclectic text seems to be called for. O'Rahilly in her edition prints the text of *Y*, giving variants from *C* in footnotes. She translates: "No one answered, for it was tabu for the Ulstermen that any of them should speak before Conchobar, and Conchobar spoke only before the three druids" (*TBC LL*, 217). In a note (*TBC LL*, 289), she says: "*Acht* has twice been added in *Y*. Here the compiler has confused *re n-*, *ria n-* with *fri* (*ri*). The original reading must have been something like *ní labrad nech díb ria Conchobar; ni labrad Conchobar riasna druídib*. This is the reading in Recension II and in *MU*." Her translation of these two clauses is an unhappy compromise between what is preserved in *Y* and what she assumes, on the basis of Recension II and *Mesca Ulad*, to have stood in the original text. In the manuscript readings, and indeed in what O'Rahilly posits as the original reading, it seems clear that the two clauses are parallel, and that they are logically (though not grammatically) dependent on *airmert*. The parallelism is lost in O'Rahilly's translation, for in the first clause O'Rahilly translates *ria* instead of *acht fri* (the reading of both manuscripts), whereas in the second clause she retains the *acht*.

Let us look at this matter afresh, paying attention to *C* as well as to *Y*, and setting aside for the moment Recension II and *Mesca Ulad*. The text of *C* is significantly different from that of *Y*, and cannot therefore be dependent upon it. The preposition *fri* occurs twice in *C* and once in *Y*: this would suggest that we are dealing with *labraithir fri* 'speaks to' and that the *ressna* of *Y* is an innovation. Crucially, however, the *re* combined with the article in *ressna* should be taken, not as *ré, ría* 'before,' but rather as the late form of *fri*. The forms *ri, re*, arising from the lenition of the initial are found already in the Milan Glosses: *DIL*, s.v. *fri*, cites *a lethe rissa n-ingraim*, "as to the persecution" (*Thes.* i, 64 [Ml. 30b2]), and *oc eregim re Abisilon*, "complaining with regard to Absalom" (*Thes.* i, 125 [Ml. 44b4]).

In Old Irish *fri* takes the accusative. In Middle Irish, however, *fri/ri/re* is frequently followed by the dative, and this is reflected in *Y*.[6] The original reading is doubtless reflected in *C*, where the reference is to speaking to one of the three druids—*fri nech dinaib trib druithibh*—which after all is in keeping with what Conchobor does in the text.

Acht occurs twice in *C*, and in *Y* it has been added in the margin and under a line. Once it is recognized that the phrase we are dealing with is *labraithir fri*, we have to retain *acht* in both instances. It would make no sense to say: "none of them used to speak to Conchobor, and Conchobor used not to speak to the three druids" (or "one of the three druids"). Since *ní . . . acht* means "only," the literal sense of what the narrator is saying here is that the people of Ulster would speak only to Conchobor, and Conchobor would speak only to a druid. Taken in the context of a public address or submission to the king, I suggest that what we are being told here is that neither the people nor the king will respond directly to a petitioner. It must be remembered that the narratorial comment is offered as an explanation of *Ní frecart nech* (*di Ultaib*), "No one (none of the Ulstermen) replied." When the druid pronounces sentence the king speaks to him in response, and then the people speak in response to the king.

There remains the variation *airmbert/airmert*. If we have to do here, as Charles-Edwards (1999, 57) has plausibly suggested, with the verbal noun of *ar-imbir*, *C* has the older spelling. On the basis of the foregoing, I propose reading:

> *Ba airmbert di Ultaib ní labrad nech díb acht fri Conchobor, ní labrad Conchobor acht fri nech dinaib trib druidib.*

The imperfect indicative is used of the actions to which *airmbert* refers, and Charles-Edwards (1999, 57) argues that in this instance it probably means "(negative) custom, practice." We may translate:

> It was the practice (?) of the Ulstermen that any one of them would speak only to Conchobor, and that Conchobor would speak only to one of the three druids.

In Recension II and *Mesca Ulad*, *fri* has been replaced by *ré*, *ría*; the *airmert* has become a *geis* and the syntax has been changed accordingly. We have seen that the sequence druid, king, people is not fully realized in either of them. Nevertheless, the observation in its revised form remains consistent with the narrative context, since the people do not speak before the king does, and he does not speak before the druid.

The role of the druid here is analogous to that of the judge as depicted in the law-text *Gúbretha Caratniad* 'The False Judgments of Caratnia'

16. *Sírrabad Súaltaim* and the Order of Speaking among the Ulaid 247

(Thurneysen 1925), which, as Fergus Kelly has remarked, points to a practice of consultation between king and judge:

> Caratnia was the judge—doubtless legendary—of King Conn Cétchathach. Whenever a request for judgement was brought to Conn he would refer it to Caratnia. In each of the 51 cases quoted (involving a wide variety of legal issues) the king challenges Caratnia's decision with the words *ba gó* 'it was false,' but Caratnia is able to defend every judgement. It is clear, therefore, that the author of the text envisaged that a law-case would normally be decided by a judge, but that a king would confirm—or perhaps overturn—the judgement. (Kelly 1988, 24)

While the actions of king and judge in this scenario are parallel to those of king and druid in *Sírrabad Súaltaim* as we find it in Recension I, there is no reference in *Gúbretha Caratniad* to the assent of the people.

For a striking instance of that, we may turn to the origin-legend of the kingship of Cashel. *Senchas Fagbála Caisil* 'The Story of the Finding of Cashel' (Dillon 1952) tells how Corc mac Luigdech came to be the first king of Cashel. Two swineherds discover Cashel, and as they sleep it is revealed to them that Corc and his descendants will reign there. One of them utters "The Sayings of Cuirirán the Swineherd," which Dillon (1952, 61) describes as "a long rhetoric . . . which is evidently archaic but very corrupt." The rhetoric is in two parts, both of which, as Fergus Kelly (1976, 72–74) has shown, contain some material from the wisdom text *Audacht Moraind* 'The Testament of Morann.' After the first part the king responds to the swineherd, saying: *Rob fír fírthar, rob bríg brígther,* "May it be a truth that is confirmed; may it be a power that is enforced," and the people answer: "Amen." The king's response is repeated after the second part, and we are presumably to understand that the people answered the king on this occasion also. What is represented here is clearly a solemn public ceremony. Building on a suggestion of Francis John Byrne's, Kelly (1976, xiv) says that "this episode may reflect the traditional inauguration procedure, i.e. the public recital of a speculum by a druid or member of the learned caste (here replaced by a swineherd) to which the king expresses his consent, followed by the people." He is followed in this by Watkins (1979, 183–84).

A somewhat similar interaction of king, druids, and people is to be found in the election of Conaire Mór as king of Tara, as it is related in *Togail Bruidne Da Derga* 'The Destruction of Da Derga's Hostel' (Knott 1936, 5).

The king of Tara has died, and it has been revealed to the druids in the course of a divinatory rite that a worthy successor will arrive at Tara naked and bearing a stone and a sling. Conaire arrives in this way and the druids recognize him as their future king. But the people object, saying that Conaire is too young to be king. Conaire answers their objection, and the people enthusiastically consent to his election. In this instance, Conaire is not yet the king and the people respond to the druids before he does. Otherwise the sequence is the same: the aspirant to kingship establishes that the druids have prophesied correctly, and it is only then that the people accept that it is so.

Súaltaim's warning at Emain is ritualistic and public, and the procedure followed has much in common with what is described in the other texts we have looked at. Súaltaim's fate is a variation on the perennial theme of "killing the messenger." The burden that Cú Chulainn places upon him is a heavy one. Ulster has suffered greatly while the king and his warriors remained in Emain helpless to confront the invaders. The defence of the province has fallen to Cú Chulainn who now lies grievously wounded. It is Súaltaim's task to bring this message to the king and his court. All that has happened to Ulster while they suffered their debility is revealed to them. The revelation is disruptive of the order and harmony that should prevail in Emain, and is an incitement of and an affront to the king. Súaltaim's intervention, as I have argued elsewhere ("*Táin Bó Cúailnge* and Early Irish Law," chap. 15 in this volume), exemplifies *géim n-áilgeso* 'a shout of importuning,' something to which a lord is entitled to respond with violence. The person who has so disturbed the peace at Emain must be slain. The king may then reassert his authority as Conchobor does in words that we have already quoted from Recension I. Here is the version of Recension II:

> "A little too loud is that cry," said Conchobor, "for the sky is above us, the earth beneath us and the sea all around us, but unless the sky with its showers of stars fall upon the surface of the earth or unless the ground burst open in an earthquake, or unless the fish-abounding, blue-bordered sea come over the surface of the earth, I shall bring back every cow to its byre and enclosure, every woman to her own abode and dwelling, after victory in battle and combat and contest." (*TBC LL*, 247)

17

Ailill and Medb
A Marriage of Equals

(2009)

The second recension of *Táin Bó Cúailnge*[1] opens with the "Pillow-Talk" (*comrád chind cherchailli*, so-called, lines 3, 297) in which Ailill and Medb argue about their marriage. They make claim and counter-claim, each of them seeking to establish that the other party is the beneficiary of the marriage. They arrive, it seems to me, at a resolution of their difficulty in every respect except the narrow one of which of them now possesses the greater wealth. They go on to compare their wealth, and find that they are equal in every respect except that Medb lacks a bull to correspond to the one called Findbennach, which is in Ailill's possession. She sends a delegation to Cúailnge in Ulster to ask Dáire mac Fiachna to lend her the bull Donn Cúailnge for a year. She promises a handsome reward, including her own sexual favors, and Dáire is happy to comply. But then he learns that one of Medb's messengers has said that if the bull were not given willingly, it would be taken by force. Dáire is enraged and declines to part with the bull. When this is reported to Medb, she intimates that she knew all along that the bull would have to be taken by force, and announces her determination to do so. This provides the basis for the cattle-raid, and (as the narrator tells us) "the basis of the invention and composition of (the *Táin*)" (*fotha a fagbála 7 a dénma*, lines 296–97, trans. 145).

Medb then sends messengers to raise an army for the invasion, and the account of this in Recension II is an expanded version of the muster by Ailill and Medb that opens Recension I (*TBC I*). No reason for the raid is offered in Recension I, and "the bull" that Medb seeks is mentioned for the first time, and without explanation, after the itinerary which the army is said to have taken: "From Findabair in Cúailnge the armies of Ireland spread out over the province in quest of the Bull (*do chuingid in tairb*)" (*TBC I*, lines 131–32, trans. 128). Some of the material in the Introduction to Recension II is found in other Ulster tales. Cecile O'Rahilly (*TBC LL*, 273) mentions, for example, the names of Medb's five sisters and of Ailill's two brothers; the statement that Medb insisted on a husband "without meanness, without jealousy, without fear" (*cen neóit, cen ét, cen omon*, line 28) and that such a one was Ailill; the two bulls, the Findbennach of Connacht and the Donn Cúailnge of Ulster, which were destined to meet in battle. Thurneysen (1921, 241) attributed the composition of the Introduction to the redactor of Recension II. O'Rahilly (*TBC LL*, 273) does not follow him in this; she is content to assert "that someone . . . wove all these strands of tradition together and invented a contention between Medb and her husband to explain why she coveted the Donn Cúailnge and mustered the forces of the four provinces of Ireland to invade Ulster and gain possession of the famous bull."

The Introduction, which I have briefly summarized, resolves itself into three parts. In the first of them, Ailill and Medb argue about their marriage; in the second they compare their wealth; and in the third Medb unsuccessfully seeks a loan of the Donn Cúailnge for a year. It is with the first part that I shall concern myself in what follows.

Ailill and Medb both have recourse to legal terminology as they describe the marriage. Medb, in particular, charges Ailill with being legally dependent upon her:

17. Ailill and Medb

"Cipé imress méla 7 mertain 7 meraigecht fort, ní fhuil díri nó eneclann duit-siu ind acht na fil dam-sa," ar Medb, "dáig fer ar tincur mná atatchomnaic."

"Whoever brings shame and annoyance and confusion upon you, you have no claim for compensation or for honour-price for it except what claim I have," said Medb, "for you are a man dependent upon a woman's marriage-portion." (lines 42–44, trans. 138)

Of the legal terms in this passage, *tinchor* is the one that is crucially important in the early Irish law of marriage, and it occurs four times in the course of the Introduction to Recension II. *Tinchor* denotes the property brought into the marriage by either partner: *lánamnas fir for bantinchur* 'a union of a man on woman-property' refers to a marriage to which a man contributes little or nothing.[2] It is reasonable to assume that Medb's *ar tinc[h]ur mná* is the equivalent of *for bantinchur*, with genitive singular *mná* used for the composition form *ban-*, and late substitution of *ar* for *for*. Medb's meaning is clear: she is the dominant party in the marriage, as she is the one who has preponderantly contributed to it. She has just reminded Ailill that she inherited Connacht from her father, and that she gave Ailill a contract of marriage and a dowry (*cor 7 coibchi*, lines 39–40). The legal underpinning for Medb's jibe is found in the law of marriage, and in particular what the relevant law text says about "a man on a woman's contribution":

Acht is fer do-r[e]anar a hinchaib na mna, mad le in tothchus uile, inge mad sofoltachu in fer oldas in ben, no mad caidiu, no mad saire, no mad airmidnechu. (Thurneysen 1936, 62)

But he is a husband who is paid honour-price in accordance with his wife's status if she holds all the property, unless he has higher property-qualifications [in his own right] than his wife or is more godly, more high-born or more estimable than she. (Ó Corráin 2002, 25)

In a commentary on this episode, Donnchadh Ó Corráin (2002, 38) says that Ailill is here humiliated. If he is, however, he shows no sign of it. It must be remembered that Medb's claims are made in the context of an argument. Ailill gives a very different account of the marriage, and the legal terms in which he couches his remarks represent him as having been a person of considerable substance in his own right before ever he married Medb. There is no particular reason for preferring Medb's avowed view of the marriage to that of Ailill's. A balanced view of the matter, based on what both partners have to say for themselves, would suggest that, legally at least, theirs is a marriage of equals.

The argument begins innocuously enough. One night as the couple lie on their "royal bed" in Ráth Crúachain in Connacht, Ailill gratuitously says to Medb: "In truth, woman, she is a well-off woman who is the wife of a nobleman" (*Fírbriathar a ingen . . . , is maith ben ben dagfhir*, lines 4–5, trans. 137). This is an unexceptional statement of the position of such a woman in early Irish society, and Medb agrees with it. But disagreement soon follows: when she asks Ailill why he should say what he has said, he applies the observation to Medb, saying that she is now better off than she was when he married her. She counters with the claim that she was already well off before that, which is not necessarily incompatible with what Ailill has said. He now contradicts her, however:

"Is maith nach cúalammar 7 nach fetammar," ar Ailill, "acht do bith-siu ar bantincur mnáa 7 bidba na crích ba nessom duit oc breith do shlait 7 do chrech i fúatach úait."

———

"It was wealth that we had not heard of and did not know of," said Ailill, "but you were a woman of property and foes from lands next to you were carrying off spoils and booty from you." (lines 7–9, trans. 137)

The meaning of the phrase *do bith-siu ar bantincur mnáa*, here translated "but you were a woman of property," will be discussed presently. It will suffice for now to observe that Medb rejects Ailill's jibe: *Ní samlaid bá-sa*, "Not so was I" (line 10, trans. 137). Her father Eochu Feidlech was high-king of Ireland, and he had six daughters. Medb tells us that she was the noblest and worthiest of them, the most generous in bounty and the bestowal of gifts (*bam-sa ferr im rath 7 tidnacul díb*, lines 15–16), and the best of them in battle. She had a large army as her standing household, and for that reason her father passed on to her the province of Connacht, here called "the province of Crúachu." The political situation envisaged for Ireland at the time of the *Táin* was that of the pentarchy, and Medb claims that the kings of the

17. Ailill and Medb

other four provinces each sought her hand in marriage. She turned them all down. For what she required in a husband was that he be without meanness, without jealousy, and without fear. And she makes it perfectly clear that in respect of these qualities (or the first two of them at any rate) what she was looking for was *equality* in a husband:

> Diambad neóit in fer 'gá mbeind, níbad chomadas dún beith maróen fo bíth am maith-se im rath 7 tidnacul, 7 bad cháined dom fhir combadim ferr-sa im rath secha, 7 níbad cháined immorro combar commaithe acht combadar maithe díb línaib.

> If my husband should be mean, it would not be fitting for us to be together, for I am generous in largesse and the bestowal of gifts and it would be a reproach for my husband that I should be better than he in generosity, but it would be no reproach if we were equally generous provided that both of us were generous. (lines 29–33, trans. 138)

A similar argument is stated in regard to their being equally courageous. As for jealousy, this would not be appropriate, since she "was never without one lover quickly succeeding another" (*ní raba-sa ríam can fher ar scáth araile ocum*, line 37, trans. 138). She then tells Ailill that he was just the man she had been looking for:

> "Fuarasa dano in fer sain .i. tussu .i. Ailill mac Rosa Rúaid do Lagnib. Nírsat neóit, nírsat étaid, nírsat déaith."

> "Now such a husband have I got, even you, Ailill mac Rosa Rúaid of Leinster. You are not niggardly, you are not jealous, you are not inactive." (lines 38–39, trans. 138)

The sting comes in the tail, however, for it is at this point that she says that she gave Ailill a marriage contract and a substantial dowry (*coibche*);[3] as we have seen, she claims that Ailill has no legal standing apart from hers, and secondly that he is dependent upon the wealth that she has brought into the marriage.

Ailill responds only to the last part of Medb's argument, and his opening words echo those of Medb's response to him: *Ní amlaid sin bá-sa*, "Not so was I" (lines 44–45, trans. 138). Two of his brothers are kings, one of Leinster and the other of Tara. (They are among the suitors that Medb claims to have rejected.) He says that he ceded kingship to them because they were older. He goes on to claim that "they were no better in bounty and the bestowal of gifts than I" (*níptar ferra im rath nó thidnacul andú-sa*, lines 47–48, trans. 138).[4] The bestowal of bounty—specifically *rath*—entails the enfeoffing of clients, which is the basis of a lord's rank. Ailill's boast is that in this respect he was the equal of a provincial king before ever he married Medb. The wording here echoes the claim that Medb made of her own preeminence among the daughters of Eochu Feidlech: "I was the most generous of them in bounty and the bestowal of gifts" (*Bam-sa ferr im rath 7 tidnacul díb*, lines 15–16, trans. 137), and indeed Medb had used the words again when she explained how she and her husband must be equal in generosity.

Medb had claimed that she inherited the province from her father. Ailill implicitly accepts this when he says:

> 7 ní chúala chúiced i nHérind ar bantinchur acht in cúiced sa a óenur. Tánac-sa dano, gabsus rígi sund i tunachus mo máthar, dáig ar bíth Máta Murisc ingen Mágach mo máthair, & gia ferr dam-sa rígan no biad ocum andaí-siu, dáig ingen ardríg Hérend atatchomnaic.
>
> ———
>
> And I heard of no province in Ireland dependent on a woman except this province alone, so I came and assumed the kingship here in virtue of my mother's rights, for Máta Muirisc the daughter of Mága was my mother. And what better queen could I have than you, for you are the daughter of the high-king of Ireland. (lines 48–51, trans. 138)

In translating this passage, O'Rahilly has adopted the reading *a dualgus* from the later (Stowe) version of Recension II (C. O'Rahilly 1961, line 53), in preference to *i tunachus*. She suggests that *tunachus* in LL, which is otherwise unattested, may be a scribal misreading of a partially illegible *tochus* 'property, possessions.' It is in any case clear that Ailill is saying that he in some sense owes to his mother his eligibility to be king of Connacht. And Medb does not question any of this: her response is to say "Nevertheless my property is greater than yours" (*Atá dano, . . . is lia mo maith-sea indá do maith-siu*, lines 52–53, trans. 138). Ailill rejects this, and there follows an elaborate comparison of their respective possessions. We have now come full circle: what started the argument was Ailill's use of *maith* with

17. Ailill and Medb

regard to Medb, first as an adjective meaning "good, well off," and secondly as a noun meaning "wealth, possessions," and it ends with a comparison of her property (*maith*) with his.

There is a remarkable degree of correspondence in the topics raised by the couple in the course of their argument. Medb dismisses Ailill's characterization of her situation before the marriage. She then boasts of her inheritance and personal qualities, declares that Ailill was just the husband she needed, and denigrates him as being entirely dependent upon her legal status and her wealth. Her description of Ailill's position in the marriage—that he is *for tincor mná*—echoes what he has said of her—that before her marriage she was *ar* (i.e., *for*) *bantinchor mná*. As we have seen, the words with which he dismisses this jibe are virtually identical with those already used by Medb. And he too goes on to speak of his personal qualities and inheritance, and to say that for his part he could find no better queen than Medb.

Ailill's allusion to his mother is consistent with what we find in great detail in the Leinster genealogies, where Ailill is said to have been the son of Russ Ruad and of Máta:

> Máta Muirisc ainm a máthar do Feraib Ool nÉcmacht; do suidib dogairder Connachta indiu 7 ro-ngabsat-side hi rríge forthu ara máthre .i. do-luid Medb ingen Echach Feidlich hí co Feraib Ool nÉcmacht impi hi crích Lagen co mbertsatar Ailill leo do rígo forthu ar ba díb a máthair 7 dano ná fríth ét ná omun inna chridiu 7rl. 7 do dénam óentad eter in dá cóiced do grés 7 do chocud fri cúiced Conchobuir conid Ailill iarum do-acht Táin Bó Cúailgne cona tríchait cét Galeán.

> Máta Muirisc was the name of his mother (who was) of the Fir Ool nÉcmacht; they are called Connachta today. And they accepted him as king over them on account of his maternal kin. That is to say, Medb—she was the daughter of Eochu Feidlech—went with the Fir Ool nÉcmacht accompanying her and they took Ailill with them to be king over them, for his mother was one of them and moreover jealousy or fear had not been found in his heart etc., and in order to effect an alliance between the two provinces for ever and to wage war on Conchobor's province. And it was Ailill afterwards who executed the Cattle-Raid of Cooley with his division of Galeáin. (M. A. O'Brien 1962, 22–23; my translation)

This passage, which has all the appearance of being very much older than the "Pillow-Talk," is incidentally of great interest, since it differs from the extant recensions of the *Táin* on the role of the Gailióin in the cattle-raid.[5] But its main value in the present context is that it shows that to the "strands of tradition" that O'Rahilly discerned in the "Pillow-Talk," we can add the notion that Ailill was accepted as king of the Connachta because his mother, Máta, was one of them. And it is inconceivable that the king of a province would not enjoy full legal rights in his realm.

Medb's view of her inheritance can be reconciled with Ailill's view of his if we pay due attention to what each of them says. Taking Medb at her word, Ó Corráin (2002, 38) says that Ailill is king by "right of wife," and it is indeed upon marriage to Medb that Ailill becomes king. The clear indication, however, both of the "Pillow-Talk" and the genealogical text, is that Medb needs Ailill as much as he needs her. She is not "a queen in her own right," as Edel (2001, 162) has claimed. Her father gave her the province of Crúachu (line 23), not its sovereignty. Her claim is territorial: as Thurneysen (1935–36, 209) pointed out, she would be described in Irish law as a *banchomarba* 'female heir.'[6] She describes herself as Medb C[h]rúachna 'Medb of Crúachu' (line 23), but never as "Queen of Crúachu." It is Ailill who uses the word for "queen" (*rígan*, line 51), and in the sense of "king's wife" rather than "woman sovereign." For all her property and royal birth, Medb only becomes queen when she marries a king. And for all her boastfulness and self-aggrandizement, she perhaps reflects the patriarchal view of marriage when she speaks of her ideal husband as *in fer 'cá mbeind* (line 35), which O'Rahilly translates as "the man with whom I should be," but which should probably be taken as "the man who would have me (as his wife)."

The marriage between Medb and Ailill was a dynastic one. Medb considered Ailill to be an ideal husband, and Ailill considered her an ideal wife. Curiously, both of them overvalue the position of women in early Ireland: a woman would not actually inherit a province, and a man would not become king because of his mother's rights.[7] While I differ in some respects from Ó Corráin's reading of the "Pillow-Talk," I would agree with him that "one of the main points of the episode" may be that "upset of the patriarchal order of society leads to conflict, even calamity" (Ó Corráin 2002, 38). The marriage of Ailill and Medb can hardly be considered ideal, but legally it seems to have been an equal one.

ADDENDUM ON *AR/FOR TINCHUR*

Tinchor, as we have seen, denotes the property brought into a marriage, and *bantinchor*, according to *DIL* (s.v. *tinchor*), denotes a "wife's preponderant contribution." The *lánamnas fir for bantinchor*, a marriage in which the man depends upon the property contributed by the woman, is alluded to by Medb when she charges Ailill with being *fer ar tincor mná*. The other three occurrences of *for/ar tinchur* in the Introduction are less straightforward, and I propose to consider them briefly here. *DIL* takes them to mean "supported by a woman, under woman's control." They are the only examples cited of the phrase in this sense, and it has to be said that the treatment of them in the dictionary is less than satisfactory. The varied ways in which our author uses the phrase exemplify the witty and adroit use of legal terminology that Ó Corráin (2002) has recognized in the text.[8]

It will be convenient to consider these instances in the reverse order of their occurrence. The last example occurs in the comparison of the couple's wealth, where the narrator uses the phrase of the Findbennach:

> Acht boí tarb sainemail ar búaib Ailella 7 ba lóeg bó do Meidb atacomnaic 7 Findbennach a ainm. Acht nírbo miad leis beith for bantinchur, acht dochúaid co mboí for búaib in ríg.

> But among Ailill's cows there was a special bull. He had been a calf of one of Medb's cows, and his name was Findbennach. But he deemed it unworthy of him to be counted as a woman's property, so he went and took his place among the king's cows. (lines 71–74, trans. 139)

O'Rahilly's interpretation of *for bantinchur* here is eminently reasonable, and Ó Corráin (2002, 40) essentially follows it: "he considered it unworthy of himself to be counted as women's property." The preposition *for/ar* in the phrase as it occurs in the Laws and is used by Medb of Ailill has the sense "relying on, depending on" (see *DIL* F, 300.6 ff.). As used here of the bull, on the other hand, it has the sense "in, amongst" (*DIL* F, 297.23 ff.). We must remember that the context is still one of a matrimonial spat, and that *ban-* here specifically denotes "woman (in marriage)." The bull resents being part of the wife's property and takes himself off to join the husband's cattle.

Ailill says of the province of Connacht (or Crúachu) that it was *ar bantinchur* (line 46), which O'Rahilly translates "dependent on a woman" and Ó Corráin (2002, 40) "being a woman's inheritance." I suggest that here too the matrimonial contract is crucial to the interpretation of the phrase. It is true that Medb is said to have inherited the province, and that before her marriage the province is therefore dependent upon her. But Ailill is explaining why he married Medb, and in that context it seems appropriate to take the phrase in its technical sense, and translate the passage: "I heard of no other province in Ireland which was included in a woman's marriage portion." Ailill is saying that he married Medb because she could bring the province to the marriage.

The first occurrence of the phrase is when Ailill uses it of Medb: *do bith-siu ar bantinc(h)ur mná* (line 8), which O'Rahilly (137) translates "you were a woman of property," and Ó Corráin (2002, 39) "you were an heiress." Thurneysen (1936a, 20n2) faulted the use of *bantinchur* to refer to the property of a woman before marriage as being legally imprecise. It may be, however, that in speaking of an unmarried woman of independent means, the phrase could be used of the property that she would bring to a marriage when the time came. But there is a complication here, since the phrase Ailill uses is actually *for ban-tinchur mná*. It has been assumed above that *for ban-tinchur* and *for tinchur mná* have the same meaning. It is just about conceivable that the occurrence of *ban-* with *mná* in the present example is pleonastic. However, given that *for ban-tinchur mná* is used of an unmarried woman here, and that this is the only example with both *ban-* and *mná*, I suggest that what Ailill is saying to her is "you were a woman subsistent upon the property which you would bring to a marriage," the implication being that it was not enough that she was an heiress: she also needed a husband.[9]

18

Cú Chulainn, the Poets, and Giolla Brighde Mac Con Midhe

(2005)

In his lecture at the First International Conference on the Ulster Cycle of Tales in Belfast in 1994, Patrick K. Ford considered the relevance of the idea of everlasting fame to the depiction of Cú Chulainn in *Táin Bó Cúailnge*.[1] He argued that "for the Irish as for the Greeks, fame was valued over life itself. And fame was bestowed on heroes by poets and consisted literally in what was heard: lofty deeds sung and told by poets."[2] The present contribution in Pat's honor will cover some of the same ground, but it has a different point of departure: it is prompted in the main by a claim made by the thirteenth-century poet Giolla Brighde Mac Con Midhe in *A theachtaire tig ón Róimh* 'O messenger who comes from Rome,'[3] to the effect that the fame of Cú Chulainn (among others) is to be put down to the survival of the praise (*moladh*) given to him by poets. There is little sign, however, that Cú Chulainn was the subject of eulogy among poets; the purpose of what follows is to explore the implications of Giolla Brighde's claim in the light of the evidence of the *Táin*.

A theachtaire tig ón Róimh takes the form of a response to a cleric who evidently has claimed that the pope in Rome had ordained that Irish poets should be suppressed, and poetic art "dethroned."[4] Giolla Brighde's reply falls broadly into three sections. In the first of them,[5] he observes that no documentary evidence has been offered in support of the cleric's claims, and he therefore declines to believe that the cleric is telling the truth. The second section[6] is a defence on largely religious grounds of the poet's role as eulogist, and particularly of his right to receive a reward for his work (*luach ar na laoidhibh*,[7] *crodh ar laoidh*[8]). In the core of this section,[9] he says that the son of Mary will give him heaven as a reward for a composition of his excellent poetry (*duais . . . ar dhuain dom dheaghdhán*).[10] He goes on to claim that a patron who is magnanimous in his payment of the poets will also go to heaven, for that is clearly what he has in mind when he says that "the generous man is free from hell."[11] Eulogy is justified since the praising of men is the praising of him who created them (*moladh daoine is dó is moladh / an neach do-ní a gcruthoghadh*).[12] The third section of the poem,[13] beginning with the well-known line *Dá mbáití an dán, a dhaoine*, "If poetry were suppressed, O people," deals with the social and cultural value of the poetic craft, mainly in terms of what would be lost if that craft were to be suppressed.

A social function has already been alluded to in a quatrain which implies that the custom of rewarding the poet for his work allows him to distinguish between the generous and the niggardly patron, thus enabling him to ennoble the one and to satirize the other.[14] Now, as he contemplates the threat of an assault on his profession, Giolla Brighde focuses on the social significance of the poet's role as historian and genealogist:

Dá mbáití an dán, a dhaoine,
gan seanchas, gan seanlaoidhe,
go bráth ach athair gach fhir
rachaidh cách gan a chluinsin.

Dá dtráigheadh an tobar fis,
ní béarthaoi muna mbeimis

do dheighfhearaibh saora a sean,
craobha geinealaigh Gaoidheal.

If poetry were suppressed, O people, so that there was neither history nor ancient lays, every man for ever would die unheard of except for the name of everybody's father.

If the well of knowledge were to dry up, but for us, noble men would not be told of the illustrious among their ancestors nor the branches of the pedigrees of the Irish.[15]

The noble men of Ireland depend on the poets for knowledge of their family history, their illustrious ancestors, and their place in the genealogical scheme of things. This is a defence not only of the contemporary poets—the *aos cumtha* as he has called them earlier in the poem[16]—but also of the literary tradition, for *dán* here encompasses not only historical lore but also ancient lays. The poet draws on the well of knowledge for his own compositions, but he also preserves the works of his predecessors. Giolla Brighde reiterates this at the end of the poem when he says to his patron that the loss of his family's *seanchas* and *dúana* would mean that the children of his kennel-keepers and his own noble progeny would be "equally high-born, equally base";[17] if the poets were expelled "every nobleman would be a churl."[18]

Warriors would be badly affected by the suppression of poetry:

Do budh ainiarmairt fhoda
do mhíleadhaibh méarbhoga;
folach a sgéal ní sgrios beag,
gan fhios na bhfréamh ó bhfuilead.

There would be lasting, evil consequences for softly-fingered warriors; the forgetting of their ancestry such that they knew not the roots from which they derive, would be no small destruction.[19]

We may read this teleologically, taking it to mean that a lack of knowledge of their ancestry would make them "soft-fingered" and hence useless in combat; alternatively, it may simply mean that "soft-fingered" warriors will remain in that condition if they are not inspired by knowledge of their ancestors. In either case, it indicates that warriors should be told about the deeds of their predecessors, and this entails an exercise of the poet's narrative function. It is possible that *folach a sgéal* here may in fact mean "keeping their stories hidden."[20] The next quatrain takes up that topic:

> Folach cliathach agus cath
> bhfear nÉireann do budh easbhach,
> dá n-éis gé madh maith a méin
> gan spéis i bhflaith ná i bhfírfhréimh.
>
> ———
>
> The suppression of encounters and battles of the men of Ireland would be a faulty matter: there would be no interest shown in prince nor in true stock after their death, though their courage had been good.[21]

There is a subtle transformation here from the effect of the loss on contemporary warriors to the notion that those of the men of Ireland who have shown courage in battle deserve to be commemorated. And now the poet changes to an enumeration of those heroes from the Irish past (whether legendary or otherwise) who have attained immortality through the praise of the poets:

> Gé tá marbh mairidh Gúaire
> 's Cú Chulainn na Craobhruaidhe;
> ón ló a-tá a nós thiar is thoir
> atá fós Brian 'na bheathoidh.
>
> Beo ó mhaireas a moladh
> Conall agus Conchobar;
> a nós 'na bheathaidh i-bhus
> nocha deachaidh fós Fearghus.
>
> Lugh do marbhadh le Mac Cuill
> ní mhairionn cnámh 'na choluinn;
> a nós ar ndul don domhan
> fós do Lugh is leasoghadh.
>
> ———
>
> Although he is dead, Gúaire lives on as does Cú Chulainn of the Craobhruadh; since his reputation is heard east and west, Brian is still alive.

Conall and Conchobhar are alive because their fame lives; with his fame alive in the world, Fearghas has not yet died.

Not a bone remains of the body of Lugh who was slain by Mac Cuill; though he has departed this world, Lugh's fame preserves him still.[22]

Giolla Brighde is unambiguous here in his assertion of the power of panegyric: praise (*moladh*) bestows fame (*nós*) and hence the dead heroes live on. And we are left in no doubt that he is talking about praise cast in the form of verse: Niall, Conn, and Cormac would be forgotten "if poems (*laoidhe*) did not preserve all they had done."[23] The two quatrains which follow expand upon this, referring (in reverse order) to the composition and performance of *dán*:

Ní bhiadh muna mbeith an dán
ag cruit téidbhinn ná ag tiompán
fios deighfhir arna dhola
ná a einigh ná a eangnomha.

Fios a seanchais ná a saoire
ní fhuighbhidis arddaoine;
léigidh so i ndán do dhéanamh
nó no slán dá seinsgéalaibh.

Were it not for poetry, sweet-tongued harp or psaltery would not know of a goodly hero after his death, nor of his reputation nor his prowess.

Noble men would have no knowledge of their traditions and nobility; allow these to be composed in poetry or else bid farewell to their ancient histories.[24]

These quatrains also reiterate the twin themes of the commemoration of the dead and the instruction of the living.

Giolla Brighde is working in what, as Calvert Watkins puts it, "must be the longest continuous tradition of encomiastic poetry in the world."[25] Eulogy and satire—poems of praise and blame—were effective instruments of social order in the hands of the poet. *Céin mair molthiar, mairg áerthiar,* "blessed is he who is praised, woe is him who is satirized": so we are told in an archaic poem, which in the Preface to the *Amra* is attributed to Colum Cille in his role as defender of the privileges of the poets.[26] In the ninth-century panegyric, *Aed oll fri andud n-áne* ("Áed great at kindling of brilliance"), the poet says of his patron, *a molad maissiu máenib / lúaidfidir láedib limmsa*, "his praise is more beautiful than treasures, it will be sung in lays by me."[27] Caerwyn Williams points out that "the Welsh *pencerdd* and the Irish ollav are equally convinced that 'praise' is the only thing that will never die," and he quotes "a very old Welsh proverb," *Trengid golud, ni threinc molud*, "Wealth vanishes, praise (fame) does not."[28]

The encomiastic and satirical functions of the Irish professional poet—two sides of the same coin—are generally taken to be an inheritance from Celtic and ultimately from Proto-Indo-European times. This view is not confined to "nativist" scholars. James Carney, who is well known for his criticism of "nativism" in the field of Irish saga, held that poetry "of praise or blame," composed in Ireland "from the earliest period of the literature down to the sixteenth and seventeenth centuries," "partook of the nature of a religious institution."[29] He said this in a context in which he observed that the origins of Gaelic institutions "are to be sought in the remote period of Indo-European unity."[30] "An ollav," he added, "is many things to a king or prince, but I would say that he is most significantly the shadow of a high-ranking pagan priest or druid."[31]

The relationship between the *ollam* and the king or prince is of course that of poet and patron. As Watkins puts it, "The two are precisely in an exchange or reciprocity relationship: the poet gives poems of praise to the patron, who in turn bestows largesse upon the poet. The institution is of Indo-European antiquity; exact parallels exist in Indic and Germanic, and it is ultimately to such a tradition that we owe the composition of the *Iliad* and the *Odyssey*."[32] This brings us back to where we began: the fame which the patron and his culture valued more than life itself, and which only the poet could confer.[33] This set of values is most famously exemplified by Achilles when he exchanges long life for imperishable fame,[34] but it is also enthusiastically embraced by Cú Chulainn.

Cú Chulainn's overweening desire for fame asserts itself at an early age. It is related in the *Táin* that one day when he was in his seventh year, Cú Chulainn overheard the druid Cathbad prophesying to his students that "if a warrior took up arms on that day his name for deeds of valour would be known throughout Ireland and his fame would last forever (*no mértais a airscéla go bráth*)."³⁵ Cú Chulainn went and asked the king for arms, and they were given to him. When Cathbad found out about this, he repeated his prophecy, but this time there was a sting in the tail: "It is certain that he who takes up arms today will be famous (*airdairc*) and renowned (*animgnaid*), but he will, however, be short-lived."³⁶ Cú Chulainn was not at all troubled by this: "'A mighty thing!' said Cú Chulainn. 'Provided that I be famous (*airderc*), I am content to be only one day on earth.'"³⁷

The heroic deeds for which Cú Chulainn deserves to be made famous are related in the *Táin*. This is an epic in a mixture of prose and verse, and it is clearly not panegyric as Giolla Brighde would understand it. What we might hope for is that the tradition of encomiastic poetry would be reflected in the world described in the *Táin*, and that the fame that the hero craves and earns would be shown to have been bestowed upon him by a poet. A distinction has long been made between epics, such as *Beowulf* and the Homeric poems, and the poetical performances that are described in them.³⁸ It has been pointed out in regard to Homer that "although the poets whose performances are described in some detail in the *Odyssey* (Demodokos at the court of the Phaiacians and Phemios on Ithaka) deliver single-episode poems of a digestible after-dinner length, the Homeric epics themselves are complex and longer by an order of magnitude."³⁹ Having said all that, however, we can now look briefly at some of the ways in which the encomiastic tradition is reflected in the sagas, and in the Ulster Cycle in particular.

Eulogy was traditionally delivered before an audience at a banquet given by a king or chieftain. In *Aed oll fri andud n-áne*, the poet gives us a brief description of the customary procedure: *Oc cormaim gaibtir duana / drengaitir dreppa dáena / arbeittet bairtni bindi / tri laith linni ainm n-Aeda*, "At ale poems are chanted: fine (genealogical) ladders are climbed; melodious bardisms modulate through pools of liquor the name of Aed."⁴⁰ This activity is also found in some of the descriptions of feasts in the sagas. In the historical tale *Orgain Denna Ríg*, we are told that when Cobthach Cóel Breg celebrated the Feast of Tara "the eulogists were out on the floor eulogising the king and the queen and the lords and the nobles" (*bátar int aes admolta for in lár oc admolad ind ríg 7 na rígna 7 na flathi 7 na n-ócthigern*).⁴¹ From the Ulster Cycle we have the following description in *Mesca Ulad* of the "festive assembly" of the Ulstermen at the house of Fintan:

> After that his drinking house was arranged by Conchobar according to exploits and divisions and kinships; according to grades and arts and gentle manners, with a view to the well-disposing of the banquet. There came portioners to apportion and cup-bearers to dispense, and door-keepers to keep the doors. Their melodies and their minstrelsies and songs of mirth were sung. Their lays and their tales and their eulogies were chanted for them (*gabtha a ndúana 7 a ndréchta 7 a n-admolta doib*). Jewels and riches and treasures were distributed to them.[42]

In the *Táin* we learn that each warrior of the Ulstermen spent a day in turn in Slíab Fúait, where they would meet any poet or warrior who might come along. The poet would be offered protection on his journey to Emain, while the warrior would be fought there and then to prevent him from reaching Emain.[43] The expression used for the poet here is "somebody with a poem" (*nech co n-airchetul*), and the poem in question is presumably a panegyric which is to be delivered at Emain in exchange for a reward. The subject of such a panegyric would of course be Conchobor: the poet's patron, after all, is the king or chief. The champion is excluded from panegyric in early Irish law: "ennoble only, make known only a king or a noble, for it is from them that is due great wealth as a result of which property increases" (*ni saora, ni sloinde acht righ, no airigh, ar as doibh dlighidh mormhainbhthe dia moaigid maoin*).[44] In the world of the *Táin*, however, such a restriction might not necessarily apply. The second recension gives a longer account of the obligations of the watcher at Slíab Fúait:

> A goodly warrior of the Ulstermen is always there, keeping watch and ward so that no warriors or strangers come to Ulster to challenge them to battle and so that he may be the champion to give battle on behalf of the whole province. And if poets (*áes dána*) leave Ulstermen and the province unsatisfied, that he may be the one to give them treasures and valuables for the honour of the province. If poets (*áes dána*) come into the land, that he may be the one who will be their surety until they reach Conchobor's couch and that their poems (*dúana*) and songs (*dréchta*) may be the first to be recited in Emain on their arrival.[45]

Here, as in the passages cited from *Orgain Denna Ríg* and *Mesca Ulad*, there are many poems, and evidently many poets. It is reasonable to assume that the king's foremost champions might expect to receive their meed of praise.

18. Cú Chulainn, the Poets, and Giolla Brighde Mac Con Midhe

Whatever may have been the normal practice in the Ulster of the sagas, we cannot expect to see it in action during the cattle-raid, for the men of Emain are all afflicted with their debility. The Connachta and their allies are accompanied by their poets and entertainers, but there is no Ulster poet at hand to praise Cú Chulainn's heroic deeds. On one occasion he makes a special effort to impress the poets of his enemies:

> Cú Chulainn came on the morrow to survey the host and to display his gentle and beautiful form to women and girls and maidens, to poets and men of art (*do filedaib 7 áes dána*), for he held not as honourable or dignified the dark magical appearance in which he had appeared to them on the previous night. So for that reason he now came on this day to display his beautiful fair appearance.[46]

The women of Connacht are duly impressed, but the poets say nothing. It is one of the Ulster exiles, Dubthach Dóel Ulad, who responds, and he does so in verse.[47] He prophesies the damage that will be inflicted upon the invaders by Cú Chulainn, and advises them to ambush and slay him. This is a tribute to the hero's ferocity and effectiveness, but it cannot be called praise poetry. Much the same can be said of the poem beginning *Atchíu fer find firfes cles*, "I see a fair man who will perform weapon-feats,"[48] in which we (and the invaders) hear about Cú Chulainn for the first time in the *Táin*. Here the Connacht poet Fedelm prophesies the destruction that Cú Chulainn will wreak on the invading army. She first describes his normal appearance, when he is so handsome that he stupefies the women-folk, and then speaks of the change that comes over him when he becomes "distorted." But this is a prophecy and not a panegyric; it is intended, not to praise Cú Chulainn, but to warn Medb. It is a response to her question, "O Feidelm Prophetess (*banfáith*), how do you see our host?"[49] and Fedelm makes it clear that she is speaking in that capacity when she says: "He will lay low your entire army. He will slaughter you in dense crowds. Ye will leave him with a thousand severed heads. The prophetess (*banfáith*) Feidelm does not conceal your fate."[50] Shortly afterwards, the invaders' sufferings at the hands of "the distorted one" are further prophesied by the aforementioned Dubthach, and all of this lends some verisimilitude to Fergus's mendacious claim that the reason why he has led the army astray is that he wishes to avoid meeting Cú Chulainn.[51]

On one occasion, Cú Chulainn praises himself in thirteen lines of verse, beginning:

> Fó mo cherd láechdachta
> benaim béimend ágmara
> for slóg síabra sorchaidi.
>
> ———
>
> Splendid is my heroic deed. I strike fearsome blows against a brilliant spectral army.[52]

Medb had duplicitously arranged to parley with Cú Chulainn, stipulating that he should come unarmed since she would be accompanied only by her woman attendants. She had concealed a number of fine warriors, and they ambushed Cú Chulainn upon his arrival. Thanks to his charioteer, Lóeg, however, Cú Chulainn does not in fact arrive unarmed, and so he is able to dispatch Medb's "spectral army." Lóeg had informed him that a warrior who is taken unawares is not entitled to his honor-price if he be without his weapons; in such a case he is entitled only to the legal due of one who does not bear arms.[53] This passage is important for the intimation it gives us of a law of war, but its relevance here lies in the role it assigns to the charioteer. Lóeg provides the warrior with the information which enables him to perform the heroic deed which the warrior then celebrates in verse.[54] Elsewhere in the *Táin*, Lóeg is directly associated with the bestowal of praise and blame.

In the course of his encounter with Fer Diad, Cú Chulainn "asked his charioteer to urge him on (*ara ngressad*) when he was overcome and to praise him (*ara molad*) when he was victorious fighting against his opponent."[55] This conveys the essence of what is expressed at greater length in the second recension:

> Therefore if it be I who am defeated this day, you must incite me and revile me and speak evil of me (*mo grísad 7 mo glámad 7 olc do ráda rim*) so that my ire and anger shall rise the higher thereby. But if it be I who inflict defeat, you must exhort me and praise me and speak well of me (*mo múnod 7 mo molod 7 maithius do rád frim*) that thereby my courage rise higher.[56]

Alf Hiltebeitel has provided an important analysis of "the uses of praise and rebuke by the two pairs of warriors and charioteer 'friends'" in this part of the *Táin*.[57] He shows that "the charioteer serves the warrior by making judicious use of the arts of eulogy and satire that have such a major place in Indo-European value systems with their emphasis on shame, disgrace, honor, and fame."[58]

The most extensive and the most lavish praise that Cú Chulainn receives in the *Táin* is of course that given to him by Fergus and the other Ulster exiles. They are responding to Ailill's request that the invaders should hear some of the adventures and stories (*ní do imthechtaib 7 airscélaib*)[59] of the people to whom they are going, and their focus throughout is on Cú Chulainn. Their account of him falls into three parts, each of which is a response to a question from Ailill or Medb: first, a brief reference to Cú Chulainn's age (seventeen years) and to what he had done in his fifth, sixth, and seventh years; secondly, an account of the many respects in which Cú Chulainn is pre-eminent among heroes and among all his coevals; and thirdly, the long section devoted to his Boyhood Deeds. The title *Inna Formolta* (plural of *formolad* 'eulogy') is used in this connection but it is not clear whether it refers to the first two sections, or only to the second one. The fact that it is plural may indicate that each of the first two sections is a *formolad*; the first of them is retrospective, since it is in fact an attenuated list of Boyhood Deeds, and the second is a list of his qualities. Cú Chulainn receives his *formolta* in prose.

It is the splendidly accomplished prose narrative of the "Boyhood Deeds" that provides the invaders with the *imthechta* and *airscéla* of Cú Chulainn. The first of Ailill's questions is very illuminating here: "What manner of man," asked Ailill, "is this Hound of whom we have heard among the Ulstermen? What age is that famous youth?" (the phrase is *in gillai sin is irdairc*, literally, "that youth who is famous").[60] We are reminded of Cathbad's prophecy about the youth who was to take up arms: his *airscéla* would live forever, and he would be famous (*airdairc*) and renowned (*animgnaid*); Cú Chulainn for his part is content to live only one day, provided he be famous (*airderc*).[61] We now learn from Ailill that Cú Chulainn is already famous (*irdairc*) among the Ulstermen; they have been heard talking about him. Ailill invites them to spread that fame among the invaders, and this they do primarily in the form of prose narrative. We do not know whether Cú Chulainn was famed in song, but he is assuredly famed in story.

Within the world of the *Táin*, then, Cú Chulainn was much praised, but not by those whose business in life it was to bestow the kind of immortal fame that he craved. What then can Giolla Brighde have been thinking of? James Carney has said of the professional poets that they "were never storytellers or entertainers: such a function would be beneath them. But they had to know so many stories that no situation could arise in their professional career but they would have a convenient analogy from the past to apply to the present."[62]

The Ulster Cycle provided many such "analogies,"[63] though it must be said that we would have a poor enough knowledge of the Ulster Cycle if we were dependent on the material in the surviving corpus of bardic poetry.[64] Giolla Brighde is not concerned with the manner in which Cú Chulainn may have been praised in the *Táin*, nor is he interested in the *Táin* as a literary work. For him, Cú Chulainn and Lugh, as much as Brian Bóraimhe and the kings of Tara, were figures from the past. The origins of the stories which are told about these figures, and the form in which the stories have been conserved and transmitted in learned and poetic circles, are irrelevant to his argument, which has to do with the way in which these stories are made available to the kings and nobles of Ireland. In essence what he is saying is that they would know nothing of these stories were it not for the compositions of the poets. The ancient lays to which he refers are earlier examples of the same mode of presenting (one might say "publishing") such stories. I have said that he is defending the literary tradition, but it is very much the tradition of the professional poet composing in verse and presenting the finished product to his patron. Within these limits, however, he places a higher valuation on the storytelling function than Carney allows. An unspoken message may be that the generous patron can look forward to being as famous as Cú Chulainn. The fact remains that in Giolla Brighde's view the hero of the past has exemplary value for the warrior of the present, and that such a hero deserves to have his name, his reputation, and his prowess commemorated in verse after his death.

19

Reflections on *Compert Conchobuir* and *Serglige Con Culainn*

(1 9 9 4)

When I began to write this paper, my interest lay in exploring the compositional character of the Ulster tales, and I had decided, quite arbitrarily, to take *Serglige Con Culainn* (*SCC*) as my specimen. For reasons which will presently become apparent I have prefaced my discussion of *SCC* with a consideration of a second Ulster tale, the (very brief) early version of *Compert Conchobuir* (*CConch*). *SCC* is much the better known of these contrasting tales, and it has received a certain amount of scholarly attention. This has mainly been of two kinds: first, thematic analysis, concerned with its description of Cú Chulainn's Otherworld journey, and with its remarkably rich material on the Otherworld; and, secondly, textual analysis, devoted to the compilatory nature of the tale in its surviving form, and to the respective contributions of the two scribes who are responsible for the text of the tale in *Lebor na hUidre*, on which that of the only other manuscript is dependent. Successive analyses, ranging from the pioneering work of Heinrich Zimmer (1887), through the classic account by Thurneysen (1921, 413–15), to a recent contribution from Trond Kruke Salberg (1992), have revealed a good deal about the compilatory and redactorial aspects of the composition of the tale as we now have it. But compilation and redaction entail the existence of narratives which are themselves the products of a compositional process, and it is probably fair to say that concern with the compilatory and redactionary processes has tended to dominate the textual study of Irish narrative to the exclusion of other aspects of composition.

One of the ways in which a compositional study of a text like *SCC* could be conducted would be by abstracting from the tale the story which it tells and then analyzing the discourse by means of which that story is realized as a tale.[1] That would be an ambitious and worthwhile undertaking, but it is not one which could be effected in the space which is at my disposal. What I want to do here is, first, to suggest another way in which we could get started on a compositional study of *SCC* and, secondly, to discuss two features of the discourse of the extant tale.

The suggestion which I wish to make is that the early version of *CConch*, which shows a relatively straightforward relationship between story and discourse, would make a suitable starting point for an analysis of more complex items of the Ulster Cycle, such as *SCC*. *CConch*, which occurs in seven manuscripts, was edited by Vernam Hull (1934), who argues that it was contained in the lost manuscript *Cín Dromma Snechta* (CDS). The text reconstructed by Hull on the basis of the extant manuscripts "is one of surprising antiquity which may with certainty be put back in the eighth century as early as the *prima manus* of the Würzburg glosses" (V. Hull 1934, 7). I reproduce the text here,[2] together with Hull's translation:

COMPERT CONCHOBUIR

Ness ingen Echach Sálbuidi boí inna ríg-suide i maig ar Emain et a ríg-ingena impe. Do-lluid in draí seccae .i. Cathboth druí di Thratraigi Maige Inis. As-bert ind ingen fris: "Cid den maith ind ór-sa indossa?" olsi.

"Is maith do dénum ríg fri rígin," ol in draí.

Iarmi-foacht ind ingen im-bo fír. As-noí in draí dar deu ba fír; mac do-génta ind úair sin for-biad Hérinn.

To-cuirestar íarum ind ingen a dochum, inna accæ ferscál cenae i n-ocus dí. Ba torrach íarum ind-í Ness. Boí a ngein fó brú trí mísa for teorib blíadnaib. Uc flid Uthir ba halachta.

FINIT

THE CONCEPTION OF CONCHOBOR

Ness, the daughter of Eochu Yellow-Heel, was on her throne outside of Emain, and her royal maidens (were) about her. A druid came past her, even Cathboth, the seer of Tratraige of Mag-Inis. The maiden said to him: "What is the present hour good for?" she said.

"It is good for begetting a king upon a queen," said the druid.

The maiden asked whether it was true. The druid swore by the gods that it was true; the son who should be begotten at that time, would rule over Ireland.

Thereupon the maiden invited him to her, since she did not see a man apart from him in proximity to her. Afterwards, the aforesaid Ness became pregnant. Three years and three months the child was in her womb. At the feast of Othar (?) she became pregnant.

THE END

This text was not included by Proinsias Mac Cana (1972, 107 ff.) in his study of the prose of CDS. Mac Cana noted that "the salient features" of the prose of CDS are well illustrated by *Compert Con Culainn*: "the spareness of the writing... suggests economy rather than abridgement: the sequence of events is clearly marked and at no point does it give an impression of serious hiatus. On the other hand, the narrative is concise to the point of abruptness and lacks those stylistic features which are most typical of traditional oral narration: alliteration, repetition, description and dialogue" (Mac Cana 1972, 109). He also notes "its relative lack of the sentence connectives which are virtually indispensable to spoken narrative" (110).

Much of this is true also of *CConch*. It contains only two sentence connectives in its approximately one hundred words: one of them, *et*, is of the type described by Mac Cana as explicit connectives, the other, *inna*, being what he calls a virtual connective. There are no clear examples of stylistic alliteration, nor is there any descriptive passage. The crucial point of the episode—the motif of the auspicious day—is conveyed in dialogue: "What is the present hour good for?" "It is good for begetting a king upon a queen." Moreover, the point is forcefully reiterated in *oratio obliqua*: Ness asks the druid if what he has said is true, and he swears that it is indeed true; the son who should be begotten at that time would rule over Ireland.

The narrative is otherwise executed with great economy: there are no attributive adjectives, no descriptive adverbs. There is however a narratorial intrusion which gives us an insight into Ness's motivation. She invited Cathbad to have intercourse with her "since she did not see a man apart from him in proximity to her." The reason why she wants to conceive is clear from the dialogue and from the reported speech. The purely opportunistic nature of her intercourse with Cathbad is what is conveyed in the narratorial comment.

This tale is concerned with the narration of a single happening. The fact that, early in the eighth century, the author of this tale, who must be assumed to be a monastic, should have been concerned to relate the circumstances of Conchobor's conception shows that the *compert* existed as a storytelling category at that date, something which is also clear from *Compert Con Culainn*. It is possible that an oral version of the story was known to the author, but there is nothing in the form or style of the extant tale to suggest that it is based on such a version. What is clear, however, is that the tale as we have it has an unspoken relationship to a narrative world, some knowledge of which must have been shared by the narrator and the reader. We are not told who Ness's son is, and he is named only in the title; in order to get the point of the tale, the reader must have some acquaintance with other stories concerning Conchobor, that is to say, with other items from what we now call the Ulster Cycle. It follows from this that, already in the early eighth century, the Ulster tales subsisted as a cycle, demanding and enabling the proliferation of tales, such as *CConch*, which are formally self-contained, but which have as their *raison d'être* an intertextual relationship with other items of the cycle.

SCC is much longer than *CConch* and it is a much more complex work than *CConch* both in terms of the story which it tells and of the discourse by means of which it does so. The plot comprises a sequence of episodes, as against the single episode of *CConch*; the narration shows stylistic and other differences from that of the earlier tale. The use of dialogue, for example, is varied and sophisticated, and the prose is interspersed with several passages of verse. Moreover, the tale as we have it combines two versions of the story, the redaction of which was complicated by the intervention of a second scribe, who altered and augmented the work of his

19. Reflections on *Compert Conchobuir* and *Serglige Con Culainn*   275

predecessor. I shall confine myself to two features of the extant tale: one of them is the creation of a narrative world (or worlds), the other being the content of two narratorial intrusions which make mention of demons.

The narrative world which is depicted in *SCC* can be described as a triptych, for we are presented with descriptions, not only of Ulster's heroic past, but also of the Otherworld, and of the conditions necessary for a Golden Age in Ireland.

An extensive treatment of the customs of Ulster's heroic past is found in the first seventeen lines of *SCC*, where there is one short narrative sentence occupying little more than a line of text: "One time a fair was held by the Ulstermen in Mag Muirthemne" (lines 7 f.).[3] The rest of the passage is devoted to describing the way (or ways) in which the Ulaid used to celebrate the fair of Samain. One of the narratorial intrusions which will be considered presently occurs at the end of this passage; the other, as we shall see, has to do with the condition of Ireland "before the faith."

When Cú Chulainn has lain in his sickness for a year, he is visited by his wife who attempts to arouse him from his stupor by uttering a poem of six quatrains, which begins *Érig a gérait Ulad!*:

> Arise, warrior of Ulster! / Awake from sleep, healthy and glad!
> Look, at dawn, upon the King of Macha. / Do not yield too long to sleep!
> Look at his shoulder girt with crystal, / look at his tankards of ale,
> behold his chariots, they come through the valley,
> behold his rows of chessmen!
> Behold his heroes with vigour, / behold his tall gentle girls,
> behold his valorous kings / and his great queens! (lines 391–402)

These quatrains offer a view of Ulster which may be said to rival the allure of the Otherworld as described in some detail in *SCC*, most notably in two poems recited by Cú Chulainn's charioteer, Lóeg: *Ránacsa rem rebrad rán*, "I came in joyous sport to a place that is wonderful though not unknown" (lines 466–537), and *Atchonnarc tír sorcha sáer*, "I saw a bright, free land where no falsehood is spoken, nor deceit" (lines 541–76).

The third panel in our triptych is provided in the account of Cú Chulainn's instructions to his foster-son Lugaid Réoderg, who has been elected King of Tara. This account, as Dillon (1953a, x) remarks, interrupts the story: it "belongs to the group of *tecosca* or 'Instructions,' of which *Tecosca Cormaic* is perhaps the best known example, and it can hardly belong to the story in its original form." In *Lebor na hUidre* it occupies all of the reverse side of leaf 46, the last words of which signal a shift of narratorial focus: *Imthúsa immurgu Con Culaind iss ed adfíastar sund coléic*, "Of Cú Chulainn, however, it will now be told here" (lines 311 f.). While Dillon is doubtless correct in his observations on this particular part of *SCC*, it is worth exploring the possibility that its inclusion in the tale, and, in particular, its precise position in the text, owe something to the Irish ideology of kingship.

In the immediately preceding section of the tale, we are told that Lóeg has returned from the Otherworld and revived Cú Chulainn with his account of it: "Lóeg set out then to Emain and told his tidings to Cú Chulainn and the others. Cú Chulainn sat up then, and passed his hand over his face; and he spoke to Lóeg clearly, and he felt his spirit strengthened by the tidings which the servant told him" (lines 229–32). It is then that we are told that the four provincial kings of Ireland other than the king of Ulster came together to elect a king of Tara; a bull-feast was held, after which it was revealed in a dream (*aislinge*) that the man to be made king was "a young warrior, noble and strong, with two red circles around his body, standing over the pillow of a sick man in Emain Macha" (lines 250–52). Messengers were sent to Emain Macha, and Conchobor identified the man in the dream as Lugaid Réoderg who was standing at the bed of his sick foster-father Cú Chulainn, whom he was comforting. Cú Chulainn arose then and began to instruct his foster-son, and the words with which he did so are called *Bríatharthecosc Con Culaind*:

Be not a seeker of fierce, uncouth quarreling.
Be not vehement, churlish, arrogant.
Be not timorous, violent, sudden, rash . . . (lines 263–65)

Much the greater part of the instruction is devoted to how the king should conduct himself. But there is also a sequence devoted to the customs which should be observed:

Prescriptive periods shall not close upon a fountain of illegality.
Memories shall determine to whom inherited land belongs.

19. Reflections on *Compert Conchobuir* and *Serglige Con Culainn* 277

> Old antiquaries shall be questioned on their conscience truthfully in thy presence ... (lines 270–72)

The election of Lugaid Réoderg is presented as an episode which follows Cú Chulainn's *aislinge* (so called, line 123), and it occurs while Cú Chulainn is in temporary remission from his *serglige* as a result of Lóeg's description of his adventures in the Otherworld. Lugaid's election is itself the result of a revelation in an *aislinge*. He is adjured by Cú Chulainn to conduct himself in accordance with gnomic instructions and he undertakes to do so. Cú Chulainn dispenses his wisdom immediately after he has acquired knowledge of the Otherworld, and I suggest that this section of *SCC* reflects the notion found elsewhere in early Irish literature that the Otherworld was the source of the righteous kingship which would ensure a Golden Age of peace and plenty in Ireland ("The Semantics of *síd*," chap. 2 in this volume).

There are two mentions of demons (*demna*) in *SCC*. The first of them occurs in the account of what used to happen at the *óenach* held annually at Samain by the Ulstermen. The warriors would proclaim their triumphs for the year, and they would bring with them to the *óenach* the tongues of everyone they had killed. Some of them, however, would include the tongues of cattle in order to boost their tally. But when they were proclaiming their triumphs, they would do so with their swords on their thighs. This latter detail is then explained by the narrator:

> Ar imsoítis a claidib fríu in tan dognítis gúchomram. Deithbir ón, ar no labraitis demna fríu dia n-armaib conid de batir comarchi forro a n-airm.

> For their swords used to turn against them when they would declare a false triumph. That was natural, for demons used to speak to them from their weapons, and thus their weapons were guarantees for them. (lines 15–17)

Dillon (1953a, 30) compares the claim made in the early modern period that the Irish used to swear on swords, while Nagy (1990, 134) cites the passage from *SCC* as an expression of "the notion of a sword as intimately connected with the speech act, and with the validity of what is said." What is significant for present purposes is that according to the narrator of *SCC* the *demna* had a regulatory role in determining the truth or falsehood of the warriors' utterances in Ulster's heroic past.

The *demna* appear again in the following words, with which the text is brought to a close:

> Conid taibsiu aidmillti do Choin Chulaind la háes sídi sin. Ar ba mór in chumachta demnach ria cretim, & ba hé a méit co cathaigtis co corptha na demna frisna doínib & co taisféntais aíbniusa & díamairi dóib, amal no betis co marthanach. Is amlaid no creteá dóib. Conid frisna taidbsib sin atberat na hanéolaig síde & áes síde.

> This is the disastrous vision shown to Cú Chulainn by the fairies. For the diabolical power was great before the faith, and it was so great that devils used to fight with men in bodily form, and used to show delights and mysteries to them, as though they really existed. So they were believed to be; and ignorant men used to call those visions *síde* and *áes síde*. (lines 844–49)

The first sentence, as punctuated by Dillon, refers to a sequence of events recounted in the foregoing narrative. It is possible, however, that this sentence contains an end-title, in which case it should be punctuated and translated as follows: *Conid "Taibsiu Aidmillti do Choin Chulaind la hÁes Sídi" sin* ("That is 'The Disastrous Vision Shown to Cú Chulainn by the Fairies'"). The reference here is taken to be to a told tale rather than to a set of events. In any case, the wording here is reminiscent of Cú Chulainn's own words. *Taibsiu* 'vision, dream, phantasm' recalls his description of his experience as an *aislinge* 'vision, dream' (line 123), while *aidmillti*, genitive singular of the verbal noun of *aidmillid* 'completely destroys,' echoes his use of a finite form, *-aidmilset*, of this verb in: "*Dó duit úaim, a Láig*," for *Cú Chulaind*, "*co airm hi tá Emer, & innis condat mná sídi rom thathigset & rom admilset*" ("'Go from me, Lóeg,' said Cú Chulainn, 'to the place where Emer is, and tell her that they are fairy women who have visited me and destroyed me,'" line 313).

The remainder of the passage seems at first sight to subvert the entire narrative by saying that it was all an illusion. I believe, however, that so far from being subversive, this narratorial commentary offers an adroit underpinning of the narrative, for its claim is that illusions, such as that visited upon Cú Chulainn in this tale, used to occur "before the faith," when demons exercised great magical power, and created illusions which were real for those who experienced them. What is condemned is the use of the words *síde* and *áes síde* for these illusions; the *anéolaig* who are accused of perpetrating this usage are presumably the narrator's less enlightened contemporaries. The integrity of the narrative is enhanced by the commentary which invites us to believe that the events recounted in *SCC* were created, not by a storyteller, but by demons, acting at a time in Ulster's past when their power had not yet been curbed by Christianity.

THE CYCLES OF THE KINGS

20

"The Expulsion of the Déisi"

(2 0 0 5)

The origin-legend of the Déisi Muman tells the story of their expulsion from Meath, their sojourn in Leinster, and finally their settlement south of Cashel. It is found under varying titles in the manuscripts, and it has become conventional to refer to it as "The Expulsion of the Déisi" (hereinafter *ED*). The different versions of the story have a common core, which may be summarized as follows: The ruling dynasty of the Déisi are said to have been Dál Fiachach Suidge—descendants of Fíachu Suidge—and to have resided in the vicinity of Tara. Fíachu Suidge was a brother of Conn Cétchathach, and the troubles of Dál Fiachach begin when a son of Cormac mac Airt, king of Tara and Conn's grandson, forcibly abducts the daughter of a member of Dál Fiachach. The task of avenging this act falls to the girl's uncle, the warrior Óengus Gaibuaifnech. He goes to Tara, kills the king's son, and inadvertently blinds Cormac himself in one eye. Óengus escapes from Tara with his niece, but the Déisi are opposed and defeated in battle by Cormac so that they leave the Tara district. They spend some years in different parts of Leinster, and when they are driven out of there they go to the southwest. They finally settle down when they form an alliance with Óengus mac Nad-Fraích, king of Cashel, who marries Eithne Uathach, a fosterling of the Déisi: on foot of this alliance, they displace the Osraige from the plain of Cashel, and take possession of their Tipperary territories.

This tale was evidently of great interest to the compilers of our manuscripts, for it is preserved in some of the earliest and most considerable of them, and the legend is reflected, in whole or in part, in a number of other sources. The popularity of the origin-legend of the Déisi among compilers of Irish manuscripts may in part be put down to the fact that the opening episode of the story—the expulsion from Tara—has to do with the legendary king of Tara, Cormac mac Airt, but it must owe something also to the pivotal role which the Déisi are said to have had in the consolidation of the Éoganacht kingship at Cashel.

It has been customary to distinguish between an early and a later version of *ED*. The "early version" is preserved in the following manuscripts:

R   Oxford, Bodleian Library, MS Rawlinson B 502, 72rb19–73rb30. 12th century.[1] Facsimile, Meyer (1909a, 131b19–133b30). Headed *Tairired na nDessi inso*. . . . Ed. Meyer (1901a).

L   Oxford, Bodleian Library, MS Laud Misc. 610, 99b2–102a2. 15th century.[2] Headed *De Causis Torche na nDéssi .i. Acuis Toirge na nDésse*. Ed. Meyer (1907a).

UM   Book of Uí Maine = Dublin, RIA MS 1225, formerly D ii 1, 91ra1–91va1. 14th century.[3] Facsimile, Macalister (1942). Incomplete. Headed *Cuis Toirchi na n[D]eise da Muigh Breagh isan Mumhain*. Ed. Pender (1947, 213–16). Corrigenda, V. Hull (1954c).

LFF   Liber Flavus Fergusiorum = Dublin, RIA MS 476, formerly 23 O 8, 51va1–51vb1.[4] 15th century. A fragment. Title frayed. Ed. Pender (1947, 216–17).

The "later version" is preserved in three manuscripts, the full text of each of which is given in the edition (with translation) by V. Hull (1958–59):

LU   Lebor na hUidre = Dublin, RIA MS 1229, formerly 23 E 25. 11th–12th centuries.[5] Incomplete. Headed *Tucait Innarba na nDessi i mMumain inso*.[6] Ed. *LU* (137–41).

H   Trinity College Dublin MS 1316, formerly H.2.15a, 67a49–68b11.[7] 14th century. Headed *Tucait Chaechta Cormaic do Aengus Gaibuaibtheach 7 Aiged Cheallaig 7 Fotha Indarbtha na nDeissi do Maig Breg andso*. Ed. Meyer (1907b).

h   Trinity College Dublin MS 1336, formerly H.3.17, cols. 720.1–723.26.[8] Probably not earlier than the 16th century.[9] Variants in Meyer's edition of H (1907b). A fresh collation was made by V. Hull (1954b).

There is ample justification for this broad distinction between an early and a later "version" of *ED*. While Meyer aptly called the early version a "tribal history,"[10] Myles Dillon said of the later version that it had "taken on the form of a tale."[11] The sojourn of the Déisi in Leinster, which is recounted in detail in the early version, is given only a brief mention in the later one. Four sons of Art Corb are named in the early version, which in R opens as follows:

Cethri maic batar la hArttchorb mac Meschuirb .i. Brecc 7 Oengus 7 Echuid 7 Forad. Forad dano mac side cumaile 7 ni ra-gaib thir 7 is he ba siniu dib. (R §1)

Art Corb son of Mess Corb had four sons, namely Brecc and Óengus and Echaid and Forad. Forad for his part was the son of a slave girl and he did not receive any land and he was the eldest of them.[12]

There is no reference to Brecc or Echaid in the later version. Echaid is said in the earlier version (R §11; L lines 36–41) to have travelled to Dyfed in Wales and founded a dynasty there. This is a matter of considerable interest, since both R and L preserve a pedigree of Echaid's descendants that bears comparison with genealogical material preserved in Welsh sources.[13] Brecc, we may infer, was king of Dál Fiachach. In R (§5), we are told that in the immediate aftermath of the abduction, Cormac's forces were routed in seven battles by Óengus together with his brother's sons Ross and Éogan (we learn in R §10 that Brecc is the brother in question). The text then relates that Óengus was king for forty days in succession to Brecc. But his people complained, for they could not endure the combined strength of the ruler and the warrior in one person. Óengus responded by relinquishing the kingship, saying that his "own strength" was best for him. Like much else in *ED*—and especially in the early version—this is ideologically significant, indicating as it does a division of labor between king and warrior within the ruling family, a functional distinction that in this case is insisted upon by the people. It would also be of some interest to the descendants of Ross and Éogan, since Óengus has given up his claim to rule them. Óengus goes a step further when he discovers that Cormac mac Airt has secretly attempted to make peace with Ross and Éogan. Óengus pleads with them as follows:

> "Na denid," ar Oengus, "nadimḟacbaid-se m'oenur! Roforbia da trian in tire araglainfem. Remthus do for clannaib for mo chlainn-se co brath. Ocus mo chlann-sa do dul i cath 7 hi crích ria cach 7 do bith fodeoid ic tudecht a crich. Ocus co n-irglantar tir remib. Nach-im-facbaid-se!" Dorigset iarum anisin 7 doretha fir fris .i. fir ciche 7 gru-aide, nime 7 talman, gréne 7 esca, druchta 7 daithe, mara 7 tire. (R §10, cf. L lines 45–50)

> "Do not do it," said Óengus, "leave me not alone! You shall have two thirds of the land which we shall clear, precedence for your children forever over my own children, and my own children to go to battle and across the border before every one, and to be the last to come out of the enemy's land. And they shall clear the land before you. Do not leave me!" Then they make that compact, and pledges (*fír*) were given for it, namely pledge of breast and cheek, of heaven and earth, of sun and moon, of dew and light, of sea and land.

The later version also omits much in regard to the settlement of the Munster territories of the Déisi. The alternation of the kingship and judgeship of Munster between the Éoganachta and Corcu Loígde (R §17; L lines 156–65) is not mentioned, nor is the name of Lugaid Loígde Cosc, who has a crucial role to play in the affairs of the Déisi according to the early version (R §18; L lines 166–76). The long lists of the "migratory bands" of the Déisi (R §§23, 27; L lines 103–56) are likewise omitted from the later version. So also is the obscure *roscad* (R §9; L lines 67–79) in which a prophet apparently tells them what lies before them.

The surviving texts of the early version fall into two groups.[14] Hull has established that "R and L represent two independent recensions of an earlier work,"[15] and he summarizes their differences as follows:

> R provides a fuller account than occurs in L; nevertheless, L includes matter, even in the lists of the Déssi migratory peoples, for which there

is no parallel in R. That R and L are mutually independent is shown likewise by the fact that they differ in their respective arrangement of the material that they share in common and that they often also differ to a marked degree in their phraseology.[16]

UM and the fragmentary LFF belong to the same recension as L, and will not be considered further here. What we have in both R and L is a compilatory text, drawing on a number of sources. A striking feature of each of them is that a fairly full account of the adventures of the Déisi is followed by some material which I have described as "supplementary notes": there are ten of these in R (§§24–27), and they add certain details which had not been included in the main narrative.[17] They seem to represent a different tradition of the expulsion story. Four of these notes are found in L, and the likelihood is that R and L ultimately owe the content and positioning of these notes to a common source. However, the L recension has evidently drawn upon yet another source in its account of the expulsion of Dál Fiachach from Meath, and in that of their acquisition of their Munster territories. It diverges from R in these accounts, and uses instead a source that also lies behind the corresponding parts of the later version. The distinction, then, between an early and a later version is a valid one, but it is not absolute.

It is not possible on present knowledge to assign a date of composition to the surviving texts. Linguistically, it is clear that much of the material in the early version was first written in the Old-Irish period, perhaps in the early eighth century. I do not propose to discuss the later version here,[18] but will confine myself instead to the main features of the expulsion, the sojourn in Leinster, and the settlement in Munster, drawing mainly on R. The story as a whole is symmetrical in that the expulsion occurs because of an improper sexual union between a son of the Dál Cuinn king of Tara and a woman of the Déisi, while the settlement is brought about on foot of a marriage alliance between the Éoganacht king of Cashel and a woman who is foster-daughter to the rulers of the Déisi.

Cormac mac Airt has a hot-blooded son, who seizes and rapes a daughter of Forad son of Art Corb. Óengus sets out for Tara to seek his niece, and when he sees her there at the right hand of Cormac's son, he expresses his indignation at their "marriage alliance" (*clemnas*). His anger is not assuaged by the terms in which certain people at Tara (according to L) or Cormac's son (according to R) defend what has been done. In L (line 9), the people say to Óengus, "The Dál Cuinn permit him to do that/grant that to him" (*Daimthi Dál Cuind do-som inní sein*).[19] The reading of R (§2) is different here: it is Cormac's son who answers, and what he says is *Daimthi dail cuind dam-sa*, which Meyer translates, "Grant me the respite of a grown-up person." However, *daimthi* is to be taken as third-person singular present indicative, with suffixed pronoun, and *dail* in R should be emended to *dál*, as in L, which preserves the correct nominative form. R should then be translated "Dál Cuinn permit me to do it/grant it to me." The sense may be that he claims the right to rape and marry Forad's daughter by virtue of his being a scion of Dál Cuinn, or more probably that the Dál Cuinn have permitted him to take her as his wife after he has raped her.[20] In any case, Óengus's response confirms that Dál Cuinn is the subject of the sentence. In L (line 9) he says, "I shall not permit it, however" (*Ni didam-sa caimme*), in R "I shall not tolerate/permit it, however" (*Nocon fodem cetumus*). This derives its point from the contrast between the permitting of the marriage by Dál Cuinn, and Óengus's declining to do so.

Óengus then proceeds to run his lance through the king's son. This "lance" was rather an elaborate weapon and had two chains attached to it. One of these chains struck the king, blinding him in one eye. This was a momentous event, for Cormac could no longer remain in Tara: he had a dwelling constructed at Skreen, which is where he resided from then on. This is explained in R (§3): *ar ni ba hada ri co n-anim do feis i Temraig*. Meyer's translation, "for it was not lawful for a king with a blemish to sleep in Tara," is unexceptionable; it is quite clear from the context that *feis* means "to sleep, spend the night" here. At the same time, we cannot altogether forget the resonance of the phrase *feis Temro/Temrach* as a mark of the legitimacy of the king of Tara.[21]

In any case, the king's son died and Óengus took the girl with him. Cormac sent his forces against the Déisi, but (as we have seen) the Déisi vanquished them (R §5).[22] Cormac then gathered "the men of Ireland" to fight the Déisi, and he did not grant them fair fight (*cert catha*), so they left their lands and went into Leinster. Fíachu ba Aiccid, king of the Laigin, was obliging enough to drive the Uí Bairrche out of their territories for the Déisi. In due course, however, one Echu Guinech of the Uí Bairrche expelled the Déisi in turn, and this time it was Crimthann son of Énnae Cennselach who came to their rescue, sending them to Ard Ladrann (Ardamine in County Wexford). Crimthann is said to have married no fewer than three daughters of Ernbrand of the Déisi. First there was Mell, who bore him four sons, and then Belc, who bore him three sons. Their sister Cuiniu bore him only one child, a daughter Eithne Uathach, "Eithne the terrible." When she was born it was foretold that on her account her maternal kin, the Déisi, would seize the land upon which they would dwell. In order that she might grow more quickly, she was given the flesh of little boys to eat, and she was called Eithne Uathach because little boys dreaded her.

After the death of Crimthann, his sons drove the Déisi out of Leinster into the lands of Osraige, where they settled at the Meeting of the Three Waters at a spot called Miledach. They were once again sent packing, this time by the king of the Osraige. They then went by sea westward until they settled at Irchuilenn "in the west."

Óengus mac Nad-Fraích was king of Cashel. His wife died and he sought the hand of Eithne Uathach in marriage. Eithne Uathach was residing with the Déisi in the west, and the three requests that she made of Óengus were all in the interests of the Déisi: that the green (*faithche*) of Cashel be given to her for the Déisi to live on, that the Déisi be permitted to drive out the Osraige and take possession of their land, and that they should be as free as the Éoganachta Raithlinn, Éoganachta Locha Léin, the Uí Fidginti, and the Uí Liatháin.

Óengus granted these requests. But the Osraige defeated the Déisi in seven battles (L line 102, reports an alternative account that puts the number of battles at thirty). Eithne then advised her maternal kin to enlist the aid of the Corcu Loígde, which they duly did. The king of Cashel was of the Éoganachta, while the judge (*brithem*) was of the Corcu Loígde. During the reign of Óengus mac Nad-Fraích, the judge was Lugaid Cosc, and it was to him that the Déisi turned for help. They promised that they would give him some of their land—the land, we must assume, that they hoped to wrest from the Osraige—and that he would have it *cen chís, cen chongbail, cen dunad, cen biathad* ("without having to pay rent or maintain them, answer a call to arms, or feed them").[23] The pledge (*fír*) of Óengus and those of Eithne and the princes of the Déisi were invoked for this.

Acting on the advice of Lugaid Cosc, the Déisi contrived to discover how they should use magical means to ensure that the Osraige would be defeated in the final battle. And so they routed them from as far as the river Lingaun, and thus acquired the territory that now corresponds to the baronies of Iffa and Offa East in County Tipperary.

Eithne had not rested once she had secured the support of the Corcu Loígde, however. She proceeded to gather every "exiled band" (*cach longas*) which she knew of in Ireland "for the Dál Fiachach Suidge had been diminished in so many battles" (*fobíth nodigbaitis Dal Fiachach Suidge isna cathaib mencib*, R §22). A division is made of the land that has been seized from the Osraige, but there are some difficulties about the text at this point:

> Rannait iarum na Dessi i cetrib rannaib na tiri sin. Cach clann tarraid in cethramaid sin ata a chuit isin tir. Coeca toirgi lasna Dessib, a .xxu. dib tarthatar raind 7 a .xxu. aile na tarthatar 7 is dona toirgib sin is ainm Dessi, ar it e fil fo chis 7 dligud 7 bothachas na ndeisse[24] dona flaithib .i. do Dail Fiachach Suidge 7 ni hainm doib-side Deisse. (R §22)

> The Déisi then divide those lands into four parts. Each family that got one of those four shares has its share in the land. There were fifty migratory bands among the Déisi: twenty-five of them got a share, while the other twenty-five did not. And those migratory bands are called Déisi, for it is they who are under the rent and legal obligation and croft-rent of vassals to lords, viz. to the Division of Fíachu Suidge and the latter are not called Déisi.

One thing is quite clear: a distinction is made between the Dál Fiachach Suidge (to whom, it will be remembered, Óengus granted the status of a free people), and the Déisi, who by definition were "subject-peoples." Moreover, the lords to whom the Déisi paid rent were not the Éoganachta of Cashel but the Dál Fiachach. But questions remain. How is a fourfold division distributed among twenty-five recipients? Are we dealing here with a numerological notion, where the four is augmented by a completive number, and the resulting five is multiplied by itself? This is perhaps reminiscent of the division of Ireland, which comprises four parts and a completive center, into twenty-five parts among the sons of Úgaine Mór.[25] Then there is the matter of the migratory bands: are they all called "Déisi"? Meyer took it that this designation applied to those who did not get land; this implies that those who got land were not "vassals" of Dál Fiachach. But this requires us to take *sin* to mean "former": Meyer translates *is dona toirgib sin is ainm Dessi* "the former are called Dessi." L (lines 215–17) suggests a different interpretation. The order is reversed, and *sin* is lacking: *Coica toirgi laisna Déisi. A cuic fichet dib tarthatar raind, a cuic fichet nach tarthatar 7 is dona toirgib is ainm Déisi,* "The Déisi had fifty migratory bands. Twenty-five of them got a division and twenty-five of them did not. And Déisi is the name of the migratory bands." Thus we have a simple distinction between the Dál Fiachach on the one hand, and all of their allies on the other. This interpretation cannot be reconciled with the solemn pledge that, as we have seen, Óengus mac Nad-Fraích, Eithne, and the lords of the Déisi gave Lugaid Cosc that he would receive some of the conquered land free of rent and of the other obligations of vassalage. It may be noted that Lugaid's sons are listed among the migratory bands (R §23; L lines 107–8). There seem then to have been three categories among these bands: those who received land without obligation, those who received land as vassals of Dál Fiachach, and those who did not receive any land at all.

In historical times Déisi Muman comprised what is now County Waterford and contiguous land in south County Tipperary, corresponding more or less to the present Diocese of Waterford and Lismore. But *ED* accounts only for the acquisition of the Tipperary territories. Eithne asked for the meadow-land of Cashel as far as Luasc, and when the routing of the Osraige is described, the territories are seen to stretch from Mullach Inneona near Clonmel to the river Lingaun, which, as we are informed in L (lines 206–7), was thenceforth the boundary between the Déisi and Osraige (*conodh i sein in choicrich co brath etir na Deisi 7 Osseirge*). To this day it is the diocesan boundary between Waterford and Lismore and Ossory.

What, then, of the Waterford territories? MacNeill observed that *ED* did not distinguish between "the Déisi settlements south of the Suir in County Waterford and those north of the Suir in County Tipperary," and therefore thought it probable that the territory of Osraige included the greater part of County Waterford.[26] The fact remains that *ED* does not deal with the Waterford territories. It may be significant that the earliest Dál Fiachach king of whom we have contemporary documentation, Bran Finn, is referred to as Bran Finn Femin—Bran Finn of the south Tipperary plain.[27] The possibility should be borne in mind that some of the migratory bands had been settled in Munster before Dál Fiachach ever entered into an alliance with the Éoganachta of Cashel.

How much history lies behind *ED*? The expulsion episode may well be "a fabrication" as O'Rahilly argued.[28] For one thing, there are very serious chronological inconsistencies in the account of the Déisi's Leinster adventures.[29] Yet there may be a historical basis for the indication in the text that the Déisi were allies of the Uí Cheinselaig in their struggle with the Uí Bairrche, and that that struggle took place or reached its height during the late fifth-century reign of Crimthann as king of Uí Cheinselaig. The story of the expulsion of the Osraige and the settlement of the Déisi in their Tipperary territories belongs to what Liam Ó Buachalla in this journal has called "the dawn of the historical period," the reign of Óengus mac Nad-Fraích as king of Cashel.[30] Ó Buachalla held it highly probable that the latter part of *ED* "contains much genuine history."[31] It is plausible—and in keeping with what seems to have been their general practice—that the Cashel kings should have employed Dál Fiachach to expel the Osraige and defend their southern flank. It is in reward for this that the Dál Fiachach enjoyed free status in Munster.[32] Indeed, Francis John Byrne has pointed to a statement that of the dues payable by the kings of Cashel to other Munster kings, the Déisi receive the particularly handsome payment of fifty *cumal*s "for it is the Dési who first established the kingdom of Cashel."[33] Ó Corráin has pointed out, however, that Byrne is here using the (unpublished) later recension of the text in question, and tentatively dates that recension to the second half of the tenth century.[34] We need not doubt, however, that the Dál Fiachach were essential allies to the Éoganachta in Cashel. And O'Rahilly may very well be right in his suggestion that the story of their banishment from Tara and their respectable descent from "an alleged brother" of Conn Cétchathach served the purpose of providing them with a respectable pedigree while at the same time stamping them as aliens.[35]

21

On the LU Version of "The Expulsion of the Déisi"

(1 9 7 6)

"The Expulsion of the Déisi" (*ED*) is the origin legend of the Déisi of East Munster.[1] It tells of their expulsion, apparently from Meath, and of their wanderings until they finally wrested their Munster territories from the Osraige. Among the texts of *ED*, Meyer (1901a, 102) distinguished two versions. Of these, the early version, as V. Hull (1954c, 266) has shown, occurs in two independent recensions which are represented respectively by the texts of Rawlinson B 502 (Meyer 1901a) and Laud 610 (Meyer 1907a).[2] The early version was aptly called by Meyer a "tribal history": as well as straightforward narrative it contains a deal of genealogical and other matter whose interest is historical rather than literary.

The later version of *ED* survives in three manuscripts: *Lebor na hUidre* (LU), H.3.17, and H.2.15; the three texts have most recently been edited by

V. Hull (1958–59) and the text of LU, which is of course the oldest MS, is also available in *LU* (137 ff.).[3] The three texts of the later version are independent of one another; they show such differences in phrasing and content that it would be impossible to establish a satisfactory critical text, and Hull's decision to print the three texts in full was the right one. It is nevertheless clear that all three texts derive substantially from an archetype. To judge from the common content of our three texts, this archetype stood in contrast to the "tribal history" of the early version: the long tribal lists and all but the most essential genealogical and topographical matter have been jettisoned. The principle of selection exercised in the composition of the later version seems to have been purely literary. Indeed, it was the late Myles Dillon (1946, 1) who characterized the later version when he observed that "it has taken on the form of a tale."[4]

The aim of the present article is to draw attention to a feature of the LU text of the later version (U). We shall see that textual comparison enables us to identify two strata in U and it will be argued that this stratification is reflected in the language of the text. These strata belong to the main text and are therefore anterior to the latest stratum in U, which Best has already isolated on palaeographical grounds as the work of the Interpolator (H). The main text was written out by the second scribe of LU, Mael Muire (M; d. 1106); the identity of H is unknown, but he has been assigned variously to the twelfth and thirteenth centuries.[5] M's text was allowed to stand comparatively unscathed by H: of the seven interpolations in his hand, five are very brief, the longest consisting of four words, the shortest of one word only; the other two take up over thirteen lines of the printed text (4388–95; 4432–37). These interpolations are distinguished from M's text in *LU* by the use of brackets and a different typeface; their content has been discussed by Hull (1958–59, 16), and they need not detain us here. It is M's text which must be examined, and in what follows U designates the main text without the interpolations.

Comparison with the other two texts of the later version shows that U contains one substantial sequence of which only a small part is represented in either of the other two. It occurs in the early part of the text, where the circumstances leading to the expulsion of the Déisi are set out. What happened, in summary, is that a son of King Cormac mac Airt abducted a daughter of one of the Déisi: in the course of avenging this deed Óengus Gaibuaifnech of the Déisi killed Cormac's son, his steward, and nine of his

21. On the LU Version of "The Expulsion of the Déisi"   295

champions, and also blinded the king in one eye, thus rendering him ineligible to retain the kingship. Cormac subsequently retired from Tara, and the Déisi were expelled into Leinster.

In its account of these events, U includes some matter which is lacking in the other texts. The matter peculiar to U occurs in the sequence covered by lines 4340–62 and comprises four passages:

(1) Is airi . . . co n-indechad (lines 4340–42)
(2) Is and . . . Oengusa (lines 4344–45)
(3) Dó dotaig . . . chend (lines 4346–59)
(4) Atchimsea . . . d'oid hé (lines 4360–62)

As for the content of these passages, (1) it is explained that Óengus used to avenge "family insults," (2) that he was performing such a mission in Connacht when the abduction occurred, and (3) that he refused to go to avenge the abduction until he had finished his Connacht mission. But he was taunted for his negligence by a lone woman, whereupon he killed her and was seized by a terrible anger. (4) In an instance of the "watchman technique," the watchman at Tara describes the appearance of a warrior who has arrived there; Cormac identifies him as Óengus and warns that he should be heeded.

These passages account for about 20 of the 23 lines in the sequence; the remaining three lines are also represented in the other two texts.[6] The short account found in the latter texts is perfectly adequate as it stands: it states the fact of the abduction, gives the words spoken by Óengus to the girl's father, and says that Óengus went to Tara. On grounds of sense alone, therefore, it is impossible to determine whether the long account is an expansion, or the short one a contraction of the original. It is, however, a general principle in Irish manuscript tradition that, when two accounts of something are of unequal length, the shorter tends to be the older. That this principle applies here is suggested by the occurrence in two independent manuscripts of the short account, against the single occurrence of the long one. More significantly, as we now turn to the language of U, we shall find that there is a much greater concentration of late forms in these twenty lines than in the remainder of the text.

In presenting the linguistic evidence, I limit myself to the verbal forms, but I may say that the inferences drawn from a study of these seem to be borne out by the other linguistic features. As for the verbs, most of the forms of the text are in accord with classical Old Irish. A full verbal system would take up too much space here, and in any case it seems adequate for my purpose to list those verbal forms which are later than classical Old Irish.[7] In what follows these forms are set out in two lists: (I) late forms in the stratum of 20 lines isolated above, and (II) late forms in the rest of the main text.

I

(1) Spread of -*m* ending to hiatus vb., indic. pres. sg. 1: *atchimsea* 4360.
(2) New simple vbb. replacing OIr compounds: Indic. pres. sg. 3 *tomlid* 4355, *tocbaid* 4356, *tócbaid* 4357; Pl. 3 *tecmait* 4358; Pret. sg. 3 -*ét* 4356 (to (*f*)*étaid*)
(3) *S*-pret. for OIr *t*-pret.: Sg. 3 -*immir* 4348
(4) Spread of OIr deponent ending to active vb., subj. pres. sg. 1: -*dernur* 4347
(5) *Andá* 4351, 4354 for OIr *oldaas, indaas, indá(a)s*
(6) Perf. pass. *tarfas* 4361, for OIr *do-árbas*

II

(1) New simple vbb. replacing OIr compounds: Pret. pl. 3 -*teilcset* 4385, -*aithniset* 4365
(2) Displacement of *s*-subj.: Sg. 3 -*maided* 4447
(3) Spread of OIr deponent ending to active vb., subj. pres. sg. 1: -*rucur-sa* 4408, 4456
(4) New ending in fut. sg. 1: *ataifetsa* 4456, *ragatsa* 4468 (the OIr fut. stem, *reg-, rig-* has been replaced by *rag-* in the latter form and in *ragait* 4459, 4462)
(5) Use of *nocho(n)* as neg. of the copula: *noco* 4449
(6) Perf. of *do-gní*: Sg. 1 *doronus* 4404; 3 *doroni* 4401, -*derna* 4412, -*dernai* 4371
(7) MIr spellings: *contule* 4464 (OIr -*i*); *atrebom* 4400 (OIr -*am*);[8] -*mebaid* 4373 (OIr -*memaid*); -*deochaid* 4377 (OIr -*dechaid*), *do-deocad-sa* 4455 (OIr *do-dechad-sa*); -*raib* 4406, 4408 (OIr -*roib*); *biait* 4461 (OIr *bieit*); *nírb* 4441 (OIr -*bo*, -*bu*)

Both of these lists contain forms which are clearly later than classical Old Irish, but it must be remembered that the first list is taken from twenty lines of text, while the second comes from more than five times that number. List I is fully representative of the language of the stratum from which it is taken; beside List II, on the other hand, we could place another one, taken from the same parts of the text, to show the retention of Old Irish features which were obsolescent or already obsolete by the Middle Irish period. The two lists, therefore, do not have the same significance. The first represents a new stratum, composed in the Middle Irish period and worked into an existing text. The second one comprises Middle Irish innovations distributed through what is otherwise an Old Irish text: these forms must represent a partial re-writing of an Old Irish exemplar. For the most part, this re-writing may already have been carried out in the common ancestor of all three texts of the later version: there are only a few cases in which either of the other two texts of that version have an early form to correspond to a later form in U.[9] We cannot be sure of this, however, for the later forms could be put down to independent innovation in each of the three texts. Moreover, the Middle Irish forms of List II may be the work of successive copyists, whereas those of List I were in all probability contributed by one person.

The two sets of Middle Irish forms represent two different aspects of the process of renovation to which what was basically an Old Irish text was subjected in the Middle Irish period. This process can be seen as part of the large-scale reworking of Irish literature which we know was being conducted around 1100 A.D. (cf. Binchy 1963, xiv). I do not attempt to supply absolute dates for the modifications in the text. The only way in which that could be attempted would be by comparing the language of the text with that of other, datable, Irish texts. The ways in which linguistic criteria have been used to date Irish texts have been cogently criticized by Mac Eoin (1961, 40 ff.; 1960–61, 193 ff.). More recently, Mac Niocaill (1968) has shown how a statistical test could be used to establish the relative dating of texts. This test cannot be applied to U, which is relatively short and does not yield a large enough sample of any relevant linguistic feature. In any case, the test in question is applied on the assumption that "linguistic usage is fairly uniform at a given period" (Mac Niocaill 1968, 49). The whole burden of my argument here, on the other hand, is that the language of U reflects two different aspects of the literary use of language in the Middle Irish period. If this is correct, it follows that significance attaches, not merely to the occurrence of late forms beside earlier ones, but also to the degree to which these forms are concentrated in different parts of the text.

In the course of the foregoing discussion, some light has been cast on the later stages in the process whereby the LU text of "The Expulsion of the Déisi" took on its present form. Even without attempting to re-trace the earlier stages of its textual history, we can see that our text is the culmination of a long process of development. Having questioned (as some would see it) the "integrity" of our text, it must be said that study of the genesis of a text is no substitute for evaluation of the text as it stands. The fact that an unknown number of persons intervened in the evolution of U does not mean that the end-product is a mere palimpsest. On the contrary, it seems to me that the text has a satisfying and ingenious structure, and that its content is full of interest for the student of Irish myth and legend.[10] What has happened is that the account of the fortunes of the Déisi has become a miniature frame-tale: within the threefold division of the tribal history—expulsion, wandering, and settlement—three distinct anecdotes or tales are narrated. We could call these the tales of Óengus Gaibuaifnech, the Birth-tale of Corc Duibne, and the tale of Eithne Uathach.

The "tale" of Óengus Gaibuaifnech has been summarized above. His position as avenging hero of the Déisi is a tragic one: to him falls the task of avenging crimes against his people, but should he attack a member of the royal household he would draw the wrath of the king upon his own people. This explains Óengus's reluctance to avenge the abduction of a girl of the Déisi by the king's son. Óengus is driven to his fate by the taunting of a lone woman: it is her words which arouse his anger (*ferg*) and drive him to a kind of frenzy. This *ferg* is the mark of the martial hero of Irish tradition: "The hero is the furious one, possessed of his own tumultuous and blazing energy" (Sjoestedt 1949, 58). It is in such a state that Óengus arrives at Tara, as the watchman observes: "*Atchimsea ... láech ... 7 tarfas dam gné fergi fair*" (lines 4360–62). At Tara, Óengus wreaks terrible vengeance on the king's household.

The sequel to all of this is briefly told: the king abandons Tara and the Déisi are expelled into Leinster. They make their way to south Leinster, and thence to Tech nDuinn off the coast of Kerry. It was at Tech nDuinn that Óengus's foster-son Corc Duibne was reared, and this provides the occasion for relating the Birth-tale of Corc Duibne, which takes up more than one-fifth of the text. This is an interesting tale of the *compert*-class, some examples of which are discussed in Rees and Rees (1961, 213 ff.).

Corc remains at Tech nDuinn, but the Déisi go to Cashel, where Óengus mac Nad-Fraích is king. Here begins what we may call the tale of Eithne Uathach, for henceforth the saga is dominated by this foster-daughter of the Déisi. In return for the hand of Eithne, Óengus mac Nad-Fraích grants the Déisi permission to seize the land of the Osraige south of Cashel. They are at first unsuccessful in their efforts to drive out the Osraige. That they eventually succeed is owed to Eithne: there is a long description of how she cunningly outwits the druid of the Osraige and thereby discovers how the Déisi may rout them. Eithne is one of the formidable women of Irish narrative tradition. It was prophesied of her that through her agency the Déisi would settle down, and she is fed on the flesh of children so that she might grow more quickly. She is the grand manipulator, gathering fighters to assist the Déisi, plotting ruses, and finally showing the Déisi how they might achieve victory.

We can discern a certain logic in the development of the LU version of *ED*. The tale of Eithne is found also in both redactions of the early version; the Birth-tale of Corc is found only in the later version; much of the material on Óengus, as we have seen, is found only in U. The person who inserted the latter not only added to the interest of the story; he also imposed a pleasing symmetry on its structure, in that each of the stages in the history of the Déisi is told in connection with the deed of a hero or heroine. It might be accounted a flaw that he did not go further and rewrite the whole story in his own words: the text he has left us is not linguistically homogenous.

It is appropriate to conclude with a word on Mael Muire, to whose labors we owe the preservation of this text. I have explained why I do not feel able to date the later stratum in M's text, but it seems not impossible that it was the scribe's own contribution. That his attitude to the text was not entirely passive is suggested by the two glosses in his hand. Whatever about that, the choice by Mael Muire of this particular text is interesting in itself. Oskamp (1966–67, 117) suggests that A, the first scribe of LU, was working to a plan. As outlined by Oskamp, A's plan may be said to be antiquarian in spirit. Mael Muire apparently did not share this antiquarian attitude, and he copied texts which would not fit into A's plan. Oskamp says that "the result is a MS. without any theme, a compilation in a pejorative sense" (1966–67, 118). This judgment is rather severe on Mael Muire. His tastes were literary rather than antiquarian, and we do not expect the library of a literary man to be informed by an antiquarian theme. Oskamp observes that *ED* "might find a place in the type of MS. which A apparently proposed to compile" (1966–67, 118); but A would doubtless have chosen to include the early version of *ED*. A and M represent two tendencies in Irish tradition: the one with an antiquarian and historical bias, the other with a stronger leaning towards literature. We are fortunate that both of these tendencies found a place in the Irish scriptoria. To one of them we owe the early version of *ED*, preserved in Rawlinson B 502 and in Laud 610; to the other, in the person of Mael Muire, the LU text of the later version, which had been shaped over the centuries into a work of literature.

22

The Déisi and Dyfed

(1984)

It has generally been accepted that the early migration from the northern half of Ireland to Scotland was paralleled by those from the southern half to Gwynedd and Dyfed in Wales. While these migrations represent what must have been more or less contemporaneous manifestations of an outward thrust from Ireland to the neighboring island, the southern migrations stand in sharp contrast to the northern insofar as they were to differ greatly in their ultimate effects. The migration to Scotland was a formative event in the history of that country, for the Irish colonists were of course the founding fathers of Gaelic Scotland. In Wales, on the other hand, the colonists were assimilated in time to the culture of their new homeland. They did leave their mark on Welsh placenames, as Richards (1960) has shown, and they left an enduring memorial in the ogam stones, which have been taken as evidence that "the Irish immigrants in Britain were still speaking Irish by the end of the sixth century" (Jackson 1950, 212). The Irish community in Wales seems also to have influenced the course of Welsh literature, though the precise extent of their influence is difficult to gauge and remains a matter of some controversy.[1]

We do not have contemporary documents at our disposal relating to the Irish migrations to Scotland and Wales, and they are in that sense prehistoric. For this reason, the testimony of documents compiled and recorded many centuries after the occurrence of the relevant events has taken on an importance which it would not otherwise have. So much is true of the origin legend now generally known as "The Expulsion of the Déisi" (abbreviated *ED*), which is constantly used as a source for the history of the Irish colonization of Dyfed. The purpose of the present article is to take a fresh look at what *ED* has to tell us about the matter. We shall see that the origin-legend claims that an Irishman, Echaid Allmuir son of Art Corb of Dál Fiachach Suidge crossed the sea to Dyfed and settled there with his children, and that it gives a pedigree of eighth-century date which shows the ruling dynasty of Dyfed to be descended from the said Echaid Allmuir. This pedigree can be compared with one which is preserved in the Welsh Harleian 3859 genealogies and which shows a considerable degree of correspondence with it. While the Harleian pedigree does not acknowledge the Irish ancestry of the Dyfed dynasty, we can add another item from early Welsh genealogy which can be interpreted as corroboration of the Irish claim as we have it in *ED*. The genealogical material and the narrative of *ED* have of course been considered in the context of other evidence on the Irish colonization of Dyfed (and of southern Britain generally), notably the placenames, the inscriptions, and, on the documentary side, the relevant observations of Cormac mac Cuilennáin, Gildas, and Nennius. What used to be more or less the received view of the matter was stated by Dillon (1977, 3): "there is no reason to doubt that the migration of the Dési did take place at the end of the third century, and that the dynasty of Dyfed in the eighth century was descended from an Irish family."

The received view has recently been challenged by M. Miller (1977–78). She accepts the Irish ancestry of the Dyfed dynasty, but argues for placing Echaid Allmuir's settlement within the years 400–425 (and thus very much later than Dillon's "end of the third century"). Miller addresses herself to the problem of the arrival of the Déisi in Dyfed and their "Cymricisation": as well as placing their arrival in the first quarter of the fifth century, she concludes that the Cymricization of the Déisi was advancing in the years around 450, that they were converted to Christianity, and that their dynasty was Christian two generations later. In constructing her argument, Miller's main recourse is naturally to the Welsh sources, but she also takes account of the Irish material, which she pronounces "reasonably straightforward." No criticism is offered here of Miller's deployment of the Welsh sources, but I fear that the Irish material, and *ED* in particular, will appear on close scrutiny to be very much less than "straightforward." What is proposed, then, is to complement Miller's study by a re-examination of the testimony of *ED*, and to balance her account of the arrival and early history of the Irish migrants in Dyfed with an investigation of what our texts may indicate regarding their departure from Ireland. I would emphasize here the primarily textual nature of the enquiry: my main endeavor will be to isolate and to assess the different strands of tradition which are entangled in the relevant texts of *ED*. The precise relationship of these strands of tradition to the facts of history will remain problematical. Of the fact of a migration (or migrations) from Ireland to Dyfed there seems to be no reasonable doubt, but, in attempting an assessment of the testimony of *ED*, we shall find ourselves faced with problems as to, first, the identity of the migrants; secondly, the source or place of origin of the migration; and, thirdly, its approximate date of occurrence.

One particularly fruitful source of confusion may be dealt with at the outset, and that is the ambiguity of *Déisi*. In historical times, the people so designated would commonly be those who were settled in the territories which now correspond more or less to the diocese of Waterford and Lismore, and which include County Waterford and an extensive contiguous area in County Tipperary.[2] They are sometimes called Déisi Muman, to distinguish them from Déisi Breg, a small group whose name is preserved in the Barony of Deece in County Meath.[3] *Déisi (Muman)*, like other Irish population-names, could refer, according to context, either to the appropriate population-group, or to their territories.

The rulers of Déisi Muman belonged to Dál Fiachach Suidge, so called because of their alleged descent from Fíachu Suidge, grandson of Túathal Techtmar.[4] We sometimes find that *Déisi* refers simply to members of Dál Fiachach Suidge and their retinues.

The Déisi are unusual (though not unique) among early Irish population-groups in that their name seems to be in origin the plural of a common noun: *déis* is "a vassal," and the original meaning of *Déisi*, as applied to population-groups, would have been "vassal or rent-paying tribes," or something of the sort. Eoin MacNeill (1932, 38 f.) has given the following explanation of the evolution of this term from common to proper noun:

> All these septs belonged to a class for which the common designation was Déis. The original significance of this term, so used, was forgotten, and Dési was thought of merely as the proper name of certain septs and the population subject to them, and so induced a notion of consanguinity.

It follows from all of this that we must be careful in drawing inferences from any statements made about the Déisi in the texts: are they referring to the people and territories of what we know today as Waterford and south Tipperary? Or to the genealogical entity known as Dál Fiachach Suidge? Or, more generally, to vassal or rent-paying tribes? As far as *ED* is concerned, this matter of the ambiguity of *Déisi* can be dealt with by giving a broad outline of the story and then going on to establish at what points in the narrative the different meanings of *Déisi* come into play.

ED tells of the expulsion of the Déisi from Meath, their sojourn in Leinster, and their settlement in Wales and Munster.[5] The story opens with the statement that Art Corb (of Dál Fiachach Suidge) had four sons, Brecc, Óengus, Echaid, and Forad. The son of Cormac mac Airt, king of Tara, ravished Forad's daughter, and Óengus went to the king's court in search of the girl. There Óengus attacked and killed the king's son, and he also inadvertently blinded the king in one eye. Óengus escaped, taking Forad's daughter with him. Since the loss of his eye was a blemish (*ainem*), Cormac was thereby disqualified from holding the kingship, and he was obliged to leave Tara. The Déisi were driven into Leinster; the account of their sojourn there is confused and chronologically inconsistent, and we shall have to return to it. For the present it will be enough to say that the Déisi were welcomed in Leinster by Fíachu ba Aiccid, who settled them in territories he had seized from the Uí Bairrche. There the Déisi remained until the time of Crimthann son of Énnae Cennselach, when the Uí Bairrche forcibly repossessed their territories, and the Déisi were taken to Ard Ladrann[6] by

Crimthann. In the meantime, Echaid son of Art Corb had gone to Dyfed with his family and settled there. Those of the Déisi who had gone to Ard Ladrann did not remain there for long, for after Crimthann's death they were driven out once more, first into Osraige, and then to the southwest. Finally, they entered into an alliance with Óengus son of Nad-Fraích, king of Cashel: Eithne Uathach of the Déisi was betrothed to Óengus, and the Déisi in return were permitted to drive the Osraige out of their territories in what is now south County Tipperary, and settle there themselves. Eithne Uathach gathered together all the exiled groups in Ireland to help the Déisi, who eventually routed the Osraige and settled in their territory.

In attempting to disentangle the different senses in which *Déisi* is used in this story, I think we can say that it was Dál Fiachach Suidge who were expelled from Meath and spent a period in Leinster, that it was one of their branches which crossed the sea to Dyfed, and that it was other of their branches which were to settle territories wrested from the Osraige in what is now south County Tipperary. It is in the course of the attempt by Dál Fiachach to drive the Osraige out of those territories that we come across *Déisi* in the sense of "vassal-tribes." The Osraige defeat the invaders in seven battles (R §16; L lines 100 f. Others give the number of battles as thirty, L line 101). Because Dál Fiachach have been depleted in many battles, Eithne gathers to them every migratory band of which she knows in Ireland (R §22; L lines 104 f.). The point in the sequence of events at which we are told of Eithne's action differs in L and R; in L, it is after the Osraige have won seven (or thirty) victories in battle but before they have been routed; in R, Eithne's action is revealed after the account of the rout. In any case, the claim of *ED* here is that Dál Fiachach acquired these tribes as allies at some stage of their settlement of their Munster territories, and that Dál Fiachach and the allied tribes henceforth constitute the Déisi. The texts go on to make a distinction between Dál Fiachach and the Déisi properly (that is, etymologically) so called: "There are fifty migratory bands among the Déisi ... and it is these migratory bands which are called Déisi, for they are under the rent and legal obligation and croft-rent (*bothachas*) of vassals to lords,[7] that is, to Dál Fiachach Suidge, and the latter are not called Déisi" (R §22; cf. L lines 215 ff.).

The account in *ED* of their settlement in East Munster purports to tell us how the Déisi were constituted; what the origin was of the relationship between Dál Fiachach and the other constituent groups, on the one hand, and of that between Dál Fiachach and the Éoganacht dynasty of Cashel,[8] on the other; and how the Déisi established themselves in their Tipperary territories.⁹ There are many other points of interest (and not a few difficulties) in the treatment of these matters in our texts, but a discussion of them must await another occasion. For present purposes, we may confine ourselves to what is relevant to the alleged migration to Dyfed of Echaid Allmuir, which is that, according to *ED*, the migration took place before Dál Fiachach settled in East Munster, and hence before Déisi Muman were constituted as a population-group and territorial entity. No claim is made in our texts that the migrants set out from what we know as Déisi Muman, County Waterford, and south County Tipperary. On the contrary, the migration is recounted in the context of the fortunes of Dál Fiachach in Leinster. I have already indicated that the Leinster section of *ED* is confused and chronologically inconsistent, and it will be necessary now to embark on a textual excursus before we go on to try to establish precisely what claims are being made in *ED* about the source and dating of the migration. The examination of the composition of the relevant texts may also perhaps give some indication of the intrinsic interest of *ED* as a specimen of early Irish historiography.

"The Expulsion of the Déisi" was evidently held in high regard by medieval Irish scribes. It is preserved (under various titles) in seven manuscripts, including some of the most important collections of traditional material. There are also numerous accounts of and references to various aspects of the Déisi story in other sources, legendary, annalistic, genealogical, and hagiographical.¹⁰ Among the seven manuscript texts of *ED*, we may follow Meyer (1901a) in distinguishing between an early and a later version. (It is only in the early version that we find any reference to the migration to Dyfed.) The early version is represented by the texts of Rawlinson B 502 (=R), edited by Meyer (1901a), and of Laud 610 (=L), edited by Meyer (1907a), as well as by an incomplete text in the Book of Uí Maine (=UM) and a fragment in *Liber Flavus Fergusiorum* (=LFF), both edited by Pender (1947). The later version is represented in three manuscripts, including *Lebor na hUidre*; the texts of all three are given in full in V. Hull (1958–59).

All the texts of *ED*, insofar as they are complete, have a common core comprising the events leading to their expulsion from Meath, their sojourn in Leinster, and their settlement of territories in East Munster. The narrative in all of them contains dramatic incidents and literary motifs of one kind and another, and, since we have to do with a political legend, there is much talk of alliances and hostilities. Meyer described *ED* as a "tribal history," and that is an apt description of the early version: here we find, within the narrative framework, a deal of non-narrative material, notably the Dyfed pedigree and the long list of tribes which were allegedly brought into alliance with the Dál Fiachach by Eithne Uathach, as well as some technical details of various political relationships. These items are lacking in the later version, which, as Dillon (1946, 1) put it, "has taken on the form of a tale." It may be added that the later version is free of those internal inconsistencies which we shall be isolating in the earlier version. These inconsistencies have their value: as Kelleher (1968, 142) said of the pre-Norman Irish genealogies, "we may take it as an axiom of historiography that in source materials of this age and kind a good, glaring contradiction is worth a square yard of smooth, question-begging consistency." The early version of *ED* exemplifies the fact that the compilation of Irish texts from disparate—and incompatible—sources is sometimes effected in such a way as to enable us to separate the different strands.

Since there is no reference in the later version to Echaid Allmuir or the colonization of Dyfed, we may concentrate our attention here on the four texts of the early version. When we do so, we find that V. Hull has established that R and L "represent two independent recensions of an earlier work" (1954c, 266), and he has summarized their differences as follows (267):

> R provides a fuller account than occurs in L; nevertheless, L includes matter, even in the lists of the Déssi migratory peoples, for which there is no parallel in R. That R and L are mutually independent is shown likewise by the fact that they differ in their respective arrangement of the material that they share in common, and that they often also differ to a marked degree in their phraseology.

The two partial texts (LFF and UM) belong with L rather than with R. LFF is a fragment, preserving only the commencement of *ED*. Enough remains, however, to show "that LFF and L derive from an exemplar different from the exemplar from which R is descended" (V. Hull 1954c, 267). UM is much more complete, and it offers ample support for Hull's conclusion that "in contradistinction to R, both UM and L stem from a common archetype"

(267). In short, L, UM, and LFF represent the one recension. Since L is the only complete text of this recension and is in every respect superior to UM and LFF, we can narrow down this discussion still further and content ourselves with an analysis of R and L.

It will be convenient to start with R. Its contents can be broadly outlined as follows, the numbered paragraphs being those of Meyer's edition (1901a):

§§1–5	Events leading to the expulsion of the Déisi
§§6–13	The sojourn of the Déisi in Leinster, and the migration to Dyfed of Echaid Allmuir
§§14	The Déisi in Osraige and in the southwest
§§15–23	The settlement of the Déisi in East Munster, and a list of the constituent population-groups
§§24–27	More on the exile, wandering, and settlement of the Déisi, and a further list of the population-groups

It is obvious from the outline that §§1–23 encompass the "tribal history" of the Déisi, and that the subsequent paragraphs cover some of the same ground. Meyer (1901a, 103) said that "towards the end of both copies (R and L) the scribes have become careless, and each has blundered in his own way." But the true nature of this final section is masked by Meyer's division of it into four paragraphs. A more logical treatment would be to set it out as a sequence of discrete items relating to successive stages in the Déisi story, and that is what is attempted in the list which follows. (Since some of this material is also represented in L, it will be economical to include the appropriate references here.)

I	Crimthann weds the three daughters of Ernbrand one after another	§24 (=L lines 224–27)
II	The Déisi are defeated and expelled by Cairbre Lifechair	§25 (=L lines 228–34)
III	After the slaying of Brecc, the Déisi are driven to Commur	§25 (=L lines 234–37)[11]
IV	The Déisi send to Cashel for aid; the origin of Carn mBrigte[12]	§25
V	The rearing of Eithne Uathach	§26

VI	The exile of the Osraige and the Corco Loígde	§26
VII	The Déisi, the Féni, and the Fothairt	§26 (=L lines 238–42)
VIII	*Forsluinte Dál Fiachach Suidge* (tribal list)	§27
IX	Etymological speculation on *Déisi*	§27
X	The duration of the Laginian sojourn of the Déisi	§27 (=L lines 243–46)

These items seem to be a set of supplementary notes rather than a fully developed alternative version of the Déisi story. (In what follows I refer to §§1–23 as the body of R, and to §§24–27 as the supplementary notes.) They would nevertheless appear to reflect a tradition different from that of the body of R. There is nothing in the latter to correspond to VI, VII, IX, or X in the above list. I, on the other hand, is a doublet of the first part of §8. There is agreement that Eithne Uathach was daughter of Cuiniu/Cinniu, daughter of Ernbrand, but in §8 Eithne's father Crimthann is said to have been previously married to Mell, daughter of Ernbrand, whereas in I he is said to have married three daughters of Ernbrand, namely, Mell, Belc, and Cinniu. Indeed, a marked feature of the supplementary notes is triplism in one form or another: in addition to the three daughters of Ernbrand, there is mention of three warriors who slay Brecc (III); a third of the Déisi are driven to Commur (III), and it is that third who rear Eithne Uathach (V); and the wanderings of the Déisi are synchronized with those of the Féni and the Fothairt (VII). The list of the *forsluinte* of Dál Fiachach Suidge contains thirty-three names (VIII). Finally, we are told that it was thirty-three years after the Déisi left Tara that the Laigin gave them battle at Gabrán and at Commur, after having routed them in seven battles (X).

The migration of the Déisi into Leinster (§6) is mentioned also in the supplementary notes (II), but the circumstances leading up to it differ in the two accounts. In the body of R we are told that after he had been blinded in one eye, Cormac had a rath constructed at Achaill outside Tara, "and he used always spend the night in it, for it was not lawful for a king with a blemish to spend the night in Tara" (§4). Cormac sent hosts against the Déisi and defeated them in seven battles (§5). Eventually, "the king of Tara" gathered the men of Ireland against them and he did not grant them fair fight, and so they left his land to him and went into Leinster (§6). Now it might seem reasonable to assume that "the king of Tara" referred to is Cormac himself, since we are told neither that he abdicated nor that he was deposed, and indeed he is shown in §§10 and 12 to have remained active in seeking vengeance on the Déisi (or at least on Óengus Gaibuaifnech). On the other hand, Cormac's retreat to Achaill could quite plausibly be taken as tantamount to abdication, since such would be required of a king who had acquired a physical blemish.[13] The relevant supplementary note (II) poses its own problems, but it is at least unambiguous as to the abdication: "Now when Cormac relinquished his kingship after he was blinded by Óengus son of Artchorp, Cairbre Lifechair assumed the sovereignty in place of his father" (R §25 = L lines 228 f.). Can we assume therefore that "the king of Tara" referred to in §6 is not Cormac, but his son Cairbre Lifechair who succeeded him? We cannot do this with complete assurance, but we may find some encouragement in the consideration that the death of Brecc, which is implicit in §5 but not actually mentioned in the body of R, is attributed in III to Fíachu Sraiphtine, Colla Uais, and Colla Menn. The death of Brecc, like the abdication of Cormac, is germane to the narrative but goes unmentioned until we come to the supplementary notes.

The items which we have been considering either have a triplistic character or add some detail lacking in the main narrative, and they would appear (as I have already noted) to represent a different tradition. The main body of R is compilatory in character: it contains items which can be shown to have existed independently of *ED*, one of these being the Dyfed pedigree, another the tribal lists which must be considered in conjunction with those of the *aithechthúatha*.[14] Moreover, the obscure "prophetic" *rosc* (R §9 = L lines 68 ff.) would seem to reflect yet another version of at least some parts of the Déisi story, the evidence for this being primarily the personal names which occur in the *rosc* but not in the remainder of the text.

If the body of R is a fair reflection of the compilatory text, then it must be said that the compilation has been maladroitly executed. In §7 it is mentioned that Crimthann sent the Déisi to Ard Ladrann. There follows some material dealing with the birth of Eithne Uathach, the migration of the Déisi to Wales, and Cormac's vengeance on Óengus (§§8–12). It is then restated that Crimthann sent the Déisi into Ard Ladrann. This structural defect may reflect the poor narrative technique of the compiler of R: it is known that linear exposition is not always well developed in early Irish writing. But there is a more serious problem about this account, one which cannot so easily be explained away. In §6 it is stated that the Déisi went into Leinster to Fíachu ba Aiccid and that they remained there, occupying territories which Fíachu had taken from the Uí Bairrche, until the time of Crimthann son of Énnae Cennselach son of Labraid son of Bressal Bélach son of Fíachu ba Aiccid. If Cormac and Óengus are portrayed as contemporaries of Fíachu ba Aiccid, they cannot live to share the stage with Fíachu's great-great-grandson Crimthann. The text convicts itself of anachronism by giving Crimthann's pedigree and showing him to be four generations removed from Fíachu. When we look to sources other than *ED* we find that the chronological problem remains. The account in *ED* of Crimthann's descent from Fíachu ba Aiccid is confirmed in the tract *Mínigud Senchassa Lagen* (M. O'Brien 1962, 10). Crimthann's obit is given at 483 in the Annals of Ulster (and repeated at 485). If we allow thirty years to a generation, the assumed date of Fíachu's death would be around 363. As for Cormac mac Airt, Byrne (1973, 65 f.) notes that "the chronographers gave Cormac a reign of forty-odd years in the third century A.D., but a synchronism interpolated into the Annals of Ulster from an eighth-century source places his obit in A.D. 366. As the chronology of the fifth-century Uí Néill dynasts has almost certainly undergone a deliberate process of pre-dating, this probably represents a more accurate tradition" (cf. Carney 1955, 369). Our text can be taken to embody the tradition that Cormac flourished in the fourth century, and by inference this would also be true of his foe Óengus Gaibuaifnech.

These observations are intended, not to establish an absolute chronology for the events depicted in the expulsion story, but rather to determine the chronological framework within which we may sift the material in *ED* itself. Now the only explicit chronological reckoning in *ED* is the mention of thirty-three years as the duration of the sojourn of the Déisi in Leinster; this occurs, as we have seen, in what I have called supplementary note X. (In the heading of the text the duration is given as thirty years.) It is clearly impossible to reconcile this figure with the story in its present form, requiring as that does a lapse of four generations between the expulsion and the reign of Crimthann, after whose death the Déisi were driven out of Leinster. It is true that chronological data of this kind cannot be taken too literally, and that they must be interpreted in the light of the numerological propensities of the Irish literati. Triplistic figures are especially suspect, and examples of triplism abound in the supplementary notes. But even when this reservation is taken into account, it is reasonable to suggest that the figure of thirty-three years cannot have been intended to cover the time-lapse required for the story in its present form.

We have seen that the body of R is chronologically inconsistent, and it remains to consider whether the same is true of the supplementary notes. In other words, is there anything in these notes which is incompatible with the thirty-three-year sojourn in Leinster here allotted to the Déisi? There is no internal criterion to help us in this instance, but, in the light of other sources, we may suspect the statement that Fíachu Sraiphtine, Colla Uais, and Colla Menn killed Brecc. Fíachu Sraiphtine is said to have been grandson, and Colla Uais and Colla Menn great-grandsons of Cormac mac Airt (O'Brien 1962, 147). As Ó Cuív (1976, 179) remarks, "Colla Mend and Colla Óss [=Uais] are best known as grandsons of Cairbre Lifechair who, together with their brother Colla Fó Chríth, killed Fiacha Sraiphtine and eventually won the Airgialla territory of Ulster for Síl Cuinn." What is suspicious in *ED*, however, is not so much the alleged collusion of this trio in slaying Brecc, who was a contemporary of the great-grandfather of the two Collas, but, once again, the chronological difficulty.

It is possible that we can account for the chronological discrepancies in the Déisi story. It will be recalled that in what I have called supplementary note II it is said that Cormac relinquished the kingship after he had been blinded by Óengus, and that Cairbre Lifechair succeeded Cormac. The burden of the rest of this note would seem to be that Cormac then proceeded to instruct his son to destroy the people of Cairbre (*muinter Chairbre*) on both sides of the Boyne, and so the Déisi went (or were driven) into exile in Leinster. Now it is unlikely that Cormac would instruct Cairbre Lifechair to destroy his own people, and *muinter Chairbre* would seem to be a designation of Dál Fiachach. Since this interpretation may be open to question, I discuss the text in some detail in the appendix to the present article, and in the meantime I shall assume that the interpretation is correct. How can *muinter Chairbre* be explained as a designation of Dál Fiachach? An answer to this may be found in the Déisi genealogies. The oldest extant tract on the genealogy of the Déisi (M. O'Brien 1962, 394 ff.) has been dated to the eighth century (Pender 1947, 210); it contains a poem which has been dated to the seventh century (Meyer 1915, 905; Pender 1947, 210). On the basis of this material the following pedigree can be set out for Art Corb, who is of course said to be the father of Óengus, Brecc, Echaid Allmuir, and Forad: Art Corb s. of Mes Corb[15] s. of Mes Gegra s. of Corb s. of Cairbre Rigronn s. of Fíachu

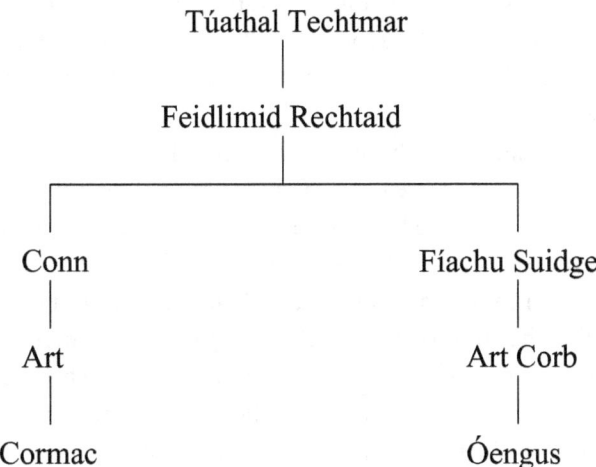

Fig. 22.1. How Cormac and Óengus are related.

Suidge s. of Feidlimid Rechtaid s. of Túathal Techtmar. Here, then, Art Corb is five generations removed from Fíachu Suidge. In a later tract (M. O'Brien 1962, 156 ff.), however, which has been dated to the eleventh century (Pender 1947, 210), Art Corb is son of Fíachu Suidge and the names of the four intervening persons have been omitted.[16] This later state of affairs is altogether appropriate to the events surrounding the expulsion of the Déisi from Meath since the excision of four generations shows Óengus to be an exact contemporary of Cormac's (see fig. 22.1).

If we restore the four lost generations, however, we find that Art's contemporary in the Dál Fiachach line is Cairbre Rigronn, and his people would be called *muinter Chairbre*. It would not be inherently anachronistic for Cormac mac Airt to use such a designation of the Dál Fiachach. If this is the correct explanation of the *muinter Chairbre* of ED, it means that the genealogical tradition represented in the eighth-century tract is reflected in the supplementary notes. It may be added that this very same tradition is also vestigially present in the main body of R where we find mention of Art Corb son of Mess Corb (§1). There is also a reference to Mess Corb in the obscure *roscad* (§9).

It is probable that the discrepancy concerning the duration of the sojourn of Dál Fiachach in Leinster is related to the foreshortening of their pedigree. The Dál Fiachach contemporaries of the Leinster king Crimthann were projected back by four generations, and it was therefore necessary to balance this by showing them to be contemporary with Crimthann's great-great-grandfather, Fíachu ba Aiccid. Thus it was that Dál Fiachach were said to have been welcomed into Leinster by Fíachu ba Aiccid. But if the revision were to be carried out in a thoroughgoing fashion Crimthann would have to be removed from the text. As happens so often in Irish tradition, however, the redactor tries to have it both ways: he introduces Fíachu ba Aiccid, but he retains Crimthann while persisting with the claim that the duration of the Leinster sojourn was a mere thirty-three years. In short, both genealogical traditions of Dál Fiachach, as represented respectively by the eighth-century and the eleventh-century tract, are required in order to explain different parts both of the main body of R and of the supplementary notes. As for the alleged intervention of Fíachu Sraiphtine and Colla Uais and Colla Menn, it is more easily reconciled with the revised than with the unrevised Dál Fiachach pedigree but it probably reflects an innocence (or defiance) of either tradition.

This discussion has been necessary not only to discover something of the nature of the material with which we have to deal, but also (as we shall see) to determine the import and the status of any claim which may be made in R, the case in hand being of course the account of the migration to Dyfed. We may now turn to a brief consideration of L. Vernam Hull (1954c, 268), who did not note the composite character of R, saw evidence of two disparate accounts in L: "the repetition of a passage which occurs once in R suggests that the common exemplar from which L and UM stem already consisted of a blend of two older accounts that have been unskilfully fused together." The relevant passage occurs in L at lines 155 f. and 215 f., of which the latter corresponds to that in R §22. A further indication of the composite character of L is provided by the discrepant accounts of the number of battles in which the Osraige are said to have defeated the Déisi (V. Hull 1954c, 268n6). In this instance, the redactor explicitly acknowledges an alternative tradition: *Muidit secht catha re nOsseirge for na Deise i lLeith Ladcind .i. Art. Asberat araile is tricha cath* (L lines 100 ff.; the corresponding passage in R §16 reads: *Dobertsat na Deisse secht catha do Osairgib 7 romaidset na secht catha sin ria n-Osairgi forsna Deissib hi Lethet Laidcind i n-Ard Chatha*). To these items may be added the supplementary notes in L which, in slightly modified form, correspond to notes I, II, III, VII, and X of R.

The obvious question which arises at this point is whether all the alternative material in L, including the supplementary notes, derives from a single source. In attempting to answer this question we must first of all consider the supplementary notes. The individual items which are common to R and L show some differences of wording but not such differences as to rule out a common source for the two sets. The set in L is not as inclusive as that in R but a crucial point is that the two sets are homotaxial: the items common to the two lists occur in the same relative sequence. Homotaxis is perhaps less than totally compelling as an argument for a common source if we have to do with events which are in any case deemed to occur in chronological sequence. It is not at all clear, however, that we are to take I (Crimthann's wedding the three daughters of Ernbrand) as being chronologically prior to II (the expulsion of the Déisi from Meath). In view of what we have already seen of the ramshackle chronography of *ED* this notion cannot be dismissed out of hand, however preposterous it may seem at first sight. The strong probability nevertheless remains that these homotaxial sets of notes derive from a common source. Finally, the fact that in both texts this material is added on to a fairly full account of the Déisi story suggests that both L and R derive from a text which was formed by adding these short notes to a compilatory tribal history.

In the course of its descent from this remote common ancestor, L appears to have acquired some material from a text which did not contribute to the tradition of R but which was used in the composition of the so-called later version. One such passage describes the expulsion episode and its immediate sequel. The account in L (lines 1–28) differs greatly from that in R (§§1–5), and they could not possibly derive from the same source. The differences are largely phraseological up to line 11 in L, but after that the texts diverge. L goes its own way in (i) recounting the escape of Óengus, who kills nine of Cormac's warriors when they pursue him; (ii) saying that Óengus was accompanied by his fosterling, Corc Duibne; (iii) telling the story of the seven battles at greater length than in R, and in different terms; (iv) explaining the names of Dumu Dér and Mag n-Inair. These latter places are not even mentioned in R; the reference to Ard na nDéise in L is also lacking in R.

The divergent account of the expulsion and its immediate sequel given in L is not to be put down to the source of the supplementary notes, since these latter, as we have seen, attribute the expulsion to Cairbre Lifechair (R §25, L lines 228–34), while in the body of L it seems certain from lines 19 ff. that it is Cormac mac Airt himself who expels them. In any case the version of the expulsion given in the supplementary notes is quite different from that in the body of L. It follows from all of this that, taken together, R and L give three different accounts of the expulsion of the Déisi from Meath, one in the body of R, one in the body of L, and the other in a note preserved in both R and L.

Since we have gone so far with the textual discussion it seems right to take it one step further and to discuss the relationship of the divergent material in L to the corresponding matter in the later version, even though this topic is not strictly relevant to a consideration of the textual basis of the migration of the Déisi to Dyfed. In addition to the expulsion episode there are two other passages in L which show major divergence from the source represented in R. The first of these is the account of the lighting of the fire and the sending of the cow over the ford by the Déisi, as it is told to the druid Díl, and the reaction of Díl to these events and the subsequent killing of the cow (L lines 193–203; cf. R §20). The second is the explanation of the origin of the Déisi Maige Breg (L lines 219–23), to which there is no corresponding material in R. These passages are remarkably close, not only in content but also in wording, to the corresponding passages in the later version. The similarity in content has already been noted by V. Hull (1958–59, 17n2): "It is worth observing that in the older version three incidents that are not in R but that are in L, UM, and may also have been in the lost portion of LFF, are likewise recorded in the later version," these three incidents being "the onomastic explanation of Dumu Dér," the dialogue between Díl and his groom, and the explanation of the origin of the Déisi Maige Breg. This observation of Hull's is an understatement. The onomastic explanation of Dumu Dér (L lines 22 ff.) occurs as part of the account of the expulsion of the Déisi from Meath. We have seen that L begins to diverge from R at line 11. The point of divergence is after *inna chind* (= *ina chind*, R §2), where R has *In tan dosreng in sleig a dochum, rodbi fochoir na sleigi triasin deogbaire, conid se conapaid prius* and L *co n-ecmaing a hirlond inn-eton in rechtaire co mboi triana chend siar. Immalle dorochratar in mac 7 in rechtairi.* The corresponding passage in *Lebor na hUidre* is at lines 4371 ff. (in *LU*), and a parallel quotation will show the close verbal correspondence between the two:

L	LU
co n-ecmaing a hirlond	Co n-ecmaing a hirlond
inn-éton in rechtaire co mboí	i n-étan ind rechtaire co mboí
triana chend siar. Immalle	triana chend síar. Immalle
dorochratar in mac 7 in recht-	dorochratar in mac 7 in recht-
airi 7 ro mebaid súil Cormaic	aire 7 ro mebaid súil Cormaic
7 ni roachtas greim fair	7 ní roacht greim fair
co rrócht a theg 7 ro marb	co rránic a tech. 7 ro marb
nonbur do churadaib Cormaic	nonbor do churadaib Cormaic
occá thafund .i. a dalta leis	oca thofund 7 a dalta leiss
.i. Corc Duibne dia tát Corco	.i. Corc Duibni 7 atrulláeside
Duibne 7 atrullai sede a giallu.	a giallai.

These excerpts are representative of the full passages from which they have been taken, and it is clear that the resemblances between the two texts cannot be fortuitous. The same can be said of the passage concerning Díl,[17] and of that recounting the origin of the Déisi Maige Breg.[18] The three passages which we find reflected in the texts of L and of LU must derive ultimately from a common source, and that source must have contained an account of the expulsion of the Dál Fiachach from Meath and of the settlement of territories which they wrested from the Osraige, this latter being the context of the passage concerning Díl. The common source therefore contained the beginning of the story and its end: how inclusive it may otherwise have been we do not know.

To sum up the textual discussion, then, we can now say that three different tellings of the Déisi story have gone into the making of R and L: (i) the source of the body of R and of much of the body of L, (ii) the source of the supplementary notes, and (iii) the source of the passages which L shares with the later version. Of these, (i) and (ii) are represented in R, while all three are represented in L. To judge from the linguistic forms, all three tellings would seem to have been written down in Old Irish in the first instance; (i) and (ii) were joined together before the addition of (iii), since the latter does not appear in the tradition of R. As for (i) and (ii), it must be borne in mind that (i) is itself a compilation, so that it is not inconceivable that the addition of (ii) was part of the compilatory process. Finally, within (i) there is an obscure *rosc* which may reflect (iv) yet another version of some parts at least of the Déisi story. The only one of these sources which can now be shown to have had any reference to the alleged migration to Dyfed is (i), though of course it should be added that this does not prove that the other sources did not make such reference. We may now turn to examine what R and L have to say about the migration.

The text of R (§11) is as follows:

Luid Eochaid mac Arttchuirp dar muir cona chlaind hi crich Demed conid ann atbathatar a maic 7 a hui. Conid dib Cenel Crimthainn allæ, dia ta Tualodor mac Rigin maic Catacuind maic Caittienn maic Clotenn maic Næe maic Artuir maic Retheoir maic Congair maic Gartbuir maic Alchoil maic Trestin maic Aeda Brosc maic Corath maic Echach Almuir maic Arttchuirp.

"Echaid son of Artchorb went across the sea with his children to the territory of Demetia (Dyfed), and there his sons and grandsons (or perhaps rather 'descendants') died. From them is descended Cenél Crimthainn over there, of which is Tualodor." L (lines 36 f.) is much the same in the brief narrative, but there is a major difference in the pedigree in that here we have Áed son of Brosc as against the single Áed Brosc of R.[19] The following is the text of L:

Luid Eochaid dar muir hi crich Demeth conid and robo marb 7 a maic 7 a hui. Conid dib Cenel Crimthain alle, dia ta Taulodar mac Rigind maic Catien maic Clothienn maic Noe maic Artuir maic Petuir maic Congair maic Goirtiben maic Alcon maic Tresund maic Aeda maic Brosc maic Corach maic Echdach Allmuir maic Airt Chuirp.

The names up to and including Trestin/Tresund can be checked against the Dyfed genealogy in the Welsh Harleian mansucript 3859 (Bartrum 1966, 9 f.). As Bartrum points out (1966, 124), Tualodor/Taulodar of *ED* corresponds to Teudos map Regin (= Tewdws ap Rhain) in the Harleian pedigree. "But Tewdws seems to have had a brother, Tewdwr (earlier *Teudubir*)," so perhaps it is he who is intended here. The relevant portion of the Harleian 3859 text is as follows:

Teudos map Regin map Catgocaun map Cathen map Cloten map Nougoy map Arthur map Petr map Cincar map Guortepir map Aircol map Triphun.

If we set the names of the Welsh version of the pedigree against those in R, we can see the first eleven names in the Irish version of the pedigree as badly transmitted variants of those in the Welsh. The twelfth, Trestin (=Tresund in L), seems hardly to be a variant of the *Triphun* of the Welsh version, but even if we accept it as such, the correspondence ends at *Trestin/Triphun*. "The Expulsion of the Déisi" is alone in claiming the rulers of Dyfed to be of Irish origin.

There is some important additional evidence in the Welsh genealogies, however. Indirect (and partial) corroboration of the Irish version of the pedigree has been found in two other Welsh genealogies (Bartrum 1966, 45.13, 106.18), in which Triphun's father is named as Ewein Vreisc. In other words, Ewein Vreisc occupies the same slot in the pedigree as does Áed Brosc, and in 1893 Zimmer identified these two with one another. The independent occurrence of the equivalents *brosc/breisc* as epithets of Triphun's father can scarcely be fortuitous: as M. Miller (1977–78, 39) has put it, it "implies some knowledge by the Welsh of some form of the material now preserved in Ireland." Moreover, the use of *breisc* as an epithet in the Welsh material is a compelling argument in favor of the authenticity of the similar use of *brosc* in R as against the Áed son of Brosc in L. Sims-Williams (1982b) has recently put forward a contrary view: notwithstanding the agreement between the Rawlinson text and the Welsh material, he thinks that it is most probable that the *Brosc* of *ED* is really a form of the personal name *Brusc* (rather than an epithet) and that it refers to a personage called *Brusc/Briscus* in Welsh hagiographical material. But on purely textual grounds the independent occurrence in the Irish and the Welsh sources of *brosc/breisc* as the epithet of a person occupying the same slot in two versions of the same pedigree is sufficient reason to accord primacy to that tradition and to regard the Áed son of Brosc of L as a secondary development. In saying this, one is of course making a textual rather than a historical point. It may well be that the *Brusc/Briscus* of Welsh hagiography is represented by the *brosc* of *ED* but, if so, he is represented primarily in the epithet of R.

The variation *brosc/breisc* is of a different order from that of the others which we can see between the names in the Irish versions of the pedigree and the corresponding ones in Harleian 3859. The use of *breisc* for *brosc* (or vice versa) must have arisen in a bilingual situation where their equivalence would have been known. It could have happened in the Irish community of Dyfed which, as we have seen, is believed to have been bilingual up to the end of the sixth century, and we must assume that this is indeed what happened if we are to take *Ewein Vreisc* as offering corroboration of the claim in *ED* that the Dyfed dynasty was of Irish descent. The possibility must also be considered, however, that the name and epithet were originally Welsh and that they were translated into Irish in Ireland by the compilers of *ED* or by their predecessors. That they might have wished to do this is suggested by their efforts to give the names that we do know to be Welsh "a more Irish look" (Meyer 1895–96, 58), and that they might well have been able to do it by the evidence that some Welsh was known in Munster in the ninth century. This evidence is of course that of *Sanas Cormaic* (Meyer 1912), the glossary compiled by Cormac mac Cuilennáin (d. 908). Cormac knew some Welsh words and their equivalents in Irish, though Jackson (1953, 155) may be pressing the evidence too far when he says that Cormac knew Old Welsh. *ED* is likely to have been compiled in Munster, though Leinster cannot be ruled out as another possibility. Now we can doubtless dismiss any notion that the Irish literati kept a record from generation to generation of the pedigree of the ruling dynasty of Dyfed. It must be assumed, therefore, that the *ED* and Harleian 3859 pedigrees (to the extent that they correspond) have their origin in a common Welsh source, and that the pedigree was transmitted to Ireland during the time of Tewdws and of his brother Tewdwr, and we know that Maredudd son of Tewdws died in 796. It was on this evidence that Zimmer (1893, 88) dated the composition of the early version of *ED* to the mid-eighth century, but, according to the chronological criteria recently proposed by M. Miller (1977–78), Teudos (and the Welsh source) would belong rather to the second half of the eighth century. In either case, the Dyfed material must have been received by the compilers of *ED* in the eighth century, and thus well before Cormac's time. But the Irish literati must have been in sufficiently close contact with their counterparts in Dyfed to obtain this material from them in the first place, and so a modest vocabulary in Welsh might reasonably be assumed also for these predecessors of Cormac's.

All of this makes it difficult to discover with absolute assurance whether Áed Brosc's name was originally Irish or Welsh. Yet I think we may suppose that he was once believed, in Wales as in Ireland, to have had an Irish name (and an Irish grandfather). From Ireland, we have the evidence of *ED*. From Wales, we have no direct evidence. But if we accept the theory, which is entirely plausible, that the Welsh would have wished to suppress the memory of the Irish origin of the Dyfed dynasty, then we have the answer to our question. The suppression theory has been offered as an explanation of the divergent versions of Triphun's ancestry in the *ED* and Harleian 3859 pedigrees (Bartrum 1966, 124). The only alternative explanation would be that the Irish ancestry was concocted in Ireland, perhaps in the interest of propaganda. The Irish literati were no strangers to this kind of activity, but the occurrence in two Welsh sources of Ewein Vreisc must give us pause before accusing them of it in this instance. Ewein Vreisc is absent from the Harleian 3859 pedigree and Triphun's ancestry is respectably Romano-British according to that account: it is hardly to be doubted that suppression is the explanation, and that the name of Ewein Vreisc need not have been suppressed had it not shown Triphun to be of Irish stock.

The argument here rests on Áed Brosc's epithet rather than his name: if we did not have the epithet it would clearly be impossible to identify Áed with Ewein. And the identification of Áed with Ewein may be illusory, for Miller has suggested that *Ewein* may be a "translation," not of *Áed*, but of *Echaid* (the name of Áed's grandfather), and that *breisc* became attached to *Ewein* in the course of transmission owing to the telescoping of three generations into one: "The appearance of Aed *brosc* and Ewein *vreisc* can ... be explained by a lacuna in which Aed's name has disappeared after Eochaid was translated as Ewein, leaving Aed's epithet as attached to Ewein's name" (M. Miller 1977–78, 39). This speculation does not in any event alter the status of the epithet, which is what concerns me here. On the other hand, I would be unhappy with Sims-Williams's tentative suggestion (1982b, 618n11) that *Ewein* is a corruption of *(A)ed m*. It would provide a convenient legitimation of the Áed son of Brosc of L, but it would require us to believe that the use of *brosc/breisc* as an epithet came about through two independent instances of scribal corruption, the one being a misreading in Wales and the other a foreshortening of a pedigree in Ireland. This is not impossible, but we are justified in reaching for Ockham's razor and confining ourselves to one instance of scribal corruption, and that in explanation of the Áed son of Brosc of L. On balance, then, we can say that the combined evidence of the Irish and Welsh sources attests to a tradition in eighth-century Wales that the Dyfed dynasty was of Irish extraction, one of the ancestors having been a person who was given the epithet *breisc* in Welsh, *brosc* in Irish. This tradition was apparently transmitted from Wales to Ireland at some time in the eighth century.

The mutual corroboration of the Irish and Welsh sources, as interpreted, is precious, but too much should not be built upon it. In particular it is important to note that the Welsh material offers no corroboration whatever of the claim that Áed Brosc was of Dál Fiachach Suidge: *ED* is quite alone in making this claim, and it is one which must be viewed with the gravest suspicion. T. F. O'Rahilly argued that the transmitted genealogy of the Déisi (that is, of Dál Fiachach) is "fictitious" (1946, 81), and he rejected the story of their banishment from Tara as "a fabrication ... suggested by the fact that there were also people called Dési in the neighbourhood of Tara," adding that "it served a useful purpose in enabling the genealogists to provide the Southern Dési with a descent from an alleged brother of Conn Cétchathach" (64).[20] E. MacNeill (1921, 57) had said that the migration of the Déisi from Meath was "told by legend alone, and yet in perfect and necessary accord with history." While it is true that O'Rahilly's reading of the material on the Déisi is characteristically speculative, the nature of that material offers ample grounds for scepticism. The expulsion episode may have at its core a reflex of an item in the heroic biography as applied to Cormac mac Airt (Ó Cathasaigh 1977, 69 f.). Moreover, migration, and particularly migration from Meath, may be a figment of the storytellers' imagination. As Pender has observed, Meath "offered unlimited possibilities to the inventors of ancestral homes and ancestors" (1947, 211). He notes also the existence of "other 'wander' tales dealing with the movements of various communities during the first centuries of the Christian era in this country" (1947, 209).

It is not being suggested that migration was always invented by the storytellers. On the contrary, migration is an important element in the early history of many countries, and Zimmer (1893, 87) suggested that the migration of the Déisi might be compared with that of the Germanic tribes on the continent. In Ireland, the distribution of tribal and placenames leaves little doubt that there was widespread migration of peoples.[21] There is no guarantee, however, that the extant accounts of population movements are based on historical fact. Migration from Meath, the central kingdom, is particularly suspect, since it may reflect traditional Irish—perhaps ultimately Indo-European—notions of territorial division and hierarchy.[22] The cosmographic significance of the territorial center is especially relevant when we are dealing with origin-legends. It may be that the theme of migration from the center in early Irish "wander tales" attests to a centripetal tendency on the part of Irish storytellers, rather than to a centrifugal movement by early Irish population-groups.

There is much in *ED* that is mythical or legendary, there is much else that lacks verisimilitude, and besides all that, we have seen that there are internal contradictions and inconsistencies. None of this goes to prove that *ED* is without historical basis, but it makes us chary of accepting claims on its sole authority. Furthermore, the origin-legend of the Déisi resolves itself readily into four parts—the expulsion from Meath, the sojourn in Leinster, the migration to Dyfed, and the settlement in Munster. One could accept or reject any one of these without necessarily accepting or rejecting all (or indeed any) of the others. Thus, any doubts which one might entertain about the expulsion episode would not automatically extend to the migration to Dyfed.

We are left, nevertheless, with the question of the genealogical affiliation of Áed Brosc. Was he grandson of Echaid son of Art Corb? Rees and Rees have placed the sons of Art Corb among the legendary families whose sons symbolize the social functions (1961, 381). Even if we abandon hope of assessing the historicity of the alleged genealogical affiliation of Áed Brosc, and content ourselves with ascertaining the nature of the claim which is made in the texts, we find ourselves confronted with a problem which may well prove intractable. The problem is why *Cenél Crimthainn* should be used of the descendants of Echaid Allmuir, since no-one of the name Crimthann occurs among the descendants of Echaid given in *ED*, and none has been found among his ascendants. An examination of this problem will lead us into a consideration of the case for a Waterford origin of the migration to Dyfed.

It has been proposed that the reference in *Cenél Crimthainn* is to Crimthann son of Fidach (Bartrum 1966, 12; Byrne 1973, 183), an Irish king of dubious historicity who is described in the much-quoted *mug eime* entry in *Sanas Cormaic* (Meyer 1912a, s.v.) as "king of Ireland and Britain as far as the English Channel." The identification of the Crimthann of *ED* with Crimthann mac Fidaig is purely conjectural, so that it is not accurate to say that *Sanas Cormaic* "adds that these Déisi represented the race of Crimthann of Munster in Britain" (M. Miller 1977–78, 36): there is no reference whatever to the Déisi in the *mug eime* entry. But there is what is taken to be a reference to the Uí Liatháin in the entry: Cormac speaks of "*Dind Map Lethain* in the land of the Cornish Britons," and he translates the name as *Dún Mac Liatháin*, "the fort of the sons of Liathán." The sons of Liathán (*Filii Liethan*) are mentioned by Nennius (cap. 14) as occupying Dyfed, Gower, and Kidwelly, and N. K. Chadwick (1965, 264) thought that Nennius and Cormac might have been using the same (lost) Welsh source. Against this there is the difference between them on the location of the sons of Liathán in Britain: this could reflect either an ignorance of Irish genealogy on Nennius's part, or of British geography on Cormac's, unless it be that we should conflate the two accounts and locate the sons of Liathán in both areas. In any case the identification of "the sons of Liathán" with the Uí Liatháin seems reasonably secure, though it is curious that it should not have been mentioned by Cormac: either it did not occur to him, or he deliberately suppressed it. We may take the observations of Nennius and Cormac as evidence that the Uí Liatháin were believed to have settled in southern Britain, either in parts of south Wales (following Nennius) or in Cornwall (following Cormac), and perhaps even in both.

Modern scholars have connected the Déisi Muman with the migration of the Uí Liatháin to Britain. There may seem to be fairly good grounds for this. In Ireland, the Uí Liatháin of East Cork and the Déisi of Waterford and south Tipperary were neighbors. Moreover, T. F. O'Rahilly (1946, 81) classed the Uí Liatháin and the Déisi as Érainn, claiming that they had both been "provided with fictitious genealogical affiliations which disguised their Ernean descent." Whatever about that, we can at least be reasonably certain that they were both non-Éoganacht. Apart from their territorial contiguity and possible genealogical affiliation, another reason has been adduced for believing that the Uí Liatháin and the Déisi migrated to Southern Britain, perhaps as "part of the same eastward movement" (Jackson 1953, 156), and that is the relatively high incidence of ogam inscriptions both in their respective Munster territories and in the parts of Britain to which our texts say they migrated.

Jackson (1953, 155) says that the Déisi migrated from Waterford; this in refutation of Collingwood's claim (and Meyer's implication) that they went from Meath. The ogam inscriptions can be taken to lend general support to this view.[23] But assuming that the distribution of the ogam inscriptions does provide an argument for the Waterford origin of an Irish colony in Dyfed, we are faced with a conflict of evidence. *ED* does not, it is true, state or imply that the Déisi migrated to Dyfed from Meath, but neither does it state or imply that they went there from Waterford. Whatever modern commentators may choose to make of it, *ED* depicts the migration as having occurred after the Déisi had been expelled from Meath and before they settled what was to become their Munster territory. As for Cenél Crimthainn, if this refers to a group of people who accompanied the Déisi to Dyfed, then the most likely candidate for the eponym in the context of *ED* is Crimthann son of Énnae Cennselach. On the other hand, if we wrench it from its context and think in terms of a migration from East Munster, Crimthann son of Fidach must be the clear favorite, in view of the passage in *Sanas Cormaic*.

It is possible that we have to do here with two quite different migrations, one from Leinster and the other from Waterford. To adapt an observation of Chadwick's, the Irish Sea, a great land-locked lake, has been, more than the land areas, the true unit of insular Celtic civilization,[24] and it is scarcely extravagant to suppose that Wexford as well as Waterford may have sent emigrants to Dyfed. We must now consider the identity of these Waterford migrants who are credited with having brought ogam to Dyfed.

The earliest British (and Dyfed) ogam inscriptions date from the mid to later fifth century (Jackson 1950, 205), so that the middle of the fifth century gives us an approximate terminus ante quem for the arrival of the bearers of the custom of inscribing in ogam. How much earlier they may have arrived must be a matter for speculation. Even if we refrained from pushing the date of their arrival backwards to any significant degree, it would have crucial implications for the identity of the migrants. If there is any truth in the account in *ED* of the settlement by Dál Fiachach of their East Munster territories, ogam must have been established in Dyfed before the arrival of Dál Fiachach in Munster, for they are said to have done so during the reign of Óengus mac Nad-Fraích whose death is recorded in the Annals of Ulster at 490 and 491, and after the death of Crimthann mac Énna Cheinselaig (AU 483, 485). The population-movement from Waterford to Wales would therefore have started some considerable time before the arrival in East Munster of Dál Fiachach.

The argument so far tends to the conclusion that Dál Fiachach had nothing to do with the export of ogam. On the other hand, MacWhite (1960–61, 296) has spoken of "a statistical correlation in the occurrences of names found on the Déisi inscriptions and those used in the Déisi genealogies," and, if well founded, that would clearly indicate a connection between Dál Fiachach and the Waterford ogams. But there is in fact no such statistical correlation, and MacWhite's claim is evidently based on E. MacNeill's comparisons (1910, passim) of the names in the Déisi genealogies with their ogam equivalents; the misunderstanding doubtless arose from MacNeill's stated reason for giving these equivalents—"because many of the ogams occur in Waterford" (E. MacNeill 1910, 46). Of the sixteen names in the genealogies identified by MacNeill with ogam forms, only three are attested in inscriptions found in County Waterford (Macalister 1945, numbers 263, 271, 302). And of these three, one occurs in the pedigree of the Mugdornai which MacNeill (1910, 44) shows to have been artificially attached to the Dál Fiachach stem. Indeed, a larger proportion of the names is to be found in the Barony of East Muskerry in Cork, though I would not attach any significance to that. It is in any case evident that there is nothing in the form of the inscriptions to link them with Dál Fiachach. Moreover, if any inference may be drawn from the incidence of the inscriptions within the Déisi territories it is rather that Dál Fiachach had nothing at all to do with them, for Dál Fiachach are said in *ED* to have settled the County Tipperary part of Déisi Muman, and there we find only two inscribed stones, one of which is quite illegible. It may be significant that both of these stones are just inside the border between County Tipperary and County Waterford.

It may be that the bearers of ogam to Wales were a group who lived in Waterford before Dál Fiachach settled in Tipperary; it is possible that they were among the population groups, such as the Semonraige,[25] who were later to be subsumed under the portmanteau term Déisi. It is of course easier to pose the problem of the identity of the migrants than to solve it, and we may perhaps never know any more precise, or less anachronistic, name than *Déisi* for the Waterford colonists of Dyfed.

We have seen above that Miller's conclusions were that the Déisi arrived in Dyfed in the first quarter of the fifth century, that their Cymricization was advancing in the years around 450, that they were converted to Christianity, and that their dynasty was Christian two generations later. It is worth pointing to the possibility that the migrants from Waterford might already have been Christian before they went to Dyfed, particularly if they went anything like as late as Miller suggests. The Life of St. Declan embodies the tradition that Ardmore was a pre-Patrician foundation (Power 1914, xvii ff.). Such traditions in the Lives of early saints must naturally be treated with caution, and they would have to be dismissed if there were not some supporting evidence. Binchy has spoken of "evidence that considerable areas in the East and South of Ireland had been Christianized by British missionaries before the sending of Palladius" (1962b, 165), and the Life of St. Declan is probably correct in its assertion that there were early Christians in what is now County Waterford.

As for the date of the migration, Miller's proposal, on the basis of her reading of the Welsh evidence, that the Déisi arrived in Dyfed in the first quarter of the fifth century is compatible with a departure from Waterford for which we have a terminus ante quem in the middle of the fifth century. On the other hand, it cannot be reconciled with a migration from Leinster by a contemporary of Crimthann's. I have already said more than enough about the chronological difficulties of the Leinster portion of *ED*, but I would hazard the opinion here that if Echaid Allmuir's migration to Dyfed is not wholly fictitious, then what is being spoken about is a migration from Leinster to Dyfed in the latter half of the fifth century. Whatever the accuracy of the account of that migration in *ED*, it cannot seriously be argued that we should take it to refer to a migration from Waterford at an earlier date. The upshot of all of this is that the account of the migration in *ED*, on the one hand, and the incidence of ogams in Waterford and Dyfed, on the other, cannot be said to be mutually corroborative, and this weakens the evidential value of each of them. That there was an Irish colony in Dyfed is beyond doubt, but our picture of it is at once fainter and fuller than before: it is fainter because of the divergence of the evidence at our disposal, but it is fuller because that same divergence of evidence offers us the possibility that the descendants of the Waterford migrants to Dyfed were joined by a fresh wave of immigrants from Wexford.[26]

APPENDIX: *MUINTER CHAIRBRE*

It has been suggested above that the *muinter Chairbre* who are mentioned in what I have called supplementary note II are the Dál Fiachach by another name. This is not certain, however, and, since Meyer's treatment (1901a) of this portion of the text is somewhat unsatisfactory, I give here the full note as it appears in R and L together with a translation of R and the significant variants in L.[27]

R O doluid iar*um* Corbm*a*c asa rige iarna gollad do Oengus mac
L Ho doluid tra Corm*a*c asa rígu iarna chaichad do Aeíngus,
R Artchuirp, gab*ais* Carp*re* Liph*e*ch*air* in fl*aith* ar belaib a athar.
L   gabais Coirp*re* Liphechair flaith ar bélaib a athar.
L Dothéided iarum Coirpre cach día co mbeired bretha ar belaib
R   Is i abairt dognid Cormac ar a belaib cach dia
L Corm*a*ic. Ba sí abreth dogniad Cormac ar a bélaib cach día
R .i. dobered a da mer immun colg ndet 7 a mer hi timchul lainne
L .i. dobeired a da mér immon cailg ndét 7 a mér timcholl lainne
R in sceith. Is *ed* noinchoisced sain slaidi mui[n]t*ire* Cairp*re*
L a scéith. Iss*ed* inrochosecht troso dani sladi muint*ire* Coirpri
R immun mBoin[n] sanchan .i. do cach leith. Is de doloinsich hi
L sainchan immon Boind di cach leith. Is de dolonget hi crich
R crich Lagen.
L Laigen.

Translation of R: "Now when Cormac relinquished his kingship after he was blinded by Óengus son of Artchorp, Cairbre Lifechair assumed the sovereignty in place of his father. This is what Cormac practised every day before him: he would put two fingers around the tusk-hilted sword and one finger around the flat of the shield. What that signified was the destruction of the people of Cairbre round about the Boyne, that is, on both sides. Hence he banished them into the territory of the Laigin."

Variants in L: The second sentence in L is lacking in R. I would tentatively translate, "Cairbre used to come every day and interpret Cormac's instructions." *Beirid breith (for)* is used of judging, passing judgment, but of dreams it can mean "interpret, expound" (*DIL* B 57.29), and our example may be an extension of that usage. From *bél* in the sense of "the mouth as the source of speech," we get by extension "word(s), subject of talk." Note in particular *roiarfaided o Fiachroig Muillethan . . . dia belaib,* "his advice was asked by F.," cited in *DIL* B 62.63 f. Perhaps then it means "advice, instructions" in our text also: this would be in keeping with Cormac's role as we see it in *Tecosca Cormaic.* It is true that in our text the instruction (if such it be) is not delivered orally: Cairbre must interpret Cormac's actions. The required semantic development, from "mouth" to "words" to "(verbal) instruction" to "instruction" in general, may be compared to that of the meaning of *longas* (*loinges*) from "fleet" to "exile, banishment overseas" to "exile, banishment" generally. The translation proposed here seems to make more sense in the context than "Cairbre used to come every day and pass judgments before his father."

The *abreth* of L seems inferior to the *abairt* of R.

For *troso dani* of L read *tre sodain* with Meyer (1907a). *Issed inrochosecht tre sodain* would mean "what was signified thereby was" as against "what that signified (lit. 'used to signify') was" in R (*Is ed noinchoisced sain*). The latter, with its verb in the imperfect, seems preferable, and it can readily be restored to Old Irish by deleting the *no-* and reading *sin* for *sain*. In his 1901a translation Meyer silently selected the reading of L and translated, "In that way he was instructed to slay." But all four examples cited in *DIL* of *in-coisig* in the sense "instructs" have *do* of the person instructed, the thing taught being the object of the verb. The likelihood therefore is that we should take *in-coisig* in its more usual sense "signifies, indicates, points out." The question remains of the force of the verbal noun *slaide* in this context. Are we to take it that Cormac is prophesying the destruction of the people of Caibre Lifechair? Or are we rather to suppose that when Cormac indicates something to Cairbre Lifechair he is instructing him to carry it out, in which case he would here be instructing Cairbre Lifechair to slay *muinter Chairbre* (?=Dál Fiachach)?

The *dolonget* of L is to be taken as 3pl. present indicative used intransitively: "they go into exile"; *doloinsich* in R could doubtless be written *doloingsig* (cf. simplex *loingsigid*) and construed as 3sg. preterite used transitively (but with object pronoun unexpressed): "he banished (them)."

To sum up, the interpretation of the whole passage depends on whether we consider Cormac's action to signify a prophecy or an instruction. Our attitude to this must depend in large measure on how we take the sentence which is peculiar to L. I have suggested that this sentence may indicate that Cormac is instructing Cairbre, but this cannot be insisted upon. If Cormac is making a prophecy, *muinter Chairpre* are the people of Cairbre Lifechair; but if Cormac is instructing his son, then *muinter Chairpre* are indeed Dál Fiachach by another name.

23

The Theme of *lommrad* in *Cath Maige Mucrama*

(1980–81)

The Book of Leinster text of *Cath Maige Mucrama* (*CMM*) has been known since the end of the last century in the editions of Whitley Stokes and Standish O'Grady, and it has recently been re-edited by Máirín O Daly for the Irish Texts Society.[1] It is a text of considerable interest, since it touches on the adventures and achievements (real or imaginary) of the prestige ancestors of the Éoganachta of Munster and of their Corcu Loígde rivals, and of the Dál Cuinn. *CMM* recounts the causes, events, and aftermath of the Battle of Cenn Abrat, of the Battle of Mag Mucrama, and of the deposal of Lugaid Mac Con in favor of Cormac mac Airt. It is, of course, only one of a number of texts dealing with its subject matter: three of these have been included with *CMM* in O Daly's Irish Texts Society volume; others have been

23. The Theme of *lommrad* in *Cath Maige Mucrama*   331

published elsewhere.² Taken together, these texts make up a rich body of material, and much work remains to be done on its elucidation and interpretation. It should be said that this work will be greatly eased by O Daly's edition and translation, which mark a considerable advance in our understanding of this material. The purpose of the present article is to consider one feature of the Book of Leinster text of *CMM*, and that is the theme of *lommrad* (literally, "the act of laying bare") as it recurs in the text. We shall see that this theme is a dominant one at various points in the story, including the opening and closing sequences, and that it provides the ultimate resolution of the plot. It will be argued that insofar as the text has a meaning (or "message"), its focal point is to be found in the exposition of the theme of *lommrad*. Moreover, the recurrence of this theme provides the text with an iterative thematic structure, counterpoised to the linear structure which is articulated in episodes.

In broad outline, the story of *CMM* is as follows. Éogan Mór was the son of Ailill Ólomm, and Lugaid Mac Con was Ailill's foster-son. A contention arose between Éogan and Lugaid about a man they had taken from a yew-tree, and they submitted the matter to Ailill for judgment. Ailill adjudged the man to be Éogan's, but Lugaid refused to accept this and challenged Éogan to do battle at Cenn Abrat. Lugaid was defeated in the battle, and he went into exile in Alba, where he was received by the king. Lugaid concealed his identity for a time, but the king of Alba discovered it by means of a ruse. Having been offered assistance by the king of Alba, Lugaid gathered a mighty host and returned to Ireland to take vengeance on the men of Ireland. Lugaid encountered no opposition until he reached Mag Mucrama, which is the plain southwest of Athenry in County Galway. (At this point the sequence of events is interrupted by the aetiology of Mac Mucrama.) When Lugaid had reached Mag Mucrama, however, Éogan son of Ailill and Art son of Conn agreed that it was time to do battle with him. At this time, Éogan was king of Munster and Art king of Tara. Éogan's son Fíacha and Art's son Cormac were both conceived on the eve of the Battle of Mag Mucrama, and Éogan and Art were both slain in the Battle. Lugaid then seized the kingship of Ireland by force and he was in Tara for seven years. He took Cormac son of Art into fosterage. On one occasion Lugaid gave a judgment on the case of some sheep which had stripped the queen's woad-garden, but Cormac protested and gave what was thereupon proclaimed by all to be the true judgment. Lugaid remained in Tara for a year after that, but the crops failed and Lugaid was deposed.³ He returned then to Ailill Ólomm, but Ailill treacherously assailed him with a poisonous tooth. Lugaid was afterwards slain at Ailill's behest.

Such, in brief, is the story of *CMM*. Its chief actors are Ailill, Lugaid and Éogan, and Art and Cormac, but it is above all the story of Lugaid—his life is a unifying thread running through it, and the story ends with his death.⁴ The only instance of *lommrad* which has found its way into our summary of the story is that of the stripping of the queen's woad-garden, and that is a crucial one since it was Lugaid's false judgment upon it which led to the failure of the crops and Lugaid's deposition from the kingship, which in turn was followed by Ailill's assault on Lugaid. This sequence of events will provide us with the key to the import of the theme of *lommrad* in *CMM*, but it is supported by two others which must also be considered in detail. The first of these concerns Ailill's experiences at Áne Chlíach and forms part of the background of the Battle of Cenn Abrat, and the second is a story of some magic pigs which is given in the aetiology of Mag Mucrama. It is on these three sequences that my case will rest, but there are other apparent instances of the theme in *CMM*, and these will be briefly discussed. For convenience of reference, the table at the end of this article lists the instances of the theme of *lommrad* and indicates their location in the text of *CMM*.

The first sequence to be attended to must be that in which Lugaid Mac Con and Cormac mac Airt gave conflicting judgments on the matter of the sheep which had consumed the queen's *glassen* or woad (§§63 ff.).⁵ When the matter was referred to Lugaid, he decreed that the sheep should be forfeited, but Cormac, who was still a little boy, protested, saying that "the shearing of the sheep for the cropping of the *glassen* would be more just, for the *glassen* will grow and the wool will grow on the sheep" (*ba córu lomrad na caírech i llomrad na glasne, ar ásfaid in glassen, ásfaid ind oland forsnaib caírib*, §63). This was proclaimed by all to be the true judgment, and Cormac was recognized as the son of the true prince. The side of the house collapsed in which the false judgment had been given. For a year after that Lugaid remained in the kingship of Tara and "no grass came through the earth, nor leaf on tree, nor grain in corn" (*ní thánic fér tria thalmain ná duil[l]e tre fidbuid ná gránni i n-arbur*, §66). So the men of Ireland expelled him from the kingship because he was an unworthy ruler (*anflaith*).

Cormac's judgment, accepted by all as the true one, was that one *lommrad* should be given for another: in this case, the shearing of the sheep for the cropping of the woad (*lomrad na caírech i llomrad na glasne*). In the early text entitled *Scéla Éogain 7 Cormaic*,[6] there is another account of this incident and Cormac's judgment is given there in general terms: *in lomrad tar héisi a chéli*, "one *lommrad* for another."[7] This is a judgment on the matter of *lommrad*, but it could be argued that it is the function of the judgment which matters, and that its content is immaterial. It is true that the function of the judgment is of primary significance, since it shows that Cormac is possessed of *fír flathemon* ("Ruler's Truth"), and hence worthy to assume the kingship of Tara, just as Lugaid's false judgment shows him to be distinguished by *gáu flathemon* ("Ruler's Falsehood"), and hence deserving to be deposed from the kingship. This being so, the subject matter of the judgment seems to pale into insignificance—what matters is that the judgment be a just one, whether it be about *lommrad* or anything else.

We can appreciate the function of Cormac's judgment, however, without dismissing its content, and we have only to look at the immediate context of the judgment in *CMM* to see that significance attaches to the fact that it is a judgment on a case of *lommrad*. It will be recalled that Cormac's judgment was given in refutation of Lugaid's false judgment. As a consequence of the latter, "no grass came through the earth, nor leaf on tree, nor grain in corn." The land has been laid waste because the king is unworthy,[8] and it is this *lommrad* of the land which leads to Lugaid's deposal. The notion that the fertility of the land was contingent upon the truth and justice of the king is central to the Irish ideology of kingship as it is expressed in early texts,[9] and this notion is a dominant one in the material on Cormac mac Airt. It is entirely appropriate, therefore, that the judgment which proves Cormac to be worthy of the kingship of Tara should concern *lommrad*, a matter which, as the text clearly shows, pertains to the relationship between the king and the fertility of the land.

The principle which underlies Cormac's judgment as it is given in *CMM*, and which is explained in *Scéla Éogain 7 Cormaic*, is that of "one *lommrad* for another," and Lugaid's destiny shows the operation of this principle. After the laying waste of the land and his own deposal, Lugaid returned to Munster. Ailill affected to welcome him, but then "Ailill touched Lugaid with a poisonous tooth that was in his head.... Within three days Lugaid's cheek had melted away" (*Don-á(i)rraill immorro co fiacail fhidba ro buí ina chind ina leccoin.... Re cind trí tráth ro legai leithchend Lugdach*, §§70 f.). The baring of Lugaid's cheek is not presented as a direct consequence of the laying waste of the land, but it could not have happened had Lugaid remained in Tara.

The laying waste of the land and the baring of Lugaid's cheek are neither of them called *lommrad* in the text, but then the cropping of the queen's woad is so called only by Cormac in his judgment. In narrating the incident itself the text merely says, "Now on one occasion sheep ate the *glassen* of Lugaid's queen" (*Fecht and didiu do-feotar caírcha glassin na rígna indí Lugdach*, §63). It is Cormac's judgment which provides us with the word, and which alerts us to the category of *lommrad*. Once that has been done, it becomes possible for us to recognize that the laying waste of the land and the baring of Lugaid's cheek are both examples of *lommrad*. The relevant elements of this sequence can be set out as follows:

A. Lugaid gives a false judgment.
B. The land is laid waste (*lommrad*).
C. Lugaid is expelled from the kingship.
D. Lugaid's cheek is laid bare (*lommrad*).

After that Lugaid is killed at Ailill's behest, which is no more than to complete the process begun in the baring of the cheek, and that is the end of the story of the Battle of Mag Mucrama.

The dominance of the theme of *lommrad* in the final sequence of *CMM* is prefigured elsewhere in the text, and indeed this dominance is already established in the opening sequence: in this respect, it may be said that the text, in the Irish fashion, ends as it begins. After a brief genealogical introduction, the story opens with an account of the unhappy adventures of Ailill at Áne Chlíach, a hill which contained an Otherworld habitation. What happened was that Ailill went one Samhain night to graze his horses on Áne Chlíach,[10] which means in effect that he was laying claim to an Otherworld habitation.[11] "That night the hill was stripped bare and it was not known who had stripped it" (*Ro lommad in tilach in n-aidchi-sin 7 ní fess cía ros lomm*, §3). This happened to him on two occasions. Ailill wondered at this and he sent for one Ferches mac Commáin. One Samhain night the two of them went to Áne Chlíach. Ailill stayed on the hill, and Ferches was aside from it. Ailill fell asleep listening to the grazing of the beasts. Then out of the *síd* came its king Éogabul son of Durgabul, and Éogabul's daughter Áne. Ferches attacked Éogabul and broke his back, killing him. Ailill raped the girl, but while he was doing so she "sucked his ear so that she left neither flesh nor skin on it and none ever grew on it from that time" (*ro den in ben a ó cona farcaib féoil na crocand fair connáro ássair fair ríam ónd úair-sin*, §3). This, we are told, is why he was called Ailill Ólomm, the implication being that *Ólomm* is compounded of *ó* 'ear' and *lomm* 'bare.' Áne also said that she would leave Ailill without any property in his possession.

The whole tragic story of *CMM* has its origin in the foregoing incident. The contention between Lugaid and Éogan, which gave rise to the Battle of Cenn Abrat, was for possession of a man whom they had taken from a yew-tree: that man was Fer Fí,[12] who was a son of the slain Éogabul. When once Lugaid and Éogan had fallen into dispute over him, Fer Fí disappeared from the scene: he had accomplished what he had come to do, which was to leave "trouble brewing between them" (*fo-rácaib drochimtel eturru*, §8).

To return to the events of Áne Chlíach, what happened there bears a remarkable similarity to the sequence of events which followed upon Lugaid's false judgment. Both sequences begin with an offence committed by a king, for Ailill Ólomm was king of Munster (§1) and Lugaid king of Tara. Just as Lugaid was to sin against the truth in giving his false judgment, so did Ailill offend the gods by laying claim to the Otherworld domain at Áne Chlíach. The offences are functionally equivalent in that they initiate the sequences in which they occur, but the comparison between them does not end there, for it would seem that they are no more than variants of one and the same offence. Dumézil has written of an old Indo-European theme which he calls "the single sin of the sovereign"; this "destroys either the raison d'être of sovereignty, namely the protection of the order founded on truth ... or the mystical support of human sovereignties, namely the respect for the superior sovereignty of the gods and the sense of the limitations inherent in every human delegation of that divine sovereignty."[13] In other words the king may offend against the truth or against the gods. According to Dumézil, "the king falls prey to one or the other of these risks, which ... are at bottom reducible to the same thing."[14] Dumézil did not find examples of this "sin"—in either of its representations—in Irish tradition, but I have argued elsewhere that in *Togail Bruidne Da Derga* Conaire Mór falls prey to both of the "risks" mentioned by Dumézil: he contrives to sin against the truth and against the gods.[15] In *CMM*, the two representations of the sin of the sovereign are also found, but they are not committed by one king: it is Lugaid who destroys the order based on truth, Ailill the respect for the superior sovereignty of the gods.

The result of the sovereign's sin is generally immediate and catastrophic.[16] In our text, the sin is in each case followed by an instance of *lommrad*. After Ailill's sin what happened was that the hill of Áne Chlíach was bared (*ro lommad in tilach*). This, incidentally, could also be taken as another example of the operation of Cormac's principle *in lommrad tar héisi a chéli*, since Ailill's offence takes the form of an attempted grazing (or baring) of the hill.

Thus far the adventures of Ailill and Lugaid have been comparable, point for point, but at this stage they diverge. Lugaid was deposed and returned to Munster. Ailill, on the other hand, returned to Áne Chlíach a second and a third time. His second visit was the same as the first, but on the third occasion he compounded his offence by raping the eponymous goddess Áne, and he was also held responsible by her for the slaying of her father Éogabul (§4). And for these offences, as we have seen, he was duly punished by Áne: she stripped his ear of flesh and skin and none ever grew on it from that time.

When Ailill first visited Áne Chlíach and attempted to graze his horses there, the gods responded by stripping the hill; this happened again on his second visit. When Ailill persisted, and committed yet more serious offences against the Otherworld, he was himself visited with a painful and permanent form of *lommrad* on his person. This punishment prefigures that inflicted upon Lugaid at the end of the story, for Lugaid too suffers the physical effects of *lommrad* when one of his cheeks is bared. It seems appropriate (and somewhat ironic) that it was Ailill whose poisonous tooth pierced Lugaid's cheek and caused it to waste away.

The structure of the Áne Chlíach sequence can now be set out as follows:

A. Ailill puts his horses to graze on Áne Chlíach (*lommrad*).
B. The hill is bared (*lommrad*).
C. Ailill rapes Áne and has Éogabul slain.
D. Ailill's ear is stripped of flesh and skin (*lommrad*).

The sequence of events at Áne Chlíach sets the action of the story in motion and, in its treatment of *lommrad*, sets the thematic key-note of the text; the Tara episode marks the climax of the story and the resolution of the plot. The third major *lommrad*-sequence is of a quite different order insofar as it is altogether external to the main plot: it is told in explanation of the name Mag Mucrama, and no attempt is made to link it to the action of *CMM*. The story of the aetiology is that magic pigs (*mucca gentliuchta*) came out of the cave of Crúachain and laid waste the land: "whatever land they traversed no corn or grass or leaf grew on it until the end of seven years" (*Nach ní immathéigtis co cend secht mblíadna ní ássad arbur na fér na duille trít*, §36). This description of the effects of the pigs' activities is very close to that which has already been quoted of the waste land after Lugaid's judgment. No explanation is given, however, for these activities, and so we must assume that they represent a gratuitous intervention by malign Otherworld animals.

It was impossible to count these pigs: wherever they were being counted they would not stay there but went into another territory. Various estimates were made of their number; some thought there were three of them, others seven, nine, eleven, or thirteen. But it proved impossible to count them. Nor was it possible to slay them, for when cast at they disappeared. It is clear from this passage that it was vital that the people should count the pigs, for then the pigs would lose their power: that is why the pigs moved on when an attempt was made to count them. This might also explain the importance which is attached in the early literature to the *búaid n-airdmiusa* 'the gift or accomplishment of estimating.'

The text goes on to say that Medb and Ailill went to Mag Mucrama to reckon the pigs and that they succeeded in counting them. But then one of the pigs jumped across Medb's chariot, and Medb was told that it was an extra one. Medb said that it would not remain so, as she seized "the pig's shank so that its skin split on its forehead and it left the skin in her hand along with the shank" (*la gabáil a colpthae na muicce co rróemid a croccend fora étan conda farggaib dano in croccand inna láim cossin cholpdu*, §37). And in conclusion we are told that it is not known where they went from that time onwards. The pigs, then, were defeated by being counted, and when one of them attempted to reverse this defeat, its skin and shank were torn off by Medb. Like Lugaid and Ailill, this pig suffers a *lommrad* of its body.

The aetiology of Mag Mucrama, like the events at Áne Chlíach, has to do with the relationship between human society and the Otherworld, but the respective roles of men and the denizens of the Otherworld are reversed. At Áne Chlíach, Ailill attempted to bare the Otherworld hill; at Mag Mucrama, the Otherworld pigs laid waste the land. In the one case,

Ailill made a wilful assault on the Otherworld, while in the other the magic pigs gratuitously encroached upon the world of men, destroying the fruits of the earth. Ailill's efforts are defeated by the king of the *síd*, and the pigs' by Medb. Ailill makes a further assault on the *síd*, while one of the pigs attempts to rob Medb of her triumph. But Ailill's ear is bared by the woman of the *síd*, while the pig's skin and shank are torn off by Medb.

These two sequences exemplify the manner in which the relationship of man with the gods is ordered in Irish tradition, and they do so by means of the theme of *lommrad*. Notwithstanding the reversal of the Áne Chlíach and Mag Mucrama sequences, the message is the same: they confirm the truth of Cormac's judgment, *in lommrad tar éisi a chéli*, and, taken together, they show that this principle holds true alike for men and for the denizens of the Otherworld when they make unwarranted encroachments on the others' domain.

The structure of the Mag Mucrama aetiology is as follows:

A. Magic pigs lay waste Mag Mucrama (*lommrad*).
B. Medb counts the pigs.
C. An extra pig appears.
D. Medb tears off the skin and shank of the extra pig (*lommrad*).

I have already pointed out that the Mag Mucrama aetiology is external to the main plot. But it will now be clear that this aetiology is no mere decoration, that it is not a gesture to antiquarianism on the part of the Irish literati. On the contrary, the aetiology deserves its place in the text since it is concerned with what we may perhaps call the primary theme of *CMM*, namely the theme of *lommrad*. It is not a mere repetition of any of the other instances of the theme, since it extends their application of it, but it does confirm the important role assigned to *lommrad* in the world-view which informs this text. Not only is *lommrad* an iterative theme which runs like a thread through the fabric of the story, but it operates also as a structural device, since it integrates the Mag Mucrama aetiology into the text as a whole.[17]

In view of the three sequences which have been discussed, it can be said that *CMM* is (among other things) a text about *lommrad* and it may therefore be significant that there are five other items in the text which seem relevant to the theme. Although none of them amounts to much in itself, they cannot be passed over without mention when they occur in such a text.

The first of them is no more than a threat, but the wording shows that the storyteller included beheading in the category of *lommrad*. In the contention between Éogan and Lugaid concerning Fer Fí, Ailill found in favor of Éogan. Lugaid rejected Ailill's judgment, but Éogan said to Lugaid that a vassal like him should not rebuke Ailill. To this Lugaid replied: "It will be a vassal like me that will shear that head off you" (*Bid aithech samlum-sa . . . lomméras a cend-sin dít-sa*, §9, where *lomméras* is future relative of *lommraid*, of which *lommrad* is verbal noun).[18] He went on to say that the beheading would be carried out at Cenn Abrat in a month's time.

Lugaid's threat proved to be an empty one, as we see when we come to the account of the battle at Cenn Abrat. When it was time for the battle, Lugaid said that Éogan would challenge him to single combat and that Éogan would overthrow him. The jester Do Déra went into battle with Lugaid's diadem on his head and wearing Lugaid's battle-dress. Éogan killed Do Déra but was not deceived. Then Éogan saw Lugaid's two calves shining through the midst of the host, so he ran after him and made a cast at him and struck him in the calf. Not only does Lugaid not carry out his threat of *lommrad* in the battle of Cenn Abrat, but he is himself injured in that battle because his calves are uncovered and hence visible to Éogan.

Lugaid leaves himself open to recognition and attack on Éogan's part because his calves are bare: what we have is an instance of the state of bareness rather than an act of laying bare. In the next item to be considered, Lugaid is again engaged in an attempt to conceal his identity. It will be recalled that after his defeat in the Battle of Cenn Abrat, Lugaid went to Alba with his followers, and that they were received there by the king. Lugaid wished to ensure that he would not be recognized by the king of Alba, and he instructed his followers to obey each other as though each of them were king and said that none of them should call him by his own name. But the king of Alba discovered Lugaid's identity by means of a ruse. What he did was to give each of Lugaid's company a mouse, "raw and with its pelt still on" (*luch . . . is sí dergg cona find*, §27), and to declare that they would be put to death unless they ate the raw unskinned mice. Lugaid's men were loath to do so, and Lugaid was the first of them to put a mouse into his mouth. The others followed his example, but when one of them failed to ingest the mouse, it was Lugaid who commanded him to do so. The king, who had already discovered that the company were of the Corcu Loígde, now knew which of them was Lugaid Mac Con. The relevance to our theme is that he obtained this intelligence by using unskinned mice: this could be described as a case of non-*lommrad*.

Finally, the aetiology of Mac Mucrama includes two instances of *lommrad* in addition to the story of the magic pigs from which the plain is said to have got its name. The magic pigs, as we have seen, are said to have emerged from the cave of Crúachain, and this gives the storyteller an opportunity to mention some other creatures which issued from the same cave, which he says is "Ireland's gate to Hell" (*Dorus iffirn na Hérend*, §34). First, there is "the swarm of three-headed creatures that laid Ireland waste until Amairgene father of Conall Cernach, fighting alone (?), destroyed it" (*in tellén trechenn ro fásaig Hérind, conidro marb Amairgene athair Conaill Chernaig ar galaib óenfir*, §34). And, secondly, out of it also had come "the saffron-colored (?) bird-flock and they withered up everything in Ireland that their breath touched until the Ulaid killed them" (*do-dechatar ind énlathi chrúan coro chrínsat i nHérind nach ní taidlitís a n-anála, condaro marbsat Ulaid dano*, §35). These Otherworld visitants differ from the magic pigs in that they could be slain, but their effect on the countryside is the same: they lay waste the land.

The threat of beheading, Lugaid's bare calves, the unskinned mice, and the defoliating creatures from the cave of Crúachain: they all contribute to the pervasiveness in *CMM* of the notions of baring, laying waste, lopping off, and these notions come within the semantic range of *lommrad*. These items confirm what has already been established on the basis of the three major *lommrad*-sequences, namely that there is an iterative principle at work in the unfolding of *CMM*, and that that principle is focussed on *lommrad*. (This information is summarized in Table 23.1.) It is of course the three major sequences which enable us to appreciate the central role of *lommrad* in this text. The message is the same in all three sequences: they show the truth of Cormac's principle of one *lommrad* for another. But they deepen and extend our understanding of this principle by exploring the theme of *lommrad* in three different ways. The Áne Chlíach and the Mag Mucrama sequences treat of the theme in terms of the relationship between man and the gods, but in doing so they show, as we have seen, a reversal of roles as between the human and the Otherworld actors. The Tara episode dispenses with Otherworld actors, for there the theme of *lommrad* is used to illuminate the role of the king. To be sure, it is a cosmic role: the fruits of the earth dry up when there is an unworthy king. (We know from other texts that there was abun-

23. The Theme of *lommrad* in *Cath Maige Mucrama*   341

Table 23.1. The incidence and distribution of *lommrad* in *CMM*.

Outline of CMM		Lommrad
1–9	Background to the Battle of Cenn Abrat	The baring of Áne Chlíach, and of Ailill's ear (3–5) A threat of beheading (9)
10–14	The Battle of Cenn Abrat	Lugaid's calves uncovered (12–13)
15–31	Lugaid's exile	The unskinned mouse (26–30)
32–33	Lugaid's return	—
34–37	Aetiology of Mag Mucrama	Land laid waste by *in tellén trechend*, by a bird-flock, and by pigs; skin and shank torn off pig (34–37)
38	Lugaid reaches Mag Mucrama	—
39–43	Eve-of-battle conception of Éogan's son Fíachu	—
44–47	Eve-of-battle conception of Art's son Cormac	—
48–58	The Battle of Mag Mucrama	—
59–62	Lugaid seizes kingship of Tara	—
63–68	The deposal of Lugaid	The sheep eat the *glassen*; the land is laid waste (63, 66)
69–77	The death of Lugaid	Lugaid's cheek is pierced and melts away (70–71)

dance in nature when a worthy king ruled the land.) Here the king is the central figure, mediating between man and nature, while in the other two sequences there is direct contact between man and the Otherworld.

Cath Maige Mucrama is not a religio-political treatise. It is a narrative text: it has a story to tell, and it tells it well, within the conventions of Irish narrative. This story, however, is about kings, and the kings in question are prestige figures for important political groups in the historical period. The terms in which the action of the story is to be interpreted are those of the Irish ideology of kingship, and in that ideology the king has a pivotal role in the determination of the fertility of the land. It is not surprising, therefore, that fertility should bulk large in our text, albeit in its negative aspect, the laying waste of the land. What is remarkable about *CMM* is the way that the narrative is combined with the literary device of iteration: as the story progresses, we are given an exploration and exposition of a central topic in the inherited religio-political ideology.[19]

24

The Theme of *ainmne* in *Scéla Cano meic Gartnáin*

(1 9 8 3)

Scéla Cano meic Gartnáin is a brief (and highly selective) biography of one Cano son of Gartnán, to whom it assigns a reign of twenty-four years as king of Scotland: the text runs to 512 lines in D. A. Binchy's edition,[1] and this includes 180 lines of verse. It is the story of a man who is destined to be king and, like many another king-tale, it falls into the pattern of Exile-and-Return. The tale opens with an account of the events which gave rise to Cano's exile (lines 1–37); he went to Ireland in order to evade the murderous attentions of Áedán mac Gabráin, who had defeated Cano's father Gartnán in a struggle for the kingship of Scotland and gone on to massacre Gartnán and all the inhabitants of the island on which Gartnán lived. Being in fosterage away from the island, Cano had escaped the massacre. *Scéla*

24. The Theme of *ainmne* in *Scéla Cano meic Gartnáin*

Cano reaches its climax with the return of its hero to Scotland, to which he has been summoned to assume the kingship (lines 367–76). The main part of the narrative is devoted to the events of Cano's exile in Ireland where he stayed, first with the joint kings of Tara, Diarmait and Bláthmac; then with Gúaire, king of Connacht; and finally with Illand, king of the Corcu Loígde. The first of these sojourns seems to have been brief, the second lasted for three months (line 220), and Cano spent three years with Illand (line 356). Two of the themes which occur in the account of Cano's exile are his love for Créd, daughter of Gúaire (lines 172 ff., 299 ff.), and his fast friendship with Illand (lines 356 ff.), and it is these two themes which are taken up again after Cano's return to Scotland. First we are told of Illand's death at the hands of his own people, and how Cano keens and then avenges him (lines 377–447). There follows a long poem on the "ales of sovereignty,"[2] and the tale ends with an account of how Cano tried to keep an annual assignation with Créd, and of how the last of these led to both their deaths (lines 488–512).

The main lines of *Scéla Cano* are clear enough, and yet it is one of the most tantalizing of the early Irish narrative texts. It has been described by James Carney as "primarily a saga of love, secondarily a saga of friendship,"[3] and, as such, we might expect it to be of timeless appeal. But its appeal and even its accessibility are greatly diminished by the condition of the extant text of the tale, for it does not readily yield up its secrets. It is true that *Scéla Cano* is a comparatively short tale, and that, since it has survived in one manuscript only, the reader may approach it directly without having to work his way through a thicket of versions and recensions. Furthermore, the text as we have it is unencumbered with the obscure rhetoric of *roscada*, the narrative is liberally leavened with passages of dialogue, and the prose is interspersed with verse. Indeed, Eleanor Knott pronounced it "the most poetic of our early tales that have survived."[4] On the other hand, the text "abounds," as Binchy put it, "in difficulties and ambiguities."[5] Many of these are doubtless to be put down to scribal corruption, and not a few have been plausibly eliminated by the scholars who have worked on the tale, notably Thurneysen, O'Brien, and Binchy.[6] A number of residual "difficulties and ambiguities" have resisted the best efforts of the scholars and remain to plague us, but it is fair to claim that, notwithstanding the imperfect transmission, we now have a reasonably adequate working text to get on with.

If it can still be said that *Scéla Cano* "is a 'text' to be studied and elucidated by scholars and cannot be read with the same ease and pleasure as some of the other sagas,"[7] some of the fault doubtless lies, not with the scribe, but with the author (or "compiler") whose work was being transmitted, and of whom Binchy remarks: "It can hardly be claimed for the compiler that he has done his work skilfully."[8] It is no part of my purpose here to argue that the author of *Scéla Cano* was possessed of any great narrative skill, which I suspect would be a futile endeavor, but I shall try to establish that, whatever his shortcomings as a storyteller, this particular product of his labors has a greater degree of thematic cohesion than has hitherto been allowed. The evidence for this will be found in an examination of the recurrence in *Scéla Cano* of the theme of *ainmne* 'forebearance, patience.' We shall see that Cano's exile in Ireland is characterized by the repeated exercise of the virtue of *ainmne* and that it is the theme also of a lengthy excursus relating to Senchán Torpéist. The iteration of this theme knits the episodes of the tale into something approaching a coherent whole.

It is in the course of Cano's sojourn with Diarmait and Bláthmac (38–147) that the theme of *ainmne* is introduced, and its crucial role in Cano's career explicitly stated: we are told that it was as a reward for his exercise of *ainmne* that Cano was granted the kingship of Scotland. What happened was that, having left Scotland, Cano repaired first to Diarmait and Bláthmac, who gave him and his retinue a great welcome. Meanwhile, Áedán had found and taken a hoard of gold and silver which had been hidden by Gartnán, and he sent emissaries to Diarmait and Bláthmac offering them a bag of silver from the hoard in return for slaying Cano. Their conversation was overheard by Diarmait's daughter, who was in love with Cano, and she alerted him to what was going on. Cano then reported back to his people:

> "People are coming to kill us all," (said Cano).
> "That has doubtless been destined for us," said the warriors.
> "It would be a good thing for us," said Cano, "to capture from the men the five houses which are in the enclosure. Let twelve swordsmen assail the entrance to each house. I shall go to the kings and ..."[9]
> "Good," said the warriors, "forebearance is better[10] (*is fearr ainmne*)."

24. The Theme of *ainmne* in *Scéla Cano meic Gartnáin* 345

"Good," said he, "I shall go to the (kings') dwelling to find out whether I shall be allowed in. If I am allowed in, there will be no killing.[11] If I am not allowed in, attack with force, and let me come out then." (lines 92–101)

Here the notions of fate and forebearance seem to be set against one another, and the implication would seem to be that awaiting the outcome of events—and indeed doing something to shape them—is better than passive assumption of an adverse fate. Cano's action had the desired effect, for he confronted Diarmait and Bláthmac and related the story of his father's treasure, whereupon Diarmait declared that Cano would not be sold, even were the whole house to be filled with silver. Cano was satisfied with that and left the company. Bláthmac followed him out and suggested that Cano should pursue the emissaries to the point on the sea where they would pass from the protection of Diarmait and Bláthmac, and that he should then assail them and take possession of his own wealth.

Cano did intercept the emissaries (here called "the warriors"), but, in the event, he did not take possession of the silver:

"It was indeed wrong of you to betray me," said Cano. "There is not a man in this boat who was not reared in the house of my father and mother."

"Well, Cano," said the warriors, "if you were the powerful one in our country, we would be subject to you. It would be a good thing for you to leave your silver behind and to allow us to go to our country."

"So shall it be, then," said he. "Go your way!"

"What is this, Cano?" said his people.

"I declare by my power," said he, "not a penny shall be removed from this boat. If it has been fated for me (*ma ra-tocad dam-sa*), I shall be the one to use this silver." (lines 129–37)

When Cano came ashore Diarmait declared that he should be made welcome, and it is explained that Diarmait had received a prophecy from God in which it was revealed that Cano's reward for the forebearance which he had shown on the sea (*lúag na hainmne do-ronnai in gillai forsin fairgi*) would be the kingship of Scotland for twenty-four years in succession to Áedán.

The burden of this sequence is that Cano's trust in his destiny inspires him to postpone the enjoyment of the wealth which had been hidden away by his father and which is now his for the taking, and that his reward for this was to be the kingship of Scotland. This, as we have seen, is the second instance of the juxtaposition in the text of the notions of fate and forebearance. In the first one, Cano finds himself in adverse circumstances and takes decisive steps to remedy the situation; in the second, Cano is in a position of strength, but he refrains from pressing his advantage. In both cases his response is described as *ainmne*, and is shown to be the correct one in the circumstances.

It is significant that God is mentioned in connection with the fulfilment of Cano's destiny. At an earlier stage in the text, the devil is likewise linked with Cano's bad fortune. It will be remembered that when Cano was warned of the arrival of Áedán's emissaries he told Diarmait and Bláthmac the story of his father's wealth. He did so in the following words:

> You have heard of my father. He wished me to have a goodly heritage, and he concealed a vat full of silver. Because Áedán's fate (*tocad*) is stronger, he found my father's wealth and sent it here to you as a reward for killing me. (lines 113–16)

The author had earlier (lines 44 ff.) reported a claim that Satan had come to Áedán and informed him of the whereabouts of Gartnán's hoard. Thus, Cano's good fortune is linked to God and his bad fortune to Satan, though in neither case is the connection made by Cano himself. Moreover, neither the divine nor the satanic intervention in his affairs is allowed to obscure the central role played by Cano himself in the working out of his destiny. Satan comes to the aid of Áedán and enables him to steal a march on Cano, but Cano nevertheless outwits Áedán; God informs Diarmait that Cano will be king, but it is Cano himself who earns the kingship by his exercise of *ainmne*.

It is in the account of Cano's first Irish sojourn, then, that the moral framework of *Scéla Cano* is established. There is no further mention of the word *ainmne* in the text, but the theme appears again in the account of Cano's relationship with Créd. Cano has two encounters with Créd in the course

24. The Theme of *ainmne* in *Scéla Cano meic Gartnáin*   347

of the next part of the text, which is devoted to Cano's journey to Gúaire's residence and his brief sojourn with Gúaire (lines 146–323). Before he meets her, however, an adventure befalls him which must be noticed here since it has to do with the moral education of Cano during his period of exile.

After his return from the sea, Cano was feasted by Diarmait for three days, and then he left his blessing with Diarmait and departed with his retinue.[12] They proceeded as far as Cernae (Carnes in County Meath), where they saw some swans. Cano's people told him to shoot at the swans, and he did so, but he missed his mark for the first time in his life, and lamented the incident in a quatrain. On the following day, they came to Lough Ennel, and Cano's people told him to shoot the ducks on the lake, but he declined to repeat his mistake of the previous day. He gave his reasons in three stanzas, of which I quote the last:

> I shall not slay the birds of the plain;
> my destructive power will not be directed at them;
> what has taken me from Skye
> is not to make war on the swans of Cernae.

What has taken him from Skye, as we know, is to preserve himself from Áedán so that he can eventually return to Scotland as its king. Cano is here rededicating himself to the single-minded pursuit of this aim, and he shows himself to have learned a lesson in self-discipline when he refrains from shooting at the ducks of Lough Ennel. This exercise in restraint can be taken as an instance of *ainmne*.[13]

After that Cano crossed the Shannon into Connacht, and he came to the residence of Marcán, whose wife was Créd the daughter of Gúaire. Créd had loved Cano before ever he crossed the sea to Ireland, and Cano had protected her home when he had accompanied Diarmait to give battle to Gúaire. Cano now sent a messenger in to Créd to seek her protection for the journey to Gúaire's residence at Durlas Gúairi. What follows in the text is somewhat obscure, but it is clear at least that Créd is loved by Marcán's son Colgu, whereas Créd's love is not for Colgu (or for Marcán, for that matter), but for Cano. But the text makes no reference to any direct contact between Cano and Créd at this point. Cano proceeded to Durlas Gúairi and was made welcome. He stayed with Gúaire for at least three months, and Gúaire, Cano, and Senchán Torpéist each occupied a third of Gúaire's enclosure. (Here there is a lengthy excursus about Senchán which will be discussed presently.) Senchán objected to the presence of Cano, saying that it was enough for the Connachta to have to maintain Gúaire and Senchán. Cano took his leave of Gúaire, and Gúaire invited him to a farewell feast.

The noblemen of Connacht came to the feast to bid farewell to Cano, and among those who came were Créd, Marcán, and Colgu. Créd served the men of Scotland and of Connacht at the feast.

> And she cast a sleep-charm on the gathering, so that they fell asleep, all except Créd and Cano. And she went to Cano and proceeded to importune him on his couch. But he could not be prevailed upon to comply so long as he was in military service; if he became king, however, he would go to meet her and she would be his wife forever. (lines 303–8)

Cano left Créd his stone in token of a tryst, and he told her that his soul was in that stone.

Scéla Cano has chiefly been attended to for its affinities to the romance of Tristan and Isolde. Among the Irish tales which have been compared to the Tristan-story, there is a sub-group, comprising *Scéla Cano*, *Tochmarc Becfola*,[14] and *Comracc Líadaine ocus Cuirithir*,[15] which "have a particular point in common that is not shared by the other tales: a union is proposed by one lover, rejected temporarily by the other until the matter of career is attended to."[16] Carney's view is that *Scéla Cano* as a whole has no connection with the romance of Tristan, but that it has borrowed motifs from a story of the Tristan-type.[17] It must also be said, however, that Cano's relationship with Créd, with its element of temporary rejection, is thematically integrated into *Scéla Cano* as a whole. In postponing the consummation of his love for Créd, Cano is exercising *ainmne* in the interest of his career, just as he has done in respect of his father's wealth. In both cases, Cano is in a position to have immediate satisfaction and rejects it in the hope that he will eventually enjoy that satisfaction when he is king of Scotland.

The account of Cano's sojourn with Gúaire is interrupted, as we have seen, by the excursus concerning Senchán Torpéist (lines 222–83). This comprises a brief description of the famous poet and three anecdotes about him. It is remarkable that each of these anecdotes centers on a theme which also occurs in the main part of the narrative. The first of them shows Senchán rejecting a young woman (lines 227–33), and in the third we are told of the inordinate demands made by Senchán on Gúaire, so that we see what a heavy burden he is upon his host (lines 275–83). We have seen how Cano rejects Créd (albeit temporarily), and the burdensomeness of entertaining Cano is underscored, as we shall see, in the account of Cano's third sojourn. The central anecdote (lines 234–74) is much the longest of the three, and the theme that is developed in this one is that of *ainmne*. The story goes that Senchán composed a poem for Diarmait son of Áed Sláine. Diarmait was pleased with the poem, but he gave Senchán a paltry reward. Senchán accepted the reward without demurral. The same thing happened in a year's time. On the third occasion, however, Diarmait rewarded Senchán with a hundred ounces of pure gold, and on the fourth he gave him thirty horses, bridled and harnessed. We might have expected Senchán to have responded to the paltry rewards which he received for his first two poems by satirizing Diarmait. Instead of this he is content to try again, and he is handsomely rewarded for his patience and restraint.

The argument which is being presented here in relation to the recurrence of the theme of *ainmne* in our text is similar in general to that which I have put forward elsewhere in relation to the theme of *lommrad* ("the act of laying bare") in *Cath Maige Mucrama*.[18] In the latter text the theme of *lommrad* occurs a number of times in the main plot. The theme of *lommrad* has an important place in the Irish conception of kingship. *Ainmne* is also relevant to kingship, for according to *Críth Gablach* the true ruler (*fírflaith*) was a repository of forebearance (*forus n-ainmnet*).[19] What is particularly to be noted in the present context is that in *Cath Maige Mucrama* the theme of *lommrad* occurs in an excursus dealing with the aetiology of Mag Mucrama, just as, in our text, the theme of *ainmne* occurs in the anecdote about Senchán. In both cases, then, we have an item which is external to the main plot but which reiterates one of the primary themes of the tale. The item in question confirms the important role assigned to its theme (*lommrad/ainmne*) in the tale. The theme, for its part, operates as a structural device and integrates the relevant item into the text as a whole.[20]

Cano's final sojourn in Ireland was at the court of Illand son of Scanlán, king of the Corcu Loígde (lines 324–76). Here once again we see Cano in single-minded pursuit of his own ends, but this time it is at great cost to his host. When Cano arrived at Illand's residence he was made welcome, but then Illand had to go and seek help from the Corcu Loígde. They undertook to give him three oxen, three flitches of bacon, and three vats of liquor each evening; his wife promised him the produce of three herds, each of twenty-seven cows, to provide his guests with rations. Illand then returned to Cano and his people and welcomed them again. Cano's reply showed his utter dependence on Illand's generosity: "'A blessing betimes,' said Cano, 'on him to whom we have come! May God make requital on our behalf, for we shall not do so.'" Nevertheless, Illand said that Cano would not have to leave in search of food until he would accede to the kingship of Scotland. And so Cano and his people remained there for three years, and Cano and Illand whiled away the time playing *fidchell*.

A brief exchange between Illand and Cano is given at this point. Illand expressed his fear that his wood would be destroyed, and he had good reason for this in that a hundred and fifty bundles of firewood were taken into the house morning and evening. Cano replied in a quatrain, saying that the wood would not fail but that Illand himself would be destroyed. But Illand said that he would pay no heed to that.

Cano was then summoned back to assume the kingship of Scotland. There was much weeping and lamenting among the followers of Cano and Illand at their parting, and when Cano took his leave of him, Illand declared that he would be dead within a year of Cano's departure. As it turned out, Illand was slain by his own people a year to that day.

We are not told in so many words why the Corcu Loígde assassinated Illand, but it is clear that he gave them cause for dissatisfaction by neglecting his affairs and depleting the resources of his people in order to attend to Cano's needs. It is true that Cano warned Illand of the danger he was in, and that Illand deliberately neglected to attend to the matter. Here there is a contrast with Cano's response to the warning he received from Diarmait's daughter: Cano, as we have seen, took decisive action and saved the day. Illand is in some measure responsible for his own undoing. Yet his misfortunes can ultimately be traced back to Cano's act of forebearance on the sea, that very act for which Cano was awarded the kingship. Cano made it clear that he could not requite Illand's hospitality, and we know that the reason he could not do so was because he had chosen not to lay hold of the "goodly heritage" which his father had hidden away for him. For Illand the consequence of this was that he impoverished himself for Cano's sake, and, so far as our text goes, this is the only reason we can see for his assassination.

24. The Theme of *ainmne* in *Scéla Cano meic Gartnáin* 351

Cano was deeply moved by Illand's death (lines 377–447): he keened him in the traditional style, beating his hands together until streams of blood flowed from them and reciting a moving lament. Then he returned to Corcu Loígde and avenged Illand's death.

The *ainmne* shown by Cano in respect of his father's wealth leads (as it would seem) to the loss of his friend Illand; that shown by him in his relationship with Créd leads to the loss of his lover and to his own death. After his return to Scotland, Cano used to have an annual assignation with Créd, but Colgu was always present with a hundred warriors. It is not clear whether Marcán prevented Cano from actually meeting Créd. It may be that Cano wished to redeem his promise to Créd and take her as his wife, and that he was frustrated in this by Marcán. In any case, Cano's final assignation with Créd was at Loch Créda. On this occasion, Cano was overtaken by Marcán and barely escaped from his ship. When Créd saw Cano's face, she shattered her head against a rock, apparently assuming him to be dead. Cano's stone broke under her body—it will be remembered that Cano's soul was in the stone—and so Cano died nine days after he had returned to the east.

Such is the tragic story of Cano son of Gartnán. Cano is not a king-hero in the classic Irish mold: he does not accede to kingship by an exercise of *fír flathemon*, or even by dint of martial prowess. But *Scéla Cano* does highlight one of the characteristics which was required of the true king, for we have seen that such a ruler is described in *Críth Gablach* as a repository of forebearance. *Scéla Cano* can thus be regarded as a moral tale, a study in the practice of forebearance as a means of accession to kingship. And for all its imperfections as a piece of narrative, the exposition of the theme of *ainmne* in *Scéla Cano* bears the hallmark of a true tragedy, for it shows the practice of a virtue in such circumstances and in such a manner that the very practice of the virtue issues in doom and destruction for the hero and for those he loves.

25

The Rhetoric of
Scéla Cano meic Gartnáin

(1 9 8 9)

Scéla Cano meic Gartnáin ("The Story of Cano son of Gartnán")[1] is a brief biography, in a mixture of prose and verse, of a Scottish prince whose life was endangered from his birth, and who fled to Ireland in order to escape the murderous attentions of his uncle, Áedán mac Gabráin, who was king of Scotland. While in Ireland, Cano stayed successively with the joint kings of Tara, Diarmait and Blathmac; with Gúaire, king of Connacht; and with the king of Corcu Loígde, Illand mac Scanláin. He secretly became betrothed to Gúaire's daughter, Créd, who was already married to Marcán, king of Uí Maine, and who was also the unwilling object of the amorous designs of Marcán's son, Colgu. Cano developed a fast friendship with Illand mac Scanláin, who was the most generous of his hosts, and it was with great sorrow that Cano parted from Illand when he was eventually

25. The Rhetoric of *Scéla Cano meic Gartnáin*   353

called home to assume the kingship of Scotland. A year later, Illand was slain, and Cano returned to Ireland to avenge his death. Once every year, he came to Ireland to try to keep a tryst with Créd, but his rival, Colgu, was always present on these occasions with a hundred warriors, and finally intervened in a way which was to lead to the death of Créd and of Cano.

    Scéla Cano survives only in the somewhat imperfect text of the Yellow Book of Lecan, and this presents several problems of interpretation at the level of the "plain sense" of the tale. Problems have been identified at other levels as well. It does not as yet seem possible, for one thing, to retrace the genesis of the tale with any degree of assurance. Its language shows a mixture of Old-Irish and Middle-Irish features, and stands in need of thorough analysis; it would seem unwise, on present knowledge, to assign a date of composition to it. What has come down to us is, in some measure, the outcome of a process of composition and transmission of the kind which I have characterized elsewhere as "comprising the expansion and contraction, reshaping and redaction of matter, much of which must have been received into the literature from indigenous oral tradition, but some of which is of learned ecclesiastical provenance."[2] The question of authorship is thus a complex one, since *Scéla Cano* is the work of more than one hand. We know that the last of them was the scribe of the Yellow Book of Lecan text (though we cannot estimate the extent of his contribution), but we do not know who the others were, or what was their number. None of this, it must be said, prevents us from studying the tale as a self-sufficient entity, and that is what I propose to do in this essay. The rhetorical and thematic features of the text which will be explored here might seem to point to the conclusion that *Scéla Cano* is essentially the work of a single author. What will not remain in question, in any case, is the integrity of *Scéla Cano* as a work of imaginative literature.

    If we are still in the dark about the author, or authors, of *Scéla Cano*, we can at least be quite certain that it was composed in the kind of literate Christian milieu which James Carney wrote about in his *Studies in Early Irish Literature and History*.[3] If, as seems likely, some of the material in *Scéla Cano* derives from oral tradition, then that material was taken and used in the creation of a written work of fiction in an early Irish ecclesiastical community. The consideration of the oral antecedents of early Irish narrative has so far generated more heat than light,[4] but the matter arises here, not least because Gerard Murphy used *Scéla Cano* to exemplify the relationship, as he saw it, between "the tales as really told to assembled kings and noblemen at an ancient *óenach*" and "the poorly narrated manuscript versions."[5] Murphy's observations on the matter have serious implications for the study of our tale, and they are best read in his own words:

> Medieval Irish manuscripts would seem . . . to be related to living storytelling much as the museum today is related to living material culture. The manuscripts contain samples from interesting specimens of genuine storytelling, particularly from out-of-date specimens, arranged without much attention to artistic requirements, just as the museum contains samples of out-of-date furniture and household utensils arranged with a view to antiquarian instruction rather than to suit the purposes of real life.[6]

A little earlier in the same work he had said:

> When we think of the well-constructed narratives which even the unlearned peasant narrator today can produce, and when we judge of the greater power of Old Irish storytellers by consideration of certain passages scattered through the inartistic manuscript versions of their tales which have been preserved, we can be fairly certain that the tales, as really told to assembled kings and noblemen at an ancient *óenach*, were very different from the poorly-narrated manuscript versions noted down by monastic scribes as a contribution to learning rather than to literature.
>
> The ninth-century story of Cano son of Gartnán [he is referring to *Scéla Cano*] offers a good example. Its opening paragraph leads the reader to expect exquisite artistry in the tale as a whole. [At this point Murphy translates the paragraph, which contains an elaborate description of Inis Moccu Chéin, the island where Gartnán lived, and Cano was born.] About page 2 of the printed text one begins to suspect that elaborate descriptions of this sort are being hinted at rather than recorded, and from page 3 on, the story begins to resemble a summary of incidents rather than a tale meant to hold the interest of an audience by its artistry.[7]

Finally, having discussed the fact that "the printed text would take about half an hour to recite,"[8] he goes on:

We should hardly be far wrong ... in conjecturing that the Story of Cano son of Gartnán as really told in the ninth century would have contained many elaborate passages reminiscent of the opening passages ... would have been much better knit than the manuscript version, and would have taken an hour or several hours to tell.[9]

Every student of early Irish literature owes a debt to Gerard Murphy, but our gratitude for his work cannot extend to the acceptance of this particular argument. There may well be a case (which would need to be argued) for seeing something of the museum-curator in the compilers of late manuscripts which preserve the early literature, though I feel that the great codices would more aptly be likened to libraries than to museums. But that is to say nothing of the authors of the works so preserved. A reading of the early Irish tale *Fingal Rónáin*,[10] to mention but one, should be enough to dispel the notion that the authors of early Irish saga were doing no more than collecting "samples from interesting specimens of *genuine* storytelling," whether "out of date" or otherwise.

Scéla Cano, admittedly, might seem more amenable to Murphy's argument than *Fingal Rónáin*. The early part of *Scéla Cano* contains two fine passages, the first of them being the one translated by Murphy, describing the beautifully decorated structures of the island, its livestock, and its way of life, with Gartnán spending his time "on his flock-bed, drinking mead" (lines 3–13), the second describing the company in which Cano set out for Ireland, a company of fifty warriors, fifty women, and fifty attendants (lines 27–37). It is indeed true that elaborate descriptions of this kind do not recur in the tale; there are several points at which such descriptions would not be out of place, and if they occurred we would be dealing with a literary work of a different order. That is not to say, however, that Murphy is justified in assuming that the two passages in question are products of oral storytelling. When he voices the suspicion, which is evidently prompted by the description of Cano's entourage, "that elaborate descriptions of this sort are being hinted at rather than recorded," the wording, taken in context, clearly implies the previous existence of an oral version of *Scéla Cano* which contained such descriptions. The existence of such a version of *Scéla Cano* is unproven.

There is a somewhat stronger case for seeing some of *Scéla Cano* as "resembling a summary of incidents." There are points in the tale at which we would dearly like to have more information. This is true, in particular, of what might be called the love-quadrangle of Cano, Créd, Marcán, and Colgu. A glaring example occurs upon Cano's arrival at Marcán's dwelling, when he is on his way to Gúaire. Cano sends a messenger to seek Créd's protection, and he instructs him to "recite these quatrains for her" (193). The quatrains are not given in the text, and we are left in the dark as to their substance. We may compare another section of the tale (234–74), in which poems are mentioned without being given to us. This tells how Senchán composed poems for Diarmait son of Áed Sláine on four successive occasions; for the first two he received niggardly rewards, but he was paid opulently for the others (234–74). As it stands, the story of Diarmait and Senchán is perfectly explicable, as we will see below, in terms of the poet's forebearance and the patron's belated generosity. The point to be made here is that we cannot say how much our appreciation of it would be deepened (not to say modified) by access to Senchán's poems; indeed, we do not even know whether those poems ever existed. The position is different with Cano's quatrains for Créd: we could do with them (or their substance), and other assistance besides, in order to understand precisely what is going on in this part of the story. It is tempting, therefore, to suppose that Cano's quatrains did exist, and that they were dropped out at some stage in the process of composition and transmission whereby *Scéla Cano* was given its present form. This need not have happened, however, in the course of the transfer of the story of Cano and Créd from a putative oral original to its written form. The fact is that at some points (though not many) *Scéla Cano* is concise to a fault: this may be due to an authorial deficiency in expository technique, an incapacity, that is to say, to translate what is in the mind into narrative on the written page; or it may have arisen as a result of defective transmission from one manuscript to another. The person who introduced the love-quadrangle into *Scéla Cano* probably had a clear conception of the story. We can say that the extant text of the tale does not convey that clear conception to the reader, and after that all is conjecture. Murphy was doubtless "not far wrong" in "conjecturing" that the extant text of *Scéla Cano* differs from how an oral version of Cano's story would have been "really told" in the ninth century—if it really was told, which it may well have been. This is consistent with the view expressed by Carney: "I find it impossible for many reasons to believe that the form of any of the fictions or entertainments preserved in our medieval manuscripts is in any way close to the form in which they would be told when they existed (in so far as they actually did) on a purely oral level."[11] What is dangerous in Murphy's argument is the implication that the manuscript tales are not "genuine" or "real." He goes so far as to make the statement, which is truly astonishing in light of what we know about *Táin Bó Cúailnge* and other tales with a rich manuscript history, that "it is unlikely that Irish story-tradition before the seventeenth century depended to any large extent upon manuscripts."[12] The manuscript text of *Scéla Cano* is genuine and real, as much in its flaws as in its many felicities, and it is a proper subject of study in its own right. Those who seek to analyze and elucidate the tale as it stands have a decided advantage, in having a real text to grapple with, over those who are concerned with what the story might have been like in an oral telling, and who must resort to conjecture as to the character of the postulated oral prototype.

Another problem which has been discussed in connection with *Scéla Cano* is that of its historicity, in the sense at least of its consistency with what little is known of the relevant historical facts. Cano himself, and most of the named persons with whom he comes into contact in the tale, are known to us from the historical record. Binchy takes a jaundiced view of *Scéla Cano* in this regard: "as in many historical novels of a later date, the author has played fast and loose with the facts of history";[13] "it is a complete travesty of the facts, full of errors and anachronisms... If we had not the contemporary witness of the annals to correct this farrago, what would we have known of the true history of Cano?"[14] Carney has taken a much more benign view,[15] but the matter continues to generate controversy.[16] I do not propose to enter the lists here, for I consider it legitimate, in a literary study, to treat the personages of the tale as characters in a work of fiction, and to examine their words and deeds, and their relations with one another, in that light. Francis John Byrne has said that "early Irish literature cannot be properly understood except as historical documentation."[17] Early Irish literature is indeed a valuable resource for the historian, and the student of the literature can learn much from what the historian has to say about the texts and their background. I would nevertheless take issue with Byrne, and say that early Irish literature cannot be properly understood except as literature, with due allowance being made for its historical dimension.

It is no part of my intention to decry the study of the genesis of *Scéla Cano*, or of its relationship to oral storytelling (provided that proper criteria can be established for such study), or of its historicity; in turning away from them now, I fully acknowledge that a rounded view of the tale would take all of these aspects into account, and many others besides. To mention but one of these others, Carney has demonstrated how fruitful it can be to consider *Scéla Cano* in conjunction with certain other early Irish tales with which it has an affinity.[18]

What I wish to do here is to examine some of the ways in which *Scéla Cano* is constituted as a literary work. In an article on *Fingal Rónáin* ("The Rhetoric of *Fingal Rónáin*," chap. 26 in this volume), the hypothesis was stated that early Irish sagas "represent the organization of the narrative lore into literary form, which implies that any given saga is more than a mere aggregation or accumulation of lore." In regard to *Scéla Cano*, this hypothesis has already been proved, to an extent, in a study of the recurrence in the saga of the theme of *ainmne* ("forebearance": see "The Theme of *ainmne* in *Scéla Cano meic Gartnáin*," chap. 24 in this volume) which contends that this feature lends the saga "a greater degree of thematic cohesion than has hitherto been allowed." The present essay is intended to complement that article, mainly by means of commentary on the text, which will attend to the ways in which certain effects are achieved by narratorial intrusion, by the selection and ordering of material, by recourse to verse, and by the use of language. For reasons of space, I have been compelled to concentrate the commentary on the first 149 lines, which is a little less than a third of the whole. But we will find that commentary on these lines leads outwards to consideration of relevant items in the remainder of the tale. Moreover, we will see that the integrity of this part of *Scéla Cano* has been called into question, and the arguments for so doing will be considered and rejected.

An unfortunate consequence of this constraint arises from the fact that the first 149 lines of text contain only one sequence of verse, amounting to twenty lines in all. *Scéla Cano* contains 180 lines of verse, and, in Binchy's edition, 332 lines of prose. It belongs to the type which Dillon describes as follows: "the form of the stories is a combination of prose and verse, the main narrative in prose, while any heightening of the mood may be marked by the use of verse, ordinarily so that the poems are spoken by one of the characters."[19] This may be unexceptionable as a general description, but it is apt to mask the complex interrelationship which can subsist, in any given tale, between prose and verse. The discussion below of the first verse-sequence in *Scéla Cano* will give some indication of how finely the verse can be integrated into the tale as a whole; for the rest, the following summary account will at least show at what points in the tale the narrator has recourse to verse.

1. 5 quatrains (lines 61 ff.): Cano is warned that his life is in danger.

2. 4 quatrains (lines 154 ff.): Cano learns to abjure the slaying of "the birds of the Son of the living God," and rededicates himself to the task of ensuring his own survival (see "The Theme of *ainmne* in *Scéla Cano meic Gartnáin,*" p. 347 in this volume).

3. 2 quatrains (lines 176 ff.): Cano had crossed the Shannon on his way to Gúaire, and he reaches the house of Marcán, who is married to Gúaire's daughter Créd. Having mentioned Créd, the narrator interrupts the sequence of his narrative to tell us that Créd had loved Cano before ever he came to Ireland—the familiar theme of *grád écmaise,* loving someone who is known only by his reputation. It was while Cano was still in Scotland that Créd uttered the two quatrains which are given here, and in which she speaks of Cano, and bewails her separation from him by the sea.

(This is the first of two items of background information which the narrator interposes here. The second is the statement that Cano had protected Créd's homestead when he accompanied Diarmait on the occasion of a battle fought by him against Gúaire. This is evidently envisaged as having taken place on an earlier visit by Cano to Ireland. Cano's sojourn with Diarmait and Blathmac, as described in *Scéla Cano,* is very short; they are enjoying tribute at a place called Collmag in Ulster when they first receive him, and they are still there when he leaves, going southwards over Mag Muirthemne to Cernae in Mag mBreg [line 149].)

4. 1 quatrain (lines 190 ff.): Having been provided with the foregoing background information, we are now returned to the narrative present. Cano tells a messenger to go into the court and seek Créd's protection for him on his way to Gúaire. Then he utters his quatrain in which he instructs the messenger to "recite these quatrains for her," quatrains which, as already noted above, are not given in the text.

5. 3 quatrains (lines 197 ff.): These are uttered by Créd, the first of them to Colgu, the others to Marcán. Colgu says to her, "These verses are given to you, Créd" (line 194). Since this is said immediately after Cano's tantalizing quatrain, the reference seems to be to Cano's verses, in which case it may be assumed that Marcán intercepted the messenger (and perhaps also that the

verses were written out). Créd replies in a quatrain, telling him that he little knows what she is chanting; she has given her love to a man whose land is not close to her. It is apparently this latter part of her address to Colgu which prompts Marcán, surprisingly, to express approval of her words,[20] adding, in a remarkable understatement, that she should not love Colgu, "seeing that he is a member of this household." In her reply Créd rounds on Marcán, and in the translation suggested by Pádraig Ó Fiannachta, says: "May you not survive your son. May it not be your son who break (poetic for 'die'); may it be you who pass away."[21] She goes on to lament the absence of Cano, and to disparage Colgu's love.

In the normal order of things, Marcán would not be expected to outlive his son. Why then should Créd expend so much passion on her wish that Marcán will indeed be the first of the two to die? The explanation must be that she expects Colgu to be accused of attempting to seduce her, and to be put to death for it. This would be a perfectly reasonable expectation, since Marcán obviously knows about it. (In *Fingal Rónáin*, Mael Fhothartaig was slain on foot of a [false] accusation that he sought to seduce his stepmother.)

6. 1 quatrain (lines 212 ff.): Spoken by Gúaire. In the brief prose introduction, the narrator once again departs from the narrative present, but on this occasion he takes us forward to an unspecified time in the future: *Roliad-si iarum a[r] C[h]olcain, dia n-ebairt Gúaire fesin dia n-etarchosaíd*. I would translate: "Colgu was afterwards accused of intercourse with her, of which (or 'when') Gúaire himself said, in order to set them at loggerheads." Thurneysen took it that it was Créd who was accused of intercourse with Colgu, and this has won universal acceptance. The older usage of *liid for* (later *ar*) would have Colgu as the accused one;[22] the reason why this has been rejected is doubtless to be sought in what Gúaire actually says in his quatrain, which is to the effect that Créd did not accept Colgu when he wooed her. But this is not a sufficient argument; Marcán knows that Colgu has attempted to seduce Créd; he also knows that she has rejected him. Créd, as we have seen, seems to expect that Colgu will be accused of his crime and executed for it. Gúaire's word would scarcely carry much weight in defence of his married daughter; on the other hand, if Colgu was the accused one, we would expect Gúaire to be believed when he said that Colgu did not in fact have intercourse with Créd. As for Gúaire's desire "to set them at loggerheads," we can only guess at what is meant: it may be that

Colgu's accusers would be locked in argument over what course to take, given Gúaire's testimony that intercourse had not taken place, but that Colgu had nevertheless wooed Créd. We do know that Colgu survived, with fatal consequences for Créd and Cano.

The verse-sequences here numbered 3–6, together with the sparse accompanying prose, form a continuum in the text, but the reason for dividing it up will now be clear. Sequence 3 is uttered earlier, and 6 later, than the narrative present. The constant factor is Créd's love for Cano: it is the theme of her own verses, and it is hinted at by Gúaire. The narrator breaks the linear sequence of the narrative to fill us in on the history of Créd's love for Cano, and her relations with her husband and stepson, but, in doing this, he neglects to inform us fully about what is happening in the present. We are not told what came of Cano's request for protection on his way to Gúaire. After Gúaire's quatrain has been given, we are returned to the narrative present only to be told that Cano and his people went to Durlas Gúairi, and that Gúaire welcomed them. (This narrative leap could well have been prompted by the fact that Gúaire has just been mentioned.) The likelihood is that Créd was prevented from seeing Cano. She speaks openly to Marcán and Colgu of her disdain for them, and of her love for Cano; that he is not present for this is implicit in her line, "Alas for her from whom Cano is absent!" (208).[23] Later, when Gúaire holds a banquet in Cano's honor, Marcán puts four men to guard Créd, evidently to prevent her from meeting Cano, but Créd contrives to put all present to sleep, save Cano and herself, and it is at this point that she importunes Cano, and they become secretly betrothed.

7. 1 quatrain (lines 319 ff.): When Créd tried to seduce Cano at Gúaire's banquet, he declined to comply while he remained in military service, but he promised that, should he become king, he would come to fetch her, and she would be his wife forever. As an earnest of his good faith, he gave her his stone of life, which contained his soul. Each day, she takes the stone from its pouch, and addresses a quatrain to it; she says, "If you are broken, only spoliation will seize and bind my soul."[24]

It is here that the seeds of the lovers' destruction are sown. Through a tragic misunderstanding, it is Créd herself who breaks the stone, while Cano is attempting to redeem his promise. When he has become king, Cano makes annual attempts to meet Créd, but he is thwarted by Colgu on each occasion. In the final attempt, three ships overtook Cano, their occupants struck him, and he barely escaped from his ship. When Créd saw his face, she evidently thought him dead, for she shattered her head against a rock, and the stone broke under her body. Cano died nine days after his return to Scotland (lines 498–510).

8. 1 quatrain (lines 362 ff.): Cano spends three years as the guest of Illand mac Scanláin, and it is made plain that the cost of the provisions required to sustain Cano and his retinue is considerable. At length, Illand complains that his wood is being destroyed, and the narrator explains that there is good reason for this, in that a hundred and fifty bundles of firewood were taken into the house morning and evening. Cano replies in a quatrain, saying that the wood would not fail, but that Illand himself would be destroyed. Illand says that he would pay no heed to that for the moment.

9. 14 quatrains (385 ff.): The forebodings expressed in the foregoing quatrain are echoed by Illand himself as Cano sets out to claim the kingship of Scotland. He foretells his own death, and he is indeed slain by his own people, one year later to the day. Cano is fishing on the sea on the same day, and he has a sea-omen (*cél tuinne*), which the narrator explains as knowledge from the sea: he sees the sea red with Illand's blood as it approaches his boat. Cano then arises and claps his hands until streams of blood are flowing from them, and he recites a splendid elegy, full of passion, ranging through desolation, anger, nostalgia, and vengefulness. Cano returns to Corcu Loígde, takes vengeance on Illand's slayers, and ensures the prosperity and safety of Illand's son.

10. 12 quatrains (lines 450 ff.): This poem, which is obscure in parts, is recited (except for one quatrain) by Cano. Thurneysen omitted this poem from his translation, as having nothing to do with the tale, and he characterized it as a catalogue of the ales drunk all over Ireland as well as among the Saxons and the Picts, but the ales which are catalogued in the first nine stanzas are "ales of sovereignty"; as Binchy points out (1963, xxvi), the poet is referring in every case to "the figurative ale of sovereignty which is drunk at the 'wedding-feast' marking the inauguration of the tribal king." Its connection with *Scéla Cano* is made plain in the remainder of the poem. In the tenth quatrain an unnamed speaker demands that Cano be given his drink, and the demand is repeated by Cano himself in the eleventh quatrain. We are witnessing the inauguration of Cano as king of Scotland, which represents the achievement of the goal which he has had before him throughout his stay in Ireland.

Binchy says that "we are in effect given a list of kingdoms over which the hero of the poem has achieved dominion"; he adds that "it is most unlikely that Cano himself is claiming to have been invested with sovereignty over them, which again suggests that the poem has been arbitrarily inserted" (1963, xxvi). I suggest a different explanation. The catalogue of the ales of sovereignty is a display of knowledge; there is no hint that the speaker claims dominion over the various kingdoms included in the list. In this inauguration ceremony, the aspirant to kingship shows himself to have some acquaintance with the political geography of Ireland, Scotland, and England, and then goes on to claim the kingship of Scotland for himself.

11. 1 quatrain (lines 501 ff.): The last quatrain is uttered by Créd on all but the last of her annual assignations with Cano. It follows immediately upon mention of the presence of Colgu with a company of a hundred warriors, and, as Binchy interprets it, it contains an oblique warning to Cano not to land.

What all of the verse passages in the saga have in common is that they have to do with critical moments in Cano's life; they accompany such moments, or portend or comment upon them. Three of them are warnings. Many of them express Créd's love for Cano, but he is never present to hear these declarations; the only quatrain which she utters to him is the oblique warning towards the end. Cano never puts his love for Créd into words, whether in verse or in prose. Cano is generally a model of restraint, in his words as in his deeds, and the outburst of passion caused by Illand's death is the more striking for that. The last remark which I would make about the verse in *Scéla Cano* is that we would have a very distorted notion of the content of the tale if we were to depend on the verse alone. We would have no idea, for example, that Créd's love was requited by the hero. It is only as an indivisible unit that the poetry and prose can be interpreted, and this proposition will be borne out in what follows, which is a commentary on the first 149 lines of the tale.

The introduction to the tale (lines 1–37) is set in Scotland. We are told that the kingship of that country was bitterly contested between Áedán son of Gabrán and Gartnán son of Áed son of Gabrán, and that Gartnán lived on an island called Inis Moccu Chéin, which, as we have seen, is described at length (lines 3–13). When his son Cano was born, Gartnán had him taken away to be fostered. Gartnán also concealed a vat of gold and silver; he killed the four men he had employed in this work, so that the whereabouts of the hoard were known only to Gartnán, his wife, and

Cano. Áedán invaded Gartnán's island, massacred its inhabitants, and razed its buildings to the ground. Cano determined to evade the murderous attentions of Áedán by going to his kinsmen in Ireland. He set out in a company of fifty warriors, fifty women, and fifty attendants, a company which is described in detail (lines 27–37).

This introduction establishes Cano as a hero whose life is endangered from the time of his birth; his life will continue to be threatened until he is summoned home to receive the kingship of Scotland (lines 367–69). The narrator does not trouble to tell us at this stage that Cano's life was in danger even while his mother was in labor; we find out later that two women from the Otherworld (*síd*) came at that time, and attempted to abscond with his soul (lines 311–13); the focus at this stage is on the threat from Áedán. Nor are we told the outcome of the contest for the kingship, but we can assume that Gartnán has already admitted defeat when he retires to his flock-bed and his mead on Inis Moccu Chéin. It is the birth of an heir to Gartnán which now poses a threat to Áedán, and it is to remove that threat that he engages in massacre and destruction. Gartnán outwits Áedán by having Cano put out to fosterage, and by concealing a vat of wealth for the boy. Cano prudently sets about securing his own survival, but we will find that Áedán's implacable hostility pursues him to Ireland, and that the wealth from the vat will figure in Áedán's further attempts to destroy Cano.

The two descriptive passages have a significant function in relation to the work as a whole. The account of Gartnán's idyllic existence on Inis Moccu Chéin serves as a contrastive backdrop to Cano's troubled career. It is the birth of Cano which leads to the destruction of Gartnán's idyll, and Cano himself is not destined to achieve the kind of tranquillity which Gartnán enjoyed, however briefly. He comes closest to it during the years he spends with Illand (lines 356–58), but the joy of those years for Cano is tainted by his awareness of the heavy price which Illand must pay for it. Even when Cano at last accedes to kingship, he is consumed by a love which cannot be consummated, and which leads to his death.

The cost to others of Cano's circumstances, and indeed of his very existence, is something which is emphasized throughout the tale. Already in the introduction we see it in the massacre at Inis Moccu Chéin. We see it too in the killing of the four men who have been employed in concealing the hoard. The function of the description of Cano's retinue is to foreground the considerable company which must be accommodated by his successive hosts: these are the numbers who strain the hospitality of Diarmait and Blathmac, and even that of the prodigiously generous Gúaire, and who deplete the resources of Illand mac Scanláin.

The only snatch of dialogue in this section is that in which Cano explains why he proposes to go to Ireland. Gearóid Mac Eoin has said of *Scéla Cano* that "motivation has to be inferred from the action itself,"[25] but it is in fact a feature of this tale that its characters are forever explaining themselves, or giving, taking, or rejecting advice or warnings. This is true in particular of Cano himself. Actions rarely go unaccounted for; if the characters do not explain themselves, the narrator is nothing loth to intrude an explanatory observation.

Cano's first sojourn in Ireland was spent with the two sons of Áed Sláine, Diarmait and Blathmac, who were joint kings of Tara (lines 38–147). We have seen that, when Cano went to them, they were enjoying due tribute at Collmag in Ulster. They received him generously, giving him a third of their food and liquor, of their living-quarters, and of their cattle. Having told us this much, the narrator turns to deal with Áedán, and he does this by intruding an account of Áedán's feelings: "Áedán was displeased when he heard how Cano had been made welcome by the sons of Áed Sláine, but what Áedán found hardest of all to bear was that he did not know the whereabouts of the vat which had been concealed by Gartnán" (lines 41–43). He then goes on to report a claim that Áedán had found out where the hoard was hidden, and had recovered it: "Now they say that Satan came to Áedán and told him where the vat was, so that it was taken by him to his own store-room, and there was not a penny of it lacking" (lines 44–47). In the first of these sentences, the narrator claims a privileged insight into Áedán's state of mind, whereas in the second, he distances himself from the content of the sentence by attributing it to unknown sources. It is evidently the satanic intervention which the narrator is reluctant to credit, for Áedán's recovery of the hoard is required for what follows. Áedán's own words are given next: "Good will come of this: this wealth of Gartnán's will be given to the sons of Áed Sláine as a reward for killing Gartnán's son Cano" (lines 47f.).

Áedán's men came, unbeknown to Cano, bearing a bag of silver, and they conveyed Áedán's proposition to Diarmait and Blathmac. Their private conversation was overheard by Diarmait's daughter (her name is not given). The narrator explains that she had loved Cano before ever he came to Ireland, because of the stories she had heard about him. She therefore set out to warn him of what was afoot. The snatch of conversation which is given in the text as having been overheard by Diarmait's daughter is simply a demand by one of Áed's sons that the silver be weighed, and the response from one of the Scotsmen that it would be done (lines 55 f.). That is all that is necessary, since the reader already knows that the silver is being offered for killing Cano. That Diarmait's daughter also knows is implied by the fact that she takes herself off to warn Cano, and it is confirmed, somewhat guardedly, in five quatrains of warning which she addresses to him, and explicitly, when she goes on to spell out the reason for her warning.

The omission from the snatch of conversation of the terms of Áedán's offer can scarcely be put down to narratorial economy, since a good deal of space is otherwise devoted to the matter. The brevity of the conversation, as given in the text, is rather to be seen as serving the important function of placing the focus fully on the response to the offer of the sons of Áed Sláine, and it lends salience to the fact that, in demanding that the silver be weighed, they seem prepared to contemplate the betrayal of their obligation in honor to protect their guest, Cano, from attack.

This brings us to the first passage of verse in *Scéla Cano*, which, together with its immediate prose context, may be translated as follows.

> The girl heard that secret conversation. She went out and took a switch in her hand, and she went onto the lintel of the enclosure. Then Cano came out with three men, each of them bearing a single spear in his hand as he came out. The girl said:
>
>> "I do not know this day
>> of any warrior in Ireland or among the Scotsmen
>> who would not be a match for Cano[26]
>> with his very slender bright spear."
>
> As he went under the lintel, she placed the rod on his head. And she said:
>
>> "Cano,
>> certain persons are watching out for you;[27]
>> if ill-fortune ensues, it will be abundant,
>> if good fortune, it will be slighter,"
>
> while she dealt him a blow as he was coming out. And as he was going away from her, she said:

> "The Scotsman is not wary,
> he goes about with (only) the strength of his hand;
> he does not take heed of
> the vigor of Áed Sláine's son.
> It is not in order to offer rebuke
> to a king who has never been reviled by satire (that I speak);
> a great many people (besides you)
> are under the protection of the sons of Áed.
> The story which I have heard through their house
> is not a beautiful melodious song,
> (but rather) a sorrowful strain for him who does not hear it;
> the Scotsman is not wary."
>
> "This is a warning, girl," said Cano.
> "If it is a warning," said she, "there is a reason for it. Silver which is to be given as a reward for killing you is being weighed in yonder dwelling." (lines 57–87)

Binchy remarks of the girl's verses that they are "couched in deliberately obscure language."[28] Cano's initial response to them may seem rather banal, but it affords an opportunity for the meaning of the girl's words to be spelled out in explicit terms, as much for the reader's benefit as for Cano's. Moreover, Cano acts on the warning and manages to retrieve the situation.

The quatrains uttered by Diarmait's daughter are at once a warning and a reproach; in delivering them, she takes the role, which is assigned to a number of female personages in Irish saga, of goading a reluctant (or, as in this case, an unwary) hero into action. The solemnity of the girl's message is seen in the choice of verse for the purpose, and in the language in which it is expressed; it is reflected also in the manner of its delivery. It is divided into three parts, two single quatrains and a unit of three, the unity of the latter being achieved by opening and closing with the same line. Its delivery is punctuated by actions with a switch. Gearóid Mac Eoin has said that the purpose of the switch was to attract Cano's attention by touching him as he passed by,[29] but I think that there is more to it than that. It is clear from the prose phrases which are interspersed with the verse, and which Pádraig Ó Fiannachta has aptly likened to stage directions,[30] that the first quatrain was uttered as Cano came out of the house which he occupied in the court, the second as he passed through the gateway of the court, and the third as he moved away from it. The girl used the rod after the first quatrain, and after the second. Since the first quatrain had been uttered before the girl touched Cano with the switch, it seems unlikely that her action was designed merely to attract his attention. It seems rather that this *rabad* is a ritual warning, delivered in verse, and divided into three parts (1+1+3) by the use of simple actions with a switch, these actions being in themselves an inherent part of the ritual.

It is significant that this warning is delivered at the very beginning of Cano's life in Ireland, for in this respect it bears comparison with Fedelm's prophetic warning to Medb as she is about to set out for Ulster in *Táin Bó Cúailnge*,[31] and with that of Cathbad to the Ulaid at the time of Deirdriu's birth in *Longes mac nUislenn*.[32]

Medb chooses to dismiss Fedelm's warning in the *Táin*, and Conchobor declines to act on Cathbad's advice in *Longes mac nUislenn*, and the tragic consequences of their folly form the substance of the respective tales. On the other hand, the hero's response to the ritual warning in *Scéla Cano* is to heed and act upon it, with consequences which are entirely benign. Within *Scéla Cano* itself, Cano's response to the warning which marks the beginning of his stay in Ireland stands in contrast with that of Illand to the brief warning, also in verse, given to him by Cano on the eve of his return to Scotland.

Diarmait's daughter is motivated by her love for Cano. We are given no indication that her love was requited: once she delivers her warning, she passes out of the story. But her love for Cano prefigures that of Créd. It too started when she knew Cano only by repute; because of it she rejects the petitions of the noblemen of Ireland (line 53), just as Créd is no longer interested in "the love of one person rather than another in the land of Ireland" (lines 206 f.). In the case of Diarmait's daughter, her love for Cano dents her loyalty to her father; in Créd's case, it destroys her fidelity to her husband. This parallelism serves to point up the contrast between the ways in which the love of these two women affects Cano's fortunes: he is saved by the first at the outset of his career in Ireland, but he is destroyed by the second when he has achieved the kingship of Scotland.

The dominant theme of the girl's warning is expressed in the repeated line, "the Scotsman is not wary." The first quatrain remarks upon the insufficiency of his armor; the first couplet of the second suggests that his life is in danger. The message of the second couplet, as Binchy remarks, is harder to interpret. It reads: *masa dodchad, is mór de, / masa sothchad, is tano*, literally, "if it is ill-fortune, it will be a great deal of it; if good fortune, it will be slight." I have essentially followed Thurneysen and Binchy in translating, "if ill-fortune ensues, it will be abundant; if good fortune it will be slighter." This probably conveys the general sense of what is being said in the Irish text, but the words rendered respectively as "good fortune" and "ill-fortune" probably have a deeper meaning in the original than emerges in translation. If we attend to that deeper meaning, we will find a solution to the problem posed by the couplet, which can be stated as follows: if we are to believe that success on the part of Áedán's emissaries would issue in "abundant" ill-fortune for Cano, why should failure on their part not issue in good fortune which would be correspondingly abundant?

Sothc(h)ad 'good luck, fortune' and *dodc(h)ad* 'ill-luck, misfortune' are compounds of *tocad* which, according to *DIL*, means "fortune, chance; good fortune, prosperity, wealth." The corresponding verb *tocaid* is used in the passive in the sense "is destined, is fated"; it is reasonable to suppose that *tocad* occasionally has the sense "fate, destiny," which incidentally is that of its Middle Welsh congener, *tynghet*. Assuming that *tocad* retains that sense in *sothchad* and *dodchad*, as used in this couplet, the message is that if it is destined for Cano that the outcome of what is going on is deleterious, it will be a disaster; if that is not the case, the outcome will nevertheless be of little benefit to Cano if he trusts to fate alone. What is implied in this is that he must take action to protect his own interests.

In the third quatrain, the girl refers again to Cano's (relatively) unarmed state, and she becomes more specific in hinting that the danger to Cano may come from Áed Sláine's son. The reference is obviously to her own father; while Diarmait and Blathmac sometimes remind us of Rosencrantz and Guildenstern, Diarmait is nevertheless the more prominent of the two. In implying that Cano should beware of Diarmait, the girl comes perilously close to impugning his honor. She is careful to disavow any such intention in her fourth quatrain, adding that the king has never been satirized—Thurneysen adds "(for his niggardliness)" at this point, and that is clearly what the girl has in mind. (We will see later that he has run the risk of being satirized for niggardliness at least once in his career.) The girl goes on to indicate that Diarmait and Blathmac now have other guests besides Cano, and in her final quatrain she tells him that she has heard something in their house that bodes ill for the unvigilant Cano.

In thus warning Cano to be vigilant, the girl introduces the two subsidiary themes of fate and hospitality, and each of these is amply represented in the prose of *Scéla Cano*. There are three references to fate in the sequel to the warning. When Cano tells his people that their lives are in danger, they reply: "That has perhaps been destined for us" (*Bés is ed ro-chindead dún*, 94), the verb which is used on this occasion being *cinnid*.[33] Cano, however, announces that he will make a peaceful approach to Diarmait and Blathmac, and commands that force should be used if he is denied admittance by them. They reply that "forebearance is better," the sense presumably being that Cano's peaceful approach is better than a precipitate response.[34] Cano is admitted by Diarmait and Blathmac, and he tells them that the wealth which is being offered to them had been hidden away for him by Gartnán, but that as Áedán's *tocad* was stronger, he found the hoard. This elicits the desired response: "We declare," said Diarmait, "that even if enough silver were to be given to fill the house up to the roof, you would not be sold for it" (lines 117 f.). Cano withdraws, and he is followed by Blathmac, who advises him to wait until the Scotsmen have passed out of the protection of the royal brothers, and then to attack them and seize his own wealth. In advising Cano to wait in that way, Blathmac shows himself to be sensitive to the obligation, in honor, of the host to protect his guests. Cano takes Blathmac's advice, but when he has overpowered the Scotsmen, he decides after all to allow them to return to Scotland with the wealth, and he explains this to his puzzled followers: "If it has been fated for me (*ma ra-tocad dam-sa*), I shall be the one to use this silver" (line 137). Cano returns ashore.

There is an interesting narratorial intrusion into the piece of direct speech which follows. Diarmait begins to speak, but only his first word has been given when the narrator intrudes an item of information. He then gives Diarmait's utterance in full, beginning with a reprise of the first word. As the nature of this passage has been obscured by Binchy's punctuation of the text, I translate it here: "'Well,' said Diarmait—he had received a prophecy from God (in which) Cano's reward for the forebearance which he had shown on the sea was revealed: the kingship of Scotland for twenty-four years after Áedán's reign—'Well,' said Diarmait, 'give welcome to the man who comes to you'" (lines 141–44). For a full three days after that, Cano and his people did not remove their belts or their brooches, and they then set out by night on the journey which would lead them to the court of Gúaire in Connacht.

25. The Rhetoric of *Scéla Cano meic Gartnáin*

We have noted the occurrence in the text of *cinnid*, *tocaid*, *tocad*, *soth-c(h)ad* and *dodc(h)ad*. Another item, *antocad*, will complete this lexical inventory. In an excursus on Senchán (lines 234 ff.), the poet's messenger twice returns from Diarmait with paltry rewards for the poems which had been sent to him. The messenger addresses Senchán disdainfully, on the first occasion calling him a *bachlach* 'churl,' and on the second an *antocad*, which is another compound of *tocad*, and of which the sense here could well be "ill-fated one." Senchán's reaction is to bide his time, and he sends Diarmait another poem, for which he is handsomely rewarded. There is a precise parallel between this episode and the exchange between Cano and his people which takes place after the girl's warning. Senchán is accused of being ill-fated, while Cano is told that he and his people are destined to suffer a murderous attack; each of them responds in a restrained manner and resorts to a verbal approach which proves successful.

It is interesting to find five references to fate in so short a text, but it should be noted that all of these references occur in dialogue. The inference is that the notion of fate has a place in the worldview of the characters of the saga, but that it does not necessarily hold any explanatory value for the narrator.

Consideration must now be given to the theme of hospitality. This is a matter of the first importance in *Scéla Cano*, since Cano is entirely dependent, while in Ireland, on the generosity of his hosts.

Cano leaves Scotland in order to escape from Áedán, and he comes to Ireland "because they are kinsmen of ours" (line 26). On grounds of kinship, as well as propinquity, one would expect him to go to Ulster, and that may be the reason why Diarmait and Blathmac are said to have been in Ulster when he stayed with them. We have seen that he was welcomed by the royal brothers, but that Diarmait soon showed signs of contemplating Cano's betrayal. Having been warned by Diarmait's daughter, Cano told the story of Gartnán's hoard, and Diarmait declared that Cano would not be sold for silver. Blathmac advises Cano to recover his wealth, but in the event Cano decides not to do so. Cano returns ashore, to be welcomed once again by Diarmait, but after three days he sets out in the dead of night, having given his blessing to Diarmait.

Cano's journey takes him to Durlas Gúairi, where Gúaire welcomes him with the words: "You will not be sold here for silver on account of the trouble of feeding you; it will not be as it was with the sons of Áed Sláine.

You will have food and protection, and you are welcome!" (217–19). He remains with Gúaire for three months, but then Senchán, who is also a guest of Gúaire's, tells the king that he has taken too much on himself, and that the Connachta have enough to do in maintaining Gúaire and Senchán. He adds that Cano and his companions should go hunting; when they do so, they fail to meet up with one another, evidently owing to magical intervention on Senchán's part. As a result of this, Cano's party decide to take their leave of Gúaire, but Cano is careful to let Gúaire know that they go without hard feelings.

Cano then sets out for Illand mac Scanláin in Corcu Loígde. Illand welcomes him, saying: "That is Cano son of Gartnáin who has come to me, having been betrayed and sold for silver by the sons of Áed Sláine, and having been reduced to hunger by Gúaire. You shall have food here; you shall not be on the road; you shall not be sold for silver" (326–30). He sets about securing provisions for the maintenance of Cano's party, and when he has done so, he declares to Cano: "By my power, you shall not go from this court in your lifetime in search of food until you have acceded to the kingship of Scotland" (354 f.). Illand is as good as his word, and Cano spends three years as his guest.

Binchy says of the "compiler" of *Scéla Cano* that "in effect he has given us three separate *scéla* in which Cano is the hero: (1) his flight to Ireland and brief sojourn with Diarmait and Bláthmac; (2) his stay with Gúaire and his love for Créd; (3) his friendship for Illand, his triumphant return to Scotland and subsequent expedition against Illand's murderers, and his final assignation with Créd" (1963, xv). This comment may have been suggested, in part, by the use of the word *scéla* in the title, but Pádraig Ó Fiannachta has pointed out that this "may be of no special significance."[35] As for Cano's successive sojourns with Diarmait and Blathmac, with Gúaire, and with Illand, it may be noted that Binchy remarks, in another connection, on "the Irish fondness for a triad of incidents" (1963, 30), and this "fondness" is reflected in the episodic character of Cano's stay in Ireland. Moreover, there is a logical development within the three sojourns: Cano moves in an ascending order of generosity on the part of his hosts, while he progresses from Ulster, through Connacht, to Corcu Loígde, putting an ever greater distance between himself and his mortal enemy, Áedán.

Binchy speaks too of "some contradictions between the three *scéla*" (1963, xv). The example he gives has to do with "the reasons for Cano's abrupt decision to leave Diarmait and Bláthmac ([lines] 146 ff.)":

25. The Rhetoric of *Scéla Cano meic Gartnáin* 373

> According to reports received by both Gúaire (217–18) and Illand (327), the royal brothers had agreed to betray him to Aedán for money; but this is in direct contradiction to the account given in the first episode (117 ff.). Indeed, no explanation of the sudden departure of Cano and his followers is even hinted at. . . . Should we conclude . . . that in an earlier version of the first episode the joint-kings of Tara had succumbed to Aedán's bribery and were on the point of betraying their guest when their treachery was accidentally discovered by Diarmait's daughter, who revealed it to Cano? This would at least provide a motive for the stealthy departure under cover of night (148), and would justify the subsequent statements of Gúaire and Illand. (Binchy 1963, xv f.)

In a discussion of these remarks of Binchy's, Seán Ó Coileáin says that "we have to do then with a passage which bears all the marks of being an interpolation of a mechanical kind";[36] he tentatively suggests that "originally the non-interpolated text ran without interruption from line 90 to line 148 of Binchy's edition and that what intervenes is the exact extent of the interpolation which we know . . . must have taken place";[37] and he remarks further that "the editor of about 1100, or some earlier editor, has clumsily tacked together two mutually contradictory accounts of the same event and in doing so disrupted the momentum and continuity of the story."[38]

There are three issues here. First, there is the contradiction between what happens in the first episode and what is said by Gúaire and Illand; secondly, the lack of a stated motive for Cano's departure from Diarmait and Blathmac; and, thirdly, the suggestion that interpolation "must have taken place." Since there is no linguistic argument for interpolation, the evidence for it resides solely in the other two considerations.

Let us look first at Cano's departure from Diarmait and Blathmac. For three whole days after their return ashore, Cano's party "did not remove their belts or their brooches" (line 145); the likelihood, as Ó Fiannachta remarks, is that this was "for purposes of defence."[39] Their stealthy departure under cover of night could well have been motivated by their desire to avoid further intervention on the part of agents of Áedán's. Blathmac showed how Cano could recover his father's wealth, and in doing so he may be felt to have absolved himself of any obligation to show further generosity to Cano. Diarmait has been a somewhat reluctant host. In the circumstances, it is natural that Cano should seek another host, and a safer (and more distant) haven.

The contradiction to which Binchy referred is between what is recounted by the narrator in the first episode, and what is said by two of the characters later in the saga. Gúaire and Illand welcome Cano with boastful rhetoric, each of them promising to outdo his predecessors in generosity. A degree of exaggeration does not seem out of place at such a moment. Indeed, Gúaire's boast is not only inconsistent with what has gone before; it also promises more than he actually delivers. It is only Illand who fulfils his promise, and in him we see "the pressing of generosity to prodigality."[40] In short, I suggest that the references, by Diarmait (lines 117f.), Gúaire, and Illand, to the selling of Cano for silver, should be seen as links among the accounts of Cano's encounters with Irish kings, punctuating his odyssey in search of a lasting source of food and protection (*biad 7 in-illius*, line 219).

Scéla Cano was not necessarily fashioned out of whole cloth; it may be that a number of separate items went into its making. My argument here is simply that present evidence does not warrant the isolation of part of the first episode as "an interpolation of a mechanical kind." On the contrary, the passage in question is an integral part of the work as a whole. In further support of this we may point to the way in which the depiction in that passage of Diarmait as a somewhat reluctant host is borne out in another episode in the tale. We have seen that, when Senchán sent some poems to Diarmait (lines 234–74), he was poorly rewarded on the first two occasions, and generously rewarded thereafter. I have interpreted this passage as an example of the exercise, on Senchán's part, of the virtue of *ainmne* ("forebearance"). But the passage has something to tell us about Diarmait as well. It will be recalled that in her *rabad*, Diarmait's daughter says that the king has never been satirized (line 78); yet in his dealings with Senchán he lays himself open to the risk of satire, on grounds of niggardliness. At length he saves his honor, by doing what is expected of a king in his role as patron to the poet. Similarly, in his treatment of Cano, there is some hesitation, but he eventually meets his obligations as host.

James Carney paid Binchy's edition the tribute of saying that he had "read it fully a dozen times with avidity and fascination";[41] he has also observed that *Scéla Cano* presents "problems of great complexity."[42] In preparing this essay in Professor Carney's honor, I have found that each reading of *Scéla Cano* reveals some fresh complexity in this densely textured tale. I cannot pretend to have touched on, let alone solved, more than a small number of the problems posed by the text; further progress will be made by following Carney's lead in attending closely, and respectfully, to the words of the transmitted text. In the study of early Irish literature, we could do worse than to take as our motto three words from *Scéla Cano* (line 98) which might well serve to characterize James Carney's own pioneering work in the field: *is fearr ainmne.*

26

The Rhetoric of *Fingal Rónáin*

(1985)

Early Irish narrative lore survives in various forms, ranging in length from brief allusions, through short anecdotes, to full-scale tales which are conventionally called sagas. It is sometimes taken for granted that the sagas represent the organization of the narrative lore into literary form, which implies that any given saga is more than a mere aggregation or accumulation of lore. This view of the sagas is eminently reasonable, but it should be seen for the hypothesis that it is. Moreover, it remains a largely untested hypothesis, for we are still at an early stage in the investigation of the nature of Irish saga.[1] Irish studies has not had enough of the cultivation of literary scholarship as an intellectual discipline, literary scholarship "conceived of . . . as a growing body of knowledge, insights and judgements."[2] There are many ways in which the literary properties of our texts may be examined. One of those which may prove fruitful is the application to Irish narrative of rhetori-

26. The Rhetoric of *Fingal Rónáin*

cal criticism, which attends to "an author's use of a variety of means—especially the authorial presence or *voice* that he projects—in order to inform, to achieve imaginative consent, and to engage the interests and guide the emotional responses of the reader to whom, whether deliberately or not, his literary work is inevitably addressed."[3] The present essay is an attempt to analyze *Fingal Rónáin* (literally, "Rónán's Act of Kin-Slaying"; conventionally, "How Rónán Killed His Son") in rhetorical terms. The analysis falls into two parts, the first dealing with overt narratorial intrusions, and the second with how the author achieves certain effects by his selection and organization of material and by his use of language. It may be worth pointing out that the reading of *Fingal Rónáin* which is presented here arises from a study, which is still in progress, of narratorial intrusion in Irish saga, *Fingal Rónáin* being one of a number of texts chosen quite at random for this purpose. One does not progress far in this kind of work, however, before one discovers that each instance of narratorial intrusion must be assessed in the context of the saga in which it occurs. Each text must therefore be examined in detail, and it must be examined whole. It seemed best, therefore, to limit oneself on the present occasion to the analysis of a single saga, but it should be added that this analysis is intended as the first installment of a study of the rhetoric of Irish saga.

Fingal Rónáin (*FR*)[4] tells the story of how Rónán, king of Leinster, killed his beloved only son Mael Fhothartaig. Following Charles-Edwards,[5] we can see five stages in the main part of the saga, up to the death of Mael Fhothartaig. In the first of these Rónán is widowed, and at length takes as his second wife the young daughter of Echaid, king of Dún Sobairche (Dunseverick, in County Antrim); her name is never given to us. In the second stage, Echaid's daughter attempts, without success, to get a message to Mael Fhothartaig, asking that he sleep with her. The third stage begins as soon as Mael Fhothartaig hears about the woman's intentions: he goes into exile to avoid her. He returns from his exile, however, when he hears that the Laigin (Leinstermen) suspect Rónán of having exiled him, and that they have threatened to kill Rónán if Mael Fhothartaig does not come back. In the fourth stage, Echaid's daughter once again tries to get her message to Mael Fhothartaig. When he hears about it, he enlists the aid of his foster-brother Congal: the next day, Mael Fhothartaig goes hunting and Echaid's daughter sets out to join him; but she finds her way barred by Congal, who upbraids her, horsewhips her, and leads her home. In the fifth stage, Echaid's daughter takes her revenge. While Mael Fhothartaig is still out hunting, she accuses him to Rónán of having attempted to seduce her. When Rónán declines to believe her she offers to prove it by capping a verse of Mael Fhothartaig's. She and Mael Fhothartaig made a practice of verse-capping, and so, when he comes inside, Mael Fhothartaig recites a half-quatrain. She caps this with a half-quatrain which convinces Rónán of Mael Fhothartaig's guilt. Rónán orders his son's immediate death, but, as he is dying from a fatal wound inflicted by one of Rónán's men, Mael Fhothartaig solemnly declares his innocence. Following Mael Fhothartaig's death there is a sixth and final stage, containing his necrology and showing how his death was avenged. Having realized his mistake, Rónán laments his son; Echaid's daughter kills herself; the warrior who killed Mael Fhothartaig is slain; and the tale ends with the death of Rónán.

When we look at how this story is unfolded in *FR*, we find that its narrator is fairly discreet, and that the story is for the most part presented dramatically. The characters speak for themselves, their dialogue being given as direct speech, and their actions are recounted in relatively objective narrative. To speak of the narrative as "objective" is to indicate that the narrator recounts the events as they are to be taken as having occurred, and without overt intervention of his own in the way of comment or judgment. The narration of *Fingal Rónáin* is not totally objective in this sense, since the narrator intrudes in three different ways: first, he comments on one of the characters; secondly, he claims knowledge of the thoughts or feelings of two of them; and, thirdly, he provides information which does not advance the action, but which helps us to understand what is going on in the saga. These three kinds of intrusion will now be considered in turn.

The narrator generally refrains from overt comment on his characters, the one exception being his description of Mael Fhothartaig as "the most wonderful boy ever to appear in Leinster" (*mac is amru tánic Laigniu riam*, lines 3–4). This, as we shall see below, has the function of providing external validation of Rónán's appraisal of Mael Fhothartaig. It is not to be taken as a subjective comment on the narrator's part, however, since it is a prolepsis of what immediately follows it in the text: "It was with him that the Leinstermen used to set out for assemblies and hostings, for games and sports, and for combats and shoots. Mael Fhothartaig was desired by all their girls and loved by all their young women" (lines 4–6).

There are two occasions on which the narrator claims access to the motivation, thoughts, or feelings of his characters. One of these is an intrusion on the narrator's part into the description of Mael Fhothartaig's last moments, which reveals Mael Fhothartaig's feelings about the spectacle offered by his Fool, Mac Glass. After Mael Fhothartaig and his foster-brother Congal had been fatally wounded, Mac Glass jumped away, but Rónán's warrior cast a spear after him and it tore out his bowels. When Mael Fhothartaig had declared his innocence to Rónán, the text continues as follows:

> A raven was taking the Fool's entrails from him on the steps; he was contorting his mouth; the churls were laughing. Mael Fhothartaig was ashamed (*Mebul la Mael Fothartaig*). Then he said:
>
> > Mac Glass,
> > gather in your bowels.
> > Why have you no shame?
> > Churls are laughing at you.
> > The three died then. (lines 153–60)

The narrator's revelation of Mael Fhothartaig's shame here anticipates the hero's own words to his Fool, so that, like the comment which we have already considered, this intrusion can be taken as proleptic.

The other example of the narrator's privileged access to a character's motivation occurs in the second stage of the saga, when Echaid's daughter has sent her maidservant to solicit Mael Fhothartaig on her behalf:

> The young woman did not dare speak of it, for fear that Mael Fhothartaig might slay her, and Echaid's daughter threatened to behead her unless she spoke of it.
>
> One time Mael Fhothartaig was playing *fidchell* with his two foster-brothers, Donn and Congal.... The young woman went to them, and she was playing *fidchell* with them. She was trying to speak of it; she did not dare, and she was blushing. (lines 28–34)

The young woman's fear that Mael Fhothartaig might slay her is revealed, not in any act or utterance of hers, but rather in the narrator's words. While these words anticipate the girl's blushing, they nevertheless remain the only instance in the saga where a character's motivation is spelt out by the narrator.

The third kind of narratorial intrusion in *FR* is that which conveys information which helps us to follow the action. Any assessment of this element in our text (or in Irish saga generally) runs up against the problem of the use, in manuscripts texts, of *.i.*, which was of course the Latin symbol for *id est*, and which in due course came to be rendered in Irish as *ed ón*. The uses of *.i.* in Irish manuscript texts have been classified in grammatical terms by Dottin.[6] What concerns us here, however, is the use of *.i.* in narrative, and in particular the question as to whether words, phrases, or sentences introduced by *.i.* represent narratorial intrusions in the text. There are, by my reckoning, fourteen instances of *.i.* in *FR*, and what I have to say in what follows is based solely on these.

Ten of the instances of *.i.* in *FR* introduce identification of persons or animals. Eight of these have to do with persons or animals who are being introduced for the first time. An example is *Rí amra ro boí for Laignib .i. Rónán mac Aeda* (line 1); similarly at lines 3, 11, 31, 59, 124, 135, 247. It seems best to regard all but one or two of these as a matter of expository technique rather than of narratorial intrusiveness. One exception to this is the identification in line 11 of a person who has been mentioned in direct speech: *Ad-fiadar dam-sa, ol Rónán, atá ingen chóem la hEchthaig (.i. rí Dúin Sobairche an-túaid)*. Since the identifying noun here (*rí*) is not in apposition to *Echthaig*, the phrase may be taken as a narratorial gloss on the words of Rónán.[7] Another possible exception is the identification in line 31 of Mael Fhothartaig's two foster-brothers as Donn and Congal, which is followed up by the information that they were the two sons of his foster-father, and that they were always with Mael Fhothartaig. This reads like a narratorial gloss rather than a piece of straight exposition.

In the two examples (lines 28, 44) where the person in question has already appeared in the saga, *.i.* is used to identify the person referred to in a pronoun or pronominal; these too can be regarded as expository rather than intrusive. (Indeed we could have wished for more identifications of this kind, since the use of insufficiently specific pronouns has given rise to differences of interpretation among modern scholars.[8] The anaphoric pronoun is of course helpful in this regard, but it is exiguously used in *FR*. The pronominal particles [*notae augentes*] do not seem to be used in any consistent way to specify the agent.[9])

The next use of *.i.* to be considered introduces an identification and explanation of a place-name. Congal advises Mael Fhothartaig to go hunting at Bae Aífe. It is then explained that Bae Aífe (The Cows of Aífe) are stones which are by the side of a mountain. From a distance they look like white cows. They are on the *aífe* (? slope) of a mountain. It is worth looking at the immediate context of the item:

> *Airg-siu ám i-mbárach*, ar Congal, *co mbé oc Buaib Aífe oc taffond.*
> (*Bae Aífi .i. clocha filet le tóeb int śléibe. It cosmaile fri bú finna do chéin. For aífe int śléibe ataat.*)
> *Eirg-siu didiu co rrabais oc mílruth and.* (lines 82–86)

What is of crucial importance here is the repetition (in different words) of Congal's advice to Mael Fhothartaig. This repetition is required (and is possible) only because of the interruption of his words by the onomastic item. Now it is not to be supposed that Congal would have any need to explain Bae Aífe to Mael Fhothartaig; the identification and explanation are intruded by the narrator for the benefit of his audience. But this onomastic item is not external or secondary—it is integrated into the text by Congal's repetition of his advice to Mael Fhothartaig, and it is as much a part of the text as the dialogue or the straight narration. Narratorial intrusion of this kind is therefore simply a feature of the narrative technique.

The enfolding of this intrusion into the text is similar to that at lines 15–16 of an item of information which is not introduced by *.i.*, and which is part of the straight narrative:

> ... *conda tuc lais i-lle. Do-chóid Mael Fhothartaig immorro co mbaí ar cuairt i ndesciurt Lagen. Tic-si a-túaid.*

Here we are told that Rónán took Echaid's daughter back to Leinster with him. It is then stated that Mael Fhothartaig, for his part, went on a visitation to South Leinster. The narrator then recapitulates, using different words to tell us what we already know—that Echaid's daughter came down from the north. Mael Fhothartaig's absence upon the arrival of Echaid's daughter, like the identification of Bae Aífe, is an integral part of the narrator's presentation of the story, and neither of them is more expendable than the other.

The item on Bae Aífe is a narratorial gloss on a place mentioned in direct speech; we have also had an instance (line 11) of what may be taken as a narratorial identification of a person so mentioned. Of a different kind are the examples in *FR* of *.i.* being used to introduce explications of words used in direct speech: in both instances the phrases thus introduced must be attributed to the speakers in question rather than to the narrator. In accusing Mael Fhothartaig to Rónán, Echaid's daughter says of him, "He does not get from me the ease he desires—to sleep with me in despite of you" (*Ni étann úam-si ám in sámchaire ass áil dó .i. comrac frim dot chindso*, lines 113–14). Her accusation would clearly lose its force if she did not specify what *sámchaire* ("ease") Mael Fhothartaig allegedly desires from her, and the explicatory phrase cannot therefore be regarded as a narratorial gloss. The same is true, *mutatis mutandis*, of the phrase introduced by .i. which is used by Mael Fhothartaig in his protestation of innocence: speaking to Rónán, he opens his declaration with the words, "By your honor and by the tryst to which I go—a tryst with death" (*Dar th'ordan-su ocus darsin dáil i tiag-sa .i. dál báis*, lines 148–49).

One further example of .i. remains to be considered, and it is the only one which introduces a fully fledged gloss of the type with which we are familiar from the Irish glosses on Latin texts as well as on certain, more or less canonical, Old Irish texts. The half-quatrain with which Echaid's daughter caps that uttered by Mael Fhothartaig, and with which she purports to establish his guilt, is glossed .i. *sech ní ránac-sa, ní thucais-siu na bú lat* ("I did not come, and you did not take away the cows," line 133). The implications of this gloss will be discussed below; here we need only consider whether it is to be regarded as a narratorial intrusion. We cannot be absolutely certain that it is not to be taken as having been uttered by Echaid's daughter with the purpose of hammering home the damaging import of her half-quatrain. The probability, however, is that the principals in the saga would understand the meaning of her half-quatrain only too well, and that in presenting this gloss the narrator obliges his audience by explaining her words to them.

Having looked now at all the examples of .i. in FR, we can see that it is used in this text as an expository device in the identification of persons and animals, in the identification and explanation of place-names, in the explication of nouns (particularizing the general), and in explaining the meaning of an obscure piece of verse. It can occur in narrative or in dialogue. The identificatory items are used mainly of characters on their first appearance in the saga. Their occurrence in connection with characters who are already known to us is random, and might have been added in the course of transmission; we have seen that it would be to our advantage to have more identifications of this kind. While the use of .i. is to be traced to "the linguistic and expository techniques established by the glossators of late Latin texts,"[10] it had become a characteristic feature of Irish saga-style by the time *FR* was composed. On occasion, *.i.* is used to introduce a narratorial intrusion of the informative kind, but here too it is not external to the text, but an integral part of the narrator's way of telling his tale.

The narratorial intrusion of information, then, and the use of *.i.* overlap, but they are not coterminous. One side of this coin we have seen in the use of *.i.* for other purposes. The other side is the narratorial intrusion of information without recourse to *.i.* An important example of such an intrusion occurs in *FR* immediately after Echaid's daughter has proposed to Rónán that she use verse-capping as a means of establishing Mael Fhothartaig's guilt: *Do-gníth-som ón cech n-aidchi do airiuc thuli di-ssi. No gaibed-som lethrand, no gaibed-si a lleth n-aill* (lines 120–21). These sentences indicate that Mael Fhothartaig used to play the game of verse-capping every night to please Echaid's daughter: he would recite a half-quatrain and she would recite the other. The question which arises is whether these activities are supposed to have occurred before Echaid's daughter has proposed the trial by verse-capping or afterwards. Charles-Edwards has favored the second possibility, taking these sentences to mean that there were several attempts by Echaid's daughter to establish Mael Fhothartaig's guilt before the verse-capping incident which finally convinced Rónán.[11] There is telling evidence against this in a speech of Mael Fhothartaig's (line 151) which shows that all the events of this part of *FR* took place on the one day.[12] The imperfect is used in these sentences of events which are anterior to the time of the main narrative,[13] and the sentences must therefore be taken as a narratorial explanation of the proposal by Echaid's daughter, in terms of events which lie outside the linear sequence of the narrative, its purpose being to show that Echaid's daughter would have no difficulty in using the verse-capping procedure. This example incidentally demonstrates that it is necessary in the interpretation of Irish sagas to attend to narratorial intrusions, and it is one which could be multiplied from other texts.

The narrator of *FR* is discreet, but he is not altogether self-effacing. He allows himself a palpable presence once in a while as he guides us through the story, intruding a comment here, a privileged insight into motivation there, and the occasional scrap of background information. The narratorial intrusions in *FR* are nevertheless modest in scope and in number, and the use of such intrusions is neither the only nor the principal way in which the author achieves his effects. It is through the selection and ordering of his material and his use of language that the author of *FR* shapes his saga and determines the audience's response to the tragic events which it unfolds.

FR opens with some necessary introductory observations:

> There was a wonderful king over Leinster, one Rónán son of Áed, and Eithne daughter of Cummascach son of Éogan of the Déisi of Munster was his wife. And she bore him a son, Mael Fhothartaig son of Rónán, the most wonderful boy ever to appear in Leinster. It was with him that the Leinstermen used to set out for assemblies and hostings, for games and sports, and for combats and shoots. Mael Fhothartaig was desired by all their girls and loved by all their young women. (lines 1–6)

This passage establishes the identity and status of Rónán and of Mael Fhothartaig, and the relationship between them. Apart from that, it performs three functions in relation to the rest of the text. In describing Mael Fhothartaig as "the most wonderful boy ever to appear in Leinster," the narrator provides external validation for Rónán's description of Mael Fhothartaig as "the best son in Leinster" (*mac as dech fil la Laigniu*, line 19); this is the first of a number of instances in the text in which Mael Fhothartaig is either praised or otherwise presented in a positive light. Secondly, Mael Fhothartaig's evidently irresistible appeal to women makes it seem inevitable that the young daughter of Echaid will also fall in love with him. Thirdly, Mael Fhothartaig's central role in the social and cultural life of the Leinstermen—their assemblies and hostings and so forth—not only shows the regard in which he is held by them, but also explains why Mael Fhothartaig has no escape from the tragic situation which develops in Leinster: we have seen that in the third stage of the saga Mael Fhothartaig goes into exile to avoid Echaid's daughter, only to be forced to return in response to the demand of the Leinstermen that he do so.

The narrator concludes his presentation of the background to the events of *FR* by informing us that Mael Fhothartaig's mother died, and that Rónán remained without a wife for a long time.

The first stage in the tragedy now begins with a dialogue in which Mael Fhothartaig unwittingly sets the chain of events in motion. "Why do you not take a wife?" he says to Rónán. When Rónán speaks of the beautiful daughter of Echaid, king of Dún Sobairche, Mael Fhothartaig objects: "'You are no husband for a girl,' said the lad. 'Will you not take a settled woman (*ben forusta*)? I should think it more appropriate for you than to take a skittish (?) girl (*scintline ingine*).'" The dialogue then gives way to narrative, and we are told that Rónán could not be dissuaded from his intention of marrying the young woman: he went and slept with Echaid's daughter in the north, and then took her home to Leinster with him. Mael Fhothartaig had gone on a visitation in South Leinster when the girl came from Dún Sobairche. The text now shifts back to dialogue:

> "Where is your son, Rónán?" said she, "I am told that you have a good son."
> "I have indeed," said Rónán, "the best son in Leinster."
> "Let him be summoned to me, then, so that he may receive me, and my people and my wealth and my treasures."
> "He will certainly come," said Rónán.
> Mael Fhothartaig came after that, and he gave her a great welcome.
> "You shall be loved," said the lad. "All the treasures and wealth that we shall obtain will be given to you for loving Rónán."
> "I am pleased," said she, "that you should act in my interests."
> (lines 17–26)

So far as possible, given that it is Rónán and Echaid's daughter who marry, the focus in this stage is on Mael Fhothartaig. It is he who suggests that Rónán remarry. He is uneasy when Rónán speaks of marrying Echaid's daughter, and he tries without success to retrieve the situation by suggesting that Rónán marry "a settled woman." This unease of Mael Fhothartaig's doubtless explains why he absents himself when Rónán takes Echaid's daughter home to Leinster as his wife, for Mael Fhothartaig might surely be expected to be present on such an occasion. In any case, we shall see of this sequence, from the point at which Mael Fhothartaig absents himself to the formal exchange between him and Echaid's daughter, that it finds a remarkably close parallel in the passage (lines 101–33) which presents the accusation and trial of Mael Fhothartaig, a passage which likewise opens with a dialogue in which Rónán and Echaid's daughter discuss Mael Fhothartaig in his absence.

While detailed consideration of the parallel passages is best deferred until we come to deal with the second one, we may attend here to the contribution by Echaid's daughter to her dialogue with Mael Fhothartaig, and show how the true significance of her utterance is gradually revealed as the text progresses. Her avowed reason for proposing a meeting with Mael Fhothartaig is that she wishes him to receive her and her people, her wealth, and her treasures. The generosity which she evinces—or affects—in this is reciprocated by Mael Fhothartaig when they meet, for he promises that she will be given all the treasure and wealth that he obtains. To Mael Fhothartaig's formal address she responds in kind, saying that she is pleased that he should act in her interests (*Is maith lim-sa, . . . mo les do dénam duit-siu*, line 26). But this semblance of formal accord is belied by the absolute incompatibility of their motives. Mael Fhothartaig makes it clear that he is motivated by love of his father: she is to be rewarded for loving Rónán (*ar grádugud Rónáin*, line 25). That his protestation of love for Rónán is sincere is borne out by everything he says and does in the saga. Echaid's daughter, on the other hand, makes no mention of Rónán, and it is not long before we discover, not only that her intentions in Mael Fhothartaig's regard are less than honorable, but also that her reply to his address contains a veiled expression of her desire to seduce him.

The account of the efforts made by Echaid's daughter to seduce Mael Fhothartaig, which immediately follow upon her dialogue with him, is given in the second stage of the saga. This stage, which is given here in translation, also introduces the important secondary characters of Mael Fhothartaig's foster-brothers, Congal and Donn, and of the unnamed maidservant of Echaid's daughter:

> There was a beautiful young woman in attendance on Echaid's daughter. She immediately sent her to Mael Fhothartaig to solicit him. The young woman dared not speak of it, for fear that Mael Fhothartaig might slay her, and Echaid's daughter threatened to behead her unless she spoke of it.

One time Mael Fhothartaig was playing *fidchell* with his two foster-brothers, Donn and Congal—they were his foster-father's two sons, and they were always with him. The young woman went to them, and she was playing *fidchell* with them. She was trying to speak of it; she did not dare, and she was blushing. The men noticed that. Mael Fhothartaig left them.

"What do you wish to say?" said Congal to the woman.

"It is not I who wishes anything," said she, "but it is the daughter of Echaid, who wishes to have Mael Fhothartaig as her lover."

"Do not say so, woman!" said Congal. "You will die if Mael Fhothartaig should hear you. Anyway, I shall see to your own interests with him (*do-gén-sa do les-su féin fris-seom*), if you wish it."

The young woman reported this to Echaid's daughter.

"I am pleased," said she, "for you will dare to deliver the message to him, provided that you sleep with him yourself; and afterwards see to my interests with him (*déna mo les-sa iarum friss*)."

It was done: the young woman slept with Mael Fhothartaig.

"Well, then," said Echaid's daughter, "you will not see to my interests now (*ni dingne-su mo-les-sa a fecht-sa*). You prefer to have that man to yourself. You shall die, however, at my hands."

One day the woman began to weep to Mael Fhothartaig.

"What is wrong with you, woman?" said he.

"Echaid's daughter is threatening to kill me," said she, "since I am not seeing to her interests with you, that she might sleep with you (*uair nach dénaim a lles frit-so, co comairsed frit*)."

"Indeed, that is likely," said he. "You have made no mistake," said he, "to take protection. If I were to be put, woman," said he, "into a burning pit of fire three times, until I became powder and ash, I should not sleep with Rónán's wife, even if it would save me from all that. Moreover, I shall go away to avoid her." (lines 27–55)

This passage is remarkable for its reiteration of the idiom *do-gní less*, which is used three times of seeing to the "interests" of Echaid's daughter in the matter of intercourse with Mael Fhothartaig (and in one instance of the like "interests" of her maidservant). Taken together with her persistence, and with her threat to the life of her maidservant, this reiteration underlines the implacable determination of Echaid's daughter to achieve her ends. The use of this idiom has the further function of pointing up the ambiguity of the words used by Echaid's daughter when she responded to Mael Fhothartaig's address in the first stage of the saga, for she used the self-same idiom in saying, "I am pleased that you should act in my interests" (*Is maith lim-sa mo les do dénam duit-siu*, line 26). The maidservant makes it quite clear to Mael Fhothartaig that the *less* Echaid's daughter has in mind is that she should sleep with him (*co comairsed frit*). Mael Fhothartaig's determination to avoid having intercourse with Echaid's daughter is as absolute as hers is to have it with him. We are left in no doubt as to his reason: she is Rónán's wife. (This is the only time she is called "Rónán's wife" in the text.) And so he decides to go into exile to avoid her.

The important point has been made by Charles-Edwards that, although Mael Fhothartaig finds out about his stepmother's intentions, her message to him is not actually delivered: "It is one thing to give the message, quite another to reveal what the message would have been had it been delivered."[14] Not having actually received the message, Mael Fhothartaig is free from the necessity either to respond to it or to confront her in person. As for Mael Fhothartaig's hasty departure, Charles-Edwards says that "it looks as though the audience can assume that the daughter of Echaid threatens to use means which will more or less compel Mael Fhothartaig to accept her advances. As Deirdriu in *Longes mac nUislenn* and Gráinne in *Tóraigheacht Dhiarmada agus Ghráinne* compel Noísiu and Diarmaid to accept their advances by threatening them with disgrace and shame if they do not, so, it seems, does the daughter of Echaid threaten Mael Fhothartaig."[15] It is well to be reminded that a work of literature does not come into being in a vacuum. The fact that there is no hint in *Fingal Rónáin* of a threat such as that envisaged by Charles-Edwards does not preclude the possibility that the audience might assume such a threat on the basis of their knowledge of other texts. It is not clear, however, that the actions of Deirdriu and Gráinne are altogether relevant to what happens in *Fingal Rónáin*. It is true of each of the three stories that we are dealing with a triangle comprising an old man, a young woman, and a young man; that the woman is either betrothed or already married to the old man; and that she sets about the seduction of the young man. But Echaid's daughter is Mael Fhothartaig's stepmother, and in this respect her relationship to him differs from that of Deirdriu and Gráinne to Noísiu and Diarmaid respectively. We cannot be sure how this difference would affect the audience's perception of the situation in which

Mael Fhothartaig finds himself. What is beyond doubt is that Mael Fhothartaig wishes to avoid a confrontation with his stepmother, and that in order to do so he goes into exile.

Mael Fhothartaig's activities during his exile in Scotland are briefly described; we hear of the hero's prowess as a hunter and a fighter, and his hounds Doílín and Daithlenn are introduced:

> Then Mael Fhothartaig went to the territory of Scotland along with fifty warriors. He received a great welcome from the king of Scotland. The king had hounds for horses, hounds for pigs, and hounds for deer. Doílín and Daithlenn, however, Mael Fhothartaig's two hounds, used to kill every quarry in turn before the king's hounds. It was Mael Fhothartaig who won every battle and every fight in which the king of Scotland was victorious.
>
> "What is this, Rónán?" said the Leinstermen. "Did you send Mael Fhothartaig away from the country? You shall die at our hands if he does not come back."
>
> That was related to Mael Fhothartaig; he came back from the east.
>
> It was to Dún Sobairche that he came from the east. He was given a great welcome.
>
> "It is bad of you, Mael Fhothartaig, that you have not slept with our daughter. We gave her to you, and not to that old churl!"
>
> "That is bad indeed!" said Mael Fhothartaig.
>
> Mael Fhothartaig came to Leinster, and the Leinstermen gave him a great welcome. (lines 56–70)

It is the threat to Rónán's life which induces Mael Fhothartaig to return from his exile. His exchange with Echaid, brief as it is, is laden with meaning. It reminds Mael Fhothartaig that Echaid's daughter awaits him in Leinster, but, much more than that, it reveals for the first time the full dimensions of her evil intent, for it is now clear that before ever she left Dún Sobairche as Rónán's wife she was fully determined to seduce Mael Fhothartaig. (It seems that, as is common in Irish saga, she loved the hero on the basis of his reputation: upon her arrival in Leinster she says to Rónán, "I am told that you have a good son.") The order of revelation here is noteworthy, for the woman's evil designs on the hero have now been peeled away like an onion: she first made an apparently innocent enquiry after Mael Fhothartaig and proposed a meeting in which he would receive her and her people and her wealth; at their meeting she greets him with what appears to be a formal and correct address; she forthwith bends all her energies to seducing him, and the ambiguity of her apparently innocuous address to him becomes clear; finally, we learn from Echaid that she married Rónán only with the intention of betraying him and seducing his son. It is no wonder that, using a common device of Irish saga-dialogue, Mael Fhothartaig echoes the word *olc*, which has been used by Echaid: "*Is olc duit-siu, a Mael Fhothartaig, nách ruí fri ar n-ingin-ni. Is duit dos-ratsam, ocus ní dont śenaithiuch ucut.*" "*Olc ón immorro,*" ol Mael Fhothartaig (lines 66–68). Not only the shift from *is olc duit-siu* to *olc ón* but also the horrifying implications of Echaid's revelation show that there is a play on the different connotations of *olc* here. Echaid, who has given Mael Fhothartaig a great welcome, is merely expressing his displeasure that his daughter has been neglected by Mael Fhothartaig. As used by Mael Fhothartaig, however, the word takes on the connotation of great evil.

At this point we may anticipate later events, in order to show the connection of Echaid's words with the rest of the saga. For this exchange between Mael Fhothartaig and Echaid has the further function of inculpating Echaid. His punishment comes later, and when it does the claim that Mael Fhothartaig has fulfilled Echaid's hopes is used to entice him to his doom. After the death of Mael Fhothartaig,

> Donn, Mael Fhothartaig's foster-brother and Congal's brother, went with twenty horsemen to Dún Sobairche, and they tricked Echaid to come to the boundary of his territory to meet Mael Fhothartaig who (they claimed) had eloped with Echaid's daughter, and they took Echaid's head and the heads of his son and his wife. (lines 162–66)

While this is going on, Rónán stands over his son for three days and nights. He then recites a lament for his son, which is interrupted by the arrival of Donn:

> Then Donn came and he threw her father's head upon her breast, and the heads of her mother and brother. She rose up then and threw herself on her knife so that it came up through her back. (lines 193–96)

In a quatrain which follows immediately upon this, Rónán remarks that the sorrow which is upon Dún Náis (in Leinster) is also upon Dún Sobairche.

In this way the story of Echaid and his family is threaded through that of Rónán and Mael Fhothartaig.

The fourth stage of *FR* is that in which Echaid's daughter once again tries to get her message to Mael Fhothartaig. He has resumed his relationship with the maidservant, and Echaid's daughter threatens to kill her if she does not deliver the message. When Mael Fhothartaig hears of this, he asks his foster-brother Congal what he should do about it. Congal undertakes to rid Mael Fhothartaig of the woman, but only if he is rewarded with Doílín and Daithlenn, and Mael Fhothartaig agrees to these terms. Congal tells Mael Fhothartaig to go hunting the next day at Bae Aífe, which, as we have seen, are rocks which look like white cows from afar. The maidservant will summon Echaid's daughter to a tryst with him there, but Congal will prevent her from reaching Mael Fhothartaig. And so it happens. Echaid's daughter cannot wait till the next day, and when it comes she sets out to meet Mael Fhothartaig, but she finds her way barred by Congal, who upbraids her, horsewhips her, and escorts her home. Three times in all Echaid's daughter attempts to keep the tryst and is repulsed by Congal. (Only two of these incidents are described in the text, but we know that there were three from references at lines 115 and 151.)

It is worth noting that it is here that Echaid's daughter is most strongly condemned. Congal calls her a whore when first he encounters her on her way to the tryst, and before he horsewhips her and sees her to her home he upbraids her in the strongest terms:

> "So!" said Congal, "you wish to put the king of Leinster to shame, you evil woman! If I see you again," said he, "I shall take your head and fix it on a stake in Rónán's presence: an evil woman putting him to shame in ditches and bushes, meeting a lad on her own." (lines 94–98)

This judgment of Echaid's daughter is not intruded by the narrator, being provided rather by one of the characters in the saga.

The hounds link this stage of the saga with the third stage, and also with Rónán's lament for his son. In the third stage we have heard of the excellence of the hounds, and we can therefore see what a heavy price Mael Fhothartaig has to pay to have Congal repel Echaid's daughter. In the lament, four quatrains are devoted to Mael Fhothartaig's hounds; of one of them, Rónán says "her head has been in the lap of everyone in turn, / seeking one whom she will not find" (lines 215–16).

When Congal finally escorts Echaid's daughter to her home she threatens to kill him, and how she achieves her revenge is shown in the fifth stage of the saga, which recounts the accusation, trial, and death of Mael Fhothartaig. It begins with a dialogue between Rónán and Echaid's daughter, and, just as she did in the earlier dialogue between them, she suggests a formal exchange between Mael Fhothartaig and herself, which on this occasion takes the form of an exercise in verse-capping:

> Rónán came to his house. Mael Fhothartaig's people came in before him; he remained outside hunting on his own.
> "Where is Mael Fhothartaig tonight, Congal?" said Rónán.
> "He is outside," said Congal.
> "Alas that my son should be outside, seeing that he gives wealth to so many."
> "You have deafened us," said his wife, "talking about your son."
> "It is right to speak of him," said Rónán, "for there is no son in Ireland who is more obedient to his father. For his concern, on my behalf, for men and for women at Áth Cliath and at Clár Daire Móir and at Drochet Cairpri is just as if his own life were at stake, so that you and I may be at ease, woman (*corop sám dam ocus duit-siu, a ben*)," said Rónán.
> "Well, he does not get from me," said she, "the ease he desires (*in sámchaire ass áil dó*)—to sleep with me in despite of you. I shall not hold out against him any longer. Congal has taken me to him three times since morning, and I barely escaped from his hands."
> "A curse on your lips, you evil woman!" said Rónán. "You are lying."
> "You shall see a proof of it now," said she. "I shall recite a half-quatrain to see if it fits what he recites."
> He used to do that every night to please her: he would recite a half-quatrain, and she would recite the other half.

Then Mael Fhothartaig came in and proceeded to dry his legs against the fire, and Congal was with him; Mael Fhothartaig's Fool, Mac Glass, was juggling on the floor of the house.

Then Mael Fhothartaig said, for it was a cold day:

"It is cold against the whirlwind
For one who herds the Cows of Aífe."

"Hear this, Rónán," said she. "Recite that again," said she.

"It is cold against the whirlwind
For one who herds the Cows of Aífe."

She said:

"It is a vain herding
Without cows, without anyone you love."

(that is, "I did not come, and you did not take the cows with you.")
"It is true, then," said Rónán. (lines 101–34)

This scene runs parallel in a number of respects to that which describes the first meeting between Mael Fhothartaig and Echaid's daughter (lines 17–26, translated above). Mael Fhothartaig has absented himself on both occasions. Rónán and Echaid's daughter discuss Mael Fhothartaig. He is praised by Rónán; Echaid's daughter proposes an encounter with him. Mael Fhothartaig arrives and addresses Echaid's daughter in a formal fashion. She responds formally, but in a double-edged way: on the first occasion we find that her words betray her seductive intentions, while on the second she purports to establish Mael Fhothartaig's guilt by her words, and indeed satisfies Rónán that she has done so. In both scenes her intentions towards Mael Fhothartaig are full of danger for him. The scenes are contrasted, however, in the attitude of Echaid's daughter to Mael Fhothartaig. On the first occasion, she expresses an interest in meeting him, on the basis of what she has heard about him. On the second, she accuses him to Rónán of having attempted to seduce or rape her.

This contrast between the utterances of Echaid's daughter in the parallel passages is one of a number of ways in which her accusation is foregrounded in the text. In its immediate context there is the play on *sám* and *sámchaire*: according to Rónán, Mael Fhothartaig wishes Rónán and

Echaid's daughter to be at ease (*sám*), while Echaid's daughter claims that Mael Fhothartaig desires the ease (*sámchaire*) of sleeping with her. The wording of her accusation also has links outside its immediate context. In the lament, Rónán says to Echaid's daughter: *ni sám lim* . . . */ aicsin Maele Fothartaig / inna léni lán fola* ("it grieves me . . . / to see Mael Fhothartaig / in his bloodstained shirt," lines 181 ff.). Furthermore, when Echaid's daughter speaks of the ease Mael Fhothartaig desires (*in sámchaire ass áil dó*), we are reminded of Congal's accusation that she wishes to put the king of Leinster to shame (*is imdergad ríg Lagen iss áil duit*, line 94), and especially of the play on *is áil do* in the passage in which the maidservant tells Congal that she herself does not wish anything, but that her mistress wishes to have Mael Fhothartaig as her lover: *Cid ass áil duit-siu do rád? or Congal frisin mnaí. Ní dam ass áil, or sí, acht do ingin Echach rop áil Mael Fothartaig na cardess* (lines 35 ff.).

We remember too Congal's reply to the maidservant, warning her that she would die if Mael Fhothartaig should hear her saying this. So far from expressing any desire, then, for the *sámchaire* of sleeping with Echaid's daughter, Mael Fhothartaig would react violently if he were to receive the message that she wished to sleep with him. The spuriousness of the woman's charge is further emphasized by the strong words which he uses in twice rejecting the notion that he would sleep with her. When the maidservant tells him of the intentions of Echaid's daughter he proclaims, "If I were to be put, woman, into a burning pit of fire three times, until I became powder and ash, I should not sleep with Rónán's wife, even if it would save me from all that" (lines 52–54). And before he succumbs to the fatal wound which has been inflicted upon him on his father's orders he swears his innocence: "By your honor and by the tryst to which I go—a tryst with death—I am no more guilty of contemplating intercourse with her than I would be of sleeping with my mother" (lines 148–50). These strategically placed proclamations provide the true perspective for the accusation, as does the only other piece of prose which rivals them for heightened language, which is that (quoted above) in which Echaid's daughter is accused and reviled by Congal.

The author of *Fingal Rónáin* went to great pains to show Mael Fhothartaig's innocence of the charge laid against him by Echaid's daughter. Rónán accuses her of lying (*Is gó duit*, line 117), but he later accepts the capping half-quatrain which she has offered as proof (*comartha*) of the charge. The words in which he does so, *Is fír són a fecht-sa*, line 134, have been translated above as "It is true, then," which seems best to convey their sense in the context. Their literal meaning is, "That is true on this occasion," and the implication is that Rónán accepts the charge now that it has been proved to be true, the force of *a fecht-sa* ("on this occasion") being to draw a contrast with the occasion when the charge was first laid and remained unproven. Rónán has no hesitation in commanding that Mael Fhothartaig be slain, and once the fatal wound has been inflicted he says, "How lucky for you that you found no woman to woo save my wife!" Mael Fhothartaig in response says that Rónán has been wretchedly deceived into killing his only son, who is without guilt (*cin*); he solemnly swears his innocence, and goes on to reveal the truth of the matter to Rónán: "She has been soliciting me since she came to this country, and Congal took her away three times today so that she would not reach me" (lines 150 ff.). This version of the events is accepted by Rónán in his lament, where he acknowledges that the *cin* ("crime") which has led to his son's death is that of Echaid's daughter: "I grieve that Mael Fhothartaig / should have been slain because of the crime of a wanton woman" (*Saeth lim-sa Mael Fhothartaig / do guin i cin mná baíthe*, lines 178–79).

The facts which are thus belatedly revealed to Rónán are already known to the audience. They must see the trial of Mael Fhothartaig as a travesty of justice, as his innocence has been underscored again and again, and they will be shocked by Rónán's use in this context of the word *fír*, with all its connotations of truth and justice and of cosmic order. The procedure used by Echaid's daughter is described by Charles-Edwards as an ordeal by verse-capping.[16] It serves her ends in that it is accepted by Rónán as proof of Mael Fhothartaig's guilt. As a trial, however, it fails of its purpose since it is taken to establish the guilt of a party who is in fact innocent. If this trial by verse-capping is indeed an ordeal, there can only be two possible explanations of its failure: we are to assume either that the ordeal was not properly conducted, or that the burden of the narrative is that ordeals are not an appropriate method for deciding the guilt or innocence of an accused person. In either case, there is no justice for Mael Fhothartaig, who dies for a crime which he has not committed.

There is an important rider to be added: the capping half-quatrain is based on fact; it tells the truth, but not the whole truth.[17] To establish this it is necessary to interpret the quatrain. It will be recalled that Mael Fhothartaig says, "It is cold against the whirlwind / For one who herds the Cows of Aífe" (*"Is uar fri clóï ngaíthe / do neoch in-gair Bú Aífe"*), and she replies: "It is a vain herding / Without cows, without anyone you love" (*"Iss ed ingaire mada, / cen bú, cen nech no chara"*). The information needed for the elucidation of this quatrain is to be found in the text. We know three things about Bae Aífe: first, the "Cows of Aífe" are not cows, but rocks which look like cows from afar; secondly, one could go hunting there, and this is what Mael Fhothartaig had been doing on the day of his death; thirdly, it is a suitable place for a tryst, and it is the spot chosen for that which was arranged between Mael Fhothartaig and Echaid's daughter. Since Bae Aífe are rocks, the "herding" of them must be a metaphor for some other activity. The two activities which suggest themselves are hunting and trysting. I take it that Mael Fhothartaig is referring to the first of these, and Echaid's daughter to the second. Mael Fhothartaig has been hunting at Bae Aífe all day, remaining there even after all the others had gathered in Rónán's house. It is a cold day, and when Mael Fhothartaig comes in he proceeds to dry his legs by the fire, and while he is doing so, he says, in effect, "It is cold against the whirlwind for one who hunts at Bae Aífe." Echaid's daughter plays on the notion of herding the Cows of Aífe, taking the phrase first in its literal sense, and then as a metaphor for trysting. What she is saying is that it is futile to set out to herd cows at Bae Aífe as there are no cows there, and it is no less futile to go trysting there if one's partner does not appear. The gloss on her second line, *sech ní ránac-sa, ní thucais-siu na bú lat* ("I did not come, and you did not take the cows with you"), adds the information that Echaid's daughter herself is the trysting partner in question.

Echaid's daughter is accusing Mael Fhothartaig of having made a tryst with her, one which she did not keep. This, as we know, accords with the facts. Rónán is therefore convinced by a half-quatrain which is true in itself; where he errs is in his hasty acceptance of it on the valuation of Echaid's daughter as proof that Mael Fhothartaig had attempted to seduce her. All of Mael Fhothartaig's attempts to evade Echaid's daughter have now come to nought, and she has finally outwitted him. It is one of the many ironies of *FR* that the tragic course of events, which was set in motion by Mael Fhothartaig's suggestion that his father remarry, and Rónán's rejection of his son's sound advice that he marry a settled woman, should be brought to a head as a result of Mael Fhothartaig's acceptance of Congal's unsound advice that he make a tryst with Echaid's daughter. In acquiescing to the making of the tryst, Mael Fhothartaig was guilty of folly at least. Perhaps his fault was greater than that: it may be that he should not in any circumstances have made a tryst with his father's wife, regardless of the innocence of his intentions. In any case, it is his tragedy that, being guilty of the lesser fault, he is convicted of the greater crime.

Mael Fhothartaig faces a final indignity immediately before his death. It is recounted in a passage which we have already looked at as an example of narratorial intrusion: the Fool's entrails are being taken from him by a raven, and the churls are laughing at him. Mael Fhothartaig reproves him in a quatrain, telling him to gather in his bowels, and saying that he should be ashamed, as the churls are laughing at him. Thereupon Mael Fhothartaig, Congal, and the Fool die. It seems to be for the sole purpose of this gruesome incident that the Fool appears in the saga. In it he fulfils his role as the purveyor of "the great primal joke of the undignified nature of the human body," which "forms a most important part of the stock-in-trade of the buffoon."[18]

The last stage of the saga contains the necrology of the hero, and tells how his death was avenged. The dead are brought into a house apart, and Rónán stands over his son for three days and three nights. Mael Fhothartaig has died without even the consolation of an acknowledgement of his innocence from Rónán. But Rónán makes some amends with the great lament for his son, which, with what Charles-Edwards rightly calls a superb stroke,[19] begins with the very quatrain which was used by Echaid's daughter to persuade him of his son's guilt. The lament contains a number of echoes of and cross-references to the prose of the earlier stages of the saga; some of these we have glanced at in passing. It runs to eighteen stanzas in all, and it includes a dialogue with Echaid's daughter, who contributes one of the stanzas. It is interrupted by a brief account in prose of the return of Donn with the heads of Echaid, his wife, and his son, and of the suicide of Echaid's daughter. Rónán commemorates Mael Fhothartaig's achievements in life, condemns Echaid's daughter, bewails his own plight now that his son is dead, and finally laments the fact that Mael Fhothartaig, "the tall bright shining tree / has found a cold dwelling" (lines 243–44).

Mael Fhothartaig's life having been celebrated in the lament, his death is avenged by his son Áed, who slays Áedán, the warrior who killed Mael Fhothartaig at Rónán's command.[20] Rónán praises Áed, and condemns Áedán. Then the Laigin come to take revenge on Rónán himself, and in the final irony the old king acknowledges that he cannot withstand them in the absence of Mael Fhothartaig:

> The fighting on the plain
> Is defective without Mael Fhothartaig;
> This old warrior cannot
> Withstand the new fight.

With that a gush of blood burst over his lips and he died at once. (lines 265–70)

The narration of *FR* can be briefly characterized on the basis of the foregoing analysis. The saga is carefully plotted, progressing in stages up to the death of the hero, and ending with the appropriate aftermath. Within the whole, every element has its function, whether it be to advance the action, to reveal character, or to equip the audience with background information. Moreover, many of the elements are related, in one way or another, to others: this is true of words and phrases, of acts and utterances, and even of whole scenes. *FR* thus exemplifies, for Irish saga, the feature which has been called "intertexture."[21] In depicting the destruction wrought in society through the sexual designs of an evil woman, the author of *Fingal Rónáin* presents us with very much more than a mere aggregation of narrative lore. Behind the narratorial intrusions, and, much more so, in the shape and texture of the saga, "we sense an organising will, an 'author,'" somebody who is "pulling the narrative strings in a very skillful manner to manipulate the reactions of his audience towards very specific goals."[22]

27

On the *Cín Dromma Snechta* Version of *Togail Brudne Uí Dergae*

(1 9 9 0)

The manuscript known as *Cín* (or *Lebor*) *Dromma Snechta* (CDS) has not survived, but its contents are not entirely lost to us; a list of items in later manuscripts which can be shown to derive from it was drawn up by Thurneysen.[1] LU is the oldest manuscript to contain material from CDS; all the others, as Tomás Ó Concheanainn has recently pointed out, "belong to the literary heritage of Connacht,"[2] and they may therefore be referred to as the Connacht manuscripts. The CDS texts in the Connacht manuscripts are very close to one another in content and in phrasing, and Ó Concheanainn takes it that they all derive from a lost manuscript written by Gilla Commáin Ó Congaláin, who is mentioned in a colophon in Egerton 88,[3] and who has been plausibly identified with Giolla Commáin Ua Conghalaigh, who is said in the *Annals of the Four Masters* to have been *fer légind* of Roscommon, and to have died in 1135.[4]

Thurneysen held the view that the contents of CDS were more faithfully represented in the later, Connacht, manuscripts than in LU.[5] A radically different opinion has recently been offered in an important article by Tomás Ó Concheanainn.[6] It has been assumed, on the basis of the colophon in Eg. 88, that Gilla Commáin Ó Congaláin derived his texts from CDS itself, but Ó Concheanainn argues that "the manuscript which Gilla Commáin had before him for the purpose of making his own collection of CDS texts was not that early codex, but one which still survives, namely LU" (1988, 9). In other words, our CDS texts are preserved either in LU itself or in manuscripts whose texts derive from LU, through the mediation of Gilla Commáin.

Thurneysen's estimation of the fidelity of the Connacht texts to those of CDS was based on considerations of language and content. Ó Concheanainn, for his part, devotes the bulk of his article to discussion of each of the nine texts which LU has in common with one or more of the Connacht manuscripts; "certain differences in narrative and style between, on the one hand, the textually superior versions of LU and, on the other, the versions found in the later manuscripts" are adduced in support of the general thesis, the argument being that the differences in question "can reasonably be attributed to a certain degree of redaction by Gilla Commáin in the course of transcribing his texts" from LU (Ó Concheanainn 1988, 9). One of the items discussed by Ó Concheanainn is the CDS text of *Togail* (or *Orgain*) *Brudne Uí Dergae* (*BUD*), and the purpose of the present article is to consider the LU and Connacht texts of this tale in greater detail than was practicable in Ó Concheanainn's wide-ranging article. We shall find that the features which Ó Concheanainn uses to show the superiority of the LU text can be otherwise explained, and that it is highly improbable that the Connacht text derives from that of LU.

In LU, the text of *Togail Bruidne Da Derga* is followed (*LU*, lines 8005–37) by a very much shorter text, which is headed *Slicht Libair Dromma Snechta inso* ("This is the version of *Lebor Dromma Snechta*"). *Slicht* could here be taken to mean "extract (from)" rather than "version (of)," but in either case the heading clearly identifies the provenance of the piece, and this is further reflected in the heading *Slicht na cíni béos*[7] which occurs later within the piece (*LU*, line 8025). The LU text opens with *Or-*

gain Brudne Uí Dergae, which is evidently intended as the title of the piece, but it also has the end title "Bruden Ui Derga." The CDS text of *BUD* also occurs in four of the Connacht manuscripts: London, British Library, Egerton 88; Dublin, Royal Irish Academy, 23 N 10; Dublin, Trinity College Dublin, H.3.18; and Dublin, National Library of Ireland, G 7.[8] There is no title in G 7; the title is *Bruiden hi Derga* in H.3.18, and *Togail Bruidne Da Derg* in the other two. What the title in CDS may have been is impossible to say. Ó Concheanainn may be correct in opting for *Orgain Brudne Uí Dergae*: *orgain* and forms of *orgid* occur frequently in both versions of the CDS text. There would nevertheless seem to be no compelling reason for departing from the customary title, *Togail Brudne Uí Dergae*.

The Connacht texts of *BUD* differ among themselves only in minor matters, and they clearly derive from a common Connacht text, which, on the evidence of the colophon in Eg. 88, may be taken to be that of Gilla Commáin. The LU text, on the other hand, contains matter which does not appear in the Connacht text, and shows significant differences in its treatment of shared matter which must derive from a common ancestor, that ancestor evidently being CDS. Thurneysen used the Connacht manuscripts as the basis for his attempt to restore the CDS text, and held that LU represented that text in a somewhat altered and greatly expanded form.[9] Ó Concheanainn, on the other hand, claims that his comparison of parts of the LU and Connacht versions of *BUD* "would suggest that the Connacht version, which is much shorter and clearly inferior in several respects, cannot be visualized as the source of the LU text (as current opinion would have it); rather it would appear that the superior text of LU, authenticated by the scribe as being the version of CDS, should be regarded as the archetype from which Gilla Commáin redacted the Connacht versions."[10] In the face of such irreconcilable views, and given that the texts are relatively short, the best procedure seems to be to place the two versions before the reader, so that items which are selected for comparison and discussion may be seen in context. The LU text is taken from Best and Bergin (*LU*); in the case of the Connacht version I have resisted the temptation to present a critical text with normalized spelling; such a text would facilitate the reader, but it could prejudice the discussion by offering a flattering view of the Connacht texts. I have therefore followed Ó Concheanainn in using G 7 as representative of the Connacht version,[11] but variants from the other manuscripts are cited when necessary or appropriate. The LU text is divided into three paragraphs by Best and Bergin and in what follows I print these paragraphs in turn, followed in each case by the corresponding matter from G 7 and by discussion. It is only in the third paragraph that the texts are quite close, and it is from that paragraph that Ó Concheanainn derived the textual evidence to support this thesis.

> LU (*LU*, lines 8006–13): Orgain Brudne Uí Dergae trá iarna remscélaib .i. iar Tesbaid Etaíne ingine Ailello 7 iar Tromdáim Echdach Airemón 7 íar nAisnéis Síde Meic Óic do Midir Breg Leith ina síd. Conaire mac Eterscéli meic meic Ier di Ernaib Muman is é ro hort isin brudin seo. Mess Búachallo dano a máthair ingen sidé Echdach Airemon 7 ingen ingine Étaine ut diximus. Conid Conaire ó máthair do Echdaig .i. Conaire úa hEcach .i. mac ingine ingine Echach hé.

> "The Destruction of Úa Dergae's Hostel" then after its prefatory tales, that is, after "The Absence of Étaín daughter of Ailill," and after "The Burdensome Company of Echaid Airem," and after "The Instruction Regarding the Síd of *Mac Óc* Given by Midir of Brí Léith in his *Síd.*" Conaire son of Etarscélae, grandson of Íar of the Érainn of Munster, he it was who was killed in this *bruiden*. His mother was Mess Búachalla and she was daughter of Echaid Airem and grand-daughter of Étaín, *ut diximus*. So that Conaire is descended through his mother [emending to *Conid úa Conaire ó máthair*][12] from Echaid, namely, Conaire descendant of Echaid, that is, he is Echaid's daughter's daughter's son.

> G 7: [C]onari mac Messi Bouchalla issne ortiu i mpruidin Huo Derce.

> Conaire son of Mess Búachalla, it is he who was killed in Úa Derge's *bruiden*.

As the title of the tale has already been discussed, we may pass on to the two texts. They stand in marked contrast: they both identify Conaire as the one who was killed in the *bruiden*, but LU contains material which is lacking in G 7 and which links the tale of Conaire's death in two ways with an episode in what we now know as *Tochmarc Étaíne*.[13] The first of these is the mention of *Tromdáim Echdach Airemón* (along with two other items) as a *remscél* to BUD. This is clearly a reference to the harrowing of the Otherworld by Echaid Airem which is described in *Tochmarc Étaíne* III,[14] and which, as we shall see, is given in the next paragraph in LU as the reason why Conaire was exiled from Mag mBreg by avenging Otherworld beings. The second link with the events of *Tochmarc Étaíne* is provided in the genealogy which shows Conaire to be descended from Echaid Airem.[15] We cannot say for certain whether or not CDS contained this material which is now peculiar to LU, but the use of the phrase *ut diximus* might indicate that we are dealing with redactorial matter contributed by the scribe, since the reference here must be the early part of *TBDD* (which immediately precedes *BUD* in LU), where Mess Búachalla's descent is set out. As it happens, the LU text of this part of *TBDD* has been lost, but we may assume that it was much the same as that of YBL.[16] It is conceivable, however, that this genealogical matter was included in the CDS text of *BUD*, as well as in *TBDD*, and that the phrase *ut diximus* was inserted by the scribe in recognition of the fact that he had already copied similar matter from his source for *TBDD*. It might therefore be supposed, in line with Ó Concheanainn's thesis, that Gilla Commáin simply jettisoned the material relating to *Tochmarc Étaíne*. But the next paragraph will cast grave doubt on that supposition.

> LU (*LU*, 8014–24): Is ed fodrúair a orcain hi cinta Echdach ar is áes síde Breg Leith dorinólsat in n-orgain fo bíth tonaidbecht forro a síd oc cuinchid Étaíne la Echdaig. Ros dolbsat iarom lucht in tsíde sin hi slúagu 7 dollotár do inriud Maige Breg 7 tarfás samlaid do Chonaire. Ecmaing ba tír dudlotar ar is hé rí insin loingside siabrai. Ar gabaissom flaith i ndíaid a athar 7 asbert Ninión druí bátar n-é aircoilte a flatha. ar ná hechtrad a Temraig cach nómaid aidche 7 ní fuinmilsed gata ina flaith. 7 na gabtha díberg. 7 ní áirsed augra in dá túathmaíl Túathmaugnae.[17] 7 ná foíed hi taig asmbad ecna soilse iar fuiniud gréne 7 r̄.

That (i.e., the fact that he was descended from Echaid) was what caused him to be killed for the crimes of Echaid, for it is the beings from the *síd* of Brí Léith who mustered (for) the slaying because their *síd* had been broken up by Echaid as he sought Étaín. The persons of the *síd* shaped themselves then into armies and they devastated Mag mBreg and thus it appeared to Conaire. That was the country they happened to come to, for he is the king whom phantoms banished. For he assumed sovereignty after his father, and the druid Ninión said that these were the prohibitions of his reign: that he should not go out from Tara every ninth night; and that he should not be indulgent of thefts in his reign; and that marauding should not be undertaken; and that he should not restrain the quarrel of the two *túathmaíl*[18] of Túathmaugain; and that he should not spend the night in a house out of which light would be visible after sunset; *et reliqua.*

G 7: Isne de-defeith trogen der Prega, et pa he pert trogein tar Pregha, ho dhu-haudfas ndou inreth cacha mentate. Cetnei-cond-ranec pruidin Hoi Dercæ co fiu i ssuthiu 7 compa hindi hourti.

It is he who came over Brega to it at sunrise ... after it appeared to him that every dwelling had been devastated. He came first to the *bruiden* of Úa Dergae and he spent the night there and in it he was killed.

LU here shows the relevance of Conaire's descent from Echaid Airem to his tragic death; it also gives five of Conaire's taboos without any explanation of their part in the story. The Connacht version also refers to the devastation in Mag mBreg, but the terms in which it does so do not suggest derivation from LU. I have followed Thurneysen in omitting to translate *et pa he pert trogein tar Pregha*. There can hardly be any doubt that Thurneysen is correct in seeing in this a gloss which has been incorporated into the text: he suggests that the glossator did not understand *do-feith* 'comes,' and that in glossing it with *bert* he was thinking of *do-fed* 'leads, brings.'[19] The reading *de-defeith* in G 7 was not available to Thurneysen when he studied BUD, but on the basis of the readings of the other manuscripts (*dodafeith, dodieich, dofeith*) he suggested that *do-difeith* stood in the archetype.[20] Vernam Hull claimed that the reading of G 7, "taken in conjunction with the readings of all the other MSS. except one," supports Thurneysen's view.[21] It seems to me, however, that *de-defeith* in G 7 points rather to an original *do-de-feith*, with preservation of sg. 3 fem. infixed *de n-* (referring to *bruden*), which had already been lost by the time of the Old-Irish Glosses. If this is so, we are dealing with a very old item, and one which may derive from CDS itself. The orthography of the Connacht texts precludes absolute certainty on a matter of this kind, and in this particular case there is the added drawback that nasalization is not shown on -*f*-. It is worth noting, however, that the same pronoun is preserved in at least one other CDS text in 23 N 10.[22]

Moreover, I suggest below that it can be detected elsewhere in the Connacht version of our text.

A different interpretation of this passage is offered by Rolf Baumgarten in the course of an article[23] in which he argues cogently that some of the forms which have been assigned to *do-feid* (< *to-fed-*) belong instead to *do-feid* (< *di-fed-*), for which he postulates a semantic range which includes "bringing (about)." This insight would not of itself rule out Thurneysen's suggestion: it could simply mean that what the glossator mistook *do-feith* for was *do-feid* (< *di-fed-*, rather than < *do-fed-*). Baumgarten,[24] however, takes it that the verb of the text is in fact *do-feid* (< *di-fed-*), and he would emend *trogain* to *torgain*, accusative of the (unattested) verbal noun of *to-org-*, a verb which in Old Irish has been replaced for the most part by *do-fúairc*, but of which some finite forms are nevertheless attested. He points out that the idiom *do-feid torgain* is paralleled by *do-feid orgain* (using the simplex *orcun*), and he translates "and it is he who causes devastation (through violating a *geis*), and it is he who brought devastation across Brega (viz. when coming from Munster)."[25] Baumgarten's suggestion, if accepted, would show that *et pa he pert trogein tar Pregha* did not arise from a misunderstanding of what now precedes it in the text; on the other hand, it would not explain why we have the successive sentences with *torgain tar Brega*. Thurneysen's explanation of the repetition remains attractive; moreover, consideration of the corresponding matter in *TBDD* suggests that Thurneysen is right in taking the verb to refer to Conaire's journey to the *bruiden*. Baumgarten compares *TBDD*, lines 236ff: *Is ed gabsait, seach Huisneach Mide co n-acus íar sin a n-indread anair 7 aníar 7 andeas 7 atúaid, 7 co n-accatar na buidne 7 na slúagu mo seach 7 na firu lomnacht 7 rop nem thened tír Húa Néill immi*. It may be added, however, that after this account of the *indread*, which corresponds to the *inreth cacha mentate* of G 7, *TBDD* goes on to describe how Conaire goes round Tara in the right-hand direction, and then through Brega in the left-hand direction; the indications in the text are that he went north-eastwards along Slige Midlúachra and then southwards along Slige Chúalann. It was this journey over Mag mBreg which was to lead to the *bruiden*, and that is in all probability referred to in *de-defeith der Prega*.

Thurneysen's view that the Connacht text contains an incorporated gloss seems to be correct. The glossed sentence was not taken over into the Connacht tradition from LU. On the other hand, it is found, together with the incorporated gloss, in all four Connacht manuscripts. Gilla Commáin's alleged redaction of the LU text can scarcely have entailed the insertion of a sentence of his own, which apparently contains an archaic pronoun, and which he then proceeded to gloss in a way which showed that he misunderstood it. It could be argued that the gloss was made and incorporated at an intermediate stage between Gilla Commáin and the extant Connacht copies, but we would then be entering upon the slippery ground of claiming that everything in the Connacht copies derives essentially from Gilla Commáin, with the sole exception of this incorporated gloss. The incorporation of the gloss may well have formed part of Gilla Commáin's own redactorial contribution, but the same can hardly be said of the sentence which the gloss was intended to explain: he must have found that somewhere, and the most economical explanation is that it derives from the copy of the CDS text which he had at his disposal.

On the other hand, if Baumgarten's reading of the passage were to be accepted, it is conceivable that it could have been substituted by Gilla Commáin for whatever lay before him in his exemplar; but there is nothing in the text to suggest that that is what happened. As for the rest of this section of the Connacht text, *ho dhu-haudfas ndou inreth cacha mentate* evidently reflects the same text as does *dollotár do inriud Maige Breg 7 tarfás samlaid do Chonaire* in LU, but there is nothing to suggest that the one derives from the other.

The final section in LU is headed *Slicht na cíni béos*. Stokes translated this "A Recension of the Codex Also," Ó Concheanainn "Still the version of the Cín." The crucial question here is the meaning of *béos* (*DIL*, s.v. *beus*). If the text of LU is no more than a continuation of the CDS version, it is difficult to know why another heading should be inserted at this point. On the other hand, if the scribe of LU had been drawing on other sources besides the *Cín* in the preceding section, and if he now proposed to return to it, there would then be good reason for the heading. The text which follows is very close to that of the Connacht manuscripts, and may therefore be accepted as deriving ultimately from CDS. It seems likely, on the other hand, that the text which precedes the heading, and which contains a deal of matter which is lacking in the Connacht manuscripts, was redacted from a source or sources other than CDS. I would therefore be inclined to take *béos* here as meaning "again" or the like.[26]

LU (*LU*, lines 8026–37): Mane Milscothach mac Carbad 7 Gér mac uí Necae 7 tri meic uí Thoigse it é nod n-ortatar Conaire tre chomarli Ingceóil. Dobreth Geer mac ui Necae hi rráith fri Ingcél im orgain no thogfad i nHére dó. Roda nertsatside do chomollod fri Ingcel a n-ebred Mani Milscothach. Asbert Mani ba liach bruden do orgain fo déig Conaire. Is de no geibed Ingcél grúad 7 fír ui Necae. Tri .lll. ba hé a llin ocund orgain. Is ed dollotár riam i nAlpain do chor a ndíbergae and ar nír léic greim Conairi doib a cor i nHere. Conid iar sin tancatar Hérind a llin cétna 7 ortatár brudin. Conid Bruden Uí Derga cona fúasaitib 7 cona slechtaib 7 cona remscélaib amal adfiadar i llebraib insin anúas a bith samlaid.

Maine Milscothach mac Carbad and Gér mac uí Necae and the three sons of Úa Toigse, it is they who killed Conaire at Ingcél's behest. Gér mac uí Necae was given as guarantor to Ingcél as regards (any) destruction he might select for himself in Ireland. They confirmed that it would be fulfilled for Ingcél when Maine Milscothach was speaking (?). Maine said that it would be a pity to destroy the *bruiden* because of Conaire. It is on that account that Ingcél used to invoke the honor and the word of úa Necae. Thrice fifty was their number at the destruction. They went to Scotland before that to perform their marauding there, for Conaire's power did not allow them to do it in Ireland. Afterwards they came, the same in number, to Ireland and destroyed the *bruiden*. So that the above is *Bruden Uí Derga* with its developments and versions and prefatory tales as books say it to be thus.

G 7: Maine Millscothach mac Caurpuith 7 Géur mac hoi[27] Nech 7 tri maic Hui Toissich it e nota-nortetar trie comairli Incéle maic Hi Conmaic. Fo-cartater i ndibirc forra o rro-ortatar a impithi lia Hincel i nt-Alpin. Do-preth Géur mac oi[28] Neuch i rraith ndo nach orcen dingóath i n-Ére nota-nertasium lais. A n-is-mbereth Mane Millscothach pa liech in cach pui isin thig di orcin, is de no-gaipeth Incel gruoith 7 fir a Hoi Necha. Tri coícait immurgu pa he i llin ican oircin. Do-lotar i nd-Alpe do chur a ndiperce ar nir-lec grem Conare doib a caur i nd-Ére. Iter Cuailin 7 Albaee ata pruiden Hui Derca.

Maine Milscothach mac Carpaith and Gér mac uí Necae and the three sons of Úa Toissich, it was they who destroyed it[29] at the behest of Ingcél mac uí Chonmaic. They inflicted their marauding upon it[30] after Ingcél had enabled them to plunder as they requested in Scotland. Gér mac uí Neuch was given to him as guarantor that they should carry out with him any destruction that he might choose in Ireland. When Maine Milscothach said that it was sad that the one who was in the house should be destroyed, Ingcél would invoke the honor and word of úa Necae in response. Thrice fifty was their number at the destruction. They went to Alba to perform their marauding, for Conaire's power would not allow them to do it in Ireland. *Bruden Uí Derga* is between Cúala and Alba.

The content, sequence, and wording of these passages leave us in no doubt that they derive from the same ultimate source, but the differences would suggest that they do so independently. The story which is summarized here is reminiscent of the events which are described at length in *TBDD*. There the Irish marauders return from Alba accompanied by Ingcél, who has afforded them the opportunity to wreak destruction there, and who insists that the *bruiden* be destroyed. In *TBDD*, Ingcél was given three guarantors, Gér and Gabor and Fer Rogain, in respect of his choice of destruction in Ireland;[31] Gér is the only guarantor mentioned in the CDS version. In *TBDD*, the Irish marauders lament the presence of Conaire in the *bruiden* which is to be destroyed, sometimes, as Ó Concheanainn has pointed out (1988, 33), using the word *liach*, as Maine does in the CDS version. When one of the Irish marauders expresses the wish that the *bruiden* would not be destroyed, Ingcél asperses Gér's word (*fír*), Gabor's honor (*grúad*) and Fer Rogain's oath;[32] the trio reassure Ingcél, and promise that the destruction will be wrought.[33] This would seem to be a version of what is involved in the CDS reference to Gér's honor and word.

The sentences which tell of Gér's appointment as guarantor give rise to Ó Concheanainn's first substantive criticism of the Connacht version. G 7 reads: *Do-preth Géur mac oi Neuch i rraith ndo nach orcen di-ngoath i n-Ére nota-nertasium lais.* Thurneysen takes this to mean: "Gér macc uí Necae was given to him as security that they would carry out with him any destruction that he might choose in Ireland." Ó Concheanainn says that "considering that LU offers the syntactically clearer text of the above passage and that the Connacht version of the summary throughout shows much corruption of the names, one must suspect that the relative -*n*- in

27. The *Cín Dromma Snechta* Version of *Togail Brudne Uí Dergae* 409

di-ngoath, as well as the strange verbal form itself, and especially the nasalization in *ndó*, are attempts at archaisation" (1988, 32). The syntax of the LU passage, as we shall see, is not at all clear; moreover, there is nothing strange in *di-ngoath* other than the characteristic Connacht spelling. Something must first be said, however, about *nota-nertasium* (v.ll. *nodaneirtisim, nodanertisim, notanoirtisium*). Thurneysen, who did not have G 7 at his disposal, took the other readings to represent an old error for *noda-ertis*, secondary future of *orgaid* (with infixed pronoun).[34] The corresponding form in LU is *roda nertsat* (with different syntax); this, together with *nota-nertasium* in G 7, would suggest that we are dealing in both versions with the verb *nertaid*. A possible emendation of the G 7 form would be to past subjunctive *-nertad*, the meaning being "as guarantor that whatever destruction he (Ingcél) might choose in Ireland, he (Gér) should confirm that he would have it" (lit., "should confirm it with him"). But the *lectio difficilior* is that of 23 N 10, *notanoirtisium*, and this may be our best clue to the original reading. It can be emended to *nonde-nortis-sium* (or *-sam*); the explicative clause, marked as such by the nasalized class C pronoun, has past subjunctive (*-ortis*) rather than secondary future; the subjunctive is used here to express purpose:[35] "that they should (rather than 'that they would') carry it out." The emendation in the form of the pronoun is justified by the following nasalization; here we seem to have another reflex of the archaic feminine pronoun discussed above.[36] (The reference is of course to *orcen*.) Thurneysen's *-ertis*, supported by two of the manuscripts, is doubtless an early variant; here too the nasalization after the pronoun is retained. *Roda nertsatside* in LU reflects re-analysis of the *-n-* as an initial, at a time when the nasalizing pronoun was obsolete. This may also be true of the reading of G 7.

Di-ngoad is also past subjunctive (for *do-ngoad*); this exemplifies the "very common" use of the subjunctive in indefinite relative clauses (Thurneysen 1946, §517; here after *nach orcen*). There is nothing wrong, then, with the syntax of G 7 at this point, and we may safely regard the relative *n* in *di-ngoad* as genuinely old, whatever about the *n* in *ndó*.

Two sentences in LU correspond to the foregoing. Of the first we need only observe that it has the Middle-Irish secondary future *-togfad*, which can hardly have served as a model for the correctly used Old-Irish subjunctive of the Connacht version. The second sentence is: *Roda nertsatside do chomollod fri Ingcel a n-ebred Mani Milscothach*. The syntax of this is not clear to me, and the translation which I have offered is entirely tentative.[37]

Ó Concheanainn translates: "They urged him to fulfil in relation to Ingcél all that Maine Milscothach had said," but it is difficult to square this with imperfect indicative *-ebred*. Moreover, Maine is the one who is saying that it would be sad to destroy the *bruiden*; the last thing that Ingcél would want would be fulfilment of Maine's words. Now LU continues with a preterite, *Asbert Mani ba liach*, but it then reverts to imperfect in *no geibed*. G 7 has *A n-is-mbereth Mane Millscothach pa liech*, which exemplifies the Old-Irish usage of *a n-* with nasalizing relative, and which is duly followed by the same tense (*no-gaipeth*) in the main clause. G 7 is consistent in its use of the imperfect; this accords with the events of *TBDD*, where, as we have seen, Conaire's foster-brothers repeatedly say of him *"Is liach a orgain."* It is difficult to escape the conclusion that *a n-ebred Mani* and the immediately following *asbert Mani* in LU arose from misunderstanding of the text which is more accurately represented by *a n-is-mbereth* in the Connacht version.

The other verb in this sentence in LU, *roda nertsatside*, presents its own difficulties. The subject is plural, but who is referred to? One would expect the reference to be to Gér, as in the Connacht version, but the plural form excludes that. I can only suppose that the redactor of the LU text was thinking of the situation in *TBDD*, in which Gér is one of three guarantors. The Connacht text would therefore seem superior on grounds of consistency as well as grammar.

Ó Concheanainn's second criticism of the Connacht version arises from Thurneysen's interpretation of the words attributed to Maine in that version. In LU Maine says that it would be a pity to destroy the *bruiden* because of Conaire; in the Connacht version the words are *pa liech in cach pui isin thig di orcin*, which Thurneysen took to mean that it would be a pity to slay all who were in the house. Ó Concheanainn rightly points to Conaire's foster-brothers' repeated *"Is líach a orgain"* in *TBDD* and, since Conaire is mentioned in the LU text, he says that "it seems . . . that the Connacht version . . . can hardly represent the original *OBUD* [*BUD*] at this point" (1988, 33). But *in cách*, as the antecedent of a relative, is frequent in the sense "he (who),"[38] and that is how it is to be translated here.

We have now looked at the main points in Ó Concheanainn's argument. He concludes his comparison of the texts with the two sentences which say that Ingcél used to invoke the honor and the word of úa Necae, and that the marauders numbered thrice fifty at the destruction. Ó Concheanainn rightly points out that the versions are here very close, but he does concede of the first sentence that "it does not of itself establish that LU is the source of the Connacht version" (1988, 33), and this concession can doubtless be extended to include the second sentence. What we can say is that at this point the versions clearly reflect a common source: the use in both of them of forms of *úa Necae* to refer to Gér makes that quite clear. It seems, therefore, that this designation of Gér and the passage in which it occurs reflect the text of CDS itself.

It remains to say a word about the end of the LU text. Mac Mathúna has taken *Bruden Uí Derga cona fúasaitib 7 cona slechtaib 7 cona remscélaib* to refer to *TBDD*,[39] but *Bruden Uí Derga* is a short form of the title of the CDS version, and we must assume that the reference is to that. Moreover, *slicht* is twice mentioned, and the *remscéla* are named, in the course of the LU text. (What *cona fúasaitib* may refer to in this context I cannot say.) It is surely significant that the redactor of the LU version should announce that what he has given us is *Bruden Uí Derga* "as it is said *in books* to be thus." Taken together with his heading *Slicht na cíni béos*, as interpreted above, this reference to books would seem to show that the redactor of the LU text did not rely on CDS as his only source for *BUD*.

Thurneysen's assessment of the extant texts of the CDS version of *BUD* remains intact. This, as I have said, is only one of the items considered by Tomás Ó Concheanainn in the course of his article, and I would stress that my examination of it is not intended as a critique of the article as a whole. All I have done is to show that his general thesis is not supported by a close analysis of *BUD*. That of itself does not prove that Gilla Commáin Ó Congaláin did not have access to LU as he made his copies of CDS texts. But if he did, he must have resolutely put it to one side when he came to copy the *Cín Dromma Snechta* version of *Togail Brudne Uí Dergae*.[40]

28

Gat and *díberg* in *Togail Bruidne Da Derga*

(1996)

Togail Bruidne Da Derga 'The Destruction of Da Derga's Hostel' (*TBDD*),[1] one of the longest and most elaborate of the early Irish sagas, recounts the tragic life and early death of Conaire Mór, a prehistoric king of Tara. According to *TBDD*, Conaire was brought up as son of Etarscélae, king of Tara, but was in reality the son of a bird. When Etarscélae died, a bird revealed to Conaire his true origins and gave him instructions which led to his being elected king of Tara. The bird also gave Conaire a set of *geisi* (taboos or injunctions, plural of *geis*) to observe during his reign. Ireland at first enjoyed a Golden Age under Conaire. But then his foster-brothers took to crime; for a time, Conaire declined to check them, and they then began to engage in *díberg* (marauding), the occurrence of which was one of the taboos laid on Conaire. He did eventually expel his foster-brothers to Britain, where British allies afforded them opportunities to pursue their marauding. Conaire, for his part, went on to infringe his other taboos. Having set out from Tara, he found that he could not return. Instead he took a path upon which he encountered a number of malevolent Otherworld beings, and which ultimately led him to Da Derga's hostel. In the meantime, his foster-brothers and their allies returned to Ireland. Conaire's foster-brothers were reluctant to assail him, but their British allies insisted that they were pledged to do so in return for their marauding in Britain. They reluctantly attacked the hostel, setting it on fire three times, and Conaire was put to death.

One of the main questions which has arisen in regard to this tale is whether Conaire is to be seen as an innocent victim or as the architect of his own tragic end. The view which I have taken is that Conaire erred fatally in not checking the initial, tentative, criminal activities of his foster-brothers, in that they then went on to perpetrate *díberg*, thereby infringing one of Conaire's *geisi*.[2] This interpretation of the text was published nearly twenty years ago, and has been challenged in the meantime by David Greene[3] and Kim McCone.[4] In a recent article on the threefold death, I had occasion to return to this matter.[5] I repeated my earlier interpretation, while acknowledging[6] that my reading of the tale was at odds with those of Greene and McCone, and of Philip O'Leary.[7] It was necessary to defer detailed discussion of the matter, and that is what I propose to enter upon in what follows.

The main recension of *TBDD* was apparently compiled in the eleventh century from two ninth-century versions of the story; it survives complete in two manuscripts of the fourteenth century, and fragmentarily in six further manuscripts, including *Lebor na hUidre* (LU). Another recension is preserved in a sixteenth-century manuscript. The earliest extant version, which is said to have been contained in the lost manuscript *Cín Dromma Snechta* (CDS), survives in two forms: first a summary account of the events leading to the death of Conaire which is contained in four late manuscripts, and, secondly, a redaction of what is essentially the same summary with other matter, which is preserved in LU.[8]

The present discussion is concerned, in the first place, with the eleventh-century recension, and *TBDD* refers to the text of that recension as edited by Eleanor Knott; we will have occasion, however, to mention the two ninth-century versions which have been combined in it, and which are known as

A and B.⁹ The CDS summary is variously known as *Bruden Uí Dergae, Orgain Brudne Uí Dergae*, and *Togail Brudne Uí Dergae*; it is convenient to refer to it as *BUD*. Important evidence will be drawn from the recension of *BUD* in LU.[10]

Samuel Ferguson, in the opening lines of "Conary," faulted Conaire for merely banishing his foster-brothers:

> Full peace was Erin's under Conary,
> Till—though his brethren by the tender tie
> Of fosterage—Don Dessa's lawless sons,
> Fer-ger, Fer-gel, and vengeful Fergobar,
> For crimes that justly had demanded death,
> By judgment mild he sent in banishment.[11]

A different view was taken by Eleanor Knott and T. F. O'Rahilly: Knott saw Conaire as "a young king foredoomed to a tragic death to which he is relentlessly urged on by fate, his kindliest deeds entangling him most inextricably in the mesh";[12] O'Rahilly described Conaire as "an innocent victim of relentless fate."[13] Máirín O Daly cited these latter remarks,[14] but she went on to propose an interpretation which is reminiscent in general of Ferguson's, but which focuses on the events immediately preceding the banishment of the marauders. She contends that Conaire's fate was not brought about by "his successive and sometimes unwitting violations" of his *geisi*, and focuses instead on the judgment pronounced by Conaire upon his foster-brothers and their companions in crime when they are finally brought before him. In his judgment, "the one act of injustice of which he is guilty,"[15] Conaire condemns the companions to death, but decrees that his foster-brothers should be spared. This is accepted by the assembly in which it is delivered, but Conaire himself recognizes its injustice and revokes it, decreeing instead that the lives of all should be spared, but that all should be banished. This "judgment mild" is not enough to save Conaire, for his foster-brothers return from their banishment to destroy him.

O Daly rightly points out that "throughout our early literature great stress is laid on the necessity for justice in the ruler,"[16] for which the term used is *fír flathemon*, "the ruler's truth (and justice)." There can hardly be any doubt that the readers for whom *TBDD* was intended would know the fatal significance of a false judgment on Conaire's part. The fact remains, however, that in *TBDD* one of Conaire's *geisi*, namely that there should be no *díberg* in his reign, has been infringed before he gives his false judgment, and indeed the judgment has to do with those who have perpetrated the *díberg*. The centrality (or otherwise) of this *geis*, and its infraction, in the fabric of *TBDD* lies at the heart of the dissension regarding Conaire's role in his own destruction.

In the context of a discussion of the relationship between the Otherworld and kingship in certain early Irish sources,[17] I have argued that Conaire brought the wrath of malevolent Otherworld beings upon himself by failing to check the unlawful activities of his beloved foster-brothers. Conaire was summoned to kingship by the bird-man Nemglan, who declared himself to be the king of Conaire's father's birds. It was Nemglan too who laid his taboos upon Conaire. Conaire's reign ("the bird-reign") was at first a Golden Age of peace and prosperity. But some time after Conaire's elevation to kingship his foster-brothers took to thieving. This they did in order to see what punishment the king might inflict upon them and how the theft in his reign might damage him. The victim of their crime complained to the king each year, but Conaire declined to punish his foster-brothers. They were therefore emboldened to advance in crime from thieving (*gat*) to marauding (*díberg*). We have seen that this was a disastrous development for Conaire, for one of the injunctions laid upon him at the beginning of his reign was that there should not be *díberg* in his reign: my argument therefore was that by failing to punish his foster-brothers for their earlier and less serious crime of theft he effectively caused the violation of one of his own taboos. It is then that Conaire violated *fír flathemon* with his unjust judgment. Where I differed from O Daly was in adding the violation of the *geis* to the false judgment as a reason for Conaire's downfall: "Conaire's offence here has two parts: he offends against the Otherworld in transgressing a taboo, and against *fír flathemon* in giving a false judgment."[18]

This seemed—and still seems—to me to offer an Irish example of the Indo-European theme which Dumézil has called "the single sin of the sovereign": "single but irreparable, for it destroys either the *raison d'être* of sovereignty, namely the protection of the order founded on truth ... or the mystical support of human sovereignties, namely the respect for the superior sovereignty of the gods and the sense of the limitations inherent in every human delegation of that divine sovereignty. The king falls prey to one or the other of these risks, which ... are at bottom reducible to the same thing."[19] Dumézil was not aware of the occurrence of this theme in Irish tradition, but his formulation stands as an excellent account of Conaire's offence in *TBDD*, except that Conaire falls prey to both of the "risks" described by Dumézil. The essence of this interpretation is as follows: "The taboos which have been laid upon him constitute in effect a contract with the Otherworld, and his transgression of one of these taboos destroys the respect of the Otherworld personages who have delegated sovereignty to him. In failing to punish his foster-brothers, and later in delivering a false judgment, Conaire destroys the respect for the order founded on truth."[20]

In an article on taboo in early Irish narrative, David Greene quoted my Dumézilian interpretation at some length; he said that I might well be right but that it seemed to him that

> O Daly was nearer the mark in seeing a great difference between the two ways in which the single sin was committed. The false judgment was indeed a classical example of the destruction of the very *raison d'être* of sovereignty, and was enough by itself to ensure the downfall of Conaire. The enumeration of eight *geasa*, and the description of the violation of each of them in turn, is a literary device of a much lower order; it is a descent from the plane of the moral to that of the magical. It seems very likely that the austerity of the original story was too simple for the storyteller who gave us the saga in its present form. While the literary men preserved the tradition of the king as judge, and the fearful doom awaiting the king who gave a false judgment, the king of their own times was a very different kind of thing. The memory of the tabus associated with the sacred kingship was called upon to supply a magical motivation for the fall of Conaire.[21]

What we are asked to believe here is that there was an original story, austere and simple, which showed that Conaire gave a false judgment which led to his downfall, but that the storytellers who gave us the saga in its present form were not satisfied with this motivation for Conaire's downfall because it entailed kingship of a kind which was very different from what they saw in their own times. It is difficult to see any justification for this conjecture. In the first place, the prevalence of judgments in Irish tales suggests that the storytellers were not worried by any differences there might have been in this respect between the kings of their own time and those depicted in the tales, and, secondly, it would have been singularly perverse of them to seek to compensate for a lack of fidelity to the contemporary role of the king by invoking a "memory" of something which must have been at least as anachronistic as the king's judgment.[22] The notion, therefore, that the narrator's recourse to *geisi* represented a decline from the moral to the magical plane has not been supported by cogent argument; moreover, it seems wholly inapplicable to Conaire's failure, as king, to punish the crimes of his foster-brothers.

Kim McCone has also addressed the question of the relative priority of Conaire's judgment and *geisi*, but his view is that the judgment is a later addition; that there were *geisi* in an early version of Conaire's downfall, but that these did not include the *geis* against the occurrence of *díberg* in his reign.[23] McCone maintains that this early version is represented by those parts of *TBDD* which derive from the ninth-century source now known as B, and by the summary of the CDS version, and that it depicted a personal tragedy in which Conaire's foster-brothers inadvertently set in motion the events which sent him to his death.[24] In this version Conaire was indeed, in O'Rahilly's words, "an innocent victim of relentless fate." As for the unjust judgment, McCone follows Thurneysen[25] in his view that it was introduced into the A version in order to provide an offence which would motivate the king's downfall.

The *geis* against the occurrence of *díberg* is an exceptional one. As McCone points out, all of the other *geisi* are personal, in the sense that they relate to actions which Conaire himself may avoid, whereas the *geis* against *díberg* has to do with public order, and the king himself would not necessarily be directly involved in an act which would infringe it. McCone argues that this *geis* is a later addition to the tale. The crime of *díberg* is of course a prominent element in *TBDD* as it stands: it is found in A, where it is in relation to *díberg* that Conaire gives his false judgment; and in B, which has a long account of the *díberg* carried out in Conaire's reign by his foster-brothers and others. Of the *díberg* in B, the text explicitly states that it was a *geis* of Conaire's. In A, the occurrence of *díberg* is mentioned in the list of *geisi*; when the crucial outbreak of *díberg* is described, however, it is not said that it was a *geis* of Conaire's, and that omission is a departure from the usual pattern in this tale. McCone says that we must therefore accept that the *díberg* was not originally regarded in A as a violation of a *geis*;[26] he thinks that this particular *geis* was added to the list by the later compiler who combined A and B.[27] Of the B version, McCone says that it is easy to suppose that this unusual *geis*, and the emphasis on *díberg* in Ireland, "slipped in" as a reason for the king's ill fate which was lacking in the story till then.[28]

The upshot of this treatment of the *geis* against *díberg* is that the notion that Conaire offended in two ways is to be put down to the work of the compiler who combined two earlier versions without regard to their different aims.[29] As for Version A, if the *geis* against *díberg* was not there before the compiler made his new version, then the unjust judgment was the only way in which the king broke his contract with the Otherworld.[30] Quoting Dumézil's observation that "the protection of the order founded on truth ... and the sense of limitations inherent in every human delegation of that divine sovereignty ... are at bottom reducible to the same thing,"[31] McCone goes on to say that they need not and cannot be distinguished from one another as domains of judgment and *geis* respectively.[32] I would agree that they need not be distinguished from one another in a single text; it would seem appropriate that a "single sin" would be committed only once by any given individual. The fact is, however, that in *TBDD*, the king sins against the order founded on truth (Old Irish *fír*) by giving a false judgment, and he also allows the conditions to develop in which one of his *geisi* is breached, these *geisi* having been given to him by the Otherworld agents who delegated sovereignty to him. We shall see presently that the LU recension of *BUD* contains an early list of Conaire's *geisi*, which contains the one against the occurrence of *díberg* in his reign, and has a further *geis*, which is lacking in the list in *TBDD*, but which is entirely consistent with what I believe to be the burden of the relevant part of the saga, namely that Conaire's failure to check the thieving activities of his foster-brothers leads on to the violation of the *geis* against the occurrence of *díberg*. This in turn is consistent in general with McCone's recent remarks on the link in *TBDD* between the taboos of the king and the fortunes of the sovereignty itself:

> Upon being made king of Tara, Conaire promulgates the prohibitions revealed to him by [Nemglan].... After unjust failure to enforce one of these, "let not plundering (*díberg*) be taken in your reign[,]" against his beloved foster-brothers, Conaire breaks his remaining taboos at an accelerating rate as a prelude to death, remarking at one climactic mo-

ment *roṁ-gabsat-sa mo gessi uili innocht*, "all my taboos have caught me tonight." As manifestations of the ruler's contract with the divine or supernatural order, the state of his *geisi* is here symptomatic of the health of his kingship.³³

TBDD is followed in LU by a recension of the *Cín Dromma Snechta* summary which, as we have seen, is conveniently referred to as *BUD*. One of the items added by the redactor of the LU recension to the material common to all manuscripts of *BUD* is a foreshortened list of Conaire's taboos. There are only five of them, as against eight in *TBDD*, and the list ends with the abbreviation for *et reliqua*. The redaction may in this case have been carried out by the main scribe of LU; the wording of the items in the list differs in certain respects from the corresponding ones in *TBDD*, and, crucially, one of them has no counterpart there. The list may therefore have been included in order to add to the comprehensiveness of the account given in *TBDD*, whereas the foreshortening may indicate that after the fifth taboo the redactor's source had little further to add to what had already been written out by the scribe in his text of *TBDD*. In this regard, we may note his use in *BUD* of *ut diximus* of matter which repeats what has been said in his text of *TBDD*.³⁴

This list has all the appearance of being early. Its fourth item is *ní áirsed augra in dá túathmaíl Túathmaugnae*,³⁵ "that he should not restrain the quarrel of the two *túathmaíl* of Túathmaugain"; this corresponds to *ní ahurrais augra do dá moghud*,³⁶ "you shall not restrain a quarrel between two of your slaves," in *TBDD*, where it is the last in the list. Proinsias Mac Cana has argued that the *BUD* version of this *geis* is the earlier.³⁷ Two features of the wording were adduced in support of this view. First there is the mention of Túathmaugain (genitive Túathmaugnae). No location is specified in the *TBDD* version of this taboo, but the violation of it in *TBDD* has to do with a quarrel between two persons *i Tuadmumain* 'in Túathmumu,'³⁸ Túathmumu being the equivalent of the less familiar Túathmaugain. Moreover, as Mac Cana further points out, *mug* (*do dá moghud*) in *TBDD* is probably to be explained as a substitution for the relatively rare *túathmáel* (*in dá túathmaíl*) of the *BUD* text. In any case, it is clear that the *BUD* list is independent of that in *TBDD*, and that it is early. Since it includes the *geis* against *díberg*, it seems very unlikely that that *geis* was added to the list in *TBDD* by the late compiler.

For the purposes of the present discussion, however, the most significant feature of the *BUD* list is the *geis* which immediately precedes that in regard to *díberg* in this list, and which has to do with *gat*. The list in *TBDD* has nothing to correspond with this *geis*, which reads *ní fuinmilsed gata ina flaith*.³⁹ Stokes's translation was "and that he should not allow (?) thefts in his reign."⁴⁰ The verb *fo-inmlig*, of which *-fuinmilsed* is past subj. 3sg., is rare; *DIL* does not suggest a meaning for it (s.v.), and the only example of the finite verb which it adds to the one in our text is *(mairg) rodafoínblig*, which is used in reference to the treatment of women in a thoroughly misogynistic passage in *Tecosca Cormaic*,⁴¹ and which Meyer translates "(woe to him) who humours them."⁴² This is followed in *Tecosca Cormaic* by *ferr a flescad a fóenblegon*,⁴³ which contains the verbal noun of *fo-inmlig*, and which Meyer translates "better to whip them than to humour them."⁴⁴ *DIL* (s.v. *foínblegon*) follows Meyer here in that it tentatively takes "humouring" to be the meaning of the verbal noun. The reason that it does not do so in regard to the finite verb may perhaps be found in Meyer's proposal that the meaning of the *geis* in which it occurs is that Conaire should not permit theft to be prosecuted in his reign, the literal meaning being "to proclaim."⁴⁵ In making this proposal, however, Meyer had evidently forgotten the occurrence of the verb, and its verbal noun, in *Tecosca Cormaic*. A notion such as humoring, indulging, or even encouraging would seem as suitable to the *geis* as it does to the context in *Tecosca Cormaic*. This is reflected in two translations of *BUD* which appeared independently in 1990: the *geis* was rendered "that he should not put up with thefts during his reign" by Máire West,⁴⁶ and "that he should not be indulgent of thefts in his reign" by me.⁴⁷

This *geis*, therefore, requires the king to act decisively if *gat* is committed in his reign. This is what Conaire fails to do in *TBDD*, and it is this failure which leads to the perpetration of the greater crime of *díberg*. Philip O'Leary has said that Conaire is hopelessly trapped by the *geis* that there should be no *díberg* during his reign.⁴⁸ He argues that what this *geis* is doing is obliging the king to be the controlling and protecting force in his realm; he agrees with McCone that this could well be beyond the power of the king to fulfil, but goes on to say that "in its impossibility it is in keeping with a central theme of this tale: that the tension on a king cannot be borne, the balancing act cannot be performed, perfect kingship is beyond human scope."⁴⁹ Another reading is possible: the king could have restored public order had he brought his foster-brothers to book for their thieving. In the law tract *Críth Gablach* we are told that the king (*rí*) is so called because he stretches (*rigid*) over his people with coercive power.[50] It has recently been pointed out that "there is a good deal of evidence in the canons and in the vernacular laws that the canon lawyers favoured strong government and urged kings to rule as well as reign."[51] A similar attitude to the duty of a king may well underlie the tragedy of Conaire Mór as it is recounted in *Togail Bruidne Da Derga*.

29

The Oldest Story of the Laigin
Observations on Orgain Denna Ríg

(2 0 0 2)

The early Irish saga *Orgain Denna Ríg* 'The Destruction of Dind Ríg' (henceforth *ODR*),[1] tells how, in prehistoric times, Labraid of Leinster killed Cobthach Cóel, king of Brega, at Dind Ríg (near Leighlinbridge in County Carlow) in revenge for the slaying of Labraid's father and grandfather. It is the origin-legend of the Laigin (Leinstermen): in the twelfth-century manuscript Rawlinson B 502 it is the first item in the *Scélshenchas Lagen,* "the narrative historical lore of Leinster," and is described there as *cetna scel Lagen 7 tuus a ngliad,* "the oldest story of the Laigin and the beginning of their fights." Cobthach Cóel and Labraid are remote ancestors respectively of the Uí Néill and the Laigin, and *ODR* narrates the origin and early stages of a feud between them which was to last for many centuries and which is a dominant theme in the abundant early literature of Leinster. The account in *Lebor Gabála Érenn* of the events which led to the slaying of Cobthach at Dind Ríg is accompanied by the observation *Is ó shein ille atá cocad eter Leth Cuind 7 Laigniu*, "it is from that time until now that there is warfare between Conn's Half and Leinster" (*LL*, line 2794).

Various events which marked this feud are related in verse as well as prose. Rawlinson B 502 contains a series of poems under the title *Laídshenchas Laigen*, "the historical lore of Leinster in verse," which is the subject of a recent study by Edel Bhreathnach (2000). Poems of this kind also occur in the Book of Leinster: one of them begins with the words *Échta Lagen for Leth Cuinn*, "The exploits of Leinster against Conn's Half" (*LL*, lines 6980–7099), an incipit which reflects a Leinster view of the feud. *Échta Lagen for Leth Cuinn*, which refers to the Laigin as *clanna Labrada Longsich* 'Labraid Longsech's descendants' (line 6983), begins with Labraid's slaying of Cobthach *i mBrudin Tuamma Tenbath* 'in the *bruiden* of Tuaim Tenbath' and, as Mac Cana (1980a, 28) has pointed out, seems in its original form to have ended with the victory of the Laigin over the invading Uí Néill at the Battle of Allen in 722. In Rawlinson B 502 we are told that *Bruiden Tuamma Tenbad* was another name for *ODR* (Greene 1955, 17), and in a poem attributed to Ferchertne, and which is included in the saga, Tuaim Tenbath is said to have been the earlier name for Dind Ríg (lines 454–55). In *Cath Almaine*, the saga dealing with the Battle of Allen, the Uí Néill are entertained on the night before the battle by the royal fool Úa Maigleine, who "proceeds to tell them of the battles and contests of Leth Cuinn and the Laigin, from the Destruction of Tuaim Tenbath, that is of Dind Ríg, in which Cobthach Cáel of Brega was slain, up to that time" (*rogab-saide oc innisin chath ocus chomrama Leithe Cuinn ocus Laigen ó Thogail Tuama Tenbath, .i. Denna Ríg, in romarbad Cobthach Cáel-breg conice in n-aimsir-sin*; Ó Riain 1978, lines 66–69). This tale, and the events depicted in it, was of crucial significance to the way in which the Laigin saw their early history.

ODR is found in three manuscripts, Rawlinson B 502 (R, twelfth century), the Book of Leinster (L, also twelfth century), and YBL (Y, in the part of the manuscript written by Giolla Íosa Mac Fhir Bhisigh about the year 1392). Stokes (1901b) made L the basis of his edition, since it is "slightly fuller" than the others. Greene (1955) followed suit, presumably for the same reason, but he adopted a number of readings from R. His editorial policy was to follow one manuscript (in this case L), "departing from it only when there was another reading which was more archaic or gave better sense"

(1955, v). He observed that "the three manuscripts point to a common source, although R often diverges verbally from LY in a way which is explicable only by assuming oral transmission" (1955, 16). Tomás Ó Concheanainn (1986), on the other hand, suggests that R is the only independent manuscript of the text, that L was copied from R, and that Y was copied from L but with sporadic readings taken directly from R. I suspect that the filiation of the texts is somewhat more complicated than that, but Ó Concheanainn's discussion clearly establishes two things: "(1) the older character of R as opposed to the later, and closely agreeing, L and Y; (2) the occasional, but striking, agreement of R and Y against L" (Ó Concheanainn 1986, 16).

The relative fullness of L as compared with R arises from the fact that the scribe of the latter includes only the opening phrases of two verse passages that are found in full in L (and Y). As Ó Concheanainn observes, "the reason for the scribal curtailment was simply economy of effort: the two passages in question are to be found earlier in the MS" (1986, 15).

ODR is a tale of considerable interest, both for its form and for its content. While Rawlinson B 502 draws a distinction between *Scélshenchas* and *Laídshenchas*, *ODR* is written in a mixture of prose and verse. It is, in fact, a singularly interesting specimen of prosimetrum, and in the latter part of this article I will consider this facet of *ODR*, and also the rhetoric of the tale, with particular reference to the replication of incidents. First, however, I want to look at the political content of *ODR*, not, I need hardly say, in relation to actual historical events, but rather with regard to the claims that are made in the tale. It will be useful at this point to give a brief summary of it: Cobthach Cóel, king of Brega, slays his brother Lóegaire Lorc, variously described as king of Leinster and king of Ireland, and Lóegaire's son Ailill Áine, who became king of Leinster after his father's death. Cobthach takes the kingship of Leinster for himself, and banishes Ailill's son Labraid "out of Ireland." Accompanied by the poet Ferchertne and the musician Craiphtine, Labraid goes to the land of Scoriath, king of the Fir Morca in West Munster. Moriath, the king's daughter, falls in love with Labraid, who wins her by means of Craiphtine's music, which sends her watchers to sleep. Thereafter Labraid marches with an army of Munstermen to Dind Ríg. Craiphtine's music puts the men who are defending the fortress to sleep, and the fortress is captured, its defenders slaughtered, and Dind Ríg destroyed. But Labraid and Cobthach make peace, and Labraid becomes king of Leinster and settles at Dind Ríg. There he secretly builds a house of iron. He invites Cobthach to a feast, and Cobthach comes accompanied by thirty other kings. They enter the iron house, and Labraid burns them all to death.

The political content of three parts of this sequence of events will concern me in what follows. I shall look first at the initial situation and at the status at that stage of Cobthach Cóel and Lóegaire Lorc respectively. Then I shall look briefly at the political implications of Labraid's sojourn in Munster. Finally, and especially, I want to discuss the happenings at Dind Ríg and the relative status, at the time of the fateful feast, of the host, Labraid, and of his guest and victim, Cobthach Cóel.

THE INITIAL SITUATION

In Greene's edition *ODR* opens as follows:

> Boí Cobthach Cóel Breg mac Úgaine Móir i rríge Breg. Baí dano Loegaire Lorc mac Úgaine i rríge Laigen. Ba formtech Cobthach fri Loegaire im ríge Laigen, corra gaib sergg[2] 7 galar de coro ṡergg a fuil 7 a feóil de, conid de ro boí Cóel Breg fair-sium. (lines 304–8)

> Cobthach Cóel Breg son of Úgaine Mór was king of Brega, while Lóegaire Lorc son of Úgaine was king of Leinster. Cobthach envied Lóegaire the kingship of Leinster, so that decline and disease afflicted him, and his blood and his flesh wasted away; and that is why he was called Cobthach Cóel Breg (Cobthach the Slender One of Brega).

RY and L differ in one important respect in this passage. In RY the office held by Lóegaire Lorc and coveted by Cobthach was the kingship of Leinster, whereas in L it was the kingship of Ireland. L thus makes a political claim which is not reflected in RY. Greene adopted the reading of RY in view of the agreement of all manuscripts that after the slaying of Lóegaire's son Ailill, Cobthach assumed the kingship of Leinster (*iar sin ro gabsom ríge Lagen*, line 332). Ó Concheanainn (1986, 19) agrees with Greene's decision here, saying that R's *Lagen* "clearly represents the original text."[3] He suggests that the substitution in L of "Ireland" for "Leinster" "may have been in the interest of Leinster propaganda."

It has to be said that Greene made the wrong editorial decision, either in the opening sequence or at line 330. The latter comes immediately after Lóegaire's death at Cobthach's hands. We are told that Lóegaire left a son named Ailill Áine. Then comes a sentence which is represented in the MSS as follows:

L: Ro gabsideríge Lagen (*LL*, line 35232).
R: *Con*gabs*ide* Laigneo fris afrithise (Meyer 1909a, 130, lines 38–39).
Y: Rogabsidhi Laigi*n*fris arisi[4] (YBL, col. 754).

Greene retains the reading of L, which can be translated "He assumed/ seized the kingship of Leinster," whereas R means something like "And he took Leinster back from him" (more literally "back in opposition to him"). The notion of taking Leinster back is consistent with the statement in R (and Y) that Cobthach killed Lóegaire because he envied him the kingship of Leinster, and serves to confirm what is in any case implicit, which is that Cobthach would have attempted to seize the office once he had killed its holder. In L, on the other hand, the first mention of the kingship of Leinster is in connection with Ailill Áine, so that there is no place there for *afrithise* 'back.' In this matter, then, R and L differ, but each of them is internally consistent. If the scribe of L has indeed changed the text in the interest of Leinster propaganda, which is quite likely, he has also taken care to change his account of Ailill's action. Having chosen to follow R in the opening passage, Greene should also have followed it in the sequel.

In according Lóegaire the kingship of Ireland, L concurs with the text of *Lebor Gabála* which is preserved in the same manuscript. T. F. O'Rahilly (1946, 105) begins his summary of this latter account as follows: "Cobthach, king of Ireland, treacherously slew Loegaire Lorc, and likewise Ailill Áine, and banished Labraid 'beyond the sea.'" In one important respect, this gives a misleading impression of what is being summarized. In the relevant part of LG, Cobthach Cóel and Lóegaire Lorc are introduced as sons of Úgaine Mór, Cobthach's descendants are mentioned, and then the text continues as follows:

Baí Cobthach .l. bliadan i rrige Herend 7 ro marb húa a brathar é .i. Labraid Longsech. Loegaire Lorc im féin is é ro gab ríge ṅHerend iar nUgaine Mór coro marb Cobthach Cael Breg é tria mebail. & dano ro marb in Cobthach cetna a mac in Loegairesin .i. Ailill Áne. (*LL*, lines 2787–91)

Cobthach was king of Ireland for fifty years, and his brother's grandson, Labraid Loingsech, killed him. As for Lóegaire Lorc himself, he assumed the kingship after Úgaine Mór, until Cobthach Cóel Breg killed him treacherously, and furthermore the same Cobthach killed Lóegaire's son Ailill Áine.

Two things are clear in this account: first, Lóegaire Lorc is supposed to have succeeded his father as king of Ireland, and secondly, Cobthach cannot have become king of Ireland until after he had slain Lóegaire. In *ODR* only L makes Lóegaire king of Ireland. On the other hand, all three manuscripts are at one in describing Cobthach as king of Brega at the beginning of the tale, and in describing him as king of Ireland only after he has slain Lóegaire and Ailill and taken the kingship of Leinster for himself.

One other thing has happened before he is designated king of Ireland in the tale: he has celebrated the Feast of Tara, which the "men of Ireland" were invited to enjoy (lines 338–53). It will not be necessary here to go into the controversial aspects of *Feis Temro*,[5] for we can assume that in this context the purpose of the feast is to mark Cobthach's achievement of the kingship of Tara and hence of the "kingship of Ireland." That he is not altogether deserving of the office is clear when, in the course of the feast, Craiphtine and Ferchertne decline to tell him that he is the most generous person in Ireland. They nevertheless acknowledge him as "king of Ireland" when, having been exiled by him, they speak about him to their host in Munster (line 359).

LABRAID'S SOJOURN IN MUNSTER

It will already be clear that *ODR* is not the only account of the events which it describes. In his analysis of the various extant accounts of Labraid's contention with Cobthach, T. F. O'Rahilly (1946, 101–17) showed that *ODR* differed from all the others in two important ways. The first of these has to do with Labraid's exile: in *ODR* the whole action of the story takes place in Ireland, but the others say that Cobthach banished Labraid from Ireland

and that Labraid spent some time overseas. The second feature which is peculiar to *ODR* is that "the capture of Dinn Ríg and the death of Cobthach in Dinn Ríg are treated as separate incidents" (O'Rahilly 1946, 109). It may be, as I shall suggest presently, that the author of *ODR* was aware of the tradition of Labraid's exile overseas; he may also have known a version of the story that had a single destruction of Dind Ríg in the course of which Cobthach was put to death. If his account of Labraid's exile is indeed a revision of an earlier one, it is to his credit that he carried it out relatively adroitly. (The significance and rhetorical value of the second destruction will concern us later.) Cobthach commands Labraid and his companions to leave Ireland, but Labraid's response is that if they cannot find a place for themselves in Ireland they will indeed leave it. And so when they are banished they go westwards on Ferchertne's advice and they are received by the Fir Morca in West Munster. The author of *ODR* shows Labraid to have been banished from Ireland, but to have found a haven within it, in defiance of Cobthach's command.

Why should the author have located the Fir Morca in West Munster? The Fir Morca are not known to history, and since the place of Labraid's exile is elsewhere said to have been in Gaul, O'Rahilly plausibly explains *tír Fer Morca* or *crích Fher Morca* as "an early popular corruption of *tír* (or *crích*) *Armorca, a borrowing of Lat. *Armorica*" (1946, 113). But while this may be so, it is not to say that O'Rahilly is correct in describing the author's location of Fir Morca in Munster as "a mere blunder on his part": "the author did not know where the Fir Morca dwelt; and as their name looked like an Irish one he chose to locate them in the remote region of West Munster" (1946, 113). But this author has consulted and used a number of sources in the construction of his narrative, and he can hardly have been unaware of the tradition that Labraid spent some time in exile overseas. Indeed in one of the quatrains cited by him from a poem by Orthanach Úa Cóellámha he is described as *mac meic Loegaire din lind*, "Lóegaire's grandson from the sea" (line 451). The author of *ODR* may have wished to suggest a certain degree of defiance in Labraid's character, but on the political level his motivation may well have been the propagandistic one of providing Labraid with Munster allies in his opposition to Cobthach. And so it is that Labraid brings an army of the men of Munster (*sluagad fer Muman*, line 396) with him when he returns to Leinster to destroy the fort at Dind Ríg.

RECHTAS AND LÁNRÍGE

There are two destructions at Dind Ríg according to *ODR*, and indeed the first of them is described as *in c[h]étorcain* (line 397); this entails the destruction of the fortress at Dind Ríg (*coro hort in dún,* "and the fortress was destroyed," line 404; similarly line 410). Cobthach, we may assume, was not in the fortress at the time, as he survived the destruction, and he went on to make peace with Labraid. This part of the text is as follows:

> Ro gab-som didiu ríge Lagen iar sin 7 batar hi córe 7 Cobthach, ocus is and ro boí a ṡossad-som, i nDind Ríg. Rechtas immorro ro gab-som 7 lánríge la Cobthach. Ro-chuirestar iarum Cobthach do dénum a menman 7 do airiuc thuile dó. (lines 412–16)

The first and last of these three sentences pose no difficulty and can be translated respectively: "Then Labraid became king of Leinster, and he was at peace with Cobthach, and his residence was at Dind Ríg"; and "Labraid afterwards invited Cobthach to come and enjoy himself and be entertained." The second sentence in the passage is less straightforward. Greene reads *rechtus* with R, where L and Y have *fechtus*. It is difficult to make anything out of the latter reading. Stokes translated "Once upon a time, however, when he had taken it, and Cobthach had the full kingship," but this entails a strained (and almost certainly ungrammatical) run-on into the next sentence which contains the adverb *iarum* 'afterwards.' It seems as if this is one of the many cases in which R preserves the better reading, but I think that the sentence in R has been misconstrued in the two translations of it that are known to me. Greene gives "authority" as the meaning of *rechtus* in his Vocabulary, but he does not translate or otherwise comment upon the sentence. Vendryes (1958–59, 17) translates "Cobthach lui reconnut autorité et pleine royauté," and Sims-Williams (1991, 54) essentially agrees: "He got authority and full kingship from Cobthach."

In interpreting this sentence we must attend to the (relative) *ro gab-som*, which echoes the (non-relative) *ro gab-som* of the preceding sentence: *Ro gab-som didiu ríge Lagen. . . . Rechtus immorro ro gab-som.* The second of these is either a modification or an amplification of the first; *immorro* can have adversative or emphasizing force (*DIL* I 159.31, 160.9), so that we can translate it either as "however" or "moreover, besides." What is decisive,

I think, is the second part, *7 lánríge la Cobthach*. The translations by Vendryès and Sims-Williams imply a clefting of **Ro gab-som rechtus 7 lánríge la Cobthach*, which would mean "He got authority and full kingship from Cobthach."[6] But in that case one would expect that *rechtus 7 lánríge* would be fronted as a unit, yielding **Rechtus 7 lánríge ro gab-som la Cobthach*. As it stands, it seems to me that the sentence draws a contrast between *rechtus* and *lánríge*, indicating that Labraid got the former and Cobthach held (or retained) the latter. *Immorro*, then, is adversative here and can be translated "however." I therefore take the meaning of the sentence to be "It was *rechtas*, however, that he assumed and Cobthach had the full kingship." The modification that is made by *immorro* here is a qualification rather than a contradiction, since Labraid's *rechtus* is contrasted not with his own *ríge* but with Cobthach's *lánríge*. In other words, Labraid did indeed achieve kingship, but it was a kingship which entailed *rechtas* rather than full kingship.

What, then, is *rechtas*? This poorly attested word is obviously an abstract from *recht* 'law' (for the etymology of which see McCone 1998, 10). According to *DIL* (s.v.), it means "authority, administration"; that it can denote the office of *rechtaire* seems to be implicit in a version of the Birth of Cormac mac Airt (*Genemain Chormaic*) in which Cormac is said to have rewarded the Fir Chúl Breg for their services to him by giving them land in Brega and the *rechtas* of Tara (V. Hull 1952, 84, line 89). Since Cormac himself is king of Tara, *rechtas* cannot here refer to a subordinate form of kingship. Donnchadh Ó Corráin (1986, 147) is surely correct in taking it to be the "stewardship of Tara." The *rechtaire*, conventionally translated "steward" or "major-domo," was the chief officer of the king, and it must have been this office which Cormac bestowed upon the Fir Chúl Breg.

In *ODR*, however, *rechtas* is used in the context of the subordination of one king to another. The model of kingship which is envisaged here finds clarification in a passage in the *dindshenchas*. A carefully crafted quatrain in the poem which Gwynn (*Met. Dind.* 1:38–45) published as "Temair V" reads as follows: *Ce beith ós Banbai brainig / ríg amrai, ard a medair, / ní fhuil rechtas ríg foraib / acht a ríg techtas Temair* (lines 69–73). Gwynn translates, "Though there be over imperial Banba / famous kings—high their mirth! / no kingly authority is binding on them / save from the king that possesses Temair." Implicit in this is a threefold hierarchy of kings, in which the lowest of the three (the *ríg amrai* here) would in some sense be subject to the authority of a king of the second rank who in turn would receive his right to exercise that authority from the king of Tara; if the authority were not granted by the king of Tara it could not be exercised at all. In the light of this quatrain, the claim in *ODR* would seem to be that the authority exercised by Labraid as king of Leinster had been granted to him by Cobthach. This notion is very far from the view of kingship which is expressed in the Irish laws. On the other hand Ó Corráin (1978, 29) has noted, among the later developments in the office of *rechtaire*, that great kings make use of subject petty-kings to fill the office. It is true that Labraid is no petty-king; moreover, the relevant development in the office of *rechtaire* is dated by Ó Corráin to the eleventh and twelfth centuries, whereas *ODR* is said to have been given its present form "not much earlier than the beginning of the tenth century" (Greene 1955, 17). Nevertheless, the arrangement which, according to *ODR*, was put in place after the first destruction at Dind Ríg is analogous to that in which the subordinate king is seen as the *rechtaire* of the over-king.

When Labraid invited Cobthach to the fateful feast in the iron house at Dind Ríg, it was an invitation to an over-king. Patrick Sims-Williams has written of "the custom of erecting temporary houses for important personages, whether over-kings or simply honored guests, as seen in literary texts like *Bricriu's Feast*, *The Destruction of Dinn Ríg*, and *Tromdám Gúaire*" (1991, 56). He points out (1991, 54) that the episode in *ODR* is a "close analogue" to that in *Branwen* in which the Irish build a house for Bendigeidfran. His reading of the text (and that of Vendryes) led him to the view that "it is the over-king Labraid, not the submissive Cobthach, who builds the house, the reverse of the position alleged for Bendigeidfran" (Sims-Williams 1991, 55). The interpretation that has been proposed here removes this discrepancy.

Labraid redeems his honor in the slaughter of Cobthach Cóel; this, at any rate, is his mother's view (line 441). His primary motivation must have been to avenge the kin-slaying of his grandfather and father by Cobthach. But he would also have been anxious to rid himself (and Leinster) of the indignity of his position as holder of *rechtas* when Cobthach held *lánríge*. This primeval rejection of the claims of an ancestor of the Uí Néill to superior kingship is presented in the literature as an exemplary act, and it was replicated by many historical kings of Leinster who claimed descent from Labraid.

ODR AS PROSIMETRUM AND FERCHERTNE'S ROLE

There are four sequences of verse in *ODR*. The first comprises four lines of rhymeless alliterative verse, beginning *Ní ceilt céis ceól do chruit Chraiphtini*, "The *céis* concealed no music from the harp of Craiphtine" (lines 384–87); they are spoken by Ferchertne after Labraid and Moriath have made love. Scoriath, having been informed by his wife that their daughter shows symptoms of having slept with a man, demands that his druids and poets discover the identity of the lover. When they fail to do so, he turns to Ferchertne and threatens to kill him if he does not tell him who is involved. At Labraid's bidding, Ferchertne obeys the king's command and reveals that it was Labraid who made love to the young woman when Craiphtine's music had put the company to sleep. In the last line he praises Labraid, saying that "he is greater than any price." (Ferchertne then repeats in plain prose the accusation he has just made in verse.) The king, as we know, is happy to accept Labraid as a husband for his daughter, but this occurs only after Ferchertne has solemnly revealed the identity of the person who, after all, has thwarted the best efforts of Scoriath and his wife to shield Moriath from all men. What is going on here is essentially a trial, and the king duly gives his judgment, which is favorable to Labraid, after he has heard what Ferchertne has to say.

A second quatrain, attributed to the poet Flann mac Lonáin, beginning *Feib con-attail Moriath múad*, "When proud (?) Moriath slept" (lines 408–11), briefly recapitulates in syllabic verse the events of the first destruction at Dind Ríg, which have been recounted in detail in the preceding prose.

The tale is "rounded off," as Mac Cana (1997, 109) puts it, by two verse passages. The first of these comprises two quatrains of syllabic verse dealing in turn with Cobthach's slaying of Lóegaire Lorc and Labraid's killing of Cobthach and his company of thirty kings. These quatrains are not attributed to a named author in *ODR*, but they are identified as a quotation by the phrase *unde dicitur*, and in fact they are taken from the poem *A chóicid choín Chairpri crúaid*, ascribed to Orthanach Ua Cóelláma, an early ninth-century bishop of Kildare (O Daly 1961–63). The opening line of Orthanach's poem, "Fair province of stern Cairbre," is addressed to Leinster; the poem is devoted to the battles fought by Leinstermen, and in Rawlinson B 502 is appropriately included in the *Laídshenchas Laigen*.

The tale ends with a poem in rhymeless alliterative verse attributed to Ferchertne, beginning *Dind Ríg / ropo Thúaim Tenbath*, "Dind Ríg was (formerly) Túaim Tenbath." This poem, which (like the other verse passage attributed to Ferchertne in *ODR*) is also preserved in the genealogies, has received a good deal of attention; its most recent editor notes that the text in *ODR* "differs in many points from the text in the genealogies, and the two versions should not be conflated" (Corthals 1990, 117). It briefly describes Labraid's actions at Dind Ríg, gives some details of his genealogy, and names some of those who were killed along with Cobthach.

When we look at the function of the verse passages in *ODR*, it is clear that the passage in which Ferchertne identifies Labraid as the illicit lover of Moriath stands apart from the others in that it is a solemn utterance which belongs integrally to the course of events recounted in the saga, whereas the others can be assigned to the type which Mac Cana (1997, 111) describes as "evidential," and which he characterizes as follows: "It serves to corroborate what has been told or mentioned in the preceding prose and consequently, if specifically ascribed, it is generally attributed to well-known poet-scholars." A distinction may be made, however, within the evidential verse of *ODR*. Whereas Flann mac Lonáin and Orthanach Ua Cóelláma are indeed poet-scholars who furnish retrospective accounts of the events they describe, Ferchertne is represented as an eyewitness. He has already participated in the events of *ODR* as eulogist, counsellor, and (in effect) officer of the court. His first appearance is at the Feast of Tara (lines 338–53), when the men of Ireland are gathered together and the eulogists (*int aes admolta*) are out on the floor "praising the king and the queen and the princes and the lords." They evidently do not praise Cobthach quite as highly as he wishes for he proceeds to ask if they know who is the most generous person in Ireland. Craiphtine and Ferchertne both say that Labraid is the most generous, with the result that Cobthach expels them along with Labraid. It is Ferchertne who tells Labraid that they should go westwards on a path which, in the event, leads to the court of Scoriath. We have seen the role that he played in Labraid's winning of Moriath, a role which complements that of Craiphtine.

Ferchertne and Craiphtine, two members of the *áes dána*, play important parts in Labraid's life. Craiphtine is the more prominent of the two. He is the first to respond to Cobthach's question about the most generous person in Ireland, and when Cobthach decides to expel Labraid, it is (surprisingly) the harpist rather than the poet who makes the portentous pronouncement: "He will be none the worse for that, and you will be none the better" (line 350). The magical efficacy of Craiphtine's music is crucial in the wooing episode and in the first destruction at Dind Ríg. But Ferchertne has the last word: when Cobthach arrives at Dind Ríg in response to Labraid's invitation he declines to enter the iron house until he has been preceded by Labraid's fool and Labraid's mother (lines 42–23). Ferchertne is not required to enter the house, and as someone who witnesses the destruction and lives to tell the tale, it is tempting to call him the *scéola orgne*. Thurneysen (1917, 34) took *scéola* as an *io*-stem meaning "Zeuge, Berichterstatter," which presumably gives the sense in the reverse order of its historical development. In *DIL* (s.v.) the meaning is given as "newsbringer, survivor (of a battle)." The sense "storyteller, newsbringer" is in all probability the primary one; if it comes to mean "survivor," this must arise from the well-attested association of the word with *orgain*, both in collocation with the genitive (*sceola/sciula orcne* occurs twice in Cormac's Glossary, Meyer 1912, 28), and in a sentence such as *ní gnáth orgain cen scéola n-eisi do innisin scél dara n-éisi*, which occurs in *Scél Tuáin meic Chairill*, and which John Carey (1984, 105) translates, "it is not usual for there to be a calamity without a fugitive (escaping) from it to tell the tale thereafter." In a note, Carey (1984, 109) passes on a suggestion made to him by John Armstrong that the expression *ní gnáth orcain cen scéola n-eisi* is proverbial and *do innisin scél dara n-éisi* an intrusive gloss, and cites in support of this the occurrence in the Rennes *dindshenchas* of *Ni bi orgain cen oensciula* (Stokes 1894, 447) as well as the phrase which occurs twice in Cormac's Glossary.

THE RHETORIC OF *ODR*

ODR is framed by two acts of kin-slaying, the second of which is carried out to avenge the first. Stokes (1901b, 1) has described *ODR* as a "tale of treachery, love, self-devotion, and vengeance," and these are indeed all closely woven into its tapestry, but it is in fact envy which is the ultimate source of the evil which is unleashed in this saga, and hence of the never-ending cycle of death and destruction which marked the feud between the descendants of Cobthach and Lóegaire. We have already seen that the envy which possesses Cobthach has the force of a disease: "Cobthach envied

Lóegaire the kingship of Leinster, so that decline and disease afflicted him, and his blood and his flesh wasted away; and that is why he was called Cobthach Cóel ('The Slender One') of Brega" (lines 305–8). The following outline will show that the underlying structure of the sequence of events leading to the slaying of Lóegaire (A) is replicated in the sequence of events leading to the slaying of Cobthach (B).

1. *Act or acts of hostility towards a kinsman*
   A. We are informed simply that "Cobthach did not manage to kill Lóegaire" (line 308)—no details are given but the clear implication is that he attempted to do so.
   B. Labraid's assault on Dind Ríg (lines 396–411) is clearly a hostile act aimed at Cobthach, who has taken the kingship of Leinster which had been held by Labraid's father and grandfather.

2. *A reconciliation is effected*
   A. "Lóegaire was summoned to Cobthach so that he might leave Lóegaire his blessing before he died" (line 309). There is an incident involving a chicken, which convinces Lóegaire that Cobthach is no longer to be taken seriously (lines 309–18).
   B. After the "first destruction," as we have seen, Labraid became king of Leinster and was at peace with Cobthach, who had "the full kingship" (lines 412–14).

3. *An invitation is issued to the victim and accepted by him*
   A. Cobthach says that he is about to die, and he invites Lóegaire to come the next day to raise his grave mound. Lóegaire promises to do so (lines 319–21).
   B. Labraid invites Cobthach to come and enjoy himself and be entertained (lines 415–16).

4. *The perpetrator secretly prepares for treachery*
   A. Cobthach instructs his wife and his steward: "Say that I have died unknown to anyone else, and let me be put in my chariot with a razor-sharp knife in my hand. My brother will come eagerly to keen me; no doubt he will get something from me as a result" (lines 322–25).

B. Labraid has a house made at Dind Ríg to receive Cobthach: "The house was very strong; it was made of iron, walls and floor and doors. The Leinstermen spent a year building it, and father concealed (the fact of) it from son, mother from daughter. From this derives the saying, 'There are as many secrets as there are Leinstermen'" (lines 416–20).

5. *A horrific killing takes place*
   A. Lóegaire's killing occurs in a chilling scene in which the solemn act of keening a kinsman is violated in the most horrifying way imaginable—the murder by the "corpse" of his brother while he is in the very act of keening him: "(In accordance with Cobthach's instructions), the chariot is taken outside. His brother comes to keen him. He goes and lies down upon him. Cobthach plants the knife into his loins and its point pierced the corner of his heart, so that he killed him with it" (lines 326–29).
   B. Cobthach's death in the iron house was brought about when Labraid and eight others seized the chain that was attached to the door and dragged it out and fastened it to a pillar. Three times fifty forge-bellows, with four warriors to each bellows, were blown, and Cobthach died in the house along with seven hundred others and thirty kings (lines 436–39, 443).

While the set of events which I have outlined accounts for all of what happens in the first of the two sequences, there is some material in the second sequence which serves to distinguish Labraid's actions from those of Cobthach which he is avenging. In the first place, Cobthach's crime is an entirely selfish one, and only his wife and steward are confided in. Labraid on the other hand is assisted (apparently) by all the adults of Leinster. Moreover, whereas Cobthach evidently has no compunctions about his bloody deed, Labraid takes to the playing field the day after Cobthach arrives:

The next day Labraid went to play with the lads on the meadow. His foster-father saw him doing that. He started to beat Labraid on the back and on the head with a one-stemmed thorn.

"It is apparent," said he, "that your notion of a valiant deed is that of a boy. It is evil of you, lad," said he, "to have invited the king of Ireland with a retinue of thirty kings and not be with them to provide entertainment for them." (lines 427–32)

Labraid's fondness, as an adult, for the playing field has been revealed earlier in the saga, and that is a point to which we shall return. With regard to the present occasion, however, it is important to note that Labraid deserts his guest only after he has discovered what a heavy price will have to be paid if he is to proceed with his planned act of vengeance. "Cobthach could not be prevailed upon to enter the house until Labraid's mother and his fool had done so. The fool chose (as his reward) the blessing of the Leinstermen and freedom for his descendants forever. The woman went for the benefit of her son" (lines 422–25). It is scarcely surprising that he should shirk from the "valiant deed" of an adult, when that entails the slaughter of his mother (and of his fool). The terms which have been set by Cobthach for his entry into the house are enough to drive Labraid away from it.

When he has been goaded into action by his foster-father, he dresses himself and he goes into the house. Two comments are made in the course of what follows. First, Labraid says to the guests that fire, drink, and food must be provided for them in the house. Cobthach's answer is curt: "It is proper (*Is cóir*)." In view of Labraid's true intention in the matter of providing fire in the house, the reader will remember the heinous crime for which Cobthach is about to be punished, and recognize that Cobthach speaks more truly than he knows. The second comment is made by Labraid's mother. When the flames are being fanned by the bellows, the Leinster warriors remind Labraid that his mother is inside. She immediately responds, "Nay, dear son, save your honor through me, for I shall die in any case." Having been called to his destiny from the playing field by his foster-father, and having been given unwitting support by Cobthach, he is now finally vindicated by his mother's invocation of the all-important concept of honor.

Replication is the most striking feature in the structure of *ODR*. Cobthach twice invites Lóegaire to come to him. Having slain Lóegaire, "he was not content with the first kin-slaying" (line 331), and he had Lóegaire's son, Ailill, killed as well. Ailill's son Labraid was dumb until a blow from a hurley made him cry out, an incident which as we have seen is echoed in a later episode. Labraid's exile is imposed upon him at the Feast of Tara, and culminates in the consummation of his marriage. There are two destructions at Dind Ríg.

The names *Labraid* and *Móen*, "The Speaker" and "The Mute," exemplify the coincidence of opposites which is often associated with mythical personages, and the first incident on the playing field explains how Labraid found his voice, and acquired the name by which he was to be most commonly known. He is classified as "an unpromising hero" by Tom Peete Cross (1952, 386). While some heroes are precocious in their childhood, others are quite the opposite: as de Vries (1963, 214) puts it, "the child is often very slow in his development; he is dumb or pretends to be mentally deficient." Given the fate of his father and grandfather, Labraid's dumbness might well be construed as a way of ensuring that the king will not regard him as a threat to his position. That it is not a purely physiological matter is revealed by his response to the shock administered on the playing field.

Art Ó Maolfabhail (1973, 57) and Michael Chesnutt (2000, 45–47) have associated this incident with that which, as Chesnutt (36) puts it, "is registered under the guises of H1381.2.2.1.1 'Boy twitted with illegitimacy seeks unknown father' and T646 'Illegitimate child taunted by playmates,'" which is rather a long shot, given that Labraid is not at this stage a child, it is clearly stated that he was Ailill's son, and there is no mention of taunting.[7] Chesnutt (47) says there is "confusion" in the text, but if the content of the text is interpreted on its own terms, rather than in relation to a motif that is not actually present in it, there is no confusion here that I can see. *Orgain Denna Ríg* is a highly accomplished work, and there is much to be said for Michael O'Brien's view (1954, 39) that it "is one of the best told Old Irish tales that have been preserved."[8]

30

Sound and Sense in *Cath Almaine*

(2004)

Cath Almaine 'The Battle of Allen'[1] is a short tale devoted to a battle that was fought in 722 at the hill of Allen (in County Kildare) between Fergal son of Máel Dúin, king of the Uí Néill (and hence overlord of Leth Cuinn), and Murchad son of Bran, king of Leinster. Pádraig Ó Riain has argued that the tale was composed in the tenth century and that the original composition is reasonably well represented in the form of an entry for 11 December 722 in the *Fragmentary Annals of Ireland*, which survives only in a seventeenth-century manuscript, now preserved in Brussels.[2] The text of this manuscript, as edited by Ó Riain, is the basis of the present study.[3] There is also a later recension, represented in three manuscripts, which Ó Riain would date to approximately 1100.[4]

The occasion of the battle of Allen was an attempt to force the men of Leinster to pay the *bórama*, a perpetual fine that had supposedly been imposed upon Leinster by Túathal Techtmar, a prehistoric king of Tara.

The *bórama* is the subject of a tract⁵ which shows that the Leinstermen frequently resisted its payment and ends with the remittal of the tribute by Fínnachta, king of the Uí Néill, to the Leinstermen in the person of Mo-Ling. *Cath Almaine* is, in effect, a sequel to the remittal episode found in the *bórama* tract and elsewhere.⁶

The Leinstermen were greatly outnumbered in the battle of Allen, but they nevertheless vanquished the invaders. This achievement is listed among "the three wonders of the battle":

Uair is iat trí inganta in chatha-sa .i. Donn Bó do rochtain 'na bethaid conice a thech dar cenn mbréithre Coluim Chille, ocus géim in drúith, uí Maigleine, trí lá ocus trí aidche 'sin áer, ocus na naí mile do foruaisligud in míle ar fichit. (lines 167–71)

For the three wonders of this battle are that Donn Bó returned alive to his house because of Colum Cille's word; that the roar of the fool Úa Maigleine was in the air for three days and three nights; and that nine thousand men overcame twenty-one thousand.

The account given in *Cath Almaine* of the actual battle is very brief; appended to the saga, however, there is a long list of the Leth Cuinn kings who lost their lives in the battle. Much the greater part of the narrative is devoted to the events that precede the battle and to those that follow. And what is most striking about those events is that they are predominantly verbal or vocal acts. We have just seen that two of them—Colum Cille's promise (given on his behalf by his successor) and Úa Maigleine's roar—are included among the wonders of the battle. But important as these are, they each take a place in the remarkable concatenation of utterances which is presented in this short saga, and which includes pledge and promise, curse and prophecy, narrative before the battle and after it, the cry of victory given by the Leinstermen and one given by the war-goddess, the Fool's roar, sweet music heard by the slain warriors, and a piteous warrior-chant heard by the victors. I shall attempt in what follows to show how these utterances constitute the very fabric of the tale.⁷

The battle has its origin in a conflict regarding a promise and a pledge. We learn in the opening sentences that those who followed Fínnachta as kings of the Uí Néill—first Loingsech, then Congal, and finally Fergal—

attempted to exact the levy, but that the Leinstermen refused to pay it, for they trusted in the words of Moling who promised that it would never again be taken from them (*uair rotairisnigset i mbriathraib Mo-Ling rogell ná bertha uathu tré bithu in bórama ó Laignib*, lines 7–8). Fergal makes war on the Leinstermen because he is annoyed that they have not fulfilled their pledge to him (*Ba trom tra la Fergal sin .i. Laigin do nemchomall a ngellta fris*, lines 9–10). But Fergal is clearly in the wrong here. No pledge was made to Fergal personally; he is invoking a pledge that the Leinstermen had indeed made to one of his predecessors but from which a subsequent king had released them. It is no longer binding, and Fergal's attempt to exact the tribute by force of arms therefore lacks just cause.

This reading of the opening lines of *Cath Almaine* is supported by the *bórama* tract,[8] according to which Fínnachta grants the remission with great reluctance and intends it to last only until the following Monday (*Luan*). But Moling chooses to interpret *Luan* here as referring to the Day of Judgment, something which the Uí Néill cleric, Adomnán, duly brings to Fínnachta's attention. Adomnán advises Fínnachta that, unless he revokes the remission of the *bórama* that day, it can never be revoked. Fínnachta sets out in pursuit of Moling, but he does not quite manage to catch him. The remission therefore is permanent.

A version of this story in given in the *Fragmentary Annals*, s.a. 677.[9] In this version, Fínnachta grants Moling's request that the *bórama* be remitted for a day and a night. For Moling this is the same as remitting it forever, "for there is nothing in time save day and night." Fínnachta intends it to be for one day and one night only, but Adomnán informs him that he has in fact remitted it for all time. The deceptive bargain here is essentially the same as that used by Óengus son of the Dagdae to gain possession of Bruig na Bóinne, according to *De gabháil in tsída* 'On the Taking of the *Síd*'[10] and *Tochmarc Étaíne* 'The Wooing of Étaín.'[11] Thomas Charles-Edwards has said of the incident in *Tochmarc Étaíne* "that it involved taking . . . a strong view on the inviolability of a contractual promise."[12] The same can be said of Fínnachta's promise to Moling: what matters is the words he utters, not what he intends. Moreover, it is implicit in these episodes that where there is ambiguity in the wording of a promise, the interpretation which holds is that which favors the person to whom the promise is made. In the remittal episode, there is the further point that a promise made in perpetuity by a king is binding upon his successors.

As for the Leinstermen, the reason they refuse to pay the tribute to Fergal, according to *Cath Almaine*, is because they trust what Moling said to them. It should be noted that Moling did not say that no attempt would ever again be made to levy the tribute; what he promised was that the tribute would not actually be taken, implying that any attempt to do so would end in failure. If Moling is to be believed, Fergal's invasion of Leinster is doomed before it begins.

Fergal musters a great army in the northern half of Ireland. This takes a lot of time: the people evidently feel no great loyalty to Fergal, for the response each of them makes to Fergal's call to arms is, "If Donn Bó goes on the hosting I will go" (*"Dia tí Donn Bó arin sluagad ragat-sa,"* lines 15–16). Donn Bó, son of a widow of the Fir Rois, is altogether remarkable in his handsome appearance and fine build, in his valor and in his many accomplishments. We are told too that "he was best in the world at composing verses for pleasure and telling the chief tales" (*is uad bud ferr rann espa ocus ríg-scéla for doman,* lines 21–22). It is all summed up in a quatrain:

> Áille macaib Donn Bó báid,
> binne a laíde luaidit beoil,
> áine ócaib Inse Fáil,
> rotócaib táin trilse a threoir. (lines 24–27)

> Most beautiful of boys is fond Donn Bó;
> men speak of the sweetness of his lays;
> he is the most splendid of the youths of Inis Fáil;
> his lead brought out a host of tressed warriors.

Donn Bó's mother does not allow him to go with Fergal until the successor of Colum Cille gives a guarantee on his own behalf and on behalf of the saint that Donn Bó will return safely. When this has been done, Fergal sets out on his journey.

We seem now to have a paradox. If Moling's promise is to be redeemed, the Uí Néill will be routed. How then will Colum Cille honor his guarantee? We shall see that he does so miraculously, by having Donn Bó's severed head restored to his body.

Fergal sets out on his journey and is soon presented with a prophecy of failure. He is led astray (geographically), and his warriors misbehave themselves by stealing the only cow of a leper and burning his house. The leper curses them, saying that the vengeance that the Lord would take upon the Uí Néill would last forever (*Co n-érbart in clam comba dígal co bráth for Uíb Néill in dígal do-bérad in Coimdid for sin,* lines 39–40). Nobody has any compassion for the leper except Cú Brettan, son of the king of Fir Rois, and Cú Brettan in two quatrains prophesies defeat for Fergal, beginning, "I fear a battle bloody and red" (*"At-ágar cath forderg flann,"* line 48). These words are reminiscent of Fedelm's prophecy regarding the ill-fated expedition of Medb and Ailill in the *Táin,* but in the case of Fergal's invasion the curse and the prophecy are directly related to an un-Christian act on the part of his army. We are told that Cú Brettan did not regret his kindness, for he was the only one of the kings on Fergal's side to escape from the battle with his life.

On the eve of battle, Fergal invites Donn Bó, as the best entertainer in Ireland, to entertain the invaders. Donn Bó is out of sorts, however, and he declares himself unable to deploy any of his artistic skills on this particular night. This is an unhappy portent, though the sting may appear to be taken out of it when he promises to entertain Fergal the next day: "Wherever you may be tomorrow, and wherever I may be, I shall entertain you" (*"cipsí airm i rabai-si imbárach, ocus i mbeo-sa do-dén-sa airfited duit-si,"* lines 63–64). A rash undertaking, this might appear, in view of Moling's promise to the Leinstermen, the leper's curse on the Uí Néill, and Cú Brettan's prophecy of defeat.

Donn Bó says that the royal Fool, Úa Maigleine, should do the entertaining in his place, and the Fool does so with stories of the battles and contests of Leth Cuinn and the Leinstermen; significantly, the only one that is mentioned by name is the account of the destruction of Dinn Ríg, in which the Leinstermen killed an ancestor of the Uí Néill.[13] If the "entertainment" offered by the Fool was intended to cheer up the Uí Néill or to stiffen their resolve, it manifestly failed to do so: "And they did not sleep much that night, because of their great fear of the Leinstermen, and because the weather was so bad" (*níba mór cotalta do-rinned leo in aidche-sin la mét ecla leo Laigen ocus la méit na doininne,* lines 69–71).

Of the Leinstermen on the eve of battle, we are told only that they went to the Hill of Clane (*Cruachan Cláenta*), for they would not be defeated if they held council there,[14] and if they went to battle from there.

The battle, as I have said, is briefly sketched. Nine thousand Leinstermen face twenty-one thousand from Leth Cuinn. Brigit and Colum Cille, brooding presences, hover silently over the Leinstermen and the Uí Néill respectively. (In the later recension, Brigit plays an active role. Colum Cille is distracted when he sees her frightening the Uí Néill, and it is at the sight of her that they are defeated.)[15] In the end the Leinstermen triumph: they kill nine thousand men and a hundred kings. Nine of the invaders go mad. Fergal is slain—we are told that he does not fall until Donn Bó falls, and also that Fergal and his Fool, Úa Maigleine, are beheaded together.

Three great utterances mark the end of the battle. First, the Leinstermen raise a cry of triumph (*Rocuirset Laigin ilaig commaídme ann d[a]no*, lines 91–92). Mention of this is immediately followed by an account in verse of the battle; the first quatrain is as follows:

Deod laithe Almaine,
iar cosnam buair Bregmaine,
ro-lá badb bélderg birach
ilach im chenn Fergaile. (lines 94–97)

At the end of the day at Allen,
after the contest for the cattle of Brega,
red-mouthed sharp-tongued Badb
raised a cry of victory about the head of Fergal.

Here it is Badb, the war-goddess in the guise of a scald-crow, who cries in triumph. Badb, as *DIL* (s.v.) succinctly puts it, is "represented as stirring up conflict, foretelling slaughter and rejoicing over the slain." I shall suggest presently that her cry of triumph here is of crucial significance and shows her to be the true victor of this battle.

The third utterance is Úa Maigleine's roar:

Rogabad ann-sain in drúth, úa Maigleine, ocus do-ratad fair géim drúith do dénam ocus do-rigne. Ba már ocus ba binn in géim-sin, co mair "géim uí Maigleine" ó sin ille oc drúthaib Éirenn. Rogatad a chenn iar tain d'Ḟergal, ocus rogatad a chenn don drúth. Roboí mac alla géime in drúth 'sin áer co cenn trí lá ocus trí n-aidche. Is de as-berar "géim uí Maigleine oc tafann na fer 'sin mónaid." (lines 106–12)

Then the Fool Úa Maigleine was seized, and they made him give a Fool's roar, and he did so. That roar was great and it was melodious, so that from that time onwards the Fools of Ireland still have "Úa Maigleine's Roar." After that Fergal's head was struck off, and so was the Fool's head. The echo of the Fool's roar was in the air for three full days and nights. From this comes the saying "the roar of Úa Maigleine pursuing the men in the bog."

This roar, one of the three wonders of the battle, is devoid of narrative or even verbal content. It memorializes a battle that failed of its purpose, and one which must be accounted a monumental act of folly.

After the battle the Leinstermen celebrate and tell stories about their contests. Murchad, their king, asks that a token (*comartha*, line 136) be brought from the battlefield, offering a chariot worth four *cumals* and his horse and his battledress to the warrior who would do so. Ó Riain infers that "the Irish had tokens, or trophies, from the battlefield at their victory-feasts. More often than not, the token would have taken the form of a severed head, since the regard in which this was held is well attested."[16] It may be added that in the later recension Murchad specifically asks for a head.[17] We may also assume that the most highly prized head would be that of the defeated king. A warrior called Báethgalach sets out to do Murchad's bidding. When he approaches the spot where Fergal lies he hears a proclamation in the air overhead:

> Timarnad dúib ó ríg secht nime; dénaid airfited do bar tigerna innocht .i. d'Fergal mac Maíle-dúin, cia do-rochrabair sunn uile in bar n-áes dána etir cuislennchu ocus cornaire ocus cruittire; ná tairmescad airfhuath nó écomnart sib d'airfited innocht d'Fergal. (lines 140–44)

> The King of the seven heavens commands all of you artists, players of flutes and horns and harps, to entertain your lord Fergal son of Máel Dúin tonight, though you have fallen here; let not terror nor weakness prevent you from entertaining Fergal tonight.

On the night before the battle Fergal had demanded entertainment from Donn Bó; now Fergal is dead, and the command comes from heaven. Báethgalach hears "plaintive whistling and music, and then he hears in the tuft of rushes next to him a warrior-chant which is sweeter than any music" (*Co cuala iaram int óclach in cúisig ocus in ceol sírechtach, co cuala dna'sin tum luachra ba nesa dó in dord fiansa ba binne ceolaib*, lines 144–46). This sound has been produced by a head which speaks to Báethgalach, telling him: "I am the head of Donn Bó, and I was pledged last night to entertain the king tonight" (*"Mise cenn Duinn Bó," ar in cenn, "ocus naidm ronaidmed form irraír airfited in ríg innocht,"* lines 148–50).

The head of Donn Bó consents to be brought back to Murchad, provided it has Christ's guarantee that Báethgalach will take it back to its body again. Báethgalach promises to take it back, and so Donn Bó's head is brought to Murchad. It is placed on a pillar, and the assembled Leinstermen ask him to entertain them. He duly obliges, but what he provides is not calculated to sustain them in their celebratory mode: "His face was turned round then and his piteous warrior-chant rose on high, so that they were all lamenting and sorrowing" (*Impaigther a aiged dno, ocus at-racht a dord fiansa attruag ar aird, co mbátar uile oc caí ocus oc tuirse*, lines 163–64).

Báethgalach finally conveys the head to its body as he has promised, and he sets it on the neck. The Leinstermen are left without a trophy after all, as Donn Bó makes his way home to his mother's house.

Cath Almaine, like so many other early Irish texts, narrative and non-narrative alike, asserts the primacy of the pledged word as an instrument of public order. Had Fergal honored the solemn word of his predecessor as king, there would have been no carnage on the Hill of Allen on that December day in 722. Verbal and vocal acts of various kinds lend emotional depth to the saga, and they also encode much of its meaning. The central message of *Cath Almaine* has to do with the futility of warfare. The victors in this battle hear a piteous war-chant, which leaves them sorrowing and weeping. It is the vanquished who hear sweet music: but they, after all, are dead. The real victor is the war-goddess, the "red-mouthed sharp-tongued" scald-crow, who "raised a cry of victory about the head of Fergal." What *Cath Almaine* shows us is that war has no victor but war itself.

THE FENIAN CYCLE

31

Tóraíocht Dhiarmada agus Ghráinne

(1995)

Is é *Tóraíocht Dhiarmada agus Ghráinne* an scéal Fiannaíochta is mó atá ar eolas ag an bpobal, agus is mó, b'fhéidir, go dtugtar taitneamh dó. Is fada siar a théann préamhacha an scéil: "the tradition of Diarmaid and Grainne descends in an unbroken line from the ninth century to the present day," adeir Gertrude Schoepperle (1913, 395). Más ea, is sa Nua-Ghaeilge atá an leagan is luaithe dá bhfuil againn de *Thóraíocht Dhiarmada agus Ghráinne*. Tá an chóip is sine le fáil i láimhscríbhinn 24 P 9 de chuid Acadamh Ríoga na hÉireann, láimhscríbhinn a dhein an scríobhaí clúiteach Dáibhí Ó Duibhgeannáin sa bhliain 1651. Deir Gerard Murphy (1955b, 14) i dtaobh an leagain seo gur beag má tá sé níos sine de mhórán ná láimhscríbhinn Uí Dhuibhgeannáin féin. Deineadh cuid mhaith cóipeanna den *Tóraíocht* ina dhiaidh sin—maireann dathad cóipeanna ar a laghad dá ndeineadh idir na blianta 1718 agus 1850 (Ní Shéaghdha 1967, xiv). D'fhoilsigh an Ossianic

Society eagrán Standish Hayes O'Grady den *Tóraíocht* sa bhliain 1855: bhain O'Grady leas as dhá láimhscríbhinn a scríobhadh in 1780 agus in 1842–43 faoi seach (O'Grady 1857, 30). Ní fios cad a thuit amach don chéad cheann acu san: maidir leis an dara ceann, tá láimhscríbhinn den *Tóraíocht* againn ón scríobhaí chéanna, ach is dealraitheach nach é sin an ceann gur bhain O'Grady leas as (Ní Shéaghdha 1967, xv). Sa bhliain 1967 d'fhoilsigh Cumann na Scríbheann nGaedhilge eagrán Nessa Ní Shéaghdha den *Tóraíocht*; tá sé bunaithe ar láimhscríbhinn Uí Dhuibhgeannáin, ach baineadh leas nuair ba ghá as cúig láimhscríbhinní eile. Is mór an dul chun cinn an t-eagrán so ar eagrán O'Grady, ach bhí Nessa cineálta, mar ba dhual di, agus í ag cur síos ar shaothar an cheannródaí: "The need for a new edition, based on manuscript material now available, has been felt for a long time, and although it is possible to improve on O'Grady's text, owing to his vagueness in the discussion of sources, nevertheless his English rendering of the story will always remain, for one in particular, a delight to read" (Ní Shéaghdha 1967, ix).

Mhair scéal Dhiarmada agus Ghráinne ar bhéalaibh na ndaoine, agus tá na leaganacha béil pléite go mion ag Ní Shéaghdha (1967, xviii–xxvi) agus Bruford (1969, 106–9). Deir Bruford (1969, 106): "Stories about Diarmaid and Gráinne are found in oral tradition, localized in different parts of Ireland and Scotland: but their relationship to the romance *Tóraidheacht Dhiarmada agus Ghráinne* is not always easy to determine." Dúirt Flower (1926, 387) i dtaobh na *Tóraíochta* gur dóichí gur Muimhneach a chum é: "The romantic tale is apparently a late medieval development of the theme, possibly based on the lost early tale and composed, if the topography may be used in evidence, in Munster." Dhein Bruford (1969, 106) Ciarraíoch de Mhuimhneach Flower, agus dúirt sé: "Though the author [of the *Tóraíocht*] may have been a Kerryman (Flower 1926, 387) the story, like the Ulster Cycle tales, seems to have been less popular in Kerry than in other areas: it may not be too much to suggest that most Kerry storytellers preferred stories more like international *märchen* and avoided those with a tragic flavour."

Dhein na scéalaithe, agus an pobal, a gcuid féin de scéal Dhiarmada agus Ghráinne:

> Local traditions about Diarmaid and Gráinne seem to have extended throughout the West of Scotland and Ireland from Cape Wrath to Cape Clear. Diarmaid's death is associated as in the literary tradition with

Beann Gulban, Benbulben in Co. Sligo, but also with a Scottish mountain of the same name, Ben Gulabin in Perthshire. Other oral accounts place it on Ben Loyal in Sutherland (S1), Benmore (Skye? *LNF:* 164), Ben Nevis (A3), Mangerton Mountain in Kerry (C2), in Lismore (A6) or at Kanturk in Co. Cork (C1), whose name *Ceann Tuirc,* "Boar's Head," suggests a connection with the boar which killed Diarmaid. The lovers' flight is also part of universal tradition: any dolmen in Ireland is liable to be called the bed of Diarmaid and Gráinne ... and oral versions of the romance locate the wood where they first hid in various parts of central Ireland. ... C4 and 5 [dhá leagan as Corcaigh] largely consist of onomastic anecdotes telling how four mountains in Co. Cork were named from incidents on the lovers' flight, and most other versions bring in place-names in the storyteller's own area. (Bruford 1969, 106)[1]

Is léir mar sin gur chuaigh scéal Dhiarmada agus Ghráinne i bhfeidhm go mór ar phobal na hÉireann agus iarthair Alban.

Cé gur i *dTóraíocht* na Nua-Ghaeilge is túisce atá teacht againn ar insint leanúnach ar scéal Dhiarmada agus Ghráinne, chonaiceamar romhainn gur mhaígh Schoepperle gur shín traidisiún na beirte ón naoú céad go dtí an lá atá inniu ann, agus gur thagair Flower do "the lost early tale." Tá an chaint sin bunaithe ar na liostaí atá tagaithe anuas chugainn de scéalta na Gaeilge sna meán-aoiseanna, agus ar ranna agus blúirí scéalaíochta atá ar marthain ón luath-ré agus a bhaineann, a bheag nó a mhór, le scéal Dhiarmada agus Ghráinne.

Dhá phríomh-liosta atá againn de scéalta na Gaeilge sna meán-aoiseanna (Mac Cana 1980), agus tugtar A agus B orthu faoi seach. Tá aicmí insna liostaí seo atá bunaithe ar theidil na scéalta, ar nós *Tána* (*Táin Bó Cúailnge,* etc.), *Togla* (*Togail Bruidne Da Derga,* etc.), *Tochmarca* (*Tochmarc Étaíne,* etc.). Áirítear *Aitheda* 'Elopements' i measc na n-aicmí seo: *Aithed* (Nua-Ghaeilge *Aitheadh*) an t-ainmneach uathu. Luaitear *Aithed Gráinne le Diarmait* san dá liosta: *Aithed Grainne re Diarmait* atá i liosta A, agus *Aithi Graine ingine Corbmaic la Diarmait ua nDuibne* i liosta B (Mac Cana 1980, 86), rud nach ionann agus a rá, i gcás *Aithed Gráinne le Diarmait,* go raibh sé ar aon dul leis an *Tóraíocht.* D'fhonn tuairim éigin fháil faoina raibh á insint mar gheall ar Dhiarmaid agus Gráinne sular cumadh an *Tóraíocht,* ní foláir dúinn breathnú ar na téacsanna luatha úd go bhfuil baint acu leis an lánúin.

Tá dhá rann fháin a mhaireann neamhspleách ar a chéile san tráchtaireacht a cuireadh le h*Amra Choluim Chille* san aonú céad déag. I gceann amháin acu labhrann Gráinne iníon Chormaic le Fionn:

> Fil duine
>   frismbad buide lemm díuterc,
> día tibrinn in mbith mbuide,
>   huile, huile, cid díupert.
>   (Murphy 1956, 160; cf. Stokes 1899, 156)

Is é tá á rá ansan aici ná go bhfuil duine ann go mba mhaith léi bheith ag féachaint air, agus go dtabharfadh sí an domhan uile air, dá olcas é sin mar mhargadh. Tugtar an rann so san tráchtaireacht ar an *Amra* mar dheismireacht ar úsáid an fhocail *díuterc*. Cuireann Murphy (1956, 160) an rann seo i leith an naoú nó an deichiú céad; deir sé: "the occurrence of the old words *díuterc, díupert*, and the citation of the quatrain in the oldest manuscripts of the commentary on the *Amra* in justification of the obsolete *díutercc* (*díuderc*), suggest that the quatrain is not later than the tenth century" (1956, 237). Deir sé freisin: "this quatrain . . . seems to be the earliest reference extant to Gráinne's love for Díarmait" (1956, 236).

San darna rann labhrann Diarmaid:

> Is maith do chuit, a Ghráinne,
>   is ferr duit inda ríge
> sercoll na cailech feda
>   la banna meda míne.
>   (Stokes 1899, 264)

Maíonn Diarmaid sa rann san gur maith an bia agus an deoch atá ag Gráinne: gur fearr di ná ríogacht feoil na gcreabhar agus an mheá mhín. Ní féidir a dhéanamh amach an bhfuil an rann so ar aon aois le rann Dhiarmada. Níl le rá ach nach déanaí é ná an t-aonú céad déag.

Tá dán san Leabhar Laighneach (*LL*, l. 58889) dar tús "Úar in lathe do Lum Laine." Is é tá ann ná agallamh idir fear agus bean, a thugann "Lom Laine" agus "Tethna" ar a chéile. Iníon is ea Tethna le mac mhic Chuinn, agus insan réamhrá a chuir Máirín O Daly (1968) lena heagrán den dán dúirt sí an méid seo leanas ina thaobh: "the circumstances indicated are so reminiscent of the story of Gráinne, not the Tóraigecht but the earlier and less romantic version in *ZCP* i 458, that I am inclined to regard 'Tethna' and 'Lom Laine' (lit. 'the bare one of L.') as pseudonyms for Gráinne and Díarmait" (O Daly 1968, 99). Seo iad na "circumstances" atá i gceist aici: "From our poem we may infer that 'Tethna' and 'Lom Laine' are in love but that there is some obstacle to their union, probably that 'Tethna' is married already, and that any relationship between them is likely to lead to the death of both. It also appears that Lom Laine is associated with Almu" (O Daly 1968, 100). Ag tagairt do aois an dáin, deir an t-eagarthóir, "I see no reason for placing it later than the ninth century" (O Daly 1968, 101).

Nuair a luaigh O Daly "the earlier and less romantic version," is ag tagairt a bhí sí do théacs ghairid atá i *Leabhar Leacáin*, agus a d'fhoilsigh Kuno Meyer (1897) faoin teideal "Finn and Gráinne." Níl na húdair ar aon fhocal maidir le haois an phíosa seo: mheas Murphy (1953, lix) gur bhain sé leis an naoú nó leis an deichiú céad. San leagan seo lorg Fionn cleamhnas le Gráinne. Dúirt sise ná glacfadh sí leis muna dtabharfadh sé dhá ainmhí fhiáine do gach saghas a bhí in Éirinn chun na Teamhrach. Le cabhair Chaoilte Chosluaith dhein Fionn an méid sin, agus tugadh Gráinne dó. Ach dob fhuath le Gráinne Fionn sa tslí gur bhuail galar í. Mhínigh Gráinne an scéal dá hathair, Cormac mac Airt. Chuala Fionn an chaint sin uaithi, agus thuig sé go raibh grá ag a bhean air. Dúirt sé gur mhithid dóibh scarúint.

Luaitear *Tochmarc Ailbe* (Thurneysen 1920) san dá liosta, A agus B, rud a chiallódh, mar a chonaiceamar, go raibh sé á insint san deichiú céad. Mheas Meyer (1910, xiv) gur san chéad chéanna san a cumadh an leagan atá ar marthain againn agus bhí Thurneysen sásta go mb'fhéidir go raibh an ceart aige. Do réir an scéil seo, thuit amach idir Fionn agus Cormac mac Airt toisc gur thug Gráinne fuath do Fhionn agus go raibh sí i ngrá le Diarmaid. Deineadh réiteach eatarthu agus scar Fionn agus Gráinne óna chéile go síochánta. Ina dhiaidh sin phós Fionn Ailbhe, an iníon ab óige a bhí ag Cormac.

Scéal a bhaineann leis an aonú céad déag is ea *Uath Beinne Étair* (Ní Shéaghdha 1967, 130). Luaitear *aithed* san abairt tosaigh: *Fechtus dia raibe Diarmait mac Duinn Í Duibne in uaim Benne Étair iar mbreith Gráinne ingine Cormaic ar aithed ó Fhind*, "Once Diarmait, son of Donn, grandson of Duibne, was in the cave of the Hill of Howth after carrying off Gráinne, daughter of Cormac[,] in elopement from Finn" (Ní Shéaghdha 1967, 130; normalú déanta agam ar an litriú). Bhí cailleach ag faire thar ceann

Dhiarmada agus Ghráinne. Tháinig Fionn chuici. Theastaigh uaidh go loicfeadh sí ar Dhiarmaid agus Ghráinne, rud a bhí sí sásta a dhéanamh mar go ndúirt Fionn léi go mba mhaith leis í a phósadh. D'aithin Gráinne cad a bhí beartaithe ag an gcailligh agus thug sí rabhadh do Dhiarmaid. Tháinig Aonghus an Bhrogha i gcabhair ar an lánúin, agus d'éirigh leo teacht slán ón ghátar.

Níl aon trácht insna téacsanna sin romhainn ar bhás Dhiarmada. Tá dhá thagairt in *Acallam na Senórach* (a cumadh thart ar an mbliain 1200) don mhuc dhraíochta a mharbhaigh Diarmaid: *Ocus luidhset as sin rompo co Leacht na Muice (co Beind nGulban) áit ar mharbh an mhuc Diarmait ó Duibhne, 7 go mullach na tulcha áit i tá Leabaidh Dhiarmada* (Stokes 1900, 43); *7 tangadur rompo ... do Lighi an Fheindida, in bail ar', marb in mucc doilfi draídechta Diarmait húa Duibne* (Stokes 1900, 191).

Tá trácht ar an mhuc agus ar bhás Dhiarmada i ndán dar tús *Éuchtach inghen Diarmatta* i *nDuanaire Finn* (Mac Neill 1908, 45–47), a cumadh, dar le Murphy (1953, 40) idir 1250 agus 1400.

Is é an léamh seo leanas a dheineann Ní Shéaghdha (1967, xiii) ar fhianaise na dtéacsanna san:

> When the *Aithed* (the probable old source) was re-cast in the Early Modern period and given its new title, *Tóruigheacht Dhiarmada agus Ghráinne*, it still retained the actual framework of the older tale, but some minor differences had crept in. Thus: (a) in the older tale Gráinne was married to Finn when she eloped with Diarmaid, but she was not married to him in the *Tóruigheacht*; (b) from the story of *Tochmarc Ailbe* we learn that because of Gráinne's hatred for Finn and her love for Diarmaid, Finn thought it best for them to part; but it was against Finn's wishes that Gráinne parted from him in the *Tóruigheacht*; (c) it was mainly in the south of Ireland that Diarmaid and Gráinne spent their time, while being pursued in the *Tóruigheacht*; the only indication we have of their whereabouts in flight in the older tale is in the east of the country, a district not included in the lovers' itinerary in our Early Modern version of the tale.

Tabharfar fé ndeara ná fuil aon trácht sa mhéid sin ar bhás Dhiarmada, eachtra a bhaineann le creatlach na *Tóraíochta*, ach nach eol dúinn ar bhain sí leis an *Aitheadh*. Shamhlaigh Murphy (1953, xxxvi) "the elopement;

Fionn's pursuit of the lovers; the death of Diarmait caused by a pig" le creatlach na *Tóraíochta* agus dúirt sé go raibh eolas maith air sin ó thús an tríú céad déag. A fhianaise san dar leis, ar *Acallam na Senórach*, ar an dán úd, *Éuchtach inghen Diarmatta*, i *nDuanaire Finn*, agus ar na tagairtí don scéal atá i ndánta Ghearóid Iarla (obit 1398). Maidir leis an *Acallam*, chonaiceamar go luaitear bás Dhiarmada ann, ach nach gceanglaítear annsan é le scéal an éalaithe. Is in *Éuchtach inghen Diarmatta* is túisce a deintear an ceangal san, agus is ann a fhaighimid don chéad uair creatlach an scéil fé mar atá sé againn sa *Tóraíocht*. Tugadh Gráinne, "lennán Diarmada déidghil" mar mhnaoi d'Fhionn, ach d'éalaigh sí uaidh i ngan fhios le Diarmaid. Chaith Diarmaid agus Gráinne seacht mbliana "i n-imlibh Banbha" agus Fionn sa tóir orthu, agus níor éirigh leis iad a mharú. Dhein Fionn síocháin go cealgach le Diarmaid agus is dá dheasca san a maraíodh Diarmaid. Ghoin Fionn Gulban, muc neimhe a bhí i mBeann Ghulban, agus chuir sé Diarmaid á fhiadhach, sa tslí gur maraíodh é. (Baineann an chuid eile den dán leis an dtréan-iarracht a dhein iníon Dhiarmada díoltas a bhaint amach.)

Maidir le Gearóid Iarla, is léir ar na tagairtí iomadúla atá ina shaothar do Dhiarmaid agus Gráinne go raibh eolas aige ar scéal faoin lánúin a bhí cosúil leis an *dTóraíocht*. Mar adeir Ní Shéaghdha (1967, xiii) i taobh leagain Ghearóid: "(a) Gráinne is always spoken of as the daughter of Cormac . . . and not as the wife of Finn; (b) we are given to understand that it was against Finn's wishes that Gráinne parted from him . . . ; (c) the places listed where Diarmaid and Gráinne lived during their flight from Finn are in the south. . . ." Tá na nithe sin ar fad ag freagairt do na "minor differences" úd a mheas Ní Shéaghdha a bheith idir an *Aithed* agus an *Tóraíocht*; dá chomhartha san deir sí (1967, xiii), "[Gearóid Iarla] shares the points of difference from the older tale with the *Tóruigheacht*."

Is fiú féachaint orthu so ina gceann is ina gceann. Déarfainn, i gcomhthéacs an scéil seo, gur miondifríocht í an chéad cheann, is é sin go bhfuil Fionn agus Gráinne pósta sna téacsanna luatha agus gur cleamhnas atá eatarthu san *Tóraíocht*. Ach is difríocht mhór í an dara ceann. Do réir "Finn and Gráinne" agus *Tochmarc Ailbe*, scarann Fionn agus Gráinne go síochanta. Is mór idir é sin agus leagan na *Tóraíochta*. Is fíor go ndeintear síocháin ansan leis idir Fionn agus Diarmaid, tar éis go dteipeann ar Fhionn breith ar an lánúin, ach is síocháin chealgach í. Maitheann Cormac mac Airt agus Fionn do Dhiarmaid *a ndearna sé orra an feadh do bhí sé fá choill*, "all he had done to them while he had been outlawed" (l. 1378). Tá sé le tabhairt fé ndeara ná fuil sé ráite anseo gur thug Fionn maithiúnas do Dhiarmaid as Gráinne a thógaint uaidh; agus d'agair sé san air in am agus i dtráth.

Is é an cúrsa a ghaibh an lánúin agus iad ar a dteicheadh an tríú "miondifríocht" a mheas Ní Shéaghdha a bheith idir an *Aithed* agus an *Tóraíocht*. Ní théann an lánúin go Beann Éadair sa *Tóraíocht*; tá sé le tuiscint as caint Ní Shéaghdha gur thugadar turas ar an áit sin san *Aithed*. Tá sé sin bunaithe, gan amhras, ar fhianaise *Uath Beinne Étair*: ar théacs den scéal san a bheith tagaithe anuas chugainn ón aonú céad déag, agus ar *aithed* a bheith luaite ina thosach. Bhí Murphy níos cáiréisí insan léamh a dhein sé ar an bhfianaise seo. Dúirt sé (1953, xxxvi), "that the story, at least in the general form of Gráinne's elopement with Diarmaid and Fionn's pursuit of the lovers, was accepted as literary matter by the learned of the 10th and 11th centuries is proved by fragments of it and references to it contained in the early literature." Is í fianaise a thugann sé mar bhunús leis an ráiteas san ná an *Aithed* a bheith luaite insna liostaí, agus *Tochmarc Ailbe* agus *Uath Beinne Étair* a bheith tagtha anuas chugainn. Is ag tagairt don dá scéal san atá sé nuair a labhrann sé ar "fragments of it," is é sin, "[of] the story at least in the general form of Gráinne's elopement with Diarmaid and Fionn's pursuit of the lovers." Ní hionann san agus a rá gur giotaí iad as an sean-*Aithed*, mar go bhfuil idirdhealú le déanamh idir *scéal* agus *insint*. Tá dhá chiall, cuirim i gcás, leis an bhfocal *Táin*: (1) eachtra nó sraith eachtraí a thuit amach nó a samhlaíodh, agus (2) saothar liteartha ina bhfuil insint ar an dtarlúint— sraith leanúnach focal in ord ar leith. Tá léiriú air sin le fáil sa dán *Éuchtach inghen Diarmatta*, áit a bhfaighimid an rann seo (Mac Neill 1908, 46):

> Ré trí lá go lánoídhche
>   nochar mhó díth na tána:
> ní tig lucht a sáraighthe
>   dia n-éis go laithe mbrátha.

> For three days and full nights the spoiling of the *Táin* had not been greater: none to surpass them come after them until doomsday.

Comparáid atá á déanamh idir trodaíocht Éuchtaigh agus *na tarlúinti* go bhfuil cur síos orthu insan saothar (nó, ba chirte a rá, insna saothair) ara dtugtar *Táin Bó Cúailnge*.

Tá *Aithed* ionchurtha le *Táin* sa mhéid sin. Luaitear *Aithed*, mar a chonaiceamar cheana, san chéad abairt in *Uath Beinne Étair: Fechtus dia raibe Diarmait mac Duinn í Duibne in uaim Beinne Étair iar mbreith Gráinne ingine Cormaic ar aithed ó Fhinn*, "Once Diarmait, son of Donn, grandson of Duibne, was in the cave of the Hill of Howth after carrying off Gráinne, daughter of Cormac[,] in elopement from Finn." Ní leor an fhoclaíocht so mar chomhartha go raibh an eachtra áirithe seo ina cuid de shaothar a fhreagródh sa deichiú ná san aonú céad déag don teideal *Aithed Gráinne le Diarmait*. Tugann na téacsanna luatha éachtaint dúinn ar na scéalta luatha a bhíodh á n-insint faoi Dhiarmaid agus Gráinne, ach, is é atá le rá sa deireadh faoin "lost *aithed*" ná go bhfuil sé caillte.

Ar leibhéal na dtarlúintí, áfach, tá fianaise ann go mb'fhéidir go raibh éaló Dhiarmada agus Ghráinne ceangailte le hoidheadh Dhiarmada ón tús. Is é atá i gceist agam ná na cosúlachtaí suaithinseacha atá ann idir scéal Dhiarmada agus Ghráinne agus scéal Adonis agus Aphrodite. Dúirt O'Grady: "It is singular that Diarmaid na m-ban should have met his death by the same beast that slew Adonis, whom he may be said to have represented in Irish legend" (*apud* Murphy 1953, xxxvi). Léirigh A. H. Krappe go bhfuil na scéalta seo an-chosúil le chéile; seo achoimriú Rees and Rees (1961, 295) ar a raibh le rá aige:

> Aphrodite, goddess of love and of nature in bloom, fell in love with the beautiful Adonis, as Gráinne did with Diarmaid, and he became her paramour, though in his case as in Diarmaid's there is a different tradition which says that he was innocent of actual congress with her. Aphrodite was the wife of Ares, the god of war, as Gráinne was the wife of the *fian* chief. Suspecting an improper relationship between Adonis and his wife, Ares sent a wild boar, or himself assumed the shape of a wild boar, which fatally wounded Adonis while he was hunting. Similarly Finn was believed to have arranged the boar-hunt to allure Diarmaid to his death at the year's end. Both Adonis and Diarmaid went hunting against his mistress's will. There is a general lament for both. Diarmaid, borne away on Mac Óc's gilded bier, recalls the annual ritual in which the image of the dead Adonis was borne away, mourned by women bitterly wailing, while the couches on which images of the god and goddess were shown may be compared with the "Beds of Diarmaid and Gráinne."

D'fhéadfaí na cosúlachtaí seo a mhíniú ar bhealaí éagsúla: (i) eascraíonn an dá scéal ón aon-fhoinse bhunaidh amháin; (ii) tá scéal Dhiarmada agus Ghráinne bunaithe ar scéal Adonis agus Aphrodite; (iii) tá siad neamhspleách ar a chéile. Is deacair liom a mheas go bhfuil na scéalta neamhspleách ar fad ar a chéile, ach ní fheicim conas a dhéanfaimis rogha idir an dá mhíniú eile. Ní gá a rá gur cnámh spairne í i measc cuid de scoláirí na Gaeilge an coibhneas atá sa luath-litríocht idir an dúchas agus anáil na hiasachta.

Tá sé ráite leis (R. A. Breatnach 1959, 150) go bhfuil bunús miotasach leis an naimhdeas idir Fionn agus Diarmaid: "the *Pursuit of Diarmaid and Gráinne* may be interpreted as a romanticized development of the myth of the rivalry of two pagan divinities"; agus gur pearsa miotasach í Gráinne chomh maith: "although there is little trace of her true nature in the literary *Pursuit*, I think Gráinne really is the ugly goddess: the loathsome crone, who becomes a radiantly beautiful maiden when she marries the sacred king in many Irish stories." Is léir ná fuil sé á mhaíomh ag Breatnach go bhfuil mórán dá rian so ar fad ar an *dTóraíocht* atá againn.

Dar le Myles Dillon (1948, 42–43), "the story of Gráinne is a variant of the story of Deirdre, the tragedy of a young girl betrothed to an old man and of the conflict between passion and duty on the part of her lover. In both cases death is the price of love." Is fíor go dtugtar tús áite san *Tóraíocht* do théama thraigéideach an ghrá, ach ina dhiaidh sin is é scéal Dhiarmada a insítear dúinn tríd síos: tá cur síos sa *Tóraíocht* ar óige Dhiarmada, ar a chuid eachtraí sa bhfiann, ar an gcaoi inar éalaigh sé le Gráinne, agus ar a bhás. Is é tá á mhaíomh agam ná go bhfuil scéal Dhiarmada agus Ghráinne neadaithe laistigh do bheathaisnéis Dhiarmada. Maidir le habhar na *Tóraíochta*, is féidir é roinnt ina dhá chuid:

(1) Tochmharc Ghráinne agus Aitheadh Ghráinne le Diarmaid.
(2) (Óige Dhiarmada, a ghníomhartha sa bhfiann agus) Oidheadh Dhiarmada.

Tochmharc atá san chéad chuid den *Tóraíocht*. Bhí Fionn *gan mhnaoi gan bheanchéile* (l. 8) agus moladh dó Gráinne iníon Chormaic mhic Airt a lorg mar mhnaoi. Ar eagla go bhfaigheadh sé *éara tochmoirc* 'a refusal of [his] suit' (l. 32), chuir sé teachtairí chuig Cormac agus Gráinne i dTeamhair. Thoilíodar san an cleamhnas a dhéanamh, agus tugadh cuireadh d'Fhionn agus don bhfiann go Teamhair d'fhonn an cleamhnas a cheiliúradh. Bhí Gráinne i ngrá cheana féin le Diarmaid, áfach, ón uair go bhfaca sí éacht aige á dhéanamh ar pháirc na hiomána: *"do chuirius rinn mo ruisg 7 mo radhairc ionnad-sa an lá sin, 7 ní thugas an grádh sin d'aoinneach eile ó sin i leith"* (ll. 186–88), adúirt sí leis, agus í ag míniú dó canathaobh gur chuir sí fé gheasa é éaló léi. Is de dheasca na ngeasa san a d'imigh Diarmaid ina teannta. Ní chuirfidh mé síos anseo ar na heachtraí a tharla don lánúin agus iad ar a dteitheadh. Ach ní miste aird a tharraingt ar an gcaoi ina labhrann an scéalaí leis an léitheoir:

> Bíodh a fhios agad, a léaghthóir, gur choimeád Diarmaid é féin fós gan chionntughadh ná cumusg lé Gráinne, 7 gur fháguibh bior d'fheóil bhruite gan aoin-ghreim do bhuain as a nDoire Dhá Bhaoth mar chomhartha d'Fhion agus d'Fhiannaibh Éirionn nár chionntaigh sé féin lé Gráinne, 7 fós gur fháguibh an dara feacht bradán ar bhruach na Leamhna bruite mar an ccéadna. Gurab uime sin do bhrosdaigh Fionn iona dhiaigh. Acht tráchtamaoid ar an ní ccéadna arís. (ll. 528–35; níl an giota seo i láimhscríbhinn Uí Dhuibhgeannáin, feic Ní Shéaghdha 1967, 110)

Ag tagairt atá sé ansan don eachtra (ll. 781–94) inar léim steancán uisce ar chois Ghráinne: dúirt sise le Diarmaid go raibh an t-uisce níos calma ná é, agus d'fhreagair seisean ná fuilngeodh sé cáineadh uaithi feasta, agus *as ann sin do-roinne Diarmaid déad-sholuis Ó Duibhne bean do Ghráinne .i. inghion rígh Éirionn, ar ttús*.

Tháinig deireadh leis an dtóraíocht nuair a d'éalaigh Diarmaid agus Gráinne go dtí Brugh na Bóinne. Dhein Aonghus an Bhrogha síocháin idir Fionn agus Diarmaid, agus chuaigh Diarmaid agus Gráinne chun cónaithe i gCéis Choruinn, toisc a fhaid a bhí san ó Chormac agus ó Fhionn. Chaitheadar sé bliana déag ansan go socair sásta, agus rugadh seisear clainne dóibh. Ansan mheas Gráinne fleadh a chur ar bun do Chormac agus d'Fhionn, agus chaith bliain á hullmhú. Ag deireadh na bliana agus é ina chodladh, chuala Diarmaid guth gadhair. D'impigh Gráinne air gan bacaint leis, ach an mhaidin dar gcionn chuaigh sé i dtreo an ghadhair. Shrois sé mullach Bheinne Gulban. Bhí Fionn roimis agus d'inis sé dó go raibh an fhiann ag teitheadh roimh thorc na Beinne. Dúirt Diarmaid nach n-imeodh sé. Is ansan a dúirt Fionn gur de gheasa Dhiarmada sealg mhuice a dhéanamh (ll. 1448–49), rud nárbh eol do Dhiarmaid go dtí sin. D'inis Fionn dó conas mar a cuireadh fé na geasa sin é (ll. 1451–1522). Mharbhaigh Donn, athair Dhiarmada, mac an reachtaire i mBrugh na Bóinne. Thairg Fionn éraic (cúiteamh) don reachtaire ach níor ghlac sé leis. Dhein sé *muc mhaol-dóite gan chluais gan iurball* dá mhac, agus dúirt, "*cuirim-se fá gheasaibh thú gurab ionann saoghal duit 7 do Dhiarmaid Ó Duibhne 7 gurab lat thuitfeas fá dheireadh*" (ll. 1516f.). Ghaibh an mhuc an doras amach, ach nuair a chuala Aonghus na geasa san chuir sé Diarmaid fé gheasa gan sealg mhuice a dhéanamh go brách.

Dúirt Fionn le Diarmaid gurbh é siúd torc Beinne Gulban agus nár chóir dó fanúint leis. Is é freagra a thug Diarmaid air: "*Do-bheirim-se mo bhriathar gurab dom mharbhadh-sa do chumais an tsealg so, a Fhinn, 7 más ann atá a ndán damh-sa bás d'fhagháil ni ffuil feidhm agum a sheachna*" (ll. 1529–31). Chuaigh Diarmaid i ngleic leis an dtorc, agus sa deireadh ghoin an torc Diarmaid agus mharbhaigh seisean an torc. Bhí Diarmaid ag saothrú an bháis nuair a tháinig Fionn agus na Fianna chuige. D'iarr Diarmaid ar Fhionn deoch uisce a thabhairt dó mar íocshláinte, ach dúirt Fionn nach raibh sé tuillte aige. Chuir Diarmaid i gcuimhne dhó an t-éacht a dhein sé tar a cheann i dtigh an Deirg mhic Dionnarthaig (ll. 1582–97). Níor leor san d'Fhionn: "*Is olc do thuillis uaim-si deoch do thabhairt duit ná aon-ní maitheasa do dhénamh dhuit an oidhche tángais leom go Teamhraigh 7 ruguis Gráinne leat uaim a Teamhraigh a bhfiaghnuisi bhfear nÉreann, 7 gurab tú féin dob fhear coimhéada agum-sa an oidhche sin a tTeamhraigh*" (ll. 1598–1603). Ansan chuir Diarmaid i gcuimhne dhó an t-éacht a dhein sé d'Fhionn i mBruidhean Chaorthainn (ll. 1606–51). Ach fós féin ní raibh Fionn toilteanach an t-uisce a fháil dó, agus fuair Diarmaid bás dá cheal.

Is mar scéalta laistigh a insítear na heachtraí a bhaineann le hóige Dhiarmada—scéal na muice dóite—agus lena thréimhse sa bhfiann—éachtanna i dtig an Deirg mhic Dionnarthaig agus i mBruidhean Chaorthainn. Tosnaíonn Oidheadh Dhiarmada sa *Tóraíocht* nuair a chinneann Gráinne ar fhleadh a sholáthar do Chormac agus do Fhionn. Is é ord na dtarlúintí, seachas ord na hinste, a bhí á leanúint agam thuas nuair a dheineas cur síos ar ábhar an dara cuid den scéal—(Óige Dhiarmada, a ghníomhartha sa bhfiann agus) Oidheadh Dhiarmada. Nuair a fhéachaimid ar ord na dtarlúintí san *Tóraíocht* ina iomláine, seo mar a chímid beatha Dhiarmada: a óige; a chuid éachtaí sa bhfiann; éalú Dhiarmada agus Ghráinne; eachtraí agus cleasanna Dhiarmada agus é *fá choill*; a bhás; é á chaoineadh agus á thabhairt go Brugh na Bóinne ag Aonghus an Bhrogha.

31. Tóraíocht Dhiarmada agus Ghráinne

Tá ceangal idir éalú Dhiarmada le Gráinne agus scéal a bháis sa mhéid ná tagann Fionn i gcabhair ar Dhiarmaid toisc go dteastaíonn uaidh an t-éalú a agairt air. Sa chás so, mar a dúirt Dillon, "death is the price of love." I gcomhthéacs bheathaisnéisiúil na *Tóraíochta*, áfach, is faide siar ina shaol a thosnaigh traigéide Dhiarmada: is uacht athar í bás Dhiarmada.

Cé go dtugtar tús áite sa *Tóraíocht*, mar adúrt, do scéal Dhiarmada agus Ghráinne, tá dhá phearsa sa scéal go bhfuil dlúthbhaint acu le Diarmaid ó thús deireadh. Aonghus agus Fionn atá i gceist agam. Dob é Aonghus athair altrama Dhiarmada (ll. 1448–49), agus bhí *cion mór* ag Aonghus air (l. 1477). Dob é Aonghus leis a chuir Diarmaid fé gheasa *gan sealg mhuice do dhéanamh go brách* (l. 1520). Nuair a d'inis Fionn dó mar gheall ar na geasa san ar Bheann Ghulban, ní raibh Diarmaid sásta gníomhú dá réir, cé go ndúirt sé ina dhiaidh sin, "ní chaillfinn-si mo gheasa ar ór na cruinne" (ll. 1605–6). Ag tagairt a bhí sé an uair sin do gheasa a chuir Gráinne air. Is í íoróin an scéil ná go bhfuil sé sásta geasa a choilleadh a shábháilfeadh ón mbás é dá ngéillfeadh sé dóibh.

Tháinig Aonghus i gcabhair ar Dhiarmaid i n-am an ghátair. Ag Doire Dá Bhaoth dúirt Aonghus go mbéarfadh sé Diarmaid agus Gráinne slán as an áit, ach b'fhearr le Diarmaid gur Gráinne amháin a thabharfadh Aonghus leis, rud a dhein sé (ll. 361–82). Shábháil sé Diarmaid ó naoi nGairbh na Féine ag Dubhros ó bhFiachrach, agus thug sé Gráinne leis go Brugh na Bóinne (ll. 1298–1329). Níorbh fhada ina dhiaidh sin gur éalaigh Diarmaid féin go Brugh na Bóinne agus is ann a d'fhan sé le Gráinne go dtí gur dhein Aonghus síocháin idir é agus Fionn agus Cormac.

Bhí an Móraltach, *claidheamh Aonghusa a' Bhrogha* (l. 638), i seilbh Dhiarmada; dhein sé cleas leis an gclaíomh sin i láthair a naimhde, muintir na Glas-Fhéinne, agus maraíodh leath-chéad acu san ag iarraidh aithris a dhéanamh air (ll. 636–57). In eachtra a bháis ar Bheann Ghulban, nuair ba léir do Ghráinne go raibh Diarmaid meáite ar imeacht leis dá hainneoin i dtreo an fhiadhaigh, molann sí dó an Móraltach (claíomh Mhanannáin, dar léi) agus an Ga Dearg a bhreith leis. Ní ghlacann Diarmaid lena comhairle: "*Ní bhéar*," ar Diarmaid, "*béarad an Beagaltach 7 Ga buidhe an Lámhaigh leam 7 Mac an Chuill ar slabhradh um láimh*" (ll. 1428–32). Theith Mac an Chuill roimh an torc: thuig Diarmaid ansan go raibh sé i mbaol a bháis, agus dúirt sé: "*Is mairg nach dén comhairle dheagh-mhná, or adubhairt Gráinne ream a mochrach an Móraltach 7 an ga Dearg do thabhairt leam*" (ll. 1536–38). Is léir gur tuigeadh do Dhiarmaid go mbeadh sé slán dá mbeadh an Móraltach aige ar an mbeann.

D'aithin Gráinne go raibh *coimhéad* (coimirce) Aonghusa ar Dhiarmaid (l. 1417). Chonaiceamar conas mar a tháinig Aonghus i gcabhair air in am an ghátair. Ach ní raibh sé ag faire air an oíche úd. Ag labhairt dó le corp Dhiarmada, dúirt Aonghus: *"Ní rabhus aon-oidhche ó do rugas leam don Brugh ós Bóinn thú a ccion do naoi míos gus anocht nach beinn dot fhaire 7 dot fhorchoimhéad ar th'easgcairdibh, a Dhiarmaid, 7 is truagh an fheall so do-rinne Fionn ort tar ceann do shíochána ris"* (ll. 1722–26). Eisean a dhein an laoi chaointe ar Dhiarmaid. Seo é a tús:

Truagh sin, a Dhiarmaid dhédla,
a hÍ Dhuibhne gheil-ghéga,
   do díobhadh do chrú fád cháil,
   do ciurrbhadh crú do chorpáin.
     (ll. 1727–31)

Alas, brave Diarmaid, / Ó Duibhne of the fair limbs, / your blood was annihilated during (?) your fame / the blood of your body was destroyed.

San rann deireanach deir sé:

A mharcraidh shíodha gan tshal,
tócthar libh Diarmaid dealbh-glan
   gusan mBrugh mbinn mbuidhneach mbuan,
   ní linn nach cuimhneach comhthruagh.
     (ll. 1744–47)

Horsemen of the fairy-mound without defilement, / let Diarmaid of the fine shape be lifted by you, / to the Brugh, (which is) sweet, full of hosts, everlasting, / we shall remember this great sorrow.

Dúirt Aonghus an laoi sin i láthair mhuintir Ghráinne. Bhíodar san tagaithe fé dhéin chuirp Dhiarmada, d'fhonn é thabhairt chuici go Ráith Ghráinne. Ach ní ligfeadh Aonghus corp Dhiarmada leo: dúirt sé go mbéarfadh sé féin leis é go Brugh na Bóinne agus, ar sé, *"ó nach éidir leam a aithbheódhughadh arís cuirfead anam aerrdha ann ar chor go mbia ag labhairt leam gach laoi"* ("and since I cannot revive him again I will put an aerial life into him so that he will talk to me every day," ll. 1752–55). Nuair a cuireadh in iúl do Ghráinne go raibh Aonghus tar éis corp Dhiarmada a bhreith leis, d'aithin sí nach raibh aon chumas aici ar Aonghus (l. 1759). Ní raibh ag Gráinne de Dhiarmaid ach iasacht; bhí sé imithe uaithi anois, agus is ag Aonghus a bheadh sé feasta.

Bhí baint ag Fionn le saol Dhiarmada ón tús freisin. Bhí sé i láthair nuair a mharbhaigh athair Dhiarmada mac an reachtaire, agus dhein sé iarracht éraic a íoc as an gcoir. Is ar mhaithe le Fionn a dhein Diarmaid gníomhartha gaile sa bhfiann. Chuir Gráinne an gaol a bhí idir Fionn agus Diarmaid as a riocht: is dá anneoin féin a d'éalaigh Diarmaid léi. Fear díoltais dob ea Fionn, rud go gcuirtear béim air arís agus arís eile san *Tóraíocht*. Sciob Gráinne Diarmaid ó Fhionn, agus sciob sí ón bhfiann é chomh maith. Bhí a chompánaigh dílis dó, agus dheineadar gach iarracht cabhrú, ach sa deireadh thiar ba threise a ndílseacht don bhfiann. Nuair a bhí Diarmaid ag fáil bháis, bhagair Osgar comhrac aonair ar Fhionn muna dtabharfadh sé uisce do Dhiarmaid. Nuair a cailleadh Diarmaid, bhí Osgar ar tí a cheann a bhaint de Fhionn, ach labhair Oisín leis: *"A mhic," ar sé, "as fíor gur thuill sé sin uait-si 7 ó Fhiannaibh Éirionn go hiomlán tré gan Diarmaid d'fhóirighthin, 7 ná déin-si an dá léan a n-áon-ló dhúinn, 7 fágbham an tulach so annois ar eagla go ttiocfadh Aonghus chuguinn 7 nách creidfeadh uainn nách sinn féin tug bás do Dhiarmaid gion gur cionntach Fionn rena bhás"* (ll. 1679–84).

Seo mar a labhrann Joseph Nagy (1985, 73) ar an gcur isteach a dhein Gráinne ar an bhfiann:

> Women in Fenian tales frequently disrupt the order of the male fían and set fénnidi against one another. The most dramatic and most famous instance of such discord is to be found in the tragic tale of Diarmaid, one of the greatest Fenian heroes, whose life and relationship with Finn are destroyed by the illicit love that Gráinne, Finn's wife, conceives for him. Despite his erstwhile affection for Diarmaid, the jealous, aged husband relentlessly pursues the eloping lovers. Even after a reconciliation has apparently been reached between husband and rival, Finn craftily sabotages his own attempt to cure the wounded Diarmaid, the victim of a hunting tragedy arranged by the rígfénnid himself.

Más ea, tá gné eile den ghaol idir Fionn agus Diarmaid nár mhiste tagairt a dhéanamh dó, is é sin gur thug Diarmaid dúshlán Fhinn os comhair an tsaoil. Nuair a chuaigh Fionn sa tóir ar Dhiarmaid agus Gráinne go Doire

Dá Bhaoth dúirt sé ná fágfadh Diarmaid an áit go dtugadh sé díol dó in gach ní dá ndearna sé air (ll. 336 f.); agus arís ná fágfadh Diarmaid Doire Dá Bhaoth go dtugadh sé éruic dó in gach masla dá dtug sé dó (l. 349). In ansan a thug Diarmaid dúshlán Fhinn: *éirghis Diarmaid ina sheasamh 7 tug trí póga do Ghráinne a ffiadhnuisi Fhinn agus na Féinne. Do ghabh doigh éda 7 anbhuana Fionn agá fhaigsin san dó, 7 adubhairt go ttiubhradh Diarmaid a cheann ar son na bpóg san* (ll. 357–59). Tá mar a bheadh ath-insint (doublet) ar an eachtra so níos déanaí sa téacs, nuair atá Diarmaid agus Gráinne i nDubhros Ó bhFiachrach (ll. 1279–85), agus deir Fionn, "*do-bhéara tú do cheann ar son na bpóg sin*" (l. 1285). Gné den choimhlint idir an t-óg agus an sean atá anso againn, agus tá an choimhlint sin le feiscint go minic nuair a labhrann Fionn agus Oisín le chéile.

Scéal Dhiarmada atá á insint i d*Tóraíocht Dhiarmada agus Ghráinne.* Is téacs fiannaíochta é, agus ar shlí is téacs faoin bhfiannaíocht chomh maith é. A fhianaise san, mar shampla, ar phearsanra an scéil. Níor chruinn ar fad a rá go bhfuil "a cast of thousands" anso, ach ní dóigh liom go mbeadh locht ag Cecil B. DeMille féin ar a bhfuil de chomrádaithe, cúntóirí, comhairleoirí, trodairí agus eile sa *Tóraíocht.* Faighimid eolas ar an bhfiannaíocht i gcuid de na scéalta laistigh, agus ba mhaith liom ceann amháin acu san a phlé anso, is é sin an scéal faoi Chonán mac an Léith Luachra agus an chnuimh (ll. 956–1127). Rugadh mac do Shadhbh bean Oiliolla Óluim: Cian dob ainm dó, agus bhí dromainn mhór treasna a chinn air. D'fhonn an dromainn a choiméad ina rún, mharaíodh Cian éinne a bhearradh é. Nuair a chuaigh Scáthán mac Scanláin i mbun a bhearrtha, áfach, ghearr sé an dromainn. Scinn cnuimh aisti, agus d'fhás go dtí go raibh céad ceann uirthi. Deineadh trén-iarracht an chnuimh a choiméad faoi smacht, ach nuair a bhain sí an chos ón cholpa síos de mhac rí Chiarraí d'ordaigh Oilill dá mhuintir an chnuimh a mharú. D'éalaigh an chnuimh uathu agus ghaibh sí siar *nó go ráinic Uaimh Dheirce Fearna a n-iarthar Chorca Dhuibhne, 7 do chuaidh asteach san uaimh 7 do-rinne sí fásach don tríocha céad sin 'na timcheall, ar chor nach lamhadh Fionn náid Fiana Éreann sealg ná fiadhach do dhénamh lena heagla* (ll. 1094–98). D'éirigh le Conán mac an Léith Luachra an chnuimh a mharú agus thug sé ceann dá cheannaibh leis.

Fillfeam anso ar liostaí na scéalta, agus go háirithe ar liosta A. Luaitear deich n-*Uatha* ansan, agus *Uath Dercce Ferna* ina measc (Mac Cana 1980, 43). I measc na n-*Eachtraí* sa liosta chéanna tá *Eachtra Fhinn i nDerc Ferna* (Mac Cana 1980, 45); "Fionn's Journey into the Cave of Dunmore, Co.

Kilkenny" atá ag Murphy air sin, agus deir sé i dtaobh *Uath Dercce Ferna* gur dóichí gur eipeasóid í de chuid an scéil eile (Murphy 1955b, 12). Deir Mac Cana (1980, 97), áfach, go mb'fhéidir gur ag tagairt don aon scéal amháin atá an dá theideal. Maidir leis an bhfocal *uath*, dob é Ó Comhraí a dúirt gur chiallaigh sé "uaimh," agus is ag leanúint dá lorg san a bhí Murphy. Áitíonn Mac Cana gurab é atá i gceist le *huath* ná "terror," "horror," "horrible being," nó "monster." Deir sé freisin: "It is true that some of the narratives in question deal with caves, and one or two with lakes, but this is hardly surprising considering that throughout Irish tradition caves and lakes have been commonly conceived of as entrances to the domain of the supernatural" (Mac Cana 1980, 96 f.).

Glactar coitianta ná fuil teacht againn ar cheachtar den dá scéal so. Ach tá scéal sa *Tóraíocht* againn a bhaineann le huaimh Dheirce Fearna, agus is díol suntais é go ndeir an scéalaí gur i gCorca Dhuibhne a bhí an uaimh sin. Ní féidir a áiteamh gur ionann an scéal so agus an ceann atá i gceist sa liosta, ach ní miste go n-aithneofaí go bhfuil a leithéid sa *Tóraíocht*. Is cuid de shaibhreas na *Tóraíochta* é, saibhreas gur beag an cuardach atá déanta air go fóill.

The Pursuit of Diarmaid and Gráinne

(translated by the author, 2011)

Tóraíocht Dhiarmada agus Ghráinne is the most celebrated tale of the Fenian Cycle, and probably the one that is most enjoyed. The tale's origins lie in the distant past: "the tradition of Diarmaid and Grainne descends in an unbroken line from the ninth century to the present day" (Schoepperle 1913, 395). Modern Irish, however, is the language of the earliest extant version of the tale. The earliest copy is preserved in Royal Irish Academy manuscript 24 P 9, written by the renowned scribe Dáibhí Ó Duibhgeannáin in the year 1651. Gerard Murphy (1955b, 14) says that the tale as we have it may not be much earlier than that date. A large number of copies were subsequently made of the *Tóraíocht*; at least forty survive that were made between the years 1718 and 1850 (Ní Shéaghdha 1967, xv). The Ossianic Society published Standish Hayes O'Grady's edition of the *Tóraíocht* in 1855: O'Grady drew on two manuscripts written respectively in 1780 and 1842–43 (O'Grady 1857,

30). What has become of the first of these in the meantime is not known; as for the second, we have a manuscript of the *Tóraíocht* in the same hand, but this does not seem to be the one used by O'Grady (Ní Shéaghdha 1967, xiv). The Irish Texts Society published Nessa Ní Shéaghdha's edition of the *Tóraíocht* in 1967; it is based on Ó Duibhgeannáin's manuscript, but draws when necessary on five other manuscripts. Ní Shéaghdha's edition is very much better than O'Grady's, but she is characteristically kind in her remarks about that pioneering scholar: "The need for a new edition, based on manuscript material now available, has been felt for a long time, and although it is possible to improve on O'Grady's text, owing to his vagueness in the discussion of sources, nevertheless his English rendering of the story will always remain, for one in particular, a delight to read" (Ní Shéaghdha 1967, ix).

The story of Diarmaid and Gráinne lived on in oral tradition; the oral versions are discussed by Ní Shéaghdha (1967, xviii–xxvi) and Bruford (1969, 106–9). Bruford (1969, 106) remarks: "Stories about Diarmaid and Gráinne are found in oral tradition, localized in different parts of Ireland and Scotland: but their relationship to the romance *Tóraidheacht Dhiarmada agus Ghráinne* is not always easy to determine." Flower (1926, 387) suggested that the *Tóraíocht* may have been composed by a Munsterman: "The romantic tale is apparently a late medieval development of the theme, possibly based on the lost early tale and composed, if the topography may be used in evidence, in Munster." For Bruford (1969, 106), Flower's Munsterman has become a Kerryman: "Though the author [of the *Tóraíocht*] may have been a Kerryman (Flower 1926, 387) the story, like the Ulster Cycle tales, seems to have been less popular in Kerry than in other areas: it may not be too much to suggest that most Kerry storytellers preferred stories more like international *märchen* and avoided those with a tragic flavour."

The storytellers, and the people, made the story of Diarmaid and Gráinne their own:

> Local traditions about Diarmaid and Gráinne seem to have extended throughout the West of Scotland and Ireland from Cape Wrath to Cape Clear. Diarmaid's death is associated as in the literary tradition with Beann Gulban, Benbulben in Co. Sligo, but also with a Scottish mountain of the same name, Ben Gulabin in Perthshire. Other oral accounts place it on Ben Loyal in Sutherland (S1), Benmore (Skye?

LNF: 164), Ben Nevis (A3), Mangerton Mountain in Kerry (C2), in Lismore (A6) or at Kanturk in Co. Cork (C1), whose name Ceann Tuirc, "Boar's Head," suggests a connection with the boar which killed Diarmaid. The lovers' flight is also part of universal tradition: any dolmen in Ireland is liable to be called the bed of Diarmaid and Gráinne . . . and oral versions of the romance locate the wood where they first hid in various parts of central Ireland. . . . C4 and C5 [two versions from Co. Cork] largely consist of onomastic anecdotes telling how four mountains in Co. Cork were named from incidents on the lovers' flight, and most other versions bring in place-names in the storyteller's own area (Bruford 1969, 106).[1]

It is clear, then, that the story of Diarmaid and Gráinne enjoyed considerable popularity in Ireland and western Scotland.

While the Modern-Irish *Tóraíocht* is our earliest continuous telling of the story of Diarmaid and Gráinne, we have seen that Schoepperle claimed that the tradition of the couple extended from the ninth century to the present day, and that Flower spoke of "the lost early tale." These observations are based on the lists of medieval Irish tales, and on quatrains and anecdotes that survive from the early period and that have to do, in one way or another, with the story of Diarmaid and Gráinne.

Two main lists have come down to us of medieval Irish tales (Mac Cana 1980), and these are respectively referred to as A and B. The lists are classified according to the tales' titles, such as *Tána* (*Táin Bó Cúailnge*, etc.), *Togla* (*Togail Bruidne Da Derga*, etc.), *Tochmarca* (*Tochmarc Étaíne*, etc.). One of these categories comprises *Aitheda* 'Elopements,' the singular being *Aithed* (Modern Irish *Aitheadh*). The "Elopement of Gráinne with Diarmaid" is mentioned in both lists: *Aithed Gráinne re Diarmait* in A, beside *Aithi Graine ingine Corbmaic la Diarmait ua nDuibne* in B. But this is not to say that the *Aithed* thus referred to was identical with the *Tóraíocht*. In order to form some impression of what the storytellers had to say about Diarmaid and Gráinne in the centuries before the *Tóraíocht* was composed, we must have a look at the extant early texts that have to do with the couple.

Two stray quatrains have survived independently of one another in the commentary added to *Amra Choluim Chille* 'The Eulogy of Colum Cille' in the eleventh century. In one of them Gráinne speaks to Fionn:

Fil duine
  frismbad buide lemm díuterc,
dia tibrinn in mbith mbuide,
  huile, huile, cid díupert.

There is one on whom I should gladly gaze, to whom I would give the bright world, all of it, all of it, though it be an unequal bargain. (Murphy 1956, 160–61; cf. Stokes 1899, 156)

The quatrain is cited in the commentary on the *Amra* as an illustration of the use of the word *díuterc*. Murphy (1956, 160) assigns the quatrain to the ninth or tenth century, and observes that "the occurrence of the old words *díuterc, díupert,* and the citation of the quatrain in the oldest manuscripts of the commentary of the *Amra* in justification of the obsolete *díuterc* (*díuderc*), suggest that the quatrain is not later than the tenth century" (237). He says further that "this quatrain . . . seems to be the earliest reference extant to Gráinne's love for Diarmait" (1956, 236).

In the second quatrain, Diarmaid speaks:

Is maith do chuit, a Gráinne
  is ferr diut inda ríge
sercoll na cailech feda
  la banna meda míne.

Good is thy share, O Gráinne; better for thee than a kingdom the dainty flesh of the woodcocks with a drop of smooth mead. (Stokes 1899, 264)

We cannot determine whether this quatrain is as old as the one spoken by Gráinne; all we can say is that it is not later than the eleventh century.

Úar in lathe do Lum Laine, "The Day is Cold for Lom Laine," is the opening line of a poem in the Book of Leinster (*LL*, l. 58889), which takes the form of a dialogue between a man and a woman, who call one another Lom Laine and Tethna. Tethna's (unnamed) father is a grandson of Conn's, as is Gráinne's father Cormac, and in the introduction to her edition of the poem Máirín O Daly says, "the circumstances indicated are so reminiscent of the story of Gráinne, not the Tóraíocht but the earlier and less romantic version in *ZCP* i 458, that I am inclined to regard 'Tethna' and 'Lom Laine' (lit. 'the bare one of L.') as pseudonyms for Gráinne and Díarmait." She outlines the "circumstances" as follows: "From our poem we may infer that 'Tethna' and 'Lom Laine' are in love but that there is some obstacle to their union, probably that 'Tethna' is married already, and that any relationship between them is likely to lead to the death of both. It also appears that Lom Laine is associated with Almu [=the Hill of Allen]." As for the date of the poem's composition, she says that she sees "no reason for placing it later than the ninth century" (O Daly 1968, 101).

The "earlier and less romantic version" mentioned by O Daly is a short text in the Book of Lecan, published by Kuno Meyer (1897) under the title "Finn and Gráinne." There has been some disagreement as to the date of this text; Murphy (1953a, lix) suggests that it may date from the ninth or tenth century. In this version, Fionn seeks Gráinne's hand in marriage, but she will not accept him unless he brings to Tara a pair of every wild animal found in Ireland. Fionn does this with the help of one Caoilte Cosluath, and Gráinne is given to him. Gráinne hates Fionn so much that she falls ill. Fionn overhears Gráinne explaining her situation to her father, Cormac mac Airt, and understands that his wife hates him. He says that they should separate.

Tochmarc Ailbe 'The Wooing of Ailbe' (Thurneysen 1920) is mentioned in the two tale-lists (A and B), indicating, as we have seen, that it was being told in the tenth century. Meyer (1910a, xiv) thought that the extant version was composed in that century, and Thurneysen felt that this was plausible. According to this tale, Fionn and Cormac mac Airt quarrel, the reason being that Gráinne hates Fionn and is in love with Diarmaid. In due course, the matter is resolved and Fionn and Diarmaid part amicably. Fionn goes on to marry Cormac's youngest daughter, Ailbe.

Uath Beinne Étair 'The Hiding of the Hill of Howth' is an eleventh-century text (Ní Shéaghdha 1967, 130). Elopement (*aithed*) is explicitly mentioned in the opening sentence: *Fechtus dia raibe Diarmait mac Duinn Í Duibne in uaim Benne Étair iar mbreith Gráinne ingine Cormaic ar aithed ó Fhind*, "Once Diarmaid, son of Donn, grandson of Duibne, was in the cave of the Hill of Howth after carrying off Gráinne, daughter of Cormac[,] in elopement from Finn" (Ní Shéaghdha 1967, 130; I have normalized the Irish spelling). A hag is keeping watch on behalf of Diarmaid and Gráinne. Fionn approaches her. He wants her to betray Diarmaid and Gráinne, and she is happy to do so because Fionn has told her that he wishes to marry her. Gráinne, however, divines the hag's intentions and warns Diarmaid. Aonghus an Bhrogha (Aonghus of the Brugh, i.e., Óengus of Bruig na Bóinne) comes to the couple's assistance and they escape unharmed.

None of the aforementioned texts mention Diarmaid's death. There are two references in *Acallam na Senórach* 'The Colloquy of the Old Men' (composed around the year 1200) to the magical pig that killed Diarmaid: the old men travel to *Leacht na Muice* 'The Pig's Tomb' on Benn Ghulban "where the pig killed Diarmait ó Duibhne"; and to the top of the hill, where Diarmait's grave is located (Stokes 1900, ll. 1514–17); and again to *Lighi an Fheindida* 'The Tomb of the *Fían*-Warrior,' "where the enchanted, magical pig killed Diarmaid húa Duibne" (Stokes 1900, ll. 6895–96).

Reference is made to the pig and to Diarmaid's death in a poem in *Duanaire Finn* 'The Poem-Book of Fionn' (E. MacNeill 1908, 45–47, 149–51) with the opening line *Éuchtach inghen Diarmatta*, "Éachtach, daughter of Diarmaid," and composed, according to Murphy (1953a, 40), between the years 1250 and 1400.

Ní Shéaghdha (1967, xiii) interprets the evidence of those texts as follows:

> When the *Aithed* (the probable old source) was re-cast in the Early Modern period and given its new title, *Tóruigheacht Dhiarmada agus Ghráinne*, it still retained the actual framework of the older tale, but some minor differences had crept in. Thus: (a) in the older tale Gráinne was married to Finn when she eloped with Diarmaid, but she was not married to him in the *Tóruigheacht*; (b) from the story of *Tochmarc Ailbe* we learn that because of Gráinne's hatred for Finn and her love for Diarmaid, Finn thought it best for them to part; but it was against Finn's wishes that Gráinne parted from him in the *Tóruigheacht*; (c) it was mainly in the south of Ireland that Diarmaid and Gráinne spent their time, while being pursued in the *Tóruigheacht*; the only indication we have of their whereabouts in flight in the older tale is in the east of the country, a district not included in the lovers' itinerary in our Early Modern version of the tale.

It will be noticed that there is no mention there of Diarmaid's death, an episode that is part of the framework of the *Tóraíocht*, but of which we cannot say whether or not it was recounted in the *Aithed*. Murphy (1953a, xxxvi) considers the framework of the *Tóraíocht* to comprise "the elopement; Fionn's pursuit of the lovers; the death of Diarmaid caused by a pig," and argues that it was well known from the beginning of the thirteenth century. His evidence is found in the references in *Acallam na Senórach*, in the *Duanaire Finn* poem, *Éuchtach inghen Diarmatta*, and in the poems of Gearóid Iarla (obit 1398). As for the *Acallam*, we have seen that it refers to Diarmaid's death, but does not connect it to the elopement story. This connection is first made in *Éuchtach inghen Diarmatta*, and it is here that we find for the first time the framework as we have it in the *Tóraíocht*. Gráinne, *lennán Diarmada déidghil* 'sweetheart of tooth-white Diarmaid,' is bestowed as wife upon Fionn, but she escapes from him unbeknown to Diarmaid. Diarmaid and Gráinne spend seven years *i n-imlib Banbha* 'in the outer bounds of Banbha [i.e., Ireland],' with Fionn in pursuit. Having failed to kill the couple, Fionn duplicitously makes peace with Diarmaid, injures Gulban, a poisonous pig on Beann Ghulban, and sends Diarmaid to hunt him, so that Diarmaid is slain. (The rest of the poem has to do with the efforts made by a daughter of Diarmaid's to avenge his death.)

As for Gearóid Iarla, it is clear from the frequent references in his poems to Diarmaid and Gráinne that he was acquainted with a story about the couple that was similar to the *Tóraíocht*.

Ní Shéaghdha (1967, xiii) characterizes Gearóid's version of the story as follows: "(a) Gráinne is always spoken of as the daughter of Cormac . . . and not as the wife of Finn; (b) we are given to understand that it was against Finn's wishes that Gráinne parted from him . . . ; (c) the places listed where Diarmaid and Gráinne lived during their flight from Finn are in the south." These features correspond with the "minor differences" that Ní Shéaghdha noted between the *Aithed* and the *Tóraíocht*; as she says, "[Gearóid Iarla] shares the points of difference from the older tale with the *Tóruigheacht*."

These differences must be considered in turn. The first one, that Fionn and Gráinne are married in the early texts, but are merely betrothed in the *Tóraíocht*, I would consider "minor" in the context of the plot as a whole. The second difference, however, is quite considerable. According to "Fionn and Gráinne" and *Tochmarc Ailbe*, Fionn and Gráinne part amicably. The *Tóraíocht* in this respect has a different tale to tell. It is true that Fionn and Diarmaid make peace when Fionn has failed to capture the couple, but in the event we find that it is a duplicitous truce. Cormac mac Airt and Fionn forgive Diarmaid for "all he had done to them while he had been outlawed" (*a ndearna sé orra an feadh do bhí sé fá choill*, l. 1378). Significantly, we are not told here that Fionn forgives Diarmaid for taking Gráinne from him; and he makes Diarmaid pay for that in due course.

The third "minor difference" that Ní Shéaghdha sees between the *Aithed* and the *Tóraíocht* concerns the couple's itinerary. They do not travel to the Hill of Howth in the *Tóraíocht*; Ní Shéaghdha implies that they did so in the *Aithed*. This is evidently based on the evidence of *Uath Beinne Étair*, taking account of the fact that a text of that tale survives from the eleventh century, and of the mention of *aithed* at the beginning of it. Murphy was more cautious in his use of this evidence. He said (1953a, xxxvi): "that the story, at least in the general form of Gráinne's elopement with Diarmaid and Fionn's pursuit of the lovers, was accepted by the learned of the 10th and 11th centuries is proved by fragments of it and references to it contained in the early literature." He bases this observation on the inclusion of the *Aithed* in the tale-lists, and on the content of *Tochmarc Ailbe* and *Uath Beinne Étair*. He is referring to these two tales when he speaks of "fragments of it," that is, "[of] the story at least in the general form of Gráinne's elopement with Diarmaid and Fionn's pursuit of the lovers." That is not to say, however, that the relevant content of the two tales belonged to the *Aithed*: we must distinguish between a story and the telling of it in a given tale. The word *táin*, for example, has two senses: (1) an event or sequence of events that occurred or was imagined, and (2) a literary work in which the events are narrated—a continuous sequence of words in a particular order. The first of these meanings is exemplified in the following quatrain from *Éuchtach inghen Diarmatta* (E. MacNeill 1908, 46, 150):

> Re trí lá go lánoídhche
> > nochor mhó díth na tána:
> ní tig lucht a sáraighthe
> > dia n-éis go laithe mbrátha.

> For three days and full nights the spoiling of the Táin had not been greater: none to surpass them come after them until doomsday.

A comparison is being made here between Éachtach's martial achievements and the events recounted in the work (or rather the works) entitled *Táin Bó Cúailnge*.

Aithed is comparable in this respect to *táin*. We have already alluded to the occurrence of *aithed* in the opening sentence of *Uath Beinne Étair*: *Fechtus diaa raibe Diarmait mac Duinn í Duibne in uaim Beinne Étair iar mbreith Gráinne ingine Cormaic ar aithed ó Fhinn*, "Once Diarmait, son of Donn grandson of Duibne, was in the cave of the Hill of Howth after carrying off Gráinne, daughter of Cormac[,] in elopement from Finn." This wording does not show that that particular episode was necessarily part of the tale that in the tenth or eleventh century would bear the title *Aithed Gráinne le Diarmait*. The early texts afford some insight into the early tales about Diarmaid and Gráinne, but when all has been said it has to be acknowledged that the "lost *aithed*" is indeed lost.

At the level of the story as a sequence of events, however, there is evidence to suggest that the elopement of Diarmaid and Gráinne was connected from the beginning with Diarmaid's death. I am thinking here of the presence of significant similarities in the story of Diarmaid and Gráinne with that of Adonis and Aphrodite. O'Grady remarked: "It is singular that Diarmaid na m-ban should have met his death by the same beast that slew Adonis, whom he may be said to have represented in Irish legend" (apud Murphy 1953a, xxxvi). A. H. Krappe showed that these stories are very similar to one another; Rees and Rees (1961, 295) offer the following summary of what Krappe had to say:

> Aphrodite, goddess of love and of nature in bloom, fell in love with the beautiful Adonis, as Gráinne did with Diarmaid, and he became her paramour, though in his case as in Diarmaid's there is a different tradition which says that he was innocent of actual congress with her. Aphrodite was the wife of Ares, the god of war, as Gráinne was the wife of the *fian* chief. Suspecting an improper relationship between Adonis and his wife, Ares sent a wild boar, or himself assumed the shape of a wild boar, which fatally wounded Adonis while he was hunting. Similarly Finn was believed to have arranged the boar-hunt to allure Diarmaid to his death at the year's end. Both Adonis and Diarmaid went hunting against his mistress's will. There is a general lament for both. Diarmaid, borne away on Mac Óc's gilded bier, recalls the annual ritual in which the image of the dead Adonis was borne away, mourned by women bitterly wailing, while the couches on which images of the god and goddess were shown may be compared with the "Beds of Diarmaid and Gráinne."

These similarities could be explained in various ways: (1) both stories derive from a single original source; (2) the story of Diarmaid and Gráinne is based on that of Adonis and Aphrodite; (3) they arose independently of one another. I find it difficult to believe that the two stories are entirely independent of one another, but I cannot see how we can choose between the other two possibilities. (There has of course been considerable disagreement among scholars on the degree to which early Irish literature was subject to external influence.)

It has been said too (R. Breatnach 1959, 150) that the enmity between Fionn and Diarmaid has a mythical basis: "the *Pursuit of Diarmaid and Gráinne* may be interpreted as a romanticized development of the myth of the rivalry of two pagan divinities"; and that Gráinne is also a mythical personage: "although there is little trace of her true nature in the literary *Pursuit*, I think Gráinne really is the ugly goddess: the loathsome crone, who becomes a radiantly beautiful maiden when she marries the sacred king in many Irish stories." It is clear, however, that Breatnach is not claiming that the mythical dimension is strongly represented in the *Tóraíocht* as we have it.

Myles Dillon (1948, 42–43) has said that "the story of Gráinne is a variant of the story of Deirdre, the tragedy of a young girl betrothed to an old man and of the conflict between passion and duty on the part of her lover. In both cases death is the price of love." It is true that pride of place is given in the *Tóraíocht* to the theme of tragic love, but it is nevertheless Diarmaid's story that we are given throughout: the *Tóraíocht* tells us of Diarmaid's youth, of his adventures in the *fiana*, of his elopement with Gráinne, and of his death. What I am saying here is that the story of Diarmaid and Gráinne is contained within the biography of Diarmaid. The content of the *Tóraíocht* can be divided in two:

(1) The wooing of Gráinne and her elopement with Diarmaid
(2) Diarmaid's (youth, deeds in the *fiana*, and) death.

The first part of the *Tóraíocht* is a *tochmarc* 'wooing-tale.' Fionn is unmarried (*gan mhnaoi gan bheanchéile*, l. 8), and it is suggested to him that he should seek Cormac mac Airt's daughter Gráinne as his wife. Fearing that he might receive *éara tochmairc*, "refusal of [his] suit," (l. 32) he sends emissaries to Cormac and Gráinne in Tara. They agree that Fionn should be accepted as Gráinne's husband, and Fionn and the *fiana* are invited to Tara to celebrate the match. Gráinne, however, is already in love with Diarmaid, having fallen for him when she saw his exploits on the hurling field:

do chuirius rinn mo ruisg 7 mo radhairc ionnad-sa an lá sin, 7 ní thugas an grádh sin d'aoinneach eile ó sin i leith, "I fixed the keenness of my eye and of my sight upon you that day, and I did not give that love to any other person from that time to this" (ll. 186–88). She says this in explanation of her having solemnly enjoined him to elope with her. Diarmaid complies with her injunction. I will not describe the adventures that befall the couple in the course of their flight. But it is appropriate to draw attention to the manner in which the narrator addresses the reader:

> Bíodh a fhios agad, a léaghthóir, gur choimeád Diarmaid é féin fós gan chionntughadh ná cumusg lé Gráinne, 7 gur fháguibh bior d'fheóil bhruite gan aoin-ghreim do bhuain as a nDoire Dhá Bhaoth mar chomhartha d'Fhion agus d'Fhiannaibh Éirionn nár chionntaigh sé féin lé Gráinne, 7 fós gur fháguibh an dara feacht bradán ar bhruach na Leamhna bruite mar an ccéadna. Gurab uime sin do bhrosdaigh Fionn iona dhiaigh. Acht tráchtamaoid ar an ní ccéadna arís.

> Let it be known to you, reader, that Diarmaid still kept himself from sinning or uniting with Gráinne, and that he left a spit of cooked flesh without a bite taken out of it in Doire Dhá Bhaoth as a sign for Fionn and for the Fiana of Ireland that he had not sinned with Gráinne, and also, that he left the second time a salmon on the bank of the Leamhain cooked likewise. Wherefore it was that Fionn hastened after him. But we will discourse on that same subject again. (ll. 528–35; this passage is not included in Ó Duibhgeannáin's manuscript: see Ní Shéaghdha 1967, 110)

He is referring here to the episode (ll. 781–94) in which a drop of water splashes on her leg: she declares that the drop of water is more daring that Diarmaid, and he says in response that he will no longer endure her reproaches, and "it is then for the first time that Diarmaid Ó Duibhne of the bright tooth made a wife of Gráinne, daughter of the king of Ireland" (*as ann sin do-roinne Diarmaid déad-sholuis Ó Duibhne bean do Ghráinne .i. inghion rígh Éirionn, ar ttús*, ll. 793–94).

The pursuit comes to an end when Diarmaid and Gráinne make their way to Bruig na Bóinne. Aonghus an Bhrogha makes peace between Fionn and Diarmaid, and Diarmaid and Gráinne go to live in Céis Choruinn

(Keshcorran, County Sligo), because it is a great distance from Cormac and Fionn. They spend sixteen prosperous and contented years there, and have five children. Then Gráinne decides to have a feast for Cormac and Fionn, and spends a year preparing it. At the year's end Diarmaid hears the voice of a hound in his sleep. Gráinne implores him to pay no heed, but the next morning he sets off in pursuit of it. He reaches the summit of Beann Ghulban. Fionn is there before him, and he tells Diarmaid that the *fiana* are in flight from the boar of the Beann. Diarmaid, however, is determined to stand his ground. It is then that Fionn announces that it is a prohibition (*geas*) of Diarmaid's to hunt a pig (ll. 1448–49), something of which Diarmaid has no previous knowledge. Fionn then tells Diarmaid how that prohibition came to be placed upon him (ll. 1451–1522). Diarmaid's father, Donn, killed the son of the steward of Brugh na Bóinne. Fionn offered to compensate the steward, but he declined to accept it. He struck his son with a magic rod and made "a singed pig without ear or tail" (*muc mhaol-dóite gan chluais gan iurball*, ll. 1514–15) of him, and addressed him, saying, "I put you under injunctions that you have the same length of life as Diarmaid Ó Duibhne and that it be by you he shall fall in the end" ("*cuirim-se fá gheasaibh thú gurab ionann saoghal duit 7 do Dhiarmaid Ó Duibhne 7 gurab lat thuitfeas fá dheireadh*," ll. 1516 f.). The pig left the Bruig, and when Aonghus heard of the injunction placed upon the pig, he solemnly enjoined Diarmaid never to hunt swine.

Fionn tells Diarmaid that the boar of Beann Ghulban is that same pig, and that he should not wait for it. Diarmaid responds: "I give my word that it is to kill me you designed this hunt, Fionn, and if it is there I am fated to die there is no use for me to avoid it" ("*Do-bheirim-se mo bhriathar gurab dom mharbhadh-sa do chumais an tsealg so, a Fhinn, 7 más ann atá a ndán damh-sa bás d'fhagháil ni ffuil feidhm agum a sheachna*," ll. 1529–31). Diarmaid assails the boar; in the end the boar wounds Diarmaid and he in turn slays the boar. Diarmaid is dying when Fionn and the *fiana* come upon him, and Diarmaid asks Fionn for a healing drink of water. When Fionn claims that Diarmaid has not deserved the drink, Diarmaid reminds Fionn of the feat he performed on Fionn's behalf in the house of Dearg son of Dionnarthach (ll. 1582–97). This does not satisfy Fionn: "[Y]ou ill-deserved of me to give you a drink or to do any other goodness for you the night you came to Tara with me and took Gráinne with you from me out of Tara in the presence of the men of Ireland, and [considering] that you were my body-guard that night in Tara" ("*Is olc do thuillis uaim-si deoch do thabhairt duit ná aon-ní maitheasa do dhénamh dhuit an oidhche tángais leom go Teamhraigh 7 ruguis Gráinne leat uaim a Teamhraigh a bhfiaghnuisi bhfear nÉreann, 7 gurab tú féin dob fhear coimhéada agum-sa an oidhche sin a tTeamhraigh,*" ll. 1598–1603). Diarmaid then reminds Fionn of the feat he performed for him in Bruidhean Chaorthainn (ll. 1606–51). But Fionn remains unwilling to fetch the water for him, and Diarmaid dies for want of it.

It is as in-tales that the adventures are recounted pertaining to Diarmaid's youth—the story of the burnt pig—and his career as a *fian*-warrior—the feats in the house of Dearg mac Dionnarthach and in Bruidhean Chaorthainn. His death-tale—*Oidheadh Dhiarmada* as it would be dubbed in Irish—begins in the *Tóraíocht* when Gráinne elects to prepare a feast for Cormac and Fionn. The outline given above of the content of the second half of the story follows the order of occurrence of events, rather than the order of revelation by the narrator. When we examine the order of occurrence in the *Tóraíocht* as a whole, we see the following pattern in Diarmaid's life: his youth; his feats as a *fian*-warrior; his elopement with Gráinne; his adventures and feats in the course of their travels; his death; the lamentation following his death; and the bringing of his body to Bruig na Bóinne by Aonghus an Bhrogha.

Diarmaid's elopement with Gráinne is connected with his death in that Fionn declines to save him because he wishes to avenge the elopement. To that extent, in Dillon's words, "death is the price of love." In the biographical context of the *Tóraíocht*, however, Diarmaid's tragedy begins much earlier in his life: Diarmaid's death is the result of his father's deeds.

While the story of Diarmaid and Gráinne, as we have seen, is given pride of place in the *Tóraíocht*, two persons—Aonghus and Fionn—are closely connected with Diarmaid from beginning to end of the tale. Aonghus is Diarmaid's foster-father (ll. 1448–49), and has great affection (*cion mór*, l. 1477) for him. It is Aonghus who enjoins him never to hunt swine (*gan sealg mhuice do dhéanamh go brách*, l. 1520). When Fionn informs him of this injunction on Beann Ghulban, Diarmaid is not prepared to comply with it, even though he later claims, "I would not violate my injunctions for the gold of the world" (*"ní chaillfinn-si mo gheasa ar ór na cruinne,"* ll. 1605–6). He is referring on that occasion to the injunctions placed upon him by Gráinne. It is ironic that he has shown himself willing to violate an injunction which would have saved his life had he been disposed to comply with it.

Aonghus helps Diarmaid in his hour of need. At Doire Dá Bhaoth, Aonghus offers to take Diarmaid and Gráinne to safety, but Diarmaid prefers that he should take only Gráinne, and this he does (ll. 361–82). He saves Diarmaid from the nine *Gairbh na Féinne* 'Rough Men of the *Fían*' at Dubhros ó bhFiachrach, and takes Gráinne with him to Bruig na Bóinne (ll. 1298–1329). Soon afterwards, Diarmaid makes his way to Bruig na Bóinne, and he remains there with Gráinne until Aonghus makes peace between him and Fionn and Cormac.

Diarmaid has possession of Aonghus's sword, the *Móraltach*, and performs a feat with it in the presence of his enemies, the people of the *Glas-Fhian*; he kills fifty of them as they seek to imitate him (ll. 636–57). In the events leading to his death on Beann Ghulban, when Gráinne sees that Diarmaid is determined to ignore her advice and go towards the hunt, she advises him to take the Móraltach—which she describes as Manannán's sword—and the Ga Dearg. Diarmaid rejects her advice: "I will not..., but I will take the Beagaltach and Ga Buidhe an Lámhaigh with me and Mac an Chuill on a chain on my hand" ("*Ní bhéar ... béarad an Beagaltach 7 Ga buidhe an Lámhaigh leam 7 Mac an Chuill ar slabhradh um láimh*," ll. 1428–32). Mac an Chuill, however, flees from the boar; Diarmaid then recognizes that his life is in danger, and says: "Woe to him who does not follow the counsel of a good wife, for Gráinne told me at dawn to take the Móraltach and the Ga Dearg with me" ("*Is mairg nach dén comhairle dheagh-mhná, or adubhairt Gráinne ream a mochrach an Móraltach 7 an ga Dearg do thabhairt leam*," ll. 1536–38). Diarmaid clearly understands that he would be safe if he had the Móraltach with him on the hill.

Gráinne recognizes that Diarmaid has Aonghus's protection (*coimhéad*, l. 1417). We have seen how Aonghus comes to Diarmaid's assistance in his hour of need. But he is not watching over Diarmaid on the night of his death. Speaking to the dead Diarmaid, he says: "I have never been for one night since I took you with me to the Brugh over the Boyne, when you had completed nine months, until tonight that I was not watching you and guarding you against your enemies, Diarmaid, and alas for treachery that Fionn has done to you notwithstanding your peace with him" ("*Ní rabhus aon-oidhche ó do rugas leam don Brugh ós Bóinn thú a ccion do naoi míos gus anocht nach beinn dot fhaire 7 dot fhorchoimhéad ar th'easgcairdibh, a Dhiarmaid, 7 is truagh an fheall so do-rinne Fionn ort tar ceann do shíochána ris*," ll. 1722–26). It was he who made the lament for Diarmaid. This is how it begins:

Truagh sin, a Dhiarmaid dhédla,
a hÍ Dhuibhne gheil-ghéga,
   do díobhadh do chrú fád cháil,
   do ciurrbhadh crú do chorpáin. (ll. 1727–31)

Alas, brave Diarmaid, / Ó Duibhne of the fair limbs, / your blood was annihilated during (?) your fame / the blood of your body was destroyed.

In the final quatrain he says:

A mharcraidh shíodha gan tshal,
tócthar libh Diarmaid dealbh-ghlan
   gusan mBrugh mbinn mbuidhneach mbuan,
   ní linn nach cuimhneach comhthruagh. (ll. 1744–47)

Horsemen of the fairy-mound without defilement, / let Diarmaid of the fine shape be lifted by you, / to the Brugh, (which is) sweet, full of hosts, everlasting, / we shall remember this great sorrow.

Aonghus speaks that lay in the presence of Gráinne's people. They have come to fetch Diarmaid's body, intending to take it to her at Ráith Gráinne. But Aonghus does not allow them to take the body; he says that he will take it with him to Bruig na Bóinne, and adds: "since I cannot revive him again I will put an aerial life into him so that he will talk to me every day" ("*ó nach éidir leam a aithbheódhughadh arís cuirfead anam aerrdha ann ar chor go mbia ag labhairt leam gach laoi,*" ll. 1752–55). When Gráinne receives word that Aonghus has taken Diarmaid's body, she recognizes that she has no power over Aonghus (l. 1759). Gráinne has had no more than a loan of Diarmaid; he is gone from her now, and henceforth will be with Aonghus.

Fionn was also involved in Diarmaid's life from the outset. He is present when Diarmaid's father kills the steward, and he attempts to pay compensation for the crime. It is on Fionn's behalf that Diarmaid performs acts of valor in the *fiana*. Gráinne disrupts the relationship between Fionn and Diarmaid: Diarmaid elopes with her against his will. Fionn is a vengeful man, something which is emphasized again and again in the *Tóraíocht*.

Gráinne snatches Diarmaid from Fionn, and from the *fiana* as well. His companions are loyal to him, and attempt to help him, but in the end their greater loyalty was to the *fiana*. As Diarmaid lies dying, Oscar threatens to challenge Fionn to single combat should he continue to refuse water to Diarmaid, and when Diarmaid dies, Oscar is about to behead Fionn. But Oisín speaks to him:

> "A mhic," ar sé, "as fíor gur thuill sé sin uait-si 7 ó Fhiannaibh Éirionn go hiomlán tré gan Diarmaid d'fhóirighthin, 7 ná déin-si an dá léan a n-áon-ló dhúinn, 7 fágbham an tulach so annois ar eagla go ttiocfadh Aonghus chuguinn 7 nách creidfeadh uainn nách sinn féin tug bás do Dhiarmaid gion gur cionntach Fionn rena bhás." (ll. 1679–84)

> "Son," said he, "it is true that he has deserved that of you and of all the Fiana of Ireland through not helping Diarmaid, but do not cause the two sorrows in one day for us, and let us leave this mound now for fear that Aonghus might come to us and that he would not believe that it was not we who brought death to Diarmaid although Fionn is guilty of his death."

Joseph Nagy (1985, 73) has the following to say about Gráinne's interference with the *fian*:

> Women in Fenian tales frequently disrupt the order of the male fian and set fénnidi against one another. The most dramatic and most famous instance of such discord is to be found in the tragic tale of Diarmaid, one of the greatest Fenian heroes, whose life and relationship with Finn are destroyed by the illicit love that Gráinne, Finn's wife, conceives for him. Despite his erstwhile affection for Diarmaid, the jealous, aged husband relentlessly pursues the eloping lovers. Even after a reconciliation has apparently been reached between husband and rival, Finn craftily sabotages his own attempt to cure the wounded Diarmaid, the victim of a hunting tragedy arranged by the rígfénnid himself.

There is, however, another aspect of the relationship between Fionn and Diarmaid to be considered, which is that Diarmaid challenges Fionn in public. When Fionn pursues Diarmaid and Gráinne to Doire Dá Bhaoth, he declares that Diarmaid will not leave that place until he gives him satisfaction (*díol*) for everything he has done to him (ll. 336–37); and again that he will not leave Doire Dá Bhaoth until he gives Fionn compensation (*éraic*) for every insult he has done to him (l. 349). It is then that Diarmaid throws down the gauntlet to Fionn:

> Rena chois sin éirghis Diarmaid ina sheasamh 7 tug trí póga do Ghráinne a ffiadhnuisi Fhinn agus na Féinne. Do ghabh doigh éda 7 anbhuana Fionn agá fhaigsin san dó, 7 adubhairt go ttiubhradh Diarmaid a cheann ar son na bpóg san. (ll. 357–59)

> With that Diarmaid rose up and he gave three kisses to Gráinne in the presence of Fionn and the Fiana. A pang of jealousy and anxiety seized Fionn on seeing that, and he said that Diarmaid would give his head for those kisses.

There is a doublet of that incident later in the text, when Diarmaid and Gráinne are in Dubhros Ó bhFiachrach (ll. 1279–85), and Fionn says "you will give your head for those kisses" (l. 1285).

Tóraíocht Dhiarmada agus Gráinne, then, tells us the story of Diarmaid Óa Duibhne. It is a Fenian tale, and in a sense is also a text about *fiannaíocht* 'fenian lore.' This is exemplified in the personnel of the tale. While it does not quite have a "cast of thousands," even Cecil B. DeMille could hardly find fault with its abundant array of companions, helpers, counselors, warriors, and so on. Some of the in-tales throw light on the *fiannaíocht*, and I should like to discuss one of them here. It is the story of Conán son of the Liath Luachra, and the Worm (ll. 956–1127). A son is born to Oilill Óluim's wife Sadhbh: he is called Cian and has a big bulge across his head. In order to keep the bulge secret, everyone who cuts Cian's hair is put to death. When one Scáthán son of Sgannlán shaves Cian, however, he rips the bulge open, whereupon a worm springs out of it. The worm grows and develops until it has a hundred heads. Every effort is made to contain the worm, but when it lops off the leg of the king of Ciarraighe Luachra from the calf down, Oilill commands his people to kill it. The worm escapes and goes westward "until it reached Uaimh Dheirce Fearna in west Corca Dhuibhne and it went into the cave and made a wilderness of that cantred round about it, so that Fionn and the Fiana of Ireland dare not hunt or chase there for fear of it" (*nó go ráinic Uaimh Dheirce Fearna a n-iarthar Chorca Dhuibhne, 7 do chuaidh asteach san uaimh 7 do-rinne sí fásach don tríocha céad sin 'na timcheall, ar chor nach lamhadh Fionn náid Fiana Éreann sealg ná fiadhach do dhénamh lena heagla*, ll. 1094–98). Conán son of the Liath Luachra contrived to kill the worm, and took one of its heads with him.

In tale-list A, ten *Uatha* are listed, among them *Uath Dercce Ferna* (Mac Cana 1980a, 43). Among the *Eachtraí* in the same list, we find *Eachtra Fhinn i nDerc Ferna* (Mac Cana 1980a, 45); Murphy translates this as "Fionn's Journey into the Cave of Dunmore, Co. Kilkenny," and says of *Uath Dercce Ferna*, which he translates as "The Cave of Dunmore," that it was doubtless an episode from the other tale (Murphy 1955b, 12). Mac Cana, on the other hand, suggests that the two titles may refer to one and the same tale. As for *uath*, Murphy's translation "cave" derives ultimately from Eugene O'Curry. Mac Cana argues that *uath* means "terror, horror, horrible being, monster." He adds: "It is true that some of the narratives in question deal with caves, and one or two with lakes, but this is hardly surprising considering that throughout Irish tradition caves and lakes have been commonly conceived of as entrances to the domain of the supernatural" (Mac Cana 1980a, 96).

It has been generally accepted that both of these tales are lost. But we have a story in the *Tóraíocht* that has to do with the cave of Derc Ferna, and it is noteworthy that the storyteller locates the cave in Corca Dhuibhne, rather than in County Kilkenny. It cannot be asserted that this story is the same as that referred to in the list, but it should be known that there is such a story in the *Tóraíocht*. It is part of the rich subject matter of the *Tóraíocht*, a tale that has as yet been little explored.

Further Reading
Compiled by Matthieu Boyd with the author's input

This section tries to orient nonspecialists while helping specialists get up to date. These two purposes are sometimes in tension—the most recent publications on a given topic may not be the most accessible, or may make questionable statements that others have not had a chance to rebut. Some readers will no doubt feel that, in the attempt to find a balance, there have been significant omissions. Also, some of the most important items in this section receive the least commentary, either because they deserve to be read in full, or because the contents are too diverse or complex to be summarized briefly. Items that antedate Ó Cathasaigh's chapters are only rarely mentioned; often the chapters themselves will have shown nonspecialists the best places to start. The Bibliography of Irish Linguistics and Literature maintained by the School of Celtic Studies, Dublin Institute for Advanced Studies, at http://bill.celt.dias.ie, and the Celtic Studies Association of North America Bibliography at http://celtic.cmrs.ucla.edu/csanabib.html are two excellent ways to keep up with the progress of research.

"INTRODUCTION: IRISH MYTHS AND LEGENDS" (2005)

Ó Cathasaigh's survey of Irish literature to ca. 800 in volume 1 of the *Cambridge History of Irish Literature* (2005b) goes into more detail on some of the topics, and the subsequent chapters by Máire Ní Mhaonaigh (2005) and Marc Caball and Kaarina Hollo (2005) complete the picture. Under the heading of "Aspects of Memory and Identity in Early Ireland," Ó Cathasaigh (2011a) has more on the role of the *filid* and their place in society. Patrick Ford (1990) is a classic take on how the early Irish understood the nature of poetic craft, and Liam Breatnach (2006) is a noteworthy recent one on the scope of the *filid*'s activities. The overview of early Irish literary criticism by Erich Poppe and Patrick Sims-Williams (2005) is invaluable.

The history of Ireland when most of the early literature was composed is covered in a magisterial survey by Thomas Charles-Edwards (2000), and Seán Duffy (1997) gives an accessible run-down of the later medieval period. For more detail on certain topics, see the hefty volumes of the *New History of Ireland* edited by Dáibhí Ó Cróinín (2005) and Art Cosgrove (1987). Katharine Simms, in her short book *Medieval Gaelic Sources* (2009), surveys all the Irish-language texts that may lend themselves to historical research, including annals, genealogies, laws, and poetry, as well as the sagas. Forthcoming books by Edel Bhreathnach (2013) and Elva Johnston (2013) should further refine our understanding of the sociohistorical context.

The status of early Irish narrative cycles has now been discussed at length by Erich Poppe (2008). Dan Wiley (2008) provides a comprehensive introduction to the King Cycle. The tradition of "synthetic pseudohistory" represented by *Lebor Gabála Érenn*, which is outside the scope of this volume, is most recently discussed in the volume of *Reassessments* edited by John Carey (2009). On saints' lives, also generally outside the scope of this volume, Kim McCone (1984b) and Richard Sharpe (1991b) are good places to start. Meanwhile, William Sayers presents the field of early Irish literature to Arthurians (2007b) and mainstream medievalists (2010).

Those not familiar with early Irish saga who would like to browse the primary texts should see the translated volumes by Tom Peete Cross and Clark Harris Slover (1969), Jeffrey Gantz (1981), Thomas Kinsella (1970), Ann Dooley and Harry Roe (1999), Patrick Ford (1999), and John Koch and John Carey (2003), not to mention the various publications of the Irish Texts Society, DIAS, and the Maynooth Medieval Irish Texts Series.

"THE SEMANTICS OF SÍD" (1977-79)

Síd and related terms are further discussed by Eric Hamp (1982) and Patrick Sims-Williams (1990); for the latest comment on the etymology of *síd*, see Matasovi (2009), s.v. **sedo-*.

The location and geography of the Otherworld are discussed in articles by John Carey (1982; 1987; 2000)—who argues that an overseas Otherworld is "foreign to the native tradition at every stage" (2000, 119)—Maxim Fomin (2004), Feargal Ó Béarra (2009), and in a recent book by Alfred Siewers (2009). William Sayers (2012) now proposes that the relocation of the Otherworld to hills or islands on the same plane as humans represents a 90-degree shift from an earlier underground or underwater Otherworld. Meanwhile, Carey (1991) discusses Hiberno-Latin perspectives on the Otherworld, and Damian McManus (2006) describes "images of the king's peace and bounty" in bardic poetry.

Catherine McKenna's (1980–81) now-classic discussion of the theme of sovereignty in *Pwyll* may also be of interest. Sayers (2007a) too makes a Welsh connection in suggesting how the semantics of *síd* can enlighten us regarding the *Joie de la Cour* episode in Chrétien de Troyes's *Érec et Énide*.

The latest take on *Echtrae Chonnlai* (last edited in McCone 2000) is an article by Kaarina Hollo (2011), who argues (with McCone and against Carey) for a Christian allegorical reading of the text.

On Conaire's relations with the Otherworld, see Tom Sjöblom (2000, 78–110) and the important new book by Ralph O'Connor (2013, esp. chaps. 2 and 7), and on the general theme of supernatural threats to kings, see Jacqueline Borsje (2009a). The concept of *fír flathemon* is discussed by Hans Hartmann (1997–2008) in a wide-ranging comparative study.

"PAGAN SURVIVALS: THE EVIDENCE OF EARLY IRISH NARRATIVE" (1984)

As a follow-up to Ó Cathasaigh's survey of possible approaches to the interpretation of early Irish texts, see R. Mark Scowcroft (1995) and Tom Sjöblom (2004); Sjöblom specifically responds to Ó Cathasaigh and recommends an approach informed by cognitive studies.

Meanwhile, the subject of "pagan survivals" has received considerable attention. A landmark, albeit controversial, work is *Pagan Past and Christian Present in Early Irish Literature* by Kim McCone (1990)—note the important review by Patrick Sims-Williams (1996)—which insists that clerical mediation and classical or biblical influence will account for material in early Irish texts that "nativists" previously thought of as pagan survivals. (McCone is comfortable, however, with the idea of persistent Proto-Indo-

European archaisms, a frequent theme in his other work; compare the broad-ranging treatment of Indo-European comparative poetics, which includes early Ireland, by Calvert Watkins 1995.) The work of J. P. Mackey (1992a; 1992b; 1999) plays on McCone's titular paradigm in various ways; Donald Meek (2000) now offers a measured assessment of the concept of "Celtic Christianity" advocated by Mackey (1989) and others. John Carey (1997) discusses the traditional qualifications of the *filid* as suspected pagan survivals; Jacqueline Borsje (2009b) discusses the character of early Irish monotheism as reflected in the literature. A recent edited collection of some interest is *Approaches to Religion and Mythology in Celtic Studies*, ed. K. Ritari and A. Bergholm (2008). Most recently, Jonathan Wooding (2009) surveys the clash of "nativist" and "anti-nativist" perspectives and subjects the "anti-nativist" position to a sharp critique (see his article for more references), while David Hutchison (2009) once more addresses the issue of pagan ritual in early Irish literature, and Mark Williams (2010) discusses astrology.

Richard Kieckhefer (1989, esp. chap. 3) and Bernadette Filotas (2005), among others, consider the issue of "pagan survivals" in European literature more generally.

"THE CONCEPT OF THE HERO IN IRISH MYTHOLOGY" (1985)

Ó Cathasaigh's treatment (1977) of the heroic biography of Cormac mac Airt is required reading; most recently, Morgan Davies (2008) invokes the concept of heroic biography in his study of Brandub mac Echach, as does Nina Chekhonadskaya in her comments on the Ulster Cycle "trickster" figure Bricriu mac Carbada (in *Ulidia 2*, 252–61).

Joseph Nagy's (1985) discussion of Finn is crucial; his further work on "the recyclable hero" (2006–7) clarifies some other important aspects of heroic identity in the Finn and Ulster Cycles. Volumes edited by Almqvist, Ó Catháin, and Ó Héalaí (1987a, 1987b), not to mention *Ulidia* and *Ulidia 2*, contain many articles of interest. Philip O'Leary (1987; 1988; 1991; 1994) covers the various demands of honor to which heroes are subject. Ann Dooley (2006) comments extensively on the concept of the hero, while Marion Deane (2003) focuses on *CCC*, the story of Cú Chulainn's conception and birth.

There is a major comparative study of the epic hero by Dean Miller (2000), who offers his own take on Cú Chulainn (2006). Connell Monette (2004; 2008) has more in the Indo-European comparative vein.

"THE SISTER'S SON IN EARLY IRISH LITERATURE" (1986)

The most complete resource on early Irish and Welsh kinship is the book by Thomas Charles-Edwards (1993); see also the article by Neil McLeod (2000). Kim McCone (1992) addresses the etymology of *amnair*. Other terms whose Common Celtic and Proto-Indo-European etymologies are discussed in this article can now be looked up in Matasović (2009).

Peter Parkes (2003; 2004; 2006) ranges widely in discussing fosterage and adoptive kinship, whereas Bart Jaski (1999) focuses on Cú Chulainn's status as *gormac* and *dalta* of the Ulstermen, and surveys the Old Irish vocabulary relating to fosterage.

Kaarina Hollo (2005) discusses the evidence for women's keening in early medieval Ireland, focusing especially on Blathmac's poetry, and Matthieu Boyd (2012) gives advice on teaching Blathmac alongside *The Dream of the Rood* in a British and Irish literature survey.

"CURSE AND SATIRE" (1986)

Major studies of early Irish satire include Róisín McLaughlin, *Early Irish Satire* (2008), and, much broader in scope, Bernard Mees, *Celtic Curses* (2009). See also Mac Eoin (1997). Liam Breatnach (2006) considers the evidence for early Irish praise-poetry, which is not well attested, and its relationship to satire (compare Mac Cana 2004); elsewhere Breatnach (2009) discusses a brief text that exemplifies the limitations of satire as a way for poets to seek redress. Dan Wiley (2001) discusses the maledictory use of psalms, and Dorothy Bray (2002) has more on curses in saints' lives. Lisa Bitel (2006–7) also revisits clerical cursing; she argues that "between about 800 and 1200, the equipment of cursers"—notably hand bells and bishops' croziers—along with the written record of curses by saints or in the name of saints, "became increasingly important in response to learned skepticism and political change" (7).

"THE THREEFOLD DEATH IN EARLY IRISH SOURCES" (1994)

Although there has been no further study of the threefold death per se, Elizabeth Gray (2005) discusses "the three sins of the warrior" in a way that resonates with Ó Cathasaigh's take on the transgressions that lead to a threefold death: she argues that in *Aided Con Roí* 'The Death of Cú Roí,' we see Cú Chulainn "as a flawed hero, different in specifics from his Indo-European brothers, but like them bound by mortal failings expressed through sins against three basic principles that uphold the world: justice, courage, and sexual fidelity" (90).

Dan Wiley (2002), Edel Bhreatnach (2005), and Michael Meckler (2008) have explored the material on Diarmait mac Cerbaill and the Uí Néill in more detail, while Mark Williams (2011) focuses on the character of Sín in *Aided Muirchertaig meic Erca*. Williams tentatively suggests that Sín "*deliberately poses as a sovereignty goddess* in order to destroy a king whom she knows to be violent and ambitious" (31), and that the manipulation of familiar tropes by an author who is a "savage ironist" causes the tale to "emerg[e] not just as a story of king versus saint, or of king and his myth-inflected marriage to a quasi-goddess, but as cunning and self-conscious exercise in literary criticism" (32). This analysis is compatible with Máire Herbert's view (1997) of *Aided Muirchertaig* as a twelfth-century original production informed by both earlier sagas and hagiography.

Neil (Cornelius) Buttimer (1987) detected an allusion to the threefold death motif in the text *Orgguin Trí Mac Diarmata Mic Cerbaill* 'The Slaying of the Three Sons of Diarmait mac Cerbaill' (Greene 1955, lines 912–13). According to Ralph O'Connor (2013, 215–16), Conaire's death in *Togail Bruidne Da Derga* "partakes of (or alludes to)" the threefold death as well.

"EARLY IRISH LITERATURE AND LAW" (2006–7)

The most significant works on early Irish literature and law to appear since Ó Cathasaigh's article are Robin Chapman Stacey's *Dark Speech: The Performance of Law in Early Ireland* (2007; also see her 2011 article) and Liam Breatnach's "Law and Literature in Early Mediaeval Ireland" (2010). Janet Sinder (2001, §§19–31) situates early Irish law in broader Irish legal history. There is a survey of the laws by Thomas Charles-Edwards (2005), and of the wisdom literature by Christopher Guy Yocum (2012). The study by Jacqueline Borsje and Fergus Kelly (2003) of the "evil eye" in legal and literary contexts is also notable.

"*CATH MAIGE TUIRED* AS EXEMPLARY MYTH" (1983)

Besides the three-part series by Elizabeth Gray on "*Cath Maige Tuired*: Myth and Structure" (1980–81; 1982–83a; 1982–83b), there is an important study of the text by John Carey (1989–90), who considers the tale's significance for audiences in the ninth and eleventh centuries. Michael Chesnutt (2001) goes further in analyzing it as a parable of the Battle of Clontarf.

In an influential article, Kim McCone (1989) anticipates his *Pagan Past and Christian Present in Early Irish Literature* (1990), emphasizing how the story may have been shaped by the Latin learning and the social agenda of the clergy, notably as regards the distinction between (clerically sanctioned) *file* and (unsanctioned) satirist.

See also William Sayers (1987) on "bargaining for the life of Bres"; Joan Radner (1992) on the combat of Lug and Balar and its afterlife in Irish folklore; and Rebecca Blustein (2007) on poets and pillar-stones in *CMT*.

Gaël Hily (2008) makes a recent contribution from the diachronic (Indo-Europeanist) perspective, whereas Karen Bek-Pedersen (2006) includes *CMT* among her analogues to the Eddic myth of Baldr, and Václav Blažek (2001) proposes an etymology for *Balar* that associates the character with the Norse god Óðinn.

Extending Ó Cathasaigh's method, Caoimhín Breatnach (2000, in Irish) suggests that the Early Modern Irish tale *Oideadh Chloinne Tuireann* 'The Violent Death of the Children of Tuireann' (which overlaps with the events of *CMT*, and describes how Lug spitefully exacts fatal compensation from the sons of Tuireann for killing his father) can also be read as exemplary myth in a negative sense, setting the Túatha Dé Danann at odds with one another, in contrast to the earlier tradition, as a warning against political discord. Ó Cathasaigh's approach in this article similarly informs Ralph O'Connor's search for the "moral" of *Bruiden Meic Dá Reo* (2006).

Ó Cathasaigh's "Three Notes on *Cath Maige Tuired*" (1989d) and Claude Sterckx's "Quand Lugh devient-il roi?" (2004) are recommended for specialists.

"THE EPONYM OF CNOGBA" (1989)

The archeological site at Knowth and its literary associations are discussed by Geraldine Stout in *Newgrange and the Bend of the Boyne* (2002, esp. 48 ff., 62 ff.). Máirín Ní Dhonnchadha (1994–95) discusses "*caillech* and other terms for veiled women in medieval Irish texts," and there is a comprehensive study of the *cailleach*, especially *Cailleach Bhéarra*, in literature and folklore by Gearóid Ó Crualaoich (1994–95; 2003, esp. part 2). Brian Murdoch (1991) and John Carey (1999) have more to say about the poem, and Carey (1995b) discusses a character in *Serglige Con Culainn* whom he associates with Bóann and the sites on the Boyne. The status of Bruig na Bóinne as "telluric womb" has been questioned by Phillip Bernhardt-House (2009, 229n11).

"KNOWLEDGE AND POWER IN *AISLINGE ÓENGUSO*" (1997)

Brenda Gray (2009) argues that the text is "an eschatological, Christian-Platonist parable on the spiritual journey of the soul, and an erotic allegory on divine love" (16). Most recently, Hugh Fogarty (2011) takes issue with the view that *Aislinge Óenguso*, in its present form, "has no more than an arbitrary connection to *Táin bó Cúailgne*" (67), pointing out some ways in which the tale functions as an effective *remscél* or prequel to the *Táin*.

"THE WOOING OF ÉTAÍN" (2008)

Alfred Siewers (2009, 40–55) offers a detailed ecocritical reading of *Tochmarc Étaíne*, while Ronald Hicks (2009) discusses its cosmography and Cozette Griffin-Kremer (2010) focuses on the yoking of oxen by Midir to build a causeway across the bog. William Sayers's article on "Fusion and Fission in the Love and Lexis of Early Ireland" (2008b) relates to many of the chapters in this volume that deal with love.

Ó Cathasaigh (2013b) himself has an article: "*Tochmarc Étaíne* II: A Tale of Three Wooings."

"*TÁIN BÓ CÚAILNGE*" (2002)

There is a more recent overview of the *Táin* by Ann Dooley (2010), author of the in-depth study *Playing the Hero: Reading the Irish Saga Táin Bó Cúailgne* (2006). Scholarship on the *Táin* is extensive, as one might expect, but the many relevant essays in *Ulidia 2* give an excellent sense of where things stand. Uáitéar Mac Gerailt (2010) revisits the dating of Recension II. Brent Miles (2011, esp. chap. 5; compare *Ulidia 2*, 66–80) discusses the *Táin*'s indebtedness to Latin epic, a topic of perennial interest previously addressed by scholars including Dorothy Dilts Swartz, Johan Corthals (1989), Joseph Nagy (1996), John Carey (2004), and Michael Clarke in *Ulidia 2* (238–51), though as Dooley (2010, 19) puts it, Miles's book now "demonstrates that classical borrowing extends much farther than anyone else has suggested and is pervasive in the work."

Doris Edel has a number of recent contributions dealing with the *Táin*: on "bodily matters," i.e., sex and elimination (Edel 2006, ranging well beyond the *Táin*; compare Ó Cathasaigh 2013); the characterization of Fergus (Edel 2007); and problems of length and fluidity, given the *Táin*'s uneasy fit with the epic genre (Edel 2011).

Pádraig Ó Néill (1999) discusses the view of early Irish literature expressed by the notorious Latin colophon to the Book of Leinster *Táin*. On the modern reception of the *Táin* and the politics of translating it, see Maria Tymoczko (1999) and Declan Kiberd (2000, chap. 23). Helen Fulton (2011) discusses "magic naturalism" in the *Táin*, and ultimately calls it "a postmodern narrative from a premodern world" (99).

See also the recommendations for the following four chapters.

"MYTHOLOGY IN *TÁIN BÓ CÚAILNGE*" (1993)

Ann Dooley addresses this topic in detail in her *Playing the Hero: Reading the Irish saga Táin Bó Cúailgne* (2006, esp. chaps. 4–5). James Carney (2008)—not the James Carney of *Studies in Early Irish Literature and History* (1955), who died in 1989—interprets Macha's curse and the Ulstermen's *ces noínden* 'debility' in terms of Dumézil's three functions and Marcel Mauss's theory of reciprocity. Matthias Egeler (2012) revisits the much-debated mythological background of Medb.

"*TÁIN BÓ CÚAILNGE* AND EARLY IRISH LAW" (2005)

Súaltaim's warning and the marriage of Ailill and Medb are studied in detail in the following two chapters in this volume, "*Sírrabad Súaltaim* and the Order of Speaking among the Ulaid" (2005) and "Ailill and Medb: A Marriage of Equals" (2009).

"*SÍRRABAD SÚALTAIM* AND THE ORDER OF SPEAKING AMONG THE ULAID" (2005)

Compare the treatment by Thomas Owen Clancy (2005) of "Court, King, and Justice in the Ulster Cycle"; and see further Ó Cathasaigh's recent article (2011b) on Conchobor and his court at Emain. On the status of druids in early Irish law, see Fergus Kelly (1988, 60–61) and Arun Micheelsen (2007); Mark Williams (2010, chap. 2) explores the literary evidence of druids as prognosticators and readers of portents. Marilyn Gerriets (1988) considers the degree to which an early Irish king would function as a judge.

"AILILL AND MEDB: A MARRIAGE OF EQUALS" (2009)

Having perhaps not had the benefit of Ó Cathasaigh's analysis, Ann Dooley (2010, 21) says that there is "a dysfunctional and doubtful legal relationship between Medb and her husband which is exploited to the full in the opening of Recension II." She comments further on Medb in chapter 6 of her book on the *Táin* (2006).

Cáin Lánamna, the principal Old Irish tract on marriage and divorce law, has been newly edited and translated by Charlene Eska (2009). See also the discussion of marriage law and women's rights by Johanna Heil (2011).

"CÚ CHULAINN, THE POETS, AND GIOLLA BRIGHDE MAC CON MIDHE" (2005)

There has been no recent reevaluation of Giolla Brighde Mac Con Midhe, but on poets' praise of the martial hero, see the article by Damian McManus,

"Good-Looking and Irresistible: The Hero from Early Irish Saga to Classical Poetry" (2009), which has a special section on Cú Chulainn (69–73).

"REFLECTIONS ON *COMPERT CONCHOBUIR* AND *SERGLIGE CON CULAINN*" (1994)

John Carey's "The Uses of Tradition in *Serglige Con Culainn*" (1994) is a valuable companion piece to Ó Cathasaigh's article; note their different readings of the colophon.

Jacqueline Borsje (1999) has more on the sword ritual as both ordeal and oracle.

The most recent discussion of *Compert Conchobuir* is by Joanne Findon (2011), who offers a comparison of the three surviving versions as "alternative 'texts' and 'stories' of a common 'fabula'" (53, borrowing the critical vocabulary of Mieke Bal to which Celtic scholars were first exposed in the work of Edgar Slotkin).

The most recent discussion of *Serglige Con Culainn* (*SCC*) is by Catherine McKenna (2011). She carefully situates *SCC* in its manuscript context before focusing on the "Christian epistemology" of the text itself.

"THE EXPULSION OF THE DÉISI" (2005)

"The Expulsion of the Déisi" has not come in for any further study as a literary text. However, it is worth remembering Donnchadh Ó Corráin's reading of the saga in "Historical Need and Literary Narrative" (1986, 142 ff.). Ó Corráin (1985b, note 32, available at http://www.ucc.ie/celt/marriage_ei.pdf) also mentions a Latin synopsis of the text in Dublin, TCD ms. H.2.7.

The characters in early Irish literature by the name of Eithne, including Eithne Uathach, are surveyed by Claire Dagger (1989). Dorothy Bray (2005) considers the appearance of a white red-eared cow in *ED* along with such appearances in other texts. Jacqueline Borsje (2007, 51–52) treats *ED* in the context of her discussion of human sacrifice in early Irish literature. Incidentally, Eithne is the subject of a Modern Irish poem by Nuala Ní Dhomhnaill, "Eithne Uathach/Eithne the Hun" (2000, 36–37).

Also see the notes to "The Déisi and Dyfed" (1984), below.

"ON THE LU VERSION OF 'THE EXPULSION OF THE DÉISI'" (1976)

See the related chapters in this volume, "The Expulsion of the Déisi" (2005) and "The Déisi and Dyfed" (1984).

"THE DÉISI AND DYFED" (1984)

Philip Rance, in "Attacotti, Déisi, and Magnus Maximus: The Case for Irish Federates in Late Roman Britain" (2001), revisits the historical question of the Déisi and Dyfed in considerable detail (252 ff.). The fact that, according to *ED*, "the crossing to Dyfed is made specifically by a branch of the Dál Fiachach Suidge ... has important implications for the size of this 'migration,' which appears now to be small-scale and familial, rather than the tribal movement often assumed" (254). Rance says we must envision a "protracted, multi-phase settlement" of the Irish in Wales; regarding "the exact date of 'the migration,'" "[a]ll that can be said with any degree of certainty from the Irish and Welsh evidence alone is that the settlement in southern Wales of certain *aithechthúatha* from Munster took place within the general period between the later fourth and very early fifth centuries. Nevertheless, this dating corresponds significantly with the date range of 360s to 390s suggested by the Roman sources for Attacotti raiding and accommodation" (256). David Thornton (1998, 87–88) likewise addresses the claim in the Harleian genealogies that the ruling dynasty of Dyfed went back to Macsen Wledig (Magnus Maximus) rather than the Déisi; he suggests that the use of Magnus Maximus would "suit the political aspirations of Owain ap Hywel (d. 988)." Compare Thornton (2003, 121–79).

The ogam inscriptions of southwest Wales and the presence of the Irish in Wales have been reexamined now by Nancy Edwards (2007) and Thomas Charles-Edwards (2013, chaps. 3–4).

"THE THEME OF *LOMMRAD* IN *CATH MAIGE MUCRAMA*" (1980–81)

The themes of "power and authority" in the tales relating to Lugaid Mac Con, including *CMM*, have been examined most recently by Clodagh

Downey (2008). Downey pays particular attention to the (false?) judgment rendered by Ailill regarding Fer Fí.

John Koch (1999) analyzes Mac Con's eating of the raw mouse as "a swallowed onomastic tale": he argues that the king of Alba would originally have sought to identify Lugaid as a man subject to a name-based taboo against eating mice (*Lugaid*—*luch* 'mouse'). Matthew Holmberg uses Ó Cathasaigh's work (1977) on the heroic biography of Cormac mac Airt to suggest that Mac Con, the "villain" of *CMM*, "likely originated as a sort of Cormac or Conn to some of Munster's people" (Holmberg 2011, 169). Sharon Arbuthnot (2012) discusses the different versions of Mac Con's death.

Sheila Boll (2005) discusses "structural symmetry and the representation of kinship" in *CMM* and *Scéla Muicce Meic Dáthó*.

"THE THEME OF *AINMNE* IN *SCÉLA CANO MEIC GARTNÁIN*" (1983)

See the following selection, "The Rhetoric of *Scéla Cano meic Gartnáin*" (1989).

"THE RHETORIC OF *SCÉLA CANO MEIC GARTNÁIN*" (1989)

No further in-depth studies of *Scéla Cano meic Gartnáin* have appeared.

Joseph Nagy (2011), however, takes up Ó Cathasaigh's observations on the poet Senchán Torpéist and suggests a parallel between Senchán and Cano: in *Scéla Cano*, he says, "the business of composing poetry and seeking patronage is not strictly the domain of professional poets like Senchán," since Cano himself does both these things, and in the end "satire and other socially transmitted viruses infect the network of relationships [he] has cultivated" (251).

Ann Dooley (2006) describes Ó Cathasaigh as having offered "some very pertinent commentary on the significant role that ritualized women's verse can play in Irish saga" (267n38, relating to chap. 6 on "the invention of women in the *Táin*"). Diarmait's daughter's ritual warning is discussed above in "*Sírrabad Súaltaim* and the Order of Speaking among the Ulaid," and we may include her alongside the many examples that Gregory Toner (2010) has gathered of "a wider motif . . . of women who play the role of knowledgeable helper to the hero and who can advise him on the most propitious course of action" (272; compare Findon 1997).

James Fraser (2009, 203 ff.) offers a recent review of the historical evidence relating to Cano and his family. Andrew Breeze (2008) is an excursus on "the mysterious *Inber in Ríg* in *Scéla Cano*," which he interprets "as 'river-mouth of the king', the Irish name of Budle Bay, a mile from the Bernician capital of Bamburgh," proposing that "the lost tenth-century *Sluagad Fiachna maic Báitáin co Dún nGúaire i Saxanaib*, 'The hosting of Fiachna son of Báitán to Dún Gúaire in the land of the Saxons', points to a legend concerning" a raid on Bamburgh, although "we can disabuse ourselves of the oft-stated belief that the Ulster hero Fiachna son of Báitán [in fact] had any part" (94) in such a raid.

"THE RHETORIC OF *FINGAL RÓNÁIN*" (1985)

There is important further analysis of *Fingal Rónáin* (*FR*) by Erich Poppe (1996), on "deception and self-deception"; by Sheila Boll (2004), on "the role of foster-kin in structuring the narrative"; by Kaarina Hollo (2004), on the text as "argumentative space"; and by Uáitéar Mac Gerailt (2006–7), who responds to a proposal by Patrizia de Bernardo Stempel (2006) that the tale is inspired by Seneca's play *Phaedra*, and also pays extremely close attention to the language of the text.

On the role of the *drúth* 'Fool, jester' in *FR* and other texts, see Ó Cathasaigh (1985c), Thomas Owen Clancy (1993), Poppe (1993), William Sayers (2008a), and Matthieu Boyd (2009a). Notably, Poppe claims that "the presence of the jester in *Fingal Rónáin* is [an] indication of Máel Fhothartaig's obvious qualification for kingship," and that "[t]he jester's death, at the same time as his master's, therefore gains a metaphorical meaning and indicates that his master, who was no king, could or even should have been king" (1993, 151).

Jürgen Uhlich (2006) examines some textual problems in Rónán's lament.

"ON THE *CÍN DROMMA SNECHTA* VERSION OF *TOGAIL BRUDNE UÍ DERGAE*" (1990)

Orgain Brudne Uí Dergae and the genesis of *TBDD* have also been studied by Máire West (1990; 1999) and Ralph O'Connor (2013, chap. 1), whereas the apparent contents of *Cín Dromma Snechta(i)* have been studied by John Carey (1995a; 2007, esp. chap. 3).

"*GAT* AND *DÍBERG* IN *TOGAIL BRUIDNE DA DERGA*" (1996)

Máire West (1997) has further explored *díberg*, while John Carey (2002) and Matthieu Boyd (2009b) discuss the relevance of this practice to depictions of werewolves in early Irish literature. Ó Cathasaigh's argument concerning the significance of *gat* is cited approvingly by Ralph O'Connor (2008), who has more in chapter 3 of his new book (2013) on *Togail Bruidne Da Derga* (*TBDD*), which will no doubt prove essential going forward.

Although not strictly connected with *gat* and *díberg*, Amy Eichhorn-Mulligan's article on "*Togail Bruidne Da Derga* and the Politics of Anatomy" (2005) is another significant recent discussion of *TBDD*, in which the bodies of the characters are related to the breakdown of the body politic.

John V. Kelleher (1965) argued that James Joyce makes crucial allusions to *TBDD* in his story "The Dead." For more on this, see Ken Nilsen (1986) and O'Connor (2013, 329–40).

"THE OLDEST STORY OF THE LAIGIN: OBSERVATIONS ON *ORGAIN DENNA RÍG*" (2002)

Bettina Kimpton (2003), responding directly to what Ó Cathasaigh says here and in his articles on *Cath Maige Mucrama* and *Scéla Cano meic Gartnáin*, argues that "the parallelism of [certain] scenes" in *Orgain Denna Ríg* (*ODR*) "suggests a thematic connection between voice and power, and the importance of speech [and concealment] for Labraid's character" (166).

She calls particular attention to the way the text uses the terms *dlomad* 'announcing, declaring; expelling' and the verbs of concealment *ceilid* and *do-ceil* (169).

Charles Doherty (2005, 22) dismisses the suggestion that Labraid remained silent to avoid seeming to be a threat to Cobthach. Rather, citing Dumézil (1973, 163), he feels that Labraid's dumbness "set him apart until he could speak," and should be interpreted as a mark of "one destined to become a great king," that is, as part of the heroic biography. But Ó Cathasaigh says precisely that Labraid may not have been *incapable* of speech ("That it is not a purely physiological matter is revealed by his response to the shock administered on the playing field"), and this would seem to answer Doherty's objection for *ODR* as we have it.

Matthieu Boyd (2009a) discusses the role of the *drúth* 'fool, jester' in *ODR*, and attempts to reconcile Cobthach's demand that the *drúth* be present in the iron house with Labraid's ability to disregard his presence. It seems that Cobthach and Labraid hold conflicting views about the relationship between king and *drúth*, with the former supposing that the death of one somehow entails the death of the other, and the latter realizing that the *drúth* is uniquely qualified to sacrifice himself on the king's behalf if circumstances require it. (Other early Irish texts can be found to support both viewpoints.)

The motif of the iron house is explored in detail by Patrick Sims-Williams (2005; 2011, 262–77), notably in relation to *Mesca Ulad* and the Second Branch of the *Mabinogi*.

Finally, specialists should note the "notes on some notes" to *ODR* by Morgan Davies (1996b).

"SOUND AND SENSE IN *CATH ALMAINE*" (2004)

There has been no follow-up to Ó Cathasaigh's article regarding either *Cath Almaine* or the subject of "sound and sense" in early Irish literature generally.

However, the article by Morgan Davies on "Kings and Clerics in Some Leinster Sagas" (1996a), cited in note 9, is particularly recommended.

Úa Maigleine is among the examples of jesters discussed by Boyd (2009a).

"*TÓRAÍOCHT DHIARMADA AGUS GHRÁINNE/ THE PURSUIT OF DIARMAID AND GRÁINNE*" (1995)

Gregory Toner (1987) reconsiders the dating of the early Irish tale-lists. According to his argument, *Aithed Gráinne re Diarmait* would have been included in a version of the list, the date of which is impossible to determine but is unlikely to have been earlier than the tenth century.

Johan Corthals (1997) offers a new edition of "Finn and Gráinne," with a German translation, including some obscure passages left untranslated by Meyer. He says that the language of the text does not allow for dating other than to say that it is neither Old Irish nor Early Modern Irish (hence it is presumably Middle Irish).

Caoimhín Breatnach (2011) suggests that O Duibhgeannáin's text may be an abridgement of an earlier narrative. The volume in which his article appears—*The Gaelic Finn Cycle*, edited by Sharon Arbuthnot and Geraldine Parsons—is the latest major publication on the Fenian Cycle.

As for the literary content, an older article by Grace Neville (1988) on the text's "literary expression of myth and folklore" deserves a look. Edyta Lehmann (2010) addresses the "perplexing presence and absence" of Gráinne, arguing that despite the story's attention to the men in the *fían*, Gráinne fully deserves her status as a title character because "her appearances and disappearances," and her intermittently active role, crucially advance the plot (126). See also William Sayers (2008b), mentioned above.

There is a survey of the *Tóruigheacht* in relation to the Tristan material by W. J. McCann (2002), and Steven Moore (2010, 130–45) discusses it in his recent "alternative history" of the novel.

Notes

1. INTRODUCTION

1. There is a useful account in Rees and Rees (1961, 112).
2. Murphy presents two further points of comparison (Knott and Murphy 1966, 147–48). Firstly, places in Europe are called after Lug (as we have seen) and after Finn; examples of the latter include *Uindobona* = Vienna in Austria, and names in Switzerland and France. Secondly, both of them appear in Welsh tradition: Lug as Lleu, and Finn as the magic warrior-hunter Gwyn ap Nudd.

2. THE SEMANTICS OF SÍD

1. Stokes (1887, 292).
2. *IEW*, s.v. *sed*. He is followed by Meid (1970, 72). *Síd* would go back to **sēdos*; the congeners may be found in *IEW* and in Meid (1970, 72). The development of the variant *síth* would not be expected in Old Irish, and so far as I know has not been explained. Cf. Thurneysen (1946, 83).
3. *LEIA* R-S (S 106). The articles on *síd* are not initialled "J.V."; on this see Bachellery, *LEIA* R-S (vi).
4. Thurneysen (1887, 154).
5. Baumgarten (1975, 23) sees the possibility of another pun on *síd* in a quatrain from Colmán's hymn.
6. Pokorny (1928), Oskamp (1974).
7. The Irish text is from Pokorny (1928, 195).

8. Pokorny (1928, 202). Quite apart from the question of a pun, *Elfenhügel* is not a happy rendering of *síd* in the wider context of *Echtrae Chonnlai*, for Síd mBoadaig, the Otherworld dwelling of Comlae's visitant, is overseas (§5); Oskamp (1974, 225) gets round this difficulty by retaining *síd* in the translation: "We live in a great *síd*, so that therefore we are called people of the *síd*."

9. Thurneysen (1887, 154). Myles Dillon translates, "We live in great peace. From that we are named People of Peace" (1948, 102); similarly, James Carney (1969, 163).

10. Oskamp (1974, 211). See also Mac Cana (1976, 96 ff.).

11. See *DIL* C 35.24. In Old Irish glosses *caínchomracc* occurs "as gloss on or suggested by *pax* etc.," *DIL* C 35.14.

12. See Mac Cana (1972, 109n1).

13. See Binchy (1970).

14. Kelly (1976); on the date, see p. xxix.

15. Kelly (1976, 6, cf. 16).

16. Byrne (1973, 59).

17. Stokes (1891a); this is a composite text, of which the *echtrae* forms a part. Another recension is edited by V. Hull (1949b). There is a summary and partial translation in Dillon (1948, 110 ff.).

18. Cf. Dillon (1947b, 137).

19. This is listed as one of a number of objects "which, in one way or another, are sensitive to an Act of Truth" (Dillon 1947b, 139).

20. On the subject of Eithne, cf. Mac Cana (1955–58, 86 ff.). In "Cormac's Dream," part of a text edited by Carney (1940, 193), Eithne is explicitly identified with the kingship of Tara.

21. Meyer (1901b; 1918; 1921), Thurneysen (1936b). Cf. Dillon (1948, 107 ff.).

22. Best (1907); cf. Dillon (1948, 122 ff.).

23. Knott (1936); references are to the lines of this edition.

24. Dumézil (1943, 33 ff.; 1969, 103 ff.). Cf. J. Williams (1972, 19).

25. *Baile in Scáil*: Meyer (1901b, 461, line 23); Thurneysen (1936b, 222, §13).

26. For an account of these and similar texts, see Patch (1950).

27. *Cath Finntrága*, Meyer (1885, 73, lines 20 f.), O'Grady (1892, 1:90). In *Geneamuin Chormaic* (V. Hull 1952), there is an account of the bounty enjoyed in Ireland during Cormac's reign, and it is said that this had been granted him from heaven through the truth of his princedom (*iarna tidnocol do nim tria fírindi a flaithiusa*, line 110). For a translation of the passage, see Dillon (1947a, 7).

28. T. O'Rahilly (1946, 120 ff.).

29. Cf. O Daly (1959, 117).

30. Dumézil (1973, 111 f.).

31. Dumézil (1973, 112).

32. Scottish Gaelic remains *sìth* 'peace.'

33. Ó Cathasaigh (1977, 81 ff.)
34. Dumézil (1973, 115).
35. Dillon (1947a; 1947b).
36. Wagner (1970). For a rejoinder to Wagner, see Dillon (1973a).
37. See the recent comment by Wagner (1975, 7n14).
38. O'Donovan (1844, 425).
39. Dillon (1973b).
40. Byrne (1973, 2).
41. Spenser (1934, 7).
42. Cf. Dillon (1948, 101). This has been the general view; the matter has recently been discussed by Dumville (1976, 80 f.), who does not accept that the term *tír tairngiri* is necessarily of Christian origin.
43. *Nem* 'Heaven' is a native word which has been taken over into ecclesiastical vocabulary; we cannot know whether in pre-Christian times it also denoted the non-terrestrial Otherworld.
44. See note 8. The Otherworld abode described in *Serglige Con Culainn* (Dillon 1953a) is also overseas, yet its people are called *áess síde* (line 844). Cf. Loomis (1956, 137 f.).
45. Liddell and Scott (1940), s.v.
46. Lewis and Short (1897), s.v.
47. Cf. *LEIA* (S 106), final paragraph of entry of *1 síd*.
48. Cf. Loomis (1956, 138).
49. An example is the name Caer Siddi, where the second element is a borrowing of the Irish *síd* in its genitive form *síde* (Loomis 1956, 148).
50. Cf. Jackson (1959, 17).
51. Pedersen (1909–13, 1:72).
52. The modern association of *gorsedd* with druids is attributed to Iolo Morganwg, but it is interesting that the Irish *forad* seems to have had an early connection with druidical functions. In an early stratum of the story of the Expulsion of the Déisi, a *forad* is opened before the druid Díl delivers a prophecy—it is not stated whether he does this within or upon the *forad* (Meyer 1907a, 140, line 178; cf. Meyer 1901a, 118, §19). Cf. *forad fis*, cited in *DIL* (F 304.78).
53. I. Williams (1951, 121).
54. Binchy (1970, 24).
55. Gruffydd (1953, 20). The text is edited by I. Williams (1951) and Thomson (1957) and translated by Jones and Jones (1993).
56. It is treated as such by Brown (1943).
57. Charles-Edwards (1970, 284 ff.).
58. Cf. Dillon (1947a, 7).
59. Loomis (1956, 131–78).
60. Loomis (1956, 135).

61. Loomis (1956, 157).
62. Bromwich (1961, cxxxv).
63. Charles-Edwards (1970, 287 f.).
64. I summarize the translation of Jones and Jones (1993, 8).
65. "Sense, intelligence," cognate with Irish *cíall*. T. F. O'Rahilly compares the name with that of Cormac's grandfather Conn (1946, 282).
66. *IEW*, s.v. *sed-*.
67. Jackson (1953, 517).
68. This would hold also for the pair *sil* 'race,' *hil* 'seed.'
69. *IEW*, x.v. *sed-*.
70. Meillet (1921, 211–29).
71. Meillet (1921, 228).

3. PAGAN SURVIVALS

1. Wood-Martin (1902, 1:viii).
2. For this purpose mention may be made of Dillon (1948) and Knott and Murphy (1966). The latter volume contains an introduction by James Carney.
3. Dillon (1947a) remains an excellent introduction to survivals in Irish literature. See also de Vries (1961), Rees and Rees (1961), and Mac Cana (1970).
4. Abrams (1960).
5. Abrams (1960, 6).
6. Abrams (1960, 6).
7. Abrams (1960, 6).
8. The earliest extant manuscript to contain Irish narrative texts is *Lebor na hUidre* (see *LU*). It is the work of three hands, and it has recently been suggested that all three scribes had completed their work by 1106: see Ó Concheanainn (1973–74b) and, for a contrary view, Oskamp (1975–76).
9. Kenney (1929, 1).
10. Kenney (1929, 1).
11. Kenney (1929, 4).
12. Kenney (1929, 2).
13. Binchy (1961, 7).
14. Carney (1955, 77 ff., 191 ff., 276 ff.). Cf. Mac Eoin (1964, 245 f.).
15. One may instance Carney's observations on *Táin Bó Cúailnge* (Carney 1955, 276 ff., 321 f.). His conclusions are that it "consists in part of traditional material, in part of imaginative reconstruction of the remote pagan Irish past in form and terms that belong to the mixed culture of early Christian Ireland. Those features which are part of the epic scale of presentation must be due to imitation of the classics or of Christian developments of them. As imitation I would include the careful drawing of character, the dramatic opening with the muster of the

hosts, the technique of dramatic description, particularly as illustrated in the device of 'the ignorant and knowledgeable watchers,' the retrospective technique by which Cú Chulainn's early deeds are narrated by characters in the drama, the purpose of rhetorical dialogues in the *Táin* as a whole" (321 f.). The assertion that these features of the *Táin must* be due to imitation of the classics or of Christian developments of them is unproven and (I suspect) unprovable. See also Murphy (1955–57, esp. 157 f.).

16. Watkins (1963, 217).
17. Watkins (1963, 212 ff.).
18. On these, see Mac Cana (1966).
19. Binchy (1979–80, 39).
20. See Byrne (1967).
21. Ó Coileáin (1977–78, 7).
22. The eleventh and twelfth centuries may together be regarded as a watershed in the history of Irish literature, as indeed in that of Irish culture in general. In literature this was a great age of compilation, and it saw the production of the three monastic codices which contain so much of our early narrative literature, these codices being *Lebor na hUidre* (on which see note 8 above), Rawlinson B 502, and the Book of Leinster. Following upon the reform of the Church in this period, custody of the manuscript tradition passed from the monasteries to the newly established lay schools which were to be conducted by hereditary learned families, and it was the members of these families who continued the manuscript transmission of the literature up to the seventeenth century. Fortunately, the hereditary lay scribes evinced a lively interest in the early material, for their manuscripts add much to what we have of it in the three great monastic codices.
23. Chadwick and Chadwick (1932, passim), Knott and Murphy (1966, 114 ff.), Jackson (1964, passim).
24. Jackson (1964, 2).
25. On these see Rees and Rees (1961, 217 ff., 246 ff., 259 f., 305 ff., 326 f., 331 ff.).
26. See Ó Broin (1961–63) and *TBC I* (241).
27. See Ross (1967, 305 f.), David Greene in Dillon (1959, 96).
28. Knott and Murphy (1966, 114).
29. Knott and Murphy (1966, 115).
30. Ó Riain (1978).
31. Chadwick and Chadwick (1932, 16): "In truth, any date which may be fixed for the end of the Irish Heroic Age must be more or less arbitrary; but for practical purposes we prefer to date it early in the eighth century. We may perhaps include the story of the Battle of Allen." Acceptance of such a date for the end of the Heroic Age in Ireland is implicit in Francis John Byrne's discussion of the Battle of Allen in Byrne (1973, 146). It has also been suggested that the Heroic Age lasted only until the end of the sixth century: see Williams and Ní Mhuiríosa (1979, 8; but cf. 12).

32. On this matter see Ó Cuív (1963), Hughes (1972; 1977).
33. Byrne (1973, 2).
34. Greene (1955).
35. Charles-Edwards (1978, 130 ff.).
36. His major work in this field is *Early Irish History and Mythology* (T. O'Rahilly 1946).
37. Murphy (1953a, passim) and (briefly) in Knott and Murphy (1966, 147 f.).
38. Rees and Rees (1961). It may be noted in passing that in this work the Rees brothers also use the work of Mircea Eliade whose comparisons are of the typological rather than of the genetic kind.
39. The arguments of some of Dumézil's critics are considered in Littleton (1966, 176 ff.).
40. See for example his treatment of *Esnada Tige Buchet* in T. O'Rahilly (1952), and of *Baile in Scáil* in T. O'Rahilly (1946, 283 f.).
41. Since O'Rahilly never presented a definitive formulation of his theory of Irish myth, it must be inferred by piecing together the relevant observations which are scattered throughout his work, and by extrapolation from his treatment of the texts. Some aspects of O'Rahilly's position are discussed in Ó Cathasaigh (1977, 11 ff.).
42. Stokes (1891b). Passages omitted by Stokes were published by Thurneysen (1918, 401 ff.). The German translation by Lehmacher (1931) includes some of the material omitted by Stokes.
43. Mac Cana (1970, 61).
44. The stemmatic theory of recension still holds the field in Irish studies, but there have been rumblings of discontent: see, for example, Ó Coileáin (1974, 89) and Melia (1978, 608). The Lachmannian position is stoutly defended by Dumville (1975–76, 273). Having noted that "over the years, it has often been said that the time has not yet come for the critical edition of an Irish text," Dumville says that "*Lebor Bretnach* is the ideal text to disprove this unfortunate maxim" (273). But *Lebor Bretnach* is a Middle Irish translation of a Latin work (the *Historia Brittonum*): it can scarcely be regarded as the ideal text upon which to base conclusions as to the relative status of the extant manuscript texts of early Irish narrative in general. The matter requires further discussion: one contribution to the debate is Slotkin (1977–79).
45. Thurneysen (1921).
46. Jackson (1961).
47. Cross (1952).
48. For a critique of the Finnish school, see A. Rees (1966, 34 ff.).
49. See Eisner (1969) and the works there cited.
50. Binchy (1963, xvii).
51. One could at least go along with Rachel Bromwich (1966, 155) when she says: "The significance of the parallel which *Cano* affords with the *Tristan* [...] consists merely in the fact that it is one among several Irish treatments of the 'eter-

nal triangle.' But for this very reason its importance ought not to be neglected. It is a version of the theme which preserves several interesting primitive features, illustrative of the type of story-material out of which we can see that the Celtic prototype of the *Tristan* must have emerged."

52. Abrams (1960, 6).

53. Mac Airt (1958, 150).

54. van Hamel (1934, passim).

55. van Hamel (1934, 5). The remainder of his definition, "or of whose example the deeds of other men must be regarded as a reflexion," need not detain us here; its relevance to *Cath Maige Tuired* is examined in "*Cath Maige Tuired* as Exemplary Myth," chap. 9 in this volume.

56. See Murphy (1963, 213 ff.).

57. "*Cath Maige Tuired* as Exemplary Myth," chap. 9 in this volume.

58. Byrne (1974, 146).

59. Introduction to Knott and Murphy (1966, 2).

60. Introduction to Knott and Murphy (1966, 17).

61. See note 44.

62. Abrams (1960, 26).

63. See note 42. The passage comprises §§33–35 of Stokes's edition. The translation is my own but draws where possible on Stokes.

64. Dían Cécht's daughter.

65. Two other tales connected with the battle are discussed in Knott and Murphy (1966, 109 f.).

66. See Flower (1926, 298 ff.) and Walsh (1947, 48).

67. Knott and Murphy (1966, 109).

68. See note 22.

69. See Ross (1967, 176 ff.) and Mac Cana (1970, 67 ff.).

70. On this latter, see Mac Cana (1970, 69) and Roberts (1975, xix).

71. On this charm and others of a very similar kind, see Ködderitzsch (1974).

72. Ködderitzsch (1974, 50).

73. Knott and Murphy (1966, 110).

74. Knott and Murphy (1966, 101).

75. Carney (1955, 277).

76. Mac Eoin (1967, 246).

77. See note 15.

78. Meid (1974, 26 f.). I am indebted to Liam Breatnach for this reference.

79. Of the vast secondary literature on this subject, one may mention Potter (1902), de Vries (1954), and van der Lee (1957).

80. See Cross (1950); Knott and Murphy (1966, 128) and the works there cited.

81. Schultz (1923, 302).

82. See de Vries (1954). This passage has also been interpreted in Dumézilian terms: see Puhvel (1970, 378 ff.).

83. Cross (1950, 180 ff.). See also Jackson (1961, 70 f.).

84. See Cross (1950, 179).

85. One may compare the structure of the well-known tale *Scéla Mucce Meic Dathó* (Thurneysen 1935). In this tale, as in *Táin Bó Cúailnge*, the Ulaid and the Connachta are in contention for the possession of a sacred animal: in the *Táin* it is the Bull of Cooley, in *Scéla Mucce* it is Mac Dathó's hound Ailbe. In the latter story, however, an account of how the Ulaid and the Connachta contend for possession of a sacred pig is given within the framing story of the contention for the hound.

4. THE CONCEPT OF THE HERO IN IRISH MYTHOLOGY

1. Quoted by Hawkes (1977, 12).
2. T. S. Eliot, quoted in Mathiessen (1959, 40).
3. Dumézil (1973, 115).
4. Leach (1969, 11).
5. van Hamel (1933); Kinsella (1970, 21–33).
6. Ó Broin (1961–63, 289).
7. Dumézil (1970, 16).
8. Text edited by Eleanor Knott (1936).
9. T. O'Rahilly (1946, 121).
10. Dumézil (1943, 33 ff.).
11. See "The Semantics of *síd*," chap. 2 in this volume.
12. Dumézil (1973, 111 f.).
13. Vendryes (1952, 233–46).
14. Dillon (1946, 11 ff.); text ed. Meyer (1901b; 1918; 1921), Thurneysen (1936b), and Murray (2004).
15. Stokes (1891b).
16. de Vries (1963, 241).
17. Dillon (1952) for text and translation.
18. Dillon (1952, 72n6).

5. THE SISTER'S SON IN EARLY IRISH LITERATURE

1. Carney (1964, 2 ff.).
2. On the basis of this ascription, Carney dates the poem at latest somewhere in the years 750–770 (1964, xix), and he is satisfied that the language of the poem is consistent with this dating. Binchy disagrees, holding that on linguistic grounds we are forbidden to regard it as having been composed before ca. 900 A.D. (1976a, 27n27).

3. Bieler (1963, 230 §6.2–5 [Bigotian Penitential], 162 §§26–29 [Canones Hibernenses]); and E. Gwynn (1914, 170 §§17 f., trans. by Binchy as "The Old-Irish Penitential" in Bieler 1963, 258–77, at 273 §§17 f.).

4. *Math mac-cleiriuch dia tecmai oen inna cinath-sa asrubartmar is diabul penne dó fri cetmuindtir*, E. Gwynn (1914, 170 §18 = Bieler 1963, 273 §18). There is nothing corresponding to this in the Canones Hibernenses. In the Bigotian Penitential the double penance is prescribed for a nun rather than a cleric: "if any nun becomes excited and shouts with sounds of this sort, she shall be corrected with double the penance prescribed above" (Bieler 1963, 230 §6.6; trans. 231). Keening is usually associated with women rather than men: see Partridge (1983, 87). But in Irish literature men are said to have engaged in keening. In *Scéla Cano meic Gartnáin*, Cano keens his friend Illann in the traditional manner: he claps his hands until streams of blood flow from them, and recites a lament for him (Binchy 1963, 14, lines 383 ff.). In *Fingal Rónáin*, Rónán utters a lament over the body of his son Mael Fhothartaig (Greene 1955, 8, lines 167 ff.). Nevertheless, too much should not be made of the *maccleiriuch* of the Old-Irish Penitential. It is conceivable that it should be amended to *maccaillech* 'nun,' and that the distinction being drawn is between the penances due respectively from a laywoman and a nun. In the Old-Irish Table of penitential commutations (ed. Binchy 1962a), it is said that, "as there is a difference between laymen and clerics and between nuns and laywomen (*eter clerichiu 7 laichiu etar maccaillacha 7 laichesa*), so too there is a difference between the [kind of] mortification and penance due from them" (60 §7, with trans. on facing page and also in Binchy's appendix to Bieler 1963, 278 f.). In the sentence which I have quoted from the Old-Irish Penitential, the *maccleiriuch* is contrasted with the married woman; in the passage which precedes it, the married woman is coupled with the *caillech aithrige* (MS *aithirgi, aithrigi*): they receive the same penance for keening, and there is also a specific penance for keening a married woman or *caillech aithrige* who dies in childbirth. It seems that the *caillech aithrige* 'penitent nun' may be a nun who, having sinned (and perhaps become pregnant), has repented of her sin and returned to religious life. There is some doubt as to whether she belongs in our text, and Binchy tentatively suggests emending to *caillech airige* 'concubine': see his trans. of §17 in Bieler (1963, 273, and note ad loc.). (I am indebted to Máirín Ní Dhonnchadha for discussing the *caillech aithrige* with me.)

5. Carney (1965a, 53; 1965b, 168).

6. On the legalistic use of this verb in religious poetry, see Quin (1981, 47 f.).

7. We find an example of the solemn "recognition" of a legal relationship between persons in the story of Cú Chulainn (see below).

8. F. J. Byrne (1973) writes of our poet's "very legalistic attitude with regard to the relations between Christ and the Jews" (44). He says that, "although Blathmac does not actually use the legal term *rath*, he illuminates for us the mode of thought which determined that even at the present day the theological concept of

the grace of God is expressed in Irish as *rath Dé* (45). The expression in the poem of the relevant "mode of thought" does in fact find lexical underpinning in the use of *-ír* and *-rathach*. It may be added that the same "mode of thought" underlies the term *céle Dé*: he was "the man who took God for his *flaith*, who entered into a contract of service with Him" (Hughes 1966, 173n3). See also Byrne (1973, 157).

9. Binchy (1976a, 24–27). [On *cobfolaid*, see now Carey (1988, 125–28).]

10. Binchy (1976a, 23–31).

11. Binchy (1976a, 29).

12. Greene (1959, 167).

13. We shall see that Christ's status as a sister's son is explicated by T. M. Charles-Edwards (1970–72, 119 f.). See further below.

14. The Jews are described as a *túath* (dat. *tuaith*) at line 385. For the designation of the Jews as *túath Dé*, see *DIL* s.v. 1 *túath*, I(b).

15. Tacitus, *Germania* 20.4; trans. Mattingly (1970, 118).

16. See, on the avunculate and on the "joking relationship," Radcliffe-Brown (1952); and, on the variety in the social environment and character of the avunculate, Lévi-Strauss (1968, 42–45). The relationship can vary even within a single society. Lévi-Strauss draws on a description of the Siuai of Bougainville: "The relationship between the nephew and his mother's brother 'appears to range between stern discipline and genial mutual dependence. . . .' However, '. . . most of the informants agreed that all boys stand in some awe of their mother's brothers, and are more likely to obey them than their own fathers'" (1968, 43, quoting from Oliver 1955, 255).

17. Lévi-Strauss (1968, 39).

18. Lévi-Strauss (1969, 431).

19. For a brief study of the controversy regarding the avunculate, and some references, see I. Lewis (1976, 56–60).

20. See Benveniste (1973, 180–92); Beekes (1976); and Szemerényi (1977, 50, 53 ff., 62, 150, 155 ff., 166 ff.). These works should be consulted for the comparative data, of which some items have been culled for what follows here.

21. The word is Szemerényi's (1977, 53).

22. See the full selection in Szemerényi (1977, 53 f.). It may be noted that Szemerényi links more of these words with the "mother's brother" than does either Benveniste or Beekes, and that he goes so far as to say that "with the uncle the reference does seem to be confined to the distaff-side" (55). This would not appear to be true of Welsh *ewythr*, for one: see Charles-Edwards (1970–72, 105n1) and *Geiriadur Prifysgol Cymru*, s.v.

23. See Bremmer (1976).

24. See, for example, Benveniste (1973, 185).

25. See again Benveniste (1973), Beekes (1976), and Szemerényi (1977).

26. Beekes (1976, 45–49); Szemerényi (1977, 157–83).

27. Bremmer (1976).

28. The notion (Szemerényi 1977, 191) that *awos* was originally "maternal uncle," and that the sense "grandfather" is secondary, is inherently improbable, given that the reflexes of unenlarged *awos* mean "grandfather," and that "mother's brother" is denoted by various enlargements of it. There is a difficulty too in Szemerényi's explanation of the shift in the meaning of *nepōts* in terms of Sol Tax's rule of terminological correlation (190–92): why did it take thousands of years for this shift to occur, and why did it not occur at all in the Aryan group? The distribution of the enlargements of *awos*, and their variety, together with the situation regarding *nepōts*, suggest that the avunculate did not figure in the kinship vocabulary of the earliest Indo-European times.

29. See van Hamel (1933, 1–8); Thurneysen (1921, 268–73); and Huld (1981).

30. Huld (1981, 240 f.).

31. Binchy (1956, 228–34).

32. See *DIL* s.v. *2 gor*, (b).

33. *TBC I* (line 3369, trans. 215). See also Binchy (1941, 98), where it is stated that *goire* "is used of the duty of supporting an aged man, which falls primarily on his sons or lineal descendants, and in default of them on other members of his kindred."

34. Charles-Edwards (1970–72).

35. Szemerényi (1977, 50).

36. Charles-Edwards (1970–72, 106).

37. Charles-Edwards (1970–72, 107–12).

38. Charles-Edwards (1970–72, 106, 112–14).

39. Charles-Edwards (1970–72, 115).

40. Charles-Edwards (1970–72, 121).

41. Charles-Edwards (1970–72, 121).

42. For a possible instance of Irish *ua* (*aue*) in the sense "ancestor," rather than "descendant; grandson," see now Ó Cuív (1981, 146 §8, and note ad loc., 148).

43. Charles-Edwards (1970–72, 121).

44. Charles-Edwards (1970–72, 115).

45. It was Charles-Edwards who established the meaning "grandson" for Common Celtic *neūss* (1970–72, 107–12).

46. See note 28.

47. s.v. *1 nia*.

48. *LEIA* (MNOP), s.v. On the semantics, see Vendryes (1929, 265–67) and Sjoestedt (1949, 58).

49. See E. MacNeill (1907–9, 369–70). In his review of MacNeill's paper, Thurneysen (1912, 185) suggested that it was not unthinkable that the two words were etymologically one and the same, with the sense "warrior," "champion," representing a change in the meaning of the word for "sister's son" but his argument is refuted by Pokorny (1915, 405–7).

50. *Néth* occurs in Adomnán's *Vita Columbae* (see *Thes.* 2:273.7); *nioth* in the Book of Armagh (*Thes.* 2:267.39, 269.34). Both E. MacNeill (1907–9, 369) and Pokorny (1915, 406) take *nioth* as genitive of *1 nia*, the form being, in their view, an early adoption of the genitive of *2 nia*. (*DIL* s.v. *1 nia* 15 f. misrepresents Pokorny on this.) I argue below that one at least of the examples of *nioth* represents the genitive of *2 nia*.

51. M. O'Brien (1973, §38) lists a number of names containing *Nia* or *Nio*, but he does not give an opinion as to the element's meaning. Ó Cuív (1986, 160) takes it to be "champion."

52. Pokorny (1915, 407).

53. *Thes.* (2:114, 61a21).

54. Ó hAodha (1978, line 27).

55. Ó hAodha (1978, lines 9, 31).

56. M. O'Brien (1938, 364).

57. For the date of the glosses on the St. Gall Priscian, see *Thes.* (2:xxiii), and for that of the Life of Brigit, Ó hAodha (1978, xxvi–xxvii).

58. "Even the terms for 'uncle' and 'aunt' have been borrowed, although some older speakers remember that the mother's brother should be *amhnair*" (Fox 1978, 73). O'Brien points out that the St. Gall glossator, at 61a19, glosses *patruus* with *bráthair athar* 'father's brother,' which would indicate that he had no word for "paternal uncle."

59. O Daly (1975, 40 §6).

60. See *DIL* s.vv. *nia, gormac*.

61. Watson (1941, lines 323 f.).

62. *DIL* s.v. *2 gor* (b).

63. *LL* ii (454, line 14204 [*Brislech Mór Maige Murthemni*]).

64. Meyer (1912a, §959).

65. Charles-Edwards (1970–72, 120).

66. *Thes.* (2:267.38 f.).

67. *Thes.* (2:369).

68. On supernatural paternity in Irish narrative see Rees and Rees (1961, 213–37, esp. 223).

69. See discussion above.

70. Binchy (1936).

71. Binchy (1936, 183).

72. Binchy (1936, 184).

73. Charles-Edwards (1970–72, 115 f., 119 f.).

74. The passages from *Táin Bó Cúailnge* listed in this connection by Charles-Edwards can now be consulted in *TBC I* (lines 1855, 4068 f., and 4123 f.).

75. McCone (1986, 11).

76. On the *cú glas* see also Charles-Edwards (1976, 46–53) and Campanile (1979).

77. Charles-Edwards (1970–72, 120).

78. Meyer (1910b); *DIL* s.v. *immathchor* suggests that the *imathchor* of the title may mean "mutual restitution." (For some observations on the curial procedure observed in this tale, see Binchy 1976a, 30–31.)

79. Binchy (1936, 185).

80. E. MacNeill (1907–9, 360) had said of NIOTTA here that "the sense of 'nephew' (perhaps 'descendant in the female line') seems apt."

81. Macalister (1945, 247 [no. 252]).

82. Charles-Edwards (1970–72, 120).

83. Macalister (1945, 283 [no. 288]).

84. Charles-Edwards (1970–72, 120).

85. *Cú* is a very important element in Irish personal names, but neither *Glaschú* nor *Cú glas* occurs in the relevant list in M. O'Brien (1973, §40) or in the index of personal names in M. O'Brien (1962).

86. Charles-Edwards (1970–72, 115–16, 119–22).

87. Charles-Edwards (1970–72, 120).

88. Some examples of the sister's son are listed in Cross (1952, 421 [motif P 253 O.1]). There is a discussion in Nitze (1912, 304–10). See also Rees and Rees (1961, 144–45, 219, 292).

89. E. Gray (1982); earlier ed., Stokes (1891b); German trans., Lehmacher (1931). Gray and Lehmacher follow Stokes's numbering of the paragraphs of the text. The full title of the tale as given in the MS is *Cath Maige Turedh ocus genemain Bres meic Elathain ocus a ríghe,* "The battle of Mag Tuired, and the birth of Bres son of Elathan and his reign," Elathan being a variant of Elatha. It has to be said that the existing translations stand in need of revision at several points. Among recent studies of the tale, mention must be made in particular of three articles by E. Gray (1980–81; 1982–83a; 1982–83b). See also S. O'Brien (1976) and "*Cath Maige Tuired* as Exemplary Myth," chap. 9 in this volume.

90. Rees and Rees (1961, 39).

91. Oosten (1985, 164). Oosten also states that "the pantheon is ordered not by the principles of the political domain but in terms of the kinship system of the Indo-Europeans" (25).

92. Oosten (1985, 126–33).

93. *CMT* §8.

94. See "*Cath Maige Tuired* as Exemplary Myth," chap. 9 in this volume.

95. Stokes (1891b, 63) translated it "if his own misdeeds (?) should so give cause"; Lehmacher (1931, 441) "falls sein schlechtes Benehmen dies veranlasse"; and Gray (1982, 29) "if his own misdeeds should give cause."

96. The text has "and."

97. Stokes (1891b, 71) translates "and he was not well-pleased (?) with them for that"; Lehmacher (1931, 444) "aber das machte ihn mittellos"; Gray (1982, 35) "and they did not regard him as properly qualified to rule from that time on."

98. *Mífholtae* (for *mífholta*), *mí-* 'ill, mis-, wrong' + nom. pl. of *folad*. On the use of the plural here, see Binchy (1976a, 23–31) as quoted above. *Sofoltach* (for *sofholtach*), *so-* 'good' + *foltach*, an adj. from *folud* + *-ach*, a suffix denoting possession. *DIL* defines *sofholtach* as "of good qualifications or deeds," and adds that it is "used of a 'flaith' and 'céle' who rightly observe their reciprocal duties" (S 313.39 ff.).

99. Thurneysen (1923a, 374). The translation is that of *DIL* s.v. *folud* (a).

100. It could also mean "as a result of that," which is implicit in Lehmacher's translation.

101. Note the remark of Rees and Rees, which relates to parts of *Cath Maige Tuired* which are not dealt with here, that "the contests, lavish hospitality, obligatory over-eating, obscenity and mockery which characterize the way in which they [Túatha Dé Danann] and the Fomoire behave towards one another in certain episodes have their counterparts in the ritual hostility and disrespectful joking which is typical of the conduct of people in many human societies towards the kin-groups from which they obtain their wives" (1961, 40).

102. See S. O'Brien (1976).

103. After the battle, Lóch Lethglas undertakes to remove from Ireland for ever the need to guard against the Fomoiri, in return for quarter from Lug (§§139 ff.).

104. See further "*Cath Maige Tuired* as Exemplary Myth," p. 140 in this volume.

105. In another incident in the tale (§124), Rúadán of the Fomoiri, whose mother was of the Túatha Dé Danann, is given a spear by his maternal kin. We are told that "that is why weavers' beams are still called 'spears of the maternal kin' in Ireland."

106. See *Compert Con Culainn*, ed. van Hamel (1933); see also, "The Concept of the Hero in Irish Mythology," chap. 4 in this volume.

107. I shall refer to *TBC I*. References to other editions may be found there (vii).

108. *TBC I* (note to line 51).

109. Fergus tells the Connachta that "women and boys do not suffer from the debility nor does anyone outside the territory of Ulster, nor yet Cú Chulainn and his father" (*TBC I*, lines 525 ff.).

110. See Rees and Rees (1961, 246–49); Melia (1974); and Nagy (1984).

111. O'Rahilly's "there" is a misprint; the Irish is *sund* (*TBC I*, line 445).

112. On the similarity here, see Melia (1974, 229).

113. See Greene (1972, 60).

114. *DIL* F 17.70 ff.

115. Sjoestedt (1949, 59).

116. Nagy (1984; 1985); McCone (1986).

117. McCone (1986, 8).

118. See "The Semantics of *síd*," chap. 2 in this volume.

119. See O'Leary (1986a).

120. Ó Riain (1973–74a).

121. Mac Cana (1985, 65).
122. Radner (1982, 47).
123. E. Hull (1898, lv).
124. The early version of this tale is edited by V. Hull (1949a).
125. Schoepperle (1913, 11–12). Rees and Rees (1961, 292) add that there is a tradition that Diarmait, who eloped with Gráinne, was sister's son to Finn.
126. Thurneysen (1935).
127. Stokes (1897, 392–95 §251).
128. Four of the relevant texts have been edited by O Daly (1975); line-references in the text refer to this edition. A fifth, *Immathchor Ailello ocus Airt* (Meyer 1910b), has already been referred to (see note 78 above).
129. McCone (1984a; 1985; 1986; 1987).
130. A short version of this paper was read at the North American Congress of Celtic Studies in Ottawa in March 1986. I am grateful to those who discussed it with me afterwards, in particular K. H. Schmidt and J. Shaw.

6. CURSE AND SATIRE

1. Elliott (1960).
2. Elliott (1960, 291). He does go on to say that magical satire is frequently in verse, the curse in prose (292). As it happens, however, the curse we shall be looking at here takes the form of an incantatory verse.
3. Elliott (1960, 292).
4. Elliott (1960, 291).
5. Stokes (1900, 14–16). There is a translation (of a slightly different text) in O'Grady (1892, 2:112 ff.). For a Modern Irish version, see Ní Shéaghdha (1942–45, 1:40–44). Except where otherwise stated my account of this anecdote is based on Stokes's text, but I am of course indebted to O'Grady's magnificent translation.
6. E. Gray (1982, 28 ff.). The satire and its context are recounted in §§24 f., 36–40. (For the textual complications here, see "*Cath Maige Tuired* as Exemplary Myth," chap. 9 in this volume.) The story of the satire is also preserved in a separate anecdote; see V. Hull (1930a). On the text of the incantation, see note 9 below.
7. See further below, p. 98 in this volume.
8. I have supplied the marks of length in Bécán. It may be noted also that the variant *séise* for *seiser* is translated by O'Grady, who also reads *dóibh* as against Stokes's *d'óibh*, and renders, "Let Becan not make mirth for them [his people]." [For *tredan* I should have read *trédán* (for earlier *trétán*), and translated along the lines of Dooley and Roe (1999, 18) "may his herd be small."]
9. Only the first four words of the incantation are written out in the extant text of *Cath Maige Tuired*. I have taken the remainder from Stokes (1899, 158), and I have essentially followed his translation.

10. Ní Shéaghdha (1942–45, 1:40).
11. See "The Semantics of *síd*," chap. 2 in this volume.
12. See Sharpe (1979, 82 ff.).
13. Byrne (1973, 15).

7. THE THREEFOLD DEATH IN EARLY IRISH SOURCES

1. It is spoken by Moling to Grác's wife, who has come to him with her child. I take the first line to mean "Wife of Grác, that (crying) is harsh," the meaning of *grácda* being "cacophonous" or the like. The word is left untranslated in *DIL*, s.v. It does not occur elsewhere, and Carney (1955, 140) translates "that is a thing like Grácc," noting that "the phrase is without importance and (was) probably added later with no other purpose than to convert a three-syllable into a seven-syllable line." Carney is doubtless correct in regarding the phrase as an addition to the original text, but this is no reason to suppose that it is virtually meaningless. I suggest that *grácda* is an adjectival derivative of *grác* 'croaking, cawing,' that a pun with Grác is intended, and that the reference is to the crying of Grác's child which is again referred to in the fourth line of the first quatrain.

2. See the chart in Radner (1983, 200).

3. For an introduction to Dumézil's work, see Littleton (1982).

4. Ó Concheanainn's work has not been noticed by Guyonvarc'h (1983, 1010).

5. In translating line 738, I have adopted the variant reading *do f[h]laitisa* (Nic Dhonnchadha 1964, 39) in preference to the pleonastic *tusa* of the edited text.

6. This interpretation of what happens in *Togail Bruidne Da Derga* is somewhat at odds with Greene (1979), McCone (1980), and O'Leary (1986a), but I believe that it is in keeping with the sequence of events in the text. [I justify this view in "*Gat* and *díberg* in *Togail Bruidne Da Derga*," chap. 28 in this volume.]

7. Two further differences are mentioned by Jackson (1940, 540). First, Grác is Moling's cowherd, Mongán his swineherd. But in *Buile Suibne*, Mongán is referred to variously as cowherd and swineherd. Secondly, Jackson says that in the *Anecdota* version the accusation against Suibne is made by the murderer's wife, whereas in *Buile Suibne* it is made by his sister. In fact, the woman who makes the accusation is not identified in the *Anecdota* version, but she is spoken of in the third person in a poem which is addressed to Grác's wife. Moreover, in his description of the incident, Moling compliments Grác's wife for her act of mercy to Suibne (*trocaire dorighnis ris*) in giving him milk. We can be reasonably certain that Grác's wife was not the accuser.

8. Pádraig Ó Riain (1973–74b, 185) suggests that the change in name from Grác to Mongán "was dictated, perhaps, by a desire to provide the episode with something like an Ulster flavour." The herdsman's wife is unnamed in the *Anecdota* poems; in the earlier version (V. Hull 1930b) she is called Crón.

9. The Irish text established by Murphy (1952, 147) reads: *flaith hó Níell co Néll; Níell cáich ua Néill; naiscther géill; dot-hetha tein; rúadgarg raithnech less; béss tress mí for bliadni bebais muir; már domain dínib dúabais, díth.* I use the acute accent here instead of the macron. The translation is Murphy's, except for *béss* which Murphy tentatively translates as "perhaps"; as it is followed by the indicative here, I have taken it to mean "surely."

10. Translation by Kelly of *tri bais aithfegar do denam don tuaith: guin 7 golo 7 crochad; arnbas do eclais .i. crochad nama* (Binchy 1978, 3:1101.27 f.). In an almost identical passage (Binchy 1978, 4:1927.20 f.), the triad is *guin 7 crochad 7 goladh,* where *goladh,* if it represents *gólad* and is not merely a late spelling of *góla,* should perhaps be translated "consigning to a pit," rather than the tentative "digging a pit" which seems to be implied in *DIL* s.v. *gólaid.*

11. A different kind of pit is envisaged in the saga *Fingal Rónáin,* in which the hero declares that he would not sleep with his step-mother even if it would save him from being put into a burning pit of fire (*i cualchlais tened*) three times and being reduced to powder and ash (Greene 1955, lines 52 ff.). This is clearly a description of the most extreme kind of suffering, but it is not a punishment for an offence.

12. This article is a modified version of a paper given in the Department of Irish Folklore at University College Dublin in March 1993, and subsequently at the Dublin Medieval Society. I am grateful to Professor Bo Almqvist for inviting me to speak on this topic, and for his helpful comments. The texts which are discussed date from different periods; except in direct quotations I have used Middle Irish forms of personal names. Translations are my own, unless the contrary is indicated.

8. EARLY IRISH LITERATURE AND LAW

1. Charles-Edwards (1999b, 1).
2. Binchy (1978).
3. Kelly (1988).
4. L. Breatnach (2005).
5. Binchy (1954, 62–63).
6. Binchy (1943).
7. Binchy (1943, 92).
8. Binchy (1943, 78n6).
9. Binchy (1943, 95).
10. Binchy (1943, 97).
11. L. Breatnach (1987, 103).
12. L. Breatnach (1990, 5).
13. *Fuithirbe* is a placename.
14. L. Breatnach (1986, 46–47).
15. L. Breatnach (1984).

16. L. Breatnach (1990, 5).
17. Binchy (1959, 39).
18. See Dillon (1932); L. Breatnach (1990, 3); and Stacey (2005, 68–75).
19. Kelly (1986, 80).
20. See Kelly (1986, 80), where the presumption is made that *ollam* in this instance refers to the highest grade of judge.
21. L. Breatnach (1987, 105). I have slightly altered Breatnach's translation for clarity in the present context.
22. Cited by L. Breatnach (1987, 123); the translation is Breatnach's.
23. See Ó Corráin, Breatnach, and Breen (1984, 400n2).
24. V. Hull (1952). Translations of this text in what follows are by me.
25. L. Breatnach (1981, 69).
26. See Ó Cathasaigh (1977).
27. E. Gray (1982).
28. Bergin and Best (1934–38); trans. Gantz (1981, 37–59).
29. See "*Táin Bó Cúailnge* and Early Irish Law," chap. 15 in this volume.

9. CATH MAIGE TUIRED AS EXEMPLARY MYTH

1. Stokes (1891b). Passages omitted by Stokes were published by Thurneysen (1918, 401–6). G. Lehmacher's German translation (1931) includes some of the material omitted by Stokes. For a discussion of other texts relating to the battle see Murphy (1955a, 19–24).
2. Murphy (1955a, 19).
3. The paragraph-numbers are those of Stokes's edition, and the translations are based on Stokes, modified where it seemed necessary or desirable.
4. For example, *LL*, lines 1049–57.
5. See Dumézil (1948, 179–88); de Vries (1961, 151–55).
6. See T. O'Rahilly (1946, 388), and authorities there cited.
7. T. O'Rahilly (1946, 388).
8. T. O'Rahilly (1946, 388).
9. Murphy (1955a, 18–19). On Dumézil's interpretation of the Indo-European theomachy see Dumézil (1948, 8).
10. Murphy (1954).
11. van Hamel (1934, passim).
12. van Hamel (1934, 5).
13. Murphy (1955a, 17). Murphy published a critique of van Hamel's argument in *Duanaire Finn* 3 (1953a, 213–17).
14. Especially by the work of Dumézil and of Rees and Rees (1961), to which I refer below.

15. More specifically it is a version of the generation conflict, which is a subset within the heroic biography. On the Irish versions of the generation conflict see Cross (1950).

16. Although the form is preterite, Lehmacher (1931) translates "Bres nun hatte die Herrschaft übernommen" (443).

17. Dillon (1952, 64). Two accounts of the discovery of Cashel have been joined together in the text edited by Dillon and, having noted that "no attempt is made to harmonize the two stories," he cites other examples of this kind of "patchwork."

18. Dumézil (1973, 111–12).

19. Dumézil (1973, 112).

20. Watkins (1979, 181); the italics are mine. McCone (1980) also brings out the importance of the verbal expression.

21. *LL*, lines 12468–70. Cf. O Daly (1975, 17). The text is edited and translated by Stokes (1908–10), who supplied the title "Scéla Conchobair Maic Nessa." The relevant passage is §10 of Stokes's edition, and has been taken by him to mean "He never delivered a judgment at a time when it was not permitted him..." rather than "He never delivered a judgment because it was not permitted him..."; but I prefer the latter translation, which is implicit in Máirín O Daly's interpretation.

22. O Daly (1975, 60).

23. Dumézil (1973, 42–43, 110–11).

24. Ed. and trans. V. Hull (1930a).

25. *LU*, lines 561–64 (Stokes 1899, 158).

26. Dumézil (1943, 230–41). Dumézil has reproduced what he wishes to retain of the earlier part of this book (*Servius et la fortune*) in his *Idées romaines* (1969, 103–24). While he does not reproduce it there, he says that "la dernière partie, sur la louange et le blâme en Irlande, reste en gros valable" (1969, 103). Greimas (1970, 117–34) recasts Dumézil's treatment of the three personages in semiotic terms.

27. Dumézil (1943, 230).

28. Dumézil (1943, 230–31).

29. Binchy (1976a, 29; see also 23–31).

30. Dumézil's interpretation is borne out by the text, but not (as he thinks) by §38, where he has been led astray by the translation of d'Arbois de Jubainville. The text reads: *Ni roan tra fochnom no ēraic dona tuathaib 7 nī tabradis sēoit na tuaithe a foicidh na tuaithe oli*. The first part of this is clear: *fochnom* is for *fognam*, and Stokes translates "Neither service nor wergild from the tribes continued," d'Arbois "Personne n'était déchargé de service ni d'amende." The difficulty arises in the second sentence. Stokes gives "and the treasures of the tribe were not delivered by the act of the whole tribe." It should be noted that in *CMT* sg. *túath* and pl. *túatha* (and the respective case-forms) are interchangeable and that Dé Danann is

frequently omitted, so that for "tribes" and "tribe" we can (and probably should) substitute Túatha (Dé Danann). But what is *i foicidh*? *Foicidh* is doubtless for *foichid*, but Stokes's "by the act" for *i foichid* is, to say the least, a long shot. *Foichid* is poorly attested, and it is suggested in *DIL*, s.v., that it may be a variant of *fochaid*. In that case we might translate "on account of the suffering of all the Túatha." For somewhat similar usage of *i n-* see *DIL* (I, 6.71–7.26): an example with *do-beir* is *ca hindeochad do-béred in rí forru ind* "(in punishment) for it" (Knott 1936, line 196). Such an interpretation is less convincing in a negative sentence, but I think it preferable to Lehmacher's rendering of *i foichid* as "für die Abwehr von Heimsuchungen" (1931, 443). (If we were prepared to amend, we might think of *fochraic* and translate "in payment, as rent," but we would expect the following genitive to denote that which is paid for, rather than those who pay.) In any case, the sentence cannot mean "pour les trésors qu'on donnait au roi personne ne recevait aucune rémunération," which rendering forms the basis of Dumézil's interpretation of the passage. In short, it is not this paragraph which shows the king to be in breach of the social contract: it is §36, which speaks of his failure to provide hospitality and entertainment. (I might add that *CMT* bristles with textual difficulties of one kind or another.)

31. Dumézil (1943, 234).
32. McCone (1980, 162).
33. McCone (1980, 162). I am not sure that McCone is correct in his interpretation of *nī boī acht meth foairi-sim ōnd uair-sin* (§39) as meaning that Bres suffered physical decay. The immediate context has been given above, where I have followed Stokes in translating "decay." But although *meth* can denote physical decline (see *DIL*, s.v.), the context would seem to indicate that what is in question here is a confirmation of Cairbre's statement about Bres's wealth, and that the reference is therefore to a decline in Bres's fortunes. This does not, of course, invalidate McCone's contention that satire tends to be manifested in its physical effects: that is beyond question. But the narrator of *CMT* does not seem to have concerned himself with that aspect of the matter: his interest was in the social implications of the story of Bres.
34. Dumézil (1943, 241–44).
35. See Robinson (1912, passim); Binchy (1941, 69, s.v. *áer*).
36. Stokes (1862, xxxvi–xl); cf. Robinson (1912, 112–15).
37. This is discussed in Ó Cathasaigh (1977, 63–68).
38. O Daly (1975, 70); Ó Cathasaigh (1977, 123).
39. On Conaire's judgment see Ó Cathasaigh (1978a, 77); McCone (1980, 145–50).
40. See "The Theme of *lommrad* in *Cath Maige Mucrama*," chap. 23 in this volume.
41. See Rees and Rees (1961, 144–45).
42. His formula has been preserved as a charm; see p. 148 in this chapter.

43. Dumézil (1941, 171–72; 1968, 289–90). See also de Vries (1961, 153–54) and Mac Cana (1970, 60–64). Steven O'Brien (1976, 304) says: "The difficulties with this approach have been brought out by Mac Cana (61). These difficulties indicate that the Second Battle of Mag Tured has no place within the rubric of the 'War of the Functions.'" On the contrary, having examined the "difficulties" (as Dumézil himself had done), Mac Cana concludes that "Dumézil's interpretation of *CMT* is not beyond controversy, but nevertheless it has the not inconsiderable merit of recovering order and purpose from apparent chaos" (S. O'Brien 1976, 304). It may be added that the analysis offered by O'Brien has no place for Lug's attainment of agricultural competence.

44. M. MacNeill (1962).

45. M. MacNeill (1962, 5).

46. Rees and Rees (1961, 211).

47. Rees and Rees (1961, 210–11). See also Mac Cana (1980a, 24–28).

48. Mac Airt (1958, 150) suggests that "the *fili*'s main business was not the mere recital of tales, but first the exposition of them ... to the noble classes. ... Secondly he was expected to use them for the purpose of illustration. ... The kind of illustration meant is exactly that exemplified by the later bardic poets in their use of incidents from heroic tales." A pertinent example is found in *Mór ar bhfearg riot, a rí Saxan*, addressed by Gofraidh Fionn Ó Dálaigh to Maurice fitz Maurice [Fitzgerald], earl of Desmond (Bergin 1970, 73–81). The poet gives a long account of the coming of Lug to Tara, and then goes on to compare Maurice to Lug.

49. Van Hamel (1934, 30).

50. Rees and Rees (1961, 210–11 and 17–19). See also Dillon (1947a, 5). The passage from *Aislinge Meic Conglinne* (ed. and trans. Meyer 1892a, 110–13) is quoted in both these works.

51. Meyer (1906, 9).

52. H. Lüders *apud* Dillon (1947a, 5).

53. Binchy (1959, 39).

54. Rees and Rees (1961, 106), where they cite Eliade (1955); see also Eliade (1963, 410–12, 429–31).

55. Angela Partridge (1978, 75) adduces evidence that in modern times the custom of keening has been validated by attributing it to the Virgin Mary.

56. See Sjoestedt (1949, 2).

57. See Ködderitzch (1974, 50).

58. See Banks (1938).

59. See the example quoted by Ködderitzch (1974, 50), and that in Banks (1938, 134). Compare the Christianizing of the keening tradition mentioned above in note 55.

60. Ó Cathasaigh (1977, 17; and cf. 5).

61. De Vries (1963, 241).

62. De Vries (1963, 5).

63. We can probably speak of the Cycles of the Saints, and when the material on the poets has been studied it may be that Cycles of the Poets will be identified. A complication here is that kings, saints, and poets tend to be closely associated in the tradition. In the present article I have confined myself to the main cycles, but I may refer here to Ó Riain (1977).

64. In *TBC I*, Lug's coming is described at lines 2088–2135. He says to Cú Chulainn (line 2109), *"Is messe do athair a ssídib .i. Lug mac Ethlend"* ("I am your father from the *síde* [the Otherworld], Lug son of Ethliu").

65. Ní Shéaghdha (1967, lines 361–82).

66. An exception to this would be the Barbarossa legend, in which the return of the hero is expected. The incidence of this legend in Irish folklore is studied by Ó hÓgáin (1974–76).

67. Cf. Sjoestedt (1949, 13).

68. Thurneysen (1936b).

69. T. O'Rahilly (1943–46, 14–21).

70. R. Breatnach (1953).

71. T. O'Rahilly (1943–46, 15).

72. T. O'Rahilly (1946, 283).

73. T. O'Rahilly (1946, 283).

74. Elsewhere Cormac's tenure of the kingship of Tara is held to have been sanctioned by Manannán mac Lir: in *Echtrae Cormaic Maic Airt* (Stokes 1891a; V. Hull 1949b) he goes to the Otherworld, where Manannán gives him a cup which distinguishes truth from falsehood.

75. Van Hamel (1933).

76. For a fuller treatment see Ó Cathasaigh (1978a, 73–75).

77. Ó Broin (1961–63).

78. Murphy (1953a, lxxi–lxxxv). He presents his argument in summary form in Murphy (1955b, 8).

79. Murphy (1955b, 8).

80. Murphy (1953a, lxxxv).

81. Murphy (1953a, iii).

82. Murphy (1955b, 8).

83. Murphy (1953a, lxxxv).

84. Cf. Rees and Rees (1961, 106).

85. On Conaire's false judgment see O Daly (1959, 117). See also "The Semantics of *síd*," chap. 2 in this volume; Greene (1979, 13–14); McCone (1980, 142–50).

86. See note 36, above.

87. T. O'Rahilly (1946, 483).

88. T. O'Rahilly (1946, 137).

89. This article is a modified version of a lecture given at University College Cork, in March 1979. I am indebted to Mark Scowcroft for some suggestions for its improvement.

10. THE EPONYM OF CNOGBA

1. For an account of the site, see Eogan (1986); see also Byrne (1968).
2. *Met. Dind.* (3:40). Bua and Buí are both found, but I generally confine myself to Buí, for the sake of convenience. On the variation in the name, see comments throughout this chapter.
3. *Met. Dind.* (3:50).
4. *Met. Dind.* (3:48).
5. *Met. Dind.* (3:48).
6. Dobbs (1931, 169).
7. Bergin (1927, 404, cf. 400).
8. See E. Gray (1982, 126 f.).
9. O'Rahilly's identification was conveyed by letter to Gerard Murphy, who reported it in Murphy (1956, 208).
10. Murphy (1953b; 1956, 74–83).
11. V. Hull (1958–59, 31–37, 51–57); *LU* (137–41, at 138–40). For a comment on the content, see Vendryes (1948, 317).
12. Byrne (1968, 386).
13. Mac Cana (1970, 94; 1988, 334).
14. Byrne (1973, 167) follows Carney in taking Buí as a placename in the poem.
15. O'Donovan (1849, 358). I have normalized the spelling of his Oileán Baie Bhérre.
16. Carney (1967b, 29).
17. Greene and O'Connor (1967, 53).
18. See Binchy (1963, xxiv).
19. Murphy (1953a, 83).
20. V. Hull (1933b, 175).
21. Meyer (1892a, 132).
22. Meyer (1892a, 132).
23. This is the name of the central hill in the cemetery, but it is given to the ridge of hills as a whole. Loch Craoibhe and Loch Craoithe are found for Loughcrew (Hogan 1910, 496). It is possible, however, that *crew* in this name is the Mod. Ir. reflex of *Cnogba*, which, if interpreted as Buí's Hill (Cnoc Buí), would be a suitable alternative for Sliabh na Caillí. (*Knowth* must have been formed on the analogy of *Dowth* [< Ir. *Dubad*].)
24. Byrne (1968, 386).
25. This is supported by the claim, in the prose introduction to "The Lament," that "her grandchildren and great-grandchildren were peoples and races" (Murphy 1953b, 84).
26. For the identity of Lug and Tadg, we are referred to Murphy (1953a, 205 f.).
27. Mac Cana (1988, 334).
28. E. Gray (1982, 38–40).

29. E. Gray (1982, 42, 60, 68).
30. van Hamel (1933, 5).
31. *TBC I* (line 2109).
32. Ed. Meyer (1901b; 1918; 1921); Thurneysen (1936b).
33. *LU* (line 4107).
34. van Hamel (1933, 5).
35. Ó Cuív (1955–57, quatrains 15, 7).
36. See again Meyer (1901b; 1918; 1921); Thurneysen (1936b).
37. T. O'Rahilly (1943–46, 14–21).
38. See "*Cath Maige Tuired* as Exemplary Myth," chap. 9 in this volume.
39. Stokes (1903); trans. reproduced in Cross and Slover (1969, 508–13). Versions in verse have been edited by Joynt (1908–10) and Ó Cuív (1983). A historian's view of the material is offered by Ó Corráin (1987, 31–33).
40. See R. Breatnach (1953). References to further work on the sovereignty-figure will be found in M. Bhreathnach (1982, 243 f.).
41. Ó Cuív (1983, quatrain 24); Joynt (1908–10, quatrain 44); Stokes (1903, §11).
42. Ó Cuív (1983, quatrain 29); Joynt (1908–10, quatrains 52 and 53); Stokes (1903, §14).
43. Ó Cuív (1983, quatrain 4).
44. *Met. Dind.* (4:134–43).
45. Stokes (1897, 316–23).
46. Stokes (1897, 320); in a replication of the incident, the woman declares herself to be *Ban-fhlaith Hérenn*, and tells Lugaid that the kingship of Ireland will be taken by him (322).
47. Even *Cóir Anmann* does not claim that Lugaid Loígde achieved the kingship of Ireland; in a brief account of the sequel to the encounter with the woman, and Dáire's prophecy, it is said of Lugaid Loígde merely that he became heir apparent in Munster (Stokes 1897, 322).
48. V. Hull (1958–59, 31–37, 51–57); *LU* (137–41, at 138–40). For a comment on the content, see Vendryes (1948, 317).
49. Meyer (1912b).
50. Müller-Lisowski (1950). On Donn, see also Lincoln (1980, 87–92; 1981).
51. T. O'Rahilly (1946, 454n4).
52. Bergin (1927, 404; cf. 400).
53. The disyllabic form may also be represented in Buíthe/Baíthe: see Binchy (1963, xxiv).
54. Quotations of text and translation are from Murphy (1956); in-text references are to the quatrains of that edition.
55. Meyer (1899, 119). I should add that Meyer did not recognize Buí in line 5 as a name; he translated "I am the Old Woman of Beare that was" (122). In Meyer (1913, 90) he left it untranslated.

56. Greene and O'Connor (1967, 8).
57. Mac Cana (1970, 94 f.) discusses Caillech Bérri under the heading "The goddess of sovereignty."
58. Ó Cuív (1983, quatrain 29).
59. Joynt (1908–10, quatrain 53). For some comments on the motif of the green cloak, see Ó Cuív (1977–78, 113–16).
60. Ó Coileáin (1974, 109).
61. Ó Coileáin (1974, 109).
62. B. K. Martin (1969).
63. B. K. Martin (1969, 251).
64. B. K. Martin (1969, 256 f.).
65. It is edited and translated in Murphy (1953b).
66. Ó Coileáin (1974, 109).
67. Murphy (1953b, 85).
68. See *DIL* s.v.
69. Krappe (1936).
70. Krappe (1936, 293).

11. KNOWLEDGE AND POWER IN *AISLINGE ÓENGUSO*

1. Shaw (1934). The text was previously edited, with a translation, by Müller (1877). Corrigenda to Müller's readings were given by Thurneysen (1918, 400) and by Shaw (1934, 31–32). There is a translation by Jackson (1951, 99–103; 1971, 93–97). In the present article, references to the Irish text are to the numbered paragraphs of Shaw's edition; translations are from Jackson (1971), unless otherwise indicated.
2. Shaw (1934, 37).
3. Flower (1926, 262).
4. Flower (1926, 286).
5. Shaw (1934, 28–29).
6. Carney (1955, 62).
7. Carney (1955, 62).
8. Carney (1955, 62).
9. Shaw (1934, 32).
10. Jackson (1971, 93).
11. Literally, "another night"; Shaw's suggestion that *in n-aidchi n-aili* (MS *hind aidqi n-aile*) means "one night" is not correct. The reference here is to *Fís Conchobuir* 'Conchobor's Vision,' which precedes the *Aislinge* in the manuscript, and which opens with the words: [B]*uí Conchopur macc Neusa aidqi n-ann ina chotlud con facco ní ind oiccbein chuicci*, "Conchobor mac Nessa was asleep one night, when

he saw a young woman coming towards him" (Flower 1926, 286). This is almost identical with the opening of the *Aislinge*; *aidchi n-and* and *in n-aidchi n-aili* are correlative.

12. Jackson (1971, 95).
13. Watkins (1976b).
14. Watkins (1976b, 24).
15. Shaw (1934, 33).
16. Shaw (1934, 20–23). Shaw substitutes *Fingen* in his normalized text; Jackson used *Fínghin*.
17. See Vendryes (1936, 162).
18. Shaw (1934, 61).
19. Jackson (1971, 96).
20. My translation.

12. "THE WOOING OF ÉTAÍN"

1. Ní Shéaghdha (1967).
2. Bergin and Best (1934–38); trans. Gantz (1981, 37–59). Quotations here (text and translation) are from Bergin and Best. *TE1* refers to the first of the three tales, and reference is to the numbered sections in Bergin and Best.
3. *TBC I, TBC LL*. See also Kinsella (1970).
4. Knott (1936); trans. Gantz (1981, 60–106).
5. E. Gray (1982).
6. Knott and Murphy (1966, 112–13).
7. Rees and Rees (1961, 271).
8. Knott (1936, lines 157–58).
9. T. O'Rahilly (1943–46, 16). See also Charles-Edwards (2002, 172–73).
10. Sayers (1986). See also L. Mac Mathúna (1999).
11. Dillon (1948, 51).
12. Dillon (1948, 51).
13. Knott (1936, line 250).
14. See "On the *Cín Dromma Snechta* Version of *Togail Brudne Uí Dergae*," chap. 27 in this volume.

13. TÁIN BÓ CÚAILNGE

1. All quotations are from *TBC I*; references in brackets are to the pages of C. O'Rahilly's translation in that volume, followed in each case by references to the corresponding page in the translation by Kinsella (1970), designated K.

14. MYTHOLOGY IN *TÁIN BÓ CÚAILNGE*

1. Chadwick and Chadwick (1932, passim); Murphy (1955a, 25–47), reproduced in Knott and Murphy (1966, 114–31); Jackson (1964, passim). Criticism of the Heroic Age theory will be found in Radner (1982); Ó Cathasaigh, "Pagan Survivals: The Evidence of Early Irish Narrative," chap. 3 in this volume; Aitchison (1987).

2. Ó Corráin (1985a, 85); Aitchison (1987).

3. T. O'Rahilly (1946, 271 and passim); Sjoestedt (1949); Rees and Rees (1961, passim).

4. Carney (1955, 276 ff., 321 f.; 1983, 128–30).

5. Kelleher (1971).

6. Puhvel (1974, 175).

7. She edited *The Stowe Version of Táin Bó Cuailgne* (1961), *TBC LL*, and *TBC I*.

8. T. O'Rahilly (1946, 271).

9. Jackson (1964, 2).

10. Abrams (1971, 49).

11. Abrams (1971, 49).

12. Thurneysen (1921, 96 f.). Thurneysen then tentatively assigned the *Grundtext* to the eighth century, but he later revised this to the middle of the seventh (1933, 209).

13. Carney (1955, esp. 321 f.; 1983, 128–30).

14. Murphy (1955–57); Mac Cana (1972–73, 86–89). See also Sims-Williams (1978–79).

15. Murphy (1955–57, 158).

16. Carney (1955, 321).

17. Murphy (1955–57, 162).

18. Mac Cana (1972–73, 89).

19. Murphy (1955–57, 158).

20. See especially McCone (1990).

21. For a judicious comment on the difficulty of assigning the ultimate origins of certain motifs which occur in the *Táin* to "either classical or biblical models as opposed to pagan Celtic or common Indo-European models," see Sayers (1986, 114 f.).

22. *TBC LL* (ix). See also Meid (1970, 67).

23. Ross (1967, 1–3).

24. de Paor (1970, 156–57).

25. Ross (1967, 302–8). For some further information on Donn, see "The Eponym of Cnogba," chap. 10 in this volume, and references there cited.

26. Dorson (1965).

27. T. O'Rahilly (1946, 270n2).

28. T. O'Rahilly (1946, 454n4 [Donn Cúailnge]; 314 [Culann's Dog]). On the latter, see Ó Cathasaigh (1977, 14–15), McCone (1984a, 8–11).

29. See Littleton (1982).

30. Lincoln (1981). See also Sayers (1985).

31. Lincoln (1981, 69).

32. Lincoln (1981, 75).

33. Lincoln (1981, 92).

34. For details, see Lincoln (1981, 87).

35. Windisch (1891), Roider (1979).

36. *TBC I* (lines 194 ff.). (There may also be an allusion in the placename *Mag Muceda* [*TBC I*, line 827], which is perhaps for Old Irish *Mucedae*.)

37. Lincoln (1981, 92).

38. Puhvel (1987, 2).

39. Ó Broin (1961–63, 288).

40. Ó Broin (1961–63, 289).

41. *TBC I* (lines 51–52, trans. 126).

42. *TBC I* (line 114, trans. 128).

43. *TBC I* (line 216, trans. 131).

44. *TBC I* (lines 524 ff., trans. 139).

45. Note ad loc.

46. V. Hull (1968, 29, lines 65–66).

47. *TBC I* (note to line 51).

48. *TBC I* (line 2138, trans. 184).

49. *TBC I* (lines 3397, 3434, trans. 216–17).

50. *TBC I* (lines 1283–84, trans. 160).

51. *TBC I* (lines 227–55, trans. 131–32).

52. *TBC I* (line 229, trans. 131).

53. *TBC I* (lines 244–55, trans. 131–32).

54. *TBC I* (lines 421–22, trans. 136).

55. *TBC I* (note to line 51).

56. Henry (1978, 33).

57. See now Slotkin (1990).

58. Radner (1982, 47).

59. Sjoestedt (1949, 59).

60. Abrams (1971, 49).

61. See Ó Cathasaigh (1977, passim).

62. See "The Concept of the Hero in Irish Mythology," chap. 4 in this volume.

63. Kelleher (1971, 121).

64. Kelleher (1971, 121 f.).

65. See "The Concept of the Hero in Irish Mythology," chap. 4 in this volume.

66. McCone (1990, 199).
67. *TBC I* (lines 608–821).
68. Dumézil (1970, 15 f.).
69. *LL* (5:1119, lines 32905 ff.).
70. Melia (1974, 215).
71. Rees and Rees (1961, 246–49).
72. Melia (1974, 215).
73. Mac Cana (1980b, 27).
74. O'Leary (1984; 1986b; 1987).
75. See "The Sister's Son in Early Irish Literature," chap. 5 in this volume.
76. See Rees and Rees (1961, 129 f.); A. Rees (1966, 53).
77. *TBC I* (lines 1039–63, trans. 154–55).
78. *TBC I* (line 1306, trans. 161).
79. *TBC I* (lines 4068–69, trans. 235).
80. *TBC I* (lines 4123–24, trans. 237).
81. *TBC I* (line 183, trans. 130).
82. *TBC I* (line 1855, trans. 177).
83. *TBC I* (lines 222–24, trans. 131).
84. Charles-Edwards (1970–72, 115–16, 119–20).
85. See "The Sister's Son in Early Irish Literature," chap. 5 in this volume.
86. Compare the remarks of Puhvel (1987, 2): "Yet in the course of human events societies pass and religious systems change: the historical landscape gets littered with the husks of dessicated myths."
87. See "The Sister's Son in Early Irish Literature," chap. 5 in this volume.
88. See "Pagan Survivals: The Evidence of Early Irish Narrative," chap. 3 in this volume.

15. *TÁIN BÓ CÚAILNGE* AND EARLY IRISH LAW

1. Kinsella (1970, xi).
2. The standard editions are, respectively, *TBC I* and *TBC LL*. I cite O'Rahilly's texts by line number, her translations by page number.
3. Carney (1971, 78). See also Carney (1983, 122–25).
4. Henry (1997, 61).
5. The passage in which this incident is narrated occurs in an interpolation in the *Lebor na hUidre* copy of Recension I. The interpolation as a whole is discussed by O'Rahilly in *TBC I* (xiv–xvi). See also *TBC LL* (304–5, note on lines 1767–71). I may add that the interpolator seems to have drawn on an early source for some of this material, including the excerpt that I shall be using here.
6. *TBC I* (lines 1929–37, trans. 179).
7. Kelly (1988, 19).

8. Kelly (1988, 19).
9. *DIL* s.v. *midlach*.
10. *TBC I* (line 419).
11. *TBC I* has "there," which must be a misprint.
12. *TBC I* (lines 439–49, trans. 137).
13. Charles-Edwards (2000, 115).
14. This is scarcely conveyed in O'Rahilly's translation, "I agree." The performative character, if not the legal force, of the Irish wording is captured in Kinsella's translation, "You have it" (1970, 78).
15. See "The Sister's Son in Early Irish Literature," chap. 5 in this volume.
16. *TBC I* (lines 450–54, trans. 137).
17. Charles-Edwards (2000, 115). For further commentary on the passage, see Ó Cathasaigh, "The Sister's Son in Early Irish Literature," chap. 5 in this volume, and Jaski (1999, 3–5).
18. Following *Lebor na hUidre* here, O'Rahilly reads *g-*; I have followed the other three manuscripts, which have *c-*.
19. *TBC I* (line 1243; trans. 159).
20. *TBC I* (lines 1253–65; trans. 160).
21. Thurneysen (1936a, 3).
22. L. Breatnach (1996, 20).
23. *TBC LL* (lines 901–7; trans. 162).
24. *TBC I* (lines 1513–19; trans. 167).
25. Kelly (1988, 50–51).
26. Kelly (1988, 51n97).
27. The form is accusative plural. O'Rahilly's translation "treasure" is perfectly acceptable, since *sét* can have a collective sense in the plural. I prefer to translate it as plural here, however, given the contrast with the singular *sét* used in the satirist's acknowledgement of Cú Chulainn's coup.
28. L. Breatnach (1986).
29. L. Breatnach (1986, 39, line 16).
30. L. Breatnach (1986, 40).
31. *TBC I* (line 3425, trans. 217).
32. *TBC I* (lines 3437–41, trans. 217).
33. See "*Sírrabad Súaltaim* and the Order of Speaking among the Ulaid," chap. 16 in this volume.
34. *Coibche* was originally the bride-price paid to the woman's family by the prospective husband. On the change in meaning, see Simms (1998, 24–25).
35. Kelly (1988, 70).
36. Ó Corráin (2002, 38).
37. *TBC LL* (lines 46–47, trans. 138). As suggested by O'Rahilly, *níp* has been emended to *níptar*.

38. Kelly (1988, 74, 104).
39. M. O'Brien (1962, 23).
40. Binchy (1941, lines 509–13; paraphrase at 106).
41. Lucas (1989, 125).
42. Bieler (1963, 179).
43. Kelly (1997, 167).
44. *TBC I* (lines 61–62, trans. 126–27).
45. *TBC I* (line 165, trans. 129).
46. *TBC I* (line 173).
47. *TBC LL* (lines 343–45; trans. 147).
48. *TBC I* (lines 1168–91, trans. 157–58).
49. On the importance of fosterage in early Irish law, see Kelly (1988, 86–90).
50. *TBC I* (lines 4108–10, trans. 236).
51. *TBC I* (line 233).
52. *TBC I* (line 229).
53. *TBC I* (line 216).
54. See "*Táin Bó Cúailnge*," chap. 13 in this volume.
55. Binchy (1941, lines 581–82); the translation is Binchy's (note to line 581).
56. *TBC I* (line 284).
57. "With their followers" is a translation of the reading of the second recension, *fer co ndáil = co ndáil fer*; the corresponding phrase in the first recension is obscure (see *TBC I*, 246, note to line 284).
58. *TBC I* (lines 282–91; trans. 132).
59. L. Breatnach (1986, 39, line 22).
60. L. Breatnach (1986, 40).
61. See O'Leary (1987).
62. *TBC I* (lines 914–15, trans. 150).
63. *TBC I* (lines 1134–36, trans. 156).
64. *TBC I* (lines 1277–86, trans. 182).
65. *TBC I* (lines 2056–57, trans. 181).
66. *TBC LL* (lines 1562–65, trans. 181).
67. *TBC I* (lines 1884–85, trans. 177).
68. *TBC LL* (lines 2541–45, trans. 209).
69. Thurneysen (1925, 327, §18).
70. O'Leary (1987, 5n13).
71. Thurneysen (1925, 327).
72. Parks (1990).
73. Bernard Martin (1994).
74. Sayers (1997).
75. *TBC I* (line 1775).
76. *TBC I* (lines 2620–86, trans. 197–98).

16. *SÍRRABAD SÚALTAIM* AND THE ORDER OF SPEAKING AMONG THE ULAID

1. *TBC I* (103–4 [text], 216–17 [translation]) and *TBC LL* (110–12; 245–47). The summary that I give here is based on the first recension. Unless otherwise indicated, the translations are Cecile O'Rahilly's.

2. I depart here from O'Rahilly's translation (*TBC I*, 217), which reads: "(I swear by) the sea before them, the sky above them, the earth beneath them that I shall restore every cow to its byre, and every woman and boy to their homes after victory in battle." The Irish text is: *Muir ara cendaib, in nem húasa mbennaib, talum foa cosaib, dobérsa cech mboin ina hindis díb 7 cach mben 7 cech mac dia tig iar mbúaid chatha* (*TBC I*, 104). This should be printed as two sentences, the second beginning at *dobérsa*.

3. O'Rahilly inserts an accent over the -*ú*- of *Súaltaim* in the first recension, but omits it in the second.

4. Spelled thus in *Scéla Cano*.

5. On this see Mac Cana (1993).

6. As it happens, *fri druídib* is one of the examples of this development cited (from *Saltair na Rann*) by L. Breatnach (1994, 240).

17. AILILL AND MEDB

1. All line and page references are to the text and translation, respectively, of *TBC LL*, unless otherwise identified.

2. Kelly (1988, 70). This form of marriage is distinguished from the "union of joint property" (*lánamnas comthinchuir*) into which both partners contribute moveable goods, and the "union of a woman on man-property" (*lánamnas mná for fertinchur*) into which the woman contributes little or nothing. See also Ó Corráin (1985b).

3. *Coibche* was originally the bride-price paid to the woman's family by the prospective husband. On the change in meaning, see Simms (1998, 24–25).

4. As suggested by O'Rahilly (note ad loc.), *níp* has been amended to *níptar*.

5. For a comment on this, see Carney (1983, 121).

6. On this see Kelly (1988, 76, 104–5).

7. The folly of giving a man the kingship of his maternal kin is exemplified in the disastrous reign of Bres in *Cath Maige Tuired* (E. Gray 1982).

8. Tristram (1993, 14–18) summarizes a 1990 lecture on the "Pillow-Talk" given by Ó Corráin in Freiburg.

9. The argument of this paper has been adumbrated in "*Táin Bó Cúailnge* and Early Irish Law," chap. 15 in this volume.

18. CÚ CHULAINN, THE POETS, AND GIOLLA BRIGHDE MAC CON MIDHE

1. Ford (1994).
2. Ford (1994, 255).
3. N. Williams (1980, 204–13), henceforth referred to as *A theachtaire*. It was first published by Lambert McKenna (1919 [with translation]; cf. 1938, 220–23 [without]), and quatrains 17 and 19–33 were published separately by Knott (1928, 78–80). Unless otherwise indicated, quotations in the present article are from Williams's text and translation.
4. *A theachtaire*, quatrain 5. *An ealadha d'aithríoghadh* is mistranslated "the poetic art should be altered" by Williams.
5. *A theachtaire*, quatrains 1–6.
6. Quatrains 7–20.
7. Quatrain 8.
8. Quatrain 11.
9. Quatrains 15–18.
10. Quatrain 15.
11. Quatrain 16.
12. Quatrain 17. The idea is developed further in quatrain 18.
13. Quatrains 21–33.
14. Quatrain 8.
15. Quatrains 21, 22.
16. Quatrain 16.
17. Quatrain 32.
18. Quatrain 33.
19. Quatrain 23.
20. Knott (1928, 79), quatrain 6, takes *folach a sgéal ní sgrios beag* as a parenthetical sentence. In that case it would be translated "To keep their stories hidden would be no small destruction," and the fourth line would be read as a continuation of the first two.
21. *A theachtaire*, quatrain 24. I have substituted "true stock" for Williams's "noble descendants," which can hardly be correct as a translation of *fírfhréamh*.
22. *A theachtaire*, quatrains 25–27.
23. Quatrain 28.
24. Quatrains 30–31.
25. Watkins (1976a, 272).
26. *LU* (13, line 355). See also Stokes (1899, 44). The translation is by Stokes (45).
27. *Thes.* (2:295, line 7). On the date of the poem, see Murphy (1940, 205n8).
28. Williams (1972, 9).
29. Carney (1967a, 5).

30. Carney (1967a, 5).
31. Carney (1967a, 7–8).
32. Watkins (1976a, 270).
33. Watkins (1976a, 270).
34. Watkins (1976a, 271); see also the references there, note 1.
35. *TBC I* (lines 613–15, trans. 143).
36. *TBC I* (lines 638–39, trans. 143).
37. *TBC I* (lines 640–41, trans. 143).
38. C. Lewis (1960, 13–14).
39. Griffiths (2000, 6–7).
40. *Thes.* (2:295, lines 16–17). Murphy (1940, 204) suggests that *bairtni*, translated "bardisms" by Stokes and Strachan, is probably to be understood in the sense of "bardic compositions," "praise-songs" here.
41. Greene (1955, 19, lines 341–42).
42. Watson (1942, 8); Irish text, Watson (1941, lines 209–16). We cannot be certain that *dréchta* meant "stories" here; for a discussion of the word, see Mac Cana (1980a, 113n122).
43. *TBC I* (lines 668–70; see also lines 674–75). O'Rahilly has mistranslated the first of these passages. It reads: *no bíth cach láth gaile a láa hi Sléib Fúait fri snádud neich dothíssad co n-airchetul nó do chomroc fri fer, combad and sin condrístá fris arná téised nech dochum nEmna cen rathugud*. She translates: "Each warrior of the Ulstermen spent a day in turn in Slíab Fúait, to protect anyone who came that way with poetry, or with challenge to battle, so that there he might be encountered and so that no one should go unnoticed into Emain" (143–44). The protection which is in question here (*snádud*) entails affording the poet safe passage to Emain (and back). No such protection is given to the warrior; the watcher fights him on the spot, in order to prevent him from reaching Emain. O'Rahilly has taken *do chomroc* to be semantically parallel to *co n-airchetul*, but I suggest that it is actually parallel to *fri snádud*. The comma after *fer* should be removed, and for the sake of clarity a comma may be placed after *n-airchetul*.
44. Cited and translated from E. Gwynn (1940–42, 17, line 20) by L. Breatnach (1987, 89).
45. *TBC LL* (lines 996–1003, trans. 165).
46. *TBC I* (lines 2336–42, trans. 189).
47. *TBC I* (lines 2372–91, trans. 190–91).
48. *TBC I* (lines 67–112, trans. 127–28).
49. *TBC I* (lines 63–64, trans. 127).
50. *TBC I* (lines 103–6, trans. 127).
51. *TBC I* (lines 248–55, trans. 131–32).
52. *TBC I* (lines 1951–63, trans. 179). Graham Isaac has kindly informed me of the existence in Welsh of a type of boasting-poem known as the *gorhoffedd*, in which the poet may describe his own martial prowess.

53. *TBC I* (lines 1934–36, trans. 179).
54. That the Irish charioteer "can be a possessor of key information" has been shown by Nagy (1997, 218).
55. *TBC I* (lines 3081–84, trans. 207).
56. *TBC LL* (lines 3271–75, trans. 227).
57. Hiltebeitel (1982, 99).
58. Hiltebeitel (1982, 99). See also Mac Cana (1992, 77–78).
59. *TBC I* (line 358, trans. 135).
60. *TBC I* (lines 358–59, trans. 135).
61. *TBC I* (lines 640–41, trans. 143).
62. Carney (1967a, 10).
63. See Ó hUiginn (1992, 30).
64. I am assuming that the published poems are reasonably representative of the corpus as a whole. See Ó Caithnia (1984, 61–73) for apologues from the Ulster Cycle. It may be noted that the authorship of the apologue on Cú Chulainn which is attributed to Giolla Brighde Mac Con Midhe (71) has been disputed by Ó Cuív (1971–72, 90–91).

19. REFLECTIONS ON *COMPERT CONCHOBUIR* AND *SERGLIGE CON CULAINN*

1. For a discussion of "story" and "discourse," see Chatman (1978).
2. V. Hull (1934) printed a text based on six manuscripts. He was made aware of the seventh manuscript and printed its text in an appendix, and suggested two minor alterations to his reconstructed text; these have been adopted here. I should add that Hull would have been justified in restoring *rígsuidiu* in the first line.
3. References are to the lines of Dillon (1953a); translations are from Dillon (1953b).

20. "THE EXPULSION OF THE DÉISI"

1. Ó Cuív (2001, 163–200).
2. Ó Cuív (2001, 22–87).
3. Mulchrone (1943, 3314–56).
4. Wulff and Mulchrone (1933, 1254–73).
5. Mulchrone and Fitzpatrick (1943, 3367–79). The dating of the three hands in LU is disputed. The present phase in the discussion was initiated in Ó Concheanainn (1973–74b). See also Oskamp (1975–76), Mac Eoin (1994), and Ó Concheanainn (1996).
6. The interpolator has added *7 aided Chormaic.*
7. Abbott and Gwynn (1921, 90–92, 340–41).

8. Abbott and Gwynn (1921, 125–29, 355–58).
9. Abbott and Gwynn (1921, 355).
10. Meyer (1901, 101).
11. Dillon (1946, 1).
12. Translations are largely based on Meyer, but are my responsibility unless otherwise stated.
13. See "The Déisi and Dyfed," chap. 22 in this volume.
14. What follows here is set out at greater length in "The Déisi and Dyfed," pp. 306–18 in this volume.
15. V. Hull (1954c, 266).
16. V. Hull (1954c, 267).
17. These are discussed in "The Déisi and Dyfed," pp. 308–10 in this volume.
18. For some remarks on the later version, see "On the LU Version of 'The Expulsion of the Déisi,'" chap. 21 in this volume.
19. I have supplied the capitals in *Dál Cuinn*. I may add that *inní sein* is probably a later addition to the original text.
20. Kelly (1988, 136) points out that in early Irish law a marriage originating in rape is regarded as being of its nature criminal.
21. See, for example, E. Bhreathnach (1996, 82–86).
22. Meyer makes a slip here, and says that the Déisi were routed.
23. R §18; similarly L line 169, where, however, *sloged* corresponds to R's *dunad*. See Gerriets (1987, 49).
24. Meyer prints *na nDeisse*; but see "The Déisi and Dyfed," 538n7 in this volume.
25. Rees and Rees (1961, 140).
26. E. MacNeill (1919, 110).
27. See Meyer (1915, 905–8) = M. O'Brien (1962, 327g50).
28. T. O'Rahilly (1946, 64). See further "The Déisi and Dyfed," pp. 322 in this volume.
29. See "The Déisi and Dyfed," pp. 310–14 in this volume.
30. Ó Buachalla (1951, 90).
31. Ó Buachalla (1954, 116).
32. Ó Buachalla (1952, 82, 86).
33. Byrne (1973, 197).
34. Ó Corráin (1980, 162–63).
35. T. Ó Rahilly (1946, 64, 394).

21. ON THE LU VERSION OF "THE EXPULSION OF THE DÉISI"

1. I am indebted to Dr. Próinséas Ní Chatháin, who read this article and made suggestions for its improvement.

2. The latter recension is also represented by fragmentary texts in the Book of Uí Maine and the *Liber Flavus Fergusiorum*, both edited by Pender (1947).

3. Except where otherwise stated, references in the present article are to the lines of *LU*. For further information on the manuscripts, see "The Expulsion of the Déisi," chap. 20 in this volume.

4. He was referring to the text of H.2.15, printed (with variants from H.3.17) in Meyer (1907b).

5. See Oskamp (1966–67, 128); to the sources there cited add Greene (1958, 110).

6. See V. Hull (1958–59, 23 ff.), where all three texts may conveniently be compared.

7. The lists are excerpted from a verbal system of U which is set out in full in my unpublished M. A. thesis on the text (NUI 1968). I have not taken account of the use of the Old Irish perfect as a narrative tense.

8. Dr. Ní Chatháin has pointed out that, since *-om* is the archaic ending, the spelling of our text could be an archaism. The form in question is imperative pl. 1, which has the same personal ending as the indic. pres. pl. 1. Archaic *-om* is attested for the indic. pres. (Thurneysen 1946, 360), but not for the impv. The variant readings are *atrebam* (H.3.17), *attraé am* (H.2.15) (V. Hull 1958–59, 32).

9. The relevant forms are given here (with corresponding readings of LU in parenthesis). H.3.17 has *dorigne* (*doroni*, line 4401); H.2.15 has *contuili* (*contule*, line 4464); both of them have *-dechaid* (*-deochaid*, line 4377). The variants of *atrebom* (line 4400) are given in note 8.

10. The end of U is lost in lacuna; its structure must be assessed on the assumption that the lost material was much the same as the end of the other two texts of the later version.

22. THE DÉISI AND DYFED

1. For a recent discussion see Sims-Williams (1982a).

2. In discussing the extent of Déisi Muman, Power (1952, 14 f.) reminds us that "the native Irish territorial boundaries ... were somewhat elastic."

3. A third group, with whom the Éoganachta are said to have colonized County Clare when they conquered it from Connacht early in the fifth century, are known as In Déis. On the relationship of Déisi Muman to In Déis, see E. MacNeill (1932, 38 f.). In Déis were divided into two, the Déis Deiscirt, comprising territories contiguous with those of Déisi Muman, and the Déis Tuaiscirt, which became known as Dál Cais. E. MacNeill (1932, 38 f.) discusses the suppression of the earlier genealogy of the latter group in favor of a fictitious attachment to the Éoganacht stem.

4. In an alternative version, the Déisi are joined to the Dál Cuinn as far back as the legendary Éremón son of Míl (M. O'Brien 1962, 17, 358).

5. The texts of *ED* are listed below (and see also "The Expulsion of the Déisi," chap. 20 in this volume). R refers to the text of Rawlinson B 502 (Meyer 1901a) and L to that of Laud 610 (Meyer 1907a).

6. Arnamine on the Wexford coast (Hogan 1910, s.v.).

7. The text of R (§22) is: *Ar it e fil fo chis 7 dligud 7 bothachas na ndeisse dona flaithib*. Meyer's treatment of *na ndeisse* is misleading. He prints *na nDeisse* in his text, and omits it from his translation. The point is therefore missed that the relationship between the tribes in question and Dál Fiachach Suidge is that of vassals (*déisi*) to lords (*flathi*). In omitting to translate his *na nDeisse*, Meyer was doubtless influenced by the consideration that it is lacking in L (lines 217 f.): *Ar itt e fil fo deisis 7 dligus 7 bodagas dona flathaib*. But L expresses the point in its own way: corresponding to *cīs* in R, it reads *deisis* which is presumably for *déisius*, an abstract noun from *déis*. Its primary meaning would be "vassalage," but we may follow E. MacNeill (1911, 63) in translating it here as "vassal-tribute." Ours is the only example cited in *DIL* s.v. *déisis*.

8. On the status of the Déisi (that is, of Dál Fiachach) in relation to the Éoganacht dynasty of Cashel, see Ó Buachalla (1952, 82, 86).

9. *ED* does not explicitly deal with the annexation of the Waterford territories of Déisi Muman.

10. Some of these are mentioned by V. Hull (1958–59, 18).

11. Only part of this item occurs in L.

12. One could alternatively take this to comprise two different items.

13. Compare (for Emain Macha) §7 of the saga of Fergus mac Léti (ed. Binchy 1952, 38, 43).

14. See p. vii of the Introduction by E. MacNeill to Ó Raithbheartaigh (1932).

15. Mess Corb occurs in the Book of Lecan and the Book of Ballymote but not in the Book of Leinster (M. O'Brien 1962, 394). Mess Corb also seems to be mentioned in what remains of the seventh-century poem (M. O'Brien 1962, 395).

16. In another pedigree, Art Corb is said to be son of Cairpre Rigronn son of Fíachu Suidge son of Feidlimid Rechtaid, with a variant in which Cairpre is omitted (M. O'Brien 1962, 253).

17. L lines 193 ff., *LU* lines 4470 ff. The reading of LU at *LU* line 4472 (*Nibo inmain ní ón*) is to be preferred to that of L line 194 (*Ni ba hí ma món*).

18. L lines 219 ff. The corresponding passage is lacking in LU as the end of its text of *ED* is lost in lacuna, but its original presence there is virtually guaranteed by its occurrence in the other two texts of the "later version" (V. Hull 1958–59, 44).

19. On the other hand, L also misses out a generation: R's *Catacuind* (gen.), corresponding to Welsh *Catgocaun*, is lacking in L.

20. Cf. also T. O'Rahilly (1946, 394), where the view is expressed that the Déisi, like the Cianachta, were provided with a respectable pedigree which at the same time stamped them as *deoraid* or aliens.

21. In considering the background to the change from the Primitive Irish of the ogam inscriptions to the Old Irish of the Glosses and law-tracts, Binchy (1958, 292) remarks that "the vague accounts in certain sagas and genealogical tracts of expulsions and migrations (e.g. of the Déisi) may point to some widespread upheaval and mixing of populations."

22. See T. O'Rahilly (1950, 387 ff.), Rees and Rees (1961, 118 ff.), and A. Rees (1966, 43 ff.).

23. The distribution-map of the ogam inscriptions (Macalister 1945, 502) suggests a continuation from Waterford into Pembrokeshire.

24. The words are those of N. K. Chadwick (1963, 47), save that I have inserted "insular."

25. On these see E. MacNeill (1919, 75).

26. A shorter version of this paper was given as a lecture at a Tionól in the Dublin Institute for Advanced Studies in March 1983. This paper had gone to press before the appearance of Coplestone-Crow (1981–82).

27. I have collated the edited texts with the facsimile edition of Rawlinson B 502 (Meyer 1909a) and with a photostat of Laud 610. (In R, I follow Meyer [1901a] in reading *noinchoisced*: to judge from the facsimile, the *e* is inked over and illegible.)

23. THE THEME OF *LOMMRAD* IN *CATH MAIGE MUCRAMA*

1. Stokes (1892b); O'Grady (1892, 1:310 ff. [text], 2:347 ff. [translation]); O Daly (1975).

2. See the list in O Daly (1975, 1 f.).

3. It is not actually stated in the text of *CMM* that Cormac succeeded Lugaid, though it is perhaps implicit in §68. The storyteller may have taken Cormac's succession for granted as something which would have been known to all, but there is also the possibility that he was embarrassed by Cormac's youth at the time when (according to *CMM*) Lugaid was deposed. The other, and probably older, tradition was that Lugaid reigned in Tara for thirty years, and this is mentioned in §77. (I use "storyteller" generically to denote those who gave *CMM* the shape in which we have it.)

4. O Daly (1975, 3) believes that the story of the battle of Mag Mucrama "in its original form had nothing to do with Cormac mac Airt or Tara, that it was a purely Munster tale which originated among the Corco Loígde and was later altered and added to by the partisans of the Connachta in order to lend support to the claim of the race of Conn to the kingship of Tara." But the story draws also on Éoganacht tradition, and the matter of Tara and Cormac may have been added in the Éoganacht interest. Cf. F. J. Byrne's discussion of the "elaborate parallelism" which "was worked out between the traditions of Dál Cuinn and Éoganacht" (Byrne 1973, 202).

5. *Glassen* is usually translated "woad" (see *DIL* s.v. *glasen*), but O Daly retains the Irish word in her translation of the text.

6. Ed. O Daly (1975, 64 ff.); Ó Cathasaigh (1977, 107 ff.).

7. O Daly (1975, 70, line 488); Ó Cathasaigh (1977, 122, line 93).

8. Cf. D. A. Binchy (1970, 10). It is worth noting that in our text Cormac is called *mac an fír-flatha* 'son of the true prince' (§64), and Lugaid *anflaith* 'an unlawful ruler' (§66), since that recalls the statement in *Audacht Moraind* (ed. Kelly 1976, 16, §54k), *To-léci do fírflaith*. In a recent article, Watkins (1979, 194 f.) argues that this statement in *Audacht Moraind* (and the series to which it belongs) is to be interpreted in agonistic terms, and translates "the un-ruler [= false ruler] yields to the true ruler." The kind of contest envisaged by Watkins is exemplified by the rival judgments of Lugaid and Cormac.

The immediate effect of Lugaid's false judgment was the collapse of the side of the house in which the judgment was given: this serves to show the destructive power of untruth, and it is the obverse side of the Act of Truth. Cf. Dillon (1947b, 137). The collapse of the side of the house could be included with the laying waste of the land in the outline of this sequence given below; moreover, it prefigures what happened to Lugaid when his cheek "melted away," which is to say that half of his face collapsed.

9. Cf. Kelly (1976, passim).

10. *Luid ... do [f]recaire* (v.l. *recire*) *a ech* (§3). O Daly (1975) translates "to attend to his horses," and discusses *frecaire* in a note to line 8 of the text. She points out that Stokes (1892b) translates "to pasture" and O'Grady (1892) "to tend," and notes that another compound of *gairid*, *in-gair*, means "herds, tends," but that no similar meaning is instanced in *DIL* s.vv. *fris-gair* or *frecra(e)*; it might be added that no instance of an unsyncopated form is given s.v. *frecra(e)*. O Daly suggests that the original reading may have been *do fáiri*. But another compound of *gairid*, *ar-gair* (vn. *airgaire*) is synonymous with *in-gair* in the sense "herds, tends," see *DIL* A 397.62, and the probability is that that is what we have here, with substitution of preverb. Ailill's intention must have been to tend, more specifically to graze, the horses, and it is that intention which was frustrated by the baring of the hill.

11. The unyoking of horses was the correct legal procedure for laying claim to the land where the act took place. Cf. Greene (1955, 15, note to line 235) and the texts there cited. (I am indebted to Angela Partridge [now Bourke] for this reference.) Cf. also "Conall Corc and the Corcu Loígde," ed. Meyer (1910a, 60), trans. V. Hull (1947, 899); and the comment by Byrne (1973, 194).

12. This name has recently been discussed by Hamp (1978, 152). The form *Fer Hí* also occurs, and *Hí* is taken by the editors of *DIL* E 145.19 f. as genitive of *éo* 'a tree,' especially 'a yew'; see also T. O'Rahilly (1946, 288). Hamp considers *Fer Fí* to have been the earlier form. But the importance of the yew in the traditions of the Éoganachta, and of the element *éo* in their nomenclature, argue decisively in

the other direction: the assumption must be that *Fer Í/Hí* is original, and that the *f-* of *Fí* has been attracted from *Fer*.

13. Dumézil (1973, 111 f.).

14. Dumézil (1973, 112).

15. "The Semantics of *síd*," pp. 26–27 in this volume. As I hope to establish in a future article ["*Cath Maige Tuired* as Exemplary Myth," chap. 9 in this volume], those who commit the "sin of the sovereign" in Human Time are repeating the sin of Bres, which was committed in the Time of the Gods.

16. Dumézil (1973, 112).

17. I suspect that close analysis of other Irish narrative texts might serve to show that certain passages which seem to be irrelevant interpolations have in all probability been included on thematic grounds.

18. *Lomméras* may be added to the list of Middle Irish verbal forms, O Daly (1975, 34(f)).

19. This article is a modified version of a paper read at the Sixth International Congress of Celtic Studies in Galway, July 1979. I thank those who participated in the discussion which followed the paper.

24. THE THEME OF *AINMNE* IN *SCÉLA CANO MEIC GARTNÁIN*

1. Binchy (1963). The references in brackets are to the lines of this edition.

2. On this poem see Binchy (1963, xxv ff.).

3. Carney (1963). I am indebted to Dáibhí Ó Cróinín for giving me a copy of this review.

4. Knott (1960, 37).

5. Binchy (1963, xxviii).

6. Thurneysen (1923b, footnotes to German trans.); M. O'Brien (1930–32, 86 f., 158); Binchy (1963, notes to ed.).

7. Mac Eoin (1964, 246).

8. Binchy (1963, xv).

9. I have left *níbat ríg na fotha* untranslated here. See Binchy's note to line 97.

10. Or "best." But *dech*, the OIr superlative of *maith*, is found elsewhere in the text.

11. See Ó Fiannachta (1964–66, 78).

12. Cano departs in the course of the night. The reason for his stealthy departure would appear to be that he is still intent on evading Áedán.

13. There may be an echo here of the taboo laid on Conaire Mór that he should not hunt *claenmíla Cernai*: see Knott (1936, note to line 173).

14. See Dillon (1946, 75 ff.) [and M. Bhreathnach (1984)].

15. Meyer (1902).
16. Carney (1955, 194 f.). See also Dillon (1945) and Eisner (1969, 106).
17. Carney (1955, 215).
18. "The Theme of *lommrad* in *Cath Maige Mucrama*," chap. 23 in this volume.
19. Binchy (1941, line 529).
20. See further "The Theme of *lommrad* in *Cath Maige Mucrama*," pp. 336–41 in this volume.

25. THE RHETORIC OF *SCÉLA CANO MEIC GARTNÁIN*

1. Binchy (1963). References are to the lines of this edition. German translation by Thurneysen (1923b). While I take responsibility for translating excerpts included here, I am of course greatly indebted to Binchy and Thurneysen, and also to an important review of Binchy's edition by Ó Fiannachta (1964–66).
2. "Pagan Survivals," p. 37 in this volume.
3. Carney (1955, esp. 77 ff., 190 ff., and 276 ff.).
4. See Ó Coileáin (1977–78).
5. Murphy (1955a, 8).
6. Murphy (1955a, 10).
7. Murphy (1955a, 8 f.).
8. Murphy (1955a, 9).
9. Murphy (1955a, 9 f.).
10. Greene (1955).
11. Carney (1955, 277).
12. Murphy (1955a, 10).
13. Binchy (1963, xvii).
14. Binchy (1962b, 67).
15. Carney (1969–70, 232–36).
16. See Ó Coileáin (1981, 116–28).
17. Byrne (1973, 2).
18. Carney (1955, 189–242).
19. Dillon (1948, 2).
20. I take Thurneysen's emendation of "*Fir a cano*" to "*Fír a canai*" to be correct, despite the objection raised by Binchy (note ad loc.). It cannot be for "*Fír, a Chano*," as Cano is not present at this stage.
21. Ó Fiannachta (1964–66, note to lines 203–5).
22. See *DIL* s.v. *liid*. Thurneysen's emendation of *a Colgain* to *ar Cholgain* seems secure. I take it that, as usual, *ar* has replaced *for* in this idiom; for a different view, see Binchy, note ad loc. In support of his emendation, Thurneysen cites, without translation, a parallel passage from Meyer (1903, 47), which should read: *Rodlia . . . ind righan . . . for mac . . . Dichoeme*; Binchy translates, "the queen was

accused of [intercourse with] the son of D.," but, while we cannot be sure, it seems to me more likely that it was the son of D. who was accused.

23. Literally, "for whom Cano is an absence," reading *dian iongnais* with Ó Fiannachta (1964–66, note to lines 208–9), in preference to Binchy's *diam ongnais*.

24. Literally, "as a result of your being broken, I shall seize with my soul only spoliation in binding."

25. Mac Eoin (1964, 244).

26. The clause is ambiguous, as *Cano* can be either subject or object; it has been taken to mean "whom Cano would not repel," or the like. It may be, as Binchy puts it, that Diarmait's daughter "combines admiration of his prowess with a jibe at the insufficiency of his armour" (note ad loc.). As against that, the translation given here lends added force to the girl's warning.

27. Thurneysen emends *faire i faile fortharo* to *faire faile fort anu*, taking *anu* as dat. of *anae* 'wealth,' and Binchy accordingly translates "'people are interested in thy store' (i.e., the treasure which his father had hidden for him)," and that would, of course, suit the context admirably. I have tentatively preferred the less radical emendation of *fortharo* to *fort aru*, taking *aru* as dative of *arae* 'temple (of the forehead),' used by synecdoche for Cano himself.

28. Note to lines 61 ff.

29. Rynne and Mac Eoin (1978, 56).

30. Ó Fiannachta (1964–66, note to lines 59–74).

31. *TBC I* (2 ff.).

32. V. Hull (1949a, 43 ff.).

33. See *DIL* C 196.21 ff.

34. This interpretation is preferable to that offered by me in "The Theme of *ainmne* in *Scéla Cano meic Gartnáin*," p. 345 in this volume.

35. Ó Fiannachta (1964–66, 77).

36. Ó Coileáin (1981, 126).

37. Ó Coileáin (1981, 127).

38. Ó Coileáin (1981, 128).

39. Ó Fiannachta (1964–66, note to line 145).

40. The phrase is used of an early king by Watkins (1976a, 272). I should add here that Myles Dillon says of Illand's greeting to Cano that it "hardly implies an alternative tradition, but may be a part of Illann's boasting" (1946, 82n2).

41. Carney (1963).

42. Carney (1968, 22).

26. THE RHETORIC OF *FINGAL RÓNÁIN*

1. For a brief (and necessarily selective) survey of the criticism of Irish saga, see "Pagan Survivals," chap. 3 in this volume.

2. Wellek and Warren (1976, 19).

3. Abrams (1971, 148).

4. Greene (1955). Meyer's edition (1892b) is accompanied by a translation, which is reproduced (with slight modification) in Cross and Slover (1969, 538–45). There is a summary of the earlier part of the saga, and a translation of the remainder (lines 101–271) by Greene (1959). Translations in the present article are my own responsibility, but are greatly indebted to Meyer and Greene. Line-references are to Greene's edition. In citing his edited text, I have substituted the acute accent for the macron, and omitted the raised point and square brackets.

5. Charles-Edwards (1978, 130 ff.).

6. Dottin (1912).

7. In his edition, Greene tends to use brackets for asyntactic items which are introduced by .i.

8. For example, in the crucial verse-capping incident, the first half-quatrain is taken by Charles-Edwards (1978, 139) to have been spoken by Mael Fhothartaig's Fool, Mac Glass, but all the indications are that it must have been spoken by Mael Fhothartaig himself. See Ó Cathasaigh (1985c, 179). For another example, see note 20, below.

9. See Greene (1973, 123) where it is observed that the use of the pronominal particles with verbal forms other than those of the copula may be emphatic, contrastive, or merely stylistic.

10. Binchy (1979–80, 39).

11. Charles-Edwards (1978, 133, 139).

12. See further Ó Cathasaigh (1985c, 179).

13. For an instance of the use of the imperfect to refer to events occurring within the narrative time, see lines 58–61.

14. Charles-Edwards (1978, 133).

15. Charles-Edwards (1978, 133).

16. Charles-Edwards (1978, 132).

17. The previous paragraph summarizes what is said on the matter in Ó Cathasaigh (1985c). I did not deal with the content of the quatrain there, except to say that the meaning of her half-quatrain and that of the accompanying explanation remain somewhat obscure to us. That it would be appropriate for this quatrain to contain a revelation of guilt has been independently suggested to me by two experts in Old Norse sagas, Gísli Sigurðsson of University College, Dublin [now of the University of Iceland], and Professor Carol Clover of the University of California, Berkeley. In view of the overwhelming evidence for Mael Fhothartaig's innocence of any attempt to seduce Echaid's daughter, I was at a loss to see how their suggestion could be accepted, but I have now come to believe that it is correct to the extent that is set out below. I record my gratitude to them here. (I should add that the interpretation offered below of the second half-quatrain is consistent with Charles-Edwards's view that "herding the Cows of Aífe" may have had "an accepted significance based upon

the use of the place for illicit trysting" [1978, 139; see also 135], but I differ from him in his interpretation of the first half-quatrain, and in his view that it would be reasonable for Echaid's daughter to claim to have "won the ordeal," if that is taken to mean that the verse-capping proves her original charge against Mael Fhothartaig.)

18. Welsford (1935, 51).
19. Charles-Edwards (1978, 134).
20. The relevant passage (lines 245–51) has been the subject of a note by D. N. Dumville (1979–80). He is unhappy with the text as transmitted, and suggests that we should mark a lacuna at a point in line 245; reverse the order of two sentences at lines 247 f.; and insert a sentence, which is not in either of the manuscripts, before l. 250. One of the problems is the use of a pronoun to identify the speaker of the words, "Let me up, warriors, unless you want to kill me." Rónán has been taken by Meyer and Greene as the speaker of these words, but Dumville favors Áedán. The difficulty is that in the transmitted text Áedán is dead at this point—hence the suggested reversal of the sentences. Leaving that aside, it is probable that the unadorned pronoun would be used of a principal in the saga, rather than a mere *aithech*. Moreover, Áedán could scarcely be in any doubt that Mael Fhothartaig's sons propose to kill him, nor would they be likely to afford him the opportunity to question them about their intentions. The text makes sense as it stands; see Greene (1959, 175 f.). Greene says of the ending, "I think we can see how natural it was to its audience that the Leinstermen, after respecting the king's mourning for three whole days, should finally break in to avenge their hero and, sweeping the king aside, seize the murderer. . . . And the old king dies then, before the maddened Leinstermen can complete their vengeance by laying hands on their own king" (176 f.).
21. Heinrichs (1976) says that "a feature . . . is 'intertextual' when it, as one part of a text, points directly to another part of the text that appears sooner or later" (127).
22. Lönnroth (1970, 188), writing of *Njáls Saga*.

27. ON THE *CÍN DROMMA SNECHTA* VERSION OF *TOGAIL BRUDNE UÍ DERGAE*

1. Thurneysen (1912–13, 1:23 ff.; 1921, 17 f.; see also 1936b, 218n2).
2. Ó Concheanainn (1988, 9). The manuscripts, twelve in all, are listed and described (9–12).
3. Text and discussion of colophon in Ó Concheanainn (1988, 5).
4. Text of obit in Ó Concheanainn (1988, 3n9).
5. Thurneysen (1912–13, 1:28).
6. Ó Concheanainn (1988).
7. The translation of this is discussed below. Stokes (1901a, 402 f.) published a translation of the LU text.

8. The text of H.3.18 was published by Nettlau (1893, 151–52). Thurneysen (1912–13, 1:27) published an edition based on 23 N 10 and Eg. 88 with some readings from H.3.18; he was not then aware of the copy in G 7, the text of which V. Hull (1954a) subsequently published. Thurneysen (1921, 622 f.) has a translation. An earlier translation was by L. Gwynn (1914, 218 f.). S. Mac Mathúna (1985, 449 f.) has an edition and translation which for the most part follow Thurneysen.

9. Thurneysen (1921, 657).

10. Ó Concheanainn (1988, 34). *BUD* is discussed on pp. 30–34.

11. I have checked Hull's readings with the manuscript.

12. Stokes translates "so that Conaire by his mother's side (belonged) to Eochaid," but an emendation seems to be required. Another possibility is *Conid Conaire úa ó máthair do Echdaig*, "so that he is Conaire, descendant through his mother of Echaid's."

13. Bergin and Best (1934–38).

14. Bergin and Best (1934–38, 139, esp. note 2).

15. There is an inconsistency in the text, as Thurneysen has pointed out (1921, 657n3); Mess Búachalla is described as Echaid's daughter, and as his daughter's daughter. If this is not a simple case of confusion, it may be that the redactor is distinguishing between Echaid Airem and Echaid Feidlech, the former being Mess Búachalla's father, the latter her grandfather. T. O'Rahilly (1946, 131) discusses a claim that Echaid Airem was married to the Étaín who was mother of Mess Búachalla.

16. Knott (1936, lines 50 ff.).

17. Best and Bergin print *túath Maugnae*. I follow Mac Cana (1955–58, 102) in taking this as genitive of *Túathmaugain*, another name for *Túathmumu*.

18. Stokes translates "tribal slaves," but *túathmáel* apparently refers to a person with a certain style of haircut known as *túathmaíle*; see *DIL* T 350.1 ff.

19. Thurneysen (1921, 622n4).

20. Thurneysen (1912–13, 1:27n8).

21. V. Hull (1954, 131n4).

22. See Murphy (1952, 151 [*Baile Chuind*]). See also Kelly (1976, xxxi [6(a)], xxv).

23. Baumgarten (1983).

24. Baumgarten (1983, 192 f.). See also his remarks, 190n9b.

25. Baumgarten (1983, 190).

26. See *DIL* B 92.18 ff.

27. MS *inahoinech*. Hull emends to *ma[c]-hoi*, which is supported by the other MSS. The original, as Ó Concheanainn observes (1988, 32n89), was probably *moccu*.

28. MS *ina oineuch*.

29. Egerton 88 has *not-nortadur*, which Thurneysen translates taking the pronoun to refer to Conaire. H.3.18 reads *notaortattar*, where the pronoun must refer to

the *bruiden*; this may be supported by the reading of G 7 and *notanortatar* in 23 N 10, both of which seem also to provide another example of archaic nasalization after the feminine class C pronoun. It should be noted, however, that Thurneysen (1946, §415) lists *da n-* as a rare form of the 3 sg. masc. class C infixed pronoun; in §418 he cites *ruda-n-ordan* 'which has dignified him' (Wb. II, 33c5). Stokes and Strachan (*Thes.* 1:710 note b) emend to *rudnordan*. Either gender would fit the present context.

30. I follow Thurneysen (1921, 623n5) in reading *forræ* here.

31. Knott (1936, lines 421 ff.).

32. Knott (1936, line 712); see note ad loc. and Thurneysen (1921, 643).

33. Knott (1936, lines 722 ff.).

34. Thurneysen (1912–13, 27n41). For the vocalism, cf. Thurneysen (1946, §665 [future 3pl. *-errat*]).

35. See Pedersen (1909–13, 2:592.2).

36. See p. 110 and note 29 in this chap.

37. Stokes translates: "Elves encouraged them to fulfil for Ingcél what Mane of the Honey-words was saying" (1901a, 403).

38. See *DIL* C 5.29 and references.

39. S. Mac Mathúna (1985, 449).

40. I am indebted to Liam Breatnach for helpful comments.

28. GAT AND *DÍBERG* IN *TOGAIL BRUIDNE DA DERGA*

1. Ed. Knott (1936); trans. Gantz (1981, 60–106).

2. "The Semantics of *síd*," pp. 23–27 in this volume. The argument is repeated in "The Concept of the Hero in Irish Mythology," pp. 59–60 in this volume, and Ó Cathasaigh (1978a, 75–78).

3. Greene (1979, 12–14).

4. McCone (1980, 146–62).

5. "The Threefold Death in Early Irish Sources," chap. 7 in this volume.

6. "The Threefold Death in Early Irish Sources," p. 516n6, in this volume.

7. O'Leary (1986a, 15–16).

8. On these matters, see Thurneysen (1921, 621–63), Knott (1936, x–xv), and West (1990).

9. See again Thurneysen (1921, 621–63) [and more recently West (1999)].

10. For the text of *BUD* with translation and discussion, see West (1990, 91–98) and "On the *Cín Dromma Snechta* Version of *Togail Brudne Uí Dergae*," chap. 27 in this volume. The text of the LU recension may also be consulted in *LU* (244–45).

11. Ferguson (1880, 62).

12. Knott (1936, ix).

13. T. O'Rahilly (1946, 130).

14. O Daly (1959, 117).

15. O Daly (1959, 117).

16. O Daly (1959, 117).
17. "The Semantics of *síd*," pp. 23–27 in this volume.
18. "The Semantics of *síd*," p. 26 in this volume.
19. Dumézil (1973, 111–12).
20. Ó Cathasaigh (1978a, 78).
21. Greene (1979, 14).
22. Eoin MacNeill's view that the early Irish king functioned as a judge in the public court has recently been rehabilitated by Gerriets (1988) and Kelly (1988, 23–25). Kelly says that "the author of *Togail Bruidne Da Derga* no doubt reflects reality when he represents King Conaire as deciding the fate of the captured brigands who had threatened the peace of the country" (24).
23. McCone (1980, 146–62).
24. McCone (1980, 147).
25. Thurneysen (1921, 622).
26. McCone (1980, 148).
27. McCone (1980, 148–49).
28. McCone (1980, 148).
29. McCone (1980, 149).
30. McCone (1980, 149).
31. Dumézil (1973, 111–12).
32. McCone (1980, 149).
33. McCone (1990, 136–37).
34. See "On the *Cín Dromma Snechta* Version of *Togail Brudne Uí Dergae*," p. 403 in this volume.
35. *LU* (line 8022).
36. Knott (1936, line 181).
37. Mac Cana (1955–58, 102).
38. Knott (1936, line 230).
39. *LU* (line 8021).
40. Stokes (1901a, 402). Russell (1988, 110) translates "that he should not ?permit theft in his reign"; it is not clear to me that he wishes this to be taken as being significantly different from Stokes's rendering.
41. Meyer (1909b, 34, line 105).
42. Meyer (1909b, 35, line 105).
43. Meyer (1909b, 34, line 106).
44. Meyer (1909b, 35, line 106). Russell (1988, 110) translates "better to whip them than to coax them."
45. Meyer (1919, 398).
46. West (1990, 95). Cf. *LEIA* MNOP (1960), s.v. *mlig-*, where *ní fuinmilsed gata* is translated "il ne subirait pas des larcins," with the explanatory note "au sens où le français pourrait employer le verbe essuyer."

47. "On the *Cín Dromma Snechta* Version of *Togail Brudne Uí Dergae*," pp. 403–4 in this volume. Cf. Lewis and Pedersen (1961, 382) where the meaning of the verb is given as "to be indulgent to."
48. O'Leary (1986a, 16).
49. O'Leary (1986a, 16).
50. Binchy (1941, 18, lines 444–45).
51. Ó Corráin, Breatnach, and Breen (1984, 390).

29. THE OLDEST STORY OF THE LAIGIN

1. Edited and translated by Stokes (1901b). This has been partly superseded by Greene (1955), which is now the standard edition, but it should be noted that Stokes is more generous in the citation of variant readings. Translations in the present article are my own, except when otherwise stated; references are to the lines of Greene's edition. The Book of Leinster text is available in the diplomatic edition (*LL* v, 1192–94); it can also be read online (see note 2). The Rawlinson B 502 text can be consulted in the facsimile (Oxford, 1909). The tale is summarized and partly translated by Dillon (1946), and M. O'Brien (1954) translates the greater part of it. The text as edited by Greene is discussed and translated into French by Vendryes (1958–59).
2. *LL* (line 35215) has *fergg* here, but the manuscript has *sergg*, as can be seen on the ISOS site [http://www.isos.dias.ie/].
3. His suggestion that *ro gab-side ríge Lagen* in line 332 refers to Lóegaire is a slip.
4. So correct Stokes's *arisin*.
5. See recently E. Bhreathnach (1996, 82–86), Etchingham (1996, 131–33), and Jaski (2000, 214–17).
6. For this use of *gaibid* with *la* cf. *Gabais caille la patric*, "[she] took the veil from Patrick" (i.e., was professed by Patrick), cited (and so explained) *DIL* L 7.63, from the Book of Armagh. [See now Sims-Williams (2011, 223)].
7. Cross (1952) does not see either of these motifs in *ODR*. On the other hand, unlike Ó Maolfabhail and Chesnutt, who seem not to have consulted him, he quite properly includes *Genemain Chormaic* among the Irish examples of T646. In this he followed Dillon (1946, 24); see also Ó Cathasaigh (1977, 58).
8. I thank the editor of *Éigse* for helpful suggestions.

30. SOUND AND SENSE IN *CATH ALMAINE*

1. Ó Riain (1978); hereafter cited as *CA*.
2. *CA*, xxvii. The entry is also to be found, with a translation, in Radner (1978, 66–81).

3. References are to the lines of Ó Riain's normalized text of the Brussels manuscript, which he gives on pp. 1–16. The translations draw heavily on Ó Riain's work but are nonetheless my responsibility.

4. *CA*, 65. Ó Riain gives the text of two of the manuscripts of the later recension on 17–31. References to the later recension in the present article are to the Yellow Book of Lecan (YBL) text (Y), as printed in *CA*.

5. Stokes (1892a); *LL* (v, 1268–1318).

6. Mac Eoin (1968, 29–30) suggests that the remittal episode was added at a relatively late stage in the development of the *bórama* story.

7. Sound, both verbal and non-verbal, is exploited with considerable effect in the early Ulster saga *Loinges mac n-Uislenn*. See Dooley (1982, 155–58) and Buttimer (1994–95, 2–9, 39–40).

8. Stokes (1892a, 98–117).

9. See Radner (1978, note to entry 67) and Davies (1996a, 49n12).

10. V. Hull (1933a, 56–57); *LL* 5:1120.

11. Bergin and Best (1934–38, 146–47).

12. Charles-Edwards (2002, 169).

13. It is the subject of the saga *Orgain Denna Ríg*. See "The Oldest Story of the Laigin: Observations on *Orgain Denna Ríg*," chap. 29 in this volume.

14. *Ní maid for Laigniu dia ndernat a comairle ann*, line 73. I take *maid* here as the Middle Irish preterite (replacing Old Irish *memaid*), used modally. Ó Riain (*CA*, "Vocabulary," s.v.) takes it as present indicative.

15. *CA*, Y, lines 59–64.

16. *CA*, note to line 136.

17. *CA*, Y, lines 117–20.

31. TÓRAÍOCHT DHIARMADA AGUS GHRÁINNE

1. Is ag tagairt do insintí béil atá na nodanna ar nós S1: tagraíonn an litir don chontae inar bailíodh í (S = Sutherland, etc.; feic Bruford 1969, 250), agus an uimhir don ord ina dtugtar na hinsintí ón chontae sin i liosta Bruford (1969, 265 f.). Is do *Leabhar na Féinne* (Campbell 1872) a thagraíonn *LNF*.

THE PURSUIT OF DIARMAID AND GRÁINNE

1. Abbreviations such as S1 refer to oral versions: the letter refers to the county in which it was collected (S = Sutherland, etc.; see Bruford 1969, 250) and the number to the order in which it appears in the list of versions from that county in Bruford (1969, 265 f.).

Bibliography of Tomás Ó Cathasaigh

1969a. "Rómánsachas Sean-Nósach." Review of *Nua-Fhilí 2 (1953–1963)*, edited by Séamas Ó Céileachair, and Séamas Ó Céileachair, *Grian na gCnoc*. *Comhar* 28 (3): 27–29.

1969b. "Bua Uí Liatháin." Review of Annraoi Ó Liatháin, *Luaithreach an Bhua*. *Comhar* 28 (7): 24–25.

1974. Review of Hubert Butler, *Ten Thousand Saints: A Study of Irish and European Origins*. *Folklore* 85:65–67.

1976. "On the LU Version of 'The Expulsion of the Dési.'" *Celtica* 11:150–57.

1977. *The Heroic Biography of Cormac mac Airt*. Dublin: DIAS.

1977–79. "The Semantics of *síd*." *Éigse* 17:137–55.

1978a. "Between Man and God: The Hero of Irish Tradition." *The Crane Bag* 2:72–79.

1978b. "Gort an Léinn." Review of *Celtica* 12. *Comhar* 37 (12): 21.

1979. Review of P. L. Henry, *Saoithiúlacht na Sean-Ghaeilge*. *Comhar* 38 (8): 20.

1980–81a. "The Theme of *lommrad* in *Cath Maige Mucrama*." *Éigse* 18:211–24.

1980–81b. Review of Pádraig Ó Riain, ed., *Cath Almaine*. *Éigse* 18:308–12.

1982–89. "Irish Literature: Saga." In *Dictionary of the Middle Ages*, edited by J. R. Strayer, 6:544–49. New York: Scribner. Also shorter entries on "Cormac mac Airt" and "Tara."

1983a. "*Cath Maige Tuired* as Exemplary Myth." In *Folia Gadelica: Essays Presented by Former Students to R. A. Breatnach*, edited by P. de Brún, S. Ó Coileáin, and P. Ó Riain, 1–19. Cork: Cork University Press.

1983b. "The Theme of *ainmne* in *Scéla Cano meic Gartnáin*." *Celtica* 15:78–87.

1984a. "Pagan Survivals: The Evidence of Early Irish Narrative." In *Ireland and Europe: The Early Church*, edited by P. Ní Chatháin and M. Richter, 291–307. Stuttgart: Klett-Cotta.

1984b. "The Déisi and Dyfed." *Éigse* 20:1–33.
1984c. "'A rather messy domestic situation. . . .'" *Nua-Aois*: 53–74.
1985a. "The Concept of the Hero in Irish Mythology." In *The Irish Mind: Exploring Intellectual Traditions*, edited by R. Kearney, 79–90. Dublin: Wolfhound Press.
1985b. "The Rhetoric of *Fingal Rónáin*." *Celtica* 17:123–44.
1985c. "The Trial of Mael Fhothartaig." *Ériu* 36:177–80.
1986a. "Curse and Satire." *Éigse* 21:10–15.
1986b. "The Sister's Son in Early Irish Literature." *Peritia* 5:128–60.
1988. Review of Doris Edel, *Helden auf Freiersfüssen: "Tochmarc Emire" und "Mal y kavas Kulhwch Olwen"; Studien zur frühen inselkeltischen Erzähltradition*. *Celtica* 20:169–77.
1989a. "The Rhetoric of *Scéla Cano meic Gartnáin*." In *Sages, Saints and Storytellers: Celtic Studies in Honour of Professor James Carney*, edited by D. Ó Corráin, L. Breatnach, and K. R. McCone, 233–50. Maynooth Monographs 2. Maynooth: An Sagart
1989b. "On the Early-Irish Prepositional Relative without Antecedent." *Celtica* 21:418–26.
1989c. "The Eponym of Cnogba." *Éigse* 23:27–38.
1989d. "Three Notes on *Cath Maige Tuired*." *Ériu* 40:61–68.
1990a. "On the *Cín Dromma Snechta* Version of *Togail Brudne Uí Dergae*." *Ériu* 41:103–14.
1990b. Review of Máire Herbert, *Iona, Kells and Derry: The History and Hagiography of the Monastic* Familia *of Columba*. *Éigse* 24:192–95.
1993a. "Mythology in *Táin Bó Cúailnge*." In *Studien zur Táin Bó Cuailnge*, edited by H. L. C. Tristram, 114–32. ScriptOralia 52. Tübingen: Gunter Narr Verlag.
1993b. Review of T. M. Charles-Edwards, *Early Irish and Welsh Kinship*. *CMCS* 33:93–94.
1994a. "Reflections on *Compert Conchobuir* and *Serglige Con Culainn*." In *Ulidia*, 85–89.
1994b. "The Threefold Death in Early Irish Sources." *Studia Celtica Japonica*, n.s. 6:53–75.
1995a. "Tóraíocht Dhiarmada agus Ghráinne." *Léachtaí Cholm Cille* 25:30–46.
1995b. "Narrativa irlandesa antigua: Tendencias recientes en la investigación." *Acta poetica* 16:257–69.
1996a. "*Gat* and *díberg* in *Togail Bruidne Da Derga*." In *Celtica Helsingiensia: Proceedings from a Symposium on Celtic Studies*, edited by A. Ahlqvist et al., 203–13. Commentationes Humanarum Litterarum 107. Helsinki: Societas Scientiarum Fennica.
1996b. "Early Irish Narrative Literature." In *Progress in Medieval Irish Studies*, edited by K. R. McCone and K. Simms, 55–64. Maynooth: Dept. of Old Irish, St Patrick's College.

1996c. Miscellaneous entries (thirty-six) in *The Oxford Companion to Irish Literature*, edited by R. Welch. Oxford: Oxford University Press.

1997. "Knowledge and Power in *Aislinge Óenguso*." In *Dán do oide: Essays in Memory of Conn R. Ó Cléirigh*, edited by A. Ahlqvist and V. Čapková, 431–38. Dublin: Linguistics Institute of Ireland.

1998. Foreword to reprint of Murphy (1956), v–vii. Dublin: Four Courts Press.

2002a. "Táin." In *The Epic Voice*, edited by A. D. Hodder and R. E. Meagher, 129–47. Westport, CT: Praeger.

2002b. "The Oldest Story of the Laigin: Reflections on *Orgain Denna Ríg*." *Éigse* 33:1–18.

2003. Miscellaneous (seven) in *The Encyclopedia of Ireland*, edited by B. Lalor. New Haven: Yale University Press.

2004. "Sound and Sense in *Cath Almaine*." *Ériu* 54:41–47.

2005a. *Táin bó Cúailnge and Early Irish Law*. The Osborn Bergin Memorial Lecture 5. Dublin: Faculty of Celtic, University College Dublin.

2005b. "The Literature of Medieval Ireland to *c*.800: St Patrick to the Vikings." In *The Cambridge History of Irish Literature*, vol. 1, *To 1890*, edited by M. Kelleher and P. O'Leary, 9–31. Cambridge: Cambridge University Press.

2005c. "*Sírrabad Súaltaim* and the Order of Speaking Among the Ulaid." In *A Companion in Linguistics: A Festschrift for Anders Ahlqvist on the Occasion of His Sixtieth Birthday*, edited by B. Smelik et al., 80–91. Nijmegen: Stichting Uitgeverij de Keltische Draak.

2005d. "Cú Chulainn, the Poets, and Giolla Brighde Mac Con Midhe." In *Heroic Poets and Poetic Heroes in Celtic Tradition: A Festschrift for Patrick K. Ford*, edited by J. F. Nagy and L. E. Jones, 291–302. *CSANA Yearbook* 4–5. Dublin: Four Courts Press.

2005e. "The Expulsion of the Déisi." *JCHAS* 110:68–75.

2005f. "The First Anders Ahlqvist Lecture: Irish Myths and Legends." *Studia Celtica Fennica* 2:11–26.

2005g. "Echtrai." In *Medieval Ireland: An Encyclopedia*, edited by S. Duffy, 139–40. New York: Routledge.

2006–7a. "Early Irish Literature and Law: Lecture Presented at the Annual Meeting of the Finnish Society of Sciences and Letters, April 27, 2007." *Sphinx*: 111–19.

2006–7b. Review of Liam Breatnach, *A Companion to the Corpus Iuris Hibernici*. *SH* 34:193–95.

2008. "Myth and Saga: 'The Wooing of Étaín.'" In *Why Irish? Irish Language and Literature in Academia*, edited by B. Ó Conchubhair, 55–69. Galway: Arlen House.

2009. "Ailill and Medb: A Marriage of Equals." In *Ulidia 2*, 46–53.

2010a. "Kingship in Early Irish Literature." In *L'Irlanda e gli irlandesi nell'alto medioevo*, 135–53. Atti delle settimane 57. Spoleto: Fondazione Centro Italiano di Studi sull'Alto Medioevo.

2010b. "King, Hero, and Hospitaller in *Aided Cheltchair maic Uthechair*." In *Bile ós Chrannaib: A Festschrift for William Gillies*, edited by W. McLeod et al., 355–64. Ceann Drochaid: Clann Tuirc.

2010c. "Textual Transmission and Variation: A Medieval Irish Case Study." In *Celtic Language Law and Letters: Proceedings of the Tenth Symposium of Societas Celtologica Nordica*, edited by F. Josephson, 169–79. Meijerbergs Arkiv för Svensk Ordforskning 38. Gothenburg: Societas Celtologica Nordica.

2010d. Review of Gregory Toner, ed., trans., *Bruiden Da Choca*. *Éigse* 37:169–74.

2010e. Review of Róisín McLaughlin, *Early Irish Satire*. *Australian Celtic Journal* 9:75–77.

2011a. "Aspects of Memory and Identity in Early Ireland." In *Narrative in Celtic Tradition: Essays in Honor of Edgar M. Slotkin*, edited by J. F. Eska, 201–16. CSANA Yearbook 8–9. Hamilton, NY: Colgate University Press.

2011b. "Conchobor and His Court at Emain." In *Language and Power in the Celtic World: Papers from the Seventh Australian Conference of Celtic Studies, The University of Sydney, September–October 2010*, edited by A. Ahlqvist and P. O'Neill, 309–22. Sydney Series in Celtic Studies 10. Sydney: University of Sydney.

2011c. Review of Peter J. Smith, ed., trans., *Three Historical Poems Ascribed to Gilla Cóemáin: A Critical Edition of the Work of an Eleventh-Century Irish Scholar*. *Speculum* 86:553–54.

2012. "Early Irish *bairdne*: 'eulogy, panegyric.'" *Studia Celtica Fennica* 9:54–61.

2013a. "The Body in *Táin Bó Cúailnge*." In *Gablánach in scélaigecht: Celtic Studies in Honour of Ann Dooley*, edited by S. Sheehan, J. Findon, and W. Follett, 131–53. Dublin: Four Courts Press.

2013b. "*Tochmarc Étaíne* II: A Tale of Three Wooings." In *The Land Beneath the Sea: Essays in Honour of Anders Ahlqvist's Contribution to Celtic Studies in Australia*, edited by P. O'Neill, 129–42. Sydney Series in Celtic Studies 14. Sydney: University of Sydney.

Forthcoming. "The Making of a Prince: *Áed Oll fri Andud n-Áne*."

Forthcoming. "On the Genealogical Preamble to *Vita Sancti Declani*."

Works Cited

Works by Tomás Ó Cathasaigh are listed in the bibliography, which precedes this Works Cited section.

Abbott, T. K., and E. J. Gwynn. 1921. *Catalogue of Irish Manuscripts in the Library of Trinity College, Dublin.* Dublin: Hodges, Figgis.

Abrams, M. H. 1960. *The Mirror and the Lamp.* London: Oxford University Press.

———. 1971. *A Glossary of Literary Terms.* 3rd ed. New York: Holt, Rinehart, & Winston.

Ahlqvist, Anders, ed., trans. 1983. *The Early Irish Linguist: An Edition of the Canonical Part of the Auraicept na nÉces.* Commentationes Humanarum Litterarum 73. Helsinki: Societas Scientiarum Fennica.

Aitchison, N. B. 1987. "The Ulster Cycle: Heroic Image and Historical Reality." *Journal of Medieval History* 13:87–116.

Almqvist, Bo, Séamas Ó Catháin, and Pádraig Ó Héalaí, eds. 1987a. *The Heroic Process: Form, Function, and Fantasy in Folk Epic.* Dublin: Glendale Press.

———. 1987b. *Fiannaíocht: Essays on the Fenian Tradition of Ireland and Scotland.* Dublin: Folklore of Ireland Society.

Anderson, Alan Orr, and Marjorie Ogilvie Anderson, eds., trans. 1991. *Adomnán's Life of Columba.* Revised by M. O. Anderson. Oxford: Oxford University Press.

Arbuthnot, Sharon J., ed., trans. 2005–6. *Cóir Anmann: A Late Middle Irish Treatise on Personal Names.* 2 vols. Irish Texts Society 59/60. London: ITS.

———. 2012. "Finn, Ferchess and the *rincne*: Versions Compared." In *The Gaelic Finn Tradition*, edited by S. J. Arbuthnot and G. Parsons, 62–80. Dublin: Four Courts Press.

Banks, M. M. 1938. "Na tri mairt, the Three Marts and the Man with the Withy." *ÉC* 3:131–43.
Bartrum, P. C., ed. 1966. *Early Welsh Genealogical Tracts*. Cardiff: University of Wales Press.
Baumgarten, Rolf. 1975. "A Crux in Echtrae Conlai." *Éigse* 16:18–23.
———. 1983. "Varia III: A Note on *Táin Bó Regamna*." *Ériu* 34:189–93.
Beekes, R. S. P. 1976. "Uncle and Nephew." *JIES* 4:43–63.
Bek-Pedersen, Karen. 2006. "Oppositions and Cooperations in the Baldr Myth, with Irish and Welsh Parallels." *JIES* 34.1–2:5–26.
Benveniste, Emile. 1973. *Indo-European Language and Society*. Translated by Elizabeth Palmer. London: Faber & Faber.
Bergin, Osborn. 1927. "How the Dagda Got His Magic Staff." In *Medieval Studies in Memory of Gertrude Schoepperle Loomis*, edited by R. S. Loomis, 399–406. Paris: Champion/New York: Columbia University Press.
———, ed., trans. 1970. *Irish Bardic Poetry*, edited by D. Greene and F. Kelly. Dublin: DIAS.
Bergin, Osborn, and R. I. Best, eds., trans. 1934–38. "Tochmarc Étaíne." *Ériu* 12:137–96.
Bernhardt-House, Phillip A. 2009. "It's Beginning to Look a Lot Like Solstice: *Snechta*, Solar Deities, and *Compert Con Culainn*." In *Ulidia 2*, 226–37.
Best. R. I., ed., trans. 1907. "The Adventures of Art son of Conn, and the Courtship of Delbchœm." *Ériu* 3:149–73.
Bhreathnach, Edel. 1996. "Temoria: Caput Scotorum?" *Ériu* 47:67–88.
———. 2000. "Kings, the Kingship of Leinster and the Regnal Poems of *Laídshenchas Laigen*: A Reflection of Dynastic Politics in Leinster, 650–1150." In *Seanchas: Studies in Early and Medieval Irish Archaeology, History and Literature in Honour of Francis J. Byrne*, edited by A. P. Smyth, 299–312. Dublin: Four Courts Press.
———. 2005. "*Níell cáich úa Néill nasctar géill*: The Political Context of *Baile Chuinn Chétchathaig*." In *The Kingship and Landscape of Tara*, edited by E. Bhreathnach, 49–68. Dublin: Four Courts Press.
———. 2013. *Ireland and the Medieval World, AD 400–1000: Landscape, Kinship, and Religion*. Dublin: Four Courts Press, forthcoming.
Bhreathnach, Máire. 1982. "The Sovereignty Goddess as Goddess of Death?" *ZCP* 39:243–60.
———, ed., trans. 1984. "A New Edition of Tochmarc Becfhola." *Ériu* 35:59–91.
Bieler, Ludwig, ed. 1963. *The Irish Penitentials*. *SLH* 5. Dublin: DIAS.
Binchy, Daniel A. 1936. "Family Membership of Women." In *Studies in Early Irish Law*, edited by R. Thurneysen et al., 180–86. Dublin: Royal Irish Academy.
———, ed. 1941. *Críth Gablach*. Mediaeval and Modern Irish Series 11. Dublin: DIAS.
———. 1943. "The Linguistic and Historical Value of the Irish Law Tracts." *PBA* 29:195–227. Reprinted 1973 in *Celtic Law Papers*, edited by D. Jenkins, 71–107.

Brussels: Editions de la Librairie encyclopédique. Page references are to the reprint.

———, ed., trans. 1952. "The Saga of Fergus mac Léti." *Ériu* 16:33–48.

———. 1954. "Secular Institutions." In *Early Irish Society*, edited by Myles Dillon, 52–65. Dublin: Colm Ó Lochlainn for the Cultural Relations Committee of Ireland, at the Sign of the Three Candles.

———. 1956. "Some Celtic Legal Terms." *Celtica* 3:221–31.

———. 1958. Review of Jackson 1953. *Celtica* 4:288–92.

———. 1959. "Echtra Fergusa Maic Léiti." In *Irish Sagas*, edited by M. Dillon, 38–50. Dublin: Mercier Press.

———. 1961. "The Background of Early Irish Literature." *SH* 1:7–18.

———. 1962a. "The Old-Irish Table of Penitential Commutations." *Ériu* 19:47–72.

———. 1962b. "Patrick and His Biographers: Ancient and Modern." *SH* 2:27–173.

———, ed. 1963. *Scéla Cano Meic Gartnáin*. Mediaeval and Modern Irish Series 18. Dublin: DIAS.

———. 1970. *Celtic and Anglo-Saxon Kingship*. Oxford: The Clarendon Press.

———. 1976a. "*Féchem, fethem, aigne*." *Celtica* 11:18–33.

———. 1976b. "Irish History and Irish Law, II." *SH* 16:7–45.

———. 1978. *Corpus Iuris Hibernici*. 6 vols. Dublin: DIAS.

———. 1979–80. "Bergin's Law." *SC* 14/15:34–53.

Bitel, Lisa. 2006–7. "Tools and Scripts for Cursing in Medieval Ireland." *Memoirs of the American Academy in Rome* 51/52:5–27.

Blažek, Václav. 2001. "*Balor*: 'the Blind-Eyed'?" *ZCP* 52:129–33.

Blustein, Rebecca. 2007. "Poets and Pillars in *Cath Maige Tuired*." In *Myth and Celtic Literature*, edited by J. F. Nagy, 22–38. CSANA Yearbook 6. Dublin: Four Courts Press.

Boll, Sheila. 2004. "Seduction, Vengeance and Frustration in *Fingal Rónáin*: The Role of Foster-Kin in Structuring the Narrative." *CMCS* 47:1–16.

———. 2005. "Structural Symmetry and the Representation of Kinship in Mediaeval Gaelic Narrative Literature: *Cath Maige Mucrama* and *Scéla Muicce Meic Dáthó*." *The Journal of Celtic Studies* 5:127–39.

Borsje, Jacqueline. 1999. "Ordeals, Omens and Oracles: On Demons and Weapons in Early Irish Texts." *Peritia* 13:224–48.

———. 2007. "Human Sacrifice in Medieval Irish Literature." In *The Strange World of Human Sacrifice*, edited by J. N. Bremmer, 31–54. Studies in the History and Anthropology of Religion 1. Leuven: Peeters.

———. 2009a. "Supernatural Threats to Kings: Exploration of a Motif in the Ulster Cycle and in Other Medieval Irish Tales." In *Ulidia 2*, 173–94.

———. 2009b. "Monotheistic to a Certain Extent: The 'Good Neighbours' of God in Ireland." In *The Boundaries of Monotheism: Interdisciplinary Explorations into the Foundations of Western Monotheism*, edited by A.-M. Korte and M. de Haart, 53–82. Leiden: Brill.

Borsje, Jacqueline, and Fergus Kelly. 2003. "'The evil eye' in Early Irish Literature and Law." *Celtica* 24:1–39.

Boyd, Matthieu. 2009a. "Competing Assumptions about the *drúth* in *Orgain Denna Ríg*." *Ériu* 59:37–47.

———. 2009b. "Melion and the Wolves of Ireland." *Neophilologus* 93.4:555–70.

———. 2012. "The Poems of Blathmac, Son of Cú Brettan, and *The Dream of the Rood*." *SMART: Studies in Medieval and Renaissance Teaching* 19.2:49–80.

Bray, Dorothy Ann. 2002. "Malediction and Benediction in the Lives of the Early Irish Saints." *SC* 36:47–58.

———. 2005. "Further on White Red-Eared Cows in Fact and Fiction." *Peritia* 19:239–55.

Breatnach, Caoimhín. 2000. "*Oidheadh Chloinne Tuireann* agus *Cath Maige Tuired*: dhá shampla de mhiotas eiseamláireach" [*OCT* and *CMT*: Two Examples of Exemplary Myth]. *Éigse* 32:35–46.

———. 2011. "The Transmission and Text of *Tóruigheacht Dhiarmada agus Ghráinne*." In *The Gaelic Finn Tradition*, edited by S. J. Arbuthnot and G. Parsons, 139–50. Dublin: Four Courts Press.

Breatnach, Liam, ed., trans. 1981. "The Caldron of Poesy." *Ériu* 32:45–93.

———. 1984. "Canon Law and Secular Law in Early Ireland: The Significance of *Bretha Nemed*." *Peritia* 3:439–59.

———. 1986. "The Ecclesiastical Element in the Old-Irish Legal Tract *Cáin Fhuithirbe*." *Peritia* 5:36–52.

———, ed., trans. 1987. *Uraicecht na Ríar: The Poetic Grades in Early Irish Law*. Early Irish Law Series 2. Dublin: DIAS.

———. 1990. "Lawyers in Early Ireland." In *Brehons, Serjeants and Attorneys: Studies in the History of the Irish Legal Profession*, edited by D. Hogan and W. N. Osborough, 1–13. Dublin: Irish Academic Press.

———. 1994. "An Mheán-Ghaeilge." In *Stair na Gaeilge*, edited by K. R. McCone et al., 221–333. Maynooth: An Sagart.

———. 1996. "On the Glossing of Early Irish Law-Texts, Fragmentary Texts, and Some Aspects of the Laws Relating to Dogs." In *Celtica Helsingiensia: Proceedings from a Symposium on Celtic Studies*, edited by A. Ahlqvist et al., 11–20. Commentationes Humanarum Litterarum 107. Helsinki: Societas Scientiarum Fennica.

———. 2005. *A Companion to the Corpus Iuris Hibernici*. Early Irish Law Series 5. Dublin: DIAS.

———. 2006. "Satire, Praise, and the Early Irish Poet." *Ériu* 56:63–84.

———. 2009. "*Araile felmac féig don Muman*: Unruly Pupils and the Limitations of Satire." *Ériu* 59:111–36.

———. 2010. "Law and Literature in Early Mediaeval Ireland." In *L'Irlanda e gli irlandesi nell'alto medioevo*, 215–38. Atti delle settimane 57. Spoleto: Fondazione Centro Italiano di Studi sull'Alto Medioevo.

Breatnach, R. A. 1953. "The Lady and the King: A Theme of Irish Literature." *Studies: An Irish Quarterly Review* 42:321–36.

———. 1959. "Tóraigheacht Dhiarmada agus Ghráinne." In *Irish Sagas*, edited by M. Dillon, 138–51. Dublin: Mercier Press.

Bremmer, Jan N. 1976. "Avunculate and Fosterage." *JIES* 4:65–76.

Breeze, Andrew. 2008. "*Scéla Cano Meic Gartnáin*, Fiachna Son of Báitán, and Bamburgh." In *Caindel Alban: Fèill-Sgrìobhainn do Dhòmhnall E. Meek*, edited by C. Ó Baoill and N. R. McGuire, 87–95. *Scottish Gaelic Studies* 24. Aberdeen: University of Aberdeen.

Bromwich, Rachel, ed., trans. 1961. *Trioedd Ynys Prydein*. Cardiff: University of Wales Press. 2nd ed. (1978). 3rd ed. (2006).

———. 1966. Review of Binchy (1963). *SC* 1:152–55.

Brown, Arthur C. L. 1943. *The Origin of the Grail Legend*. Cambridge, MA: Harvard University Press.

Bruford, Alan. 1969. *Gaelic Folk-Tales and Mediaeval Romances*. Dublin: Folklore of Ireland Society.

Buttimer, Cornelius G. 1987. "*Un joc grossier* in *Orgguin Trí Mac Diarmata Mic Cerbaill*." *Celtica* 19:128–32.

———. 1994–95. "*Longes mac n-Uislenn* Reconsidered." *Éigse* 28:1–41.

Byrne, Francis John. 1967. "Seventh-Century Documents." *Irish Ecclesiastical Record* 108:164–82.

———. 1968. "Historical Note on Cnogba (Knowth)." *PRIA* 66 C: 383–400.

———. 1973. *Irish Kings and High-Kings*. London: Batsford.

———. 1974. "*Senchas*: The Nature of Gaelic Historical Tradition." In *Historical Studies IX: Papers Read before the Irish Conference of Historians*, edited by J. G. Barry, 137–59. Belfast: Blackstaff Press.

Caball, Marc, and Kaarina Hollo. 2005. "The Literature of Later Medieval Ireland, 1200–1600: From the Normans to the Tudors." In *The Cambridge History of Irish Literature*, vol. 1, *To 1890*, edited by M. Kelleher and P. O'Leary, 74–139. Cambridge: Cambridge University Press.

Campanile, Enrico. 1979. "Meaning and Prehistory of Old Irish *cú glas*." *JIES* 7:237–47.

Campbell, John Francis, ed. 1872. *Leabhar na Féinne: Heroic Gaelic Ballads Collected in Scotland Chiefly from 1512 to 1871*. London: Spottiswoode.

Carey, John. 1982. "The Location of the Otherworld." *Éigse* 19:36–43. Reprinted as Carey (2000).

———, ed., trans. 1984. "Scél Tuáin meic Chairill." *Ériu* 35:93–111.

———. 1987. "Time, Space, and the Otherworld." *PHCC* 7:1–27.

———. 1988. "Three Notes." *Celtica* 20:123–29.

———. 1989–90. "Myth and Mythography in *Cath Maige Tuired*." *SC* 24/25:53–69.

———. 1991. "The Irish 'Otherworld': Hiberno-Latin Perspectives." *Éigse* 25:154–59.

———. 1994. "The Uses of Tradition in *Serglige Con Culainn*." *Ulidia*, 77–84.

———. 1995a. "On the Interrelationships of Some *Cín Dromma Snechtai* Texts." *Ériu* 46:71–92.
———. 1995b. "Eithne in Gubai." *Éigse* 28:160–64.
———. 1997. "The Three Things Required of a Poet." *Ériu* 48:41–58.
———. 1999. "Transmutations of Immortality in Lament of the Old Woman of Beare." *Celtica* 22:30–37.
———. 2000. "The Location of the Otherworld." In *The Otherworld Voyage in Early Irish Literature*, edited by J. Wooding, 113–19. Dublin: Four Courts Press.
———. 2002. "Werewolves in Medieval Ireland." *CMCS* 44:37–72.
———. 2004. "The Encounter at the Ford: Warriors, Water and Women." *Éigse* 34:10–24.
———. 2007. *Ireland and the Grail*. Aberystwyth: Celtic Studies Publications.
———, ed. 2009. *Lebor Gabála Érenn: Textual History and Prehistory*. Irish Texts Society Subsidiary Series 20. Dublin: ITS.
Carney, James Patrick. 1940. "Nia son of Lugna Fer Trí." *Éigse* 2:187–97.
———. 1955. *Studies in Irish Literature and History*. Dublin: DIAS.
———. 1963. "Iseult of Ireland." Review of Binchy (1963). *The Irish Press*, 1 June.
———, ed., trans. 1964. *The Poems of Blathmac Son of Cú Brettan: Together with the Irish Gospel of Thomas and a Poem on the Virgin Mary*. Irish Texts Society 47. Dublin: ITS.
———. 1965a. "Poems of Blathmac, son of Cú Brettan." In *Early Irish Poetry*, edited by J. Carney, 45–57. Cork: Mercier Press.
———. 1965b. "Old Ireland and Her Poetry." In *Old Ireland*, edited by R. McNally, 147–72. New York: Fordham University Press.
———. 1967a. *The Irish Bardic Poet*. Dublin: Dolmen Press.
———, ed., trans. 1967b. *Medieval Irish Lyrics*. Berkeley: University of California Press.
———. 1968. "Two Poems from *Acallam na Senórach*." In *Celtic Studies: Essays in Memory of Angus Matheson*, edited by J. Carney and D. Greene, 22–32. London: Routledge and Kegan Paul.
———. 1969. "The Deeper Level of Irish Literature." *Capuchin Annual* 36:160–71.
———. 1969–70. "The So-Called 'Lament of Créidhe.'" *Éigse* 13:227–42.
———, ed., trans. 1971. "Three Old Irish Accentual Poems." *Ériu* 22:23–80.
———. 1983. "The History of Early Irish Literature: The State of Research." In *Proceedings of the Sixth International Congress of Celtic Studies*, edited by G. Mac Eoin et al., 113–30. Dublin: DIAS.
Carney, James. 2008. "The Pangs of the Ulstermen: An Exchangist Perspective." *JIES* 36.1–2:52–66.
Chadwick, Hector Munro, and Nora Kershaw Chadwick. 1932. *The Growth of Literature*, vol. 1, *The Ancient Literature of Europe*. Cambridge: Cambridge University Press.
Chadwick, Nora Kershaw. 1963. *Celtic Britain*. London: Thames and Hudson.

———. 1965. *The Colonization of Brittany from Celtic Britain*. Sir John Rhŷs Memorial Lecture. London: Oxford University Press. Reprinted from *PBA* 51:235–99.

Charles-Edwards, Thomas M. 1970. "The Date of the Four Branches of the Mabinogi." *The Transactions of the Honourable Society of Cymmrodorion*, 263–98.

———. 1970–72. "Some Celtic Kinship Terms." *BBCS* 24:105–22.

———. 1976. "The Social Background to Irish *peregrinatio*." *Celtica* 11:43–59.

———. 1978. "Honour and Status in Some Irish and Welsh Prose Tales." *Ériu* 29:123–41.

———. 1986. "*Críth Gablach* and the Law of Status." *Peritia* 5:53–73.

———. 1993. *Early Irish and Welsh Kinship*. Oxford: Clarendon Press.

———. 1994. "A Contract between King and People in Early Medieval Ireland: *Críth Gablach* on Kingship." *Peritia* 8:107–19.

———. 1999a. "Geis, Prophecy, Omen, and Oath." *Celtica* 23:38–59.

———. 1999b. *The Early Mediaeval Gaelic Lawyer*. Quiggin Pamphlets on the Sources of Mediaeval Gaelic History 4. Cambridge: Dept. of Anglo-Saxon, Norse, and Celtic, University of Cambridge.

———. 2000. *Early Christian Ireland*. Cambridge: Cambridge University Press.

———. 2002. "*Tochmarc Étaíne*: A Literal Interpretation." In *Ogma: Essays in Celtic Studies in Honour of Próinséas Ní Chatháin*, edited by M. Richter and J.-M. Picard, 165–81. Dublin: Four Courts Press.

———. 2005. "Early Irish law." In *A New History of Ireland* 1: *Prehistoric and Early Ireland*, edited by D. Ó Cróinín, 331–70. Oxford: Oxford University Press.

———. 2013. *Wales and the Britons, 350–1064*. The History of Wales 1. Oxford: Clarendon Press.

Chatman, Seymour. 1978. *Story and Discourse: Narrative Structure in Fiction and Film*. Ithaca, NY: Cornell University Press.

Chesnutt, Michael. 2000. "The Fatherless Hero in the Playground: Irish Perspectives on the Norse Legend of Sigurd." *Béaloideas* 68:33–65.

———. 2001. "*Cath Maige Tuired*: A Parable of the Battle of Clontarf." In *Northern Lights: Following Folklore in North-Western Europe*, edited by S. Ó Cathain, 22–33. Dublin: University College Dublin Press.

Clancy, Thomas Owen. 1993. "Fools and Adultery in Some Early Irish Texts." *Ériu* 44:105–24.

———. 2005. "Court, King, and Justice in the Ulster Cycle." In *Medieval Celtic Literature and Society*, edited by H. Fulton, 163–82. Dublin: Four Courts Press.

Cohen, David J. 1977. "Suibne Geilt." *Celtica* 12:113–24.

Colish, Marcia. 1997. *Medieval Foundations of the Western Intellectual Tradition, 400–1400*. New Haven: Yale University Press.

Coplestone-Crow, Bruce. 1981–82. "The Dual Nature of the Irish Colonization of Dyfed in the Dark Ages." *SC* 16/17:1–24.

Corthals, Johan. 1989. "Zur Frage des mündlichen oder schriftlichen Ursprungs der Sagen *roscada*." In *Early Irish Literature: Media and Communication/ Mündlichkeit und Schriftlichkeit in der frühen irischen Literatur*, edited by S. N. Tranter and H. L. C. Tristram, 201–20. Tübingen: Gunter Narr Verlag.

———. 1990. "Some Observations on the Versification of the Rhymeless 'Leinster' Poems." *Celtica* 21:113–25.

———. 1995. "Affiliation of Children: *Immathchor nAilella 7 Airt*." *Peritia* 9:92–124.

———. 1997. "Die Trennung von Finn und Gráinne." *ZCP* 49/50:71–91.

Cosgrove, Art, ed. 1987. *A New History of Ireland*, vol. 2, *Medieval Ireland 1169–1534*. Oxford: Oxford University Press.

Cross, Tom Peete. 1950. "A Note on 'Sohrab and Rustum' in Ireland." *The Journal of Celtic Studies* 1:176–82.

———. 1952. *Motif-Index of Early Irish Literature*. Bloomington: Indiana University Press.

Cross, Tom Peete, and Clark Harris Slover, trans. 1969. *Ancient Irish Tales*. 2nd ed. New York: Barnes & Noble.

Dagger, Claire. 1989. "Eithne: The Sources." *ZCP* 43(1): 84–124.

Davies, Morgan T. 1996a. "Kings and Clerics in Some Leinster Sagas." *Ériu* 47:45–66.

———. 1996b. "Protocols of Reading in Early Irish Literature: Notes on Some Notes to *Orgain Denna Ríg* and *Amra Coluim Cille*." *CMCS* 32:1–23.

———. 2008. "The Somewhat Heroic Biography of Brandub mac Echach." In *Essays on the Early Irish King Tales*, edited by D. Wiley, 170–212. Dublin: Four Courts Press.

Deane, Marion. 2003. "Dangerous Liaisons." *PHCC* 23:52–79.

de Bernardo Stempel, Patrizia. 2006. "Phaedra und Hippolytos in irischem Gewand: Die mittelalterliche *Fingal Rónáin*, 'Der Verwandtenmor des Rōnān', als Theaterstück." In *Nachleben der Antike—Formen ihrer Aneigung: Fesftschrift anlässlich des 60. Geburtstages von Klaus Ley*, edited by B. Besold-DasGupta, C. Krauß, and C. Mundt-Espín, 237–66. Berlin: Weidler.

de Paor, Liam. 1970. Review of Ross (1967). *SH* 10:156–57.

de Vries, Jan. 1954. "Das Motiv des Vater-Sohn-Kampfes im Hildebrandslied." *Germanisch-romanische Monatsschrift* 34:257–74.

———. 1961. *Keltische Religion*. Stuttgart: W. Kohlhammer.

———.1963. *Heroic Song and Heroic Legend*. Translated by B. J. Timmer. London: Oxford University Press.

Dillon, Myles, ed., trans. 1932. "Stories from the Law-Tracts." *Ériu* 11:42–65.

———. 1945. "The Wooing of Becfola and the Stories of Cano, Son of Gartnán." *Modern Philology* 43:11–17.

———. 1946. *The Cycles of the Kings*. Oxford: Oxford University Press.

———. 1947a. *The Archaism of Irish Tradition*. Sir John Rhŷs Memorial Lecture. London: Oxford University Press. Reprinted from *PBA* 33:245–64.

———. 1947b. "The Hindu Act of Truth in Celtic Tradition." *Modern Philology* 44(3): 137–40.
———. 1948. *Early Irish Literature*. Chicago: University of Chicago Press.
———, ed., trans. 1952. "The Story of the Finding of Cashel." *Ériu* 16:61–73.
———, ed. 1953a. *Serglige Con Culainn*. Mediaeval and Modern Irish Series 14. Dublin: DIAS.
———, trans. 1953b. "The Wasting Sickness of Cú Chulainn." *Scottish Gaelic Studies* 7:47–88.
———, ed. 1959. *Irish Sagas*. Dublin: Mercier Press.
———. 1973a. *Celt and Hindu*. The Osborn Bergin Memorial Lecture 3. Dublin: University College Dublin.
———. 1973b. "The Consecration of Irish Kings." *Celtica* 10:1–8.
———. 1977. "The Irish Settlements in Wales." *Celtica* 12:1–11.
Dobbs, M. E., ed., trans. 1931. "The Ban-shenchas." *RC* 48:163–234.
Doherty, Charles. 2005. "Kingship in Early Ireland." In *The Kingship and Landscape of Tara*, edited by E. Bhreathnach, 3–31. Dublin: Four Courts Press.
Dooley, Ann. 1982. "The Heroic Word: The Reading of Early Irish Sagas." In *The Celtic Consciousness*, edited by R. O'Driscoll, 155–59. Mountrath: Dolmen Press.
———. 2006. *Playing the Hero: Reading the Irish Saga Táin Bó Cúailgne*. Toronto: University of Toronto Press.
———. 2010. "*Táin Bó Cúailgne*." In *A Companion to Irish Literature*, edited by J. M. Wright, 1:17–26. Chichester: Blackwell.
Dooley, Ann, and Harry Roe, trans. 1999. *Tales of the Elders of Ireland: Acallam na Senórach*. Oxford: Oxford University Press.
Dorson, Richard M. 1965. "The Eclipse of Solar Mythology." In *Myth: A Symposium*, edited by T. A. Sebeok, 25–63. Bloomington: Indiana University Press.
Dottin, Georges. 1912. "Sur l'emploi de .i." In *Miscellany Presented to Kuno Meyer*, edited by O. Bergin and C. Marstrander, 102–10. Halle a. S.: Max Niemeyer.
Downey, Clodagh. 2008. "Women, the World and Three Wise Men: Power and Authority in Tales Relating to Niall Noígiallach and Lugaid Mac Con." In *Essays on the Early Irish King Tales*, edited by D. Wiley, 127–47. Dublin: Four Courts Press.
Duffy, Seán. 1997. *Ireland in the Middle Ages*. New York: St. Martin's Press.
Dumézil, Georges. 1941. *Jupiter, Mars, Quirinus*. Paris: Gallimard.
———. 1943. *Servius et la fortune: Essai sur la fonction sociale de louange et de blâme et sur les éléments indo-européens du cens romain*. Paris: Gallimard.
———. 1948. *Mitra-Varuna*. 2nd ed. Paris: Gallimard.
———. 1968. *Mythe et épopée*, vol. 1, *L'idéologie des trois fonctions dans les epopées des peuples indo-européens*. Paris: Gallimard.
———. 1969. *Idées romaines*. Paris: Gallimard.

———. 1970. *The Destiny of the Warrior*. Translated by Alf Hiltebeitel. Chicago: University of Chicago Press.

———. 1971. *Mythe et épopée*, vol. 2, *Types épiques indo-européens: un héros, un sorcier, un roi*. Paris: Gallimard.

———. 1973. *The Destiny of a King*. Translated by Alf Hiltebeitel. Chicago: University of Chicago Press. A translation of Dumézil (1971), pt. 3.

———. 1983. *The Stakes of the Warrior*. Translated by David Weeks. Berkeley: University of California Press. A translation of Dumézil (1971), pt. 1.

Dumville, David N. 1975–76. "The Textual History of *Lebor Bretnach*: A Preliminary Study." *Éigse* 16:255–73.

———. 1976. "*Echtrae* and *immram*: Some Problems of Definition." *Ériu* 27:73–94.

———. 1979–80. "The Conclusion of *Fingal Rónáin*." *SC* 14/15:71–73.

Edel, Doris. 2001. *The Celtic West and Europe: Studies in Celtic Literature and the Early Irish Church*. Dublin: Four Courts Press.

———. 2006. "'Bodily Matters' in Early Irish Narrative Literature." *ZCP* 55:69–107.

———. 2007. "Charakterzeichnung in der *Táin bó Cúailnge* am Beispiel des exilierten Fergus." In *Kelten-Einfälle an der Donau: Akten des vierten Symposiums deutschsprachiger Keltologinnen und Keltologen*, ed. H. Birkhan, 183–93. Vienna: Österreichische Akademie der Wissenschaften.

———. 2011. "Off the Mainstream: A Literature in Search of Its Criteria." *ZCP* 58:23–44.

Edwards, Nancy, et al. 2007. *A Corpus of Early Medieval Inscribed Stones and Stone Sculpture in Wales*, vol. 2, *South-West Wales*. Cardiff: University of Wales Press.

Egeler, Matthias. 2012. "Some Thoughts on 'Goddess Medb' and Her Typological Context." *ZCP* 59:67–96.

Eichhorn-Mulligan, Amy. 2005. "*Togail Bruidne Da Derga* and the Politics of Anatomy." *CMCS* 49:1–19.

Eisner, Sigmund. 1969. *The Tristan Legend: A Study in Sources*. Evanston, IL: Northwestern University Press.

Eliade, Mircea. 1955. *The Myth of Eternal Return*. Translated by Willard R. Trask. London: Routledge and Kegan Paul.

———. 1963. *Patterns in Comparative Religion*. Translated by Rosemary Sheed. New York: World.

Elliott, Robert C. 1960. *The Power of Satire: Magic, Ritual, Art*. Princeton: Princeton University Press.

Eogan, George. 1986. *Knowth and the Passage-Tombs of Ireland*. London: Thames & Hudson.

Eska, Charlene, ed., trans. 2009. *Cáin Lánamna: An Old Irish Tract on Marriage and Divorce Law*. Medieval Law and Its Practice 5. Leiden: Brill.

Etchingham, Colmán. 1996. "Early Medieval Irish History." In *Progress in Medieval Irish Studies*, edited by K. R. McCone and K. Simms, 123–53. Maynooth: Dept. of Old Irish, St. Patrick's College.

Ferguson, Samuel. 1880. *Poems*. Dublin: William McGee.
Filotas, Bernadette. 2005. *Pagan Survivals, Superstitions and Popular Cultures in Early Medieval Pastoral Literature*. Toronto: Pontifical Institute of Mediaeval Studies.
Findon, Joanne. 1997. *A Woman's Words: Emer and Female Speech in the Ulster Cycle*. Toronto: University of Toronto Press.
———. 2011. "Fabula, Story, and Text: The Case of *Compert Conchobuir*." In *Narrative in Celtic Tradition: Essays in Honor of Edgar M. Slotkin*, edited by J. F. Eska, 37–55. CSANA Yearbook 8/9. Hamilton, NY: Colgate University Press.
Flower, Robin. 1926. *Catalogue of Irish Manuscripts in the British Museum*, vol. 2. London: British Museum. Reprinted 1992 as *Catalogue of Irish Manuscripts in the British Library [formerly British Museum]*, Dublin: DIAS.
Fogarty, Hugh. 2011. "*Aislinge Óenguso*: A *Remscél* Reconsidered." In *Narrative in Celtic Tradition: Essays in Honor of Edgar M. Slotkin*, edited by J. F. Eska, 56–67. CSANA Yearbook 8/9. Hamilton, NY: Colgate University Press.
Fomin, Maxim. 2004. "On the Notions of Death, Navigation and the Otherworld." *CMCS* 47:73–80.
Ford, Patrick K. 1979. Review of Ó Cathasaigh (1977). *Speculum* 54:836–39.
———. 1990. "The Blind, the Dumb, and the Ugly: Aspects of Poets and Their Craft in Medieval Ireland and Wales." *CMCS* 19:27–40.
———. 1994. "The Idea of Everlasting Fame in the *Táin*." In *Ulidia*, 255–61.
———, trans. 1999. *The Celtic Poets: Songs and Tales from Early Ireland and Wales*. Belmont, MA: Ford & Bailie.
Fox, Robin. 1978. *The Tory Islanders*. Cambridge: Cambridge University Press.
Fraser, James E. 2009. *From Caledonia to Pictland: Scotland to 795*. The New Edinburgh History of Scotland 1. Edinburgh: Edinburgh University Press.
Frykenberg, Brian. 1984. "Suibhne, Lailoken, and the *Taídiu*." *PHCC* 4:105–20.
Fulton, Helen. 2011. "Magic Naturalism in the *Táin bó Cúailgne*." In *Narrative in Celtic Tradition: Essays in Honor of Edgar M. Slotkin*, edited by J. F. Eska, 84–99. CSANA Yearbook 8/9. Hamilton, NY: Colgate University Press.
Gantz, Jeffrey, trans. 1981. *Early Irish Myths and Sagas*. Harmondsworth: Penguin.
Gerriets, Marilyn. 1987. "Kingship and Exchange in Pre-Viking Ireland." *CMCS* 13:39–72.
———. 1988. "The King as Judge in Early Ireland." *Celtica* 20:29–52.
Gray, Brenda. 2009. "Reading *Aislinge Óenguso* as a Christian-Platonist Parable." *PHCC* 24/25:16–39.
Gray, Elizabeth A. 1980–81. "*Cath Maige Tuired*: Myth and Structure (1–24)." *Éigse* 18:183–209.
———, ed., trans. 1982. *Cath Maige Tuired: The Second Battle of Mag Tuired*. Irish Texts Society 52. London: ITS.
———. 1982–83a. "*Cath Maige Tuired*: Myth and Structure (24–120)." *Éigse* 19:1–35.

———. 1982–83b. "*Cath Maige Tuired:* Myth and Structure (84–93, 120–167)." *Éigse* 19:230–62.

———. 2005. "The Warrior, the Poet and the King: 'The Three Sins of the Warrior' and the Death of Cú Roí." In *Heroic Poets and Poetic Heroes: A Festschrift for Patrick K. Ford*, edited by J. F. Nagy and L. E. Jones, 74–90. CSANA Yearbook 3/4. Dublin: Four Courts Press.

Greene, David, ed. 1955. *Fingal Rónáin and Other Stories*. Mediaeval and Modern Irish Series 16. Dublin: DIAS.

———. 1958. "The Analytical Forms of the Verb in Irish." *Ériu* 18:108–12.

———. 1959. "Fingal Rónáin." In *Irish Sagas*, edited by M. Dillon, 167–81. Dublin: Mercier Press.

———. 1972. "The Responsive in Irish and Welsh." In *Indo-Celtica: Gedächtnisschrift für Alf Sommerfelt*, edited by H. Pilch and J. Thurow, 59–72. Munich: Hueber.

———. 1973. "Synthetic and Analytic: A Reconsideration." *Ériu* 24:121–33.

———. 1979. "Tabu in Early Irish Narrative." In *Proceedings of the Third International Symposium Organized by the Centre for the Study of Vernacular Literature in the Middle Ages*, edited by H. Bekker-Nielsen et al., 9–19. Odense: Odense University Press.

Greene, David, and Frank O'Connor, trans. 1967. *A Golden Treasury of Irish Poetry A.D. 600 to 1200*. London: Macmillan.

Greimas, Algirdas Julien. 1970. *Du sens: Essais sémiotiques*. Paris: Editions du Seuil.

Griffin-Kremer, Cozette. 2010. "Wooings and Works: An Episode on Yoking Oxen in the *Tochmarc Étaine* and the *Cóir Anmann*." *Eolas* 4:54–85.

Griffiths, Alan. 2000. "The Homer of Kosovo." *Times Literary Supplement*, 8 September, 6–7.

Gruffydd, W. J. 1953. *Rhiannon: An Inquiry into the Origin of the First and Third Branches of the Mabinogi*. Cardiff: University of Wales Press.

Guyonvarc'h, Christian-J., trans. 1983. "La mort de Muirchertach, fils d'Erc: Texte irlandais du très Haut Moyen Age; La femme, le saint et le roi." *Annales* 38:985–1015.

Gwynn, Edward J., ed., trans. 1914. "An Irish Penitential." *Ériu* 7:121–95.

———, ed. 1940–42. "An Old-Irish Tract on the Privileges and Responsibilities of the Poets." *Ériu* 13:1–60, 220–36.

Gwynn, Lucius. 1914. "The Recensions of the Saga *Togail Bruidne Da Derga*." *ZCP* 10:209–22.

Hamp, Eric P. 1978. "Varia II: 1. Conjoining *os*. 2. *Gwion* and *Fer Fí*. 3. *iomna* and *udhacht*." *Ériu* 29:149–54.

———. 1982. "Varia X: Irish *síd* 'tumulus' and Irish *síd* 'peace.'" *ÉC* 19:141–42.

Hartmann, Hans. 1997–2008. "Was ist 'Wahrheit'?: Ein Vergleich französischer, keltischer, indischer, iranischer und griechischer Vorstellungen von der Verwirklichung der Wahrheit; eine kulturgeschichtliche Analyse." *ZCP* 49/50

(1997): 287–310; *ZCP* 52 (2001): 1–101; *ZCP* 53 (2003): 1–19; *ZCP* 54 (2004): 31–53; *ZCP* 55 (2006): 1–17; *ZCP* 56 (2008): 1–56.

Hawkes, Terence. 1977. *Structuralism and Semiotics*. Berkeley: University of California Press.

Heil, Johanna. 2011. "Marital Law and Women's Rights in Early Christian Ireland." In *Allerlei Keltisches: Studien zu Ehren von Erich Poppe, Studies in Honour of Erich Poppe*, edited by F. Bock, D. Bronner, and D. Schlüter, 61–77. Berlin: Curach Bhán.

Heinrichs, Anne. 1976. "'Intertexture' and Its Functions in Early Written Sagas." *Scandinavian Studies* 48:127–45.

Henry, P. L. 1978. *Saoithiúlacht na Sean-Ghaeilge*. Dublin: Stationery Office.

———. 1997. "*Conailla Medb Míchuru* and the Tradition of Fiacc Son of Fergus." In *Miscellanea Celtica in Memoriam Heinrich Wagner*, edited by S. Mac Mathúna and A. Ó Corráin, 563–70. Uppsala: Uppsala University Press.

Herbert, Máire. 1997. "The Death of Muirchertach mac Erca: A Twelfth-Century Tale." In *Celts and Vikings: Proceedings of the Fourth Symposium of Societas Celtologica Nordica*, edited by F. Josephson, 27–39. Meijerbergs arkiv för svensk ordforskning 20. Göteborg: Göteborgs Universitet.

Hicks, Ronald. 2009. "Cosmography in *Tochmarc Étaíne*." *JIES* 37.1–2:115–29.

Hiltebeitel, Alf. 1982. "Brothers, Friends, and Charioteers: Parallel Episodes in the Irish and Indian Epics." In *Homage to Georges Dumézil*, edited by E. Polomé, 85–111. Journal of Indo-European Studies Monographs 3. Washington: Journal of Indo-European Studies.

Hily, Gaël. 2008. "Le trio Goibne, Lug et Balor: un héritage de la tradition cosmogonique indo-européenne." *ÉC* 36:119–33.

Hogan, Edmund. 1910. *Onomasticon Goedelicum*. Dublin: Hodges, Figgis.

Hollo, Kaarina. 2004. "*Final Rónáin*: The Medieval Irish Text as Argumentative Space." In *Cín Chille Cúile. Texts, Saints and Places. Essays in Honour of Pádraig Ó Riain*, edited by J. Carey, M. Herbert, and K. Murray, 141–49. Aberystwyth: Celtic Studies Publications.

———. 2005. "Laments and Lamenting in Early Medieval Ireland." In *Medieval Celtic Literature and Society*, edited by H. Fulton, 83–94. Dublin: Four Courts Press.

———. 2011. "Allegoresis and Literary Creativity in Eighth-Century Ireland: The Case of *Echtrae Chonnlai*." In *Narrative in Celtic Tradition: Essays in Honor of Edgar M. Slotkin*, edited by J. F. Eska, 117–28. CSANA Yearbook 8/9. Hamilton, NY: Colgate University Press.

Holmberg, Matthew. 2011. "A Sheep in Wolf-Son's Clothing? Lugaid Mac Con and Pseudo-Historical Etiology." *PHCC* 31:158–72.

Hughes, Kathleen. 1966. *The Church in Early Irish Society*. London: Methuen.

———. 1972. *Early Christian Ireland: Introduction to the Sources*. London: Hodder & Stoughton.

———. 1977. *The Early Celtic Ideal of History and the Modern Historian*. Cambridge: Cambridge University Press.
Huld, M. E. 1981. "Cú Chulainn and His IE Kin." *ZCP* 38:238–41.
Hull, Eleanor, ed. 1898. *The Cuchullin Saga in Irish Literature*. London: David Nutt.
Hull, Vernam. 1930a. "Cairpre mac Edaine's Satire upon Bres mac Eladain." *ZCP* 18:63–69.
———, ed., trans. 1930b. "Two Anecdotes Concerning St. Moling." *ZCP* 18:90–99.
———, ed., trans. 1933a. "*De gabáil in tšída*: Concerning the Seizure of the Fairy Mound." *ZCP* 19:53–58.
———. 1933b. "The Old Woman or Nun of Beare." *ZCP* 19:174–76.
———, ed., trans. 1934. "The Conception of Conchobor." *Irish Texts* 4:4–12.
———, ed., trans. 1947. "Conall Corc and the Corcu Luígde." *PMLA* 62:887–909.
———, ed. 1949a. *Longes mac nUislenn*. New York: Modern Language Association.
———, ed., trans. 1949b. "Echtra Cormaic maic Airt, 'The Adventure of Cormac mac Airt.'" *PMLA* 64:871–83.
———, ed. 1952. "Geneamuin Chormaic." *Ériu* 16:79–85.
———. 1954a. "Togail Bruidne Da Derga: The Cín Dromma Snechta Recension." *ZCP* 24:131–32.
———, ed. 1954b. "A Collation of Tucait Innarba na nDessi." *ZCP* 24:132–34.
———. 1954c. "The Book of Uí Maine Version of the Expulsion of the Déssi." *ZCP* 24:266–71.
———, ed., trans. 1958–59. "The Later Version of the Expulsion of the Déssi." *ZCP* 27:34–63.
———, ed., trans. 1968. "Noínden Ulad: The Debility of the Ulidians." *Celtica* 8:1–42.
Hutchison, David A. 2009. "Links to Pagan Ritual in Mediaeval Irish Literature." *Études Irlandaises* 34.1:113–43.
Jackson, Kenneth Hurlstone. 1940. "The Motive of the Threefold Death in the Story of Suibhne Geilt." In *Féilsgribhinn Eóin Mhic Néill*, edited by J. Ryan, 535–50. Dublin: At the Sign of the Three Candles. Reprinted 1995, Dublin: Four Courts Press.
———. 1950. "Notes on the Ogam Inscriptions of Southern Britain." In *The Early Cultures of North-West Europe*, edited by C. Fox and B. Dickens, 199–213. Cambridge: Cambridge University Press.
———, trans. 1951. *A Celtic Miscellany: Translations from the Celtic Literatures*. London: Routledge and Kegan Paul.
———. 1953. *Language and History in Early Britain*. Cambridge, MA: Harvard University Press.
———. 1959. "Arthur in Early Welsh Verse." In *Arthurian Literature in the Middle Ages: A Collaborative History*, edited by R. S. Loomis, 12–19. Oxford: Oxford University Press.

———. 1961. *The International Popular Tale and Early Welsh Tradition*. Cardiff: University of Wales Press.

———. 1964. *The Oldest Irish Tradition: A Window on the Iron Age*. Rede Lecture. Cambridge: Cambridge University Press.

———, trans. 1971. *A Celtic Miscellany*. 2nd ed. Harmondsworth: Penguin.

Jaski, Bart. 1999. "Cú Chulainn, *gormac* and *dalta* of the Ulstermen." *CMCS* 37:1–31.

———. 2000. *Early Irish Kingship and Succession*. Dublin: Four Courts Press.

Johnston, Elva. 2013. *Literacy and Identity in Early Medieval Ireland*. Cambridge: Boydell & Brewer.

Jones, Gwynn, and Thomas Jones, trans. 1993. *The Mabinogion*. New rev. ed. London: Everyman.

Joynt, Maud, ed., trans. 1908–10. "Echtra Mac Echdach Mugmedóin." *Ériu* 4:91–111.

Kelleher, John V. 1965. "Irish History and Mythology in James Joyce's 'The Dead.'" *The Review of Politics* 27.3:414–33.

———. 1968. "The Pre-Norman Irish Genealogies." *Irish Historical Studies* 16:138–53.

———. 1971. "The *Táin* and the Annals." *Ériu* 22:107–27.

Kelly, Fergus, ed., trans. 1976. *Audacht Morainn*. Dublin: DIAS.

———, ed., trans. 1986. "An Old-Irish Text on Court Procedure." *Peritia* 5:74–106.

———. 1988. *A Guide to Early Irish Law*. Early Irish Law Series 3. Dublin: DIAS.

———. 1997. *Early Irish Farming*. Early Irish Law Series 4. Dublin: DIAS.

———. 2010. "Cauldron Imagery in a Legal Passage on Judges (*CIH* IV 1307.38–1308.7)." *Celtica* 26:31–43.

Kenney, James F. 1929. *The Sources for the Early History of Ireland*, vol. 1, *Ecclesiastical*. New York: Columbia University Press. Reprinted 1997, Dublin: Four Courts Press.

Kiberd, Declan. 2000. *Irish Classics*. Cambridge, MA: Harvard University Press.

Kieckhefer, Richard. 1989. *Magic in the Middle Ages*. Cambridge: Cambridge University Press.

Kimpton, Bettina. 2003. "Voice, Power and Narrative Structure in *Orgain Denna Ríg*." *PHCC* 23:165–71.

Kinsella, Thomas, trans. 1970. *The Táin*. London: Oxford University Press.

Knott, Eleanor. 1928. *An Introduction to Irish Syllabic Poetry of the Period 1200–1600*. Cork: Cork University Press.

———, ed. 1936. *Togail Bruidne Da Derga*. Mediaeval and Modern Irish Series 8. Dublin: DIAS.

———. 1960. *Irish Classical Poetry*. 2nd ed. Dublin: Colm Ó Lochlainn for the Cultural Relations Committee of Ireland, at the Sign of the Three Candles.

Knott, Eleanor, and Gerard Murphy. 1966. *Early Irish Literature*. London: Routledge and Kegan Paul.

Koch, John T. 1999. "A Swallowed Onomastic Tale in *Cath Maige Mucrama*?" In *Ildánach Ildírech: A Festschrift for Proinsias Mac Cana*, edited by J. Carey, J. T. Koch, and P.-Y. Lambert, 63–80. Andover, MA and Aberystwyth: Celtic Studies Publications.

Koch, John T., and John Carey, trans. 2003. *The Celtic Heroic Age: Literary Sources for Ancient Celtic Europe and Early Ireland and Wales*. 4th ed. Aberystwyth: Celtic Studies Publications.

Ködderitzsch, R. 1974. "Der Zweite Merseburger Zauberspruch und seine Parallelen." *ZCP* 33:45–57.

Krappe, Alexander H. 1936. "La Cailleach Bheara. Notes de mythologie gaélique." *ÉC* 1:292–302.

Leach, Edmund. 1969. *Genesis as Myth and Other Essays*. London: Cape.

Lehmacher, G. 1931. "Die zweite Schlacht von Mag Tured und die keltische Götterlehre." *Anthropos* 26:435–59.

Lehmann, Edyta. 2010. "The Woman Who Wasn't There: Preliminary Observations on the Perplexing Presence and Absence of the Character of Gráinne in the *Tóruigheacht Dhiarmada agus Ghráinne*." *PHCC* 30:116–26.

Lévi-Strauss, Claude. 1968. *Structural Anthropology*. Translated by Claire Jacobson and Brooke Grundfest. London: Allen Lane.

———. 1969. *The Elementary Structures of Kinship*. Translated by James Harle Bell, John Richard von Sturmer, and Rodney Needham. London: Eyre & Spottiswoode.

Lewis, C. S. 1960. *A Preface to Paradise Lost*. Rev. ed. London: Oxford University Press.

Lewis, Charlton T., and Charles Short. 1897. *A Latin Dictionary*. Oxford: Oxford University Press.

Lewis, Henry, and Holger Pedersen. 1961. *A Concise Comparative Celtic Grammar*. 3rd ed. Göttingen: Vandenhoeck & Ruprecht.

Lewis, I. M. 1976. *Social Anthropology in Perspective*. Harmondsworth: Penguin.

Liddell, Henry George, and Robert Scott. 1940. *A Greek-English Lexicon*. 9th ed. Oxford: Oxford University Press. Reprinted 1996 with supplement.

Lincoln, Bruce. 1980. *Priests, Warriors, and Cattle: A Study in the Ecology of Religions*. Berkeley: University of California Press.

———. 1981. "The Lord of the Dead." *History of Religions* 20:224–41.

Littleton, C. Scott. 1966. *The New Comparative Mythology*. Berkeley: University of California Press.

———. 1982. *The New Comparative Mythology*. 3rd ed. Berkeley: University of California Press.

Lönnroth, Lars. 1970. "Rhetorical Persuasion in the Sagas." *Scandinavian Studies* 42:157–89.

Loomis, Roger Sherman. 1956. *Wales and the Arthurian Legend*. Cardiff: University of Wales Press.

Lucas, A. T. 1989. *Cattle in Ancient Ireland.* Kilkenny: Boethius Press.
Mac Airt, Seán. 1958. "*Filidecht* and *coimgne.*" *Ériu* 18:139–52.
Macalister, R. A. S., ed. 1942. *The Book of Uí Maine.* Dublin: Stationery Office.
———. 1945. *Corpus Inscriptionum Insularum Celticarum,* vol. 1. Dublin: Stationery Office.
Mac Cana, Proinsias. 1955–58. "Aspects of the Theme of King and Goddess in Irish Literature." *ÉC* 7 (1955–56): 76–114, 356–413; *ÉC* 8 (1958): 59–65.
———. 1966. "On the Use of the Term *retoiric.*" *Celtica* 7:65–90.
———. 1970. *Celtic Mythology.* London: Hamlyn.
———. 1972. "Mongán mac Fiachna and *Immram Brain.*" *Ériu* 23:102–42.
———. 1972–73. "Conservation and Innovation in Early Celtic Literature." *ÉC* 13:61–119.
———. 1976. "The Sinless Otherworld of *Immram Brain.*" *Ériu* 27:5–118.
———. 1980a. *The Learned Tales of Medieval Ireland.* Dublin: DIAS.
———. 1980b. *Literature in Irish.* Aspects of Ireland 8. Dublin: Dept. of Foreign Affairs.
———. 1985. "Early Irish Ideology and the Concept of Unity." In *The Irish Mind,* edited by R. Kearney, 56–78. Dublin: Wolfhound Press.
———. 1988. "Placenames and Mythology in Irish Tradition: Places, Pilgrimages and Things." In *Proceedings of the First North American Congress of Celtic Studies,* edited by G. W. MacLennan, 319–41. Ottawa: Chair of Celtic Studies, University of Ottawa.
———. 1992. "*Laíded, Gressacht* 'Formalized Incitement.'" *Ériu* 43:69–92.
———. 1993. "Ir. *Buaball,* W. *Bual* 'Drinking Horn.'" *Ériu* 44:81–93.
———. 1997. "Prosimetrum in Insular Celtic Literature." In *Prosimetrum: Cross-cultural Perspectives on Narrative in Prose and Verse,* edited by J. Harris and K. Reichl, 99–130. Cambridge: D. S. Brewer.
———. 2004. "Praise Poetry in Ireland before the Normans." *Ériu* 54:11–40.
Mac Eoin, Gearóid. 1960–61. "Das Verbalsystem von Togail Troí (H. 2. 17)." *ZCP* 28:73–136, 149–223.
———. 1961. "Smaointe ar stair litríocht na Meán-Ghaeilge." *Irisleabhar Muighe Nuadhat,* 39–44.
———. 1964. Review of Binchy (1963). *SH* 4:244–49.
———. 1967. Review of Knott and Murphy (1966). *SH* 7:246–47.
———. 1968. "The Mysterious Death of Loegaire mac Néill." *SH* 8:21–48.
———. 1994. "The Interpolator H in Lebor na hUidre." In *Ulidia,* 39–46.
———. 1997. "Satire in Medieval Irish Literature." In *Celts and Vikings: Proceedings of the Fourth Symposium of Societas Celtologica Nordica,* edited by F. Josephson, 9–25. Meijerbergs arkiv för svensk ordforskning 20. Göteborg: Göteborgs Universitet.
Mac Gerailt, Uáitéar. 2006–7. "The Making of *Fingal Rónáin.*" *SH* 34:63–84.

———. 2010. *On the Date of the Middle Irish Recension II of Táin bó Cúailnge*. Quiggin Memorial Lectures 11. Cambridge: Department of Anglo-Saxon, Norse, and Celtic, University of Cambridge.
Mackey, J. P. 1989. *An Introduction to Celtic Christianity*. Edinburgh: T&T Clark.
———. 1992a. "Christian Past and Primal Present." *ÉC* 29:285–97.
———. 1992b. "Magic and Celtic Primal Religion." *ZCP* 45:66–83.
———. 1999. "Mythical Past and Political Present: A Case-Study of the Irish Myth of the Sovereignty." *ZCP* 51:66–84.
Mac Mathúna, Liam. 1999. "Irish Perceptions of the Cosmos." *Celtica* 23:174–87.
Mac Mathúna, Séamus, ed., trans. 1985. *Immram Brain: Bran's Journey to the Land of the Women*. Tübingen: Max Niemeyer.
MacNeill, Eoin. 1907–9. "Notes on Irish Ogam Inscriptions," *PRIA* 27 C: 329–70.
———, ed., trans. 1908. *Duanaire Finn*, vol. 1. Irish Texts Society 7. London: ITS.
———. 1910. "The Déisi Genealogies from the Book of Ballymote." *Journal of the Waterford and South-East Ireland Archaeological Society* 13:44–51, 81–87, 151–57.
———. 1911. "Early Irish Population Groups." *PRIA* 29 C: 59–114.
———. 1919. *Phases of Irish History*. Dublin: Gill & Son.
———. 1921. *Celtic Ireland*. Dublin: M. Lester.
———. 1932. "The Vita Tripartita of St Patrick." *Ériu* 11:1–41.
MacNeill, Máire. 1962. *The Festival of Lughnasa*. London: Oxford University Press.
Mac Niocaill, Gearóid S. 1968. "The Proportional Method in Dating Irish Texts." *SC* 3:47–52.
MacWhite, Eóin. 1960–61. "Contributions to a Study of Ogam Memorial Stones." *ZCP* 28:294–308.
Martin, B. K. 1969. "*The Lament of the Old Woman of Beare*: A Critical Evaluation." *Medium Aevum* 38:245–61.
Martin, Bernard. 1994. "Flyting and Fighting in the Irish *Táin Bó Cúailgne*." In *The Epic in History*, edited by L. S. Davidson, S. N. Mukherjee, and Z. Zlatar, 40–55. Sydney Studies in Society and Culture 11. Sydney: University of Sydney.
Matasović, Ranko. 2009. *Etymological Dictionary of Proto-Celtic*. Leiden: Brill.
Mathiessen, F. O. 1959. *The Achievement of T. S. Eliot*. 3rd ed. New York: Oxford University Press.
Mattingly, Harold B., trans. 1970. *Tacitus: The Agricola and the Germania*. Revised edition edited by S. A. Handford. Harmondsworth: Penguin.
McCann, W. J. 2002. "Tristan: The Celtic and Oriental Material Re-Examined." In *Tristan: A Casebook*, edited by J. T. Grimbert, 3–36. New York: Routledge.
McCone, Kim R. 1980. "Fírinne agus Torthúlacht." *Léachtaí Cholm Chille* 11:136–73.
———. 1984a. "*Aided Cheltchair maic Uthechair*: Hounds, Heroes and Hospitallers in Early Irish Myth and Story." *Ériu* 35:1–30.
———. 1984b. "An Introduction to Early Irish Saints' Lives." *Maynooth Review* 11:26–59.

———. 1985. "OIr. *Olc, Luch-* and IE **wlk^w^s, *lúk^w^os* 'wolf.'" *Ériu* 36:171–76.

———. 1986. "Werewolves, Cyclopes, *díberga*, and *fíanna*: Juvenile Delinquency in Early Ireland." *CMCS* 12:1–22.

———. 1987. "Hund, Wolf und Krieger bei den Indogermanen." In *Studien zum indogermanischen Wortschatz*, edited by W. Meid, 101–54. Innsbrucker Beiträge zur Sprachwissenschaft 52. Innsbruck: Universität Innsbruck.

———. 1989. "A Tale of Two Ditties: Poet and Satirist in *Cath Maige Tuired*." In *Sages, Saints and Storytellers: Celtic Studies in Honour of Professor James Carney*, edited by D. Ó Corráin, L. Breatnach, and K. R. McCone, 122–43. Maynooth: An Sagart.

———. 1990. *Pagan Past and Christian Present in Early Irish Literature*. Maynooth: An Sagart.

———. 1992. "OIr. *aub* 'river' and *amnair* 'maternal uncle.'" *Münchener Studien zur Sprachwissenschaft* 53:101–11.

———. 1998. "'King' and 'Queen' in Celtic and Indo-European." *Ériu* 49:1–12.

———, ed., trans. 2000. *Echtrae Chonnlai and the Beginnings of Vernacular Narrative Writing in Ireland*. Maynooth Medieval Irish Texts 1. Maynooth: Dept. of Old and Middle Irish, NUI Maynooth.

McKenna, Catherine. 1980–81. "The Theme of Sovereignty in *Pwyll*." *BBCS* 29:35–52. Reprinted 1996 in *The Mabinogi: A Book of Essays*, edited by C. W. Sullivan, 303–30. New York: Garland.

———. 2011. "Angels and Demons in the Pages of Lebor na hUidre." In *Narrative in Celtic Tradition: Essays in Honor of Edgar M. Slotkin*, edited by J. F. Eska, 157–80. *CSANA Yearbook* 8/9. Hamilton, NY: Colgate University Press.

McKenna, Lambert, ed., trans. 1919. "A theachtaire tig ón Róimh." *Irish Monthly* 47:679–82.

——— [as Láimhbheartach Mac Cionnaith], ed. 1938. *Dioghluim Dána*. Dublin: Stationery Office.

McLaughlin, Róisín. 2008. *Early Irish Satire*. Dublin: DIAS.

McLeod, Neil. 2000. "Kinship." *Ériu* 51:1–22.

McManus, Damian. 1991. *A Guide to Ogam*. Maynooth Monographs 4. Maynooth: An Sagart.

———. 2006. "'The Smallest Man in Ireland Can Reach the Tops of Her Trees': Images of the King's Peace and Bounty in Bardic Poetry." In *Memory and the Modern in Celtic Literatures*, ed. J. F. Nagy, 61–117. *CSANA Yearbook* 5. Dublin: Four Courts Press.

———. 2009. "Good-Looking and Irresistible: The Hero from Early Irish Saga to Classical Poetry." *Ériu* 59:57–109.

Meckler, Michael. 2008. "The Assassination of Diarmait mac Cerbaill." In *Law, Literature, and Society*, edited by J. F. Nagy, 46–57. *CSANA Yearbook* 7. Dublin: Four Courts Press.

Meek, Donald E. 2000. *The Search for Celtic Christianity*. Edinburgh: Handsel Press.

Mees, Bernard. 2009. *Celtic Curses*. Woodbridge: Boydell & Brewer.
Meid, Wolfgang, ed., trans. 1970. *Die Romanze von Froech und Findabair*. Innsbrucker Beiträge zur Kulturwissenschaft 30. Innsbruck: Universität Innsbruck.
———. 1974. "Dichtkunst, Rechtspflege und Medizin im alten Irland." In *Antiquitates Indogermanicae*, edited by M. Mayrhofer et al., 21–34. Innsbrucker Beiträge zur Sprachwissenschaft 12. Innsbruck: Universität Innsbruck.
Meillet, Antoine. 1921. *Linguistique historique et linguistique générale*, vol. 1. Paris: Champion.
Melia, Daniel F. 1974. "Parallel Versions of 'The boyhood deeds of Cuchulainn.'" *Forum for Modern Language Studies* 10:211–26.
———. 1978. Review of *TBC I*. *Speculum* 53:607–9.
Meyer, Kuno, ed., trans. 1885. *Cath Finntrága*. Anecdota Oxoniensia, Mediaeval and Modern Series 1(4). Oxford: Clarendon Press.
———, ed., trans. 1892a. *Aislinge Meic Conglinne*. London: David Nutt.
———, ed., trans. 1892b. "Fingal Rónáin: How Rónán Slew His Son." *RC* 13:368–97. [There is a more recent edition of this text by David Greene (1955).]
———. 1895–96. "Early Relations between Gael and Brython." *Transactions of the Honourable Society of Cymmrodorion*, 55–86.
———, ed., trans. 1897. "Finn and Gráinne." *ZCP* 1:458–61. [There is a more recent edition of this text by Johan Corthals (1997).]
———, ed., trans. 1899. "Stories and Songs from Irish Manuscripts." *Otia Merseiana* 1:113–28.
———, ed., trans. 1901a. "The Expulsion of the Dessi." *Y Cymmrodor* 14:101–35.
———, ed. 1901b. "Baile in Scáil." *ZCP* 3:457–66. [See also Meyer (1918; 1921). There is a more recent edition of this text by Kevin Murray (2004).]
———, ed., trans. 1902. *Liadain and Curithir: An Irish Love-Story of the Ninth Century*. London: David Nutt.
———, ed., trans. 1903. "King Eochaid Has Horse's Ears." *Otia Merseiana* 3:46–50.
———, ed., trans. 1906. *The Triads of Ireland*. Todd Lecture Series 13. Dublin: Royal Irish Academy.
———, ed. 1907a. "The Expulsion of the Déssi." *Ériu* 3:135–42.
———, ed. 1907b. "Tucait indarba na nDessi." In *Anecd.* 1:15–24.
———, ed. 1909a. *Rawlinson B. 502. A Facsimile Edition with Introduction and Indexes*. Oxford: Clarendon Press.
———, ed., trans. 1909b. *The Instructions of King Cormac mac Airt*. Todd Lecture Series 15. Dublin: Royal Irish Academy.
———, ed., trans. 1910a. *Fianaigecht*. Todd Lecture Series 16. Dublin: Royal Irish Academy.
———, ed. 1910b. "Imathchor Ailello ocus Airt." In *Anecd.* 3:27–29. [There is a new edition of this text by Johan Corthals (1995).]
———, ed. 1910c. "Conall Corc and the Corco Loígde." In *Anecd.* 3:57–63.

———, ed. 1912a. *Sanas Cormaic* (=*Anecd.* 4). Halle a. S.: Max Niemeyer.
———. 1912b. "Der irische Totengott und die Toteninsel." *SPAW*, 537–46.
———, trans. 1913. *Selections from Ancient Irish Poetry*. London: Constable & Co.
———, ed., trans. 1915. "Ein altirisches Gedicht auf König Bran Find." *SPAW*, 905–8.
———, ed. 1918. "Das Ende von Baile in Scáil," *ZCP* 12:232–38.
———. 1919. "Zur keltischen Wortkunde IX." *SPAW*, 374–401.
———, ed. 1921. "Der Anfang von Baile in Scáil." *ZCP* 13:371–82.
Micheelsen, Arun. 2007. "King and Druid." *PHCC* 20/21:98–111.
Miller, Dean A. 2000. *The Epic Hero*. Baltimore: Johns Hopkins University Press.
———. 2006. "Cú Chulainn and Il'ya of Murom: Two Heroes, and Some Variations on a Theme." In *Parallels between Celtic and Slavic: Proceedings of the First International Colloquium of Societas Celto-Slavica Held at the University of Ulster, Coleraine, 19–21 June 2005*, edited by M. Fomin and S. Mac Mathúna, 175–84. Studia Celto-Slavica 1. Coleraine: The Stationery Office.
Miller, Molly. 1977–78. "Date-Guessing and Dyfed." *SC* 12/13:33–61.
Miles, Brent. 2011. *Heroic Saga and Classical Epic in Medieval Ireland*. Woodbridge: D. S. Brewer.
Monette, Connell. 2004. "Indo-European Elements in Celtic and Indo-Iranian Epic Tradition: The Trial of the Champions in *Táin bó Cúailnge* and the *Shahnameh*." *JIES* 32.1–2:61–78.
———. 2008. "Heroes and Hells in *Beowulf*, the *Shahnameh*, and the *Táin bó Cúailnge*." *JIES* 36.1–2:99–147.
Moore, Steven. 2010. *The Novel: An Alternative History; Beginnings to 1600*. New York: Continuum.
Mulchrone, Kathleen. 1943. *Catalogue of Irish Manuscripts in the Royal Irish Academy* 26. Dublin: Royal Irish Academy.
Mulchrone, Kathleen, and Elizabeth Fitzpatrick. 1943. *Catalogue of Irish Manuscripts in the Royal Irish Academy* 27. Dublin: Royal Irish Academy.
Müller, Edward, ed., trans. 1877. "Two Irish Tales. I. Aislinge Oengusso: The Dream of Oengus." *RC* 3:342–50.
Müller-Lisowski, Käte. 1950. "Contributions to a Study in Irish Folklore: Traditions about Donn." *Béaloideas* 20:142–99.
Murdoch, Brian. 1991. "In Pursuit of the *Caillech Bérre*: An Early Irish Poem and the Medievalist at Large." *ZCP* 44:80–127.
Murphy, Gerard. 1940. "Bards and Filidh." *Éigse* 2:200–207.
———. 1952. "On the Dates of Two Sources Used in Thurneysen's *Heldensage*." *Ériu* 16:145–56.
———. 1953a. *Duanaire Finn*, vol. 3. Irish Texts Society 42. Dublin: ITS.
———, ed. 1953b. "The Lament of the Old Woman of Beare." *PRIA* 55 C: 83–109.
———. 1954. "Notes on *Cath Maige Tuired*." *Éigse* 7:191–98.

———. 1955a. *Saga and Myth in Ancient Ireland*. Dublin: Colm Ó Lochlainn for the Cultural Relations Committee of Ireland, at the Sign of the Three Candles.

———. 1955b. *The Ossianic Lore and Romantic Tales of Medieval Ireland*. Dublin: Colm Ó Lochlainn for the Cultural Relations Committee of Ireland, at the Sign of the Three Candles.

———. 1955–57. Review of Carney (1955). *Éigse* 8:152–64.

———, ed., trans. 1956. *Early Irish Lyrics*. Oxford: Oxford University Press.

Murray, Kevin, ed., trans. 2004. *Baile in Scáil*. Irish Texts Society 58. Dublin: ITS.

Nagy, Joseph Falaky. 1984. "Heroic Destinies in the *macgnímrada* of Finn and Cú Chulainn." *ZCP* 40:23–39.

———. 1985. *The Wisdom of the Outlaw*. Berkeley: University of California Press.

———. 1990. "Sword as *audacht*." In *Celtic Language, Celtic Culture: A Festschrift for Eric P. Hamp*, edited by A. T. E. Matonis and D. F. Melia, 131–36. Van Nuys, CA: Ford & Bailie.

———. 1996. "The Rising of the River Cronn in *Táin Bó Cúailgne*." In *Celtica Helsingiensia: Proceedings from a Symposium on Celtic Studies*, edited by A. Ahlqvist et al., 129–48. Commentationes Humanarum Litterarum 107. Helsinki: Societas Scientiarum Fennica.

———. 1997. *Conversing with Angels and Ancients: Literary Myths of Medieval Ireland*. Ithaca, NY: Cornell University Press.

———. 2006–7. "Heroic Recycling in Celtic Tradition." *PHCC* 26/27:1–36.

———. 2011. "(Im)purity, Horror, and a Legendary Poet." *PHCC* 31:242–52.

Nettlau, Max. 1893. "On the Irish Text Togail Bruidne dá Derga and Connected Stories (suite et fin)." *RC* 14:137–52.

Neville, Grace. 1988. "Mythe et folklore et leurs expressions littéraires dans la légende de Diarmuid et Gráinne." In *Mythe et folklore celtiques et leurs expressions littéraires en Irlande*, edited by R. Alluin and B. Escarbelt, 53–68. Villeneuve d'Ascq: Études Irlandaises, Université de Lille III « Pont-de-Bois ».

Nic Dhonnchadha, Lil, ed. 1964. *Aided Muirchertaig Meic Erca*. Mediaeval and Modern Irish Series 19. Dublin: DIAS.

Ní Dhomhnaill, Nuala. 2000. *The Water Horse: Poems in Irish*. Translated by Medbh McGuckian and Eiléan Ní Chuilleanáin. Winston-Salem, NC: Wake Forest University Press.

Ní Dhonnchadha, Máirín. 1994–95. "*Caillech* and Other Terms for Veiled Women in Medieval Irish Texts." *Éigse* 28:71–96.

Nilsen, Ken. 1986. "Down among the Deda: Elements of Irish Language and Mythology in James Joyce's *Dubliners*." *The Canadian Journal of Irish Studies* 12.1:23–34.

Ní Mhaonaigh, Máire. 2005. "The Literature of Medieval Ireland, 800–1200: From the Vikings to the Normans." In *The Cambridge History of Irish Literature*, vol. 1, *To 1890*, edited by M. Kelleher and P. O'Leary, 32–73. Cambridge: Cambridge University Press.

Ní Shéaghdha, Nessa, ed. 1942–45. *Agallamh na Seanórach*. 3 vols. Dublin: Stationery Office.

———, ed., trans. 1967. *Tóruigheacht Dhiarmada agus Ghráinne*. Irish Texts Society 48. London: ITS.

Nitze, William A. 1912. "The Sister's Son and the *Conte del Graal*." *Modern Philology* 9:291–322.

Ó Béarra, Feargal. 2009. "The Otherworld Realm of *Tír scáith*." In *Festgabe für Hildegard L. C. Tristram*, edited by G. Hemprich, 81–100. Berlin: Curach Bhán.

Ó Briain, Máirtín. 1996. "The Conception and Death of Fionn Mac Cumhaill's Canine Cousin." In *Celtica Helsingiensia: Proceedings from a Symposium on Celtic Studies*, edited by A. Ahlqvist et al., 179–202. Commentationes Humanarum Litterarum 107. Helsinki: Societas Scientiarum Fennica.

O'Brien, Michael A. 1930–32. "Varia." *Ériu* 11:86–93, 154–71.

———. 1938. "Miscellanea Hibernica." *ÉC* 3:362–73.

———. 1954. "Irish Origin-Legends." In *Early Irish Society*, edited by Myles Dillon, 36–51. Dublin: Colm Ó Lochlainn for the Cultural Relations Committee of Ireland, at the Sign of the Three Candles.

———, ed. 1962. *Corpus Genealogiarum Hiberniae*, vol. 1. Dublin: DIAS.

———. 1973. "Old Irish Personal Names." Posthumously edited by Rolf Baumgarten. *Celtica* 10:211–36.

O'Brien, Steven. 1976. "Indo-European Eschatology: A Model." *JIES* 4:295–320.

Ó Broin, Tomás. 1961–63. "What Is the 'Debility' of the Ulstermen?" *Éigse* 10:286–99.

Ó Buachalla, L. 1951. "Contributions towards the Political History of Munster, 450–800 A.D." *JCHAS* 56:87–90.

———. 1952. "Contributions towards the Political History of Munster, 450–800 A.D." *JCHAS* 57:67–86.

———. 1954. "Contributions towards the Political History of Munster, 450–800 A.D." *JCHAS* 59:111–26.

Ó Caithnia, Liam P. 1984. *Apalóga na bhFilí, 1200–1650*. Dublin: An Clóchomhar.

Ó Coileáin, Seán. 1974. "The Structure of a Literary Cycle." *Ériu* 25:88–125.

———. 1977–78. "Oral or Literary: Some Strands of the Argument." *SH* 17/18:7–35.

———. 1981. "Some Problems of Story and History." *Ériu* 32:115–36.

Ó Concheanainn, Tomás. 1973–74a. "The Act of Wounding in the Death of Muirchertach mac Erca." *Éigse* 15:140–44.

———. 1973–74b. "The Reviser of Leabhar na hUidhre." *Éigse* 15:277–88.

———. 1986. "The Manuscript Tradition of Two Middle Irish Leinster Tales." *Celtica* 18:13–33.

———. 1988. "A Connacht Medieval Literary Heritage: Texts Derived from *Cín Dromma Snechtai* through *Leabhar na hUidhre*." *CMCS* 16:1–40.

———. 1996. "Textual and Historical Associations of Leabhar na hUidhre." *Éigse* 29:65–120.

O'Connor, Ralph. 2006. "Searching for the Moral in *Bruiden Meic Da Réo*." *Ériu* 56:117–43.

———. 2008. "Storytelling and the Otherworld in *Togail Bruidne Da Derga*." In *Approaches to Mythology and Religion in Celtic Studies*, edited by K. Ritari and A. Bergholm, 54–67. Newcastle: Cambridge Scholars Press.

———. 2013. *The Destruction of Da Derga's Hostel: Kingship and Narrative Artistry in a Mediaeval Irish Saga*. Oxford: Oxford University Press.

Ó Corráin, Donnchadh. 1978. "Nationality and Kingship in Pre-Norman Ireland." In *Nationality and the Pursuit of National Independence*, edited by T. W. Moody, 1–35. Belfast: Appletree Press.

———. 1980. Review of Byrne (1973). *Celtica* 13:150–68.

———. 1985a. "Irish Origin Legends and Genealogy: Recurrent Aetiologies." In *History and Heroic Tale: A Symposium*, edited by T. Nyberg, 51–96. Odense: Odense University Press.

———. 1985b. "Marriage in Early Ireland." In *Marriage in Ireland*, edited by A. Cosgrove, 5–24. Dublin: College Press.

———. 1986. "Historical Need and Literary Narrative." In *Proceedings of the Seventh International Congress of Celtic Studies*, edited by D. E. Evans, J. G. Griffith, and E. M. Jope, 141–58. Oxford: Oxbow Books.

———. 1987. "Legend as Critic." In *The Writer as Witness: Literature as Historical Evidence*, edited by T. Dunne, 23–38. Cork: Cork University Press.

———, trans. 2002. "Early Medieval Law, c. 700–1200." In *The Field Day Anthology of Irish Writing*, edited by A. Bourke et al., 4:6–44. Cork: Cork University Press.

Ó Corráin, Donnchadh, Liam Breatnach, and Aidan Breen. 1984. "The Laws of the Irish." *Peritia* 3:382–438.

Ó Cróinín, Dáibhí. 2005. *A New History of Ireland*, vol. 1, *Prehistoric and Early Ireland*. Oxford: Oxford University Press.

Ó Crualaoich, Gearóid. 1994–95. "Non-Sovereignty Queen Aspects of the Otherworld Female in Irish Hag Legends: The Case of Cailleach Bhéarra." *Béaloideas* 62/63:147–62.

———. 2003. *The Book of the Cailleach: Stories of the Wise-Woman Healer*. Cork: Cork University Press.

Ó Cuív, Brian, ed., trans. 1955–57. "A Poem in Praise of Raghnall, King of Man." *Éigse* 8:283–301.

———. 1963. *Literary Creation and Irish Historical Tradition*. Sir John Rhŷs Memorial Lecture. London: Oxford University Press. Reprinted from *PBA* 49:233–62.

———. 1964–66. Review of Nic Dhonnchadha (1964). *Éigse* 11:146–50.

———, ed., trans. 1971–72. "An Appeal on Behalf of the Profession of Poetry." *Éigse* 14:87–106.

———. 1973–74. "The Motif of the Threefold Death." *Éigse* 15:145–50.

———, ed., trans. 1976. "Comram na Cloenfherta." *Celtica* 11:168–79.

———. 1977–78. "The Wearing of the Green." *SH* 17/18:107–19.

———, ed., trans. 1981. "A Middle-Irish Poem on Leinster Dynasties." *ÉC* 18:141–50.

———, ed., trans. 1983. "A Poem Composed for Cathal Croibhdhearg Ó Conchubhair." *Ériu* 34:157–74.

———. 1984. "Ireland's Manuscript Heritage." *Éire-Ireland* 19 (1): 87–110.

———. 1986. "Aspects of Irish Personal Names." *Celtica* 18:151–84.

———. 2001. *Catalogue of Irish-Language Manuscripts in the Bodleian Library and Oxford College Libraries. Part 1: Descriptions*. Dublin: DIAS.

O Daly, Máirín. 1959. "Togail Bruidne Da Derga." In *Irish Sagas*, edited by M. Dillon, 107–23. Dublin: Mercier Press.

———, ed., trans. 1961–63. "A chóicid choín Chairpri crúaid." *Éigse* 10:177–97.

———, ed., trans. 1968. "Úar in Lathe do Lum Laine." In *Celtic Studies: Essays in Memory of Angus Matheson*, edited by J. Carney and D. Greene, 99–108. London: Routledge and Kegan Paul.

———, ed., trans. 1975. *Cath Maige Mucrama*. Irish Texts Society 50. Dublin: ITS.

O'Donovan, John. 1844. *The Genealogies, Tribes and Customs of Hy-Fiachrach*. Dublin: Irish Archaeological Society.

———. 1849. *Miscellany of the Celtic Society*. Dublin: Goodwin, Son, and Nethercott.

Ó Fiannachta, Pádraig. 1964–66. Review of Binchy (1963). *Éigse* 11:76–79, 156.

———, ed. 1966. *Táin Bó Cúailnge*. Dublin: DIAS.

O'Grady, Standish Hayes, ed., trans. 1857. *Tóruigheacht Dhiarmada agus Ghráinne*. Transactions of the Ossianic Society 3 [for 1855]. Dublin: John O'Daly.

———, ed., trans. 1892. *Silva Gadelica: A Collection of Tales in Irish*. 2 vols. London: Williams & Norgate. [There is a more recent translation of *Acallam na Senórach* by Dooley and Roe (1999), with the episode discussed in "Satire and Curse" appearing on 16–17.]

Ó hAodha, Donncha, ed., trans. 1978. *Bethu Brigte*. Dublin: DIAS.

Ó hÓgáin, Dáithí. 1974–76. "An é an t-am fós é?" *Béaloideas* 42–44:213–308.

Ó hUiginn, Ruairí. 1992. "The Background and Development of *Táin Bó Cúailgne*." In *Aspects of the Táin*, edited by J. P. Mallory, 29–67. Belfast: December Publications.

O'Keeffe, J. G., ed., trans. 1913. *Buile Suibhne Geilt*. Irish Texts Society 7. London: ITS.

———, ed. 1931. *Buile Ṡuibne*. Mediaeval and Modern Irish Series 1. Dublin: DIAS.

O'Leary, Philip. 1984. "Contention at Feasts in Early Irish Literature." *Éigse* 20:115–27.

———. 1986a. "A Foreseeing Driver of an Old Chariot: Regal Moderation in Early Irish Literature." *CMCS* 11:1–16.

———. 1986b. "Verbal Deceit in the Ulster Cycle." *Éigse* 21:16–26.

———. 1987. "*Fír Fer*: An Internalized Ethical Concept in Early Irish Literature." *Éigse* 22:1–14.

———. 1988. "Honour-Bound: The Social Context of Early Irish Heroic *geis*." *Celtica* 20:85–107.
———. 1991. "Magnanimous Conduct in Irish Heroic Literature." *Éigse* 25:28–44.
———. 1994. "Choice and Consequence in Irish Heroic Literature." *CMCS* 27:49–59.
Oliver, D. L. 1955. *A Solomon Island Society: Kinship and Leadership Among the Siuai of Bougainville.* Cambridge, MA: Harvard University Press.
Ó Maolfabhail, Art. 1973. *Camán: 2000 Years of Hurling in Ireland.* Dundalk: Dundalgan Press.
Ó Néill, Pádraig. 1999. "The Latin Colophon to the *Táin bó Cúailnge* in the Book of Leinster: A Critical View of Old Irish Literature." *Celtica* 23:269–75.
Oosten, J. G. 1985. *The War of the Gods: The Social Code in Indo-European Mythology.* London: Routledge and Kegan Paul.
O'Rahilly, Cecile, ed., trans. 1961. *The Stowe Version of Táin Bó Cuailgne.* Dublin: DIAS.
O'Rahilly, Thomas Francis. 1943–46. "On the Origin of the Names *Érainn* and *Ériu*." *Ériu* 14:7–28.
———. 1946. *Early Irish History and Mythology.* Dublin: DIAS.
———. 1950. "Notes on *Early Irish History and Mythology*." *Celtica* 1/2:387–402.
———. 1952. "Buchet the Herdsman." *Ériu* 16:7–20.
Ó Raithbheartaigh, T., ed. 1932. *Genealogical Tracts*, vol. 1. Dublin: Stationery Office.
Ó Riain, Pádraig. 1973–74a. "The 'crech ríg' or 'regal prey.'" *Éigse* 15:24–30.
———. 1973–74b. "The Materials and Provenance of 'Buile Shuibhne.'" *Éigse* 15:173–88.
———. 1977. "Traces of Lug in Early Irish Hagiographical Tradition." *ZCP* 36:138–56.
———, ed. 1978. *Cath Almaine.* Mediaeval and Modern Irish Series 25. Dublin: DIAS.
Oskamp, Hans P. A. 1966–67. "Notes on the History of *Lebor na Huidre*." *PRIA* 65 C: 117–37.
———, ed. 1974. "Echtra Condla." *ÉC* 14:207–28. [There is a more recent edition of this text by Kim McCone (2000).]
———. 1975–76. "Mael Muire: Compiler or Reviser?" *Éigse* 16:177–82.
Parkes, Peter. 2003. "Fostering Fealty: A Comparative Analysis of Tributary Allegiances of Adoptive Kinship." *CSSH* 45.4:741–82.
———. 2004. "Fosterage, Kinship, and Legend: When Milk Was Thicker than Blood?" *CSSH* 46.3:587–615.
———. 2006. "Celtic Fosterage: Adoptive Kinship and Clientage in Northwest Europe." *CSSH* 48.2:359–95.
Parks, Ward. 1990. *Verbal Dueling in Heroic Narrative: Homeric and Old English Traditions.* Princeton: Princeton University Press.

Partridge [Bourke], Angela. 1978. "Caoineadh na dTrí Muire agus an chaointeoireacht." In *Gnéithe den chaointeoireacht*, edited by B. Ó Madagáin, 67–81. Dublin: An Clóchomhar.

———. 1983. *Caoineadh na dtrí Muire*. Dublin: An Clóchomhar.

Patch, Howard Rollin. 1950. *The Other World According to Descriptions in Medieval Literature*. Cambridge, MA: Harvard University Press.

Pedersen, Holger. 1909–13. *Vergleichende Grammatik der keltischen Sprachen*. 2 vols. Göttingen: Vandenhoeck & Ruprecht.

Pender, Séamus, ed. 1947. "Two Unpublished Versions of the Expulsion of the Déssi." In *Féilscríbhinn Torna: Essays and Studies Presented to Professor Tadhg Ua Donnchadha (Torna) on the Occasion of His Seventieth Birthday*, edited by S. Pender, 209–17. Cork: Cork University Press.

Picard, Jean-Michel. 1989. "The Strange Death of Guaire Mac Áedáin." In *Sages, Saints and Storytellers: Celtic Studies in Honour of Professor James Carney*, edited by D. Ó Corráin, L. Breatnach, and K. R. McCone, 367–75. Maynooth: An Sagart.

Plummer, Charles, ed., trans. 1922. *Bethada Náem nÉrenn: Lives of Irish Saints*. 2 vols. Oxford: Oxford University Press.

Pokorny, Julius. 1915. "Zur irischen Etymologie und Wortkunde." *ZCP* 10:403–7.

———, ed. 1928. "Conle's Abenteuerliche Fahrt." *ZCP* 17:193–205. [There is a more recent edition of this text by Kim McCone (2000).]

Poppe, Erich. 1993. "A Note on the Jester in *Fingal Rónáin*." *SH* 27:145–54.

———. 1996. "Deception and Self-Deception in *Fingal Rónáin*." *Ériu* 47:137–51.

———. 2008. *Of Cycles and Other Critical Matters: Some Issues in Medieval Irish Literary History*. Quiggin Memorial Lectures 9. Cambridge: Department of Anglo-Saxon, Norse, and Celtic, University of Cambridge.

Poppe, Erich, and Patrick Sims-Williams. 2005. "Irish Literary Theory and Criticism." In *The Cambridge History of Literary Criticism 2: The Middle Ages*, edited by A. Minnis and I. Johnson, 291–309. Cambridge: Cambridge University Press.

Potter, Murray Anthony. 1902. *Sohrab and Rustem: The Epic Theme of a Combat between Father and Son*. London: David Nutt.

Power, Patrick C., ed., trans. 1914. *Life of St Declan of Ardmore and Life of St Mochuda of Lismore*. Irish Texts Society 16. London: ITS.

———. 1952. *Log-ainmneacha na nDéise*. 2nd ed. Cork: Cork University Press.

Puhvel, Jaan. 1970. "Mythological Reflections of Indo-European Medicine." In *Indo-European and Indo-Europeans*, edited by G. Cardona, H. M. Hoenigswald, and A. Senn, 369–82. Philadelphia: University of Pennsylvania Press.

———. 1974. "Transposition of Myth to Saga in Indo-European Epic Narrative." In *Antiquitates Indogermanicae*, edited by M. Mayrhofer et al., 175–84. Innsbruck: Universität Innsbruck.

———. 1987. *Comparative Mythology*. Baltimore: Johns Hopkins University Press.
Quin, E. G. 1981. "The Early Irish Poem *Ísucán*." *CMCS* 1:39–52.
Radcliffe-Brown, A. R. 1952. *Structure and Function in Primitive Society*. London: Cohen & West.
Radner, Joan Newlon, ed., trans. 1978. *Fragmentary Annals of Ireland*. Dublin: DIAS.
———. 1982. "'Fury destroys the world': Historical Strategy in Ireland's Ulster Epic." *Mankind Quarterly* 23:41–60.
———. 1983. "The Significance of the Threefold Death in Celtic Tradition." In *Celtic Folklore and Christianity: Studies in Memory of William W. Heist*, edited by P. K. Ford, 180–200. Santa Barbara: McNally & Loftin.
———. 1992. "The Combat of Lug and Balor: Discourses of Power in Irish Myth and Folktale." *Oral Tradition* 7 (1): 143–49.
Rance, Philip. 2001. "Attacotti, Déisi, and Magnus Maximus: The Case for Irish Federates in Late Roman Britain." *Britannia* 32:243–70.
Rayner, Lee J., trans. 1988. *Legends of the Kings of Ireland*. Cork: Mercier Press.
Rees, Alwyn D. 1966. "Modern Evaluations of Celtic Narrative Tradition." In *Proceedings of the Second International Congress of Celtic Studies*, edited by H. Lewis, 31–61. Cardiff: University of Wales Press.
Rees, Alwyn D., and Brinley Rees. 1961. *Celtic Heritage*. London: Thames & Hudson.
Richards, Melville. 1960. "The Irish Settlements in South-West Wales: A Topographical Approach." *The Journal of the Royal Society of Antiquaries of Ireland* 90:133–62.
Ritari, Katja, and Alexandra Bergholm, eds. 2008. *Approaches to Religion and Mythology in Celtic Studies*. Newcastle: Cambridge Scholars Press.
Roberts, Brynley F., ed. 1975. *Cyfranc Lludd a Llefelys*. Mediaeval and Modern Welsh Series 7. Dublin: DIAS.
Robinson, Fred Norris. 1912. "Satirists and Enchanters in Early Irish Literature." In *Studies in the History of Religions Presented to Crawford Howell Toy*, edited by D. G. Lyon and G. F. Moore, 95–130. New York: Macmillan.
Roider, Ulrike, ed., trans. 1979. *De Chophur In Da Muccida*. Innsbrucker Beiträge zur Sprachwissenschaft 28. Innsbruck: Universität Innsbruck.
Ross, Anne. 1967. *Pagan Celtic Britain*. New York: Columbia University Press.
Russell, Paul. 1988. "The Celtic Preverb **uss* and Related Matters." *Ériu* 39:95–126.
Rynne, Etienne, and Gearóid Mac Eoin. 1978. "The Craggaunowen crannog: Gangway and Gate-Tower." *North Munster Antiquarian Journal* 20:47–56.
Salberg, Trond Kruke. 1992. "The Question of the Main Interpolation of H into M's Part of the *Serglige Con Culainn* in the Book of the Dun Cow and Some Related Problems." *ZCP* 45:161–81.
Sayers, William. 1985. "Fergus and the Cosmogonic Sword." *History of Religions* 25:30–56.

———. 1986. "'*Mani Maidi an Nem* . . .': Ringing Changes on a Cosmic Motif." *Ériu* 36:99–117.

———. 1987. "Bargaining for the Life of Bres in *Cath Maige Tuired*." *BBCS* 34:26–40.

———. 1992. "Guin & Crochad & Golad: The Earliest Irish Threefold Death." In *Celtic Languages and Celtic Peoples: Proceedings of the Second North American Congress of Celtic Studies*, edited by C. J. Byrne, M. Harry, and P. Ó Siadhail, 65–82. Halifax: D'Arcy McGee Chair of Irish Studies, Saint Mary's University.

———. 1997. "Contracting for Combat: Flyting and Fighting in *Táin Bó Cúailgne*." *Emania* 16:49–62.

———. 2007a. "*La Joie de la Court* (*Érec et Énide*), Mabon, and Early Irish *síd* [peace; Otherworld]." *Arthuriana* 17.2:10–27.

———. 2007b. "Medieval Irish Language and Literature: An Orientation for Arthurians." *Arthuriana* 17.4:70–80.

———. 2008a. "Deficient Royal Rule: The King's Proxies, Judges, and the Instruments of His Fate." In *Essays on the Early Irish King Tales*, edited by D. Wiley, 104–26. Dublin: Four Courts Press.

———. 2008b. "Fusion and Fission in the Love and Lexis of Early Ireland." In *Words of Love and Love of Words in the Middle Ages and Renaissance*, edited by A. Classen, 95–109. Tempe: Arizona Center for Medieval and Renaissance Studies.

———. 2010. "Irish Studies." In *Handbook of Medieval Studies: Terms, Methods, Trends*, edited by Albrecht Classen, 727–38. Boston: de Gruyter.

———. 2012. "Netherworld and Otherworld in Early Irish Literature." *ZCP* 59:201–30.

Schoepperle [Loomis], Gertrude. 1913. *Tristan and Isolt: A Study of the Sources of the Romance*. Frankfurt: J. Baer.

Schultz, Wolfgang. 1923. Review of Thurneysen (1921). *ZCP* 14:299–305.

Scowcroft, R. Mark. 1995. "Abstract Narrative in Ireland." *Ériu* 46:121–58.

Sharpe, Richard. 1979. "Hiberno-Latin *Laicus*, Irish *Láech* and the Devil's Men." *Ériu* 30:75–92.

———, trans. 1991a. *Adomnán of Iona: Life of St Columba*. Harmondsworth: Penguin.

———. 1991b. *Medieval Irish Saints' Lives: An Introduction to* Vitae sanctorum Hiberniae. Oxford: Clarendon Press.

Shaw, Francis, ed. 1934. *The Dream of Óengus: Aislinge Óenguso*. Dublin: Browne & Nolan.

Siewers, Alfred K. 2009. *Strange Beauty: Ecocritical Approaches to Early Medieval Landscape*. Basingstoke: Palgrave Macmillan.

Simms, Katharine. 1998. "The Contents of Later Commentaries on the Brehon Law Tracts." *Ériu* 49:23–40.

———. 2009. *Medieval Gaelic Sources*. Dublin: Four Courts Press.

Sims-Williams, Patrick. 1978–79. "Riddling Treatment of the 'Watchman Device' in *Branwen* and *Togail Bruidne Da Derga*." *SC* 12/13:83–117.

———. 1982a. "The Evidence for Vernacular Irish Literary Influence on Early Medieval Welsh Literature." In *Ireland in Early Medieval Europe: Studies in Memory of Kathleen Hughes*, edited by D. Whitelock, R. McKitterick, and D. N. Dumville, 235–57. Cambridge: Cambridge University Press.

———. 1982b. "The Significance of the Irish Personal Names in *Culhwch ac Olwen*." *BBCS* 29(4): 600–620.

———. 1990. "Some Celtic Otherworld Terms." In *Celtic Language, Celtic Culture: A Festschrift for Eric P. Hamp*, edited by A. T. E. Matonis and D. F. Melia, 57–81. Van Nuys, CA: Ford & Bailie.

———. 1991. "The Submission of Irish Kings in Fact and Fiction: Henry II, Bendigeidfran, and the Dating of the Four Branches of the Mabinogi." *CMCS* 22:31–61.

———. 1996. Review of McCone (1990). *Éigse* 29:179–96.

———. 2005. *The Iron House in Ireland*. H. M. Chadwick Memorial Lectures 16. Cambridge: Dept. of Anglo-Saxon, Norse, and Celtic, University of Cambridge.

———. 2011. *Irish Influence on Medieval Welsh Literature*. Oxford: Oxford University Press.

Sinder, Janet. 2001. "Irish Legal History: An Overview and Guide to the Sources." *Law Library Journal* 93.2:231–60.

Sjöblom, Tom. 2000. *Early Irish Taboos: A Study in Cognitive History*. Comparative Religion 5. Helsinki: Dept. of Comparative Religion, University of Helsinki.

———. 2004. "Mind-Stories: A Cognitive Approach to the Role of Narratives in Early Irish Tradition." *CMCS* 47:59–72.

Sjoestedt[-Jonval], Marie-Louise. 1949. *Gods and Heroes of the Celts*. Translated by Myles Dillon. London: Methuen.

Slotkin, Edgar M. 1977–79. "Medieval Irish Scribes and Fixed Texts." *Éigse* 17:437–50.

———. 1990. "*Noínden*: Its Semantic Range." In *Celtic Language, Celtic Culture: A Festschrift for Eric P. Hamp*, edited by A. T. E. Matonis and D. F. Melia, 137–50. Van Nuys, CA: Ford & Bailie.

Spenser, Edmund. 1934. *A View of the Present State of Ireland*. Edited by W. L. Renick. London: Scholartis Press.

Stacey, Robin Chapman. 2005. "Law and Literature in Medieval Ireland and Wales." In *Medieval Celtic Literature and Society*, edited by H. Fulton, 65–82. Dublin: Four Courts Press.

———. 2007. *Dark Speech: The Performance of Law in Early Ireland*. Philadelphia: University of Pennsylvania Press.

———. 2011. "Learning and Law in Medieval Ireland." In *Tome: Studies in Medieval Celtic History and Law in Honour of Thomas Charles-Edwards*, edited by F. Edmonds and P. Russell, 135–44. Woodbridge: Boydell.

Sterckx, Claude. 2004. "Quand Lugh devient-il roi?" *Ollodagos* 18.2:301–5.

Stokes, Whitley, ed. 1862. *Three Irish Glossaries.* London: Williams & Norgate.
———. 1887. "Irish Feminine Stems in *i* and *u*, and Neuter Stems in *s*." *KZ* 28:289–94.
———, ed., trans. 1891a. "The Irish Ordeals, Cormac's Adventure in the Land of Promise, and the Decision as to Cormac's Sword." In *IT* 3:1, 183–229.
———, ed., trans. 1891b. "The Second Battle of Moytura." *RC* 12: 52–130, 306–8. [There is a more recent edition of this text by Elizabeth Gray (1982).]
———, ed., trans. 1892a. "The Boroma." *RC* 13:32–124, 299.
———, ed., trans. 1892b. "The Battle of Mag Mucrime." *RC* 13:426–74.
———, ed., trans. 1894. "The Prose Tales in the Rennes Dindshenchas." *RC* 15:272–336, 418–84.
———, ed., trans. 1897. "*Cóir anmann.*" In *IT* 3:2, 285–444. [There is a more recent edition of this text by Sharon Arbuthnot (2005–6).]
———, ed., trans. 1899. "The Bodleian Amra Choluimb Chille." *RC* 20:30–55, 132–83, 248–89, 400–437.
———, ed., trans. 1900. "Acallamh na Senórach." In *IT* 4:1, 1–438.
———, ed. 1901a. "The Destruction of Da Derga's Hostel (appendix)." *RC* 22:390–437.
———, ed., trans. 1901b. "The Destruction of Dind Ríg." *ZCP* 3:1–14. [There is a more recent edition of this text by David Greene (1955).]
———, ed., trans. 1903. "Echtra Mac Echach Muigmedóin." *RC* 24:190–203. [There is a more recent translation of this text by John Carey in Koch and Carey (2003, 203–8).]
———, ed., trans. 1907. *The Birth and Life of St. Moling.* London: Harrison.
———, ed. 1908. "Poems Ascribed to St. Moling." *Anecd.* 2:20–41.
———, ed., trans. 1908–10. "Tidings of Conchobar mac Nessa." *Ériu* 4:18–38.
Stout, Geraldine. 2002. *Newgrange and the Bend of the Boyne.* Cork: Cork University Press.
Strachan, John, and J. G. O'Keeffe, eds. 1913. *Táin Bó Cúailnge from the Yellow Book of Lecan. With Variant Readings from the Lebor na Huidre.* Dublin: School of Irish Learning.
Szemerényi, Oswald. 1977. "Studies in the Kinship Terminology of the Indo-European Languages with Special Reference to Indian, Iranian, Greek and Latin." *Acta Iranica* 16 (= *Textes et mémoires VII. Varia*): 1–240.
Thomson, R. L., ed. 1957. *Pwyll Pendeuic Dyuet.* Mediaeval and Modern Welsh Series 1. Dublin: DIAS.
Thornton, David E. 1998. "Orality, Literacy and Genealogy in Early Medieval Ireland and Wales." In *Literacy in Medieval Celtic Societies*, edited by H. Pryce, 83–98. Cambridge: Cambridge University Press.
———. 2003. *Kings, Chronicles and Genealogies: Studies in the Political History of Early Medieval Ireland and Wales.* Prosopographica et Genealogica 10. Oxford: Unit for Prosopographical Research, Linacre College.

Thurneysen, Rudolf. 1887. "Irisches." *KZ* 28:145–54 [esp. "IV. Irisch *síd*," 153–54].
———. 1912. "Erschienene Schriften." *ZCP* 8:184–85.
———. 1912–13. *Zu irischen Handschriften und Litteraturdenkmälern*. 2 vols. Berlin: Weidmann.
———. 1917. "Irisches." *ZCP* 11:30–38.
———. 1918. "Zu irischen Texten." *ZCP* 12:398–407.
———, ed. 1920. "Tochmarc Ailbe." *ZCP* 13:251–82.
———. 1921. *Die irische Helden- und Königsage bis zum 17. Jahrhundert*. Halle a. S.: Max Niemeyer.
———, ed. 1923a. "Aus dem irischen Recht." *ZCP* 14:335–94.
———. 1923b. "Eine irische Parallele zur Tristan-Sage." *Zeitschrift für Romanische Philologie* 43:385–402. [Addenda and corrigenda in *ZCP* 16 (1926): 280–82.]
———, ed. 1925. "Aus dem irischen Recht III." *ZCP* 15:302–76.
———. 1933. "Colmán mac Lénéni and Senchán Torpéist." *ZCP* 19:193–209.
———, ed. 1935. *Scéla mucce Meic Dathó*. Mediaeval and Modern Irish Series 6. Dublin: DIAS.
———. 1935–36. "Ir. Eneclann." *ZCP* 20:205–12.
———, ed. 1936a. "*Cáin Lánamna*: 'Die Regelung der Paare.'" In *Studies in Early Irish Law*, edited by R. Thurneysen et al., 1–80. Dublin: Royal Irish Academy. [There is a more recent edition of this text by Charlene Eska (2009).]
———, ed. 1936b. "Baile in Scáil." *ZCP* 20:213–27. [There is a more recent edition of this text by Kevin Murray (2004).]
———. 1946. *A Grammar of Old Irish*. Translated and revised by D. A. Binchy and O. Bergin. Dublin: DIAS.
Toner, Gregory. 1987. "Reconstructing the Earliest Irish Tale Lists." *Éigse* 32:88–120.
———. 2010. "Wise Women and Wanton Warriors in Early Irish Literature." *PHCC* 30:259–72.
Tristram, Hildegard L. C., ed. 1993. *Studien zur Táin Bó Cuailgne*. ScriptOralia 52. Tübingen: Gunter Narr Verlag.
Tymoczko, Maria. 1999. *Translation in a Postcolonial Context: Early Irish Literature in English Translation*. Manchester: St. Jerome.
Uhlich, Jürgen. 2006. "Some Textual Problems in Rónán's Lament I: Two Quatrains Concerning Echaid's Daughter." *Ériu* 56:13–62.
van der Lee, Anthony. 1957. *Zum literarischen Motiv von der Vatersuche*. Verhandelingen der Koninklijke Nederlandse Akademie van Wetenschappen, Afd. Letterkunde; n.s. 63(3). Amsterdam.
van Hamel, A. G., ed. 1933. *Compert Con Culainn and Other Stories*. Mediaeval and Modern Irish Series 3. Dublin: DIAS.
———. 1934. *Aspects of Celtic Mythology*. Sir John Rhŷs Memorial Lecture. London: Oxford University Press. Reprinted from *PBA* 20:207–48.
Vendryes, Joseph. 1929. "Remarques de vocabulaire." *RC* 46:252–67.

———. 1936. Review of Shaw (1934). *ÉC* 1:159–62.

———. 1948. "La religion des Celtes." *Mana: Introduction à l'histoire des religions* 2(3): 237–320.

———. 1952. "L'unité en trois personnes chez les Celtes." In *Choix d'Études linguistiques et celtiques*, 233–46. Paris: C. Klincksieck.

———. 1958–59. "La destruction de Dind Ríg." *ÉC* 8:7–40.

Wagner, Heinrich. 1970. "Studies in the Origins of Early Celtic Civilisation." *ZCP* 31:1–58. Reprinted 1971 in *Studies in the Origins of the Celts and of Early Celtic Civilisation*, Tübingen: Max Niemeyer.

———. 1975. "Studies in the Origins of Early Celtic Traditions." *Ériu* 26:1–26.

Walsh, Paul. 1947. *Irish Men of Learning*. Edited by Colm Ó Lochlainn. Dublin: At the Sign of the Three Candles.

Ward, Donald J. 1970. "The Threefold Death: An Indo-European Trifunctional Sacrifice?" In *Myth and Law Among the Indo-Europeans*, edited by J. Puhvel, 123–42. Berkeley: University of California Press.

Watkins, Calvert. 1963. "Indo-European Metrics and Archaic Irish Verse." *Celtica* 6:194–249.

———. 1976a. "The Etymology of Irish *dúan*." *Celtica* 11:270–77.

———. 1976b. "Sick-Maintenance in Indo-European." *Ériu* 27:21–25.

———. 1979. "*Is Tre Fír Flathemon*: Marginalia to *Audacht Morainn*." *Ériu* 30:181–98.

———. 1995. *How to Kill a Dragon: Aspects of Indo-European Comparative Poetics*. Oxford: Oxford University Press.

———. 2000. *The American Heritage Dictionary of Indo-European Roots*. 2nd ed. Boston: Houghton Mifflin.

———. 2008. "What Makes the Study of Irish Worthwhile." In *Why Irish? Irish Language and Literature in Academia*, edited by B. Ó Conchubhair, 43–53. Galway: Arlen House.

Watson, J. Carmichael, ed. 1941. *Mesca Ulad*. Mediaeval and Modern Irish Series 13. Dublin: DIAS.

———, trans. 1942. "Mesca Ulad." *Scottish Gaelic Studies* 5:1–34.

Wellek, René, and Austin Warren. 1976. *Theory of Literature*. 3rd ed. Harmondsworth: Peregrine.

Welsford, Enid. 1935. *The Fool: His Social and Literary History*. London: Faber & Faber.

West, Máire. 1990. "*Leabhar na hUidre*'s Position in the Manuscript History of *Togail Bruidne Da Derga* and *Orgain Brudne Uí Dergae*." *CMCS* 20:61–98.

———. 1997. "Aspects of *díberg* in Early Irish literature." *ZCP* 49/50:950–64.

———. 1999. "The Genesis of *Togail Bruidne Da Derga*: A Reappraisal of the 'Two-Source' Theory." *Celtica* 23:413–35.

Wiley, Dan M. 2001. "The Maledictory Psalms." *Peritia* 15:261–79.

———. 2002. "Stories about Diarmait mac Cerbaill from the Book of Lismore." *Emania* 19:53–59.
———. 2008. "An Introduction to the Early Irish King Tales." In *Essays on the Early Irish King Tales*, edited by D. Wiley, 13–67. Dublin: Four Courts Press.
Williams, Ifor, ed. 1951. *Pedeir Keinc y Mabinogi*. 2nd ed. Cardiff: University of Wales Press.
Williams, J. E. Caerwyn. 1972. *The Court Poet in Medieval Ireland*. Sir John Rhŷs Memorial Lecture. London: Oxford University Press. Reprinted from *PBA* 57 (1971): 85–135.
Williams, J. E. Caerwyn, and Máirín Ní Mhuiríosa. 1979. *Traidisiún Liteartha na nGael*. Dublin: An Clóchomhar. Printed in English as J. E. Caerwyn Williams and Patrick K. Ford, 1992, *The Irish Literary Tradition*, Cardiff: University of Wales Press.
Williams, Mark. 2010. *Fiery Shapes: Celestial Portents and Astrology in Ireland and Wales 700–1700*. Oxford: Oxford University Press.
———. 2011. "'Lady Vengeance': A Reading of Sín in *Aided Muirchertaig meic Erca*." *CMCS* 62:1–33.
Williams, N. J. A., ed., trans. 1980. *The Poems of Giolla Brighde Mac Con Midhe*. Irish Texts Society 51. Dublin: ITS.
Windisch, Ernst, ed. 1891. "De Chopur in dá muccida." *IT* 3:230–47.
Wood-Martin, William Gregory. 1902. *Traces of the Elder Faiths of Ireland*. 2 vols. London: Longmans, Green.
Wooding, Jonathan M. 2009. "Reapproaching the Pagan Celtic Past—Anti-Nativism, Asterisk Reality and the Late-Antiquity Paradigm." *Studia Celtica Fennica* 6:61–74.
Wulff, Winifred, and Kathleen Mulchrone. 1933. *Catalogue of Irish Manuscripts in the Royal Irish Academy*, vol. 10. Dublin: Royal Irish Academy.
Yocum, Christopher Guy. 2012. "Wisdom Literature in Early Ireland." *SC* 46:39–58.
Zimmer, Heinrich. 1887. "Keltische studien 5: Über den compilatorischen Charakter der irischen Sagentexte im sogennanten Lebor na hUidre." *KZ* 28:417–689.
———. 1893. *Nennius Vindicatus: Über Entstehung, Geschichte und Quellen der Historia Brittonum*. Berlin: Weidmann.

Index

This index also serves as a glossary of Irish words introduced in the book, and as a reminder of the significance of people and places.

Modern scholars are included in the index only when their views are presented in the body of the book (not in notes or Further Reading); mere parenthetical citations of a scholar's work without commentary, especially in the notes, are not normally included in the index.

For texts mentioned many times, also see the main entries "dating" and "manuscripts" for a shortcut to discussion of those aspects.

An equal sign (=) is used for corresponding pages of chapter 31, which appears in Irish and English; the numbers to the left of the equal sign refer to the Irish.

Abrams, M. H.: 36, 44, 46, 203–4
Acallam na Senórach ("The Colloquy of the Old Men"): 9, 95–100, 454–55=471–72
Achilles: like Cú Chulainn, 264
Act of Truth. See *fír flathemon/fír flatha*
Adomnán, hagiographer of Colum Cille/Columba: 2, 14–15, 102, 104–5, 107, 110 character in *Cath Almaine*, 441

Adonis: like Diarmaid, 457–58=474–75
Áed, son and avenger of Mael Fhothartaig: 397
Áed, son of Fidga, slain by Finn mac Cumaill: 11
Áedán, slayer of Mael Fhothartaig: 397–98
Áedán mac Gabráin, king of Scotland and enemy of Cano mac Gartnáin: 242, 342, 344–47, 352, 363–66, 369–73

Áed Brosc, of uncertain genealogy: 318–23. *Cf.* Ewein Vreisc
Áed Dub, slayer of Diarmait mac Cerbaill: 14–15, 102, 104–12, 115, 119–20. *See also* three: threefold death
Áed (Goll) mac Morna, enemy of Finn mac Cumaill: 10, 153
áer '(poetic) satire.' *See* satire
áes dána 'men of art,' i.e., poets and musicians: 2, 266–67, 433, 445. *See also fili*
áes síde 'people of the *síd*' ("fairies"): 20–21, 29, 278–79, 403, 433. *See also síd*; Túatha Dé Danann
Ahlqvist, Anders: 2
aided 'violent death' (as a class of tale), pl. *aitte/aideda*: 3, 175–76. *See also Aided Con Roí; Aided Diarmata meic Cerbaill; Aided Muirchertaig meic Erca*
Aided Con Roí ("The Violent Death of Cú Roí"): 489
Aided Diarmata meic Cerbaill ("The Violent Death of Diarmait mac Cerbaill"): 102, 110–12, 117. *See also* Diarmait mac Cerbaill; three: threefold death; Uí Néill dynasty
Aided Muirchertaig meic Erca ("The Violent Death of Muirchertach mac Erca"): 103, 106–10, 116–17. *See also* Muirchertach mac Erca; three: threefold death; Uí Néill dynasty
Ailbe, daughter of Cormac mac Airt: 456=470. *See also Tochmarc Ailbe*
Ailill, brother of King Echaid Airem: 177
Ailill, father of Étaín: 177, 180, 402
Ailill Áine, son of Lóegaire Lorc and father of Labraid Loingsech: 424–27, 437–38

Ailill mac Máta, Ulster Cycle king of Connacht: 7, 175
in other texts, 166, 170–72, 337
relationship with wife Medb, 195, 216–17, 229–30, 249–58
in the *Táin*, 187–90, 192, 194–95, 199–200, 216–17, 219, 224, 226, 229–30, 232, 234–36, 240, 249–58, 269, 443
Ailill Ólomm, Munster king, foster-father and killer of Lugaid Mac Con: 79, 92, 139, 331–39, 341, 496
meaning of epithet *Ólomm*, 335
as *Oilill Óluim*, 464=482
Aillén mac Midna, supernatural burner of Tara: 10
ainem 'blemish.' *See* blemish
ainmne 'forbearance': 342–51, 358, 374–75. *See also Scéla Cano meic Gartnáin*
Airmed, daughter of Dían Cécht: 47
aislinge 'dream, vision.' *See* dreams
Aislinge Meic Conglinne ("The Vision of Mac Conglinne"), satirical MidIr text: 147
Aislinge Óenguso ("The Dream of Óengus"): 165–73, 491. *See also* Óengus the Mac Óg
aithed 'elopement' (as a class of tale), pl. *aitheda* (do not confuse with *aided* 'violent death,' pl. *aideda*): 3, 175–76, 451–57=468–74
Alba 'Scotland; Britain': 26, 109, 160, 331, 339, 408, 496. *Cf.* Britain; Scotland, *according to term used in text*
Almu 'the Hill of Allen,' gen. *Almaine*: 10, 453, 470. *Cf. Cath Almaine*
ambue 'one who possesses no cattle' (person from Ireland living outside *túath* of origin): 78–79. *Cf. cú glas*

amnair 'mother's brother': 70, 76, 79, 488. *See also* avunculate
Amra Cholm Cille ("The Eulogy of Colum Cille"): 2, 140, 263–64, 452=468–69. *See also* Colum Cille; Dallán Forgaill
Áne Chlíach, hill in Munster: 334–36
Áne daughter of Éogabul, *síd*-woman raped by Ailill Ólomm: 335–36
Anglo-Irish literature: xi, 51–52
animals: general reference, 453=470. *See also* birds; bulls; cows; dogs; horses; mice; pigs; sheep; wolves; worms
annals: 117–18, 213, 230, 306, 311, 357, 485
  Annals of the Four Masters, 399–400
  Annals of Ulster, 311, 325
  Fragmentary Annals of Ireland, 439, 441
Annwfn, the Welsh Otherworld: 30–34. Cf. *síd*
antocad 'ill-fated one': 371. Cf. *tocad*
Aonghus an Bhrogha (Óengus the Mac Óg in earlier tales): 150, 454=471, 459–63=476–81
Aphrodite: like Gráinne, 457–58=474–75
Arawn, king of Annwfn: 31–33
Art buidhe Mac Murchadha Caomhánach, ms. patron: 166–67
Art Corb son of Mess Corb, of Dál Fiachach Suidge: 285, 287, 302, 304–5, 312–13, 323
artist, the: 36–40. *See also* critical approaches to early Irish literature
Art mac Cuinn, king of Tara, father of Cormac mac Airt: 12, 23, 76–77, 79, 129, 331–32, 341
assignation. *See* tryst
athardae 'paternal kin': 85

Audacht Moraind ("The Testament of Morann"): 12–13, 22, 247, 540n8. *See also fír flathemon/ fír flatha*
audience, the: 36, 44–45. *See also* critical approaches to early Irish literature
avunculate: 69–75, 223–24. *See also* Indo-European

Badb, war-goddess (one of three along with the Morrígan and Nemain): 444–46
Bae Aífe 'The Cows of Aífe,' trysting-place referenced in *Fingal Rónáin*: 380–81, 391–96
Báethgalach, Leinster warrior in *Cath Almaine*: 445–46
Baile Chuinn ("The Vision of Conn"): 115–18
Baile in Scáil ("The Phantom's Vision/[Prophetic] Frenzy"): 23, 61–63, 150–51, 158–60
Balar, evil-eyed Fomoire champion: 5, 10, 81, 85, 136, 144–45, 152–53, 490
banchomarba(e) 'female heir': 230, 256
Bear-son legend: 28
beauty, descriptions of: 144, 159
Bhreathnach, Edel: 423, 485, 536n21, 549n5
Binchy, D. A.: 2, 30, 38–39, 43, 67, 72, 78–79, 83, 122–23, 125–26, 128, 141, 147, 242, 297, 327, 342–44, 357–58, 362–63, 367–70, 372–74, 542n1, 543n27
birds:
  birds from Otherworld cause devastation, 7–8, 53–54, 58, 152, 212–13, 340–41
  choice or obligation not to kill birds, 23–24, 26, 347, 359

birds (*cont.*)
    crows/scald-crows, 444–46
    Otherworld beings manifest as birds, 13, 23–24, 57–58, 171–72, 412, 415
Blathmac, poet, son of Cú Brettan: 36–37, 65–69, 77, 80, 82, 87, 91, 119, 217–18, 488. *See also* Cú Brettan
Blathmac son of Áed Sláine, joint-king of Tara with Diarmait in *Scéla Cano meic Gartnáin*: 242, 343, 344–46, 352, 359, 365, 369–73
blemish (*ainem*): causing removal from kingship. *See* blinding: of Midir; blinding: of Cormac mac Airt; Núadu
blinding:
    of Balar, 5, 10, 81, 85, 136, 144–45, 152–53, 490
    of Cormac mac Airt, 283–84, 288, 294–95, 304, 309–10, 312
    of Midir, 179–81
Boann, goddess of the Boyne, mother of Óengus: 165, 169, 178, 180
boar of Beann Ghulban. *See* pigs
Bodb, brother of Óengus: 169–70
Book of Leinster, Trinity College Dublin ms.: 214–15, 330–31, 423, 452=469, 492. Contents incl. *Cath Maige Mucrama; Orgain Denna Ríg; Táin Bó Cúailnge*
Book of the Dun Cow. *See Lebor na hUidre*
Book of Uí Maine, Dublin, RIA ms.: 284, 287, 306–8, 314, 316. Contents incl. "*Expulsion of the Déisi*"
bórama, tribute imposed on the Leinstermen: 439–41
Boyne (river): 54, 106–8, 155, 177–79, 312, 328, 462=479. *See also* Boann; Bruig na Bóinne

Bran Finn Femin, Dál Fiachach king: 291
Breatnach, Liam: 122, 226, 228, 234, 485, 488–89, 507n78
Breatnach, R. A.: 151, 458=475
Brecc, son of Mess Corb: 285, 304, 308–10, 312
brehon law. *See* law
Bresal, druid, foster-father of Fuamnach: 181–83
Bres son of Elatha, *gormac* and failed king of the Túatha Dé Danann:
    conception and relationship to Túatha Dé Danann, 4, 6–7, 76–77, 80–85, 135, 137–48, 177
    contrasted with Lug, 6, 84–85, 143, 147, 153–54, 176
    and Dumézil's third function, 5, 85, 145, 148
    target of satire, 96–100
Bretha Nemed ("Judgments Concerning Privileged Persons," law-text): 125–26, 227
brideprice. *See coibche*
brigands. *See díberg*
Brigit, keening woman in *CMT*: 147
Brigit (saint): 76, 443–44
Britain: 14, 104, 155, 301–2, 323–24, 413, 495. *See also* Alba
Bromwich, Rachel: 32, 506n51
Bruford, Alan: 450–51=467–68
Brugh na Bóinne. *See* Bruig na Bóinne
bruiden 'hostel,' gen. *bruidne*: of Da Derga, 14, 56, 110, 175, 413. *See also Togail Bruidne Da Derga*
Bruig Mac ind Óaic. *See* Bruig na Bóinne
Bruig na Bóinne: 7–8, 53–55, 58, 86, 106, 152, 155–58, 164, 166, 172, 177–83, 441, 459–62=476–80
búaid, pl. *búada*:
    'duty, prescription,' 63 (*cf. geis*)
    'gift, special ability,' 57, 61, 337

Buí: 155–164. *See also cailleach*; Cnogba
Buile Suibne ("The Madness of Suibne"). *See* Suibne Geilt
bull-feast, divinatory rite: 57, 259.
    See also Conaire Mór; prophecies
bulls: 207–9, 229.
    in *Táin Bó Cúailnge* (*see* Donn Cúailnge, Finnbennach)
    See also cattle-raiding; cows; sacrifice
Byrne, Francis John: 6, 28, 41, 45, 103, 116–17, 156–57, 247, 292, 311, 323, 357

Cáer Ibormeith, Óengus's love interest in *Aislinge Óenguso*: 165–68, 170–72
Caier, Connacht king and target of satire: 142, 154
Cailb, supernatural hag in *TBDD*: 110. *Cf.* Sín
Cailleach Bhéarra 'Old Woman of Beare.' *See also* Cnogba; "Lament of the Old Woman of Beare"
cailleach 'old woman; (supernatural) hag': 110, 156–57, 159–64, 470–71, 491
cáin '(rule of) law': 27, 60, 98–99, 220–21. *Cf.* law; *síd*
caíned. *See* keening the dead
Cáin Fhuithirbe ("The Law of Fuithirbe"), earliest datable law-text: 124–25, 228, 234
Cairbre Lifechair, son of Cormac mac Airt: 308, 310, 312, 315–16, 328–29
Cairbre Músc: 160–61. *See also* Corc Duibne; incest
Cairbre Nia Fer, Ulster Cycle hero: 77–78, 90, 200
Cairbre Rigronn, ancestor of *muintir Chairbre*: 313
Cairbre son of Étaín/Etan, poet of the Túatha Dé Danann: 82, 96–100, 137, 140–42 (mac Étaíne/Étain)

cairdes 'formal union' (political alliance, sex, etc.): 169, 172. *Cf. cerennyd*
"The Caldron of Poesy": xix–xx
Cano mac Gartnáin, hero of *Scéla Cano meic Gartnáin*: 43–44, 242, 342–75
Carney, James: 6, 38, 40, 45, 48–49, 66, 68, 87, 113–14, 157, 166, 202, 204, 220, 264, 270, 311, 343, 348, 353, 356–58, 374–75
Cashel, Munster seat of kingship: 53, 63, 163, 247, 283–84, 287, 289–92, 299, 305, 308, 519n17, 538n8
    kings of (*see* Corc mac Luigdech/ mac Láire; Óengus mac Nad-Fraích)
cath 'battle' (as a type of tale), pl. *catha*: 3, 175–76. *See also Cath Almaine; Cath Maige Mucrama; Cath Maige Tuired*
Cath Almaine ("The Battle of Allen"): 41, 423, 439–446, 499
Cathbad, Ulster Cycle druid, father of Conchobor: 226, 241, 243, 264–65, 272–74, 368
Cath Maige Mucrama ("The Battle of Mag Mucrama"): 330–41, 349, 495–96
Cath Maige Tuired ("The [Second] Battle of Mag Tuired"): 4–7, 42–49, 61–62, 76, 80–85, 95–100, 129–30, 135–54, 158, 176–77, 184, 217, 490. *See also* Bres; Fomoiri; Lug mac Céin; Túatha Dé Danann
cattle-raiding, incl. to inaugurate a reign (*crech ríg*): 88, 205, 230–31, 444. *See also* cows; *táin*; *Táin Bó Cúailnge*
cauldrons:
    of the Head of Annwfn, 31–32 (*cf.* Cormac mac Airt: relations with the Otherworld)
    of poetic knowledge, xix–xx

Celestine, Pope: 1, 174
Cenn Abrat, battle of (Éogan Mór vs. Lugaid Mac Con): 330–32, 335, 339, 341
W. *cerennyd* 'friendship, formal alliance': 32–33
Cernae, place in Meath: 347, 359, 541n13. *Cf.* birds
cert catha 'fair fight': 288. *Cf. fír fer*
ces noínden 'debility (of the Ulstermen)': xiv, 86, 175, 188–89, 198, 209–13, 216, 219, 239, 248, 267
Cet mac Mágach, Ulster Cycle champion of Connacht: 91. *See also Scéla Mucce Meic Da Thó*
Chadwick, Hector Munro, and Nora Kershaw Chadwick: 40, 201, 324–25, 505n31, 527n1, 539n24
champion's portion (*mír curad*): 91
charioteers: 53, 188, 191–92, 216, 220–22, 224–25, 234, 243, 268–69, 275, 535n54. *See also* Lóeg
chariots: 275, 337, 435–36, 445
 in challenge, 233
 in royal inauguration, 57, 179–81
Charles-Edwards, Thomas: 6–7, 31, 42, 73–75, 77–79, 217, 223–24, 246, 377, 383, 388, 395, 397, 441, 485, 488, 490, 495
Christ. *See* Jesus Christ
Christians/Christianity: xiii, 1–3, 7, 38–39, 49, 103, 113, 163, 174, 204, 214, 303, 326–27, 353, 486
 contact with paganism, 35–36, 48, 53, 63, 118, 148
 and law, 123–24, 230–31, 443
 See also God (Christian); Jesus Christ; Latin literacy and learning; monastic churches/culture/scools; saints; *cf.* paganism

Church. *See* Christians/Christianity; saints; three: threefold death
Cian, father of Lug: 5
Cian, son of Ailill Ólomm: 464=482
Ciarán (saint), of Clonmacnoise: 111–12
Cín Dromma Snechta(i), lost ms.: 272, 399–421
client (*céile*), clientship (*céilsine*): 2–3, 66–69, 83, 88–89, 212, 224–25, 229–30, 254
Cnogba (Knowth): 155–64, 491. *See also* Bruig na Bóinne
Cobthach Cóel, fratricidal king of Brega in *Orgain Denna Ríg*: 265, 422–38, 499
coibche 'bride-price; dowry': 180–81, 229, 251, 253, 453=470, 530n34
coire sois 'the Cauldron of Knowledge': xix–xx
Colgu, son of Marcán, suitor of Créd in *Scéla Cano meic Gartnáin*: 347–48, 351–53, 356, 359–61, 363
Colla Uais and Colla Menn, grandsons of Cormac mac Airt: 310, 312, 314
Colmán mac Lénéni, poet: 2–3
Columba (saint). *See* Colum Cille
Colum Cille (Columba) (saint): 2, 14–15, 104–6, 111, 263–64. *See also Amra Choilm Cille*
Common Celtic:
 language, 73–75, 488
 law and social institutions, 30, 124
 narrative survivals, 38–39, 174
compert 'conception, birth' (as a type of tale), pl. *comperta*: 3, 8, 175, 274. *See also Compert Con Culainn; Compert Conchobuir*
Compert Conchobuir ("The Conception and Birth of Conchobor"): 271–74, 494. *See also* Conchobor mac Nessa

Compert Con Culainn ("How Cú
    Chulainn Was Begotten"): 7–8,
    53–56, 72, 152, 158, 164, 274. *See
    also* Cú Chulainn
Conailla Medb míchura (early poem:
    "Medb enjoined evil contracts"):
    220
Conaire Mór 'the Great,' king of
    Tara, son of Mess Búachalla
    and a bird-man, putative son
    of Étarscelae: 12–14, 175,
    402–3, 498.
    conception, birth, accession, 57–58,
        63, 100, 144, 148, 181, 183,
        247–48, 404 (*see also* birds; *geis*;
        inauguration)
    exemplary rule, 24–25, 33, 54–56,
        58–59, 88 (*see also fír flathemon/
        fír flatha*; Golden Age; *síd*
    failure and death, 26–27, 59–62,
        98–99, 154, 335, 405, 407–8, 410,
        412–21, 489 (*see also díberg*;
        "single sin of the sovereign")
    See also Togail Bruidne Da Derga
Conall, son of Niall Noígiallach: 116
Conall Cernach, Ulster Cycle hero:
    8–9, 91, 197, 216–17, 262–63, 340
conception: by swallowing fly, 176–77.
    See also compert; *cf.* heroic
    biography
Conchobar Ruadh Mac an Bháird
    (bardic poet): 100
Conchobor mac Nessa, Ulster Cycle
    king of Ulster: 7, 175, 188–89,
    210, 219–220, 266, 493
    his birth-tale (*Compert Conchobuir*),
        272–74, 494
    children, 90, 200 (*see also* Cormac
        Conn Loinges; Follomon)
    and Cú Chulainn, 53–54, 71–72, 77,
        86–89, 93, 152, 193, 211–12,
        215–16, 222–26, 243–44, 276
    and Deirdriu, 90–91
    and Fergus mac Roích, 90–91,
        196–97, 219
    as judge, incl. taking the advice of
        druids, 139, 199–200, 222–24,
        228–29, 238–48, 368
    meaning of his name, 8
    and sister Dechtine, 8, 53,
condalbae 'love of kindred' (esp. as a
    decisive factor in the *Táin*): 9,
    89–90, 192–194, 200, 210–11,
    217, 232
Congal, Mael Fhothartaig's foster-
    brother: 377, 379–81, 386–87,
    390–97
Congal, Uí Néill king: 440
Connacht, province of: 170, 192–93,
    229–30, 251–52, 254–58, 295,
    343, 347–48, 352, 369
    manuscripts associated with,
        399–401, 404–6, 408–11
    rulers of (*see* Ailill mac Máta; Caier;
        Gúaire; Medb)
    See also Connachta
Connachta (Connaughtmen): 7, 54,
    86, 88, 91, 111, 175, 189–90,
    192–200, 203, 211, 215, 219, 231,
    256, 267, 372. *See also* Ailill mac
    Máta; Medb; *Táin Bó Cúailnge*
Conn Cétchatach 'of the hundred
    battles,' king of Tara, grandfather
    of Cormac mac Airt: 12, 21–23,
    61, 115–16, 128–29, 150–51, 158,
    247, 263, 283, 292, 322, 423,
    452=469. *See also Baile Chuinn*;
    Baile in Scáil; sovereignty; Uí
    Néill dynasty
contracts (*cor, córaidecht*, etc.):
    of clientship, or king and people,
        66–67, 82–83, 87, 90, 94, 98, 130,
        141, 147, 176, 519n30 (*see also*
        client; *fír flathemon/fír flatha*;
        folad; *frithfolad*)
    combat, 236 (*see also fír fer*)

contracts (*cor, córaidecht*, etc.) (*cont.*)
  love and marriage, 171–72, 229, 251–53, 258
  misleading yet binding, 180, 220, 441 (*see also bórama*; Bruig na Bóinne)
  with the Otherworld, 6, 24, 60, 110, 416, 418–19 (*see also fír flathemon/fír flatha*; *geis*; *síd*; "single sin of the sovereign")
conversion. *See* Christians/Christianity
Corc Duibne (from *Corcu Duibne*), incestuous son of Cairbre Músc: 157, 160–61, 164, 298–99, 317
Corc mac Luigdech/mac Láire 'son of the Mare,' first king of Cashel: 53, 63, 247
Corcu Duibne (Mod. Ir. *Corca Dhuibhne*), people of the Dingle Peninsula in modern Co. Kerry: 160, 464–65=482–83
Corcu Loígde, people of West Munster: 92, 160–63, 286, 289–90, 309, 315, 330, 339, 343, 349–52, 362, 372, 539n4. *See also* Dáire Donn; Illand mac Scanláin; Lugaid Mac Con
Cork, Co.: 324, 326, 451, 468
Cormac Conn Loinges, son of Conchobor: 194, 196–97
Cormac mac Airt/Ua Cuinn, legendary king of Tara: 10, 22, 58, 62, 88, 148–49 (*cf.* Lug mac Céin), 151–54 (*cf.* Lug mac Céin), 263, 487
  birth-tale, 128–29, 331–32, 341, 430
  and the Déisi, 283–88, 294–95, 304, 309–13, 315–16, 322, 328–29
  judgment correcting Lugaid Mac Con, 12, 139–40, 142, 144, 153–54, 330, 332–34, 336–38, 340–41
  relations with the Otherworld, 22–25, 31–33 (Cormac's Cup) (*see also Echtrae Chormaic*)
  wife and children, 22–23, 287–88, 308, 310, 312, 315–16, 328–29, 452–53=469–70, 455=472, 457–58=474–75, 459–61=477–79 (*see also* Ailbe; Cairbre Lifechair; Colla Uais and Colla Menn; Eithne Thóebfota; Gráinne)
Cormac mac Cuilennáin, author of *Cormac's Glossary*: 77, 302, 320, 323–24, 434
Cormac's Glossary. *See* Cormac mac Cuilennáin
cosmos: 22, 56, 64, 182, 208
cotach 'bond': 236
cows: 25, 97, 113–14, 161, 164, 189, 199, 239–40, 248, 257, 316, 350, 442. *Cf.* Cows of Aífe; *see also* cattle-raiding
Cows of Aífe (*Bae Aífe*), in *Fingal Rónáin*: 380–82, 391, 393, 396
Craiphtine, Labraid's harpist in *Orgain Denna Ríg*: 424, 427, 432–34. *See also* Ferchertne
Créd, beloved of Cano mac Gartnáin: 43–44, 343, 346–53, 356, 359–63, 368, 372
Crimthann, Leinster king, great-great-grandson of Fíachu ba Aiccid: 288–89, 292, 304–5, 308–11, 314–15, 323, 325, 327. *Cf.* Déisi
Críth Gablach ("The Branched Purchase"), law-text: 6–7, 230, 349, 351, 421
critical approaches to early Irish literature: ix–xvii, 36–52, 376–77
crows/scald-crows: 444–46
Crúachu/(Rath) Crúachain, seat of Connacht kingship: 7, 89, 171, 175, 252, 256, 258
  cave of, 337, 340

Cú Brettan, king of Fir Rois: 443.
  See also Blathmac, poet
Cú Chulainn 'the Hound of Culann,'
  gen. Con Culainn, Ulster Cycle
  hero, named Sétantae at birth:
  7–8, 40, 175, 219–220, 259–60
  'Boyhood Deeds' and relationship
    to uncle Conchobor and the
    Ulstermen: 8–9, 53–54, 71–72,
    76–77, 86–89, 93, 152, 190–91,
    193, 210–12, 215–16, 222–26,
    243–44, 264–65, 269–70, 276
  and charioteer Lóeg, 191–92,
    220–22, 224–25, 243, 268–69, 275
  conception, birth, and relationship
    to fathers Lug and Súaltaim, 7–8,
    53–56, 61–62, 85–87, 89,
    149–50, 152–53, 158, 189–90,
    197–98, 213–14, 248, 487
  defense of Ulster in the *Táin*, 7–9,
    14, 89–90, 175, 188–93,
    196–200, 203, 210, 215, 217,
    219–222, 226–28, 231–37, 240,
    248, 267–69,
  and Fergus mac Roích, 190–91,
    194–98, 216, 224, 232–36, 267,
    269
  as fertility symbol, Christ figure, etc.,
    x, 54, 152, 202, 209, 212–16, 262
  vs. Finn mac Cumaill, 10–11, 88
  his Otherworld journey (*Serglige
    Con Culainn*): 271, 275–79
cú glas 'gray dog, wolf' (person from
  outside Ireland living in a *túath*):
  78–79, 93. *Cf. ambue*
Cúl Dreimne, battle of: 111
cumachtae' (magic) power': 171–72,
  178, 181
Cúr mac Da Lath, unusually disgusting
  Ulster Cycle warrior: 188
curses, notably by clerics: 95–100 (*cf.*
  satire), 107–9, 111, 113–15, 120,
  392, 442–43, 488

cycles:
  Cycles of the Gods and Goddesses
    (Mythological Cycle), 3–7,
    129–30, 133–84
  Cycles of the Kings, 12–14, 41,
    281–446
  Fenian Cycle, 9–12, 42, 447–83
  in general, xviii, 3, 174–75, 485
    (*cf.* tale types)
  Ulster Cycle, 7–9, 40, 43, 49, 89–91,
    185–279

Da Derga 'Red God': 56, 175.
  See Togail Bruidne Da Derga
Dagdae, the, a.k.a. Eochaid Ollathair,
  of the Túatha Dé Danann: 130,
  138, 165, 168–72, 178–80, 182,
  184, 441
Dáire Donn, ancestor of the Corcu
  Loígde: 156, 160–61
Dáire mac Fiachna, owner of the bull
  Donn Cúailnge: 249–50
Dál Cais: 537n4
Dál Cuinn, descendants of Conn
  Cétchathach (incl. the Uí Néill):
  22, 61–62, 92, 149–51, 158–60,
  288, 330
Dál Fiachach Suidge, Déisi kindred
  descended from Fíachu Suidge:
  283, 287, 290–92, 303–7, 309,
  312–14, 317, 322, 325–27,
  329, 495. *See also* Áed Brosc;
  Cairbre Rigronn; *muintir
  Chairbre/Chairpre*
Dallán Forgaill, poet: 2. *See also Amra
  Choluim Chille*
dalta(e) 'fosterling.' *See* fosterage *and
  entries beginning with* "foster–"
dating:
  of *Aislinge Óenguso*, 166–67
  of *Cath Almaine*, 439
  of *Cath Maige Tuired*, 47–48, 135
  of early Irish literature in general, 1

dating (*cont.*)
  of "The Expulsion of the Déisi," 283–87
  of inscriptions, 2
  of the laws, 121–22
  of *Orgain Denna Ríg*, 423–24
  of *Táin Bó Cúailnge*, 220, 492
  of *TBDD* and *BUD*, 413
  of *Tóraíocht Dhiarmada agus Ghráinne*, 449–52=466–69
  See also *manuscripts* (early texts in late mss. are common)
debility (*ces*) of the Ulstermen. See *ces noínden*
De Chopur in da Muccida ("The Quarrel of the Two Swineherds," who become the bulls Finnbennach and Donn Cúailnge): 205, 208
De gabháil in tsída ("On the Taking of the *síd*"): 441
Deirdriu, Deirdre: 61, 194, 458=475. See also *Longes mac n-Uislenn*
Déisi, Munster people, and "The Expulsion of the Déisi": 160, 283–329
  cause of expulsion, 287–88
  settlement in Ireland, 288–92, 298–99, 303–6
  settlement in Wales, 285, 301–27
demons (*demna*): 277–79
  Satan himself, 346, 365
Derc Ferna, cave of (*Uaimh Dheirce Fearna*): 464–65=482–83
devil(s). See *demons*
de Vries, Jan: 62, 149, 438
Dían Cécht, Túatha Dé Danann physician: 47–49, 81, 137, 148, 179
Diarmaid Ó Duibhne, gen. Diarmada, Fenian Cycle hero: 150, 388, 449–465=466–483
Diarmait mac Cerbaill, Uí Néill king of Tara: 14, 102–3, 110–13, 115, 117. See also *three: threefold death*

Diarmait son of Áed Sláine, joint-king of Tara with Blathmac in *Scéla Cano meic Gartnáin*: 242, 343–47, 352, 356, 359, 365–74
díberg 'marauding': 12–14, 26, 98–99, 113, 403–4, 412–21
Díl, druid in *ED*: 316
Dillon, Myles: 28, 63, 138, 183, 247, 275–78, 285, 294, 302, 307, 358, 458=475, 461=478, 502n9, 503n36, 504n3, 519n17, 543n40
dinnshenchas 'place-name lore': 155–57, 160, 430, 434
disability. See *blemish*; *blinding*; *ces noínden*; *Labraid*; *leper*; *ríastrad*
dogs: 205, 225–26, 389, 391–92, 459=477
  in law, 226
  in metaphors, 15, 90, 93, 105, 200
  in personal names: 8–9, 11, 208, 225–26, 269
Donn, father of Diarmaid Ó Duibhne: 453=470, 457=473–74, 460=477
Donn, foster-brother (with Congal) of Mael Fhothartaig: 379, 390–91
Donn, perhaps equivalent to Dáire Donn or Donn Cúailnge, perhaps a god of the dead: 161
Donn Bó: 440, 442–46
Donn Cúailnge 'the Brown [Bull] of Cúailnge,' owned by Dáire mac Fiachna and sought by Medb in the *Táin*: 7, 161, 187–89, 205, 207–8, 219–220, 229–30, 249–50. Cf. *Finnbennach*; see *swineherds*
Donn Désa, sons of, foster-brothers of Conaire Mór. See *foster-brothers*
dowry. See *coibche*
dreams (*aislinge, taibsiu*, etc.): 8, 57, 107–9, 165–69, 259, 278, 328
drink. See *sovereignty*
drowning. See *three: threefold death*

druids: 76, 299, 316
  as pagan priests, champions of paganism: 63, 264
  in a parental role, 161, 181, 226, 273–74
  as prophets, diviners, interpreters of dreams and signs, 63, 108–9, 111–12, 233–34, 248, 264–65, 273–74, 403–4, 432, 493
  in (quasi-)legal proceedings, 199, 228, 238–47, 403–4, 493
Dublin, Co. and city: 56–57
Dubthach Dóel Ulad, Ulster exile: 208, 267
Dumézil, Georges:
  and animals: 205
  and the gods, 5–6, 61–62, 139–42, 145
  and Indo-European myth (esp. trifunctionalism), ix, 3, 42–43, 52, 208, 492
  and kings: 26–27, 58–62, 139–42, 335–36, 415–18
  and threefold death, 15, 103–6, 119–20
  and warrior heroes: 55, 62, 83, 115, 214, 499
Dumville, David N.: 503n42, 506n44, 545n20
Dyfed, southwest Wales: 31–33, 285, 301–27. *See also* Déisi; *Mabinogi*

Echaid Airem, king of Ireland: 177, 183, 402–4, 546n15
Echaid Allmuir, son of Art Corb, who settled in Dyfed: 285, 302, 304–8, 312–13, 318, 321, 323, 327
Echaid/Eochu Feidlech, king of Ireland: 23, 252, 254–55, 546n15
"Echaid's daughter," unnamed second wife of Rónán in *Fingal Rónáin*: 377–79, 381–97

echtra(e) 'expedition [to the Otherworld]' (as a class of tale), pl. *echtrai*: 3, 25, 31, 175–76. *See also Echtrae Airt; Echtrae Chonnlai; Echtrae Chormaic*
Echtrae Airt 'The Adventure of Art': 23
Echtrae Chonnlai 'The Adventure of Conlae': 19–22, 29, 486
Echtrae Chormaic 'The Adventure of Cormac': 22–23, 27–32
Egerton 88, London, British Library ms.: 21, 399–401. Contents incl. *Togail Brudne Uí Dergae*
Egerton 1782, London, British Library ms.: 166–67. Contents incl. *Aislinge Óenguso; Táin Bó Cúailnge*
Eithne, daughter of Balar (Fomoire champion) and mother of Lug: 81
Eithne daughter of Cummascach, first wife of Rónán in *Fingal Rónáin*: 384
Eithne Thóebfota, wife of Cormac mac Airt: 22–23, 502n20
Eithne Uathach 'E. the Terrible,' cannibalistic Déisi fosterling: 284, 289–91, 298–99, 305, 307–10, 494
Elatha(n) of the Fomoiri, father of Bres: 4, 67, 80–82, 98, 137–38
Elcmar, original possessor of Bruig na Bóinne: 130, 178–80
Emain Macha 'the Twins of Macha,' seat of Ulster kingship: 7, 53–54, 86–87, 93, 152, 175, 190–91, 193, 197, 211–13, 222, 239, 242, 276
Emer, wife of Cú Chulainn: 8, 56, 190, 278
énflaith 'bird-reign' (of Conaire): 24, 58, 415. *See also* birds; Conaire Mór
Énnae Cennselach, great-grandson of Fíachu ba Aiccid: 304, 311, 325
Éogabul son of Dergabul, Munster *síd*-dweller, father of Áne: 335–36

Éogan, son of Niall Noígiallach: 116
Éoganachta, Munster people
 descended from Éogan Mór: 92,
 162–63, 284, 287, 289 (incl.
 subgroups), 290–92, 305–6, 324,
 330. See also Cashel
Éogan and Ross, nephews of Óengus
 Gaibuaifnech in *ED*: 285–86
Éogan Mór mac Ailella, foster-brother
 of Lugaid Mac Con in *CMM*: 12,
 76–77, 331–32, 335, 339, 341
epic, as genre: 86, 203, 208–9, 212,
 237. See also *Táin Bó Cúailnge*
Érainn, Munster people: 324, 402
Ériu of the Túatha Dé Danann,
 mother of Bres: 4, 81, 137
Ernbrand of the Déisi, with three
 daughters married by Crimthann:
 288–89, 308–9, 315
Étaín, gen. Étaine, of the Túatha Dé
 Danann: 23, 130, 173–74,
 176–84, 402–4
Etarscélae, king of Tara, putative father
 of Conaire Mór: 13, 23–24, 57,
 183, 402, 412
Ethal Anbúail, Connacht *síd*-dweller,
 father of Cáer Ibormeíth: 165,
 170–72
eulogy (*formolad*)/praise (*molad*): 2–3,
 124, 141–42, 147, 190, 259–60,
 262–70, 432–33. Cf. satire; see also
 Amra Choluim Chille
evil eye. See Balar
Ewein Vreisc: 319–21. Cf. Áed Brosc
exemplary myth: 44–45, 62, 129,
 135–54, 431. See also *Cath Maige
 Tuired*; Lug mac Céin
exile:
 of Cano mac Gartnáin, 342–47
 of the Déisi and others, 290, 305,
 308–9, 312
 of Labraid Loingsech, 428, 437
 legal terms, 79–80, 328–29
 of Lugaid Mac Con, 92, 331, 341
 of Mael Fhothartaig, 377, 384,
 388–89
 of other kings, 111, 161, 403
 from Ulster, 86, 90–91, 175,
 194–97, 219, 222, 231, 267, 269
 (see also *Longes mac n-Uislenn*)
exile-and-return formula: 161,
 342–43. See also Cano mac
 Gartnáin; Cormac mac Airt;
 Lugaid Mac Con
"The Expulsion of the Déisi." See Déisi

fairies, fairy hills. See *síd*; Túatha Dé
 Danann
Falartach, dispossessed young man
 helped by St. Patrick: 96–99
Fearghas. See Fergus mac Roích
Fedelm (Feidelm), poet-prophetess in
 the *Táin*: 188, 210, 267, 368, 443
Fedelm Nóichride, daughter of
 Conchobor and Cú Chulainn's
 lover: 190, 217
Feradach Find Fechtnach, addressee of
 Audacht Moraind. See *Audacht
 Moraind*; "Mirror of Princes"
Ferchertne, Labraid's poet in *Orgain
 Denna Ríg*: 423–24, 427–28,
 432–34
Ferches mac Commáin, warrior-poet,
 henchman of Ailill Ólomm:
 334–35
Fer Diad, Cú Chulainn's foster-brother:
 9, 14, 189, 192–93, 236, 268
Fergal son of Máel Dúin, Uí Néill
 king: 439–46
Fergne, Conchobor's physician: 168–69
Fergus mac Roích, Ulster Cycle hero,
 exiled former king of Ulster: 86,
 219, 262–63 (as Fearghas)
 relationship with Conchobor and
 the Ulstermen, 90–91, 190,
 194–95, 199–200, 210–11, 232,
 240, 267 (see also *condalbae*;
 warning)

relationship with Cú Chulainn, 190–91, 196–98, 216, 224, 232–36, 267, 269 (*see also* *fír fer*)
relationship with Medb, 86, 89, 188, 195, 211, 216–17, 231
Fíachu ba Aiccid, Leinster king: 288, 304, 311, 314
Fíachu Muillethan, son of Éogan Mór: 341
Fíachu Sraiphtine: 310, 312, 314
Fíachu Suidge, Déisi ancestor, brother of Conn Cétchathach: 283, 290, 292, 303, 313, 322
fían 'warband': 9, 11–13, 88–89, 175, 463=481
Fíana 'Finn's warband': 9–11, 458–60=475–77, 463–64=480–83
fief. *See* rath
fili 'poet,' pl. *filid*: 2–3, 38, 44–45, 95–100, 124–26 (*see also* law), 129, 140–42, 485. *See also* Blathmac, poet; eulogy; satire
Findchán, priest and lover of Áed Dub: 14–15, 104–6
Fingal, James Macpherson's character corresponding to Finn mac Cumaill: 10
fingal 'kin-slaying': 6–7, 68–69, 78–80, 107–10. *See also* Fingal Rónáin
Fingal Rónáin ("How Rónán Slew His Son"): 335, 358, 360, 376–98, 497
Fíngen. *See* Fergne
Finnabair, daughter of Ailill and Medb: 192
Fínnachta, Uí Néill king: 116, 440–41
Finnbennach 'the White-Horned [Bull]' belonging to Ailill of Connacht: 229. *Cf.* Donn Cúailnge; *see also* swineherds

Finn mac Cumaill (Fionn Mac Cumhaill, Finn McCool): xii, 9–11, 148–49, 153, 175, 452–65=468–483. *See also* *Tóraíocht Dhiarmada agus Ghráinne*
Fionn Mac Cumhaill. *See* Finn mac Cumaill
Fir Bolg, inhabitants of Ireland before the Túatha Dé Danann: 4, 81, 136
fír catha 'truth of battle': 152. *Cf.* *fír fer*
fír fer 'ordeal by battle, fair play in combat' (lit. 'truth of men'): 31, 196–97, 221–22, 234–37. *Cf.* *cert catha*; *fír catha*
fír flathemon/fír flatha 'the truth and justice of the ruler': 12–13, 22, 26–28, 56, 58, 62, 129, 138–40, 333, 351, 414–15. *Cf.* *gáu flatha/flathemon*; "single sin of the sovereign"
Fir Morca, people of West Munster: 424, 428
Fir Rois, people of what is now Co. Monaghan. *See* Blathmac, poet; Cú Brettan
Fís Conchobuir ("Conchobor's Vision"): 525–26n11
fóesam. *See* protection
folad '(legal or social) obligations': 6, 67, 83–84, 141
Follomon, son of Conchobor mac Nessa: 211
Fomoiri, sg. Fomoire, opponents of the Túatha Dé Danann: 4–5, 46, 80–82, 84–85, 98, 135–38, 143–45, 147–48, 152, 174. *See also* Balar; Elatha(n) of the Fomoiri
fool. *See* jester
forad 'mound, seat': 30, 33, 503n52. *Cf.* W. *gorsedd*
Forad son of Art Corb, in *ED*: 285, 287–88, 304, 312

fosterage:
  of Cano mac Gartnáin, 342–43, 363–64
  as a social institution, 71, 488, 531n49
foster-brothers:
  of Conaire Mór, 13–14, 26, 57, 59–61, 99, 410, 412–21
  of Cú Chulainn (*see* Fer Diad)
  of Mael Fhothartaigh (*see* Congal, Mael Fhothartaig's foster-brother; Donn, foster-brother)
foster-daughters:
  of the Déisi (*see* Eithne Úathach)
  of herdsmen (*see* Mess Búachalla)
foster-fathers:
  of Cormac mac Airt, 128–29, 331 (*see* Lugaid Mac Con)
  of Cú Chulainn (*see* Fergus mac Roích)
  of Diarmaid Ó Duibhne (*see* Aonghus an Bhrogha; Óengus the Mac Óg)
  of Labraid Loingsech, 436–37
  of Lugaid Mac Con (*see* Ailill Ólomm)
  of Óengus (*see* Midir of Brí Léith)
foster-mothers: 163
  of Lugaid Mac Con (*see* Sadb)
foster-sons:
  of Ailill Ólomm (*see* Lugaid Mac Conn)
  of Cú Chulainn (*see* Lugaid Réoderg)
  of Fergus (*see* Cú Chulainn)
  of Óengus Gaibuaifnech (*see* Corc Duibne)
fratricide. *See* Cobthach Cól; *fingal*
friendship:
  of Cano mac Gartnáin and Illand mac Scanláin (*see* Illand mac Scanláin)
  of Pwyll and Arawn (*see* Pwyll)
  See also cairdes, condalbae

frithfolad '(legal or social) counter-obligations.' *See folad*
Fuamnach, first wife of Midir: 176–77, 181–83

gae bolga, Cú Chulainn's special weapon: 9
Gailióin, Leinster contingent on the *Táin*: 194–95, 231–32, 256
Galway, Co.: 331
gat 'thieving': as a prelude to *díberg* in *TBDD*, 26, 98–99, 412–21
gáu flatha/flathemon 'ruler's falsehood': 139, 333. *Cf. fír flathemon/fír flatha*
Gearóid Iarla, poet: 455=472
géim n-áilgeso 'a shout of importuning': 228, 233–34, 248
geis 'taboo, (supernatural) prohibition,' pl. *gessi/geisi*: 13–14, 24–27, 33, 57–61, 63, 99, 110, 238, 241–43, 404–5, 412–20
genealogy, genealogical tracts: 55, 92, 230, 255–56, 260–61, 265, 334, 403, 433
  of the Déisi, 285, 292, 293–94, 302–7, 311–14, 318–22, 325–26, 495
  of the Uí Néill, 117–18
Generation Conflict: 46–49
generosity. *See* gift-giving; hospitality
genres. For the generic classification of early Irish literature, *see* tale types
gift-giving: 66–67, 69, 141, 192, 224–25, 229–30, 252–54, 349, 445. *See also folad*; *cf.* hospitality
Giolla Brighde Mac Con Midhe, bardic poet: xiv, 259–65, 269–70
Giolla Commáin Ua Conghalaigh, medieval scholar: 399–400
Giolla Íosa Mac Fhir Bhisigh, scribe: 423
Giolla Riabhach Ó Cléirigh, scribe: 47–48

God (Christian), direction intervention by: 63, 66, 162–63, 345–46, 370, 445
goddesses. *See* Badb; Boann; Étaín; Eithne Thóebfota; Morrígan. *See generally síd*; sovereignty; Túatha Dé Danann
classical (*see* Aphrodite)
gods. *See* Da Derga; Dagdae; Dían Cécht; Donn, perhaps equivalent to Dáire Donn; Elcmar; Lug mac Céin; Manannán mac Lír; Midir of Brí Léith; Núadu; Óengus the Mac Óg. *See generally síd*; Túatha Dé Danann
"Otherworld God" theory of T. F. O'Rahilly, 207–8
See also Fomoiri; theomachy
Gods and Goddesses, Cycles of. *See under* cycles
goire 'filial support and devotion': 72, 85, 87, 91–94, 511n33. *See also gormac*
Golden Age:
under Conaire Mór, 12–13, 24–25, 27, 29, 57–59, 88, 110, 175, 412, 415
under Cormac mac Airt, 62, 88, 151–52, 175
under Lug or in Otherworld, 151–52, 275–77 (*see also síd*)
Goll mac Morna. *See* Áed (Goll) mac Morna
gormac 'adopted son (to support the adopter); sister's son': 72–73, 75–77, 80–82, 85, 92–94. *See also* Bres, Cú Chulainn; *cf. nia*
W. *gorsedd* '(Otherworldly) mound': 30–34. *Cf. forad; see also síd*
Grác, herdsman of Moling: 112–15
Gráinne, daughter of Cormac mac Airt: 388, 449–65=466–83
Gray, Elizabeth: 4, 489–90, 513n89

Greene, David: 157, 162, 413, 416, 423, 425–26, 429, 431
Gúaire, king of Connacht in *Scéla Cano meic Gartnáin*: 262, 343, 347–49, 352, 356, 359–61, 365, 370–74, 431
Gúbretha Caratniad ("The False Judgments of Caratnia"), law-text: 246–47

Hafgan, king of Annwfn, rival of Arawn: 31–32
hand, loss of. *See* Findchán; Núadu
hanging. *See* three: threefold death
Harley 5280, London, British Library ms.: 47–48, 136–36. Contents incl. *Cath Maige Tuired*
harpists. *See* Craiphtine
heads:
of animals on humans, 107
other beheading, 113, 130, 183, 338–39
other trauma, 47, 108, 111–12, 145, 227, 351, 362, 464–65=482–83
polycephalic monsters, 340, 464–65=482–83
severed, as trophies, 171, 267, 390, 397, 445
severed yet speaking, 14, 60, 199, 239, 241, 443–446
struck in warning, 242, 366, 436
with three faces, 55
W. *hedd* 'peace,' contrasted with *sedd* 'seat': 30–34
herald. *See* Mac Roth
hero:
concept of, xii, 8, 31–32, 44–45, 51–64, 93, 145–54, 175, 197–98, 215–17, 259, 262–65, 270, 298, 487–88
conforms to mythological pattern, 10, 53–54, 62, 85, 136–54, 208–9, 212–17 (*see also* Dumézil; heroic biography)

hero (cont.)
  king hero vs. warrior hero, 8, 52–54, 56, 76, 200, 212, 298, 351
  major examples (see Bres; Conaire Mór; Cormac mac Airt; Cú Chulainn; Finn mac Cumaill; Lug mac Céin)
  "of the tribe" vs. "outside the tribe," 11–12, 88, 93, 175 (see Sjoestedt)
  and the Otherworld (see síd)
Heroic Age: 3, 7, 40–41, 89, 125, 201–2, 204–5, 275, 277–78. See also epic
heroic biography (esp. conception, birth, and childhood): 8–13, 31–32, 53–58, 84–86, 93, 137, 148–49, 152–54, 189–90, 215–17, 322, 364, 438
  major examples (see Bres; Conaire Mór; Cormac mac Airt; Cú Chulainn; Finn mac Cumaill; Lug)
Homer: 204, 236, 264–265
homosexuality: 14–15, 104–6
honor: 42, 88, 269, 370, 437, 487
  fear of losing, 192–93, 197, 227, 369, 374 (see also satire)
  honor-based pledges, 171–72, 190, 382, 394, 407–8, 410, 441
  violations of, 111, 175, 183, 366 (see also hospitality; protection)
honor-price (díre, eneclann, lóg n-enech), i.e., possession of legal rights: explicitly referenced, 217, 221–22, 251, 268
horses: 54, 61, 199, 233, 239, 334–36, 389
  as gifts, 349, 445
  in legal proceedings, 540n10
  in metaphors, 89, 159, 188

hospitality: 53, 114, 192, 225, 242–43, 314, 344–50, 361, 364–65, 370–74, 385, 389–90
  failure to provide, 82, 96–99, 137–38, 141
  prelude to killing, 92, 333, 436–37
Hound of Culann. See Cú Chulainn
hounds. See dogs
Hull, Vernam: 272, 284–87, 293–94, 306–7, 314, 316, 404, 535n2
hunters/hunting: 3, 9, 11, 106, 159, 175, 221, 372, 377–78, 380, 389, 391–92, 396, 457=474, 459–61=477–79, 464=481

.i. ('i.e., id est; ed ón'): 379–83
Iliach, grandfather of Ulster Cycle hero Lóegaire Búadach: 72
Iliad. See Achilles; Homer
Illand mac Scanláin, king of the Corcu Loígde in *Scéla Cano meic Gartnáin*: 343, 349–53, 362–65, 368, 372–74
imbas forosnai 'great knowledge which illuminates' i.e. prophetic power: 210. Cf. prophecies
Imbolc (February 1): end of the *ces nóinden*, 86, 210
immram 'sea-voyage' (as a type of tale), pl. *immrama*: 3, 24–25, 175–76. See also *Immram Brain*
Immram Brain 'The Voyage of Bran': 24
inauguration, royal: 24, 28, 57, 88–89 (see cattle-raiding), 181, 247, 362, 427 (see Tara: Feast of Tara), 433. See also sovereignty
incest: 160, 183
Indo-European:
  kinship system, 70–75 (see also avunculate)
  language, 33, 70–71, 73–75, 123, 207–8, 488

law, mores, social structure, 6, 28, 123, 204, 264, 269
mythology, esp. tripartite ideology (*see* Dumézil; heroic biography; oral tradition/orality)
ritual practices (*see* sacrifice)
Ingcél, British marauder in *TBDD*: 407–10. *See also díberg*
Irish language: literacy in, 1–2, 38, 297. *See also* Cormac mac Cuilennáin; manuscripts; *cf.* Latin literacy and learning

Jackson, Kenneth: 33, 40, 43, 101–3, 105, 108, 167–68, 171, 203, 301–2, 320, 324, 516n7, 525n1, 527n1
jester (*drúth, oinmid*): 339, 379, 393, 397, 423, 434, 437, 440, 443–45, 497
Jesus Christ:
and Cú Chulainn, xiii, 202, 213–14, 217–18
as "sister's son" of the Jews or humanity, 6–7, 65–69, 77–80, 82, 87, 91, 217–18, 260 (*see also* Blathmac, poet)
and threefold death, 119
Jews, as characters in Biblical narrative: 66–69, 77, 80, 82, 91, 509n8, 510n14

keening the dead: xi, 65–66, 108, 147, 343, 351, 378, 390–92, 394–95, 397–98, 435–36, 446, 457=474, 461–63=478–80, 509n4
Kelleher, John: 163, 202, 213–14, 307
Kelly, Fergus: 22, 119–20, 122, 227, 231, 247, 490, 493, 518n20, 536n20, 548n22
Kenney, James F.: 38

Kerry, Co.: 298, 450–51=467–68
kings (*rí*, pl. *ríg*), kingship:
and the Church (*see* saints; three: threefold death; *cf.* druids)
disqualifying features (*see* blemish; *gáu flatha/flathemon*; satire; "single sin of the sovereign"; three: threefold death)
law and ideology, 6, 21–22, 41, 45, 58–60, 69, 76, 83, 126–30, 141–42, 146, 151–52, 181, 212, 214–16, 221, 430–31 (*see also rechtas*), 349, 351, 416–18, 421 (*see also* hero; inauguration; Tara)
negative models (*see* Bres; Conaire Mór; Lugaid mac Con)
and Otherworld (*see síd*; sovereignty)
positive features (*see ainmne; búaid; fír flathemon/fír flatha; folad*; gift-giving; hospitality)
positive models (*see* Cormac mac Airt; Lug mac Céin; Pwyll)
kinship: 6, 66, 68–94 (*see* avunculate; sister's son), 189, 192, 195, 200, 488
foster-kin (*see* fosterage *and entries beginning with* "foster–")
kin-love (*see condalbae*)
legal terms (*see ambue; amnair; athardae; cú glas; gormac; máithre; nia*)
Knott, Eleanor: 343, 413–14
Knowth (Cnogba). *See* Bruig na Bóinne; Cnogba

Labraid Loingsech, originally Labraid Móen 'the Dumb,' king of Leinster: 422–38, 498–99
Labraid ('Speaker') Móen ('Mute') Loingsech, protagonist of *Orgain Denna Ríg*: 432–38, 498–99
Laídshenchas Laigen 'historical lore of Leinster in verse': 423–24, 432

Laigin (Leinstermen): 41, 378, 384, 389 (*see also Fingal Rónáin*), 422–38 (*see also Orgain Denna Ríg*), 439–46 (*see also Cath Almaine*)
   and the Déisi: 288, 309, 328
lament. *See* keening the dead
"Lament of the Old Woman of Beare," poem: 156–57, 159, 161–64. *See also caillech*
lánríge 'full kingship' (in contrast to *rechtas*): 429–31
Latin literacy and learning: 1–3, 38–39, 95, 124, 163, 174, 380, 382–83. *See also .i.; ut diximus* formula
Laud Misc. 610, Oxford, Bodleian Library ms.: 284–88 (as L), 293, 300, 306–18 (as L). Contents incl. "The Expulsion of the Déisi"
law: 6, 121–30, 176, 247, 489–90
   archaism of, 122–24 (*cf.* Christians/Christianity; Indo-European)
   vs. civil unrest (*see cáin*)
   of kinship, 78–80, 200, 217
   of marriage, 249–58 (*see also coibche*)
   and poets, 124–28
   punishments, 119–20, 226
   specific principles cited (*see ambue; banchomarba;* blemish; *coibche; cú glas; fingal; fír fer; fír flathemon/ fír flatha; folad; géim n-áilgeso;* honor-price; hospitality; protection; *rath; rechtas;* sureties; *tinchor; wergild*)
   specific texts (*see Bretha Nemed; Cáin Fhuithirbe; Críth Gablach; Gúbretha Caratniad; Senchas Már; Uraicecht Bec; Uraicecht na Ríar; cf. Audacht Morainn*)
   in *Táin Bó Cúailnge*, 219–58

Lebor Gabála Érenn ("The Book of the Taking of Ireland/Book of Invasions"): 4, 136, 422–23, 426, 485
Lebor na hUidre, Dublin, RIA ms.: 156–57, 271–72, 276, 284, 293–300, 306, 316–17, 400–11, 413, 418–19. Contents incl. "Expulsion of the Déisi," *Táin Bó Cúailgne, Togail Bruidne Da Derga, Togail Brudne Uí Dergae*
   scribes (A, H 'the Interpolator,' and M 'Mael Muire'), 294, 299–300, 504n8
   sources (*see Cín Dromma Snechta[i]*)
Leinster, Leinstermen. *See* Laigin
leper: 442–43
Leth Cuinn 'Conn's Half, i.e. the northern half of Ireland,' named for Conn Cétchathach: 423, 439–40, 443. *Cf.* Uí Néill dynasty
Liber Flavus Fergusiorum: 284, 287, 306–8, 316. *See* manuscripts: of "The Expulsion of the Déisi"
literacy. *See* Irish language; Latin literacy and learning
literary criticism. *See* critical approaches to early Irish literature
litotes (understatement for rhetorical effect): 193
Lóeg, Cú Chulainn's charioteer: 191–92, 220–22, 224–25, 243, 268–69, 275
Lóegaire, son of Niall Noígiallach: 117
Lóegaire Búadach 'the Victorious,' Ulster Cycle hero: 72
Lóegaire Lorc, King Cycle king of Leinster/Ireland: 424–28, 432, 434–37
Lóegaire mac Néill, king of Tara at the time of Patrick: 119

Loingsech, Uí Néill king: 440
Lom Laine: 452–53=469–70. *Cf.* Diarmaid Ó Duibhne
lommrad 'laying bare': 144, 330–41, 349
Longes mac n-Uislenn ("The Exile of the Sons of Uisliu"): 61, 90–91, 194, 368, 388
love:
  as a basis for providing help, 242
  for foster-kindred, 14, 26, 59, 189
  for Ireland, 92
  for kindred (*see condalbae*)
  love-pairings (*see* Cano mac Gartnáin *and* Créd; Cú Chulainn *and* Emer; Deirdriu *and* Noísiu; Diarmaid Ó Duibhne *and* Gráinne; Étaín *and* Midir of Brí Léith; Labraid *and* Moriath; Óengus the Mac Óg *and* Cáer Iborméith)
  love-sickness, 167–69, 177
  love triangle/quadrangle, 91, 348, 356
  for a person one has never met (*serc écmaise* 'a love of absence' in *Aislinge Óenguso*), 169–70, 347, 359, 365–66, 368, 389
  sexual pairings (*see* homosexuality; sex)
Lugaid (Loígde) Cosc, Corcu Loígde judge: 286, 289–91
Lugaid Loígde, ancestor of the Corcu Loígde: 160, 524n47
Lugaid Mac Con: 330–41
  his false judgment as king of Tara, 12, 139–40, 142, 144, 153–54, 332–34, 337
  his killing by Ailill Ólomm, 92, 332–34, 336
  texts legitimizing his reign, 151, 160
Lugaid mac Nóis (Munster king, in the *Táin*): 232

Lugaid Réoderg (Cú Chulainn's foster-son): 275–77
Lugh: 262–63, 270 (*see also* Lug mac Céin)
Lughnasadh, festival on August 1: 145
Lug mac Céin 'son of (father) Cían'/mac Eithlenn 'son of (mother) Eithliu'
  compared to Finn mac Cumaill, 10, 149, 153
  contrasted with the negative model of Bres, 84–85, 143, 147, 153–54, 176
  as Cú Chulainn's father and prototype, 7–8, 53–56, 62, 86–87, 89, 148–49, 150, 152, 190, 197–98, 213–14
  as a legitimator of sovereignty and model for kings, 61–62, 148–52, 154, 158–60 (*see also Baile in Scáil*)
  as a pre-Christian/pan-Celtic god, 4, 54–55, 136, 148, 155–61, 182
  as a Túatha Dé Danann hero in his own right, 4–6, 62, 81, 84–85, 136, 138, 140, 143–48, 176, 182, 262–63, 270, 490

W. *Mabinogi*, Four Branches of the: 30–34
Mac Airt, Seán: 44
Mac Cana, Proinsias: 4, 156–58, 204, 215–16, 273, 419, 423, 432, 433, 451=468, 464–65=483
Mac Con. *See* Lugaid Mac Con
Mac Glass, Mael Fhothartaig's jester: 379, 393. *See also* jester
Mac Mathúna, Liam: 240
MacNeill, Eoin: 77, 291, 304, 322, 326, 512n50, 513n80, 537n3, 538n7, 548n22
MacNeill, Máire: 145
Macpherson, James: 10

macrad 'boy-troop' (of Ulster): 86, 222–24
Mac Roth, Ulster Cycle Connacht herald: 88, 193, 224–25, 234–35
Mael Fhothartaig, son of King Rónán of Leinster: 360, 377–98
Mael Muire mac Célechair, scribe: 294, 299–300. See also *Lebor na hUidre*
Mag Mell 'Plain of Delights': 29. See also *síd*
Mag Mucrama:
  battle of (Art mac Cuinn and Éogan Mór vs. Lugaid Mac Con), 12, 92, 330–31, 334, 341
  supposed origin of name, 332, 337–38, 340–41
Mag nInis, in County Down, home of Étaín's father Ailill and of Bres: 177, 180
Mag Rath, battle of: 115
Mag Tuired (Moytirra):
  first battle of (Túatha Dé Danann vs. Fir Bolg), 4, 136
  second battle of (Túatha Dé Danann vs. Fomoiri) (*see Cath Maige Tuired*)
Maine Milscothach 'Honey–Words,' son of Ailill and Medb: 407–10
máithre 'maternal kin,' 68, 77, 81–82
Manannán mac Lír, king of *Tír Tairngiri*: 23–24, 29, 31–32, 461=479
manuscripts (incl. recensions, transmission): 37–39, 42–43, 46, 121–22 (*see also* law), 295, 353–57, 505n2 (*cf.* oral tradition/orality)
  of *Aislinge Óenguso*, 166–67
  of *Cath Almaine*, 439, 444–45
  of *Cath Maige Mucrama*, 330–31
  of *Cath Maige Tuired*, 47–48, 135–36,
  of "The Expulsion of the Déisi," 283–87, 293–300, 306–18
  misc. variants in, 21, 55, 75–76, 157
  of *Orgain Denna Ríg*, 423–27
  of *Scéla Cano meic Gartnáin*, 342–43, 353–57
  significant examples (*see* Book of Leinster; Book of Uí Maine; *Cín Dromma Snechta[i]*; Egerton 88; Egerton 1782; Harley 5280; Laud Misc. 610; *Lebor na hUidre*; *Liber Flavus Fergusiorum*; Rawlinson B 502; Yellow Book of Lecan)
  of *Táin Bó Cúailnge*, 166–67, 220, 239, 244–46 (*see also Táin Bó Cúailnge*: recensions of)
  of *TBDD* and *BUD*, 399–411, 413, 419,
  of *Tóraíocht Dhiarmada agus Ghráinne*, 449–52=466–69, 459=476
  use of *.i.*, 379–83
  See also dating
Marcán, father of Colgu in *Scéla Cano meic Gartnáin*: 347–48, 351–52, 356, 359–61
marriage. *See coibche*; law; love
Martin, B. K.: 163
Martin, Bernard: 236
Mary, mother of Jesus: 6–7, 65–66, 68–69, 77–78. *See also* Blathmac, poet
Máta Muirisc, mother of Ailill mac Máta: 254–55
McCone, Kim: xvi, 12, 70, 88, 93, 109, 113, 142, 214, 413, 417–18, 420, 430, 485–88, 490
McManus, Damian: 2, 486, 493–94
Meath, Co., and early province: 86, 155, 157, 177, 197, 232, 283, 287, 293, 303–6, 313, 315–17, 322–25, 347
Medb, Ulster Cycle queen of Connacht: 7, 86, 175
  attitude to Cú Chulainn, 191, 267–69
  in other texts, 166, 170–72, 337–38
  relationship with Fergus mac Roích, 86, 89, 188, 195, 211, 216–17, 231

relationship with husband Ailill, 195, 216–17, 229–30, 249–58
in the *Táin*, 89, 187–95, 198–200, 205, 210, 216–17, 219–21, 224, 226, 229–30, 231–32, 234–36, 240, 249–58, 267–69, 368, 443
Meid, Wolfgang: 49
Meillet, Antoine: 33
Mess Búachalla 'the Herdsman's Fosterling,' mother of Conaire Mór: 23, 57, 402–3
Mess Corb: 285, 313
Meyer, Kuno: 161–62, 288, 290, 293, 306–7, 312, 320, 324, 327, 329, 420, 453=470, 545n20
Míach, son of Dían Cécht: 47–49, 137, 148
mice: 339, 496
Midir of Brí Léith, of the Túatha Dé Danann, husband of Étaín: 130, 174, 176–84, 402
midlach 'non-warrior; coward, weakling': 222
Miller, Molly: 302–3, 319–21, 323, 326–27
mimetic approach. *See* critical approaches to early Irish literature
"Mirror of Princes" (*Speculum Principum*): 12–13, 247. *See also Audacht Moraind*
Moling (saint): 102–3, 113–14, 441–43
monastic churches/culture/schools: 15, 38–39, 44–45, 47–48, 62–63, 274, 354, 505n22. *Cf.* Christians/Christianity; saints
Mongán, Moling's swineherd: 114, 516n7
Móraltach, the, Aonghus's (or Manannán's?) sword that Aonghus gives to Diarmaid: 461=479
Morann mac Moín, legendary judge. *See Audacht Moraind*

Moriath, daughter of Scoriath, Labraid's love interest in *Orgain Denna Ríg*: 424, 432–33
Morrígan 'the Spectral Queen,' war-goddess (one of three along with Badb and Nemain): 196, 217
muintir Chairbre/Chairpre 'Cairbre's folk': 313, 327–29. *See also* Cairbre Lifechair; Cairbre Rigronn
Muirchertach mac Erca, Uí Néill king of Tara: 103–4, 106–12, 115, 117. *See also* three: threefold death
Munster, Munstermen: 126, 139, 162, 165, 169–70, 177, 330–36, 384, 402, 405, 424, 427–28, 450=467, 495–96
and the Déisi, 286–87, 291–93, 304–6, 308, 320, 323–25
on the *Táin*, 175, 195, 200, 219, 231–32
See also Cashel; Corcu Loígde; Éoganachta
Murchad son of Bran, Leinster king: 439, 445–46
Murphy, Gerard: 4, 10, 42, 48–49, 116, 136, 153, 156, 163, 176, 204, 353–57, 449=466, 452–54=469–71, 456=474, 464–65=483
music, musicians: 243, 424, 432–34, 440, 445–46. *See also* Craiphtine
myth/mythology: 4, 29, 51–52, 125, 184, 438, 458=475
comparative, 5, 28, 208 (*see also* Dumézil; Indo-European)
mythological criticism, 42–44 (*see also* critical approaches to early Irish literature; Dumézil)
in *Táin Bó Cúailnge*, 201–18
See also exemplary myth; Generation Conflict; Golden Age; hero; sovereignty; theomachy; Waste Land theme

Mythological Cycle. *See* cycles: Cycle of the Gods and Goddesses

Nagy, Joseph F.: xvi, 10–11, 277, 463=481, 487, 492, 496, 535n54
Navan Fort. *See* Emain Macha
Nechta Scéne, sons of: killed by Cú Chulainn, 55, 214
Nemglan, king of Conaire's father's birds: 13, 24, 26–27, 57–58, 415, 418
Ness, mother of Ulster king Conchobor mac Nessa: 272–74
nia 'sister's son': 70, 73–80, 87, 94. *Cf. gormac*
Niall Caille, Uí Néill king: 118
Niall Noígiallach 'of the Nine Hostages,' ancestor of the Uí Néill dynasty: 116–18, 151, 159, 263
Ninión, druid in *BUD*: 403–4
Ní Shéaghdha, Nessa: 449–50=466–67, 454–56=470–73
Nodons, Celtic god: 48. *See also* Núadu
Noísiu: 61, 90–91, 388. *See also Longes mac n-Uislenn*
Núadu, king of the Túatha Dé Danann: 4–5, 46–49, 81, 84–85, 97, 137, 140, 143–45, 148, 150, 152
W. Nudd/Lludd: 18. *See also* Núadu

O'Brien, M. A.: 76, 117, 255, 311–13, 343, 438, 512n51, 513n85
Ó Broin, Tomás: 209–13
obscure speech: 128–29
Ó Coileáin, Seán: 162–63, 373
Ó Concheanainn, Tomás: 399–403, 406, 408, 410–11, 424–25, 504n8
O'Connor, Frank: 157, 162
Ó Corráin, Donnchadh: xvi, 201, 229, 251, 256–58, 292, 430–31, 494

Ó Cuív, Brian: 2, 115–18, 312
O'Donovan, John: 28
Odyssey. *See* Homer
Óengus Gaibuaifnech son of Art Corb, Déisi avenger: 283–86, 294–95, 298, 304, 310–13, 315, 328
Óengus mac Nad-Fraích, king of Cashel: 284, 289–92, 299, 305, 325
Óengus the Mac Óg ('Young Son'), son of the Dagdae: 130, 165–73, 176–84, 441
 as Aonghus an Bhrogha 'A. of Bruig na Bóinne,' 150, 454=471, 459–63=476–81
ogam inscriptions: 1–2, 75, 77, 79, 173, 232–33, 236–37, 301–2, 324–27, 495
Ogmae, champion of the Túatha Dé Danann: 147–48, 182
Oilill Óluim: 464=482. For the same character in earlier tales, *see* Ailill Ólomm
Oisín (Oisean, "Ossian"), son of Finn mac Cumaill: 9, 463–64=481–82
O'Leary, Philip: 216, 236, 413, 420, 487
ollam(h) 'chief poet': xx, 124–27, 264. *See also fili*; Senchán Torpéist
O'Rahilly, Cecile: 72, 197, 202, 205, 210–12, 233, 239–40, 245, 250, 254, 256–58, 532n2, 534n43
O'Rahilly, T. F.: 25–26, 42, 136, 148, 151, 153–54, 156–59, 181, 201, 203, 207, 216, 291–92, 322, 324, 414, 417, 426–28, 504n65, 506nn36, 40, 41, 538n20, 546n15
oral tradition/orality:
 and Christian literacy, 7, 37–40, 45–46, 48, 50, 63, 120, 174, 201–2, 204, 206, 217–18, 273–74, 353, 355–57, 450–51=467–68
 and law, 124, 328–29

and manuscript transmission, 356–57, 424
modern-day, 148, 450–51=467–68
orgain 'slaughter, destruction' (as a type of tale), pl. *oircne*: 3, 175–76. See also *Orgain Denna Ríg*
Orgain Denna Ríg ("The Destruction of Dinn Ríg"): 265, 422–38, 498–99
Ó Riain, Pádraig: 439, 445
Orthanach Ua Cóelláma, bishop of Kildare and poet: 432
Oscar, grandson of Finn mac Cumaill: 10, 463=481
Oskamp, Hans: 20, 299, 502n8, 504n8
Osraige, Munster region and people: 163, 284, 289–93, 299, 305, 308–9, 314, 317. *Cf.* Déisi
"Ossianic" poems of James Macpherson: 9–10
Ossianic Society: 449–50=466–67
Otherworld. *See síd*

paganism (pre-Christian beliefs specific to the Irish), reflected in literature: 29, 35–50, 63, 204–7, 264, 458=475. See also demons; druids; goddesses; gods; *cf.* Indo-European
Palladius: 1, 327
Parks, Ward: 236
Patrick (saint): 39, 95–100. *Cf.* Palladius
peace. *See cáin; fír flathemon/fír flatha; síd*
pedigree. *See* genealogy
penitentials: 65, 230–31
pigs: 22–23, 54, 205, 332, 337–41, 389, 508n85. See also *Scéla Mucce Meic Da Thó*; swineherds
  boar that killed Diarmaid Ó Duibhne, 454–55=471–72, 460=478
poets. *See fili*

Pokorny, Julius: 19–21, 75–76, 512n50
polygamy: 130, 155–56
praise. *See* eulogy
prohibition. *See* geis
propaganda, political claims: xvi, 41, 45, 162–63, 307, 321, 341, 424–28. See also Déisi; sovereignty; Uí Néill dynasty
prophecies: 38, 91, 172, 286, 299, 310, 329, 503n52
  of birth, 77, 81
  of death, 460=477
  of defeat in battle, 89, 188–89, 208, 210, 231, 267, 368, 442–44
  of heroic deeds, 264–65, 269
  of kingship, 23–24, 57–58, 128–29, 151, 160, 181, 248, 345, 370
  of own death, 362
  of threefold death, 15, 101–12, 114–17, 120
protection (*fóesam, snádud*, etc.):
  legal sense, 86–87, 91, 111, 130, 183, 222–24, 266, 345, 347, 356, 359, 361, 367, 370, 372, 374, 387, 534n43
  other senses, 147
  of society by *fír flathemon*, 26–27, 59–60, 139, 335, 415, 418
Proto-Indo-European. *See* Indo-European
Prthu, Hindu king: 24
Puhvel, Jaan: 202, 209, 507n82, 529n86
purity, required of poets: 127–28
"The Pursuit of Diarmaid and Gráinne." *See Tóraíocht Dhiarmada agus Ghráinne*
Pwyll, Prince of Dyfed: 30–34

queens: 12, 93, 176, 265, 273, 275, 331–34, 433
  in Irish law, 254–256
  See also "Echaid's daughter"; Étaín; Medb

Radner, Joan: xvi, 89, 101–3, 105, 110, 112, 115, 118, 120, 212, 490, 527n1
rape: 23–24, 57, 287–88, 304, 335–36, 393, 536n20
rath 'fief; grace': 2–3, 66–68, 229–30, 252–54. *Cf.* gift-giving
Rawlinson B 502, Oxford, Bodleian Library ms.: 284–88 (as R), 293, 300, 306–18 (as R), 422–24, 432, 505n22. Contents incl. "The Expulsion of the Déisi," *Orgain Denna Ríg*
recensions:
  of the *Táin* (*see Táin Bó Cúailnge*: recensions of)
  of other texts (*see* dating; manuscripts)
rechtaire 'steward.' *See* stewards
rechtas 'stewardship/subordinate kingship': 429–31
Redg, Ulster Cycle satirist: 226–28
Rees, Alwyn, and Brinley Rees: 3–4, 8, 10, 42, 110, 146, 201, 215, 298, 323, 457=474, 504n3, 505n25, 506n38, 512n68, 514n101, 515n125, 518n14
regicide: 15, 106, 109–110, 112, 436
remscéla 'prefatory tales (esp. of *Táin Bó Cúailnge*)': 7, 166, 172, 189–90, 194, 205, 208, 214–15, 402, 407, 411. *See also Compert Con Culainn; Compert Conchobuir; De Chopur in da Muccida; Longes mac n-Uislenn*
rhetoric:
  retoiric, gnomic verse, 247 (*see also rosc[ad]*)
  in sagas (*see* critical approaches to Early Irish literature; and esp. *Fingal Rónáin; Orgain Denna Ríg; Scéla Cano meic Gartnáin*)

rí 'king.' *See* kings
ríastrad '(Cú Chulainn's) distorting battle frenzy': 8, 191
ritual. *See* inauguration; sacrifice; Tara: Feast of Tara; three: threefold death; warfare; warning; *cf.* Dumézil; Indo-European; paganism
Rónán (saint): 115
Rónán mac Áeda, king of Leinster: 377–98. *See Fingal Rónáin*
rosc(ad) 'unrhymed alliterative gnomic verse,' pl. *roscada*: 39, 125, 211, 286, 310, 313, 317, 343. *Cf.* obscure speech
Roscommon, Co.: 7, 60, 175
Ross and Éogan. *See* Éogan and Ross
Rúadán (saint): 111–12
Rúadán of the Fomoiri: 514n105

sacrifice:
  animal, 161, 208–9
  human, 103–4, 118–20, 208, 499 (*see also* Dumézil; jester)
Sadb (Sadhbh), wife of Ailill Ólomm: 76–77, 79, 92, 464=482
saints: 3, 326–27. *See also* Adomnán; Ciarán; Colum Cille; Moling; Patrick; Rónán, Rúadán
sám(chaire) 'ease' (with sexual connotations, in *Fingal Rónáin*): 382, 392–94
Samain (November 1, "Hallowe'en"): 10–11, 54, 86, 107, 171, 179, 210, 275, 277
  start of the *ces noínden* and the *Táin*, 210, 219, 228, 241
Sanas Cormaic ("Cormac's Glossary"). *See* Cormac mac Cuilennáin
satire (*áer*): 95–100, 124, 127–28, 138, 140–42, 147, 154, 227, 263–64, 268–69, 367, 374, 488

satirists (sg. *cáinte*): 95, 140–41, 192, 226–28, 490. *See* Cairbre son of Étaín/Etan; Redg
Sayers, William: xvi, 15, 104, 119–20, 236, 240, 485–86, 490–91, 498, 527n21
Scáthach, woman-warrior, trainer of Cú Chulainn and Fer Diad: 9, 190
Scéla Cano meic Gartnáin ("The Story of Cano son of Gartnán"): 43–44, 242, 342–75, 496–97
Scéla Mucce Meic Da Thó ("The Story of Mac Da Thó's Pig"): 91, 107, 203, 205, 508n85
Scélshenchas Laigen 'narrative historical lore of Leinster': 422, 424
Scoriath, king of the Fir Morca in *Orgain Denna Ríg*: 424, 432–33
Scotland (*Alba*): 10, 148, 160, 301–2, 363 (*see also* Cano mac Gartnáin), 389, 407–8, 450–51=467–68. *See also* Alba
scriptoria. *See* manuscripts; monastic churches/culture/schools
Senchán Torpéist, chief poet (*ollam*) of Ireland: 344, 347–49, 356, 371–72, 374, 496
senchas 'tradition, traditional lore.' *See dinnshenchas; Laídshenchas Laigen; Scélshenchas Laigen*
Senchas Fagbála Caisil ("The Story of the Finding of Cashel"): 247. *See also* Cashel
Senchas Már ("The Great Tradition"), collection of law-texts: 124
Senchas na Relec ("The History of Burial Places"): 158
Serglige Con Culainn ("The Wasting Sickness of Cú Chulainn"): 271–79, 494. *See also* Cú Chulainn
sét 'treasure; unit of value': 227–28
Sétantae, Cú Chulainn's birth name. *See* Cú Chulainn

sevens, events or time intervals in: 81–84, 107, 126–27, 163, 182, 190, 195, 231–32, 285, 289, 305, 309, 331, 337, 436, 455=472
sex:
  attempted seduction: 192, 361, 386–90
  false accusations, 113–14, 360–61, 378, 393–97, 459=476
  as metaphor for assuming sovereignty, 151, 161–64 (*see also caillech*; sovereignty)
  nonconsensual (*see* rape)
  sexual pairings, ad hoc to conceive a child (*see* Boann *and* Dagdae [*conceiving* Óengus the Mac Óg]; Cathbad *and* Ness [*conceiving* Conchobor]; Cú Chulainn *and* Aífe [*in* Tochmarc Emire]; Elatha(n) *and* Ériu [*conceiving* Bres]; *by* Éogan Mór mac Ailella [*conceiving* Fíachu Muillethan] *and* Art mac Cuinn [*conceiving* Conaire Mór] *with their hosts' daughters before the battle of* Mag Mucrama)
  sexual pairings, ongoing (*see* Áed Dub *and* Findchán; Fergus mac Roích *and* Medb; Muirchertach mac Erca *and* Sín; *cf.* love: love-pairings)
  sexual sin (*see* three: threefold death)
shame (*imdergad, mebul*, etc.): 8, 53, 160–61, 192, 227, 251, 269, 379, 388, 391, 394, 397. *See also* satire; *cf.* honor
Shannon (river): 347, 359
sheep: 12, 331–34, 341
síd 'Otherworld/peace; "fairy hill,"' gen. and pl. *síde*, abode of the Túatha Dé Danann:
  definition, 19–22, 27–30, 485
  location, 20, 28–29, 184, 486 (*see also* Bruig na Bóinne; Cnogba)

síd 'Otherworld/peace; "fairy hill,"' gen. and pl. *síde*, abode of the Túatha Dé Danann (*cont.*)
  relations with humans, 19–34, 57–58, 168–71, 183–84, 197, 212, 277, 334–38, 402–3, 461–2=479–80 (*see also fír flathemon/fír flatha*; Lug mac Céin; Óengus the Mac Óg; sovereignty)
  threatens humans, 10–11, 106–110, 278, 364 (*see also* birds; pigs)
  Cf. Annwfn; Tech nDuinn; *Tír Tairngiri*
Síd mBoadaig 'the *síd* of Boadach': 20, 29, 502n8
Sims–Williams: xvi, 319, 321, 429–31, 485–87, 489, 499, 527n14, 537n1, 549n6
Sín 'Storm,' woman who destroys Muirchertach mac Erca: 106–10
"single sin of the sovereign": 26–27, 58–62, 139–42, 335–36, 415–19. See also Bres son of Elatha; Conaire Mór; Dumézil; *fír flathemon/fír flatha*
Sírrabad Súaltaim ("Súaltaim's Long/Repeated Warning"). *See* Súaltaim; *cf.* Conchobor mac Nessa; druids
sister's son: 65–94, 216–18
  examples (*see* Bres son of Elatha; Cú Chulainn; Noísiu)
  Cf. gormac
Sjoestedt, Marie-Louise: 8, 11, 88, 201, 212, 298, 511n48
Sligo, Co.: 4, 46, 62, 80, 100, 135, 451=467, 459=477
slings:
  of Conaire Mór, 13, 57, 248
  of Lug, 5, 85, 145
socht 'stupor': 168. *Cf.* wasting sickness

sons of Donn Désa. *See* foster-brothers: of Conaire Mór
sons of Nechta Scéne. *See* Nechta Scéne
sovereignty:
  drink metaphor, 61–62, 150–51, 158–60, 343, 362–63
  female personification ("goddess") of, 23, 61–62, 150–51, 157–60, 162–64, 181, 216, 489, 502n20 (*see also caillech*; Étaín; Lug mac Céin; Medb)
  righteous exercise of (*see fír flathemon/fír flatha*)
  ship metaphor, 108–9
spears: 11, 213, 226–27, 242, 288, 366, 379
  in metaphors, 66, 190, 514n114
  and the threefold death, 15, 105, 107–8, 112–15
speculum. *See* "Mirror of Princes"
Spenser, Edmund: 28
Springmount Bog tablets: 2
stewards: 294–95, 430–31, 435–36, 460=477, 463=480
stones:
  containing soul of Cano mac Gartnáin, 348, 351, 361–62
  "The Cows of Aífe" (*see Bae Aífe*)
  "of destiny" or of royal inauguration, 28
  inscribed stones (*see* ogam inscriptions)
  pillar stones, 232, 490
  sling-stones (*see* slings)
Súaltaim, Cú Chulainn's human father: 7–8, 53, 55, 86–87, 152, 189–90, 193, 197–98, 213
  his warning to the Ulstermen in the *Táin*, 89, 198–200, 228–29, 238–48 (*see also* warning)
Suibne, king of Dál nAraide, father of Áed Dub: 111

Suibne Geilt 'the Mad,' king of Dál nAraide: 102–4, 113–15
sureties: 91, 97, 182–83, 196, 231, 235, 266
survivals. *See* paganism
swineherds: 63, 205, 208, 247, 516n7. *See also* bulls; *De Chopur in da Muccida*; Grác; Mongán
swords: 47, 147–48, 197, 216, 220–21, 277–78, 328, 416=479 (*see* Móraltach), 494
  in metaphors, 120, 193, 200
Szemerényi, Oswald: 71, 73, 75, 510n20, 511n28

taboo. *See geis*
táin 'cattle raid' (as a type of tale), pl. *tána bó*: 3, 175–76, 456=473. *See also Táin Bó Cúailnge*
Táin, the. *See Táin Bó Cúailnge*
Táin Bó Cúailnge ("The Cattle-Raid of Cooley"): 7–9, 14, 40, 49, 54, 56, 72–73, 78, 86, 88–90, 93, 130, 150, 152, 158, 166, 175, 187–258, 259–60, 264–70, 357, 456=473, 492–94
  benefits of reciting, 147
  as epic (*see* epic)
  historical accuracy (*see* Heroic Age)
  main characters (*see* Conchobor mac Nessa; Cú Chulainn; Fergus mac Roích; Medb)
  message, 9, 89–90 (*see also condalbae*)
  pre-tales (*see remscéla*)
  recensions of, 166, 210–11, 214–15, 220, 226, 229–31, 235, 239–42, 244–51, 254, 256, 266, 268, 492 (*cf.* Book of Leinster; Egerton 1782; *Lebor na hUidre*)
tale-lists: 146, 451=468, 453=470, 456=473, 464–65=483. *See also* tale types

tale types: 3, 146, 150, 175–76 456=473. *See also* tale-lists
Tara (*Temair/ Teamhair*, gen. *Temro*): 458–60=475–78
  Feast of Tara (*Feis Temro*), 265, 427, 433 (*see also* inauguration; sovereignty)
  royal election (*see* bull-feast)
  seat of preeminent human kingship in Ireland, 10, 12–13, 22–23, 27, 56–58, 60–62, 84, 92, 108, 129, 139, 150–52, 154, 159–60, 177, 181, 183, 248, 254, 283–84, 288, 294–95, 298, 322, 331–37, 340–42, 343, 404–5, 413, 430
  seat of Túatha Dé Danann kingship, 4–5, 143–44, 158
Tech nDuinn 'Donn's House,' an abode of the dead: 160–61, 298–99
Temair. See Tara
Tethna: 452–53=469–70. *Cf.* Gráinne
Tethra, Fomoire king: 147–48
Teudos map Regin (Tewdws ap Rhain/Tualodor/Taulodar): 318, 320
textualist approach. *See* critical approaches to early Irish literature
theomachy (the Indo-European theme of "the War of the Gods"): 5, 62, 129–30, 135–36, 145. *See also Cath Maige Tuired*; Dumézil
"the third kills the triple": 55, 214. *See also* Dumézil
three:
  events/motifs in threes, 14, 23–24, 53, 58, 60, 85, 93, 100, 108, 125, 140, 145, 172, 196–97, 199, 213, 216, 217, 228–29, 232, 234, 240–42, 288–89, 291, 298, 340, 348–49, 350, 366–68, 387, 391–95, 440, 444–45, 464=482
  legal triads, 120, 227, 230, 430–31

three (*cont.*)
  periods of three days, months, or years, 47, 55, 213, 273, 311–14, 333, 343, 362, 371–73, 390–91, 397, 445, 456=473
  threefold conception (*see* Compert Con Culainn)
  threefold death, 14–15, 55, 60, 101–20, 413, 489
  three functions, ix, 5, 15, 62, 103–4, 106, 109–10, 115, 118–20, 140, 145, 147, 154 (*see* Dumézil)
  three months of winter (*see ces nóinden*)
  "Three Sorrows of Storytelling," xi
  tripartite cosmos, 82
  triplicity of gods and heroes, 55–56, 60–61, 213–14, 309–312, 407–8, 413
tinchor 'property brought into a marriage': 229, 251, 255, 257
Tipperary, Co.: 162, 284, 289, 291–92, 303–6, 324, 326
Tír na mBéo 'Land of the Living': 20–21, 29. *See also síd*
Tír Tairngiri 'Land of Promise': 23, 25, 29, 31, 66 (=Palestine), 503n42. *Cf. síd*
tocad 'destiny, fate': 169, 172, 345–46, 369–71. *Cf.* prophecies
tochmarc 'wooing' (as a type of tale), pl. *tochmarca*: 3, 175–76, 451=468, 458=475. *See also* Tochmarc Ailbe; Tochmarc Becfola; Tochmarc Emire; Tochmarc Étaíne
Tochmarc Ailbe ("The Wooing of Ailbe"): 453–56=468–73
Tochmarc Becfola ("The Wooing of Becfola"): 348
Tochmarc Emire ("The Wooing of Emer [by Cú Chulainn]"): 8

Tochmarc Étaíne ("The Wooing of Étaín"): xii, 130, 173–74, 176–84, 402–4, 441, 451=468, 491
togail 'destruction' (as a type of tale), pl. *togla*: 3, 175–76, 451=468. *See also* Togail Brudne Uí Dergae; Togail Bruidne Da Derga
Togail Brudne Uí Dergae ("The Destruction of Úa Dergae's Hostel"):
  contents and ms. transmission, 399–411
  See also Togail Bruidne Da Derga
Togail Bruidne Da Derga ("The Destruction of Da Derga's Hostel"): 13, 22–28, 56–63, 98–99, 110, 144, 175, 181, 247–48, 335–36, 412–21, 489, 498.
  relationship to *Togail Brudne Uí Dergae*, 403, 405, 408, 410–11
  See also Conaire Mór
Tóraíocht Dhiarmada agus Ghráinne ("The Pursuit of Diarmaid and Gráinne"): 150, 173, 449–65=466–83, 500
Tóruígheacht Dhiarmada agus Ghráinne. See Tóraíocht Dhiarmada agus Ghráinne
Trifunctionalism. *See* Dumézil; three: three functions
tripartite ideology. *See* Dumézil; three: three functions
Triphun: 318–19, 321
Tristan and Iseult/Isolde: 43–44, 91, 348, 500
tryst, assignation: 190, 217, 343, 348, 351, 353, 363, 372, 382, 391, 394, 396–97. *See also* Bae Aífe; love; sex
túath 'tribe, petty kingdom': 6, 78, 83, 510n14

Túatha Dé Danann (notionally, 'Tribe(s) of the Goddess Danu'), inhabitants of the *síd*: 4–6, 46, 77, 80–85, 89, 97–98, 135–45, 152, 158, 174, 176, 178, 181–82, 490
   kings (*see* Bres son of Elatha; Lug mac Céin; Núadu)
   main texts (*see Aislinge Óenguso; Cath Maige Tuired; Tochmarc Étaíne*)
   rival groups (*see* Fir Bolg; Fomoiri)
   in singular (*Túath Dé Danann* or *Túath Dé* 'people of God'), 6, 83, 510n14. *Cf.* Jews
   See also gods; goddesses
Túathal Techtmar, king of Tara: 303, 313, 339

Úa Maigleine, jester of Fergal son of Máel Dúin: 423, 440, 443–45. *See* jester
"Uar in lathe do Lum Laine," poem: 452–53=469–70
Úgaine Mór, father of Cobthach Cóel and Lóegaire Lorc: 290, 425–27
Uí Bairrche, Leinster people: 288, 292, 304–5, 311. *Cf.* Déisi
Uí Liatháin, Munster people: 289, 323–24. *Cf.* Déisi
Uí Néill dynasty, descended from Niall Noígiallach: 12, 41, 102–3, 106–7, 112, 116–18, 151, 158–60, 311, 405, 422–23, 431, 439–44
   prominent members (*see* Diarmait mac Cerbaill; Fergal son of Máel Dúin; Fínnachta; Muirchertach mac Erca)
Ulaid (Ulstermen). *See ces nóinden*; Cú Chulainn; Conchobor mac Nessa; *Táin Bó Cúailnge*

universe: in literary criticism, 36–37, 40–44. *See also* cosmos; critical approaches to early Irish literature
Uraicecht Bec ("Small Primer"), law-text: 126
Uraicecht na Ríar ("Primer of Stipulations"), law-text: 126
ut diximus formula: 402–3, 419

vassal. *See* client
Vico, Giambattista: xii, 51
Vita Columbae. See Adomnán; Colum Cille

Wagner, Heinrich: 28, 503n37
Wales. *See* Dyfed; *Mabinogi*; Welsh language/terminology
warfare:
   attitudes regarding, 89, 196, 204, 212, 216, 423, 444–46 (*see also fír fer*)
   between the Túatha Dé Danann and the Fomoiri (*see Cath Maige Tuired*; theomachy)
   between the Uí Néill and the Laigin (*see Cath Almaine*)
   between Ulster and Connacht (*see Táin Bó Cúailnge*)
   See also cath 'battle,' *and specific battles:* Cenn Abrat; Cúl Dreimne; Mag Mucrama; Mag Rath; Mag Tuired
warning, esp. formal or ritualistic: 89–90, 190, 195, 198–200, 210–11, 228–29, 232, 238–48, 344, 350, 363, 365–71, 394
War of the Gods. *See* theomachy
"warp-spasm." *See ríastrad*
Waste Land theme: 54, 152, 212–13, 332–34, 337–38, 340–41. *Cf. lommrad*
wasting sickness (*serg*)/stupor (*socht*): 107, 275
   caused by love, 167–68, 177

Waterford, esp. as origin point for Déisi migration: 291, 303–4, 306, 323–27
weapons. *See gae bolga*; slings; spears; swords
Welsh language/terminology: 4, 30, 32–34, 48, 70–71, 73–74, 102, 206, 264, 285, 301–3, 318–24, 327, 369
werewolves: 89, 93
wergild (*éraic* 'body-fine'): 78, 141, 519n30

wolves: 12
  in metaphors (incl. legal), 68–69, 78, 90–93, 194
  in personal names, 8–9, 91
  See also dogs; werewolves
work, the: 36, 45–46. *See also* critical approaches to early Irish literature
worms: 181–82, 464=482–83

Yellow Book of Lecan, Trinity College Dublin ms.: 21, 156, 161, 403, 423–24, 426

www.ingramcontent.com/pod-product-compliance
Lightning Source LLC
Chambersburg PA
CBHW071215290426
44108CB00013B/1188